HISTORY OF THE GREAT WAR
BASED ON OFFICIAL DOCUMENTS

OPERATIONS IN PERSIA
1914—1919

Compiled, by arrangement with the Government of India,
under the direction of the
HISTORICAL SECTION OF THE COMMITTEE OF IMPERIAL DEFENCE,

BY

BRIG.-GEN. F. J. MOBERLY,
C.B., C.S.I. D.S.O., *p.s.c.*

The Naval & Military Press Ltd

Published by

The Naval & Military Press Ltd
Unit 5 Riverside, Brambleside
Bellbrook Industrial Estate
Uckfield, East Sussex
TN22 1QQ England

Tel: +44 (0)1825 749494

www.naval-military-press.com
www.nmarchive.com

In reprinting in facsimile from the original, any imperfections are inevitably reproduced and the quality may fall short of modern type and cartographic standards.

PREFACE.

Persia, as Sir Henry Rawlinson, Lord Curzon and other men of note reminded us at different times during the nineteenth century, was destined by her geographical situation to play a part in the future history of the East altogether disproportionate to her size or her rank in the scale of nations, while the condition of her people and the temper of her government were further factors, which, for good or ill, might powerfully affect the fortunes of our Indian Empire. At the beginning of the present century these factors, losing none of their importance, had been considerably affected by the great development in the East of European international rivalry and by a growing local demand for reform in government. By 1914 the establishment of Persian constitutional government and the Anglo-Russian Convention of 1907 may be said to have entirely dominated the situation.

No authoritative Russian account bearing on these questions has yet been produced, but the opinions expressed by the late M. Sazonoff (the Russian Minister for Foreign Affairs from 1910 to 1916) in his recently published memoirs are interesting. He says that the Anglo-Russian Convention removed many obstacles to the Triple Entente and that up to the last Russia and Great Britain both showed a sincere desire not to allow Persian affairs to become an apple of discord. He attributes much of the misunderstanding, which arose subsequently to the Convention, to the opposite views the two countries held regarding political reform in Persia. The British Government and British public opinion, he says, saw salvation in a representative form of government. But they were, in Russian eyes, applying to Persia a standard but little adapted to the degree of civilisation which she had attained or to the ethnographical diversion or nomadic state of her races. Russia had no faith in the miraculous effects of a parliamentary system but did not oppose stubbornly the earnest British efforts to introduce it, though the consequent anarchical state of Persia was detrimental to Russian interests. But as the scepticism of the Russian Foreign Office was, he explains, even more acutely felt by the Russian consular representatives in Persia, it was found extremely difficult to bring their activities into accord with those of their British colleagues and with the new course of Russian policy in Persia. It also seemed to the Russians that many British officials concerned shared this Russian scepticism.

The experiences of our officials and officers in Persia during the war—and apparently those of our enemies also—tend to show that the Russians had good ground for their opinion. The rise of a national spirit in Persia, which local enthusiasts and foreign sympathisers had professed to discern, proved in effect to be a delusion. The governing classes, the clergy and the politicians were swayed more by self-interest than by patriotism; the merchants and traders were either insufficiently interested or organised to influence events; and the lower classes were passive or impotent. In fact, only a radical national regeneration could have given representative institutions any chance of success. For this a leader or leaders were necessary. But no one appeared having the requisite enlightenment, ability and strength of character; and the term nationalism became a catchword for agitators, actuated either by anti-Ally hostility or by their own material desires.

In considering what actually occured in Persia, it is very necessary to bear in mind that, throughout the war, India was faced by the possibility of danger from the Alsatia on her north-west frontier and from the hostility of a considerable section of the Afghan nation, and also that, during and especially towards the end of the war, the authorities in India, in consultation with His Majesty's Government, were faced with the necessity of investigating and discussing the extent of representative government which it was possible or desirable to apply to India herself. This refers especially to the period after the summer of 1917, when the military advantages in Persia which we gained from the Russian alliance ceased to have effect.

The situation in Persia always affected, or was affected by, our operations in Mesopotamia. In fact, in some areas the operations in Persia were carried out under the orders of the General Officer Commanding in Mesopotamia. The narrative of the operations in North-West Persia and in Arabistan has consequently been already included in the history of the Mesopotamia Campaign. But, though the British force at Bushire was also for a time included in the Mesopotamia Command, the account of the operations there, or from there, are for the sake of continuity given in this volume.

In addition to his indebtedness to Colonel F. E. G. Talbot for valuable co-operation, the author desires to take this opportunity of expressing his acknowledgment and gratitude for the assistance which many officials and officers have given him in various ways and which has greatly facilitated his task. For the majority of the photographs reproduced the author is indebted to Lieutenant-Colonel W. P. Pakenham-Walsh, R.E.

The spelling of place names is that decided on by the Permanent Committee on Geographical Names of the Royal Geographical Society.

F. J. M.

CONTENTS.

	PAGES
CHAPTER I.	1–43

INTRODUCTORY.

GEOGRAPHICAL 1
   Physical characteristics—Rainfall—Deserts—Coasts and ports—Climate—Road communications—Railways—Telegraphic communications—Population—Resources.

SOCIAL, MILITARY AND RELIGIOUS 10
   Persian characteristics—Classes—Distribution of population — Races — Tribal irregular cavalry — Persian military forces in 19th Century—Foreign military missions—Persian army, 1914—Cossack Brigade—Gendarmerie—Religion.

HISTORICAL 17–41
   Early history—Commencement of English relations with Persia—Russian aggression—Persia under Nadir, 1736–1747—Foundation of Qajar dynasty—British diplomacy, 1800—France and Persia, 1807—Anglo-Persian treaty, 1814—Russo-Persian Treaty of Gulistan, 1813—War with Russia and Treaty of Turkomanchai, 1828—Revision of Anglo-Persian Treaty of 1814—England and the Persian Gulf—Persian designs on Afghanistan—Attack on Herat, 1837–38—British action—Persian troubles, 1838–48—Accession of Nasir-ud-Din Shah, 1848—Break with England, 1856—Anglo-Persian War, 1856–57—Perso-Afghan boundary—British work in the Persian Gulf—Perso-Turkish relations—Russia's expansion in Central Asia—Commencement of concessions—Conditions in Persia, 1857–96—Concessions to foreigners and growth of discontent—Accession of Muzaffar-ud-Din Shah, 1896—England and the Persian Gulf—The Constitutional movement, 1905 onwards—Accession of Muhammad Ali Shah, 1907—Anglo-Russian Convention, 1907—Shah's *coup d'état*—Abdication of Shah Muhammad Ali, 1909—Political parties—Financial difficulties—Mr. Shuster's mission, 1911—Russian opposition and action — Chaotic situation — Russian dominance — British policy, 1914.

SUMMARY OF RUSSIAN, BRITISH AND TURKISH POLICY .. 42–3

CONTENTS—*continued.*

	PAGES
CHAPTER II.	44–84

AUGUST, 1914 TO JUNE, 1915.
ENEMY EFFORTS TO BRING PERSIA INTO THE WAR.

General situation ; August, 1914	44
Russian forces in North-West Persia ; August, 1914	45
Attitude of Turkey ; August–October, 1914	45–7
The gendarmerie and South Persia ; August–Sept., 1914	47
Effect of Turkey's entry into the war ; November, 1914—January, 1915	48–51
Muscat and Chahbar ; October, 1914—January, 1915	51–3
Defence of Muscat ; 11th January, 1915.	
Arabistan ; January, 1915	53–4
Enemy emissaries in Persia ; February, 1915	54–5
Arabistan and South Persia ; March, 1915—Bushire	55–6
Increasing enemy activity and Persian inaction ; February—March, 1915	57–9
Situation in West and South Persia—British protests—Change of Premier—Wassmuss at Shiraz backed by Swedish officers of gendarmerie.	
North-West Persia ; March, 1915	59
Massacre of Christian Assyrians.	
Doubtful attitude of new Persian Cabinet ; March–April, 1915	59–62
German and Turkish intrigues—British protests—Disturbed conditions at Kermanshah and Isfahan.	
Turkish invasion of West Persia ; April, 1915	62
Change of Persian Government ; April, 1915	62–4
Their continued failure to check enemy activities.	
Bushire ; April, 1915	64
Increase of British Residency escort.	
Views of Government of India ; March–April, 1915	64–66
Jask and Chahbar ; April–May, 1915	66
General situation ; May, 1915	66
Bushire ; May, 1915	67
Question of Russian reinforcements ; May, 1915	67
British and Allied policy ; May, 1915	68–9
Critical situation in Fars ; May, 1915	69
Bakhtiaris and the Arabistan oil-field ; May, 1915	70
British policy ; May, 1915	70
Swedish officers of gendarmerie ; May, 1915	70–1
German action and its effect ; June, 1915	71–3
Progress of German emissaries and inaction of Persian Government.	
Bushire, June, 1915 ; enemy activity and increase of British escort	73
Persian Gulf littoral ; June, 1915—Makran	73
Turks retire from Karind to Qasr-i-Shirin ; June, 1915	74
Situation in India ; June, 1915	74
German account of activities of their emissaries in Persia ; August, 1914—June, 1915	74–84

vii

CONTENTS—*continued.*

	PAGES
CHAPTER III	..85–130

JULY–NOVEMBER, 1915.
ENEMY ACTION AND PERSIAN WEAKNESS NECESSITATE ALLIED INTERVENTION.

Inception of the East Persia Cordon ; July, 1915..	85–6
Bushire ; July, 1915, attack on British	87
General situation, events and British policy ; July, 1915	87–9
Further British reinforcement of Bushire.	
East Persia ; July, 1915	89–93
Allied action to prevent enemy ingress into Afghanistan.	
East Persia ; August, 1915..	93–4
German mission crosses Persian frontier into Afghanistan—German accounts of same..	94–6
Kerman ; August, 1915	96
Zugmayer's activities.	
East Persia ; August, 1915	96–7
Central and South-West Persia ; August, 1915	97
Bushire ; August, 1915	98
British occupation.	
Operations at Dilbar ; August, 1915	98–101
Bushire ; August, 1915	101–2
British dispositions.	
Change of Persian Government ; August, 1915	102–3
Fails to check German activities.	
Situation at end of August, 1915	103
Strong position of Germans.	
Isfahan ; July–August, 1915	104
Activities of Seiler.	
Central Persia and Allied policy ; September, 1915	105
Attempt to murder British Consul-General at Isfahan, 1st September.	
Isfahan ; September, 1915	105
British policy ; September, 1915	106–8
Murder of British Vice-Consul at Shiraz, 7th September—Improvement in situation as result of a Russian landing at Enzeli.	
Bushire ; September, 1915	108–111
Action of 9th September—Heavy tribal defeat.	
Shiraz ; September, 1915	111
Governor-General recalled to Tehran.	
General events and British policy ; September, 1915	112–3
Intensified German activities ; British evacuate Isfahan, 14th September.	
Kerman ; September, 1915	113
East Persia ; September, 1915	113–4
Movements of German emissaries checked—Completion of Anglo-Russian Cordon.	

CONTENTS—*continued.*

CHAPTER III—*continued.*

	PAGES
South Persia; October, 1915	114-5

Temporary improvement of situation at Shiraz—Persians resume administration of Bushire town; 16th October—Increasing unrest in Makran.

East Persia; October, 1915 115
British reinforcements and movements of German parties.

Germans at Kabul; October, 1915 116-7
Niedermayer's account.

General events and Allied policy; October 1915.. .. 117-9
Serious situation at Tehran caused by German efforts—Russian reinforcements land at Enzeli—Kiesling's account of German activities.

General events and Allied policy; November, 1915 ..119-124
Russian troops' advance towards Tehran saves situation and causes exodus of enemy legations.

Seizure of British consul and colony at Shiraz; November, 1915 124-5

Improved attitude of Persian Government; 20th November, 1915 125

Russian military action; end of November, 1915 .. 126-7
British policy; end of November, 1915 127-8
Turco-German plans 128
Bushire; November, 1915 129
East Persia; November, 1915 129-30
Enemy movements and British dispositions.

CHAPTER IV. 131-172

DECEMBER, 1915–MAY, 1916.

SUCCESSFUL RESULTS OF ALLIED OPERATIONS.

Central and West Persia; December, 1915 .. 131-136
Confused political situation at Tehran—Successful advance of Russians under Baratoff—Farman Farma becomes Premier, 24th December—Enemy designs and action—Divergence of Turkish and German aims—The German military mission.

Bushire; December, 1915 136
East Persia; December, 1915 136-7
Allied consuls forced to evacuate Kerman.

Central and West Persia; January, 1916.. 137-8
South Persia; January, 1916 138-9
Revolted gendarmerie drive out acting governor—Inception of British mission under Sir P. Sykes.

Central and West Persia; January, 1916.. .. 139-140
Question of Russo-British alliance with Persia—the German mission at Kermanshah.

South Persia; January–February, 1916 141-143
Discussion regarding British policy.

CONTENTS—*continued.*

CHAPTER IV—*continued.*

	PAGES
Central and West Persia ; February, 1916	143–144

Baratoff ordered to occupy Kermanshah—British agreement with Bakhtiaris for protection of oilfields — Local intrigues undermine Persian Premier's position—Weakness of German position at Kermanshah, Goltz's appreciation of 16th February—Baratoff captures Kermanshah, 25th February.

South Persia ; February, 1916 144
Discussion regarding rôle of the Sykes mission.

Bushire ; January–February, 1916 145
British prisoners at Ahram.

East Persia ; January, 1916 145–8
British dispositions—Unsuccessful German attempt to break through British cordon into Afghanistan—Affair at Deh Salm, 18th January—German account—Zugmayer sends agents to Bam and Bampur.

East Persia ; February, 1916 149
General Dyer appointed to command.

Makran ; December, 1915—February, 1916 149
Unrest owing to German propaganda—British counter-measures.

East Persia ; February, 1916 150
Zugmayer in the Bam area—German position at Kerman deteriorates.

British policy ; February–March, 1916 150–1
H.M. Government authorise more active policy to counter enemy measures in South and East Persia.

South Persia ; March, 1916 151–2
Assistance in arms and ammunition given to Qawam—Sykes to start his mission at Bandar Abbas.

General situation ; March, 1916 152
Resignation of Farman Farma, 2nd March—Sipahsalar becomes Prime Minister—German propaganda losing ground.

Bushire ; March, 1916 153
Decision not to undertake operations inland.

Central and West Persia ; March, 1916 153
Allied policy—Russians occupy Isfahan, but advance west of Kermanshah hampered by snow.

Sykes Mission at Bandar Abbas ; 16th March 154

East Persia ; March, 1916 154–8
Evacuation of Kerman by Germans—General Dyer assumes command of Seistan Force and decides on action against Sarhaddis—British and Russian dispositions—Zugmayer abandons Baluchistan project.

CONTENTS—*continued*.

CHAPTER IV—*continued*.

PAGES

South and East Persia ; April, 1916 158–9
    Collapse of German activities—Qawam and Saulat gain Shiraz—Capture of Seiler's and Zugmayer's parties.

South Persia ; April, 1916 159–160
    Plans for Sykes Mission.

Bushire ; April, 1916 160–1
    The British prisoners at Ahram—Affair at Chaghadak, 27th April.

West Persia ; April, 1916 161–2
    Baratoff ordered to advance on Khaniqin—Death of F.M. von der Goltz at Baghdad—The German Persian mission.

East Persia ; April, 1916 162–7
    Dyer's operations in Sarhad—Affair of 13th April—Submission of Sarhaddi leaders—Occupation of Khwash, 18th April.—Affair of Lirudik, 13th April—Affair of Kundi, 17th–18th April.

East Persia ; May, 1916 167–8
    Treachery of Sarhaddi leaders—Dyer again occupies Khwash—Raising of Sarhaddi levies—Attempts to improve Nushki-Robat line of communication.

Makran ; April–May, 1916 168–170
    Missions under Colonel Dew and Major Keyes.

German Mission to Afghanistan 170–2
    Departure from Kabul, 21st May—Adventures and fate of members of the mission.

CHAPTER V. 173–216

MAY TO DECEMBER 1916.

TURKISH INVASION OF WESTERN PERSIA AND BRITISH MEASURES IN SOUTH AND EAST PERSIA.

West Persia ; May, 1916 173–5
    Russian occupation of Qasr-i-Shirin and Turco-German retreat—Turkish reinforcements from Tigris and inception of Turkish expedition into Persia—Return of British consul and community to Isfahan.

Shiraz ; May, 1916 175–6

The Sykes Mission ; May, 1916 176
    Sykes prepares to move on Kerman.

The British prisoners at Ahram ; May, 1916 176–7

The Sykes Mission ; May–June, 1916 177–8
    Sykes starts from Bandar Abbas, 17th May—The march to Kerman.

Bushire ; May—June, 1916 178–9
    Discussion of plans for effecting relief of prisoners at Ahram.

CONTENTS—*continued.*

CHAPTER V—*continued.*

	PAGES
General situation; June, 1916	179–180
Russian obstruction prevents conclusion of Anglo-Russian agreement with Persian Government.	
West Persia; June, 1916	180
Baratoff, defeated at Khaniqin, 3rd June, forced to retreat followed by Turks.	
Shiraz situation, June, 1916, unsatisfactory	181
The Sykes Mission; June, 1916	181–2
Arrival at Kerman, 11th June—Future plans.	
East Persia; June, 1916	183
Dispositions and strength of British "Seistan Force."	
Sarhad; June, 1916.	183–6
Dyer's operations against Sarhaddi tribes.	
Sarhad; July, 1916	186–9
Dyer's operations—Affair of the Gusht defile, 19th–21st July—Progress of Major Keyes's Makran Mission.	
Sarhad; August, 1916	189–191
Dyer's further operations—His junction with Keyes.	
East Persia; July–August, 1916	191–3
Difficulty of supply and transport problem—Railway extension from Nushki decided on.	
West Persia and the general situation; July, 1916	194–7
Turkish capture of Kermanshah, 1st July, causes alarm at Tehran and apprehension in India.	
Shiraz; July, 1916	197
Unsatisfactory situation.	
Kerman; July, 1916	197–8
Sykes' column starts for Shiraz, 27th July.	
Anglo-Russian Agreement with Persia, August, 1916	198–9
West and Central Persia; August, 1916	199–200
Turkish capture of Hamadan and Russian retirement to Sultan Bulag pass raises prospect of evacuation of Tehran by Allied legations—New Persian Government formed under Vossuk-ud-Daula.	
The Sykes Mission; August, 1916..	200–2
Arrives Yezd, 14th August and after discussion as to further movements leaves on 28th August for Isfahan.	
Kerman; August, 1916	202–4
Escape of enemy prisoners at Saidabad.	
Bushire; July–August, 1916	204
Release of British prisoners from Ahram.	
West and Central Persia; September, 1916	204
Turkish halt at Hamadan—Improved situation at Tehran and Isfahan.	
Fars situation; September, 1916	204–5
Refusal of Saulat and Qawam to recognise Farman Farma as Governor-General.	

CONTENTS—*continued.*

CHAPTER V—*continued.*

	PAGES
The Sykes Mission ; September, 1916	205–7

Sykes halts at Isfahan—His Mission placed under orders of British Minister at Tehran.

Isfahan ; September–October, 1916	207
Shiraz ; September, 1916	207

Saulat and Qawam withdraw opposition to Farman Farma.

Kerman September–October, 1916	207–8

Capture of Saidabad, 28th September.

Reserve of Indian troops at Muscat, October–November, 1916	208–9
Shiraz ; October–December, 1916	209–10

Arrival of Farman Farma and Lt.-Col. Gough, 15th October—Discussion regarding policy towards hostile Khans of Bushire hinterland.

South Persia Rifles ; November–December, 1916	210–11

Organisation—Recognition by Persian Government.

Shiraz ; November–December, 1916	211–12

Situation on Bushire-Shiraz road—Treacherous attack on South Persia Rifles post at Kazerun, 17th December—Rebels capture South Persia Rifles post at Dasht-i-Arjan, 21st December—British action.

Kerman ; November–December, 1916	212–13

Improved situation.

West Persia ; October–December, 1916	213–14

Turks at Hamadan.

East Persia ; September–December, 1916	214–16

Affair of Kalmas, 26th September—General Tanner relieves General Dyer in command—Makran Mission moves southward on Chahbar—Reduction in size of Seistan Force.

British troops in Persia ; 31st December, 1916	216

CHAPTER VI. 217–53

DECEMBER, 1916–AUGUST, 1917.

EFFECTS OF BRITISH SUCCESS IN MESOPOTAMIA.

South Persia ; December, 1916	217–21

Affair of Dasht-i-Arjan, 25th December.

Bushire–Shiraz road ; December, 1916	221–2

Operations from Bushire vetoed.

Control of operations in South Persia ; December, 1916—January, 1917	222–5
South Persia ; January, 1917	226

Situation at Shiraz—Arrangements to reinforce Sykes from India.

CONTENTS—*continued*.

CHAPTER VI—*continued*.

	PAGES
Bakhtiari territory ; December, 1916–January, 1917	226–7
West Persia ; January–February, 1917	227
East Persia ; December, 1916–February, 1917	227

Nushki railway extended to Dalbandin—Makran Mission arrives Chahbar.

West Persia ; February–March, 1917 228
Retirement of Turks and Russian advance to Qasr-i-Shirin.

South Persia ; February–March, 1917 228–30
Reinforcements from India—Effect of capture of Baghdad, 11th March—Progress of organisation of South Persia Rifles.

Kerman ; January–March, 1917 230
Situation quiet—Good progress with South Persia Rifles.

Control of operations in South Persia ; February–March, 1917 230–2
Further discussion and decision—Persian Government officially recognise Sykes' appointment.

Bushire ; February–March, 1917 232

General situation ; March–May, 1917 232–3
Effect of Russian revolution on political conditions at Tehran—Resignation of Vossuk-ud-Daula, 27th May.

West Persia ; April–May, 1917 233–4
Deterioration of Russian troops owing to effect of revolution—Pavloff relieves Baratoff—Scheme for Bakhtiari levy corps abandoned.

South Persia ; April–May, 1917 234–5
Improved situation—Agreement with Saulat—Arrival of Indian reinforcements at Shiraz—Scope of duties of South Persia Rifles.

Scheme for organisations of the South Persia Rifles ; May, 1917 235–8

Control of operations in South Persia ; May–June, 1917.. 238–9
Further discussion.

Bushire ; April–May, 1917 240–1

East Persia ; February–May, 1917 241–2
Complete submission of Damanis—Reduction of British force—Disquieting situation in Russian Turkestan, April,1917.

North-West Frontier of India ; May, 1917 242

Persian and British Policy ; June–August, 1917.. .. 242–4
New Persian Government under Ala-es-Sultaneh, June—Refusal to recognise South Persia Rifles—Discussion as to Russo-British policy.

CONTENTS—*continued.*

CHAPTER VI—*continued.*

PAGES

General situation ; June–August, 1917 244–5
    Deterioration of Russian troops—Russian retirement enables Turks to re-occupy Qasr-i-Shirin—Baratoff replaces Pavloff, but Russian demoralisation continues—Extremist anti-British agitation at Tehran.

Operations of the Sykes Mission ; June–July, 1917 ..246–52
    Distribution of Indian troops, 1st June—Operations of troops and South Persia Rifles to suppress brigandage—Affair of Kafta, 5th July, 1917—Sykes' improvement of road communications.

Bushire Force ; June–July, 1917 252

East Persia ; June–August, 1917 252–3
    Railway extension from Dalbandin to Persian frontier sanctioned.

CHAPTER VII. 254–296

SEPTEMBER, 1917–APRIL, 1918

THE FAILURE OF PERSIA TO MAINTAIN HER NEUTRALITY NECESSITATES FURTHER BRITISH INTERVENTION.

The Russian situation ; September–November, 1917 .. 254–5
    Continuous deterioration—Bolsheviks gain power.

The Caucasus ; September–November, 1917 255
    Chaotic situation—Spread of anarchy.

Enemy intentions ; September–November, 1917 .. 255–7
    Threat of Turco-German eastward thrust.

British policy ; October–November, 1917 .. 257–60

Persian policy ; October–November, 1917 260–1
    Formation of new Persian Government under Ain-ud-Daula, 24th November.

Bushire ; September–November, 1917 261

Punitive operations by the Sykes Mission ; September–October, 1917 262–6

The Sykes Mission ; October, 1917 266–7

East Persia ; September–November, 1917 267

General situation ; December, 1917 267–8
    Suspension of hostilities between Russia and Central Powers, 2nd December—British policy in regard to Russia and Trans-Caucasia.

CONTENTS—*continued.*

CHAPTER VII—*continued.*

PAGES

Persian politics and British policy; December, 1917 . . 268–71
    Weakness of Ain-ud-Daula's Government—The Jangali revolt—Extremist agitation in Tehran—British Minister recommends despatch of British force to secure Kermanshah-Hamadan road—Inception of the Dunsterville Mission.

British policy; January, 1918 271–3
    Mustaufi-ul-Mamalik forms new Persian Government; 19th January.

North-West Persia and British policy; January, 1918 273–4
    Failure to get Russian volunteers to protect Persian frontier—Jangalis and Bolsheviks in control at Enzeli.

East Persia; December, 1917–January, 1918 274–8
    Chaos in Russian Turkestan—Russian withdrawal from East Persia Cordon—British Cordon extended northward—Question of a British mission to Turkestan.

South Persia; December, 1917—January, 1918 278–80
    Tribal raids in Fars—Affair of Gumun.

British policy; January, 1918 280
    British negotiations with Persian Government.

British policy; February, 1918 280–5
    Continuous discussion—Persian procrastination—Failure of Dunsterville to reach the Caucasus—Increasing seriousness of situation at Tehran and in N.W. Persia.

British policy; March, 1918 286–9
    H.M. Government decide to send troops into N.W. Persia and to reinforce Sykes—Anti-British action of Jangalis—Small British detachment reaches Hamadan.

British policy; April, 1918 289–91
    Turco-German aims and progress in N.W. Persia and the Caucasus—Persian Government's hostility to England—Chaotic situation in Trans-Caucasia—Orders to General Marshall to strike in Kirkuk direction.

South Persia; February–April, 1918 291–3
    Move of reinforcements from India to join Sykes—Inception of disaffection in South Persia Rifles—Distribution of troops with the Sykes Mission at end of April.

East Persia; February–April, 1918 293–6
    Extended British cordon reaches Meshed, 14th March—Increased British strength—Events in Turkestan and question of despatch of British mission—Question of further railway extension.

CONTENTS—*continued*.

	PAGES
CHAPTER VIII.	297–341

MAY–JULY, 1918.
THE EFFECT IN PERSIA OF THE GERMAN SUCCESSES IN FRANCE; AND THE ANTI-BRITISH OUTBREAK IN FARS.

Causes of Fars outbreak in May, 1918 297–8
Inception of anti-tribal operations; May, 1918 298
The Caucasus and North-West Persia; 1st–11th May, 1918 299–300
   Turco-German aims and progress.
Persian politics and British policy; May, 1918 300–3
   Samsam-es-Sultaneh becomes Prime Minister, 3rd May—Situation at Tehran—British policy.
Operations in Northern Fars; May, 1918.. 303–9
   Colonel Grant's operations—Affair at Chinar-i-Naz, 10th May—Affair of Ziarat, 13th May—Affair of Kuh-i-Khan, 16th May—Return to Shiraz, 23rd May.
South Persia; May, 1918 309–12
   Tribal attack on Khan-i-Zinian, 10th May—Loss of South Persia Rifles' outpost at Timouri—Open declaration of hostilities by Saulat on 23rd May.
Qashqai operations; May, 1918 312–19
  Action of Deh Shaikh; 25th May, 1918 313–17
  Mutiny at Khan-i-Zinian; 25th May, 1918 317
Shiraz; 26th–31st May, 1918 317–20
   Situation—Reinforcements to Bushire—British measures at Shiraz—Sykes placed under control of Commander-in-Chief, India.
East Persia; May, 1918 320–1
   British cordon reinforced—H.M. Government sanction reconnaissance for railway extension beyond Mirjawa—Turkestan situation.
Persian politics and British policy; 1st–20th June, 1918.. 321–4
   British policy—Turks occupy Tabriz; 14th June—Slight improvement in general situation, 20th June.
Shiraz; 1st–16th June, 1918 324–6
   Situation—India's proposals for relief of pressure on Sykes—Sykes' appreciation of situation, 5th June—Decision to send reinforcements to Sykes via Bandar Abbas—Discussion of future policy regarding the South Persia Rifles.
Qashqai operations; June, 1918 326–7
  Action of Ahmadabad; 16th June 328–30
Shiraz; 17th–21st June, 1918 330–1
   Anti-British agitation necessitates British occupation of city, 18th June, with excellent results.

CONTENTS—*continued.*

CHAPTER VIII—*continued.*

	PAGES
British policy ; 21st–30th June, 1918	331–3

Discussions—H.M. Government, on 28th June, direct General Marshall to devote his main attention to our objects at Tehran, Baku and on Caspian.

East Persia ; June, 1918 333–5
  Bolsheviks dominate Turkestan—Active Turco-German propaganda there—Instructions of Commander-in-Chief, India, for the Malleson Mission Bolsheviks defeated by Mensheviks near Askabad—General Malleson leaves Simla for Meshed, 28th June.

South Persia ; 21st June–July, 1918 335–41
  Affair near Bulvardi ; 27th June—Sirdar Ehtesham appointed chief of Qashqais vice Saulat, 5th July.
  Affair of Chenar-i-Rahdar, 7th–8th July, 1918 .. 336–7
  Defence and relief of Abadeh ; 28th June–17th July, 1918 337–40
  Situation in Kerman province.. 340–1
  Arrival of reinforcements at Bandar Abbas, 27th June 341

CHAPTER IX. 342–78

JULY TO SEPTEMBER, 1918.
THE TIDE TURNS IN FAVOUR OF THE ALLIES.

British policy ; July, 1918 342–4
  Efforts to secure Persian friendliness.
The Caucasus and North-West Persia ; July, 1918 .. 344
  Turkish progress towards Baku—Bolsheviks decline British assistance—The Jelus at Urmia—*Coup d'état* at Baku and appeal for British assistance.
British occupation of Baku, 4th August, 1918 344–5
Tehran situation ; end of July, 1918 345
Fars and Kerman ; end of July, 1918 345–6
Bushire ; June and July, 1918 346–7
  Preparations for autumn offensive.
East Persia ; July, 1918 347–9
  Situation in Trans-Caspia—The " Turkestan Union "—Malleson arrives Meshed and his appreciation of situation—Bolsheviks defeated by Mensheviks and driven eastward—Move of British detachment to Perso-Russian frontier—Instructions to the Malleson Mission.
Summary of the general situation at the end of July, 1918 349–50
Persian Policy ; August, 1918 350
  Vossuk-ud-Daula becomes Prime Minister.
British and Persian policy regarding the South Persia Rifles ; August, 1918 350–4
  Varying views.
Fars ; August, 1918 354–5

CONTENTS—*continued.*

CHAPTER IX—*continued.*

	PAGES
Bushire ; August, 1918	355

Progress of preparations for autumn offensive.

North-West and North Persia ; August, 1918 356
  Turks capture Urmia ; 3rd August—Flight of Jelus to Hamadan—Turkish advance southward from Tabriz causes diversion of British troops towards Mianeh.

The Malleson Mission and Trans-Caspia ; August, 1918. . 356–60
  Decision to support Mensheviks—Action by Malleson —War Office instructions—Machine guns of 19th Punjabis join Trans-Caspians at Bairam Ali.

  Trans-Caspian defeat at Bairam Ali ; 13th August. . 359–60
  Detachment 19th Punjabis join Trans-Caspians at Dushak, 20th August.

Affair of Kaahka ; 28th August, 1918 361–2
  Further British reinforcements reach Kaahka.

East Persia ; August, 1918 362–3
  East Persia Cordon Force reinforced—Difficulties of Line of Communications—Government of India recommend railway extension from Mirjawa via Duzdab to Neh.

Suggestion for unifying the command of all British forces east of Suez ; August, 1918 363–4

North Persia and adjacent territory ; September, 1918. . 364–6
  Turks capture Baku, 14th September—Apparently critical situation, 17th September—Commodore Norris's action on Caspian—General Thomson assumes command of North Persia Force—Withdrawal of a Turkish division from Trans-Caucasia to Constantinople, end of September.

Trans-Caspia ; September, 1918 366–7
  Affairs at Kaahka ; 11th and 18th September.

British policy and Persian politics ; September, 1918 . . 367–70
  Sir P. Cox relieves Sir C. Marling ; 16th September— Politics and diplomacy at Tehran—Effect of victories in Palestine and Bulgaria.

North Persia ; end of September, 1918 370–1
  Norris pushes on measures to control Caspian— British occupation of Krasnovodsk—Favourable Allied war situation.

East Persia ; September, 1918 371–3
  Measures to strengthen British position at Meshed— New organisation of British forces in Trans-Caspia and East Persia—The East Persia Line of Communication.

Fars ; September, 1918 373
Bushire ; September, 1918.. 373–8
  Political situation in hinterland—Commencement of British operations—Instructions to General Douglas—Advance across the *mashileh* and affair at Chaghadak, 29th September.

xix

CONTENTS—*continued.*

	PAGES
CHAPTER X.	379–417

OCTOBER TO 11TH NOVEMBER, 1918.
THE EFFECT OF OUR VICTORIES.

British and Persian policy ; October, 1918 379–84
Situation in North-West Persia and Caspian ; end of October, 1918 384–5
British and Persian policy ; October–November,1918 .. 385–6
Armistic with Turkey ; 31st October, 1918 386
Preparations to occupy Baku 387
British and Persian policy ; 1st–11th November, 1918 .. 387–8
    Persia and the Peace Conference.
Situation at Baku ; 1st–11th November, 1918 388–90
Trans-Caspia ; October, 1918 390–8
    Action of Dushak, 14th October, 1918 394–6
    Occupation of Merv, 1st November, 1918.
Trans-Caspia ; November, 1918 398–403
    The question of British policy.
East Persia ; October–November, 1918 403–8
    General Dickson and the line of communication.
Operations from Bushire ; October–11th November, 1918 408–14
    Progress of operations—Influenza epidemic.
    Affair of Lardeh ; 31st October, 1918 410–13
    Distribution of troops, end of October .. 413
Operations based on Shiraz ; October–11th November, 1918 414–17
    Despatch of column to Firuzabad.
    Relief of Firuzabad ; 24th October, 1918 417
British troops in Persia ; 15th November, 1918 417

CHAPTER XI.	418–471

CONCLUSION.

General situation at end of war 418–19
Terms of Armistice with Germany 419
Trans-Caucasia, the Caspian and North-West Persia ; November, 1918–January, 1919.. 419–24
    Occupation of Baku ; 17th November—Decision for British troops to remain in West Persia—Naval affair off Chechen ; 8th December, 1918 .. 422–3
    Events at Baku and in Caucasia—General Milne takes over control in Trans-Caucasia on 15th January, 1919 424

CONTENTS—*continued.*

CHAPTER XI—*continued.*

	PAGES
Trans-Caspia ; November, 1918–March, 1919 ..	424–51
Question of British policy—Local developments.	
Action of Annenkovo ; 16th January, 1919.. ..	442–4
General Milne's review of situation ; 1st February, 1919 ..	444–6
H.M. Government decide to withdraw from Trans-Caspia ..	447
Coming British withdrawal publicly announced ; 11th March, 1919 ..	450
Evacuation of Trans-Caspia, end of March, 1919 ..	450
East Persia Line of Communication ..	450–1
Bushire Field Force ; November–December, 1918 ..	452–5
Mallu Pass occupied ; 18th November—Occupation of Kamarij ; 20th December, 1918—Visit to Khurmuj ; 31st December, 1918.	
Fars ; November, 1918—January, 1918 ..	455–6
Bushire Field Force ; January–March, 1919 ..	456–60
Discussion as to policy.	
Occupation of Kazerun, 27th January 1919, and opening up of through communication with Shiraz.	
Instructions for withdrawal of troops, end of March, 1919.	
Bushire situation ; April, 1919 ..	460–1
Kerman ; November, 1918—March, 1919 ..	461–2
Policy ; November, 1918—April, 1919 ..	462–71

APPENDICES.

		PAGES
Appendix I.—Views of Field-Marshal von der Goltz on the situation in Persia, 16th February, 1916		472–3
,, II.—British troops in Persia, 31st December, 1916		474
,, III.—Distribution and strength of the troops with the Sykes's Mission 30th April 1918		475–7
,, IV.—East Persia Cordon Field Force. Distribution of troops, 31st March 1918		478
,, V.—British troops in Persia, Persian Gulf and Trans-Caspia; 15th November, 1918		479–81
Index		482-90

LIST OF MAPS.

Map of Persia	⎫
Map 1.—Operations at Bushire 1915	⎬ In pocket.
,, 2.—Portion of Perso-Afghan frontier.	⎭
,, 3.—Operations at Dilbar, 13th–15th August 1915	To face p. 100
,, 4.—Operations of General Dyer in Sarhad; April–August 1916.	⎫ In pocket.
,, 5.—Wanderings of German parties in Persia and Afghanistan.	⎭
,, 6.—Affair of Dasht-i-Arjan; 25th September, 1916	To face p. 220
,, 7.—Affair of Kafta; 5th July, 1917	,, 250
,, 8.—Northern Fars	,, 308
,, 9.—Action of Deh Shaikh; 25th May, 1918	,, 316
,, 10.—Shiraz	,, 338
,, 11.—Operations from Bushire; September, 1918–January, 1919	In pocket.
,, 12.—Plan of East Persia L. of C.	To face p. 408
,, 13.—Operations for relief of Firuzabad; October, 1918	,, 416

ILLUSTRATIONS.

Kacha Tangi	⎫ To face p. 92
Kacha	⎭
Saindak Camp	⎫ ,, 155
Robat	⎭
Summit of Asadabad Pass in March	,, 286
Road between Kazvin and Hamadan in March	,, 288
Floods between Duzdab and Robat; 27th March, 1918	,, 293
Birjand, from the North-East	⎫ ,, 404
Dehani Sulaiman Pass (North-West of Kain)	⎭

BIBLIOGRAPHY.

Official War Diaries and Records of the War Section, Army Headquarters, India.

Official War Diaries and Records of the various forces and units operating in Persia.

Official Records of the Government of India, Foreign Office, War Office, Admiralty and Committee of Imperial Defence.

Official Despatches.

"The Campaign in Mesopotamia, 1914–1918." Official History of the War.

"Persia." The Hon. G. Curzon.

"The Persian Revolution of 1905–1909." Edward G. Browne.

"The Middle Eastern Question." Sir Valentine Chirol.

"The Strangling of Persia." W. M. Shuster.

"A History of Persia." Brigadier-General Sir Percy Sykes.

"The Adventures of Dunsterforce." Major-General L. C. Dunsterville.

"The Raiders of the Sarhad." Brigadier-General R. E. H. Dyer.

"East Persia." Brigadier-General W. E. R. Dickson.

"With the Persian Expedition." Major M. H. Donohoe.

"Unter der Glutsonne Irans." Oskar von Niedermayer.

"Mit Feldmarschall von der Goltz Pascha in Mesopotamien und Persien." Lieutenant-Colonel H. von Kiesling.

"Meine Diplomatenfahrt ins Versehlossene Land." Legations-Sekretär Dr. W. O. von Hentig.

"Vom Balkan nach Baghdad." Major-General von Gleich.

CHAPTER I.

INTRODUCTORY.

(General Map of Persia.)

Except for low-lying strips adjacent to its sea coasts and for its great salt and sand deserts, the country which we know as Persia—and which in the East is generally termed Iran (the country of the Aryans)—lies at a mean altitude of from three to five thousand feet. The greater part of this plateau consists of mountains, which run in numerous parallel ranges generally from north-west to south-east. These, while attaining in many parts a mean altitude of eight thousand feet, seldom rise to really great heights; Demavend in the Elburz, with its volcanic cone of 18,549 feet covered with perpetual snow, being almost the sole exception. The most common characteristic of the land is its bare aridity. Though there are many well-watered and fertile valleys between the rugged and bleak ridges, the country is for the most part treeless and without verdure outside its irrigated areas. Physical characteristics.

To this general aridity, however, the region immediately south of the Caspian presents a complete contrast. Owing to the heavy annual rainfall, the land here is so abundantly clothed with trees and dense undergrowth as to be often almost impenetrable. The main centres of population lie hidden on the lower mountain slopes among trees and surrounded by rich orchards and gardens, or in the considerable cultivated clearings in the midst of the dense jungle of the low levels. The coast is fringed with a chain of sandhills, piled up by the surf and winds, which have everywhere forced the rivers and the many streams to spread themselves out in wide morasses or lagoons. These damp low levels with their luxuriant growth and malarious swamps are in the summer so close and unhealthy that all who can manage to do so migrate to the mountains.

An inland sea once extended over a great part of the central plateau; and the lakes, deserts or marshes which remain, many of them salt, still absorb about three-fifths of the drainage of the country. The remaining two-fifths drain into the sea by rivers, which follow remarkably devious courses through close-set valleys and gorges splitting the mountains transversely. There are very few rivers of any importance; the Karun, which is the largest, being the only one that is navigable. Many of the minor streams exist only during the melting of the snows or after rain and, moreover, are frequently salt or brackish.

Rainfall. The general aridity of the country is due to the scanty rainfall, which, owing to the fact that the moisture-laden clouds are intercepted by the high mountain ranges in the north-west and north, is much less in the eastern provinces than it is in the west. For instance, in the Caspian provinces the average annual fall varies from about fifty-six inches in the west to seventeen in the east; at Urmia there are about twenty-one, at Tehran about ten, and at Bushire about thirteen inches; while in the south-eastern provinces and Seistan it generally amounts to only four inches or less. Fortunately, except in the Caspian provinces, most of the moisture falls in the winter in the form of snow and feeds perennial springs, on which the irrigation of the country is chiefly dependent. The water from these springs is taken to the lower levels in artificial subterranean aqueducts, or *qanats*, which are sometimes as much as fifteen miles in length. The mounds of earth, which surround the vertical shafts sunk in their construction and which mark the course of the *qanats*, are a notable feature in the landscape of all irrigated areas.

Deserts. The eastern half of Persia consists largely of salt or sandy desert, the Dasht-i-Kavir in the north and the Dasht-i-Lut in the south being the two chief desert areas.

Dasht-i-Kavir. The former extends for about four hundred miles from east to west and for eighty to one hundred and fifty miles from north to south. Edged with sand, its greater portion is impregnated with salt; and the rapid evaporation in the intense heat of summer of the large volume of water draining into it from streams which are practically all saline constantly increases the proportion of salt. When dry, the surface of the desert is generally passable, though sometimes it is so honeycombed as to make it very difficult to traverse. When wet, it becomes a quagmire in which men and animals sink and cannot move. Caravans cross it from north to south during the winter, but only at the utmost speed, owing to the great danger of being caught by rain. In summer the great heat prevents any traffic.

DESERT AND COAST LINE

The Dasht-i-Lut extends for about four hundred miles **Dasht-i-Lut.**
from north to south and for eighty to one hundred and fifty
miles from east to west. Though in one part there are large
salt marshes and almost everywhere some eight or nine inches
below the surface a substratum of hard rock salt, this desert
is mainly covered with expanses of sand or gravel and with
curiously shaped clay bluffs. It differs from the *Kavir* in
that it is sprinkled in places with thorny shrubs which afford
grazing for camels. Blown by the wind, its sand is formed
into billows, mounds and hills which are constantly shifting
and eddying, and its surface is heated by the sun till it feels
like incandescent metal. The lack of water is, moreover,
aggravated by the almost constant hot wind which sucks
every atom of moisture from man and beast. In spite of its
difficulties and dangers, however, there are a few recognised
caravan routes across it.

Notwithstanding her two sea frontiers, Persia really has few **Coasts and**
natural facilities for maritime traffic. The coast line of the **ports.**
Caspian stretches in a series of shallow indentations without
a break and is devoid of natural harbours. The lagoons,
with the exception of that at Enzeli, are shallow, and the
mouths of the rivers are obstructed by sand-bars. The only
important port is Enzeli (Pahlevi as it is now called), whose
artificial harbour requires constant dredging to keep it open.
Besides Mohammerah on the Shatt-al-Arab, the chief ports
on the south coast are Bushire, Lingeh and Bandar Abbas,
where, owing to the gradual shelving of the muddy or sandy
sea floor, ships have to anchor three to seven miles out in
open roadsteads.

At the head of the Persian Gulf the coast line is low and
marshy, liable to flood and fringed with mud-banks caused
by the river silt which is gradually and slowly encroaching
on the sea. To the southward of this alluvial plain, except
for a short distance where the mountains fall directly into
the sea, there is a belt of low-lying land of varying width
situated between the sea and the southern rim of the main
plateau. The surface of this plain is frequently broken up
by a series of subsidiary ridges of hills, and its character varies
from great fertility to extensive mud-flats, salt marshes or
sandy wastes. It is one of the hottest regions in the world.

The climate of Persia naturally varies with the locality **Climate.**
and, although some of the chief characteristics of different
areas are given below, they can only be taken as a very general
guide.

Climate. In the Caspian provinces, though the range of temperature is moderate, the rain is variable and the climate is very changeable. In the damp heat of summer the swarms of mosquitoes render the unhealthy lowlands almost uninhabitable, while on the lower slopes of the mountains the horse flies practically forbid travelling except at night. From November to the middle of April, however, the climate is temperate and healthy. Above 3,000 feet the climate is good, being cooler in summer and milder in winter than at the same altitudes elsewhere in the country. The prevailing winds are northerly, that from the north-west usually bringing rain.

In the northern half of the Persian plateau there are extreme ranges of temperature, but the atmosphere is dry, clear and generally invigorating. The transition from spring to summer and from summer to autumn is very sudden, while from December to February snow falls everywhere at frequent intervals and lies on the higher mountain ranges till June or July. Up to an altitude of about 6,000 feet, however, the sun is so powerful that, even in the coldest weather, it raises the temperature above freezing point and thaws the snow. Travelling in winter is arduous and difficult, while during the thaw in early spring much of the country is so waterlogged and deep in mud as to be impassable for anything but the lightest traffic. The hottest months are July and August, when the average maximum shade temperature is 105° F. But the dryness of the atmosphere somewhat mitigates the heat, and the nights, when the temperature usually drops at least thirty degrees, are cool. The worst features of the summer are the dust, glare and flies. The rainfall, which is scanty and very variable, generally occurs in November, March and April and the prevailing winds follow the direction of the mountain ranges, namely north-west and south-east. Cold gales are frequent in the winter, and throughout the summer there is usually a breeze except in the early mornings.

In Southern Persia the country is divided by the inhabitants into two regions, *sardsir* and *garmsir* (i.e., cold and hot areas), the latter consisting of the belt of land between the sea and the inland plateau. In the former region the general climatic characteristics are much as they are farther north, with the differences in temperature due to the more southern latitude. In the *garmsir*, which includes the Persian Gulf littoral, the intense heat of summer and autumn is aggravated by the humidity of the atmosphere and the dust raised by every wind. All movement by day is to be avoided as far as possible, though at night the temperature drops only a few degrees. In the winter the cold is never great, snow seldom falls and it is then and in the early spring that the rain, which is almost always accompanied by a south-east wind, generally falls. At sea, bad weather generally prevails during January and February and during the monsoon from the middle of June to the middle of September.

In Persian Baluchistan also the climatic conditions are most varied, the coast district of Makran being extremely hot, steamy and unhealthy, while the farther north and higher one goes the cooler and healthier it becomes.

Seistan has practically only two seasons, for the transition between summer and winter is extraordinarily rapid. Summer sets in about the beginning of April. May and the first half of June are very hot and trying, especially as, in the total absence of wind, mosquitoes and other winged insects abound. At the beginning or middle of June " the wind of 120 days " sets in and blows almost continually till about the end of September. In direction north by west, its velocity has been registered up to seventy-two miles an hour. Its effect is, however, beneficent for, although causing great discomfort from dust and noise, it blows away all the insects, mitigates the heat and clears away much disease. The cold in winter is often very severe, and blizzards are frequent from January to March. During the winter there are occasional showers of rain, but the total fall averages less than three inches annually.

With the exception of the northern and southern coasts, Persia is not unhealthy and the sun is a powerful disinfecting agency. A water supply almost invariably polluted and a total disregard for sanitary precautions cause a considerable amount of disease, whose infection is spread by flying insects and vermin, while in several areas the bite of the latter causes severe fever or blood-poisoning. Under these conditions epidemics frequently cause great mortality and the death rate among infants and children is always very high. Consequently, to obtain any immunity from disease, precautionary measures —such as inoculation, sterilisation of water, milk, vegetables and fruit, the use of mosquito nets and vermicides—are absolutely necessary.

The fact that mountain ranges, desert areas, harbourless coasts and climatic extremes all combine to render Persia not too easy of access, renders the position and extent of the communications in the country of special importance. In

_{Road communications.}

Road communications.

ancient times the chief highway between west and east ran from the Mediterranean via Babylonia through the defiles of the Zagros mountains to Hamadan and past what is now Tehran to Bactria (Northern Afghanistan). During the reign of Darius a royal road ran from Sardes in Asia Minor to Susa,* the Persian capital; and remains can still be traced of roads which evidently connected the chief cities of the Achaemenian Empire. But little appears to have been done by subsequent rulers to maintain these roads, and in mediaeval times the main trade thoroughfare from Europe entered Persia by what is still the line of easiest access from Europe, namely via Tabriz, whence it passed Yezd and Kerman on its way to the great trade market at Hormuz.

In more modern times Persian rulers have shown little inclination to improve communications, though without such improvement a real development of the country and its resources is impossible. For this, no doubt, the great initial financial outlay and the small immediate return, which the great distances, engineering difficulties and sparse population involve, are largely reponsible; as well as the fact that made roads would be distinctly unpopular as implying tolls.

In 1914 the metalled roads in the whole of Persia did not exceed a total of one thousand miles, and of that total Russian effort and Russian money were responsible for the greater proportion. Practically all such roads were in the northern parts of Persia, which, besides being in the so-called Russian sphere, included the richest provinces in the country. The following were the main roads which were suitable for wheeled traffic, and on two or three of them motor vehicles had begun to ply:—Julfa–Tabriz, Tabriz–Urmia, Enzeli–Kazvin–Tehran, Kazvin–Hamadan, Tehran–Shahrud–Meshed, Askabad–Meshed, Meshed–Afghan frontier towards Herat, and Tehran–Qum–Isfahan–Shiraz. In addition there were various good camel roads which were practicable for field artillery and passable in places for wheeled traffic, as for instance the roads from Kashan to Yezd and Kerman, and from the Indo-Persian frontier through Seistan to Meshed. But the remaining roads were either caravan routes or mule tracks which had been in existence from time immemorial and were frequently only natural paths worn smooth by generations of traffic. In both cases long stretches of sand, loose boulders and stones, slippery rocks, narrow defiles and steep gradients were common

---

* Its ruins are some forty miles in a north-westerly direction from Shushtar.

characteristics; and traffic was seldom able to deviate from the road owing to the mountain slopes or the irrigation cuts. The only made caravan road was one from Ahwaz to Isfahan, which was generally called the Lynch road, after the British firm who made it and who maintained it in partnership with the chiefs of the Bakhtiari tribes.

<small>Railways.</small> The only railway, save for a short line from Tehran to a shrine six miles distant, was the one from Julfa to Tabriz which the Russians had begun to construct in 1913. From 1865 onwards many railway concessions in Persia had been granted to foreigners, but attempts to develop them had all been unsuccessful, generally owing to Russian opposition.

On the 16th September 1888, the Shah in an autograph rescript—which he directed the Minister for Foreign Affairs to hand over to the British Minister—confirmed a former promise by which H.M. Government were to receive a priority over others in the construction of a southern railway to Tehran, and he said positively that no southern railway would be granted to any foreign country without consulting with the British Government. By the Russo-Persian agreement of the 11th November, 1890, the Persian Government engaged that no railways should be constructed in Persia for ten years; and the term of this engagement was prolonged till near the outbreak of war. But, in April, 1900, the British Chargé d'Affaires at Tehran received an assurance, in reply to an official note to the Persian Minister for Foreign Affairs, that, though for the next ten years the question of railway concessions would not arise owing to the agreement with Russia, the Shah regarded the rescript of 1888 as binding. The British position was strengthened by the Anglo-Russian Convention of 1907, under which Russia undertook not to oppose concessions supported by H.M. Government in the British sphere, nor in the neutral zone without discussion. Up till the outbreak of war neither Great Britain nor Russia made any use of their privileges, though Russia had agreed with Germany to link up the Baghdad-Khaniqin railway with Tehran, and was talking of constructing a line from Baku, through Resht, Tehran and Isfahan, to Yezd and Kerman.

<small>Telegraphic communications.</small> In comparison with her other means of communication Persia is well equipped with telegraph lines, an advantage which she owed in the first place to the pressing need for more rapid communication with India which Great Britain experienced at the time of the Indian Mutiny. An attempt to lay a cable down the Red Sea in 1859 having failed, the

Telegraphic communications. British Government arranged with Turkey and Persia to continue to India the line which the former country was about to construct to Baghdad. By 1864, in face of considerable obstacles, depredations and local obstructions—which were only surmounted by the tact and capacity of the British engineers—a single line was laid via Kermanshah, Hamadan and Tehran, and thence via Isfahan and Shiraz, to Bushire where it connected with a submarine cable from India via Jask. In the same year a non-British line from Tehran to Tabriz was continued to Julfa, thus affording an alternative route through Russian territory. The Persian Government and people were quick to realise the great benefit which the telegraph lines conferred on the country, and considerable extensions in them have since taken place.* Timely information of the situation in distant provinces has minimised the danger from revolts and has enabled the Government to maintain more effective control, while to the people generally, as a means of representing their views to the Shah and his Ministers, the telegraph has meant some security against tyranny and oppression. The British telegraph officials scattered through the country have, moreover, been a distinct power for good, and their services to the Persian Government in cases where accurate information has been of value can hardly be exaggerated. It is interesting to note that, owing to the popular supposition that the telegraph wires end at the foot of the Shah's throne, telegraph offices share the privilege with shrines, mosques, royal stables and foreign legations or consulates of being places of sanctuary, where, according to the Persian custom, malefactors and political refugees can claim immunity from arrest.

Population. With an area about three times the size of France, Persia has a population which has been roughly estimated at ten millions. Of these about a quarter reside in something like one hundred towns, a quarter are nomads and the remaining half inhabit villages. The proportion of cultivated land to wilderness and desert is small and is, moreover, said to be shrinking. There is no doubt that in former days the land maintained a much larger population; and experts consider that, under more scientific methods of water conservancy,

---

* In 1914, there were nearly 7,000 miles of line open, of which about 4,000 were Persian, worked by a Persian staff. The Tehran–Julfa line was worked by the Indo-European Telegraph Company; and the remainder were worked by the Indo-European Telegraph Department (a Government of India concern) either on behalf of the British Government under certain conventions or on behalf of the Persian Government.

irrigation and cultivation, an enormous development of agriculture is possible. At present, wheat, rice and barley are grown in more than sufficient quantities for the country's needs, and the constant famines are due to transportation difficulties and not to crop failures or shortage. Cotton, tobacco, opium, grapes, dates and melons are also grown in considerable quantities and there is a little maize, millet, sugar, indigo and henna. Agricultural supplies.

The Russian garrisons of Trans-Caspia and Turkestan drew most of their supplies from Persia, and there was a considerable export of grain and sheep from Azerbaijan. It was thus evident that a large military force could easily find subsistence in Northern Persia, while it was also estimated that a force of some size could supply itself while traversing South Persia.

No satisfactory estimate is possible of the number of animals in the country. But very many horses, mules, camels, donkeys and bullocks are bred for transport purposes, cattle are kept wherever there is sufficient grazing, and there are large numbers of sheep and goats. Animals.

Manufactures are practically limited to carpets and shawls and the domestic trade of the country is unimportant. Manufactures

The unit of money is the kran, whose value varies with the price of silver. It was worth about fourpence-halfpenny in 1914 and twenty-two krans went to the gold toman, which was, however, seldom in circulation. The Imperial Bank of Persia, one of the two banks in the country, was incorporated by Royal British Charter in 1889. It had the right to issue bank notes and to advance money to a limited extent to the Persian Government. It had branches in all the important towns and was the most important British institution in the country. The other bank was Russian, virtually a Russian Government institution and, also with branches in all the important towns, filled an important part in Russian policy. Finance.

Persia is said to be very rich in minerals, of which the most important are coal, copper, lead, iron, manganese, zinc, nickel, cobalt and petroleum. Owing, however, to scarcity of water and transport difficulties, attempts by Europeans to work the mines have not been successful, with the sole exception of the petroleum field east-south-east of Shushtar. This is worked by the Anglo-Persian Oil Company under a concession from the Persian Government and subsidiary financial arrangements with the Bakhtiari khans and the Shaikh of Mohammerah. The British Government, with a considerable financial interest in the company, has a voice in the direction of its general policy. Minerals.

Social, Military and Religious.

Persian characteristics. In spite of the many waves of conquering invaders who in the past have swept over Persia leaving their mark on the inhabitants, the descendants of the original Caucasian stock still form about seven-tenths of the population; and, though they show some of the physical characteristics of the invaders, they have retained in a great degree the strongly marked idiosyncracies of the original national character. Herodotus described the ancient Persians as brave, lively, spirited, capable of sharp sayings and repartees, but vain, weak, impulsive and hopelessly servile towards their lords. We are also told that in those days the Persian youth was brought up to ride, to speak the truth and to draw the bow. The late Lord Curzon, in the best general account that has been written of the country, speaks of the Persian character as presenting many complex features, elsewhere rarely united in the same individual, and he says that the Persians present a marked racial difference to the inhabitants of neighbouring countries. It is probably for these reasons that opinions regarding their character have varied and that many Europeans who have lived in the country find it rather difficult to explain why they like its people.

All authorities admit their wit, quickness of mind, pleasant manners, agreeable address, amusing conversation, hospitality,* dignity and ready assimilation of new ideas. But most people who have had dealings with them have come to the conclusion that they lack many of the qualities which are elsewhere held most honourable; and there appears to be little doubt that, generally speaking, they are vain, unpractical and lacking in energy and stability of purpose, while it is quite unsafe to rely on their words and actions. As Lord Curzon says, the one gift with which they can be credited on a truly heroic scale is their faculty for imaginative utterance. It must be remembered, however, that in few oriental countries have the standards of integrity and morality kept pace with those of western civilisation, and that the corrupt and despotic form of government and landlordism to which Persians have been long subjected explains the almost universal habit of prevarication, whose use in self-defence is, moreover, not confined to Persia. Many modern Persians are what we should term cowards, as they have adopted a line of philosophy which

---

* The Persian, of whatever rank in life, shines most as a host. He is ideal in this respect, as he delights in dispensing hospitality, and it is this trait in the Persian character, combined with a strong sense of humour, which has usually most attracted visitors to the country.

POPULATION

justifies them in their own eyes in fleeing from danger, both physical and moral. Lord Curzon says that, while as individuals they present many attractive features, as a community they are wholly wanting in elements of real nobility or grandeur. He offers the opinion, however, that history shows that their irrepressible vitality, imitativeness and freedom from prejudice or bigotry, hold out for the country possible chances of redemption. One of the most apt illustrations of the Persian character is furnished by General Dunsterville in "The Adventures of Dunsterforce," when he says that though all Persians are brought up on the wisdom of Saadi and other deep and attractive thinkers—and there is not a problem in life that has not its solution in their writings—they only quote, and are never guided by, them.

Generally speaking, the inhabitants of the country may be divided into five classes:—the courtiers, nobles, large landowners and provincial governors; the religious leaders; the merchants; the artisans and shopkeepers; and the peasants and labourers. The strength of the nation lies chiefly in her enterprising mercantile class, her ingenious and industrious artisans and her hardy and laborious peasants. Men of humble origin frequently rise to high position, a fact which, combined with the brotherhood of Islam, has given rise to a strong democratic instinct in the country. On the other hand, it has also conduced to the toleration of a corrupt administration, as every man has felt that it might be his turn one day to benefit thereby. *Classes.*

There are no proper statistics of the numbers of the population, but, as the normal annual increase is said to be less than one per cent., the estimate made in 1910 of a total population of 10,300,000 is still generally accepted. The distribution of population varies greatly, depending mainly on the water supply, the most thickly populated districts in 1914 being Urmia and the Caspian deltas. Tehran and Tabriz, the two largest towns, each had populations of over 200,000; Isfahan, Kermanshah, Meshed, Kerman, Shiraz, Yezd and Khoi populations of sixty to eighty thousand; about fifteen other towns had each over twenty thousand inhabitants; and the largest villages contained about three hundred houses, averaging four or five persons to a house. *Distribution of population.*

The aboriginal races number some seven and a half million, which include, besides the Persians proper who speak a modern form of the ancient Indo-Germanic Persian language, about a million Kurds, Laks and Lurs who speak various old Persian *Races.*

dialects. Of immigrant races there are about two million Turki, over three hundred thousand Arabs, about a hundred thousand gipsies and a considerable number of Baluchis, Hazaras, Chaldaeans, Armenians and Jews, with some negroes and a small colony of Hindus (in Kerman).

Persians proper. Of the Persians proper, or Farsi, who are practically all *Shiahs*, the upper classes and townspeople are of poor physique, due to their indolent and sedentary habits and to their addiction to opium and vice. Of medium height and pale complexion, they are frequently handsome. The peasantry, coarser featured, possess great physical strength and endurance, resemble the townspeople in mental qualities and intelligence, and are hardworking and patient. Although their manner of life has remained unaltered for generations, their material prosperity compares very favourably with that of the peasantry of neighbouring countries.

Kurds. The Kurds are a warlike, pastoral and semi-nomadic people, residing for the most part in the north-west. Their generally discordant relations with their Persian masters are as much due to the religious hatred which as *Sunnis* they bear to the *Shiahs* as to Persian persecution and misgovernment. They are governed by the chiefs of their tribes and pay very few taxes, but are expected to furnish armed contingents for Government service whenever demanded. Inter-tribal feuds cause frequent strife, brigandage is common, and Turkish frontier officials constantly stirred them up against the Persian Government. They are good riders and marksmen, but require training and discipline to make efficient soldiers.

Laks. The Laks, who are kindred to the Kurds, are nomads dispersed about Kazvin, Mazanderan and Fars, and are chiefly distinguished as being expert thieves.

Lurs. Also akin to the Kurds and under tribal government are the Lurs inhabitating the mountainous districts of the west and south-west, their chief tribes being the Faili, the Bakhtiari, the Kuhgalu and the Mamassani. Wiry, enduring and warlike, they are constantly fighting among themselves, and their marauding habits render their districts unsafe for travelling. Like the Kurds they dislike and despise the Persians. While they all profess to trust the word of the British, the Bakhtiaris especially have generally not only maintained friendly relations with us, but have come to rely on our support.

Turki. The Turki, who predominate in the districts between Gilan and Kurdistan, are found in all parts of the country as nomads, cattle-breeders and cultivators and also in the towns under chiefs appointed by the Shah. Turki landowners and peasantry alike differ from the Farsi and show their Turco-Tartar origin by their broad faces, sturdy build and by their manners and ways which savour more of the Mongol than of the Aryan. Except that they are not as addicted to opium, they have all the bad without the redeeming qualities of the Farsi, between whom and them there is a strong mutual antipathy. They are accustomed to arms and take readily to military service, but have a greater taste for raiding than for sustained fighting. The majority of them are *Shiahs*.

Arabs inhabit the shores of the Persian Gulf and Arabistan as far as Dizful; two of the five Khamseh tribes in Fars are Arab; and there are Arab tribes scattered in Khurasan and elsewhere. They are mobile to a remarkable degree and are fairly well armed, but are more renowned as marauders than soldiers. *Arabs.*

It was from these tribes, aboriginal and immigrant, that came the irregular cavalry which from time long past have formed the main part of Persia's military strength. The tribal chieftains, preserving a nominal independence on the feudal basis of a military contribution, kept up large studs of well-bred horses and encouraged horsemanship, warlike training and patriotism among their followers till Fateh Ali Shah, at the beginning of the nineteenth century, set himself to disintegrate their power and authority. He succeeded only too well. Subsequent Shahs generally followed the same policy, with the result that this tribal military reserve has practically ceased to exist. Moreover, the sympathies of the tribesmen were so alienated by the methods adopted towards them that by 1914 many of them, and especially those who cherished the traditions of their foreign origin, were ready to welcome foreign assistance if it enabled them to throw off the Persian yoke. *Tribal irregular cavalry.*

Fateh Ali's action was partly due to the reliance he placed on organising a regular Persian army, trained and disciplined on the European model. Two centuries previously the Sherley brothers had organised a large force of infantry armed with muskets, but for the most part the army remained a loose collection of irregular cavalry contingents, such as that with which Nadir invaded India. Fateh Ali's heir Abbas Mirza, Governor-General of Azerbaijan, came to the conclusion that without foreign assistance his military forces could make no headway against the Russians; and he personally did much to promote the efforts of the foreign military instructors. *Persian military forces in 19th Century*

Neither he nor any of the Shahs who succeeded him, however, appear to have realised that many other reforms, besides one in military training, were necessary before the army could become efficient.

Foreign military missions. In 1810 the French military mission sent by Napoleon was replaced by a British mission from India, among whose officers Christie, Lindsay-Bethune, Monteith and Willock have left a distinguished record. Majors D'Arcy Todd and Hart also did fine military service in Persia about this period, the latter's influence over the Shah, the heir-apparent and the Persian soldiery being so great that he held a position in the country, till his death there in 1830, which was unequalled by any other foreign officer. Persia, however, gained almost nothing in military strength from their employment; not from the fault of the British personnel or of the Persian rank and file—who proved to be docile, intelligent and sufficiently courageous—but owing to the uselessness and inefficiency of the Persian officers and to the corruption and lack of proper system of the administration. In 1815 a dispute between the two Governments over the subsidy led to the departure of most of the British personnel; but in 1834 another large military mission from India arrived in Persia, among its officers being Shiel, Rawlinson, Passmore, D'Arcy Todd and Stoddart, all of whom gained distinction there. Within six months of their arrival, however, Muhammad became Shah and, actuated by Russian influence and his own desire to invade Afghanistan, not only failed to give them the necessary support but treated them with growing hostility and contumely till they all left the country with Mr. McNeill in 1838, without having been able to effect as much good as they might have. The different British officers and non-commissioned officers who had so far served Persia left a fine military tradition behind them, which in 1861, 1870 and 1874, after the efforts of other European military officers had proved unsuccessful, prompted further Persian requests for British military instructors. But the Governments in India and London, displaying indifference, refused the requests. In 1879 an Austrian military mission arrived in the country, and the Russians started to organise the Persian Cossack force which was to become a significant emblem of Russian ascendancy.

Most European military officers who have been employed in Persia have held but a poor opinion of the military quality of its inhabitants. They all agree as to the lack of the necessary moral and military attributes of the officer class. Some of those best qualified to judge consider that the real remedy lies in the formation of irregular tribal corps.

In 1914 the regular infantry numbered about 13,000 under arms and scattered in many detachments. The rank and file were generally unpaid, untrained and badly clothed, being consequently compelled to eke out a livelihood by casual labour, while the officers were useless, their appointment being solely due to purchase or patronage without any regard to their age or efficiency. The cavalry was organised almost entirely on a tribal basis, the men serving under their own leaders and supplying their own horses, arms and equipment. They served in detachments in their own districts and, though part of them were permanently employed to protect the main routes, the majority were only called out as their services were required. Their numbers amounted to about 38,000—only a fraction of the total force the tribes could collect if they desired —and though most of them were armed with breech-loading rifles, these were frequently in bad repair, while ammunition was generally scanty. They were unlikely, in any case, to agree to serve out of their own districts, but would certainly not do so to repel a foreign invader. The artillery consisted of about five or six thousand men and there were in the country about fifty breech-loading and one hundred muzzle-loading field and mountain guns, but of these probably only half would be found fit for service. There were a few machine guns. In fact, the regular army, maintained on a form of conscription, was entirely negligible as a military instrument. *Persian Army, 1914.*

The Persian Cossack Brigade, with about thirty Russian officers and non-commissioned officers, totalled 3,500 or more. It was organised in four cavalry regiments, four infantry companies, one horse and two mountain batteries and a machine gun detachment, and its armament was modern. Its headquarters were at Tehran, but it furnished many detachments and a considerable proportion of the men were always on furlough. It was fairly well disciplined and drilled, but did little field training and had no transport. Consequently, though useful for garrison duties, it was hardly capable of taking the field and was, in any case, unfit to cope with foreign regular troops. Though, in 1914, the best military force in Persia, it had been created by Russia as a political rather than a military weapon. Its Russian officers ensured that its military efficiency should not become so high as to constitute a danger to Russian plans and that its standing as a personal force of the Shah, directly subordinate to him and not to his *Cossack Brigade.*

Ministers, should be maintained. Though it thus gained strong support, as affording security for the Royal person and throne, it was disliked by Persian politicians as furthering Russian dominance and by the Persian public owing to the overbearing conduct of its Russian officers and the extortionate habits of its men. Its maintenance expenses were a first charge on the northern customs duties.

Gendarmerie. The gendarmerie, whose reorganisation under Swedish officers commenced in 1911, consisted of six regiments, three of which had two battalions. At the beginning of 1914 their numbers totalled 36 Swedish officers and about 6,000 mounted and dismounted Persians, armed with Mauser carbines, four mountain guns and about a dozen machine guns. Their duty was to maintain internal security and to collect the revenue, and they were located in the districts of Tehran, Fars, Kerman, Isfahan and Kazvin. The Swedish officers were keen and capable, but their lack of knowledge of the people and the language led them to make several mistakes. They got insufficient assistance and support from the Persian officers, who if left to themselves frequently practised tyranny and extortion and were generally useless as leaders. In spite of financial stringency and Russian hostility the force became fairly efficient and, though its discipline left something to be desired, conducted itself well in fights with tribesmen in 1913 and 1914. In the spring of the latter year, however, the senior Swedish officer, Colonel Hjalmarsen, left Persia and was followed in the next three or four months by most of his Swedish regular officers. Those who remained developed at any rate anti-Russian if not pro-German sentiments, and the force as a whole deteriorated.

Religion. The great majority of Persia's inhabitants belong to the *Shiah* sect of Islam. They look to the resurrection of the Twelfth Imam, who disappeared from earth without leaving a successor in A.D. 873–4, to restore and establish the pure Mahomedan faith; and the question of the Caliphate had no religious interest for them. In fact, there is a vital difference of principle between them and the *Sunnis*. Though always prevalent in Persia, the *Shiah* doctrine was by no means universal till about A.D. 1500, when Ismail Shah established it as a means of giving the country unity, coherence and a strong motive for resisting Turkish aggression. Consequently, by interposing a religious barrier between the *Sunnis* to west and east of her respectively, Persia proved a hindrance to Pan-Islamic schemes till, after the revolutions in Turkey and Persia, Pan-Islamism made use of anti-foreign propaganda to lessen the antagonism to it. Pending the reappearance of the Twelfth Imam, his authority is vested in *mujtahids*, of whom the leading ones reside in Najaf, Karbala and Samarra in Mesopotamia. There are, however, many minor *mujtahids* residing in Persia whose influence generally suffers by association with the Government, more especially as since the extinction of the Safawi dynasty no Shah has been admitted to have any claim to religious control. Owing to this the *mujtahids* have attained considerable independent power and jurisdiction, which had in fact been one of the few checks on the autocratic rule of the Shahs. Anti-foreign motives impelled them to support the Constitutional movement, but their reactionary and religious impulses have been a hindrance to their profitable participation in the administration.

Other Mahomedan sects in the country are the *Bahais* (formerly *Babis*), the *Ismailis* (the "Assassins" of the Middle Ages), the *Sufis* (or mystics), and the *Ali Elahis* (dissenters). The first named and most important was founded by a pretended *Mahdi*, known as the *Báb*, the revolt of whose followers gave considerable trouble in the reign of Nasir-ud-Din. Since those days the movement has grown considerably, not only in Persia but in Europe, and especially in the United States of America. Though the sect is now immune in Persia from Government persecution, the hostility between its followers and the *Shiah* priesthood has continued to be a frequent source of disorder.

Historical.

Few nations can lay claim to as long and as stormy a history as Persia or have in the past contributed as much to the spiritual, intellectual and artistic wealth of the human race. Frequently overrun by invading armies and held in long-enduring subjection, Persia as frequently recovered, regained lost territory and maintained her independence; though, when external aggression ceased, she generally fell a prey to internal warfare. It is all the more noteworthy that in the arts of peace her influence was so considerable. Christianity, Judaism and Islam are all indebted to a greater or less extent to Zoroaster and other Persian spiritual leaders and thinkers; her art and poetry are world-renowned; mediaeval Europe and Asia owed to her nearly all that was known of philosophy and medicine; and even to-day the language, thought and culture of the Eastern Mahomedan are redolent of Persia.

Early history.
Persia first rose to greatness in the sixth century B.C. when Cyrus I founded the Achaemenian dynasty, under which the boundaries of the Empire were extended from the Punjab in the east to the frontiers of European Greece in the west. After the defeats of Marathon, Plataea and Salamis and the death of the last Darius, Persia was invaded and conquered by Alexander the Great, and remained under Greek and then Parthian rule for over five hundred years. In the third century A.D. Ardashir drove out the Parthians, restored the power and religion (Zoroastrian) of the Persians and founded the Sasanian dynasty. Under Sasanian rule Persia regained the Achaemenian empire almost in its entirety, disputed with Rome the sovereignty of the Middle East with considerable measure of success, and broke the power of the Arabs by the conquest of Yemen.

In the seventh century, however, Persia, showing signs of disintegration, succumbed to the Arabs and the new-found faith of Islam. Nevertheless, the intellectual superiority of the Persians enabled them before long to assert and maintain a considerable influence at the court of the Caliphs, till the advent in the eleventh century of the Seljuk Turks. Under the Seljuk princes Islam was again united beneath a single powerful sway, which governed from Samarkand to the Mediterranean and endured till the middle of the thirteenth century. Hulagu and his Mongols then captured Baghdad and, devastating the country, dealt the Moslem world a blow from which it never recovered.

Hulagu became the first Il-Khan of Persia. He was succeeded by four generations of his offspring. These, prompted in the first place by their enmity to Islam, maintained a friendly intercourse with the crusading Powers of Europe, and, in their desire to repair the devastation wrought by the invasions of their forbears, opened their dominions to foreigners. Among notable visitors to Persia at this period were Marco Polo and the mission, under Geoffrey de Langley, despatched by Edward I of England. The Mongols settled in Persia, became gradually absorbed by its inhabitants and, following the lead of Ghazan, Hulagu's great-grandson, turned Moslem. Ghazan himself was a good and enlightened ruler who instituted many administrative reforms. But the power of his successors gradually decayed and they had been replaced by several minor dynasties by the end of the fourteenth century, when the second great Turco-Tartar invasion under Timur the Lame devastated Western Asia. Timur's descendants were, however, unable to hold the vast Empire he had created, and a great part of it fell under Turkoman dominion till, at the beginning of the sixteenth century, Ismail founded the Safawi dynasty and re-established Persia as an independent kingdom.

The Persian *Shiahs* have always held that the true succession to Muhammad descended through the house of Ali (cousin and son-in-law of the Prophet), and they consequently welcomed with delight the accession to power of a Shah who was descended from Ali through the Seventh Imam. Ismail, whom they regarded both as Saint and King, established the *Shiah* doctrine as the State religion, an act which has had many important political results. It at once brought Persia into conflict with her *Sunni* neighbours, the Uzbegs and the Ottoman Turks. With the latter, indeed, the feud thus originated has been the cause of intermittent warfare or discordant relations practically ever since, while at the time it also had the effect of leading certain European Powers to look to Persia as their main hope against Turkish aggression. Among Ismail's successors, his great-grandson Abbas I (1587–1629) stands out as a courageous, great and enlightened ruler, whose memory is more respected and beloved in Persia than that of any other of her monarchs. It was during his reign that there began between England and Persia those commercial relations which for over two hundred years " superseded and filled the place of diplomatic communications, factors and agents acting the part of envoys and plenipotentiaries, and firmans and charters being substituted for treaties and alliances . . . . . and worthy of remembrance for the lustre which they shed upon the English name."* {Commencement of English relations with Persia.}

The trade ventures to Persia through Russia of the British Moscovy Company in the middle of the sixteenth century had been abandoned as too difficult and dangerous to be profitable, and the Portuguese still held their eastern monopoly, when the factors of the East India Company in 1614 obtained from the Shah firmans to trade, largely owing to the influence at the Persian Court of Sir Robert Sherley. He and his brother (Sir Anthony), arriving in Persia in 1598, had taken service under Shah Abbas, who utilised their services in reorganising his army and in political and trade missions to Europe. Sir Anthony Sherley only remained in Persian service for a few years, but Sir Robert gained great distinction, during the course of nearly thirty years, both in the wars with Turkey

---

* " Persia " by Hon. G. N. Curzon.

English relations with Persia. and in other ways. In 1627, however, his connection with the second British embassy to Persia, under Sir Dodmore Cotton, was largely responsible for its failure; and in the same year both he and Cotton died at Kazvin.

The Portuguese strove by arms to prevent British interference with their monopoly in the Persian Gulf, but in 1620 the Portuguese fleet was beaten off Jask by the ships of the East India Company; and in 1622 a combined Anglo-Persian naval and military force captured the Portuguese forts at Qishm and Hormuz. Then followed an agreement with the Shah under which the East India Company undertook "to keep two men of war constantly to defend the Gulf," and Bandar Abbas became the headquarters of the foreign trade in the Gulf. The Portuguese, whose power and influence were on the wane, were succeeded first by the Dutch and then by the French, both to become for a term keen trade competitors with the British.

Towards the close of his reign Shah Abbas, in fear of deposition by one of his sons or of other capable male members of his family, was guilty of great cruelty towards them. He also ordered that they were to be brought up in the harem and not to be trained to arms. This policy proved fatal to his dynasty, for his successors in his own line proved inept and degenerate, and it was only owing to the reverence felt by the Persians for the sacred Safawi house that their cowardice, effeminacy and corruption were at all tolerated. Further results were that the Afghans, throwing off their allegiance to the Shah, successfully invaded Central Persia in 1722, the Russians occupied part of the Caspian provinces and the Turks invaded Georgia.

Russian aggression. From their very commencement the transactions of Russia with Persia have been disingenuous. The contemptuous dismissal in 1664 by Shah Abbas of a Russian mission—in reality a party of merchants posing as an embassy to evade customs dues—led to reprisals in the shape of a Cossack raid on Mazanderan. In 1708 and 1715 semi-commercial embassies sent by Peter the Great, though regarded with suspicion, met with an honourable reception. In 1722, on the pretext of redressing Russian grievances and of aiding the Shah against the Afghans, Peter occupied Derbend with a Russian army, being only kept from further aggression by the wrecking of his flotilla and fear of the Turks. His forces then, at Persian request, occupied Resht and part of Gilan to save them from the Afghans; but in 1723 he bombarded and seized Baku, forestalling the Turks, who in agreement with Russia had invaded Georgia. In the same year, in return for the cession to Russia of the Caspian provinces, Peter pledged himself to expel the Afghans from Persia. But he made no attempt to fulfil his pledge, and in 1724 he came to an agreement with Turkey for the partition between them of some of the most valuable Persian provinces. Turkey duly seized the greater part of Western Persia which had been allotted to her, but Russia, owing to Peter's death in 1725, took no steps to occupy her portion, i.e., the Caspian provinces. As his action showed, Peter the Great had very clearly defined ideas of Russian expansion in Central Asia and it is, therefore, scarcely to be wondered at that the document known as his will is to this day regarded in Persia as genuine and a true presentment of Russian aspirations.*

In 1730 the Afghans were finally expelled from Persia by Nadir, an adventurer who had risen to the command of the Shah's army and who after six years more of anarchy, during which he consolidated his position, proclaimed himself Shah. Before he was assassinated in 1747 he had regained the provinces lost to Turkey, reconquered Afghanistan, invaded India and captured Khiva, while he also induced the Russians to evacuate the Caspian provinces which they had found to be most unhealthy. He also made a bid, with some measure of success, for sea power both in the Persian Gulf and the Caspian. He was a great leader who did much to restore the power and prestige of Persia, but he was never popular owing to his intense hostility to the *Shiah* doctrine, which as a *Sunni* he regarded as heresy. [Persia under Nadir, 1736-1747.]

On his death another period of anarchy ensued, in which the three rival clans, Zand, Qajar and Bakhtiari contended for the throne. The first of these finally gained the upper hand and its representative, the humane and enlightened Karim Khan, reigned for nearly thirty years and gave the country a much needed rest. During his reign the British East India Company, which had been obliged to close its trading establishments at Isfahan and Bandar Abbas during the anarchy following the Afghan invasion, opened factories at Bushire and Basra, the latter being in Persian possession from 1776 to 1779. Internal feuds in the Zand family following on Karim Khan's death gave the Qajar tribe its opportunity. After

---

* It contained these words: "Hasten the decadence of Persia, penetrate to the Persian Gulf, re-establish the ancient commerce of the Levant, and advance to the Indies, which are the treasure-house of the world."

22 OPERATIONS IN PERSIA

Foundation of Qajar dynasty. fifteen years of strife its representative, the eunuch Agha Muhammad Khan, crushed the Zand leader and founded the Qajar dynasty, which was still in power in 1914.

On the death of Nadir, Georgia, throwing off the Persian yoke, had annexed territory up to the river Aras and in 1793 had formed an offensive and defensive alliance with Russia. Two years later, Agha Muhammad Khan retook the country before Russia could come to its assistance. Though the Empress Catherine recovered it in the next year just before her death, her son Paul abandoned it again as soon as he came to the throne. Agha Muhammad Khan, a sagacious and courageous ruler with a justifiable reputation for vindictive cruelty and avarice, was assassinated in 1797, and was succeeded by his nephew Fateh Ali.

British diplomacy, 1800. Soon after the latter's accession, the British in India, apprehensive of an Afghan invasion and of French designs, started negotiations to induce the Shah to continue hostilities against the Amir of Kabul. Captain Malcolm, the first English diplomatic envoy to Persia since the reign of Charles II, was successful in 1800 in concluding a political and commercial treaty. The Shah agreed to make no peace with the Amir of Kabul unless he renounced his designs on the British possessions in India, while the British envoy agreed to furnish munitions of war to the Shah in the case of Afghan or French attack ; French subjects were not to be allowed to settle in Persia ; and British and Indian merchants were to be granted certain trade privileges.

In the same year the Emperor Paul of Russia, who with Napoleon was discussing plans for the invasion of India, sent Georgia military assistance against Persia. The feeble King of Georgia, much against the wishes of his subjects, was induced to renounce his crown in favour of the Czar ; and in 1801 Paul started the Don Cossacks on a march to India, which his death, however, stopped at the Volga. For a short time after this there was a cessation of Russian activity in Trans-Caucasia ; but in 1804 they sent a force against Erivan, **France and Persia, 1807.** and Napoleon, on the eve of declaring war with Russia, proposed a Franco-Persian alliance against her. Fateh Ali, who had rejected French overtures two years previously owing to his agreement with the British and who had by this time applied to both Calcutta and London for assistance against Russia, temporised. But the East India Company, no longer afraid of Afghanistan or France, was indifferent, and the British Government procrastinated. On the other hand, Russia

ANGLO-PERSIAN TREATY 1814

continued her aggression and began to invade Gilan. Fateh Ali, reluctant though he was to ally himself with a regicide nation, accordingly felt obliged in the spring of 1807 to accept Napoleon's offer of military assistance in Georgia and a subsidy, in return for the repudiation of the British alliance and the assistance of Persian troops in an invasion of India. A few months later a military mission of seventy French officers arrived and started to train the Persian army which Napoleon hoped to utilise against India. But the news of the Convention of Tilsit, in which there was no mention of the restoration of Georgia to Persia, led to a reaction against the French which gave the British an opportunity of which they were fortunately able to avail themselves.

The authorities in Calcutta and London had been seriously alarmed at the increase of French influence at Tehran and they both sent missions there, under General Malcolm and Sir Harford Jones-Brydges respectively. The former arrived first and met with no success, but Sir Harford Brydges was able in 1809 to negotiate a preliminary treaty and to effect the dismissal of the French Mission. Further negotiations led to the signing in 1814 of the final treaty, which was specially declared to be defensive. All alliances between Persia and European nations hostile to Great Britain were declared null and void; no European army, hostile to the British, was to be allowed to enter Persia; and the Shah was to induce certain rulers in Turkestan to oppose any armies attempting to traverse their territories on the march to India. Persia and Great Britain were to render one another mutual assistance in case of attack and the limits between Persia and Russia were to be determined by Great Britain, Russia and Persia. Great Britain was to grant Persia an annual subsidy of 200,000 tomans (i.e., about £150,000) and would endeavour to include Persia in any treaty of peace with a European Power with whom they were both at war, or, failing this, would afford Persia military and financial support. Finally, Great Britain was not to interfere in case of war between Persia and Afghanistan, while Persia agreed to attack Afghanistan if she went to war with Great Britain. *Anglo-Persian Treaty, 1814.*

In the meantime the Persian army, thanks to the ineptitude of the heir-apparent who commanded it, had suffered a severe defeat at the hands of the Russians; and the Shah, faced by internal risings and unable to get assistance from Great Britain (then at peace with Russia), was constrained in 1813 to sign the Treaty of Gulistan. By this he ceded to Russia a large *Russo-Persian Treaty of Gulistan, 1813.*

part of Trans-Caucasia and also agreed not to maintain a navy on the Caspian. In return Russia merely bound herself to secure the succession of Abbas Mirza, the Persian heir-apparent. From this time forward, British and Russian diplomatic representatives resided at the Persian Court.

War with Russia and Treaty of Turko-manchai, 1828.
After this, internal risings and wars with Afghanistan and Turkey—the latter due to Russian intrigues—caused almost continuous fighting till 1823. The anger felt by the Persians at the loss of rich provinces to Russia, intensified by the overbearing attitude of the Russian representatives and by the accounts of the ill-treatment of Moslems in the lost territories, reached its climax when the Russians in 1825 occupied by force the Gokcha district, whose cession to them by treaty was in dispute. There was a national uprising led by the priests, and the Shah was forced to declare war. The Persian forces at first met with some success, but finally, owing once more to the military incapacity of the heir-apparent as well as to the parsimony of the Shah, they encountered defeat in 1827. Under the ensuing treaty of Turkomanchai (1828) Russia took further territory in Trans-Caucasia, obtained an indemnity of about three million sterling, acquired a right to appoint consuls or commercial agents as trade required and, besides other concessions, gained extra-territorial rights in Persia for her officials and subjects.

Persia thus lost something of her independent status, and since then all other European nations have claimed similar extra-territorial rights.

Revision of Anglo-Persian Treaty of 1814.
Persia's claim that, under the treaty of 1814, Great Britain should have come to her assistance against Russia, though disallowed, alarmed the authorities in London at their latent obligations under that treaty. They consequently negotiated a further agreement under which Great Britain paid a fifth of the war indemnity to Russia on the condition that she at once evacuated Persian Azerbaijan and that Persia agreed to the elimination, from the 1814 treaty, of the clauses binding Great Britain to intervene in the Russo-Persian boundary settlement and to give military or financial assistance in case of an invasion of Persia.

England and the Persian Gulf.
The reign of Fateh Ali Shah saw the final suppression by the British of the piracy in the Persian Gulf to which the Arab tribes inhabiting the coast between the Straits of Hormuz and the peninsula of Qatar had been addicted from time immemorial. During the eighteenth century they had formed, under Wahabi influence, such a formidable aggressive

confederation that the limited naval resources of the East India Company experienced great difficulty in coping with them. In 1798 the British concluded a treaty with the Sultan of Muscat, the main object of which was the exclusion of French agents and influence from Oman, upon which Napoleon had designs as a naval base for an attack on India. At this time the Sultan also held Qishm, Hormuz and the Persian coast from Bandar Abbas to Lingeh under a lease from the Shah of Persia, and in 1805, when the capture of two British vessels by the pirates forced Great Britain to send a punitive expedition against them, he co-operated with a force from Oman. The resulting treaty binding the pirates to respect the flag and property of the East India Company was not adhered to, and further attacks on British ships and property necessitated a second expedition in 1809–10, when several piratical strongholds and fifty of their largest vessels were destroyed. But they still persisted in their lawlessness and a third expedition, consisting of a naval squadron of twelve ships of war and about 3,500 soldiers, was despatched against the pirate coast in 1819. The expedition was so successful that in 1820 a general treaty was concluded with the combined Arab chieftains. This, though it imposed a decisive check on piracy and kidnapping, placed no ban on the traffic in slaves nor on inter-tribal maritime warfare. To stop the latter, which continued to afford an excuse at times for piracy, the British in 1835 induced the Arab chiefs to sign a maritime truce pledging themselves not to engage in hostilities by sea for six months, provided the British did not interfere with them by land. This proved to be so successful that it was renewed annually for some years and then for periods of ten years at a time. By these treaties the British Resident at Bushire became the arbiter of all disputes among the chiefs and Great Britain has ever since assumed the responsibility for enforcing observation of the treaties, an arduous task which has involved considerable sacrifice of lives and money.

In 1832, Fateh Ali started on the first of a series of attempts to gain compensation for the territory lost to Russia by recovering the Afghan provinces which at one time belonged to Persia, the primary Persian objective being the independent principality of Herat. The Russians, animated by the desire to gain a commercial footing in Afghanistan (as they were entitled to do by treaty as soon as it became Persian territory), did all they could to encourage this policy, while the British, hampered as they were by their treaty agreement not to

Persian designs on Afghanistan.

Persian designs on Afghanistan. intervene in a Perso-Afghan conflict, did what they could to oppose it. In 1833, Muhammad Mirza, the commander of a Persian force before Herat, hearing of the death of his brother the heir-apparent, raised the siege hurriedly and concluded a treaty by which the ruler of Herat agreed to pay tribute to the Shah. Muhammad then returned to Tehran and secured his proclamation as heir-apparent a year before his father's death, when he was able, thanks to the assistance given him by the British and Russian representatives backed by a Persian force under the command of British officers, to overcome the opposition of two other brothers and gain the throne.

Muhammad Shah soon began to display pro-Russian and anti-British tendencies. He started to organise a large force for an Afghan campaign. This the British opposed, but the Shah had the justification that the ruler of Herat had not only failed to pay tribute but had annexed Seistan, which was regarded as a Persian province. In spite of the efforts of Mr. McNeill, the British envoy, to bring about the suspension of the operations, the Persian army arrived before Herat in **Attack on** November, 1837. The Persian attacks, however, met with **Herat,** little success, largely owing to the great assistance rendered **1837-38.** to the defence by the young English artillery officer, Eldred Pottinger. In the spring of 1838 Mr. McNeill arrived at Herat and, at the disheartened Shah's request, entered the city and on his behalf drew up an agreement with its ruler. Meanwhile the Russians had offered the Shah military assistance and he refused to ratify the agreement, though he soon entered into further negotiations which had to be broken off by Mr. McNeill owing to the Shah's extortionate demands. The Shah's consequent hostility led to Mr. McNeill's departure in June, just before a great final Persian assault, planned by the Russian General Simonich, met with decisive defeat.

British action. Lord Auckland, the Governor-General of India, had in the meantime been negotiating with the Amir of Kabul, but—disregarding the advice of the British envoy—had only succeeded in causing Dost Muhammad to side with Persia. Then ensued a period of great anxiety for the British, owing to the constant reports of the imminent fall of Herat and of a coming Moslem invasion of India. These led Lord Auckland to organise British forces to relieve Herat, to occupy the island of Kharij in the Persian Gulf and to drive Dost Muhammad from Kabul. The reports of these military movements so influenced the dejected Shah that at Herat in August 1838 he signified his agreement to all the demands of a British ultimatum. But though he raised the siege and left Herat, he did not carry out his word for another three years and it was only then that Mr. McNeill returned to the Persian capital.

From 1838 to 1848 the country passed through a most troubled time. In spite of Persian protests the Russians occupied Ashurada island, in the Caspian, as a naval station in 1839, on the grounds that the Shah had invoked their assistance against the Turkoman pirates; there was a rebellion in 1842 of the Ismaili religious sect, whose chief the Agha Khan found refuge in India; relations with Turkey during 1842–43 were very strained, war only being averted by the intervention of British and Russians, acting for once in accord; and the Babis (religious revivalists) rebelled in 1844. When Muhammad Shah died, the ignorance, ineptitude and indolence of his Vizier had brought the country to the verge of bankruptcy and the brink of revolution, while its power of self-defence had almost vanished, for the army, with its pay several years in arrears, was grossly inefficient and the mounted forces of the tribes had practically ceased to exist. *Persian troubles, 1838–48.*

On the accession of Nasir-ud-Din, Muhammad's sixteen year old son, the general discontent gave rise to disorder which only subsided when the unpopular Vizier resigned. His successor, entitled Amir-i-Nizam,* proved himself to be one of the greatest and most upright statesmen that Persia has ever seen; and he set himself, with considerable success, to reform existing abuses and to reorganise the country's finances. But the reactionary and corrupt elements among the population were too strong for him and, by effecting his removal from office in 1851 and then his execution, did the country irreparable injury. *Accession of Nasir-ud-Din Shah, 1848.*

The Persians still hoped to recover some of their lost provinces and from 1851 to 1853 nursed the idea of re-occupying Herat, till induced by the British, much against their own wishes, to conclude a treaty engaging not to send troops into Herat territory except in the event of attack from without. In 1853 the Shah saw in the Crimean War a chance for the recovery of territory lost to Russia, and, rejecting an invitation to join that country against Turkey, made overtures to Great Britain and France. These Powers, realising their inability to ensure Persia against subsequent Russian reprisals, advised the Shah to remain neutral. He so disliked this counsel *Break with England, 1856.*

---

* All officials in Persia assume high-sounding titles by which they are known to the total abrogation of their real names.

that he displayed a growing hostility to Great Britain, revived the idea of retaking Herat and at the end of 1855, by his insults, forced the British Minister to break off diplomatic relations and leave Tehran. In 1856 the Shah despatched an army which succeeded in re-occupying Herat; and Great Britain, who in the previous year had concluded a treaty of peace and friendship with Dost Muhammad, Amir of Kabul, most reluctantly declared war on Persia.

Anglo-Persian War, 1856-57. There were many ways in which Great Britain could have enforced her will on Persia, for Dost Muhammad, the Khan of Kalat, the Sultan of Muscat and most of the tribes of South Persia were all ready and anxious to join in taking up arms against the Shah. But Great Britain, with no desire to exercise more than sufficient force to compel the evacuation of Herat, contented herself with sending in December 1856 a small expeditionary force to the Persian Gulf. There it occupied Kharg island, captured Bushire and Borazjan and, re-embarking in March 1857, took Mohammerah and Ahwaz. On the fall of Bushire the Shah sued for and obtained peace,* the sole conditions imposed by the British being the evacuation of Herat and Afghan territory, the recognition of their independence and an agreement that, in future disputes with them, Persia should have recourse to British advice before resorting to force. The Persians were amazed and gratified at the British magnanimity, which had the most beneficial results on their subsequent mutual relations.

But for his death within the week, Dost Muhammad's capture of Herat in 1863 would have caused fresh trouble between Persia and Afghanistan. Both these countries also laid claim at this period to Seistan. But Great Britain refused Persia's invitation to intervene in the dispute and, as Sher Ali was engaged in establishing himself as Amir of Afghanistan, Persia was able to secure the greater part of the disputed province.

Perso-Afghan boundary. In 1870, however, to avert war between Afghanistan and Persia on this question, Great Britain suggested arbitration; and this led to the appointment of Sir Frederic Goldsmid,† who had just succeeded in delimiting the Makran boundary, to adjudicate on the rival claims. His award gave Seistan proper to Persia and outer Seistan (i.e., the district then on the right bank of the Helmand) to Afghanistan.

---

* Owing to the time which news then took in transit, the operations continued after the peace agreement had been signed at Paris.

† He was the first Director of Telegraphs in Persia.

In the meantime, Great Britain's self-assumed responsibilities in the Persian Gulf, where she alone carried out the work of policing, surveying, charting, lighting and buoying, had much increased. The work included sanitary control and quarantine administration, as well as protection of the Gulf pearl fisheries and the maintenance of the submarine cables between Fao, Jask and Muscat. British commercial interests in the Gulf now far exceeded those of any other nation and her influence in these waters became as preponderating as it was unquestioned. *British work in the Persian Gulf.*

Relations between Persia and Turkey were still strained owing to the boundary question, which, though nominally settled in 1847 by the Treaty of Erzerum, was actually still a cause of acute dispute. From 1857 to 1865 a map was compiled, under British and Russian auspices, of the debateable land—a strip twenty to fifty miles wide running from Mount Ararat to the Persian Gulf—and when this was completed the two countries were left to mark the boundary within these limits. As it turned out, no agreement was found possible. *Perso-Turkish relations.*

About 1840 Russia had started the forward movement in Central Asia which was to advance her boundary east of the Caspian up to that of Persia. Between 1865 to 1868 she occupied Tashkend, Khojand, Samarkand and Bokhara and in 1869 she established herself, in spite of Persian protests, at Krasnovodsk and near the mouth of the Atrek river. In 1873 she took Khiva and in 1875, when she occupied Khokand, the only independent area remaining was that of the Turkomans, over which Persia had for many years exercised an ineffective suzerainty, having been content for some time past to leave to Russia the operations required to check Turkoman raids. After the Russo-Turkish war of 1877–8, the failure and losses attending a Russian attack on the Turkoman stronghold at Geok Teppe were followed by Skobeleff's operations in 1881, the final crushing of the Tekke Turkomans and the annexation of Merv and the surrounding country. A good deal of the territory which Russia had annexed since 1869 had been Persian, and the new frontier line from the Caspian to the Tejend river, in addition to giving Russia many more Persian villages, completed the strategical envelopment of Persia from the north which Russia had evidently envisaged for some time past. *Russia's expansion in Central Asia.*

In 1871 the Shah granted to a British subject, in return for the customs dues and other resources of the country, a concession which was in effect a railway, mines and banking monopoly. But finding, on his first European tour, that this *Commencement of concessions.*

concession was regarded in Russia with hostility and in England with apathy, the Shah gained popularity with his own subjects by rescinding the concession on his return to Tehran.

<small>Conditions in Persia, 1857-96.</small> From the conclusion of the Anglo-Persian war till the end of Nasr-ud-Din's reign Persia enjoyed a period of peace, brigandage decreased greatly and the country was as prosperous as was possible under a bad and corrupt administration. Every post and appointment in the kingdom was farmed out to individuals who, as long as they paid the presents and annual amounts agreed on, were generally left alone to conduct their duties as they pleased. The result was that not only were extortion, injustice and cruelty rife, but some authorities actually connived at crime for their own personal gain. The Shah's authority, uncontrolled by any council, was almost absolute, though he was obliged to follow the established usage and law of the land and his powers were to some extent limited by the religious jurisdiction exercised by the *Shiah* leaders residing in Mesopotamia. He was very susceptible to European opinion; and, though he bears the reputation of having been reactionary and despotic, it is only just to remember that the exigencies of his position made it very difficult for him to obtain disinterested advice and that he had little actual control either over the execution of his orders or over the work of his governors and other officials. He was the first Shah to venture to leave his dominions for friendly visits to foreign countries. But his trips to Europe in 1873, 1878 and 1889 were opposed by the priesthood and unpopular in the country owing to the great expenditure they involved.

<small>Concessions to foreigners and growth of discontent.</small> During Nasr-ud-Din's reign a wave of unrest among Moslem communities in the Near East led to revolts in Egypt and Turkey. This had little effect at first among educated Persians, as, although they admitted the advantages of European forms of government, they showed little desire for their adoption in Persia. Western education and western ideas, however, spread gradually through the country at the same time that the movement for the regeneration of Islam as a world power began to gain ground. During the same period the Shah was granting to foreigners a series of concessions which placed in their hands, for a relatively small pecuniary benefit to himself and his courtiers, a great part of the actual or potential sources of the country's wealth. Foreign sympathisers, Pan-Islamic agents and agitators all helped to foment the discontent which bad government had caused, and their advice and action did much to increase the hostility aroused by these

concessions. Matters came to a climax in 1890 when a tobacco monopoly was granted to a British company. Tobacco is used in Persia probably to a greater extent than in any other country, and, led by the priests who successfully forbade the consumption of tobacco until the concession was rescinded, the popular clamour, emphasised by disturbances and riots in many places, finally forced the Shah to cancel the concession. Incidentally, it may be remarked that the half million sterling, which he paid the British company as compensation, laid the foundation of a National Debt, which constantly increased and added greatly to the difficulties and anxieties of the administration. It is also noteworthy that there was still no generally expressed desire among the population for reform in government.

In 1896 Nasir-ud-Din was assassinated by a disciple of Sayad Jamal-ud-Din, one of the chief protagonists of Pan-Islamism and a vehement critic of the Persian administration. *Accession of Muzaffar-ud-Din Shah, 1896.*

Muzaffar-ud-Din, who, largely owing to support from Russia, succeeded his father as Shah, was quite unfitted to cope with the difficult situation he inherited; and the unchecked extravagance and oppression of his officials and followers added to the general discontent and disorder. To replenish his empty treasury, he obtained, in 1900, a loan of about two and a half million sterling from Russia on the security of the recently increased customs dues. This amount was soon spent in paying off debts and the expenses of a royal visit to Europe. The Shah then obtained in the following year another loan from Russia of over a million sterling. For this second loan Russia took advantage of the British pre-occupation in South Africa to obtain several valuable concessions and an increase in the customs tariff which was as favourable to Russian trade as it was unfavourable to British. Great Britain was only able to mitigate the effect of the latter by the Anglo-Persian Commercial Convention of 1903, by steps taken by Lord Curzon (then Viceroy of India) to foster and support British trade in Persia, including the opening of the Nushki–Seistan trade route, and by the successful termination of a second Seistan Boundary Commission.

The British were faced by the fact that in Tehran and Northern Persia Russian influence had become predominant and that Russia was making every effort to extend her influence to Seistan and to the Persian Gulf, where she was attempting to obtain a naval footing. Here also for a few years past Germany had been making organised efforts to achieve political *England and the Persian Gulf.*

England and the Persian Gulf

ascendancy by commercial penetration. German warships began to visit the Gulf in 1899; members of the German firm of Wonckhaus, which was a subsidised Government agency, established themselves at various points; various attempts were made to rent, purchase or seize a site at the head of the Persian Gulf for a railway terminus; and the Baghdad Railway Convention of 1903 brought German activities into special prominence. In consequence of these different movements, the British Foreign Secretary made an unequivocal declaration in the House of Lords in 1903 that H.M. Government would regard the establishment by any other Power of a naval base or a fortified port in the Persian Gulf as a very grave menace to British interests which they would resist with all the means at their disposal. In the following winter this declaration was further affirmed by a visit to the Gulf of the Viceroy of India (Lord Curzon), escorted by the East India naval squadron.

The Constitutional movement, 1905 onwards

The Russo-Japanese War and the revolution which gained a constitution for Russia in 1905 reacted on the situation in Persia, where there was great discontent among all classes owing to the extravagance of the administration, the Shah's costly foreign tours, the increased customs tariff and its tactless enforcement by foreign officials, the tyranny of the Grand Vizier and provincial governors, and the exploitation of the country by foreigners. The popular feeling found expression at Tehran in December 1905 in the movement known as the "First *Bast*."* In this, priests, merchants, tradesmen and students took sanctuary in a shrine, where they maintained a passive resistance by which they brought sufficient pressure to oblige the Shah to concede their demands, namely the dismissal of the Grand Vizier and the foundation of a House of Justice. It is noteworthy that this movement obtained much financial and other support from prominent reactionaries, including the Crown Prince, whose main incentive was their personal desire to effect the dismissal of the Grand Vizier.

The Shah, however, took no steps to give effect to his promises and the Grand Vizier, taking advantage of a royal illness, started on a campaign of active repression. This led in May 1906 to another *bast*, which failed owing to the authorities cutting off supplies. In July, however, learning from the British chargé d'affaires that force would not be used to expel them, some twelve thousand Persians of all

---

* *Bast* is the Persian word for sanctuary.

classes took sanctuary in the grounds of the British Legation and finally in August forced the Shah, not only to fulfil his previous promises, but also to grant a constitution and a national assembly. The prominent part taken by the priests in these *basts* is specially worthy of remark as they were really reactionaries. Apparently, however, they considered that foreign intervention was more dangerous to their power and influence than any administrative innovations; they had never regarded the Qajar dynasty, whose origin was Turkish, as having any real title to rule over a *Shiah* community; and being recruited from the general population they understood and sympathised with the popular discontent. In spite of several attempts by the Shah, the Grand Vizier and the Crown Prince to evade the promises made, the first *Majlis* (assembly) met in October 1906 and drafted a Constitution and Fundamental Law, which were signed by the Crown Prince, Muhammad Ali, in December and by the Shah a few days before his death in January 1907.

The Turks meanwhile took advantage of the troubled state of the country to revive the unsettled boundary question and, after maintaining a threatening attitude for some months, moved troops across the frontier in August 1906 and forcibly occupied Persian territory about Urmia and Sauj Bulag. Here they remained, defeating the Persian troops sent against them until evicted by the Russians, and continuing the dispute until the final demarcation of the boundary by a mixed Commission in 1913–14.

Muhammad Ali, an oriental despot of the worst type, showed from the first that he had no intention of submitting to the control of the Assembly. He soon recalled the Grand Vizier, whom his father had been forced by popular clamour to dismiss; and it was unfortunate for the country that his intrigues were facilitated by the internal discord which prevailed in the *Majlis*. This was due to the lack of experience, the visionary or anarchical ideas, and the low standard of integrity of many of the deputies. An emotional people, the Persians are easily swayed by mere rhetoric, and in this case the general result was to allow the political party with extreme anarchical ideas to gain the upper hand. The other party, imbued with more moderate views, included most of the clerical deputies; but these rather foolishly demanded that a clerical committee should invariably ratify all laws as conforming with the ecclesiastical code of Islam. Generally, in fact, the spirit of compromise, one of the main essentials of successful democratic

Accession of Muhammad Ali Shah, 1907.

control, was entirely lacking. The local provincial councils also proved unequal to their task and neither they nor the central assembly were able to obtain the money required to enable them to enforce their authority.

<small>Anglo-Russian Convention, 1907.</small> It was in this critical year (1907), when Persia was in special need of judicious and disinterested advice, that Great Britain, by signing the Anglo-Russian Convention, lost the popularity and influence which she, more than any other foreign nation, enjoyed in Persia. For over three hundred years, except for a few short interludes, British intercourse with Persia had been uniformly of a most friendly character. Since the days of the Sherley brothers, many British soldiers, merchants and diplomatists had been honoured in Persia for their distinguished service in the country. British naval and military forces had cleared the shores of the Persian Gulf of the invading Portuguese and the sea of marauding Arabs; and British officers had fought on the side of Persia against Turks, rebellious subject-tribes and Russians. Moreover, for the services she rendered, Great Britain had only asked for the right to trade, and her innocence of aggressive intention had been confirmed by her generous conduct after the one small war between the two countries. Ever since then, Persia had come to rely on Great Britain as her main stand-by against Russia, while the popular respect and admiration for the British had been much enhanced by the support and sympathy which they had afforded the recent constitutional movement.

Of the causes which led Great Britain to sign this convention and which have been given in his book " Twenty-five Years " by Lord Grey, the following appear the most important. He says that the cardinal object was to secure ourselves against further Russian advances in the direction of the Indian frontier and against further interference with our interests which concerned India. Not only had Russian action brought us at times to the verge of war, but it obliged the Government of India to incur expenditure on defence which they desired to utilise on other growing needs of the country. To India an independent Persia* offered the advantage of a buffer state, but her internal condition so attracted and invited foreign intervention as to become at any time the cause of conflict, more especially as it had become the policy of Persia to play off one Government against the other. It seemed evident to the British Government that nothing short

---

* The Convention dealt also with Afghanistan and Tibet, but here we are only considering its relation to Persia.

ANGLO-RUSSIAN CONVENTION, 1907

of a clear understanding with Russia would prevent matters getting worse. Moreover, an agreement with her was the natural complement of our *entente* with France, who was Russia's ally. On the other hand, Russian despotism was so repugnant to British ideals that, had it not been for the recent institution of the Duma in Russia, H.M. Government would have found it difficult to justify the Convention to the British public.

By the terms of the Convention both countries agreed to respect Persian integrity and independence and stated their desire for the preservation of order in Persia and its pacific development, as well as the permanent establishment of equal advantages for the commerce and industry of other nations. Having geographical and economic reasons for the maintenance of peace and order in the Persian provinces conterminous with their respective frontiers and being desirous of avoiding all motives for conflict between their respective interests in these regions, they agreed on the following arrangement. Great Britain would not seek for herself, for her own subjects, or for the subjects of a third power, any political or commercial concessions north of a line running from Qasr-i-Shirin and including Isfahan, Yezd and Kakh to the point on the Persian boundary where the Russian and Afghan frontiers intersected. Russia similarly bound herself in regard to the area south of a line running from Bandar Abbas and including Kerman and Birjand to Gazik on the Afghan frontier.* Both nations also agreed not to oppose, without previous discussion, any concession which the subjects of the other Power might seek in the neutral zone between these lines.

Owing to the alarm caused in Persia by the news of this convention, the British Minister at Tehran found it expedient to send at once to the Persian Foreign Minister a reassuring memorandum. This repudiated in the most explicit manner any aggressive designs or desire to interfere in Persian affairs and it guaranteed the independence and integrity of Persia. It concluded by declaring that not only did Great Britain and Russia not seek a pretext for intervention, but that their

---

* This line was a compromise between the views of the Government of India, who urged that it should include the Lower Karun Valley and the head of the Persian Gulf, and those of Lord Kitchener (then Commander-in-Chief in India) who considered that we should limit our responsibilities to the semi-desert areas of Persian Baluchistan, Kain, Seistan and Kerman and that it would be a strategical advantage to us if Russia and Germany were to establish ports in the Persian Gulf or the Arabian Sea where we could attack them. The Germans, it may be noted, were still continuing their efforts to gain a footing on the shores of the Gulf.

Anglo-Russian Convention, 1907. aim in these friendly negotiations was not to permit one another to intervene on the pretext of safeguarding their own interests.

The Persians, however, put little faith in these assurances, as they regarded the terms of the convention as quite incompatible with Persian independence and integrity. They realised that they could no longer rely on one Power to assist them in resisting the demands of the other and they considered that in consequence the agreement would facilitate interference, the appointment of officials and even the despatch of military forces by either country. The sequel was to prove that the Persians had considerable justification for their apprehensions. For, while Great Britain was inspired by a genuine desire to maintain Persia's independence and to help her, Russian officials, if not the Russian Government, regarded the agreement as a preliminary to partition. Russia began almost immediately to take advantage of the agreement to absorb gradually her so-called sphere, and continued to do so. Great Britain, endeavouring to co-operate closely with Russia and to avoid dissensions with her, felt obliged to remonstrate. But as her protests were generally without effect, she got no credit for them and became more and more implicated in Persian minds with responsibility for Russian aggressive action.

Lord Grey contends—with some justification—that Persia's integrity and independence did not in fact exist in 1907 and that we gained considerably by the greater prospect of peace which the convention achieved. On the other hand, however, it had effects which were subsequently to handicap or embarrass us. It resulted in the reduction of military expenditure in India, both in 1907 and 1912; it displeased the Amir of Afghanistan and thereby facilitated the acquisition of arms by the tribes on the North-West Frontier of India; and it changed the not unfriendly attitude of the inhabitants of the buffer states covering India into one of suspicion or worse.

Shah's coup d'état. In December 1907, the Shah initiated a *coup d'état* having as its aim the abolition of the constitution. But his hesitation at a critical moment gave the *Majlis* and the populace time to counteract the stroke and to force the Shah to surrender and swear, for the fifth time, that he would observe the constitution. Attempts to bring about better relations between the Shah and the *Majlis* were checked in February 1908 when a bomb was thrown at the Shah, who believed that it was the work of his political enemies. Consequently the situation became more strained than ever and in June the Shah, ordering the bombardment of the *Majlis* by Colonel Liakhoff and his Persian Cossacks, abolished the constitution and re-established an autocracy. Popular risings at once took place at Tabriz and elsewhere. Finally in July 1909 the combined forces of the Nationalists and the Bakhtiaris captured Tehran after a few days fighting, followed two days later by Muhammad Ali's abdication. The constitution was restored and Sultan Ahmad, Muhammad Ali's twelve-year old son, succeeded to the throne. *Abdication of Shah Muhammad Ali, 1909.*

During the popular rising at Tabriz the Russians had sent troops there for the protection of foreign subjects, and their arrival had proved beneficial in that it put an end to the fighting round Tabriz and saved the Nationalists from royal reprisals. But the Russians proceeded to send more troops to Enzeli and to Kazvin on the pretext that the lives of foreigners were endangered, which was untrue. The British protested. But it was not till the *Majlis* assembled in November that the Russians began to withdraw part of the troops they had sent into the country; and even that they ceased to do as it became evident that the new Cabinet was imbued with great hostility to Russia.

The political party styling itself Democrat—really formed of extremists with strong anti-foreign views—obtained and maintained ascendancy over the Moderates mainly by methods of intimidation and assassination; and the Cabinet it appointed was controlled by an irresponsible body of Young Persians, whose preposterous behaviour forced Ministers to resign time and again. As none of the Young Persians had the executive experience, character or authority to govern a province, they had to fall back on officials of the old *régime*, and these found themselves checked and thwarted at every turn by the young inexperienced officials and by the local provincial assemblies. Animosities and dissensions increased and the whole country suffered from disorder. *Political parties.*

The Democrats had hoped to put an end to the dominating Russian influence, but the great hostility they displayed towards the Russians was so resented by the latter that they felt no hesitation in raising difficulties to embarrass the new Government. Rebel leaders found refuge or support in Russia; Russian officials connived at an armed attempt by the ex-Shah and his brother Salar-ud-Daula to regain the throne; and the prevalent dissensions and disorders gave the

Russians many other opportunities, of which they took full advantage. In South Persia the insecurity on the Bushire-Isfahan road was paralysing British trade and in 1910 Great Britain found it necessary to inform the Persian Government that, unless they restored order there within three months, Great Britain would herself make the necessary police arrangements at Persian expense. This, of course, rendered Great Britain more unpopular than ever.

Financial difficulties. The Treasury was empty, and, as the central and provincial Governments had not the necessary military or police forces to ensure collection of revenue, they found themselves in a very difficult financial situation. The national debt, though relatively small, had not only involved the mortgaging to Russia and Great Britain of important sources of revenue, but had introduced a measure of foreign (Belgian) control; and it was the special desire of the Government to raise the loans which were now urgently required without further pledging the national resources or giving fresh occasion for foreign intervention. Their attempts to do so in 1910, however, almost all failed, chiefly owing to the action of Russia, who was unwilling that Persia should borrow, except from herself or Great Britain at the price of fresh concessions. It then became clear to the most enlightened Persians that their only chance of financial salvation lay in obtaining the services of disinterested foreign financial advisers and of foreign officers to organise the Treasury gendarmerie required to collect revenue and to maintain order. Both Great Britain and Russia were apprehensive lest Germans, who for some years past had taken every opportunity for intervention, should be invited and they accordingly suggested that nationals of small Powers should be engaged. Those of the latter, however, who were approached refused, and in 1911 the Persian Government entered into a private arrangement with an American, Mr. W. Morgan Shuster, to come as Financial Adviser, while they obtained officers for gendarmerie from Sweden and some professors from France. They also tried to obtain Swedish officers to organise a Persian military force, but failed owing to Russian objections.

Mr. Shuster's mission, 1911. Mr. Shuster, with a small staff, reached the country in May 1911 and, after a brief examination of the situation, asked for and obtained extra-ordinary powers. These he wielded, from the very first, with an attitude of complete disregard of British and especially Russian interests which, while it gained him the support and confidence of the Persians, enhanced the hostility already felt by the Russians towards an appointment regarding which they had not been consulted. He showed by many of his acts that he failed to realise that nothing short of force would oblige Russia to relax her grip on Persia and that there was no power existing to exercise that force. This was all the more unfortunate that the progress made by his reorganisation showed that it might have gone far towards making the experiment in government a success if he had been able to complete his task. But, in November 1911, the Russians, exasperated at his indifference to their interests, issued an ultimatum to the Persian Government, demanding (i) Mr. Shuster's dismissal, (ii) an agreement to engage no more foreigners without Russian or British consent, and (iii) the payment of the expenses of the Russian military force sent to Enzeli to enforce the ultimatum. Great Britain protested against this action at St. Petersburg, but without avail; there was a great popular outcry in Persia against Russia and also against Great Britain; the *Majlis* refused to comply with the ultimatum; and three to four thousand Russian troops advanced to Kazvin, en route to Tehran. Some fighting took place between Persians and Russians at Enzeli, Resht and Tabriz and, in order to avoid further disaster, the Regent and the Cabinet forcibly dissolved the *Majlis* and dismissed Mr. Shuster. Russian opposition and action.

The *Majlis* remained in suspense for the next two and a half years; the Regent, who had taken the post unwillingly and found little favour in Russian eyes, was absent from the country for half that period; and there were constant changes of Cabinet, owing to the impossibility of forming one that met with both Russian and Persian approval. The Treasury was generally empty and, though some increase in revenue was obtained by the efforts of Belgian officials, there was practically no reform in the financial administration. Effective government in fact proved impossible, and the situation in the provinces became chaotic. Chaotic situation.

Russia, whose troops continued to occupy Tabriz, Kazvin, Resht, Meshed and other cities, was all-powerful in the most important part of the country, continually found pretexts for political, military, commercial and economic intervention and openly showed her desire for a complete partition of the country. It is only possible here to give a few instances of the action taken by the Russians. They carried out severe reprisals in Tabriz for the resistance they encountered in 1911 and they installed as Governor a notorious reactionary, who maintained for many months a reign of terror characterised by shocking Russian dominance.

Russian dominance. barbarities and who, with Russian support, prevented the Belgian officials from collecting the taxes. The ex-Shah and his brother Salar-ud-Daula, who remained in the country, counting on Russian support, continued to give trouble till 1912 and 1913 respectively, when, with pensions from the Persian Government, they went to Europe, only, however, to threaten fresh raids from there. In March 1912 the Russians intervened in Meshed in civil disturbances connected with the ex-Shah's rebellion and bombarded the most sacred shrine in the country, killing many innocent people—an outrage which the Persian nation and *Shiah* Moslems elsewhere have never forgotten nor forgiven. The only loans that the Persian Government could obtain were from Russia or with Russian sanction, in exchange for some disadvantageous concession, while every opportunity was taken to press for increases in the Russian-officered Persian Cossack force.

The Russians also usurped to an increasing extent in the five northern provinces and in Isfahan the civil and financial functions of the governors, and any attempt on their part to maintain Persian rights against Russian intervention led inevitably to their dismissal. In addition to great commercial interests, large landed estates had passed into the hands of Russians and Russian-protected persons or had been mortgaged to the Russian bank; and such estates were treated by the Russians as no longer being under Persian jurisdiction. Russian consuls collected taxes and, paying the money into the Russian bank, refused to hand it over to the Persian Government, while their demands for money due to Russia or for the expenses of the Persian Cossack force always more than absorbed anything which the central Government could collect. In face of this Russian action the Persian Government and the Belgian Treasurer-General were helpless, and the latter in July 1914 suggested to the Persian Cabinet that the only way to avert bankruptcy, get rid of the incubus of Russian and British debt and make a fresh start was to sell territory in the north to Russia and some islands in the Persian Gulf to Great Britain.

Before the conclusion of the Anglo-Russian Convention, by far the larger portion of the British interests established in Persia had been in the so-called neutral zone. But the Russian occupation of Isfahan and the closure of the southern trade routes owing to disorders enabled the Russians to oust British trade almost completely. Not content with this, Russian officials constantly put obstacles in the way of legitimate British attempts to trade. H.M. Government were anxious to avoid new and incalculable commitments in Persia, but Russian infringements of the Convention, as displayed by her attitude both to Persian independence and British interests, were so flagrant that several British remonstrances were addressed to St. Petersburg. These were without avail, and one result was that Great Britain became associated in the Persian mind with the distrust and hatred felt towards Russia. In Fars, which was for the time without a governor, insecurity became so menacing that in October 1911 an Indian cavalry regiment was sent there and to Isfahan to reinforce the British consular guards, and remained in the country till April 1913. Otherwise, British action was for the most part directed towards securing the appointment of strong governors with British sympathies in South Persia and towards encouraging—and to a large extent financing—the newly formed gendarmerie officered by Swedes.

The whole situation in the country got to such a state by May 1914, that a considerable movement started in England for the revision of the Anglo-Russian Convention. In June 1914 the Foreign Office in London found it necessary to hand the Russian Ambassador another strong remonstrance against the manner in which the Russian representatives in North Persia were undermining the principle of Persian independence and integrity on which the Anglo-Russian Convention was based. As a result of this and of French representations to Russia, both the Czar and his Foreign Minister declared that they would not allow Persia to stand in the way of the maintenance of good relations between Great Britain and Russia. Nevertheless Russian officials in Persia showed little intention of altering their methods.

British policy, 1914.

On the 3rd August 1914, Sir Walter Townley, British Minister at Tehran, in mooting the abrogation of the Convention to the Foreign Office, wrote : " I presume that H.M. Government are of opinion that British interests are best served by a Persia sufficiently strong to act as a buffer state between Great Britain and Russia in the Middle East. Such a Persia can never, it has been clearly demonstrated, be created under the 1907 Convention. Half the country is directly under Russian influence, a portion is undecided, and the insignificant remainder from the point of view of Tehran politics owns British allegiance. Meanwhile, the central Government has no authority and never can have any authority so long as its hands are tied by the necessity of considering the wishes of one or other Power, or of both."

Summary of Russian, British and Turkish Policy.
From the foregoing brief summary, which is necessarily incomplete in many respects, some indication is afforded of the main reasons for the decline of the Persian Empire and for the inability of the Persians to defend their inheritance. Among these reasons, the policy and actions during the last hundred years or so of her three most powerful neighbours,—Russia, Great Britain and Turkey—have been most important factors.

It was Russia's declared policy, of which she gave us repeated assurances, to observe the integrity and promote the peaceful development of Persia. But Russia's record of a steady and continued expansion of territory at the expense of Persia, and her action, in successfully opposing all efforts to form a stable constitutional government and to bring about financial, administrative and military reforms, pointed instead to her desire either to render Persia impotent and subservient or to absorb her northern provinces into the Russian Empire.

British efforts till the commencement of the nineteenth century were entirely directed towards obtaining a commercial footing in Persia, while our growing maritime ascendancy gained for us control of the commerce of the Persian Gulf. This commercial control led to a naval supremacy which the interests of India obliged us to maintain as a cardinal principle of our Imperial policy. It is noteworthy, however, that the policy we have adopted on land has been very different. Persia's geographical situation, midway between Europe and India with the ancient highways between West and East running through her richest provinces, has predestined her to play an important part in the history of the East. Napoleon's perception of this and his plan for the invasion of India drew British attention seriously to the advisability of ensuring the independence of Persia so as to form a buffer state to India. At the time of the Treaties of Gulistan and Turkomanchai (1813–28) the Russian army was little superior to the Persian military forces, and the subsequent history of Persia might have been very different if we had afforded her the modicum of support and assistance which she required to resist Russia successfully and which our treaty obligations implied if they did not actually compel. We adopted instead a policy of inaction which we have practically ever since continued to follow in face of constant Russian aggression and a growing deterioration in the ability of Persia to defend herself. Hence we were faced at the beginning of the present century with a situation to which we endeavoured to find a solution by signing a convention with Russia,—a convention which proved in effect to be better adapted to the requirements of the current European situation than as a means of securing Persian independence.

The Turks, ever since the founding of the Ottoman Empire, have been the foes of the Persians, and the traditional enmity between the two nations has been exacerbated by the religious feud between *Sunnis* and *Shiahs*. Consequently the Pan-Islamism fostered by Sultan Abdul Hamid of Turkey to create a community of political and religious interests among all Moslem people found little response in Persia, till it was found useful by the Young Persians as a political weapon. Meanwhile, however, the Young Turks had rejected the original Pan-Islamic ideals and were evolving from them and from the Pan-Turanian movement a new Pan-Turkish policy, whose aims were to recreate the Ottoman Empire by extending it to include the races akin to Turk who inhabited Trans-Caucasia, Turkestan and the north west, if not the greater part, of Persia. In 1914 these aims were hardly understood and received little attention outside Turkey, if only for the reason that the way to their achievement seemed to be definitely barred by Russia, while the recent encroachments along the Persian frontier by the Turks were regarded as due merely to a desire to strengthen their position vis-à-vis Russia.

CHAPTER II.

AUGUST 1914 TO JUNE 1915: ENEMY EFFORTS TO BRING PERSIA INTO THE WAR.

(General Map of Persia.)

General situation; August 1914. The eighteen-year old Shah had only been crowned for a fortnight and the Persian National Assembly was still in abeyance when war broke out in August 1914. Thus the weak Cabinet which was in power possessed neither royal nor popular support.

Lacking effective national government, on the verge of bankruptcy and without the military means to preserve its territorial integrity, the country found itself in a truly unenviable position. For this state of affairs the great majority of the Persian people held, and with some justice, that Russian intervention was largely responsible and that the Anglo-Russian Convention had furthered rather than restrained Russian aggression. It is, therefore, not surprising that Germany, even though aided by Turkey, Persia's traditional foe, was able to take immediate advantage of the situation.

There are good grounds for the belief that most of the leading men in Persia desired to avoid any chance of being involved in the war. But it is not easy, in the atmosphere of intrigue, personal animosities and self-interest in which they lived and moved, to discern any definite plan or policy which they strove to follow. Their strong dislike of Russia undoubtedly induced hopes that she would be defeated by Germany and would consequently be obliged to loosen her military and political hold on Persia. This dislike, however, was tempered by a very real fear of Russia, by nervous uncertainty regarding the future and by the feeling that the British alliance, which was universally regretted or condemned, minimised the chances of the wished-for defeat. On the other hand, though Turkey was not yet at war, the proceedings of the Turco-Persian boundary commission, then concluding its work, were a reminder that Turkey might take advantage of British and Russian preoccupation to resume her old policy of territorial expansion at Persia's expense.

AGGRESSIVE TURKISH ACTION

Many of the Europeans in the country left early in August to join their national forces, and a considerable portion of the Russian troops in Persia also withdrew to join the field armies. Among the Russian units which remained were some at Maku, Khoi and Urmia which had been moved there a few years previously to prevent the Turks from occupying the district; and Turkish troops still occupied, to the west of Lake Urmia, important strategical positions which constituted a threat to the Russian flank. Persian objections to this Russian occupation had been modified by the benefits it conferred in the way of increased security, trade and prosperity and by its consequent local popularity, especially among the considerable Christian community. The question, however, assumed a different aspect after the outbreak of war, when Turkish mobilisation and military preparations stopped trade into Persia and when reports came in that the Turks were preaching a holy war against Russia and were threatening to attack Persia if she did not join Turkey. *Russian forces in N.W. Persia; August 1914.*

At the end of August, on receipt of the draft of the official *communiqué* which Great Britain proposed to publish in the event of war with Turkey, the British Minister at Tehran took advantage of a visit by the Persian Prime Minister and one of the chief *mujtahids* to explain to them Turkey's improper action in regard to the *Goeben* and the *Breslau*. Sir Walter Townley also asked that steps should be taken to put a stop in Persia to expressions of open hostility to Great Britain and her allies and that the Shiah *mujtahids* might be warned not to encourage anti-Ally hostility. The Prime Minister agreed to take this action and added that, if it were a question only of hostilities between Great Britain and Turkey, the British could rely on active Persian sympathy. But, he said, the hatred for our ally Russia was so great that he could not promise more than neutrality. *Attitude of Turkey; August–October 1914.*

At this time, Turco-German agents in Persia were busy propagating all sorts of lying stories and preaching a *Jahad*. But though the Allied Ministers considered an anti-Christian outbreak possible, to the British at any rate it seemed highly improbable that Persia would join in the war against us. If, however, this were to happen, it was felt that we could bring considerable pressure to bear on her by occupying the ports in the Persian Gulf and thus close one of her chief sources of revenue.

During September Turkish agitation and instigation were responsible for a series of hostile incidents in the frontier region

46 OPERATIONS IN PERSIA

Attitude of Turkey; August–October 1914.
near Urmia in which Russians, Kurds, and at times Turks were concerned. Russia, genuinely anxious, because of the complications in the Balkans that would ensue, that Turkey should not be drawn into the war, withdrew most of her troops from Urmia. But the incidents continued, and early in October Persia, desiring to prevent her territory becoming a theatre of war, decided to proclaim her neutrality, at the same time protesting to Turkey against the action of her local officials. The Turkish Ambassador gave an assurance in the name of his Government that, if the Russian troops withdrew from Persia, Turkey would respect her neutrality, would withdraw Turkish troops from the frontier and would also possibly demobilise them. The Persian Government, thereupon, requested the Russians to withdraw their troops and asked the British and Russian Governments to advance about £200,000 each, being the cost of a tribal force which the Persian Government proposed to organise under their own officers to secure order in the areas to be evacuated by the Russians. In view of the warlike action Turkey was taking in the Dardanelles, Syria, Arabia, Mesopotamia and elsewhere, however, neither the British nor the Russian Government put any faith in the Turkish assurances. The Persian Government were notoriously incapable of organising any force competent to maintain order or neutrality; and, although they assured the British Minister that their request had not been prompted by outside influences, it was felt that the Persian motives were doubtful.

It was true that the Persian Government had taken some steps to try to counteract the effect in the country of the Turco-German Pan-Islamic propaganda. But this still continued unceasingly, and the enemy's intentions were further indicated by the receipt in September and October of reports from two different sources of a Turco-German mission, which was said to be leaving Baghdad with a letter from the German Emperor to the Amir of Afghanistan.

During October, owing to a serious attack by Kurds accompanied by some Turks, the Russians were obliged to send back troops to Urmia to restore the situation, which was aggravated by a Turkish proclamation calling on the Kurds to join the other Moslem nations and races in a *Jahad* and by the reported presence of the exiled and rebellious Salar-ud-Daula.*

The war and Turkish action had by this time stopped nearly all trade into North Persia, and the consequent loss of customs

---

* See Chapter I., pp. 37 and 40.

dues added greatly to the financial difficulties of the Persian Government. They asked the British and Russian Governments for a year's grace in respect of repayments of debt and also for a further advance of about half a million sterling. But, in the complete absence of any financial control by the Persian Government and the uncertainty regarding the results of the increasing hostile propaganda in Persia, neither Government felt justified in lending the country any more money.

Soon after the outbreak of war, the anti-Russian sentiments of the Swedish officers of the Persian gendarmerie led them to adopt a strong pro-German attitude. Even before the war this force had begun to deteriorate, as Russian opposition, lack of money, loss of popular confidence in the force and local intrigues led to the resignation of many of the best Swedish officers, to the disbandment of part of the Persian personnel and to an announcement by the Swedish Government that all their officers would leave the country on the 1st March 1915. H.M. Government had considered it politically inexpedient to replace these Swedes by British officers, and in the spring and early summer of 1914 there had been much discussion as to how security was to be maintained in South Persia in the absence of an efficient gendarmerie. This referred especially to Fars, where the existence of the two great nomad tribal groups, the Qashqai and the Khamseh (the former composed entirely and the latter largely of Turco-Tartar races), had always rendered the province specially liable to disorder. Security depended almost entirely on the goodwill and support of Saulat-ud-Daula and Qawam-ul-Mulk, the respective chiefs of these two groups. But there was constant dissension and jealousy between them, frequently aggravated deliberately by the Persian Governors-General of the province for their own purposes.

The gendarmerie and South Persia; August–September 1914.

The state of the gendarmerie and the total inability of the Persian administration to control these two chiefs had at last impelled the British in July 1914 to offer them inducements to keep inter-tribal peace and to assist the Persian administration to maintain order and collect the revenue. But, as it still remained to be seen whether this arrangement would prove successful, the effect on the gendarmerie of the pro-German sentiments of its Swedish officers caused us considerable concern, especially as it was ascertained that, owing to the war, India was quite unable to spare any British officers to replace them.

As regards the Gulf ports, the position was more favourable. The necessity for checking the traffic in arms from the Arabian coast to the North-West Frontier of India and for providing escorts for the British consular officials had led to the location some time previously of small detachments of Indian infantry at Muscat, Bushire, Jask, Chahbar and Hangam island. These also furnished guards for the British cable and telegraph stations and could, if required, assist or support the local Persian officials in the maintenance of order.

Effect of Turkey's entry into the war; November 1914–January 1915. The entry of Turkey into the war at the end of October added to Persian anxieties and difficulties. The Government at once published a declaration of their neutrality and issued a special warning to the leading notables, priests and press to maintain an impartial attitude. This was all the more necessary because a considerable party in the country with Pan-Islamic tendencies was gaining strength owing to the lavish bribes of the enemy, the vigour of his propaganda and a proclamation by Shiah *mujtahids* in Mesopotamia calling on their Persian followers to join in the *Jahad* against the Allies. Regarding this proclamation, however, these *mujtahids* were informed by the Persian Government that neither they nor the local priests were in favour of a Turkish-inspired *Jahad*.

Great Britain, aware of the strain on many of her own Moslem subjects which the war with Turkey created, urged on Russia the necessity for a more conciliatory attitude towards Persia. This Russia agreed to, realising that it was in her own interests to remain on friendly terms with Persia, if only because of the supplies that she drew from there. But she pointed out that she must protect her flank against Turkish attack through Azerbaijan, although in doing so she had no intention of menacing Persian integrity. Both Governments explained this to the Persian Government, and Russia also promised to pay compensation for any damage arising from Russian military operations. It is worthy of note that both Great Britain and Russia felt at this period that they could probably, if they so desired, bring Persia into the war on their side; but they saw no advantage in doing so, while on the other hand it would have the disadvantage of involving them in the undesirable military commitment of defending Persia.

Acting in conjunction with an offensive movement by the Caucasus Army towards Erzerum, a Russian force advanced early in November towards Van from Khoi. But a Turkish force entered Persia further to the south, outflanking the Russians and threatening Khoi and Tabriz. The Persian Government protested to both Turkey and Russia against this infringement of her neutrality; and then suggested, under threats from the Turkish Ambassador, that, although it might be too late for Russian troops to evacuate Azerbaijan, those in the provinces of Mazanderan and Khurasan should be withdrawn. The Russians, who learnt of the reason for this suggestion, declined to agree to it, as they pointed out that the Persian Government were quite unable by themselves, in face of the growing hostile propaganda, to maintain order or to protect foreigners in those provinces. In the light of subsequent events it seems probable, though it does not appear to have been suspected at the time, that the enemy hoped to open the road to Afghanistan.

At this period, the Russians were also faced by trouble in Trans-Caucasia. Turkish troops, invading the Batum district, had induced local Moslem tribes to join them; German agents were exploiting the considerable German influence in Georgia to embarrass Russia; and the Daghestanis were showing signs of unrest. Consequently the arrival of refugees from Urmia and Tabriz and of Germans deported from Tabriz by the Russians, indicating a successful Turkish advance through Azerbaijan, accentuated the general feeling of uncertainty.

In Persia, the Turkish success also had its effect. Moreover, telegrams from Baghdad and other holy places in Mesopotamia continued to pour in exhorting the Persians to join in a holy war and calling on the Persian Government to stop the Shaikh of Mohammerah from assisting the British in Mesopotamia. The Persian Government, however, maintained a correct attitude. They prohibited the publication in the press of the Turkish declaration of *Jahad;* they informed the Shiah *mujtahids* in Mesopotamia that, while deeply imbued with the necessity for maintaining the Islamic faith, they did not consider it in the interest either of that faith or of Persia to adopt anything but a neutral attitude, in which they hoped for the *mujtahids'* support; and they said that the action of the Shaikh of Mohammerah had their full approval as he had done nothing without consulting them.

The *Majlis* reassembled on the 5th December with the " Moderate " party, which included a strong clerical element, in a majority. It was, therefore, most unfortunate that, a few days later, the Russians, faced by a strong Turkish offensive towards Kars and by unrest in Trans-Caucasia, decided to supplement their own lack of troops by utilising the services of the much hated Shuja-ud-Daula* to organise a Persian force

---

*Appointed to govern Tabriz in 1911 by Russian influence, his subsequent administration there had been marked by such cruelty, corruption and disregard of central Persian authority as to cause his banishment from the country.

Unpopular Russian action; December 1914.

in Azerbaijan to oppose the Turkish invasion. The Persian Government, distrusting Shuja himself and fearing embroilment with Turkey as well as a rising of the Persian tribes of Turkish origin, protested strongly. The British, feeling that the Persian protests were justified, also urged the Russians not to employ Shuja. But the Russians, acutely alive to their own dangers and resenting the strong anti-Russian feeling in Persia, which inclined them to believe the Turkish announcement that they had been invited by the Persians to expel the Russians, would not be dissuaded. In the third week of December their action in ordering a force of Persian Cossacks to join Shuja so exasperated the Persian public that the British Minister reported that anti-Russian sentiment was growing so strong that he feared lest a religious movement should ensue of which it was impossible to foresee the results. At the same time Sir Walter Townley said that, although the country was greatly affected to the disadvantage of the Allies by Turco-German propaganda,* he personally was convinced that the Persian Government were not only not pro-Turk but that they had really protested strongly against the Turkish invasion.

At the end of December, Shuja's force was defeated a short distance to the south of Tabriz by Turks, Kurds and other Persian tribesmen; and Shuja himself fled. His employment had thus proved useless.

At the beginning of January 1915 the Russians inflicted a decisive defeat on the Turkish Third Army at Sari Kamish. But they had no troops available to reinforce their troops in Persian Azerbaijan, and they decided to withdraw from both Urmia and Tabriz rather than risk a reverse at the hands of the Turco-Kurdish forces. The Russian Minister at Tehran, learning of this decision but attributing it to anxiety regarding the safety of Trans-Caucasia, asked Sir Walter Townley to inform the Persian Government, as he himself was unwilling to do so. The result of this news and of the subsequent Turkish occupation of Tabriz was to give a great impetus to enemy propaganda all through Persia. At Tehran the German Legation took advantage of it to renew their lavish offers of money, munitions and military instructors; at Isfahan, Pugin, a Chilean adventurer in German employ, redoubled his anti-Ally activities, which had already met with considerable

---

*Among other fiction, circulated by our enemies and believed by many Persians, was the statement that the German Emperor and his people had embraced Islam.

success; and in Fars the gendarmerie became still more affected by the openly expressed pro-German sympathies of their Swedish officers.

The reports they received seemed to the British Government to show that the apparent Russian inability to cope with the Turkish invasion might lead to Persia siding with the enemy. Sir Edward Grey accordingly suggested to Russia that she should, as a conciliatory measure, withdraw all her troops from Persia and that, if the Turks then failed to keep their promise to evacuate Persia also, Russia and Great Britain should give Persia financial assistance to help her to organise a force to defend herself. In reply, however, Russia intimated that she had every intention of reoccupying Tabriz as soon as reinforcements were available; and in any case she had no faith in Turkish assurances or in Persian ability to organise effective resistance. This discussion, which was entirely due to the Russian Minister's imperfect acquaintance with Russian military intentions and the state of affairs in Trans-Caucasia, had rather unfortunate results. For it revived Persian hopes of getting rid of the Russian troops only to dissipate them again, thus accentuating the anti-Russian feeling; and it inclined Russia to suspect Great Britain's intentions. Fortunately, the effects were to some extent modified by the resentment aroused by Turkish and Kurdish outrages in the Urmia area and by reports that the adherence of the Mesopotamian Shiah *mujtahids* to the Turkish *Jahad* had been due to strong coercion.* The Persian public, it was said, began to recall the constant tyranny and extortion, which in the past the Turks had practised towards Shiah pilgrims and which they compared unfavourably with the religious tolerance which Moslems of all sects enjoyed under British rule. It was an indication of the general feeling that, at the end of January, 1915, the leading priests in Tehran volunteered the statement to Sir Walter Townley that they looked forward with pleasure to the British securing control of the holy places in Mesopotamia.

Muscat and Chahbar; October 1914-January 1915.

In October and November 1914, it had appeared that enemy propaganda was likely to cause trouble at Muscat and at Chahbar. The Sultan of Muscat was under British protection;

---

* Although Turco-German pressure may have been partly responsible, these *mujtahids* gave us constant trouble. They thought that British control meant a loss of their power and influence, which was always greater under a weak and corrupt government.

Muscat and Chahbar; October 1914– January 1915. and when, after the outbreak of war with Turkey, it was reported that Turkish agents were instigating a rebel force to attack the Sultan, the British had no option but to assist him. The 95th Infantry (less one company at Jask and Chahbar) from Bombay, and headquarters and one hundred rifles of the 102nd Grenadiers from Bushire, were accordingly sent to reinforce the half-battalion 102nd already at Muscat. In November it was also found necessary to reinforce the 95th Infantry guard at Chahbar in view of a threatened attack by tribesmen on the telegraph station there.

Defence of Muscat; 11th January 1915. The threatened rebel attack on Muscat took place on the 11th January 1915. The British garrison there consisted of about one thousand rifles of the 95th Infantry and 102nd Grenadiers, under command of Colonel S. M. Edwardes of the Grenadiers, who had received instructions from India that he was not to take the offensive but that, if he was attacked, he was to inflict severe punishment on his assailants.

To cover the three coastal towns of Matrah, Muscat and Sidab as well as the residence of the Sultan at Bait-al-Falaj (about two miles west of Muscat), Colonel Edwardes held, with a line of piquet posts, the hill ridges to the southward and westward, which rose to a height of 300 to 860 feet and commanded the main approaches at distances of one to four miles from Muscat, the central of the three towns. The total length of the line that should have been held was about eight miles. But, owing to a considerable reduction in the strength of his force through sickness, Colonel Edwardes was only able to man widely-extended piquets for about three-quarters of this distance. Moreover, he could obtain little or no assistance from the Sultan's local troops, who declined to fight beyond the walls of the towns.

About 2 a.m. on the 11th, the enemy's force, estimated at about 3,000 tribesmen, started its main attack against the right centre of the British outpost line on a frontage of about two miles. Close fighting ensued, but the piquets held their own with the exception of one on the extreme right, held by twenty-five rifles, which was forced to retire about 4 a.m., when its position was occupied by the enemy. As soon as it was light, Colonel Edwardes launched a counter-attack with his main force, the 102nd advancing westward towards the British right centre and the 95th, who were about $1\frac{1}{2}$ miles to the south, advancing northward after clearing their immediate front. By noon the enemy was in full retreat having suffered about five hundred casualties, while those of the British force only totalled twenty.

ARABISTAN

As the enemy remained in the vicinity, arrangements were made to send British naval and military reinforcements. But it was soon seen that these would not be required, as the tribesmen proved to be so disheartened by their losses that they dispersed to their homes abandoning all idea of further hostilities. Clear proof was obtained that Turco-German influence had caused the attack, which had been carried out in an unusually determined fashion under the stimulus of the Turkish declaration of *Jahad*.

In the third week of January the Turks again violated Persian neutrality by sending troops into Arabistan with the avowed intention of making a flank attack on the British at Basra and of injuring the British by destruction of the oil-pipe line. At first it was hoped that the Shaikh of Mohammerah and the Bakhtiaris would be able to protect Ahwaz, the oil-pipe and the oil-field. But the Turkish bribes and cry of *Jahad* proved to be too strong for some of the Shaikh of Mohammerah's tribesmen, who threw off their allegiance and joined other Persian Arab tribes who were assisting the Turks. At the same time they destroyed portions of the pipe line. Up to this period, the British had been very careful, in their operations against the Turks in the Basra *vilayet*, to respect Persian neutrality. But, as the Shaikh of Mohammerah now said that he could no longer control his tribesmen or guarantee the security of foreigners or foreign property, the British were obliged to detach a small body of troops from the Shatt-al-Arab to proceed up the Karun to Ahwaz, which the foreign colony had been forced to evacuate.*

Arabistan; January 1915.

The Persian Government had already, acting on representations from the Shaikh of Mohammerah, protested strongly to the Turkish Government against this violation of Persian neutrality; and the Persian Prime Minister at first told Sir Walter Townley that Persia would resist this Turkish aggression even if it meant war. It is uncertain how far he was influenced in making this statement by the fact that the Russians, advancing again from Julfa, had defeated the Turks and driven them out of Tabriz and by the belief that the tribes under the Shaikh of Mohammerah and the Bakhtiaris would be able to resist the Turkish invasion successfully. But he soon changed his tone. Sir Walter Townley kept him informed of the military

---

* For further details see "The Campaign in Mesopotamia 1914–18," Volume I., Chapter VIII.

action we were taking, and though the Prime Minister regretted that we had been obliged to send troops into Persia he admitted that we had no other course open to us.* He pointed out, however, that our action made the task of government more difficult, as so many of the people were pro-Turkish and were growing more so under the ceaseless activity of enemy agents. For this reason Persia could not declare war against Turkey nor adopt an openly hostile attitude towards her.

It seemed evident to Sir Walter Townley that Persian Ministers realised that Persia had everything to lose if she was driven to take sides against us but that they could not see how to persuade the Persian public of this, lacking any tangible advantage to be gained by joining us. The only tangible advantage that the British could offer would be financial assistance. But to give this would, it was felt, be unwise, as the Cabinet's tenure of office was most uncertain and money we gave to friends one day might be used the next by enemies. Moreover, though for some time past the Russians, incensed by the demands made for withdrawal of Russian troops and the whole anti-Russian movement in the country, had been trying to get rid of this Cabinet, it was doubtful if they were any longer in a position to influence the appointment of its successors.

Enemy emissaries; February 1915. At the beginning of February the Persian Government professed alarm at the number of consuls which the Germans were introducing into the country. It had become clear that the German and Turkish diplomatic and consular officials, already in the country, were abusing the privilege of their appointments by their vigorous attempts to bring Persia into the war, so that the Persians had complete justification for opposing the establishment of any new consulates. But though German agents, styling themselves consuls without Persian permission, and Turkish agents, began to arrive in increasing numbers, the Persian Government were afraid or unable to stop them. From this time forward enemy activity increased greatly in most parts of the country, its chief aim and object being to induce priests, notables, warlike tribes and the general public to bring pressure in various ways on the Government to declare war against the Allies. For this purpose, in

---

* Three or four weeks later, however, the Persian Foreign Minister, just before handing over to a successor, considered it expedient to send the British Minister a formal protest against our action.

ARREST OF GERMAN AGENTS 55

addition to mendacious propaganda, their agents made skilful use of bribery, religious feelings, the prevalent anti-Russian sentiment and local intrigues and quarrels.

When the British troops from Mesopotamia reached Ahwaz they found a German employé of Wonckhaus there in active communication with the enemy and arrested him. They also learnt that three Germans, who had reached Shushtar from Baghdad via Pusht-i-Kuh in the middle of February, were inciting the local notables and priests to declare a *Jahad* against the British. One of these Germans, an ex-consul for Bushire, Wassmuss by name, was on his way to Shiraz, where the openly expressed pro-German sympathies of the Governor-General and the Swedish officers were already causing us concern. It was also learnt that the Bakhtiari chiefs, who had been considering the despatch of a tribal force against the Turks in Arabistan, had decided not to do so ; apparently as the result of a communication they received from an unknown source. The situation generally appeared critical and its seriousness was accentuated by the wide circulation of a report that exaggerated the seriousness of the retirement, on the 3rd March near Ahwaz, of a small British-Indian force before superior numbers of Turks and Arabs. In the circumstances General Barrett, commanding in Mesopotamia, and Sir Percy Cox, who was combining the office of British Political Resident* in the Persian Gulf with that of Chief Political Officer with the Mesopotamia Force, agreed that it was a necessary military measure to arrest all Germans within their reach.

[margin: Arabistan and South Persia; February–March 1915.]

On the 9th March, two Germans, including Dr. Listermann the consul, were arrested at Bushire. This action was fully justified by the documentary evidence we found in the consulate records. There was a telegram from the German Legation at Tehran, despatched in December 1914, giving orders for the destruction of the British cable to India, and a copy of Listermann's reply that he had not the means of doing so. There was another telegram from the Legation, sent in January, announcing Wassmuss' impending departure from Baghdad to make preparations at Shiraz for an undertaking towards Afghanistan and against India, while a third telegram of recent

---

* British political relations with Persia were conducted by the Foreign Office in London, but those with the Persian Gulf ports were to a great extent controlled by the Government of India, who provided most of the consular officers for South Persia.

date gave instructions that an attack on the British Residency at Bushire, which Listermann was inciting the Chief of Dilbar* to make, should synchronise with other anti-Ally hostilities initiated at Tehran. It had been due to reliable information regarding Listermann's incitement of the Dilbar chief to attack the Bushire Residency that we had decided on his arrest. At that time the guard at the Residency and cable station consisted of about one hundred and eighty rifles of the 102nd Grenadiers.

Bushire and South Persia; March 1915. The information regarding Wassmuss rendered it more than ever desirable to arrest him. But though a friendly tribal chief captured one of his companions† (Dr. Lenders) and the baggage of the party, Wassmuss himself escaped. From documents found in this baggage it was learnt that Wassmuss had been in Cairo shortly before the war and in Constantinople when war broke out; and that he had been appointed leader of a mission to induce Persians, Afghans and Indians to start hostilities against the British. This mission, composed of Germans, Turks and Indian revolutionaries and deserters, was to work in several directions, Wassmuss himself being originally destined for Afghanistan and India. His intentions were further indicated by a mass of inflammatory pamphlets, in English and in various Indian dialects, which called on Indian soldiers to mutiny, the Moslem soldiers among them being exhorted to join in the *Jahad*.

To cope with possible trouble at Bushire, British warships were sent there and to Dilbar; arrangements were made to divert a detachment of Indian infantry, on its way to Basra, to land at Bushire if necessary; and the Persian Governor was informed of the unneutral activities of the German consul. The result was so satisfactory that it was found unnecessary to land any troops.

At Shiraz, however, the welcome which Wassmuss met from the Governor-General, the Swedish officers and the gendarmerie seemed to show that they were all ready to subserve German plans; and it soon became evident that the Germans expected that their efforts, combined with the effect of the *Jahad*, would shortly either force the Persian Government to join the Central Powers or would leave Persian Ministers powerless to prevent the gendarmerie from joining other forces, organised by Turco-German agency, in anti-Ally hostilities. It was reported that one of their first acts would be to seize the British consul and consulate at Shiraz.

---

* About twenty-five miles south of Bushire.

† The other German, Bohnstorff, had already started to return to Baghdad.

PERSIAN INACTION

During February and March 1915 the British Minister at Tehran had a most anxious and trying time, not the least difficult of his tasks being the endeavour to bring about better relations between the Russians and the Persian Government.

In Western Persia there was increased enemy activity, and Sir Walter Townley was told by the Persian Prime Minister that he had received information that the Turks intended shortly to advance via Kermanshah and Hamadan on Tehran. Nevertheless, the Persian Government took no effective measures to guard against such a movement. The Russians, whose force in the north-west was still insufficient to drive the Turks out of Persia, were much concerned at the state of affairs in Kermanshah, where Schönemann, a self-styled consul for Sultanabad, was carrying out an energetic agitation. Our own consul at Kermanshah saw no cause for immediate anxiety; but several apparently reliable reports that the *Vali* of Pusht-i-Kuh had espoused the Turkish cause, and the success of Pugin's anti-Ally activities in Isfahan, were indications that there existed many elements of danger. H.M. Government, however, would not agree to a proposal that we should use our influence among the many tribes friendly to us in the Kermanshah area to rouse and assist them to oppose the Turks, unless the Persian Government asked us to do so.

The Swedish Government had agreed, at the special request of the British Government, to allow one of the senior officers, Colonel Folke, to remain with the Persian gendarmerie. But he left Tehran on the 21st February on leave to Sweden, and we felt that his departure at this critical juncture, when there was more reason than ever for judicious control of the ten or twelve Swedes remaining, was most untimely.

Towards the end of February Sir Walter Townley warned the Persian Government that in South Persia we should arrest Germans, whether consuls or private persons, if they persisted in violating Persian neutrality by endeavouring to incite tribesmen to rise against us. But in spite of the evidence we gave them of the guilt of the Germans we had arrested, the Persian Government protested formally against our action, and the Swedish officer commanding the gendarmerie at Shiraz sent the British Resident at Bushire an impudent telegraphic ultimatum demanding their release.

In the second week of March Mustaufi-ul-Mamalik resigned the post of Prime Minister which he had held since the middle of August 1914. At the time it was felt that his tenure of office had been generally marked by weakness, avoidance of

Increasing enemy activity and Persian inaction; February–March 1915.

action likely to arouse public opposition, and a total lack of constructive policy beyond an overwhelming desire to rid Persia of Russian troops. But, judged by subsequent events, he appears to have been no weaker than any of his successors. On the 14th March 1915 he was succeeded by Mushir-ud-Daula, who had the advantage of possessing the confidence of the *Majlis* and who, it was hoped, would adopt a strong attitude towards breaches of Persian neutrality.

British protests; March 1915. The state of affairs at Shiraz and in the Bushire hinterland led the British Minister on the 16th March to make a strong remonstrance to the Persian Foreign Minister against the bias in favour of our enemies which the Persian Government appeared to be displaying. Recapitulating the proofs obtained of the schemes of the German Minister and German agents to involve Persia in hostilities against us, Sir Walter Townley pointed out that the Persian Government had done nothing to stop the progress of these agents, whose action had laid them as open to restraint as if they had been belligerents with arms in their hands. He urged that immediate and energetic instructions should be sent to the authorities in the south to take all necessary steps to check the subversive movement which had sprung up in the gendarmerie-protected footsteps of Wassmuss.

On the same day, hearing from the British consul at Shiraz that Wassmuss' plan to seize the British consul and consulate there might be carried out at any moment, Sir Walter Townley gave Major W. F. T. O'Connor permission to destroy all but one of his cipher codes. Next day Major O'Connor sent another telegram saying that he had definite evidence that the Swedish officers were parties to the German conspiracy and that there were many unmistakable indications that the gendarmerie were prepared to assist actively in the German plans. These were ripe for execution, and he understood that Wassmuss, having grounds for the belief that the whole country and the gendarmerie were behind him, was only awaiting instructions from the German Minister to start hostilities. Sir Walter Townley at once made a vigorous protest to the Persian Prime Minister, demanding that instructions be immediately sent to the Governor-General and the gendarmerie at Shiraz to preserve order, and adding that the Persian Government would be held responsible for any damage to British interests if a disturbance with violence should occur. The Prime Minister agreed to send the necessary orders, and these were so far successful that the Governor-General and the senior Swedish officer at Shiraz both assured Major O'Connor that they intended to maintain neutrality.

Unfortunately, however, it soon became apparent that little reliance could be placed on these assurances. It appeared to the British that the Swedish officers, who had openly expressed their conviction that Sweden would soon join Germany, were co-operating with the Germans in Persia with the definite object of creating at a given moment some situation which would force Persia into war against us. H.M. Government brought the unneutral conduct of the Swedish officers in Persia to the notice of the Swedish Government. But the latter insisted that the allegations made were quite untrue, and at the same time pointed out that as these men were not officers of the Swedish army, but were private individuals, their employment or discharge was entirely a matter for the Persian Government.

On the 6th March Russian troops drove Turks and Kurds out of Dilman. Soon after this, reports began to reach Tabriz and Tehran of the very serious situation, in the Dilman and Urmia districts, of the local Christian communities and of some ten thousand Assyrian Christian refugees who had fled from Turkish territory. Many Christian villages had been totally destroyed and their inhabitants massacred by Kurds, instigated either by Turks or by a local Persian Governor. The greater part of the Urmia district was still in possession of the Turks, and the American and French missionaries at Urmia feared that a general massacre of the refugees in their charge was imminent. One of these missionaries, Dr. Shedd, who estimated that eight hundred Christians had been killed in the Urmia district since its occupation in January by the Turks, appealed for assistance to the United States consul at Tabriz. But he had no means of helping them; and, little reliance being placed on the efficacy of the orders which the Turkish Government were said to have issued to safeguard the Christians, the Russians were asked to despatch a force to relieve Urmia, as being the only other possible solution. *North-West Persia; March 1915.*

Soon after the new Persian Cabinet assumed office it became evident to the British Minister that the Government, the *Majlis*, the press and the public, believing that Germany was certain to win the war, were all hostile to the Allies. The landing of some Russian frontier guards at Enzeli to relieve the regular troops at Kazvin, a movement which the Persians professed, *Doubtful attitude of new Persian Cabinet; March–April 1915.*

Doubtful attitude of new Persian Cabinet; March-April 1915. in spite of assurance to the contrary, to believe to be a preliminary to a Russian occupation of Tehran, led to a vigorous agitation for the total withdrawal of Russian troops from Kazvin and Ardebil. In several frank exchanges of view on the situation with Sir Walter Townley during the third week of March, the Persian Prime Minister, evidently speaking with the strong support of the *Majlis* and of the German and Turkish Legations, insisted on such a withdrawal to pacify and ease the public mind. Persian public opinion, he said, would not allow Persia to side with the Allies; and the Persian Government, having no intention of joining the Central Powers, wished to remain neutral. For this she must have the assistance of neighbouring countries. Sir Walter Townley replied that it appeared clear to him that the prevailing uneasiness in the country was due, not to the presence of the Russian troops, but to the German and Turkish intrigues which were stirring up the country against the Allies. He had already on several occasions remonstrated against the inaction of the Persian Government, who had done nothing to restrain the hostile activities of enemy agents and Persian subjects. To the instances which he had formerly given of these activities at Shiraz, Isfahan, Pusht-i-Kuh and elsewhere he must now add Kermanshah, where the so-called German consul had started to enrol and arm a hostile force. It was only natural, continued Sir Walter Townley, that, seeing no signs of disapprobation, the disaffected elements presumed that the Persian Government approved of these activities. The Prime Minister had been unable to suggest any measures to ensure security if the Russians withdrew, so that it was useless to suggest such a course. In fact, in face of the evident Persian unwillingness or inability to maintain neutrality, it might become necessary for Russia and Great Britain to despatch more troops into Persia. If the Persian Government really meant to remain neutral, they should take steps to recall the pro-German Governor-General and Swedish officers from Fars and replace them by others who could be relied on to adopt an impartial attitude.

The Persian Government appeared, reported Sir Walter Townley, to be wilfully shutting their eyes to a situation intended to lead to an incident that would force Persia into the war, either against her will or at the bidding of an unenlightened populace who did not realise the catastrophic consequences. A suggestion by the Persian Government to recall the Governor-General and Swedish officers from Fars on the sole condition that the Russians would agree to withdraw their troops was another confirmation of the evident unwillingness to face facts; and this, combined with information that the Governor-General at Shiraz was persisting in his close association with the Germans, forced the British Minister on the 2nd April to remonstrate in very plain terms to the Persian Government. This seems to have had some effect. For within a week the Persian Prime Minister, expressing a desire not to forfeit the goodwill of H.M. Government, agreed to drop the question of a Russian withdrawal and to send telegraphic instructions which at once had the effect of bringing about a temporary improvement in the Fars situation. At the same time the Prime Minister asked that the British and Russian Governments would agree to a suspension of the Persian debt service for a period of two years with effect from the 1st August 1914.

In the meantime, the situation at Kermanshah had become more threatening. A Turkish force was reported to be on its way to take Qasr-i-Shirin; German emissaries were displaying increased activity in propaganda and were enlisting and arming local ruffians; and the Persian garrison professed to have no orders either to oppose the invasion or to stop German hostile activities. The town was consequently in a very disturbed state and Sir Walter Townley authorised the British consul to leave there if necessary for Hamadan.

Disquieting news also came from Isfahan, to which place a German named Zugmayer, accompanied by a Captain Griesinger, was said to be on his way. Zugmayer was reported to be a Bavarian reserve officer and a professor of natural history, who had spent four months in British Makran in 1911. As he was well informed about that country it seemed very probable that he was on his way to cause trouble there.

Owing to the assurances and actions of the Persian Prime Minister, Sir Walter Townley believed that the Persian Government really intended at last to take proper steps to maintain neutrality. It also seemed to him that the German propaganda was losing ground and that if left alone it was more likely to lose effect than if Persian public opinion was excited by his bringing constant pressure to bear on the Government. It was for these reasons that on the 12th April he deprecated a suggestion that he should ask the Persian Government to demand the recall of Wassmuss and to prevent German emissaries at Isfahan and elsewhere from leaving those places to proceed eastward. He also disagreed with a proposal from the Foreign Office in London that British officials in South Persia should try to arrange with friendly local chiefs to capture and deport the German emissaries there. He was strongly of the opinion that such action would have precisely the opposite effect to that desired. For the moment, he said, it seemed essential to await developments. News of the occupation of Qasr-i-Shirin by Turkish troops had just arrived; and this unprovoked violation of Persian territory, without even the excuse of the presence in the neighbourhood of either British or Russian troops, had aroused great indignation in the Persian Cabinet.

Further Turkish invasion; April 1915. The Turkish force, which occupied Qasr-i-Shirin on the 12th April, consisted of a few thousand Turkish irregulars and Kurdish tribesmen under the command of Hassan Raouf Bey, who about a month previously had been forced to retire from the Persian frontier by Sinjabi tribesmen aroused to retaliation by Turkish outrages. The news of the Turkish arrival at Qasr-i-Shirin caused a panic at Kermanshah, and the British and Russian consuls and colonies found it advisable to leave there for Hamadan.

Prince Reuss, the German Minister returning from leave to Tehran, and the Austrian Minister had passed across the frontier a few days before the Turkish invasion. They had a very large following and an inordinate amount of baggage, which amongst other things contained rifles, ammunition and a considerable sum in gold; and their journey through Persia was as ostentatious and as much advertised as a royal progress. The Turkish invasion, with its tale of robbery and violence in many Persian villages, however, was difficult to reconcile with the Moslem unity invoked by the *Jahad* which the enemy representatives were advocating so vigorously. It was evidently a considerable embarrassment to them, especially as it came at a time when doubts were again arising in Persian minds of the truth regarding the attitude to the *Jahad* of the Shiah leaders in Mesopotamia, and when circumstantial reports were reaching Tehran of the exactions which the Turks had carried out during their brief occupation of Tabriz. For a short time indeed it seemed quite possible that Persian resentment would lead her to join the Allies. But the Germans, realising the urgent necessity for stopping Raouf Bey's advance, got the Turkish Ambassador at Tehran to represent the situation to his Government, who then sent orders which stopped the Turkish advance at Karind.

Change of Government; April 1915. Soon after receipt of the news of the Turkish invasion and possibly owing to it, or to his realisation that he was not equal to the task of keeping Persia out of the war,

Mushir-ud-Daula resigned the post of Prime Minister. The question of his successor was a difficult one, owing to the many conflicting powerful influences that had to be considered, not the least among them being that of the Allied representatives on whose financial goodwill so much depended. At this stage Mr. Marling* learnt from the Manager of the Imperial Bank of Persia that, owing to the recent unusually large demands by the German Legation and by others, the bank would be unable to make further payments in silver and would have to pay out notes only. This would mean a run on the bank and a financial crisis. As Tehran, where the police were the only force on which the Government could rely, was already in a panic-stricken state owing to wild rumours of imminent Turkish and Russian attacks on the town and of an Armenian rising, serious disorders would certainly ensue. These, our enemies, with the aid of the approaching German Minister with his train of agitators and with an ample command of silver drawn from the bank itself, would easily be able to turn to account against us. The British, Russian and French Ministers decided, therefore, to approach the Shah at once and urge him to appoint a new Prime Minister, whose name they suggested. There were two or three days of discussion and on the 26th April the Shah appointed Ain-ud-Daula, a selection in which—though it was not theirs—the Allied representatives concurred.

While this discussion was proceeding, Sir Edward Grey telegraphed to the British Ambassador at Petrograd that a proposed despatch of Russian troops to Kazvin seemed to him to be inexpedient, unless it was by request of the Persian Government. In view of the recent Turkish aggression and its possible consequences, the Allies should, he considered, give the new Cabinet all possible assistance but should refrain from military movement unless the situation imperatively demanded it.

One of the first acts of the new Cabinet was to pass a bill rapidly through the *Majlis* authorising the Imperial Bank of Persia to pay notes instead of silver for the next sixty days.† But in the matter of maintaining Persian neutrality against German and Turkish violations their conduct proved less satisfactory. This was not altogether surprising. The

---

* Mr. (afterwards Sir Charles) Marling relieved Sir Walter Townley on the 15th April, 1915.

† The Cabinet first obtained a British Government guarantee that the bank would then resume silver payments.

Majlis had only accepted Ain-ud-Daula's appointment as being preferable to that of the alternative candidate and, moreover, considered that it was the work of the Russian and British Legations. In these circumstances Prince Reuss, with considerable money and several competent agents at his command, was able to create an atmosphere very unfavourable to the new Cabinet ; and in consequence, though the Government were well aware of the danger to which they were allowing the country to drift, they could not find heart for the moment to take any steps in opposition to German action and intrigue.

Bushire; April 1915. To return to South Persia. On the 5th April the Commander-in-Chief in India sent telegraphic instructions to General Nixon, due at Bushire that day on his way to take over command in Mesopotamia, to discuss the situation there with Sir Percy Cox's deputy. There was a possibility that the Khans of the interior, instigated by Wassmuss, might attack the Anglophile chief, Haidar Khan of Bandar Rig.* General Nixon was, however, to bear in mind the objections to our becoming entangled on the mainland and the importance of avoiding a rupture with Persia. It was not our policy, he was told, to interfere in tribal quarrels ; and our action should be limited to protecting the life and property of British subjects at Bushire. On the 7th April half the 96th Infantry landed at Bushire and relieved the double-company 102nd Grenadiers as Residency guard. This increase in strength, the instructions from the central Persian Government already alluded to, and the news of our victory at Shaiba in Mesopotamia all combined to ease the situation.

Lord Hardinge's intervention; March–April 1915. At the end of March the Viceroy of India had authorised the Persian Consul-General there to send to his Government a telegraphic message expressing Lord Hardinge's personal friendly feelings (based on his former residence at Tehran) and hopes that Persia would not allow the selfish machinations of Turks and Germans to plunge her into a useless war. The reply, received by the Consul-General on the 11th April, was most satisfactory in tone. It asserted Persia's determination to maintain neutrality and stated that a *moratorium* would assist her. A week later, however, a second telegram was

---

* In addition to other past services, Haidar Khan's co-operation had given us timely revelation of the German plans.

received by the Consul-General from his Government, for communication to the Viceroy, which was couched in anything but conciliatory terms. It intimated that if the British Government, to avoid danger to themselves, desired Persia to remain neutral, they should abstain from such questionable actions as closing telegraph offices in Arabistan and arresting German consuls. They should withdraw all British troops from Persia and send no more there and should also request Russia to vacate Persia, thus leaving her free to organise her own army under Persian officers for the preservation of neutrality. Great Britain should, further, allow Persia a *moratorium*. For disturbances, which might endanger British possessions and which were due to difficulties created by British and Russians, the Persian Government would, they said, accept no responsibility. Lord Hardinge, who repeated the correspondence to London, asked the Consul-General to thank the Persian Government on his behalf for this frank exposition of their views and to make it clear to them that his own previous message had been a purely personal expression of friendly concern and that the questions mentioned by them in their second telegram were matters for the Foreign Office in London to deal with through the British Minister at Tehran.

This second telegram was despatched about the time of Mushir-ud-Daula's resignation and before the appointment of his successor; and it coincided with a marked recrudescence of enemy activity in Fars. The British troops then in South Persia consisted of a half-battalion 96th Infantry at Bushire and about a company 95th Infantry scattered in detachments at Jask, Chahbar, Lingeh, Bandar Abbas, Bahrein and Hangam At Jask the telegraph guard had been raised to the strength of 130 rifles at the beginning of April, owing to tribal unrest in Persian Makran and a reported imminent attack by a force under a well-known arms-dealing *mullah*, which, materialising on the 17th April, was repulsed without difficulty and without loss to our men. At Ahwaz, there was a mixed brigade from Mesopotamia, which General Nixon had just decided to reinforce so as to clear the Turks out of Arabistan.

On the 22nd April, the Government of India telegraphed their view of the Persian situation to London. It appeared to them that the Persian Government, with an exaggerated idea of the importance of their neutrality and really embarrassed by the public hatred of Russia with its consequent anti-British feeling, were inclined under Turco-German pressure to make impossible demands on us. To offer further inducements to

Views of Government of India; April 1915.

them to preserve neutrality would, therefore, probably be construed as a sign of weakness. Consequently we should at the most concede them a *moratorium*. We should also relax pressure on them in regard to Fars and South Persia, as it was unlikely to do any good. Moreover, so long as Bushire was safe, our interests in those parts were not paramount for the time being.

<small>Jask and Chahbar; April–May 1915.</small> The unrest in Makran, fomented by enemy agents from Shiraz, threatened further trouble ; and in the third week of April it was considered advisable to reinforce the guards at Jask and Chahbar from Muscat.* But the *mullah's* party contented itself for the time being with wrecking the telegraph line between Chahbar and Jask ; and Sir Percy Cox, whose views were asked for, deprecated any attempts on our part to take the offensive against the raiders. He hoped to induce the local Khans, whom we subsidised to guard the telegraph line, to restore order without our assistance and thus enable parties to go out and repair the line. Chahbar, which was held by one hundred men of the 95th Infantry under Lieutenant C. M. Maltby, was attacked on the 3rd May. But although, after a few hours' fighting, the raiders were repulsed with loss,† the *mullah* remained in the neighbourhood preaching *Jahad*. Consequently further attacks seemed probable.

<small>General situation; May 1915.</small> At this stage, the British, Russian, French and Belgian diplomatic representatives at Tehran all agreed that the increasing dangers of the situation called for the early despatch, from Russia, of troops to Enzeli. Trouble threatened from many directions. Raouf Bey was still at Karind with his force of irregulars. German emissaries at Kermanshah, Sultanabad, Hamadan and Isfahan were recruiting and arming followers, intriguing with the neighbouring tribes and inducing priests, officials, gendarmerie and " democrats " by lavish bribes and propaganda to agitate and urge the Government to declare against the Allies. At Shiraz the Governor-General was lending himself unreservedly to the schemes of Wassmuss, whose lavish bribery and lying propaganda only required this support to create a strong current of public opinion against the British. The noisy

---

* The 95th Infantry (less detachments) and half the 126th Baluchistan Infantry were at Muscat.

† They left 20 dead behind them. Our casualties were 4 killed and 3 wounded.

BRITISH ACTION AT BUSHIRE

and mischievous " democrats " were specially amenable to his overtures ; *Jahad* was being openly preached in the town ; and all British employés or adherents were being threatened and intimidated. As the only means of averting serious trouble, Major O'Connor urged the immediate removal of the Governor-General and the temporary appointment in his place of Qawam-ul-Mulk. At Bushire, an attack on Bandar Rig still seemed probable and Wassmuss was visiting Saulat-ud-Daula, evidently with a view to enlisting his support.

The Persian Governor of Bushire, hearing that the headman of a neighbouring village was collecting armed men to attack the British Residency, despatched a force which included some gendarmerie to apprehend this headman. But the defection of the gendarmerie forced the Governor to apply for British military assistance. This was at once afforded. On the 7th May, a detachment of about two hundred rifles 96th Infantry, moving to carry out the Governor's request and meeting with resistance, rushed the village and captured the headman, dispersing his following.* Bushire was then reinforced from India by the remaining half-battalion 96th Infantry, which dropped fifty men *en route* to strengthen the post at Chahbar. [Bushire; May 1915.]

On the 10th May Sir Edward Grey asked Mr. Marling whether the Russian troops, whom it was proposed to send to Enzeli, were required to protect Allied Legations and subjects or whether their presence was meant to create a diversion in our favour by establishing a situation favourable to us. If the latter was the intention, it seemed to him that their arrival might precipitate a declaration by Persia against us. Mr. Marling replied, two days later, that Allied Legations and subjects were in no personal danger and that the object of asking for Russian troops was to show that our patience had limits and also that we had the means to support a Persian Ministry which took firm measures to preserve neutrality. He was convinced that the appearance of Russian troops would not provoke the Persian Government into abandoning neutrality. No Persian desired this, but the country might be jockeyed into it unless we showed unmistakably that we were in earnest. Two or three thousand Russian troops sent to Enzeli would suffice ; and reinforcements should also be sent to Bushire. Sir Edward Grey then telegraphed to Petrograd, asking for the views of the Russian Government. [Question of Russian reinforcements; May 1915.]

---

* Twenty-eight of them were killed, wounded or captured. Our casualties were three.

British and Allied policy; May 1915. In England and India it was clear that the chances of Persia being drawn into the war, even unwillingly, were appreciably greater; and it became necessary to determine what action we should take in such an eventuality, especially as India had practically no troops available. After some telegraphic discussion between London and Simla, it was agreed that it should be our policy to leave the interior of Persia alone, and limit ourselves to holding the Bushire peninsula.

On the 16th May, Mr. Marling reported that there had been a very marked improvement in the situation during the last week. He and the Russian Minister thought that, provided they were given reasonable support, the Persian Government would succeed is maintaining neutrality and independence in spite of Turco-German activities. The Allied Ministers three days previously had discussed the situation and the best manner in which the Allies could help the Prime Minister. They had told him that they knew that the Persian Government required money, but that they could not hold out hopes of their two Governments granting anything more than moderate advances from time to time to tide over the period of the war. The Prime Minister said that he quite understood, that he wished to work with the Allies and he asked for a small sum required for urgent expenses. The British and Russian Ministers agreed to a small immediate advance by the Imperial Bank of Persia and this met the wishes of the Prime Minister, who hoped that if the Allies were satisfied with the results they would continue to give similar support. He seemed to be confident that he could master the situation and he had hopes of obtaining full powers from the *Majlis* or of inducing them to adjourn for a long holiday.

On the same day Mr. Marling also reported that the Russian Minister had just heard that the Russian military authorities proposed the despatch of two divisions to seize the personnel of the enemy missions at Tehran, whence, after a short stay, they would again withdraw. But all the Allied Ministers considered that such severe measures were unnecessary and inadvisable. They considered that, provided a small Russian force was held in readiness at Enzeli in case the course of events rendered its presence at Tehran necessary, the best policy to pursue would be that outlined in the telegram mentioned above.

In a despatch to the Foreign Office of the 18th May Mr. Marling, describing the previous month's events in the country, said that the senior Swedish officer in Fars was being relieved and that Ain-ud-Daula had promised to recall the Governor-

General from Shiraz and, pending the selection of a successor, to appoint Qawam-ul-Mulk as acting Governor. One of the most interesting features of the despatch is the opinion Mr. Marling expressed of the effect of the Turco-German propaganda in Persia and of the views generally held there. He considered that the considerable success of the Turco-German propaganda was due entirely to Persian hatred for Russia and was no proof of any affection for Germany. The desire of the average Persian to see Russia defeated had been encouraged by Swedish reports of Germany's military might and, though he might not always believe them, by the German accounts of their glorious victories. No thinking Persian wanted to go to war with Russia and Great Britain owing to the inevitable consequences. But most of them felt acute satisfaction at seeing Russia flouted by Germany; and such public opinion as there was disliked and opposed any Government action which interfered with German activity. The Persians did not expect to gain by our defeat, as Germany was too far away; and they believed that Turkey would be encouraged by Germany to recoup herself in Asia for the expenses of the war. They did not realise, however, that they were in danger of being hustled into the war by Germany and so they continued to play with fire by hampering Ministers in their endeavours to maintain Persian neutrality. This would not have mattered if the Persian Cabinet had been strong. But it was not, and the Allies were consequently obliged to rely on their own strength.

On the night of the 18th May, the manager of the Russian Bank (and Russian Vice-Consul) at Isfahan, was murdered, an outrage which was strongly suspected to be due to German instigation. Next day, possibly as a result of this, Ain-ud-Daula, whose position was extraordinarily difficult, tendered his resignation. But the Shah persuaded him to remain in office; and two days later a small Russian force landed at Enzeli, affording him proof that the Allies were prepared to support him. *Murder of Russian bank manager at Isfahan; May 1915.*

On the 19th May the Russians, having defeated the Turks at Dilman a fortnight previously, reached Van, where they relieved a garrison of insurgent Armenians, who had been holding that place against the Turks; and on the 25th they re-occupied Urmia. But as Turkish forces remained in the Ushnu–Sauj Bulag and Karind–Qasr-i-Shirin areas, German emissaries still had unopposed access to Kermanshah and Isfahan.

Ain-ud-Daula showed no sign of fulfilling his promise to recall the Governor-General of Fars, where the situation was still critical. Major O'Connor reported on the 22nd May that *Critical situation in Fars; May 1915.*

Qawam and Saulat had composed their differences and had agreed to do all they could to preserve Persian neutrality so long as this was the policy of the Government. But Wassmuss was at Borazjan doing his utmost to incite the Khans of the Bushire hinterland to start hostilities against Bushire and Bandar Rig.

Bakhtiaris and the Arabistan oil-field; May 1915. Owing to the possibility of Persia declaring against us, Sir Percy Cox arranged a meeting with the Bakhtiari chiefs to discuss the situation and especially the security of the Anglo-Persian oil-field. The meeting took place on the 23rd and 24th May and, although the chiefs did not consider it probable that Persia would declare against us, they stated that in such an eventuality they would be unable to afford us support. For, if they did so, the tribal hostages at Tehran would be killed. They gave their word, however, that they would give us twenty days' warning before withdrawing their guarantee for the safety and security of the oil-field and the foreigners employed there.

British policy; May 1915. On the 29th May the Government of India recommended to H.M. Government that, in the event of war with Persia, the following should be the policy which we should definitely adopt :—

(a) We should leave Persia as a whole severely alone, taking what steps were possible to extricate our Legation and consuls. Russia should be left to take such action in North Persia as she desired.

(b) We should try, by subsidising local tribes, to safeguard the oil-field and pipe-line in Arabistan.

(c) We should, if possible, continue to hold Bushire and the telegraphic stations at Jask and Chahbar. For this it would be essential that our troops holding those places should be supported by warships, which should also blockade the Persian ports.

In forwarding these recommendations for Mr. Marling's views Sir Edward Grey told him that, in case of war with Persia, the situation on the Indian frontier would so tax the military resources remaining in India as to preclude operations in South Persia on anything but a very small scale. Mr. Marling replied that he concurred fully in the Indian recommendations.

Swedish officers of gendarmerie; May 1915. The discussion between the British and Swedish Governments regarding the Swedish officers of the gendarmerie resulted in May in the Swedish Government saying that they were prepared to advise these officers to resign in consideration of suitable financial compensation. But Mr. Marling and the Russian Minister at Tehran had by this time both come to the conclusion that it would on the whole be better for the Swedes to remain at their posts. Though, by the incautious expression of their anti-Russian feelings and their equally imprudent intimacy with the German Legation and agents, they had enabled the German propaganda to make great headway, they now appeared to realise the results of their intervention and were displaying greater readiness to carry out the orders of the Persian Government to maintain neutrality. Most of them could be relied upon, said Mr. Marling, to prevent the Germans bringing about any serious act of violence calculated to force Persia into war. Whereas if they resigned, the Germanophile Persian officers would become formidable German instruments and chaos would result on the southern trade routes. The attitude of the Swedish officers towards the Allies was not likely, continued Mr. Marling, to be friendly and they would probably in consequence be troublesome to our consuls. But it was best to tolerate this, especially as their anti-Russian attitude had endeared them to the *Majlis*, whose protests if they were withdrawn would certainly embarrass Ain-ud-Daula.

During June the German hostile activities in Persia continued. Zugmayer and Griesinger were reported to have left Isfahan for Kerman about the 6th; and two other Germans (Wagner and Paschen) were also reported to have left there with a party of eight Austrian soldiers, thirty-two Persian levies, a machine gun and twelve mule loads of ammunition on the 16th, ostensibly for Yezd and Meshed, but really for Afghanistan via Nain and the desert. Further, a party of two German officers, twelve German or Austrian soldiers and forty-three Turks and Caucasians was said to have reached Isfahan on the 20th June, and another party of two Germans with several Indians, including Pathan sepoy deserters from the British army, was said to have left Kermanshah, destined for Afghanistan, on the 13th June. [German action and its effect; June 1915.]

At the end of the month Mr. Marling telegraphed that there were disquieting elements in the situation at Isfahan, which had become the main centre of German activities since the arrival of Russian troops at Kazvin. There were four or five German agents at Isfahan, with about thirty Austrian prisoners of war who had escaped from Trans-Caspia and two hundred armed retainers who had been recruited locally. The British and Russian consuls might possibly be in danger, but Mr. Marling deprecated their withdrawal as a sign of weakness. The Persian Prime Minister, though full of promises

German action and its effect; June 1915. to check the German intrigues and disarm their followers, actually took no effective action. He was in a difficult position, being the object of constant attack for his Anglo-Russian sympathies by the strong pro-German elements in the *Majlis* and the press ; and he consequently met all representations by the Allied Ministers with threats to resign and demands for the withdrawal of the Russian troops. As any other Cabinet would probably be worse, the British and Russian Ministers could see nothing for it but to support him. Persia would not, thought Mr. Marling, join the enemy intentionally, but the German parties were too strong to be arrested without actual fighting and for this no Persian Cabinet cared to be responsible. Mr. Marling also considered that the German mission would possibly be able to reach Afghanistan and that other Germans would create a situation at Kerman similar to that at Isfahan. To authorise British consuls to recruit guards for themselves would, he thought, be useless, as it would tend to precipitate a serious incident such as the Germans appeared to desire. Mr. Marling could only suggest that the British and Russian Governments, when informing the Persian Government of the advances which it was intended to grant them, should give them a very strong warning regarding their responsibility for any untoward results of their supineness.

On the 26th June information was received from Meshed that Wagner and Paschen had proceeded eastward from Nain, evidently bound for Seistan or Baluchistan. On the previous day the Secretary of State for India, referring to the reports from Persia, telegraphed to the Viceroy, enquiring if the consuls at Meshed, Birjand and Kerman were alive to the importance of preventing the entry into Afghanistan of the Germans and of otherwise neutralising their efforts, and asking whether arrangements could not be made with the Amir to arrest any German crossing the Afghan frontier. On the 28th Mr. Marling reported that the Persian Government, at last displaying some signs of energy, had disarmed the followers of a German agent on his way to Meshed and had sent him back to Tehran. They had also got the German Minister to promise to recall Wassmuss.* During June, Russian officials in Persia and Persian Ministers also displayed some anxiety regarding reports of the state of Afghanistan and of the Amir's intentions. The Government of India was,

---

* Whether this was done or not is unknown. But Wassmuss appears to have been prepared to disobey any such order.

however, able to reassure them. It was also reported that the well-known German secret service agent Baron Oppenheim had left Constantinople for Afghanistan with a large sum in ready money.

Throughout June, Wassmuss continued his efforts, from the neighbourhood of Borazjan, to organise attacks on Bushire by bribes and by promises of support from a German warship. Three other Germans with a quantity of arms and ammunition were said to have joined him towards the end of the month; and he looked so like being successful that the Persian Governor appealed to his Government to prevent trouble by getting Wassmuss recalled. His action, said the Governor, gave the British justifiable grounds for military intervention. *Bushire; June 1915.*

In Mesopotamia and India the situation was being closely watched. From Basra, General Nixon sent two captured Turkish 13-pounder guns with instructors to train gun-crews from the Indian infantry at Bushire; and just afterwards (on the 24th June) he was warned by India that he might be called on to send troops there at short notice. On the 28th, receiving orders that he was to be responsible for its defence, he was told that our sole aim was to protect Bushire and that no operations outside that place were to be undertaken without sanction from India. H.M. Government desired to avoid any military action that might serve as an excuse for Persia to abandon her neutrality and also any military commitment in that country. The troops at Bushire would henceforward form part of Force "D," the other troops in the Persian Gulf and the Gulf of Oman coming under the command of the senior officer present, then Colonel W. H Wooldridge of the 126th Baluchistan Infantry at Muscat.

Enemy propaganda was also active along the Persian Gulf littoral, but it had little effect and at Muscat the arrest of four Arabs acting as German agents had a tranquillising effect. In Makran, however, the Khan of Bampur was reported to be collecting a force to join the *mullah*, who had previously attacked Jask and Chahbar, in further hostilities against the British; and in the last week of June the *Dalhousie* was sent to Gwadur to meet an attack there which was reported to be imminent. Before the ship could arrive, however, the attack had been definitely repulsed by a party of the Makran Levy Corps. *Persian Gulf littoral; June 1915.*

OPERATIONS IN PERSIA

Turkish retirement; June 1915. At the end of June Mr. Marling reported that, following an affair at Karind between Turks and Persian tribesmen, the German Minister had intervened with the result that Raouf Bey's force was to withdraw to Qasr-i-Shirin.

Situation in India; June 1915. About the same time, Lord Kitchener asked the Commander-in-Chief in India if he could not release more regular British battalions from that country. Sir Beauchamp Duff in reply said that he could not do so. He had already had to meet three heavy frontier raids and would have had to meet more if it had not been for the correct attitude adopted by the Amir of Afghanistan. The latter, however, was in a difficult position and might find himself forced to declare against us by the arrival in his country of the several German parties which the Persians would not, and we could not, stop.

German account of activities of their emissaries; August 1914–June 1915. Before concluding this chapter, it will make the situation clearer to give a short account (derived from German sources*) of the activities of some of the German agents in Persia up to the end of June 1915.

In August or September 1914, the German Government, concurring in a suggestion by Enver Pasha to send an expedition to induce the Amir of Afghanistan to invade India, sent about twenty-five Germans to Turkey to lend support to the enterprise. Of these Niedermayer says that only one† knew anything at all about Persia, the remainder being mainly men with African experience. On the 16th–19th September, Niedermayer and Zugmayer, who were both to take part in the expedition, attended a conference on the question at the Berlin Foreign Office, at which three Indians were also present.

German money, arms and organisation and a declaration of *Jahad* by Turkey, would, it was hoped, enable the Central Powers to raise Moslem Asia against the Allies and divert much of Great Britain's attention from Europe. Turkey was not yet ready to join in the war, but when she did she would form an alliance with Persia so as to afford the expedition a secure base.

Niedermayer, who had only returned from a trip to India in the spring of 1914, put little faith in the stories of revolutionary

---

* " Unter der Glutsonne Irans " by Oskar von Niedermayer ; " Meine Diplomatenfahrt ins Verschlossene Land " by Legations-Sekretär Dr. W. O. von Hentig ; and diaries and other documents captured by us in Persia.

† Presumably Wassmuss.

GERMAN ACCOUNTS

unrest in India, in the power or capacity of Indians to overthrow British rule or even in the probability of internal risings on the appearance of an enemy on the Indian frontier. Nevertheless, thinking that much could be done in Persia and Afghanistan to divert British attention, he agreed to take part in the enterprise. But he did not like the manner in which it was being organised. Dual control by the Foreign Office and the General Staff, combined with lack of control in the expedition itself, whose members were all of equal status, seemed likely to allow the political and commercial aspects of the project to overshadow its military objects. The lack of definite instructions as to the procedure to be followed or the action to be taken soon led both him and Zugmayer to the conclusion that, to do any good, the expedition must be organised on a military basis.

By the end of September, most of the members of the expedition under the leadership of Wassmuss were at or nearing Aleppo, while Niedermayer and Zugmayer in Constantinople were discussing plans, including that of moving through Persia in parallel columns, with Enver Pasha. He was confident that the Amir of Afghanistan would fall in with their plans, but, as these would be carried out under the banner of *Jahad*, it was undesirable that the expedition should be accompanied by too many obviously Christian Germans. Consequently, said Enver, these must have Turkish officers' commissions and wear Turkish uniform. To this the Germans agreed, though they did not like the idea it suggested of Turkish control.

On the 16th October Zugmayer, Paschen* and Schönemann left Constantinople for Aleppo with some of the baggage and £60,000 in gold. Niedermayer, his doctor brother, Consten (a commercial expert†) and Griesinger remained in Constantinople waiting for the arrival of stores and equipment which had been sent off some time previously from Berlin, labelled "Travelling Circus." But the sight of wireless masts among the stores aroused the suspicions of the Rumanian authorities, who, finding on closer inspection that the so-called fireworks included machine guns and rifle ammunition, confiscated the whole consignment. Niedermayer had, therefore, to send to Berlin for more equipment and to despatch Consten to facilitate its transit through Rumania by bribery.

Niedermayer had many troubles and difficulties to overcome. There was constant friction between Germans and Turks; and

---

* Two Germans of this name took part in the expedition.

† Consten subsequently left the expedition, i.e., after it reached Baghdad.

German account of activities of their emissaries; August 1914–June, 1915. there was also dissension among the Germans themselves over the proposal to organise the expedition on a military basis, owing to the loss of individual liberty which this would involve. Moreover, Wassmuss, who appears to have been rather arbitrary, uncultured and eccentric,* was an unpopular leader; and the superior attitude which he and Zugmayer adopted as experts on oriental conditions did not improve matters. Eventually some of the objecting members were dismissed for misbehaviour and others were allowed to join the column fitting out for an attack on the Suez Canal.

At this stage, learning of the British intention to attack Basra, Niedermayer, who knew the locality, proposed to use the Turkish gunboat and the German steamship *Ekbatana* to form a block in the river below Abadan and to set on fire the oil tanks and refinery at that place. The Turkish authorities agreed, and Niedermayer was setting out for Basra to supervise the arrangements when orders came from Berlin not to destroy Abadan but to retain it for Turco-German use. Niedermayer was to await the arrival of a mission with special equipment that was being sent for the purpose. But Niedermayer declined to have anything to do with the new proposal, which he implies was responsible for preserving Abadan for the British.

On the 5th December, the second consignment of stores and equipment having arrived, Niedermayer, his doctor brother, Consten and Griesinger, with twenty-seven men left Constantinople, reaching Aleppo eight days later. From Aleppo they were to go to Mosul to join the expedition which Halil Bey was organising for an advance into Persia. Niedermayer also says that they learnt then for the first time that the Turks some weeks before had sent a small diplomatic mission† to Afghanistan under Obeidulla Effendi. The suspicion thus aroused that the Turks were not keeping faith with them was not lessened by the passive obstruction they and several of the other members encountered in their journeys to Aleppo and beyond. About this time the mission under Klein destined to defend Abadan reached Aleppo, but, as the British had already secured Abadan, Klein proposed to proceed to Karbala and induce the Shiah *mujtahids* there to start anti-Ally propaganda in Persia.

In the meantime, Wassmuss, who had failed to persuade the Turks to agree to his own plan to move through South-West and South Persia, had decided to go there himself and work

---

* He was believed by several of his companions to have turned Moslem.
† This never reached its destination.

independently, as from his knowledge of the area he felt confident of speedier chances of success there than elsewhere in Persia. Niedermayer, sorry to lose the benefit of his expert knowledge, but unable to oppose him, took over control of the main expedition and left with him on the 21st December for Baghdad, where Niedermayer wished to consult with Raouf Bey, who was to lead the Turkish expedition from there. The remainder of the mission, consisting of about a dozen Germans,* was to leave later for Mosul.

At Baghdad, meeting Schönemann, whom the British occupation of Basra had stopped from taking up the post of consul there, Niedermayer learnt from Raouf Bey that he had just received orders to abandon the Afghan expedition and to hand over his men and material to Sulaiman Askari, commanding in Mesopotamia, for the attack on the British at Basra. Raouf also said that he had failed to get into communication with the Amir of Afghanistan and doubted if Turks or Germans could get permission to enter that country. He also considered that the only way they could get through Persia would be in disguise or in considerable force. So that ultimate success in Afghanistan was doubtful. Niedermayer, unpleasantly surprised at these opinions, tried to ascertain Raouf's immediate intentions. But he only obtained evasive replies, though he understood that Raouf was trying to make arrangements to enter Persia with the assistance of Kurdish tribes. Niedermayer decided, however, to carry out his orders from Berlin, if necessary without help from the Turks, whose motives he was uncertain of and the value of whose assistance from a political point of view he was doubtful about. He realised by this time that the Turks regarded the Turco-Persian border area, and indeed all eastern Islamic countries, as a political domain in which they must preserve for themselves a predominating influence ; and that any German activities therein, which did not confine themselves within very narrow limits and were not based on purely military considerations, would be stoutly opposed by the Turks.

Reviewing the situation, Niedermayer decided that the German expedition would not be able to enter Persia in one body and that all things considered it would make their task easier if they were to split up into small parties, working at some distance from one another. As, in the absence of Turkish assistance, they would thus be very weak, it would be necessary

---

* No complete list of the German members of the expedition is available, but the names of fourteen to twenty-two are given in different documents covering the period from December 1914 to June 1915.

German account of activities of their emissaries; August 1914–June 1915.

for them not only to avoid all hostilities but to make it appear that their entry into Persia was in that country's own interests. Niedermayer telegraphed these views to the Embassy at Constantinople for orders from Berlin and at the same time directed the main body of the expedition, which had left Aleppo on the 7th January 1915, to move to Baghdad by the shortest route.

Raouf, on his return visit to Niedermayer, was evidently bent on dissuading the Germans from their intention to continue with the expedition. He expatiated on the countermeasures which the Russians and British were taking in Persia, especially at Hamadan and Kermanshah, and of the great difficulties he anticipated in getting into Persia, even with the support of the Karbala clergy and of Kurdish tribes. To Niedermayer it seemed clear that in any case Raouf's proposed procedure, with its obvious annexationist designs, did not fit in at all with Pan-Islamic propaganda and was consequently unlikely to open the way to Afghanistan. This was all the more unfortunate that, having left everything to the Turks, the Germans had made no previous arrangements in the Persian frontier provinces, where, even though not taken in conjunction with the Turks, their action would appear to be taken in Turkish military interests.

At the same time, Sulaiman Askari, professing concern at the unrest among the Arabs which he said the presence of Germans in Mesopotamia was causing, requested them to dress themselves to look as little like Germans as possible. Moreover, although he said that he had received no instructions from his Government regarding this German expedition, he maintained that he was entitled to take over its equipment to supplement the deficiencies of his own force.

The news from Persia at this period was so good that an early start seemed to Niedermayer to be most advisable. Though the Russians had retaken Tabriz, the general situation had obliged them and the British to adopt a more conciliatory tone to the Persians; and the tribes of Pusht-i-Kuh, the Bakhtiaris and the Qashqais, all of them hitherto considered pro-British, were said to be desirous of negotiating with the Germans. Niedermayer decided after much deliberation to push some of his companions forward into and through Persia by stages, creating as they went a favourable atmosphere (by bribery and propaganda) for the subsequent passage of his main body and for a line of communication by which he could receive telegrams or letters, stores and such support or reinforcements as were available. Kermanshah was to be the first stage; Isfahan via Daulatabad the second stage; and from there his people were to feel their way forward cautiously to Yezd and Kerman, getting into communication with Wassmuss at Shiraz. Niedermayer himself would go to Tehran to direct matters from there and to obtain information regarding conditions in southern Khurasan. On the 23rd January he sent Schönemann off to the Persian frontier area to start arrangements for the move to Kermanshah and on the 28th Wassmuss, Dr. Lenders and Bohnstorff, with some Persians and Indians, left Baghdad *en route* to Borazjan via Kut-al-Amara and Pusht-i-Kuh.

About this time, after an official intimation that the Turkish expedition to Afghanistan had been abandoned, Niedermayer and Klein received written orders from Sulaiman Askari, then lying wounded in hospital,* detailing the German members of the two expeditions to posts on the Turkish Mesopotamian lines of communication. This was followed by a further order stopping all German activities in Mesopotamia, a step which was due apparently to Klein's recent mission to Karbala, which the Turks had regarded with much disfavour. Both Niedermayer and Klein replied that, as their men and material could only be placed at the Turks' disposal by orders from Germany, they had referred the question to the Embassy at Constantinople. In the meantime they both resigned their Turkish commissions. Further coercive action by the Turks soon increased the tension between them and the Germans. Wagner, Paschen and Griesinger, who had just reached Baghdad from Aleppo and who had been sent off by Niedermayer on the 30th January to join Schönemann, were stopped by the Turks at Qizil Ribat, disarmed and sent back to Baghdad; and Sulaiman Askari, without asking Niedermayer's permission, took possession of all the expedition stores and equipment which had just arrived. This action led to all the German members of the expedition taking refuge with their personal belongings in the German consulate and telegraphing requests for assistance to the Embassy at Constantinople. In reply Niedermayer was told that there had evidently been some misunderstanding and that he was to await at Baghdad the arrival of the German Minister on his way back to Tehran. In the meantime, the machine guns should join the Turkish Basra force and the other Germans of the expedition should assist the Turks in military administrative work in connection with that force.

---

* He had been wounded in an affair with the British near Qurna on the 20th January.

German account of activities of their emissaries; August 1914– June 1915. Niedermayer was of opinion that the military situation did not justify the diversion of his men and material to the defence of Mesopotamia, where the Turks were in no immediate danger either from the Russians or the British. In any case he considered that the limited support which his expedition could afford was less likely to be useful in Mesopotamia than in causing a diversion elsewhere by creating Anglo-Indian strife. He was convinced that Sulaiman Askari's action had only been prompted by the desire to paralyse German activity and to prevent their interfering with Raouf Bey's project.

Pending the Minister's arrival, Niedermayer continued his plans and preparations. The Turks would not, however allow any but German consular officials to travel by the Khaniqin-Kermanshah route, although they agreed grudgingly to allow Niedermayer to send P. Paschen and Voigt into Persia via Mosul and Sauj Bulag. The necessity for avoiding opposition by Russians, British or pro-Ally tribes had led Niedermayer to select Isfahan as the most suitable place for the main Persian base of his expedition. But as the Persian Government were evidently incapable of assuring the safety of his expedition he would have to arrange himself for its security. This would not be easy to reconcile with Germany's professed friendly intentions in face of the remonstrances which the Persian Government, under pressure from the Russian and British Legations, were already making against Schönemann's activities in the Kermanshah area. More of what Niedermayer terms " preliminary arrangements " would, therefore, be necessary ; and he arranged to send Zugmayer and Griesinger (who were really destined eventually for work at Kerman and in South Persia), under the guise of consul and consulate secretary respectively, to Isfahan via Kermanshah. They and Paschen and Voigt, who were to start activities at Hamadan, left Baghdad on the 26th February with strict orders to avoid hostilities.

At the beginning of March, Niedermayer was annoyed to learn that the force under Raouf Bey had suffered a defeat near Mandali at the hands of the Sinjabi Kurds and had been forced by its losses to retire. It was what he had feared, and his feeling that it could hardly fail to have a bad effect in Persia was soon confirmed by the unwelcome news that the Persians were collecting a force to defend their frontier. A further unpleasant surprise was the British attempt to capture Wassmuss, and the loss of the cipher code and of some important papers in Wassmuss' baggage. It is interesting to note that

Niedermayer says that Wassmuss had done nothing to justify the British action; and he says that Wassmuss himself swore to be revenged on the British for their " treacherous " conduct.

The German Minister, reaching Baghdad about the middle of March, agreed that further Turco-Persian hostilities must be prevented and that Niedermayer's expedition must pose as a peaceful mission. Without further opposition from the Turks, the expedition crossed the Persian frontier with the German and Austrian Ministers on the 3rd April and was met near Qasr-i-Shirin by twenty-five armed and mounted levies recruited by Schönemann. Here the local Persian Governor appealed to Prince Reuss to stop Raouf Bey who, having concentrated about 3,000 irregular troops at Khaniqin, had sent the Governor-General of Kermanshah an ultimatum. Desirous of conciliating the Persians, of preventing a Turkish embroilment with Persian tribes and of improving Turco-Persian relations, the German Minister got Raouf to agree to delay his advance pending negotiations at Kermanshah by Prince Reuss and also induced the Persians to withdraw their forces.

On arrival at Kermanshah, Niedermayer found that the activities of Schönemann, Zugmayer and others of his party had met with gratifying success. On the other hand it was most embarrassing to hear that Raouf Bey's force, meeting with no Persian opposition and disregarding his agreement with the Minister, had occupied Qasr-i-Shirin and Sar-i-Pul.

Soon after this, Niedermayer himself hurried ahead of the others to Tehran, instructing Seiler and Zugmayer to get to Isfahan as soon as possible, leaving Winkelmann at Kermanshah and taking Voigt,* whom he met at Daulatabad, on with him. Everywhere on his way to Tehran Niedermayer found the Persians most amenable to German overtures, with the single exception of Qum, where the clergy refused to have anything to say to a *Jahad* or to Turco-German propaganda. At Tehran, however, where the Cabinet had just resigned (owing, he says, to Anglo-Russian pressure on the Shah), he found a most unpleasant situation with German influence at a discount.

Niedermayer admits that, in her own interests, Persia ought to have kept out of the war at any rate till peace was imminent, when she might have benefitted by joining the winning side. But for German purposes it was desirable to bring Persia in as soon as possible, and his book and the other German accounts

---

* Voigt had come from Hamadan, where Paschen had been detained by sickness.

German account of activities of their emissaries; August 1914-June 1915.

show how at various centres they all worked to this end by lavish bribery, propaganda, encouragement of agitation and organising runs on the British and Russian banks. They stirred up tribal leaders, clergy, "democrats" and others to make demonstrations of protest against the Allies and to send telegrams to the central Government calling on them to take armed action against Russians and British. They recruited and armed a considerable number of retainers, whom they utilised to back up their propaganda, when necessary, by a show of force; and they subsidised some of the robber tribes, whom they used as intelligence agents, escorts and guides. The Persian Government, says Niedermayer, were helpless in face of his own and his subordinates' activities and could only make strong protests.

The arrival of Russian reinforcements at Enzeli and Kazvin, betokening a possible Russian occupation of Tehran, impelled Niedermayer to send his stores, arms, ammunition and money to his advanced base at Isfahan. From there he intended to move eastward to Afghanistan across the desert, which he had explored in 1913.

In organising his expedition, which he appears to have done very well and thoroughly, he had anything but an easy task. Rumania's refusal, after Italy's entrance into the war, to allow the passage through her territory of German warlike stores deprived him of all hope of getting the arms and equipment he desired. The Russian re-occupation of Urmia and the British advance to Amara (Mesopotamia) threatened his line of communication and reacted on the whole Persian situation. Raouf Bey's hostile action aroused strong resentment among the Persians* and, when the Germans remonstrated, Raouf destroyed part of the telegraph line, cutting them off from communication with Turkey and Europe for about three weeks. Moreover, though the Persians professed to look to Germany to liberate them from Russian and British domination, they would give no active assistance. Realising that the self-seeking tendencies of Persian notables and priests and the lack of arms, money and an efficient military force all stood in the way of any real uprising in the country, Niedermayer came to the conclusion about the end of May that it was hopeless to expect Persia to join in the war.

Though the German propaganda was, he considered, infinitely superior to that of the Allies, and the gendarmerie

---

* German documents captured by us confirm other accounts of the devastation of the country between the frontier and Karind by Raouf's men.

preserved a friendly attitude towards the Germans, Niedermayer foresaw that the British and Russians would soon employ force to stop the German activities. In anticipation, therefore, of his own departure eastward, he had to consolidate the German position in Persia generally, but especially along his line of communication with Turkish territory. For this it was necessary to obtain complete control of the whole area from Kermanshah to Isfahan and to extinguish every hostile influence in it. He realised that this could not be done altogether by peaceable means, but he had to ensure that his subordinates did not go too far. To further his plans in this respect he did all he could to induce the German, Austrian and Turkish Legations to persuade the Shah to move with them to Isfahan, so as to be away from Russian and British influence.

In addition to controlling the work in the provinces of his subordinates and gaining information regarding his route to Afghanistan and the chances of enemy interference, Niedermayer had to collect stores, arms, animals and men (whom he had to train) and to maintain an intelligence and counterespionage organisation. To escape detection he had himself, he says, to do much of his work at night and in disguise. He also sent agents into Turkestan to carry out destructions and demolitions and to promote and assist the escape from there of Austro-German prisoners of war. He hoped to stop the traffic in munitions which, he says, the British were conducting to Turkestan from India through East Persia ; * and he made special efforts to win over the Shah Sawan tribe, which occupied the area in North-West Persia through which lay the Russian lines of communication.

At the beginning of June, when his preparations were nearly complete, he took the following steps. He despatched P. Paschen on a special mission to Khurasan ; † he sent Wagner to Isfahan with orders to proceed from there, with W. Paschen and thirty armed mounted retainers, and reconnoitre the route Nain–Tabas–Kain in advance of the main expedition ; he instructed Zugmayer to start off for Yezd and Kerman ; he ordered the men and equipment left at Baghdad to move at once to Isfahan ; he arranged for Klein's party to take over the line of communication from the Turkish frontier to

---

* No such traffic in munitions was, in actual fact, taking place.
† The Persian Government disarmed and detained Paschen's men and forced him to return to Tehran, as reported by Mr. Marling on 28th June, see *ante*.

Kermanshah and so relieve Niedermayer's men for urgent work farther east; and with the object of preventing interruptions to the line of communication he appointed a *liaison* officer to remain with the Turkish forces on the frontier.

In the middle of June, Hentig, who had been on the staff of the Tehran Legation when war broke out and had been recalled from military service in March 1915 to take diplomatic charge of a mission to conclude an Afghan alliance, arrived at Tehran. The main body of Hentig's party with Becker and Röhr and a few Pathan sepoy deserters had gone straight to Isfahan, but Hentig with two Indians, " Prince " Mahendra Partap and Professor Moulvi Barkatullah,* had come to discuss matters with the Minister. Niedermayer says that, as the dangers and difficulties of the journey of this mission to Afghanistan would be considerable, it was arranged that it should accompany his expedition and that he would be in military command of the whole party. By the end of June they had all assembled at Isfahan and preparations for the movement to Afghanistan were complete. On the 1st July Niedermayer sent off the first échelon to await him at Anarak.

---

* Mahendra Partap, an eccentric megalomaniac, was a small land-holder with no right to any such title as Prince. He had left India in December 1914 and after visiting Switzerland had joined the Berlin " Indian Committee."

Barkatullah, a native of Bhopal State, had been pursuing revolutionary activities for the previous twelve years in America, Japan, Egypt and Turkey. At one time he had been a news-agent for the Amir of Afghanistan and from 1909 to 1913 was Professor of Hindustani at Tokyo University. He joined the Berlin " Indian Committee " in November 1914.

CHAPTER III.

JULY–NOVEMBER 1915:

ENEMY ACTION AND PERSIAN WEAKNESS NECESSITATE ALLIED INTERVENTION.

(Maps 1, 2, and 3.)

On learning that German parties had left Isfahan for Afghanistan, the authorities in India on the 2nd July authorised British consuls and officials in East Persia and on the frontier to take such preventive measures as the India Office telegram of the 25th June seemed to imply.* Our consuls at Meshed, Kerman and Seistan and our political officers on the Perso-Baluch frontier were instructed to obtain and transmit information of the progress of these parties and also to rouse local opinion against the German action, which was compromising Persian neutrality. In addition, Lieut.-Colonel T. W. Haig, the Consul-General at Meshed, was to try to arrange for Russian troops to capture any German parties attempting to enter Afghanistan via Meshed or Birjand; the political officers on the Baluch border were to employ the local militia and other available local forces against any German agents approaching the frontier; Major F. B. Prideaux in Seistan was to act in close co-operation with Major G. A. Dale (commanding a half-battalion 19th Punjabis stationed at Kacha, near Robat, for the suppression of the arms traffic); and Major Dale, who was given the latest news regarding five different German parties moving eastward across Persia, was if possible to intercept and capture, or destroy, any entering Seistan. At the same time, orders were issued for the headquarters and two squadrons 28th Light Cavalry, with two machine guns, to move from Quetta and reinforce Major Dale's detachment. As their march of 370 miles, from railhead at Nushki to Kacha, and the operations they might have to undertake across the frontier would be over waterless desert country, officers and men were to be mounted on camels instead of horses.

Inception of the East Persia Cordon; July 1915.

---

* See p. 72.

Inception of the East Persia Cordon; July 1915. Mr. Marling, however, surprised that the Afghan situation should call for the use of British troops in Persia, deprecated such a course as calculated to bring about results which we desired to avoid. Moreover, Ain-ud-Daula, whose inaction had hitherto disappointed and rather perplexed Mr. Marling, had just made some real efforts, including strong instructions to the Governors of Kerman and Seistan, to check the German hostile activities. The effective execution of these instructions would depend, said Mr. Marling, on the financial support we afforded the Persian authorities concerned. But, provided he could sanction expenditure on the same scale as the Germans, he considered that we should try to effect our purpose through Persian agency before resorting to more drastic measures.

The Government of India, while allowing the orders for the reinforcement of Kacha to stand, at once modified the other instructions they had issued and thus anticipated orders sent from London after receipt of Mr. Marling's views. The Viceroy pointed out, however, how difficult it would be for the Amir of Afghanistan, faced as he was by a fanatical and inflammable pro-Turkish population, to maintain neutrality if German armed parties entered his country. It was to obviate the critical situation which might result and which would strain their remaining resources to the fullest extent that the Government of India had prepared as a last resort to employ their own troops to try to intercept the German parties. The Persian authorities, they pointed out, had hitherto displayed neither inclination nor ability to deal with these, so that if we waited till the Seistan authorities failed similarly we should be too late.

This explanation and a Cabinet crisis at Tehran, brought about by German and Democrat intrigues, combined to alter Mr. Marling's views. Learning on the 10th July that the Cabinet had definitely resigned at the bidding of a minority in the *Majlis*, Mr. Marling realised that enemy influence was predominant and that there was consequently little chance of the country observing real neutrality. The political crisis was likely to continue; and, as it would prevent any action being taken to stop the German emissaries, Mr. Marling telegraphed that day to India and London that both the Russian Minister and he were of opinion that no time should be lost by the Allies in taking their own measures. In reply, he was requested on the 12th July by Sir Edward Grey to inform India what steps he considered it desirable to take.

On that day the British at Bushire were attacked by tribesmen. (See Map 1.) For some time past Wassmuss had been inciting the local Khans* to attack, and had lately increased his efforts in view of the commencement on the 15th July of the fast of *Ramazan*. On the 8th July General Nixon had telegraphed, however, that, though Wassmuss (with about one thousand armed tribesmen, one field and one machine gun, fourteen miles east of Bushire) was urging the necessity of an early attack on the pretext that he himself was under orders for Tehran, no immediate attack was anticipated. A report on the 12th that three or four hundred hostile tribesmen had gathered in *nalas* two miles south of the British Residency was, therefore, not altogether credited by Major E. H. Oliphant, commanding the outposts. To verify it, he and Captain J. G. Ranking of the Political Department took out a reconnoitring party of five sowars of the Residency escort and twenty-seven rifles 96th Infantry. Unfortunately these two officers and the advanced patrols got too far ahead of their main body and ran into an ambush. Both officers were killed and three sepoys killed or wounded, Major Oliphant himself losing his life in a heroic attempt to rescue Captain Ranking. At 7 p.m. and again at 4 a.m. on the 13th the tribesmen, mainly men from Dilbar, attacked the outpost line from the south. But they were driven back without difficulty, and early on the 13th the British advanced to find all the tribesmen gone. It transpired subsequently that this attack was intended to synchronise with one from the east, but that owing to the premature discovery of the southern party the eastern attack never materialised.

Bushire; July 1915.

On the 12th July Mr. Marling telegraphed that the Democrats were experiencing great difficulty in forming a Cabinet, that there was a chance of Ain-ud-Daula resuming office, and that the Russian Minister had recommended his Government to reinforce Enzeli—a procedure which Ain-ud-Daula also advocated—and to send more troops into Khurasan. Mr. Marling also said that he agreed with Major Prideaux that, as the local Persian authorities would be unable to stop the German parties, the Indian troops at Kacha should move into Seistan before it was too late. They would, he thought, be able to deal with parties moving

General situation, events, and British policy; July 1915

---

* The principal ones hostile to us were:—Shaikh Husain of Chah Kutah, Ghazanfar of Borazjan, Rais Ali of Dilbar, and Zair Khidar of Tangistan.

British policy; July 1915. eastward via Khabis or Bam, though not with those reported to be going via Tabas. To intercept these, the Russian Minister had recommended that a Russian force should be despatched to Rui Khaf. Next day Mr. Marling telegraphed that the attack on Bushire, of which he had just heard, seemed to justify the despatch into Persia of any British force considered requisite to prevent German missions from entering Afghanistan; and the death of two British officers as the result of German intrigues also justified us in using similar means, i.e., in employing tribesmen to attack German agents. Continuing on the 14th, Mr. Marling said that it was hopeless to expect that anything would be done to check German activities during the existing political crisis. It was, therefore, imperative for the Allies to take decisive action at once. Russia should reinforce Enzeli, while we should occupy Bushire, Bandar Abbas, Lingeh, Mohammerah and Hormuz till reparation was made and till the various German agents in Persia were arrested

The Government of India, while agreeing that the time had come for strong action, regarded the occupation of the four last-named places as politically inexpedient and as an ineffective dissipation of military strength. They recommended the assumption by us of the administration of Bushire town, with the control of the Customs House, the holding of the revenue and the prohibition of mercantile traffic with the interior. The Persian Government should be informed that, as they were unable or unwilling to check the German unneutral activities, H.M. Government were forced to adopt such measures for the protection of their own interests as they thought necessary. If the Persian Government were then ready to take effective action with regard to the matters to which their attention had been frequently drawn, we should disclose our terms. These should be:—punishment of the Khans concerned in the attack on Bushire; compensation for our casualties; the arrest, disarmament and internment, or deportation, of the German agents in Persia; and the recall of the Governor-General of Fars. Failing compliance we should take such further action as might seem desirable. The Government of India did not, for the time being, contemplate any military operations outside Bushire except a bombardment of Dilbar. In conclusion they drew attention to the fact that if, in consequence of our action, Persia were to declare war against us, this would make it much more difficult for the Amir of

Afghanistan to remain neutral and would also probably induce unrest and bitter feelings among many of our own Moslem subjects.

It is noteworthy that at this time India had practically no troops which she could make available for employment in Persia, a factor which rendered a military diversion there more than ever undesirable. On the 16th July General Nixon was informed that, if H.M. Government accepted the proposal to occupy Bushire, he would at once have to reinforce that place with a squadron of cavalry and half a battalion of infantry. It was not intended, he was told, to carry out any operations inland; and he was asked if he considered these reinforcements sufficient and also if, in view of the Nasiriya operations in progress, he could spare them.

Mr. Marling considered that the Government of India's proposals erred on the side of moderation and might be taken by the Persians as implying our inability to do more. In any case they made it more than ever necessary for the Russians to send troops to act in the north, which was a more effective sphere of operations. He did not believe that Persia desired to go to war with Russia and ourselves. But, having regard to the indifferent military situation of the Allies in practically all the theatres of war, Allied failure to show strength at this juncture brought nearer the possibility of Persian participation in the war.

H.M. Government accepted India's proposals and informed Mr. Marling to that effect on the 21st July. One squadron 16th Cavalry and two* more captured Turkish guns were at once sent to Bushire from Basra, but it was not till about a week after the capture of Nasiriya on the 25th that it was found possible to send the 11th Rajputs. Arrangements were also made for the co-operation of a naval force. In the meantime the tribal gatherings had all dispersed on the commencement of the *Ramazan*, and Wassmuss with the other Germans were said to have left for Shiraz. A few days later, however, the Khans stopped all caravan traffic and cut the telegraph wires between Bushire and the interior.

Frequent reports of the movements and composition of seven armed German parties which had recently left Isfahan in an easterly direction had enabled the General Staff in

East Persia; July 1915.

---

* Three were sent, but one was in replacement of one found unserviceable.

East Persia; July, 1915. India to form a fairly accurate estimate of their numbers and of the approximate dates by which they would be likely to reach localities in East Persia where we or the Russians might hope to intercept them. On the 17th July it was learnt that 120 Russian Cossacks had left Meshed the previous day for Turbat-i-Haidari, with a view to intercepting these parties, whose numbers and dispositions were estimated as follows. A party under Zugmayer and Griesinger, consisting of a Bengali and thirty-two Persian sowars, was still at Kerman, where it had arrived on the 4th July; Wagner's and Paschen's party of eight Austrians, thirty-two Persian sowars and one or two machine guns, had left Nain about the 25th June for Tabas, Wagner being bound for Birjand and Paschen for Tun; two parties under Hentig and Niedermayer—consisting of seventeen Germans or Austrians, one Afghan, thirty-one Persian sowars and four machine guns—had left Nain about the 6th July for Tabas, where they were to await another party (of four Germans or Austrians, three Indians or Afghans and about twenty Afridi deserters) which had left Nain on the 10th July; and two more parties, totalling eleven Germans or Austrians, ten Caucasians and thirteen Persian sowars had left Isfahan between the 11th and the 13th bound for Tabas.

Summarising this information in a telegram to London on the 17th July, the Government of India said that, as they were powerless to deal with the northerly group of these parties, they trusted that the Russians would be able to do so. As regards the southerly group, the 400 Indian rifles and two machine guns at Kacha would be increased by the 6th August to two cavalry squadrons, 450 rifles and four machine guns. But, until definite information of the approach of Germans was received, no part of this force would enter Seistan owing to the risk that their continued presence might excite fanatical sections of the local population and create an embarrassing situation.

In addition to the above-mentioned reinforcements, twenty men of the 106th Hazara Pioneers were being sent at Major Prideaux's request to join him; and Colonel Haig and he had been authorised to enlist and arm locally up to one hundred and fifty Hazara ex-soldiers of the Indian Army and other suitable men.* On the 22nd July about seventy more Russian Cossacks left Meshed for Turbat-i-Haidari, but two days later a report was received that the leading

---

* There was some delay in enlisting men at Meshed until Russian objections had been withdrawn.

BRITISH PLANS

German party was within a day's march of Kain. Its arrival there on the 26th was reported the same day by Major Prideaux, who considered that it would probably reach Birjand on the 27th.

Major Prideaux had more than once urged that the detachment at Kacha should move immediately into Seistan, where he did not believe that its presence would be resented by the local inhabitants. But the Government of India did not agree for the following reasons, which on the 25th they telegraphed to London. The Germans concentrating at Tabas apparently meant to cross into Afghanistan via Kain and Gazik, in which case the troops from Kacha could not arrive in time to stop them. Merely to move troops into Seistan would not improve matters, and their presence there, in view of the attitude of the Persian Baluchis and Sayads, might create an embarrassing situation which would react on the Afghan frontier population. Consequently, the risks of sending part of the Kacha detachment, before reinforcements arrived, on a long and unsupported march and of weakening the garrison of Kacha, did not seem to be justified; especially as the strength of the united German parties* might enable them to command considerable support from local malcontents. It was inadvisable to risk a reverse, as this would have a deplorable effect locally and in Afghanistan. The Government of India, therefore, preferred, they said, to keep the troops at Kacha so as to intercept any Germans who might move in that direction from Kerman, and to trust to the northerly parties of Germans being dealt with by our consuls—by means of promises of handsome rewards to tribal leaders and the use of local forces—in addition to measures the Russians might take. The Viceroy was informing the Amir of Afghanistan of the numbers and composition of the German parties and was asking him to contradict the wild rumours then current that they were the vanguard of a Turco-German army advancing eastward. Owing to these rumours there was considerable unrest on the North-West Frontier of India.

In addition to factors mentioned in the above telegram there were others which militated against the chances of British troops being able to prevent the Germans from entering Afghanistan. The long road (370 miles) from railhead at Nushki to the post at Kacha lay over a desert of sand devoid

---

* Further parties had been reported as leaving Isfahan for the east, and the Germans at Kerman and Tabas had been recruiting more men locally.

East Persia; July 1915. of supplies, where water was only procurable in small quantities at long intervals and where there was not even sufficient grazing for camels. It was 340 miles or so by road from Kacha to Birjand, the southern limit of the practicable Russian sphere of action; and the greater part of this road lay through an area of barren and rugged mountains or hills, in which water, supplies, grazing and fuel were all either lacking altogether or were scanty in the extreme. The only exception was Seistan, which, owing to the Helmand river and the Hamun (great lakes) formed by the overflow of its snow-fed waters, was a most fertile area. (See Map 2.) At this time there was no mechanical transport available in India and as, consequently, transport for this region was restricted to camels, the number of troops that could be maintained in East Persia was definitely limited. The mountain and hill area abounded in hiding places and there were many of the inhabitants who could be counted on, for a consideration, to guide the Germans. So that it would in any case be very difficult, even with a much larger force than the British could hope to maintain, to watch the whole line effectively. Moreover, at this time of year the difficulty was much increased by the heat and the " wind of 120 days." This wind General Dickson describes in " East Persia " as " a hurricane when an effort is needed to stand upright, the heat that of a furnace-room in a foundry and the air filled with sand to the consistency and darkness of a November fog in London . . . . "

On the 27th July the India Office telegraphed to India that one thousand more Russian Cossacks with four machine guns were on their way to attack the Germans advancing from Tabas and that the Russian authorities asked that we should protect the southern area in East Persia which was beyond their reach. It appeared to the India Office that there was a risk that the Germans, hearing of this Russian Cossack movement, might try to evade it by entering Afghanistan through Seistan unless we moved troops there to intercept them.

Major Prideaux had just reported that it looked as if the Germans from Kain did not mean to go to Afghanistan but intended to come as consuls to Birjand and Seistan and to pursue there the policy they had carried out elsewhere in Persia; that they knew of the presence of Russian troops at Turbat-i-Haidari; and that the Governor of Birjand was obstructing Major Prideaux in his attempts to recruit men locally and to take action through tribal agency.

Kacha Tangi.

Kacha.

BRITISH MOVE INTO SEISTAN

In consequence of the above, orders were at once sent to Major Dale that he was to leave Kacha on the 30th July with 300 rifles and two machine guns and march by the shortest route to Nasratabad (Seistan), where he was to take steps, in co-operation with the local Persian officials, to prevent the establishment of German agencies in Seistan. Two squadrons 28th Light Cavalry with two machine guns, the party of Hazara Pioneers, a few Sappers and Miners and two machine guns of the 12th Pioneers, all of whom had left Nushki in three parties on the 12th, 16th and 25th July and were due at Kacha on the 2nd, 6th and 15th August, would follow him as soon as possible. In informing H.M. Government of this action, the Viceroy said that if the German parties meant to enter Afghanistan via Birjand, avoiding Seistan, neither the British nor the Russians could stop them, so that the matter must be left to the Amir of Afghanistan, who was being acquainted with the German movements.

On the 30th July the Governor of Birjand informed Major Prideaux that in accordance with orders from Tehran—which Mr. Marling had induced one of the permanent officials to issue—he was sending a force to apprehend the Germans at Kain and disarm their followers. The necessity, however, did not arise, as these Germans and their followers, after a short and indecisive fight with the leading detachment of Cossacks on the morning of the 30th, fled hurriedly during the night abandoning their baggage, which was said to contain gifts for presentation, in addition to arms, ammunition and bombs. On the 1st August, forty Cossacks, who had moved southward through Tun and to the westward of Kain, but had seen no signs of the Germans retiring from there, arrived at Birjand having learnt that a small enemy party had reached Tabas from the west and was being followed closely by other parties whose numbers totalled one hundred and fifty. On the 1st August the 1st Semirechia Cossacks, about seven hundred strong, reached Meshed and left there four days later for Turbat-i-Haidari.

On the 4th August Major Dale's detachment reached Nasra-tabad, where he was joined on the 14th by Lieut.-Colonel J. M. Wikeley with one squadron 28th Light Cavalry, two machine guns and a few Hazaras and Sappers and Miners. About half their riding camels, however, required either ten days' rest or replacement as a result of their 500-mile desert march. Since the 1st August the information of the German movements

East Persia;
August 1915.

East Persia;
August 1915.

had been rather indefinite, but showed that they had left Tabas and indicated that they were bound for the area north of Birjand, where the Cossacks were patrolling. On the 20th, however, news was received that some Germans and about two hundred Persians were moving from Khur towards Neh; and Major Dale was sent off there at once with fifty sabres and one hundred rifles. Next day Major Prideaux reported that a party of Russian Cossacks had ascertained definitely that, on the night 19th–20th, a party of six Germans, two Indian Princes, two or three Turks, six Afridis and some sixty armed retainers had crossed the Afghan frontier at Chah Rig. A few days later it was reported that this party had reached Herat.

The German accounts show that parties under the leadership of Hentig and Niedermayer left Isfahan on the 1st and 6th July and, moving via Nain, Anarak and Mihrjan, concentrated for rest and reorganisation, after a very trying march, at Chehar Deh and Tabas between the 22nd and 25th July. At Tabas, where they were unable to get transport animals but managed to enlist twenty armed retainers, the reports they received of the strength of the Russo-British cordon on the Meshed-Seistan road dispelled any idea they had of trying to fight their way through. Niedermayer, evidently discounting the fighting qualities of most of his armed Persian following, asserts that his fighting strength was only fifteen to twenty, without any guns, machine guns or wireless. After sending a party of about thirty armed sowars under Wagner to reconnoitre in the Tun–Gunabad direction, the remainder of the expedition, leaving Chehar Deh on the 26th and 28th July, moved via Deh Muhammad to Aspek. Here, having learnt that some Russian troops were at Tun and that others were moving from Turbat-i-Haidari towards Birjand, a conference was held to discuss future action. It was decided to divide the expedition into three parties, of which two would endeavour to divert the enemy's attention from the area which the third party would traverse to reach Afghanistan. Becker, forming an advanced base with sick men and animals near Aspek, was to move a short distance northward and spread false information so as to induce the Russians to concentrate towards Bushruyeh and the area north of it, while Wedig, with a convoy of camels laden with boxes filled with stones, was to carry out a similar rôle in regard to the British in the south. The third party, i.e., men and animals destined for Afghanistan, was divided into two portions, one a lightly laden mule column in which every animal was led by a man, and the other a camel column carrying food and water, which could be abandoned if necessary.

On the 1st August Becker left for Nagina and the remainder for Bushruyeh. They had hitherto received no news of Wagner's party, but at Bushruyeh they learnt of his encounter with the Russians at Kain and of the loss of his baggage, including £600 in gold and 18,000 tomans in silver. Wagner and his men had taken refuge at a point about twenty-five miles east of Bushruyeh, and Niedermayer sent out a party to bring them in. Wagner's horsemen proved to be so demoralised as to necessitate not only their own dismissal but also that of many of Niedermayer's sowars, who on hearing of the affair with the Russians refused to proceed. After getting from Becker, who had to be recalled for the purpose, munitions, money and clothes to refit Wagner and Paschen, Niedermayer and Hentig with the main body of the expedition, including Wedig's column, started from Bushruyeh at sunset on the 7th August in the direction of Tun. During their halt on the 8th, they released some local inhabitants and a small caravan which they had detained, feeling sure that some of these men would carry the news of their move towards Tun to the Russians. They learnt during the afternoon that there were 150 Russian troops at Kain, 150 at Tun, and 300 moving on Nagina-Aspek from Turbat-i-Haidari, while Indian troops were thought to be moving on Duhak from the Birjand direction. A little later, Russian troops being seen in the distance, the Germans started off to the south straight across the desert for a point half-way between Bushruyeh and Duhak. Halting there for the day, they marched next night to Duhak, having first ascertained that there was no enemy party there.

From Duhak the party started off on the Birjand road, but, after marching a short distance and leaving Wedig to continue in that direction so as to attract the attention of the British,* Niedermayer left the road and moved due east. From this time on he marched day and night with little rest and consequently soon had to abandon his camels. On approaching the Birjand-Kain road, Paschen was detached with a small party to act as a left flank guard at some distance off and was told to rejoin the main column a few days later

---

* Wedig, when certain that he had attracted British attention, was to abandon his camels and make for Kerman. He arrived there on the 23rd August.

near the Afghan frontier. After crossing the road, passing near Duruksh and being rejoined by Paschen, who had moved via Sehdeh, the whole party crossed the Afghan frontier near Yazdan on the night 19th–20th August.

Niedermayer says that the Amir of Afghanistan subsequently informed them that their pursuers reached the frontier half a day after them and that 10,000 Anglo-Indian troops and a mixed Russian brigade had been set in motion against them! They arrived at Herat on the 24th August, being treated virtually as prisoners for the first few days there. But they then experienced more friendly treatment and left with an escort for Kabul on the 7th September. Of the 140 men and 236 animals, the maximum strength he had altogether enrolled in his own expedition, Niedermayer says that 37 men and 79 animals reached Herat. His passage of the desert had certainly been a fine exploit.

In the meantime, our anxiety regarding Afghanistan had been lessened considerably by the receipt, by the Viceroy, of a most satisfactory letter from the Amir, saying that if German armed parties entered Afghanistan they would be disarmed and interned till the end of the war and that the Amir fully intended to remain neutral.

**Kerman;
August 1915.** Reports from the British consul at Kerman at the beginning of August stated that Zugmayer, with all the disorderly elements of the town at his disposal, had obtained such a dominating position that the Governor was afraid to carry out the orders from Tehran to stop the German activities. Zugmayer's diary confirms this and shows how he managed by bribery and intimidation to overawe the Governor and to win over a large section of the population, including many of the clergy. Throughout August he continued his propaganda and intrigues, not only with the local notables but also with the chief of Bam and other tribal leaders to the north of Makran, and he increased his armed following considerably by local enlistment. At the end of August our consul reported that pro-German enthusiasm had lessened, as a result of the scattering of Wagner's party.

**East Persia;
August 1915.** The apparent intention of Zugmayer's party to extend its operations eastward, the frequent reports of other German parties leaving Isfahan for an easterly destination and the fact that at least one party was known to be still in the vicinity of Tabas, all made it probable that more of the enemy

contemplated entering Afghanistan. Consequently, Major Dale's party, which reached Neh on the 29th August, left there next day for Birjand so as to gain touch with the Russians and complete the cordon. It was true that Colonel Wikeley's force of some 700 men,* of whom only about a third were mounted, was obviously too small to watch the whole line. But, with the aid of the various British consuls a fairly good intelligence service had already been organised, and it was hoped, by improving this and with the co-operation of the local Persian officials, to obtain accurate and timely news of the German movements. Small lightly-equipped bodies of troops kept ready at different centres to move out at any hour of the day or night on receipt of news should, therefore, stand a good chance of intercepting or capturing enemy parties trying to get past. A special watch would be also kept on the more important watering places.

To return to the situation in Central and South-West Persia. On the 3rd August Mr. Marling telegraphed that it looked as if there would soon be some three hundred Germans and Austrians at Isfahan, being mainly prisoners of war who had escaped from Trans-Caspia. Such a concentration implied more than a mere attack on our consulates, and it was popularly rumoured that the Germans meant to combine with the Democrats and carry off the Shah and the Government to Isfahan in furtherance of the German plan to involve Persia in the war. But the doubtful attitude of the Bakhtiaris and a report that they contemplated an alliance with the Qashqais, combined with the movement of a number of small German parties towards the Persian Gulf from Isfahan, made Mr. Marling wonder whether a threat to our position at Basra, or an attack on the Anglo-Persian oil-field, was not contemplated. Both he and the Russian Minister considered that our only remedy lay in the early arrival at Enzeli of Russian reinforcements. They also both realised that the position of the Allied consuls and colonies at Shiraz and Isfahan was decidedly dangerous, as we had no means of affording them effective assistance. But it might precipitate trouble if we withdrew them, and such action would in any case be interpreted as a sign of weakness.

Central and South-West Persia; August 1915.

---

* Major Prideaux had enlisted and armed a few men locally, but had not yet been joined by the men from Meshed.

Unfortunately the Russian commander in the Caucasus had just been obliged to divert a militia brigade, previously destined for Tabriz, to reinforce the left of his main front (to meet the Turkish offensive which followed the Russian evacuation of Van on the 3rd August) and could for the time being spare no men for Persia.

**Bushire;
August 1915.**
The British occupation of Bushire had been delayed by the Nasiriya operations in Mesopotamia and by the effect of the intense heat on the crew of H.M.S. *Juno*, which reached Bushire from Aden on the 5th August. But it was carried out on the 8th August without opposition; and, although it substituted British for Persian administration, the publication of our reasons for the step had an excellent effect in the town and its vicinity. In the interior the tribesmen remained hostile and at once started to raid the Bushire peninsula, while at Shiraz the situation continued critical. The active part which the Persian gendarmerie officers there were taking in the German campaign, and the acquiescence of their Swedish officers, obliged H.M. Government to cease giving the force financial support. At the same time Mr. Marling was authorised to subsidise the Bakhtiaris so as to secure both their adherence to the declared Persian policy of neutrality and their co-operation in the protection of the oil-fields.

**Dilbar;
August 1915.
(See Map 3.)**
On the 10th August a small expedition left Bushire to carry out punitive measures at Dilbar. The force consisted of the ships *Juno, Pyramus, Lawrence* and *Dalhousie** under the command of Captain D. St. A. Wake, R.N. (Senior Naval Officer, Persian Gulf) and half the 96th Infantry with two machine guns under Major C. E. H. Wintle. Doubts as to the depth of water and a strong breeze which created a heavy surf prevented a landing before the 13th and gave the tribesmen time to complete their fortification of the beach line, though the ships' guns put a stop to their work during daylight.

Although the weather was favourable on the 13th August, visibility was so poor that the covering party (fifty Royal Marines, one hundred and seventy rifles 96th Infantry, two machine guns and medical personnel, under command of

---

* Their gun armament was :—*Juno*, eleven 6-inch, eight 12-pr. and one 3-pr.; *Pyramus*, eight 4-inch and eight 3-pr.; *Lawrence*, four 4-inch and four 6-pr.; and *Dalhousie*, six 6-pr.

Captain G. Carpenter, R.M.L.I.), did not start for the shore till 11 a.m. It advanced in three lines of boats, under an effective covering fire from the ships' guns and from four naval machine guns in the boats, so as to land well to the north of the enemy's line of trenches. But the strong tide carried the boats towards the enemy's right, whence as they got to close range the hostile fire caused some sixteen British casualties. As soon as the troops began to jump ashore, however, the 150 to 200 tribesmen manning the trenches retired hastily inland for about two thousand yards. The landing, which was in charge of Commander Viscount Kelburn, R.N. (*Pyramus*), was made good; reconnoitring parties were sent forward; a base was established near the beach; and the remainder of the landing force with the necessary stores were brought ashore. The total force ashore, under Major Wintle who had landed with the covering party, totalled fifty Marines with five naval machine guns, twenty seamen for demolition work and two hundred and eighty rifles 96th Infantry with two machine guns.

The village of Old Dilbar lay over a mile away to the east surrounded by flat open country in which the only cover consisted of a few scattered palm groves. The exact location of New Dilbar and its fort was unknown. Ascertaining by reconnaissance that about three hundred tribesmen were holding Old Dilbar and a palm grove fifteen hundred yards to the south of it, Major Wintle decided to capture the latter in the hope that from it he would be able to locate New Dilbar. So as to reduce casualties, however, he made arrangements to launch his attack under cover of darkness.

Leaving the five naval machine guns and seventy rifles 96th Infantry to hold his base camp, Major Wintle advanced with the remainder at 3.30 a.m. on the 14th August and surprised the enemy in the palm grove (about 2,500 yards distant). The tribesmen fled hurriedly without firing a shot. As day broke, New Dilbar and its fort could be seen about 1,400 yards away to the north-east across a bare and open plain. The fort, a massive structure with walls thirty feet high and a large tower over the gateway, was evidently strongly held; and the enemy began to open a hot fire from it, from both the villages and also from the east and south of the palm grove. His numbers were estimated at three to four hundred.

Not wishing to risk heavy casualties by a daylight attack, Major Wintle decided to remain for the time being in the palm grove, where he started his men cutting down date-palms, a

Dilbar; part of the punitive measures he had been ordered to carry out.
August About two hours later, at 6.40 a.m., he sent a signal message
1915. to the Senior Naval Officer asking that the guns should open
fire on Old Dilbar, which the enemy had been reinforcing.
Through some mistake the message was understood in the *Juno*
to refer to New Dilbar, which was supposed to lie immediately
to the east of, and close to, the palm grove occupied by the
landing party The result was that the shells from the salvo
fired by the *Juno*—three rounds of lyddite from her 6-inch guns
at 11,500 yards range—fell into the palm grove. Though no
one was hit, the shells caused some confusion and impeded the
dispositions for defence against the continuous enemy fire.
Major Wintle at once decided that, to avoid casualties which
further shelling was likely to cause before he could stop it, he
would withdraw to his base camp. This movement was immediately perceived by the enemy, who started to advance boldly
in spite of losses, causing the British a number of casualties.
The retirement proceeded in good order, however, and the
battle casualties grew less, though before the base camp was
reached the intense heat caused further losses. The remainder
of the day was occupied in reconnaissance work and in directing
the fire of the naval guns against the two villages with very
good effect. Major Wintle decided to attack New Dilbar
village and fort at daybreak next day.

Leaving the base camp at 3.30 a.m. on the 15th August, the
force, marching on a compass bearing, reached the southern
end of Old Dilbar without opposition. Half a company 96th
Infantry* having been left there to cover the approaches from
the south and south-east, the remainder advanced towards
New Dilbar till they could just discern the fort through the
darkness. Major Wintle then issued instructions for the
volunteers from the naval demolition party to move forward
as soon as they could see, to make a breach in the wall. But
just then a revolver discharged by accident dissipated all
chance of surprise and the demolition party, advancing at once,
succeeded in blowing a breach in the wall, when the fort was
rushed and occupied

There had been no opposition, as the enemy, anticipating
another attack on the palm grove to the south, had concentrated in strength there during the night and did not realise
their mistake till they heard the explosion at the fort. They
then streamed out of the grove and advanced on New Dilbar,

---

* i.e., a company in the then-existing organisation. Indian battalions were still organised in eight companies.

SKETCH MAP
TO ILLUSTRATE OPERATIONS AT DILBAR.
13th – 15th August, 1915.

Enemy's beach position shown in Green.

MAP 3

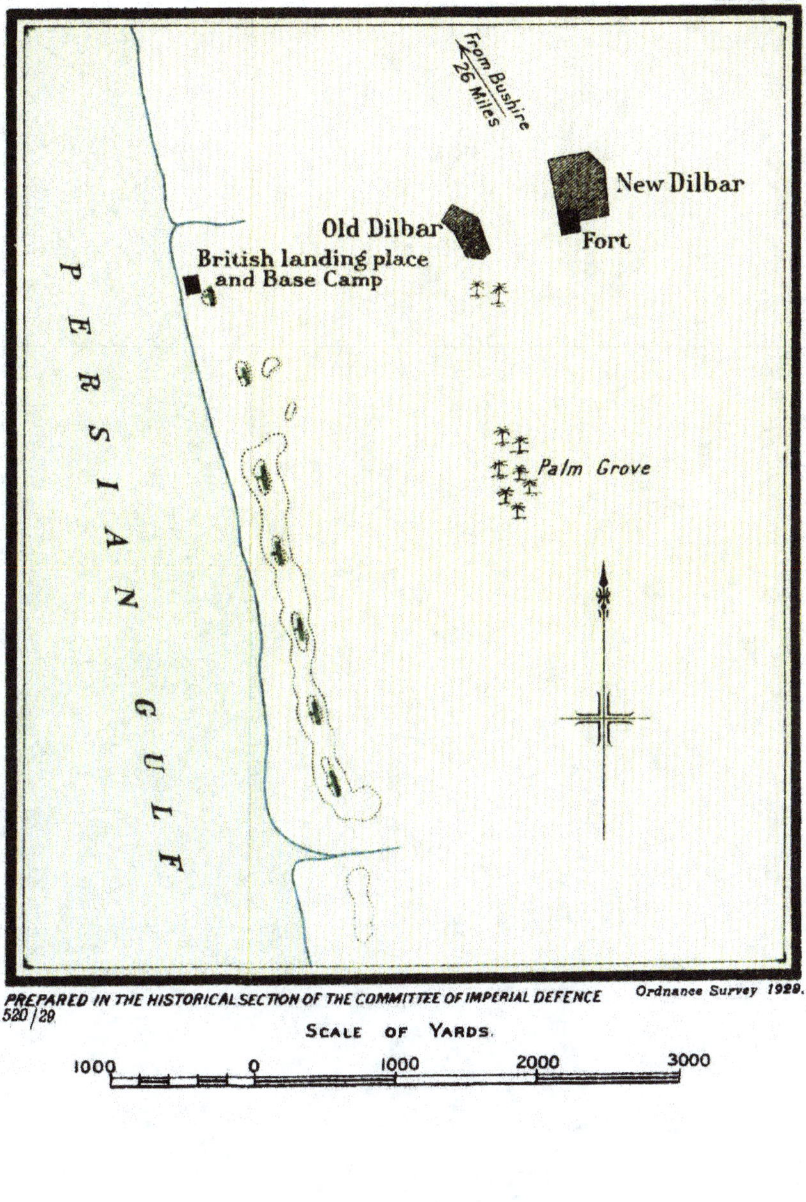

From Bushire 26 Miles

Old Dilbar
British landing place and Base Camp

New Dilbar
Fort

PERSIAN GULF

Palm Grove

PREPARED IN THE HISTORICAL SECTION OF THE COMMITTEE OF IMPERIAL DEFENCE
520/29
Ordnance Survey 1929.

SCALE OF YARDS.
1000   0   1000   2000   3000

incurring considerable casualties on coming into the open. The enemy's strength was estimated at five to six hundred, which showed that tribesmen from elsewhere had joined the men of Dilbar. Their attack against New Dilbar gradually developed from south, east and north, but it was held in check without difficulty.

As soon as the fort had been captured, Major Wintle had begun to destroy both it and the village; and when this was completed, he started to withdraw to the base camp. The retirement by the north end of Old Dilbar was well carried out, being covered by the detachment which had been left there during the advance and by the fire of the naval guns. Our total casualties for the day amounted to only six wounded. Re-embarking that night without enemy opposition, the force returned to Bushire.

The operations had been carried out in great heat and under very trying conditions and, as General Nixon said in his Despatch, reflected great credit on all concerned. The total casualties* amounted to 66 (including 11 from heatstroke), most of them having been incurred during the fighting which followed the unfortunate mistake on the 14th.

The Bushire peninsula, which is some twelve miles long and from one to four miles wide, is practically an island, as the flats which connect it with the mainland, and which are known as the *mashileh*, are covered at times by the tide. These flats extend eastward for about twelve miles, are open and waterless and, except when covered by the sea, are passable by all arms. The town of Bushire is at the northern apex of the peninsula, but the cable-house, telegraph station, British Residency and other buildings occupied by the foreign colony lie in a wide circle round the old fort of Rishahr about halfway down the peninsula. Between the slight ridge on which the British Residency is situated and Bushire town the sandy plain is dotted with villages, houses and palm groves.

[Bushire; August 1915. (See Map 1.)]

To defend this area against attack from the mainland with the small force available was, therefore, not an easy task. To cover Bushire, Rishahr and the important buildings, the British troops had taken up an outpost line six miles long, which

---

* 1 naval officer (Commander T. C. A. Blomefield, R.N.), 5 seamen, 1 marine and 8 Indian ranks killed; 1 naval officer, 12 seamen, 12 marines and 15 Indian ranks wounded. Major Wintle had a bullet through his helmet and three bullet grazes on legs and arms.

102   OPERATIONS IN PERSIA

Bushire; August, 1915. extended from the northern coast along the eastern edge of the peninsula to a point about 1¾ miles east-south-east of the Residency and then turned westward to the sea. To the east of this line there was an excellent field of view and fire, but to the south the country was broken and intersected by numerous *nalas* and by a line of cliffs which lay along the eastern edge of the peninsula.

Between the 11th and 16th August the tribesmen, passing through our outposts, carried out no less than four bold night raids, in which our troops suffered eleven casualties; while the raiders, after capturing or killing about forty horses and mules, escaped with very slight loss. General Nixon, realising the disadvantages of our passive defence, suggested that we should carry out offensive operations across the *mashileh*. He himself, however, required all the troops in Mesopotamia for the impending advance on Kut; and the Indian authorities, who also had no troops to spare for the purpose and were most anxious to avoid any further commitments in Persia, did not agree. On the 20th August a party of fifty to one hundred raiders were overtaken by daylight close to our outpost line and were attacked in their hiding place by about three hundred Indian infantry. But the latter were not well handled and most of the raiders escaped, while we sustained thirteen casualties. On the same day Brigadier-General H. T. Brooking, commander of the 33rd Infantry Brigade in Mesopotamia, arrived at Bushire, having been sent by General Nixon to investigate the situation, which seemed likely to get more threatening as Wassmuss was reported to have returned to the neighbourhood.

General Brooking characterised the British dispositions as being altogether of too passive a nature and he criticised the action of some of the senior officers, with the result that changes were decided on and General Brooking himself was ordered to remain at Bushire and take over command. By the end of August he had with him his 33rd Brigade staff, one squadron 16th Cavalry, 11th Rajputs, 96th Infantry, fifty men of the 2/7th Gurkhas sent by General Nixon to lay ambushes for raiders, four ex-Turkish guns (two field and two mountain) and two field searchlights. He also had authority to call on the warships for a landing party if required.

Change of Government; August 1915. On the 19th August a new Cabinet was formed at Tehran with Mustaufi-ul-Mamalik as Prime Minister. After seven weeks without a Government the Democrats, who had completely failed to form a Ministry, appear to have realised that if the country was not to relapse into anarchy some sort of government was necessary to check the German intrigues which had caused the British and Russians to take counter-measures. Mustaufi-ul-Mamalik was consequently allowed to form a Cabinet, whose heterogeneous composition can have pleased no party. In the meantime, however, the Germans had made the most of the interval to further their two main immediate objects, i.e., to reach Afghanistan and to rouse the tribes to attack Bushire. Schönemann, nominally a German consul, had used armed force to prevent the return, from Hamadan, of the British and Russian consuls to Kermanshah. Large quantities of arms and ammunition had been smuggled into Isfahan, the main German centre, where new German agents were constantly arriving and where at least two hundred Austro-Hungarian escaped prisoners of war were being trained for use against the Allies. Parties under Wustrow and others had been sent to Shiraz and to assist Wassmuss; and agents had been sent to other centres so as to spread German propaganda right through the whole country.

The new Prime Minister was nominally a Democrat, but any hopes that the Allies might have held that he would prove equal to dealing with the difficult situation were soon dispelled by his vacillating procedure. The Government had no force on which they could depend except the Cossack Brigade or a Bakhtiari tribal force. But, as these were generally regarded as pro-Russian and pro-British forces respectively, Mustaufi-ul-Mamalik apparently feared to utilise their services against the Germans lest he should arouse the antagonism of the Democrats. The prestige of the gendarmerie as well as their strength had suffered considerably from two recent defeats incurred at the hands of Shah Sawan and Lur tribesmen, while their strong pro-German sympathies also rendered them unreliable. In effect nothing was done to check the Germans; and only in his attempts to use their presence to wring concessions out of the British and Russians, as a means of conciliating the Democrats, did the Prime Minister appear to follow any consistent policy.

At the end of August the Germans were virtual masters of Kermanshah, Isfahan and Shiraz and were trying to obtain the upper hand at Tehran. They were apparently endeavouring to undermine all Persian authority and to force the Allies to withdraw their Legations, consuls and subjects from the country. The British consuls and subjects at Shiraz and

Situation at end of August 1915.

Isfahan were evidently in considerable danger; but it was considered necessary for them to remain as long as possible; and it was hoped that the warnings sent by H.M. Government, that they would hold the Persian authorities concerned responsible for their safety, would enable them to do so.

Isfahan ; July–August 1915. German accounts and especially Niedermayer's book throw an interesting light on German methods in Persia, and we may take the following brief summary of Seiler's activities in Isfahan as being generally applicable to the other emissaries. Finding that most of the people who had at first espoused the German cause so warmly had done so mainly for the material advantages which they hoped to gain by a change of government, Seiler devoted his attention to winning over the leading men of all classes. Niedermayer denies that he did this by lavish bribery, as he says that for the three months or so that Seiler was in Isfahan he was only given some £700 to spend. He found that the priests would have nothing to do with the Turkish *Jahad*, but he succeeded by other means in gaining their sympathy in increasing numbers. The prominent merchants he was able to ignore as, unless they were Democrats, they were unorganised and generally indifferent to politics. The gendarmerie were always friendly, but the great landowners though apparently sympathetic really remained neutral. With the Bakhtiaris he was unable to obtain any definite results, though one of their Khans gave him much assistance in the hope of thus obtaining reinstatement of his lost status. Seiler also endeavoured to win over Saulat-ud-Daula and his Qashqai tribesmen and to bring about a reconciliation between them and the Bakhtiaris. But here again he met with little success and he was compelled to undertake acts of direct injury to the Allies, such as destruction of the English telegraph lines and the subornment of their consulate guards. The escaped Austro-Hungarian prisoners of war were an extraordinary mixture of Poles, Hungarians, Croats, Ruthenians, Rumanians and Bohemians, incessantly fighting with one another and difficult to train into a useful body of men. But they eventually gave valuable and faithful assistance. By the end of August, says Niedermayer, the German position at Isfahan was so strong, with so much public opinion in its favour, that the enemy consuls and subjects were reduced to a state of impotence which enabled Seiler to work directly for their complete expulsion.

Though Mustaufi-ul-Mamalik at first told Mr. Marling that he would recall the Governor-General from Shiraz, he soon began to try to impose conditions which we could not accept. Sir Edward Grey, realising that Mr. Marling was in a very difficult position owing to the German armed menace and the lack of Allied military support, then gave Mr. Marling considerable latitude in conducting the negotiations for the restoration of Bushire. The Persian Government, however, persisted in their unreasonable attitude and, even after the attempt to murder Mr. Grahame, the British Consul-General at Isfahan, and the murder of his Indian orderly, on the 1st September—the fourth of a series of attempts against Allied consular officials—Mr. Marling failed in two interviews with Persian Ministers on the 2nd and 3rd September to obtain any effective assurance that such outrages would be prevented in the future. He warned them of the possible results of their acquiescence in the German scheme of rendering the Allied position in Persia impossible, and on the 3rd he reported that, in view of the evident impotence of the Persian Government, both the Russian Minister and he considered that even the drawbacks entailed in the departure from Isfahan of their respective consuls and colonies did not justify the risks involved in their remaining there. *[margin: Central Persia and Allied policy September 1915.]*

On the 4th September the Russian Minister had an unsatisfactory interview with the Shah, who seemed to be very much under enemy influence. It appeared to all the Allied representatives at Tehran that the Persian Government's inaction, in face of the German efforts to bring about a rupture with the Allies and a Turco-Persian alliance, created such a critical situation that—unless drastic measures were taken by the Allies or unless they obtained a military success sufficient to shake Persian belief in German invincibility—neither Allied officials nor Allied subjects would be able to remain in Persia much longer. As there was no time, even if they had the troops available, for either British or Russians to bring sufficient military pressure to bear, they considered that the only course was to give Persia the choice of declaring herself within, say, forty-eight hours, either for or against the Allies. They believed that there was a chance that Persia would declare, on terms, for the Allies.

On the 5th September Sir Edward Grey authorised the withdrawal of the British consul and colony from Isfahan if it became imperative. On the 6th, Mr. Marling, learning that the Persian Prime Minister had replied to a telegraphic enquiry *[margin: Isfahan; September 1915.]*

from the *mujtahids* at Isfahan in terms which almost invited them to continue anti-British agitation, reported that he had authorised the British to withdraw if danger should demand it; and on the same day he further reported that the officer commanding the gendarmerie at Isfahan had informed Mr. Grahame that the agitation was becoming very serious, that there was a plot to assassinate the British and Russian consuls and bank managers and that the gendarmerie were powerless to prevent it. Mr. Marling again warned the Prime Minister, who was also Minister of the Interior, that he would be held personally responsible for any harm that might occur.

British policy; September 1915.
On the 6th September the Government of India telegraphed to London and Tehran expressing disagreement with Mr. Marling's proposal to present an ultimatum to the Persian Government. This seemed to them to be playing the German game, and they considered that Persia was more likely to declare against than for us. Moreover, as India had no troops to spare to give an allied Persia the support she would require to stamp out German intrigues, the situation would be likely to deteriorate rather than improve if Persia joined us. If Persia sided against us, the measures necessary for the defence of the oil-fields and pipe line would impede our operations in Mesopotamia, while the moral effect of a second Moslem nation declaring against us would have a most disadvantageous effect in Afghanistan and among our own Moslem subjects. In either case the positions of our consuls and communities would become more precarious. The Government of India therefore preferred, for the time being, a policy of drift as having a much less serious effect and they trusted that success in the Dardanelles would soon alter the whole position in our favour.

With reference to these views, Mr. Marling telegraphed on the 7th admitting that the proposals, which the Russian Minister and he had made, offered only a slight chance of success. But the situation was so critical owing to the strength of the German position that he preferred to take this chance, which utilised the one element in our favour, namely the reluctance of the Persian Government to see the two Legations leave the country, rather than follow a policy of drift. He considered that the arrival that day of a Russian regiment at Enzeli—an insufficient force to inspire respect—was not likely to improve matters, and he offered the opinion that the capture by us of Baghdad would be more likely to alter the situation in our favour than the forcing of the Dardanelles. The only

EFFECT OF RUSSIAN ACTION

other alternative was to submit to Persian demands for large sums of money and arms in the hope that this might induce them to abstain from encouraging the pro-German feeling. It might, however, he said, just as well have the contrary effect, as it would show Persia that we were wholly dependent on her good-will.

On that day the Persian Government had again intimated to Mr. Marling that they would not agree to the British terms for the restoration of Bushire; and the serious nature of the situation was further confirmed by news that the British vice-consul at Shiraz (Ali Quli Khan Nawab) had been attacked and mortally wounded on the 7th and that the German consular agent at Hamadan, with one hundred and fifty men in his pay, was threatening to drive British and Russians out of the town. On the 8th September, however, Mr. Marling telegraphed a more reassuring report. He had just visited the Persian Prime Minister at the latter's request and had come to an agreement with him respecting Bushire, which was in effect an acceptance of the British terms and which was largely due, in Mr. Marling's opinion, to the landing of Russian troops at Enzeli. The Governor-General was to be recalled immediately from Shiraz and Qawam, appointed as acting Governor-General, was to select a suitable person to act as Governor of Bushire and take over the administration there from the British military authorities. The British troops were to remain at Bushire as long as required in order to ensure the safety of the British consulate and community, and the Persian Government undertook to punish the guilty Khans and to endeavour to put an end to German intrigues.

On the 9th September Sir Edward Grey telegraphed to Mr. Marling that H.M. Government approved these terms and did not therefore consider it desirable to present the suggested ultimatum to the Persian Government. Mr. Marling was, however, authorised to inform the Persian Prime Minister in the most earnest manner of the surprise and concern of H.M. Government at recent events in Persia, and that they found it difficult to believe that the Persian Government had ever contemplated the serious consequences to their country of alienating the very friendly feelings of Great Britain. H.M. Government felt justified, therefore, in asking if the Persian Government were prepared forthwith to assert themselves to protect British consular officers and subjects in Persia, and if so, what steps they proposed to adopt for the purpose. In the event of a satisfactory reply, Mr. Marling was authorised to say that H.M. Government would be willing to ease the financial position of the Persian Government by granting them a monthly subsidy.

This telegram crossed one from Mr. Marling which reported that 1,200 Russian troops had disembarked at Enzeli. Though the Russian Minister did not know the full numbers of the force that would eventually arrive, the presence of a General Officer to command it and a telegram from the Russian Foreign Office speaking of the possibility of sending troops to Isfahan appeared to indicate that its strength would suffice to restore the situation.

Bushire; September 1915. It is now necessary to return to Bushire, where, since his assumption of command on the 23rd August, General Brooking had been working hard at the reorganisaton of the defensive arrangements. So as to have a force ready to move in any direction to meet attacks or raiders at the shortest notice, he had made various changes of which the following are notable. Beyond the outpost line, where the searchlights gave great assistance, ambush parties of Gurkhas lay out every night. In addition to supports, an outpost reserve of two companies,* four guns and four machine guns had been established at Imamzadeh. The communications in rear of the outposts were being improved and made passable for the four ex-Turkish guns (two field and two mountain), which had been rendered mobile by hitching them to mule-drawn army transport carts. Telephone and signalling communications had been improved and extended. The general reserve at Rishahr had been strengthened by a company taken from the garrison of Bushire town and by machine gun parties from H.M.S. *Juno* and *Pyramus*. Arrangements had been made with the Senior Naval Officer by which the fire of the *Juno's* guns could be directed on to any part of the peninsula; and the *Lawrence* patrolled the creeks and shallow water east of Bushire town.

On the 3rd September General Brooking, estimating that the enemy's main forces, amounting at most to 2,000, were at Dilbar and Borazjan, reported that any attack or raids would probably be attempted during the dark nights between the 4th and 16th. An attack, however, took place that very

---

* At that time the Indian infantry battalions were organised each in eight companies and four double-companies.

ATTACK ON BUSHIRE

night and was repulsed without loss to the British, while among the enemy casualties was Rais Ali, the hostile Khan of Dilbar, who was killed.

The next attack came on the morning of the 9th, an intensely hot day. General Brooking, who was starting out to see a gun practice, learnt from a patrol, which he met near Imamzadeh at 6.30 a.m., that about twenty of the enemy were in a four or five hundred yard-wide belt of broken ground which extended southward from Zangina and lay immediately east of the cliffs. As, in addition to its broken nature, this piece of ground contained several water-holes and many palm trees, General Brooking had always realised that it afforded the enemy an excellent position of assembly for an attack. (See Map 1.)

Defence of Bushire; 9th September 1915.

On reaching the outpost support at No. 10 Post at 6.45 a.m. the volume of fire indicated that a considerable number of the enemy must have collected, and General Brooking at once issued the following orders:

The company 11th Rajputs in support at No. 10 Post was to move to No. 6 Post and thence work southwards through the palm trees on the edge of the *mashileh* and attack the enemy's right;

the company 96th Infantry in support at the Residency was to move to No. 3 Post;

the outpost reserve at Imamzadeh (one company 11th Rajputs, one company 96th Infantry, four machine guns and the four ex-Turkish guns) under Major C. H. Ward, 11th Rajputs, was to move to No. 10 Post;

a machine gun detachment from H.M.S. *Pyramus*, which was doing a route-march, was also ordered to No. 10 Post;

the general reserve at Rishahr (two companies 11th Rajputs and two companies 96th Infantry) under Lieutenant-Colonel H. P. Lane, 96th Infantry, was to prepare to move out;

a company from the Bushire town garrison was to be sent to join the general reserve; and

the 16th Cavalry squadron was to move north of Zangina out on to the *mashileh*.

The outpost reserve reached No. 10 Post at 7.40 a.m. General Brooking then ordered the guns to come into action, the field guns at a point half a mile to the south and the mountain guns at No. 4 Post; the 96th Infantry company was to advance southward directly against the enemy; the

Defence of Bushire; 9th September 1915. 11th Rajputs' company with two machine guns was to move round to a point marked B on the map and attack the enemy's left; and the other two machine guns were sent to Zangina to support the attack from that flank.

The companies of infantry were all only about fifty to sixty strong and, by 8.15 a.m., General Brooking realised that he had insufficient troops to push the attack home. He, therefore, ordered the *Pyramus* detachment forward (they came into action soon after near Zangina) and the general reserve to march from Rishahr to No. 10 Post. At 8.45 a.m. he ordered the support company 96th Infantry to move from No. 3 Post to point B; and at 9.10 a.m. he ordered the Gurkhas up from Rishahr.* The enemy's fire was heavy and had caused a number of British casualties, but the Indian infantry had closed in, pinning the tribesmen to their ground.

On the arrival of the general reserve at No. 10 Post at 9.25 a.m., General Brooking ordered Colonel Lane to move round under cover to Point B and to assault from there with the bayonet. This assault started at about 10.25 a.m. and at once encountered a heavy enemy fire. But it did not last, as the tribesmen, unable to stand the sight of the steadily advancing bayonets, first retired through the palm trees and then broke all along the line and fled out on to the *mashileh* to the number of about six hundred.

Here the squadron 16th Cavalry under Major W. H. Pennington, which had been in observation about three thousand yards east of Point B, had just received orders to close in towards the enemy. Owing to the mirage their view was limited and they started to move slowly westward covered by a line of dismounted men, when suddenly they sighted at close range the stream of enemy fugitives, on whom they at once opened fire. The order to mount and charge followed immediately and this was carried out quickly and gallantly with effective results, but at the expense of casualties among the cavalry which totalled a third of their strength. The two British officers, Major Pennington and 2nd Lieutenant L. I. L. Thornton, two Indian officers and 11 rank and file were killed and 10 rank and file wounded.

These heavy losses rather disorganised the cavalry, and the tribesmen continued their flight across the *mashileh*, outdistancing the Indian infantry though a good many of them

---

* The Gurkhas had been out all night and General Brooking did not want to utilise them if it could be avoided.

SITUATION AT SHIRAZ

were hit by our guns. They left 43 dead and 14 wounded behind them, which were believed to represent only a small portion of their losses, and we took four unwounded prisoners.

In addition to the 25 casualties of the 16th Cavalry, there were 5 in the naval detachment, 34 in the 11th Rajputs and 22 in the 96th Infantry.

In forwarding General Brooking's report on this affair, General Nixon commended the bravery and the endurance in most trying heat of officers and men; and he endorsed General Brooking's mention of several cases of individual gallantry, including those of Major Pennington, Lieutenant-Commander T. S. L. Dorman, R.N., and Lieutenant E. C. Staples, 11th Rajputs.

On the 13th September General Nixon reported that the effect of this action on the tribes of the Bushire hinterland had been great, and he recommended that we should utilise the services of pro-British Khans to attack and finally disperse the hostile elements. The Government of India, however, decided that it was better to avoid getting involved in inter-tribal disputes. On the 13th General Brooking left for Mesopotamia, the command at Bushire being taken over by Colonel S. M. Edwardes from India.

At Shiraz, the British occupation of Bushire gave the Germans and their sympathisers a good pretext for increased agitation; and the Governor-General, with German assistance, raised a corps of local volunteers under gendarmerie officers to retake Bushire. The situation became very critical and it was only the presence of Qawam with a following of his tribesmen and the belief that Saulat also, who was in the vicinity, was friendly to the British which prevented an anti-British outbreak. In the middle of September Saulat signified to the British and Russian Ministers that, in return for a letter of personal protection from both Powers, he would guarantee to maintain order in Southern Persia, to protect Allied interests and to take active steps against German agents. Though to do this would be a great innovation in our policy, it was felt that, as the Russian Minister at once agreed to grant the request, it was most undesirable for us to refuse. At the end of the month the Governor-General left Shiraz on recall to Tehran, his place being temporarily taken by Qawam.

Shiraz; September 1915.

General events and British policy; September 1915. The arrival of the Russian troops at Enzeli and the advance of General Townshend's force towards Kut-al-Amara in Mesopotamia, while they sensibly lightened the situation, also seemed to have the effect of causing the Germans to redouble their activities. At Hamadan they made no secret of their intention to attack and drive out the British and Russians; at Kermanshah not only did they receive large additional consignments of arms and ammunition and reinforcement by some three hundred Turkish troops (wearing Persian caps with German badges*), but the German consul was openly enlisting as many men as he could to assist the Turks in Mesopotamia; and at Isfahan the position was so dangerous that the Allied consuls and communities were all leaving. The British left there on the 14th September for Ahwaz, where they arrived safely at the beginning of October. The attitude of the Bakhtiaris, whose power and influence in the Isfahan area was considerable, had been disappointing and was evidently a result of the failure of the Persian Government to send them orders to stop the German agitation. Consequently, though most of them appear to have refused German bribes, they remained passive spectators.

About the middle of September Persian Ministers began to profess great anxiety to protect Allied consuls and to put an end to German intrigues, the danger of which they seemed at last to have realised and to be alarmed at. But their change of policy was unwelcome to the Democrats, and the Prime Minister had not sufficient strength of character to enforce the fulfilment of his promises to the Allies. It is true that he could not rely on the gendarmerie and was still afraid to use the Persian Cossacks and the Bakhtiaris, but he could at least have prevented and restrained the pro-German action of some of the leading permanent officials at Tehran.

In reply to the urgent request of the Persian Government for financial assistance and arms, the British and Russian Governments arranged during September to grant them a monthly subsidy, but neither Power was in a position to give them arms.

On the 30th September Mr. Marling telegraphed that the German position in Persia depended entirely on their keeping open the road to Baghdad via Kermanshah. The German Minister had, on the previous day, told the newly-appointed

---

* These were possibly the levies under Captain Klein which German accounts mention as being intended to support Niedermayer.

DESPOTIC GERMAN ACTION

Persian Governor of Kermanshah that, if there was any intention of his bringing about the return to Kermanshah of the British and Russian consuls, the Governor's own arrival would be forcibly prevented, as German interests could not permit the possibility of closing their only means of communicating with the outer world, through which they received news, money, etc. Mr. Marling added that if the Grand Duke Nicholas* could send enough troops to hold Kazvin and Kermanshah until our own troops reached Baghdad† and could control Khaniqin, the Germans would be left *en l'air*. Kermanshah, said Mr. Marling, was virtually in German possession, as the greater part of Raouf's irregulars had been surreptitiously brought in and the German consul, who was still busy proselytising, had over one thousand men in his pay.

Zugmayer's party were still at Kerman at the end of September. With them, besides a few Europeans, were about forty armed Persian retainers, and they had enlisted many other local ruffians who were to turn out when called upon. They had established such a hold on the town that Zugmayer had not hesitated to inform the Governor of his plans—which he intended to carry out whether the Governor liked it or not—to start a *Jahad* locally and to drive out Allied subjects. His intrigues in regard to Baluchistan and Makran had so far prospered that Bahram Khan of Bampur was again attacking the Makran Levy Corps.

Kerman; September 1915.

In East Persia the Russians captured the greater part of Becker's party near Tabas on the 1st September, Becker himself escaping with one Austrian, who died soon afterwards at Isfahan from the results of exposure. Becker, some days previously, had buried most of the expedition baggage and the treasure; and he wandered about in the neighbourhood, suffering great privations, waiting for reinforcements from Isfahan, which he apparently expected would include a large body of Bakhtiaris. On the 17th, however, Winkelmann arrived with fifteen Austrians only and they all remained on in the vicinity waiting for a chance to recover the buried

East Persia; September 1915.

---

* Recently appointed to command the Russian Caucasus armies.
† At this time it had not been decided that our troops should advance to Baghdad.

baggage and treasure. The latter they recovered on the 21st October, but the former seems to have been found and taken away either by the Russians or by local inhabitants.

Colonel Dale with his detachment reached Birjand on the 7th September and, although he had insufficient men to do all that the Russians (half of whose men were sick with fever) desired, arranged to hold the cordon as far as Sehdeh. News having been received on the 9th that Paschen had returned from Herat and was in Persia, measures were taken to intercept him; and it was soon reported that owing to these measures he had recrossed the frontier.* Beyond news of the arrival of a party of about twenty Germans at Nain and then at Mihrjan—evidently Winkelmann's party—there were no signs of any others attempting to follow Niedermayer's mission. The reports of the latter's reception at Herat did not seem to indicate that they were meeting with much encouragement from the Afghans; and, soon after their reported departure for Kabul from Herat on the 7th September, a letter was received by the Viceroy in which the Amir said that, though he had sent for the Germans to ascertain their object, this did not imply any departure from a neutral attitude.

The small size of the force under Colonel Wikeley, the area it had to watch and the limit on its action which the scarcity of water and fodder and the nature of the country imposed, rendered its reinforcement necessary. In the middle of the month eighty Hazara ex-soldiers left Meshed to join the force, and on the 20th September a double-company 19th Punjabis left railhead at Nushki for the same purpose. It had been arranged that a third squadron 28th Light Cavalry with horses for all three squadrons should also be sent from Quetta to East Persia, but their departure was delayed as it was found impossible to collect, in the Quetta area, sufficient camels for their transport.

Shiraz, Bushire, Kerman and Makran; October 1915. The appointment of Qawam to act as Governor-General of Fars at once brought about an improvement in the situation at Shiraz, though it proved to be only temporary. His nominee for the governorship of Bushire, Darya Begi, took over the

---

* Although Paschen himself, after his capture in 1916, said that he succeeded in reaching Isfahan with a letter and in returning to Herat, Niedermayer in his book confirms Paschen's failure and pays a tribute to the skilful watch kept by the East Persia Cordon.

administration of that town from the British on the 16th October and throughout the month the British garrison there remained undisturbed, though there were occasional rumours of an impending tribal attack. At Kerman also, October saw little change in the situation. The Germans under Zugmayer continued their agitation, which the Persian Governor was quite unable to check and which had the effect of increasing unrest in Makran. Our naval ships were consequently obliged to patrol the coast line and the Government of India took steps to increase the Makran Levy Corps, to arm villagers and to organise a better local intelligence system. But as the area was of no great political importance they decided to take there no other steps of a military nature.

The British force in East Persia was reinforced by a third double-company 19th Punjabis, which reached Kacha in the middle of October, by a third squadron 28th Light Cavalry with horses for all three squadrons, which left Nushki on the 12th October, and by twenty more Hazara ex-soldiers from Meshed. Colonel Wikeley, whose difficult task was enhanced by the necessity of avoiding any appearance of waging war against neutral Persians, had received his orders and instructions in a series of telegrams sent to Colonel Dale and himself since the end of July. These, collated and defined in a letter issued by the Chief of the General Staff in India on the 6th October, were to the following effect. Colonel Wikeley, while keeping in closest touch with the British consul in Seistan, was solely responsible for the military measures necessary to carry out his mission of intercepting and capturing, or destroying, any German parties who attempted to enter Afghanistan* or Seistan. By the end of the month, the regular force at his disposal would consist of three squadrons of cavalry, three double-companies of infantry and six machine guns. As it was undesirable to run the risk involved in splitting this force up into a number of small detachments, Colonel Wikeley was authorised to spend money freely in organising a good system of intelligence and in obtaining timely information of enemy movements. As regards the distribution of his force, for which he was authorised to build huts, the Chief of the General Staff suggested the location of three parties, each of equal strength, at Birjand, Nasratabad (Seistan) and Kacha, respectively.

East Persia; October 1915.

---
* It may not be amiss here to point out that we had the right, by treaty, to conduct Afghan relations with any other Power.

Information was received during October that Seiler intended shortly to leave Isfahan for Afghanistan, via Tabas, taking with him a large amount of arms, ammunition and treasure. It was said that his party would travel in two portions by different routes. The first portion under Major von Versen would include an Austrian doctor, eight Austrian soldiers and some Afghans or Pathans; and the second, whose composition was uncertain or unknown, would be under Seiler himself. The Niedermayer-Hentig party was reported to have reached Kabul early in October, but was said to be located outside the town, more or less as prisoners without intercourse with the public.

The Germans at Kabul; October 1915. Niedermayer says that on their arrival at Kabul on the 2nd October they were well received and lodged in the Amir's guest-house " Baber-Shah " outside the city. But they were painfully surprised to find that they were kept as honourable prisoners, and they received no reply to two letters which they soon sent to the Amir. To attract attention they started a hunger-strike, whereupon they were visited by a Turkish doctor, who informed them that, though the Amir himself was a strong Anglophile, his brother Nasrulla, many high officials and a large section of the populace were pro-German. On the 10th October they received a letter from the Amir bidding them welcome and promising to receive them shortly. About a fortnight later the Amir Habibulla Khan gave them a long audience, at which the Amir's brother, Nasrulla, and the Amir's two sons, Inayatulla and Amanulla, were present, in addition to several Ministers and a number of high officials. Habibulla, who was in no way the semi-barbarian chieftain pictured by many in Germany, impressed the Germans by his outstanding ability, his knowledge of men and affairs and his judgment. They realised that he exercised control over even the smallest matters in his realm, that they could not hope to induce him to come to any decision rashly and that he was evidently very much under British influence. His political sagacity, which had enabled him to maintain the status of his country, would, says Niedermayer, have brought all honour to a German. Though the general impression regarding their chances of success which the Germans gained from this audience was not encouraging, there seemed to be several factors in the situation which made it worth their while to persevere. Nasrulla, who was anti-British owing to resentment at what he considered his humiliating treatment in England in 1895, showed his sympathy with the Germans in every way and, though intellectually inferior to the Amir, proved to be a most valuable tool in German hands. Of the two sons, Amanulla seemed to the Germans to have the stronger character and greater ability and to be influenced by Nasrulla rather than by his father.

General Townshend's victory at Kut and his subsequent advance towards Baghdad seemed to Mr. Marling to be stimulating the Germans to still further efforts to strengthen their position in Persia. How far they were really actuated by the threat to their communications and by the influence on Persia which a British occupation of Baghdad would involve, appears, however, to be uncertain. At the beginning of October the Russians were in a critical situation in Europe and were still short of munitions; their Caucasus army, since its evacuation of Van in August, had showed no signs of recovery; and the small Russian force in Persia evidently only sufficed for the protection of Azerbaijan. Bulgaria was mobilising to co-operate with an Austro-German invasion of Serbia which promised to open unobstructed communication with Turkey; and the British attempt to force the Dardanelles had come to a standstill. Consequently, with the sole exception of Mesopotamia, the situation in the East generally favoured the Central Powers rather than the Allies. *[margin: General events and Allied policy; October 1915.]*

On the 15th October Mr. Marling reported that, owing to the increase of German activities, the situation was serious. The Germans appeared to him to be meditating a *coup* not only at Tehran, but also at Hamadan, to which place the Russian Minister was asking permission to send a regiment of Russian Cossacks from Kazvin. Sir Edward Grey at once telegraphed to Petrograd suggesting an increase of the Russian troops in Persia and was told in reply that reinforcements would be sent to Kazvin as soon as possible, but that a Cossack regiment could not be spared as yet to go to Hamadan. At the same time he learnt that the German Government expected to conclude a convention with Persia within a few days. This information he sent to Mr. Marling, and it crossed a telegram from Tehran reporting that powerful anti-Allied influence was being brought to bear on the Persian Government, that they were hesitating to accept financial assistance from the Allies and that they might possibly be constrained to join Germany.

This serious state of affairs contributed to the decision of H.M. Government to allow General Nixon to advance on

General events and Allied policy; October, 1915. Baghdad; and on the 24th October, when informing Petrograd of the British intention, Sir Edward Grey suggested that if the Russians could act simultaneously in North Persia, the situation might be saved. By this time the Germans were virtually masters of Tehran. In addition to large quantities of arms and ammunition, they had there about two hundred Austro-Hungarian soldiers,* several hundred locally recruited followers and six or seven hundred Persian gendarmerie under Swedish officers, on whom they could rely for support. Against these the Persian Government might possibly be able to count on about five hundred Persian Cossacks and one thousand police, but their loyalty was very doubtful. Mr. Marling and the Russian Minister received reports daily of an intended attack on them and the Legations, and in many ways it was clearly indicated that the Germans meditated a *coup d'état*.

On the 23rd October two members of the British consular staff at Shiraz were shot at and wounded, and two days later Major O'Connor informed Mr. Marling that, unless steps were taken at once to set matters right, the British colony would find it impossible to remain any longer at Shiraz. They and Qawam were constantly threatened with assassination and Major O'Connor feared that neither Qawam nor Saulat was capable of dealing with the situation. In consequence of this state of affairs Major O'Connor was authorised to leave Shiraz if necessary, but, as his departure would be hailed as a German success and would render the position of Qawam and Saulat much more difficult, he was instructed to remain there as long as possible.

A most unsatisfactory interview which Mr. Marling had with the Persian Prime Minister on the 26th October and information which he acquired during the next two days all seemed to indicate that Persian Ministers were deceiving him and were in reality negotiating with the Germans; and on the 29th he heard that a convention with Germany had actually been signed. But this was followed the same day by news that 4,000 Russian cavalry had just disembarked at Enzeli and on the 30th by a visit from the Persian Foreign Minister, who absolutely denied that any convention had been suggested or signed and who adopted altogether a much more amenable attitude.

About the same time three hundred Persian Cossacks, whom the Russian Minister had insisted on despatching in spite of

---

* It was found that Persian officials had been implicated in assisting their escape from Trans-Caspia and their journey to Tehran.

Persian protests, reached Hamadan, with the result that most of the German consul's armed retainers at once deserted him.

Lieutenant-Colonel H. von Kiesling, in his account* of the German efforts to organise an Islamic federation—Turkey. Persia and Afghanistan—against the Allies, furnishes an explanation of the increased German activities. He says that the organisation of a German line of communication across Persia was at first carried out cautiously and unostentatiously. Post commandants were established under the guise of consuls at the most important towns, and local Persian authorities were won over by German gold. He further says that, when the Hentig-Niedermayer expedition moved to Afghanistan, a second expedition under Klein was prepared at Baghdad to follow and support Niedermayer's party. But when Count Kanitz arrived at Tehran as military attaché in June 1915 he overrode all Prince Reuss' objections on the score of military necessity and insisted on hastening matters regardless of consequences. Henceforward the German campaign of intrigue and agitation was intensified and carried on openly without regard to Persian neutrality or Persian feelings. As the chief Persian supporters of the German plans were the Democrats, who were only pro-German because of their hatred for Russia, and as they proved really to have little influence in Persia as compared with that of the conservative landowners, this acceleration of activity was, in Kiesling's opinion, productive of much harm. In September 1915 Captain Klein's party reached Kermanshah, where it formed a strong military supporting point at a time that Prince Reuss was negotiating with Mustaufi-ul-Mamalik for a Persian alliance. In exchange for this alliance Germany was to provide Persia with arms and money; and negotiations on this basis, and on the understanding that the command of all forces in Persia would be given to Field-Marshal von der Goltz, were still in progress at the end of October.

On the 1st November the Persian Government accepted the Russo-British offer of a subsidy, but instead of saying at the same time that they agreed to the conditions on which it had been made, namely that they would take steps to stop German intrigues, they suggested an agreement under which Persia would formally adopt an attitude of actively benevolent neutrality. For this they intimated that they would require

General events and Allied policy; November 1915.

---

* " Mit Feldmarschall von der Goltz Pascha in Mesopotamien und Persien."

General events and Allied policy; November 1915.
terms, which they only defined by saying that they involved stipulations calculated to conciliate public opinion. Neither the British nor the Russian Minister considered it likely that the Persian Cabinet was really strong enough to carry through such an agreement in face of German and Democrat opposition, and it appeared to them that in reality the only possible means of restoring the situation was the immediate reinforcement of the Russian force at Kazvin. Their views were confirmed in the next few days by reliable information that, soon after the commencement of the *Moharram* festival on the 9th, the Germans intended a *coup* at Tehran, which they would initiate by the creation of anti-Ally disorders. Consequently, the Allied Ministers asked that at least two Russian regiments should move at once to Tehran from Kazvin.

Russian troops left Kazvin accordingly for Tehran on the evening of the 7th November, with the result that the next day the nervous young Shah was only dissuaded with difficulty from following the German advice to leave Tehran and that two Persian Ministers visited the Russian and British Ministers to protest and threaten that, unless the troops were stopped, the Cabinet would resign or leave Tehran. They were told, however, that, in view of the open preparations for a *coup* by the Germans, the two Powers considered it essential to protect their Legations and subjects at Tehran from attack and murder such as the Persian Government had quite failed to prevent, or even to inflict punishment for, elsewhere. The troops had no hostile designs and would only enter Tehran in the case of disorders. Both Persian Ministers, thereupon, promised that the safety of Allied officials and subjects would be ensured, that the Persian retainers enlisted by the Germans would be removed, the German arms and bombs seized and the Austrian prisoners of war escorted out of Tehran and kept under strict watch at a safe distance. Mr. Marling and the Russian Minister acknowledged that, if these measures were carried out, their Governments would doubtless feel reassured. But they doubted, they said, if the Persian Government had power to carry out their promises. The gendarmerie, the only force capable of acting, was known to be in German pay; the force the Cabinet were trying to form was to be under Persians who had received their military training at Constantinople and were therefore most unlikely to be ready to act against Germans, Austrians and Turks; and it was known that the Germans expected to conclude a convention, if not with the present Cabinet, with another which they would put into office by a *coup d'état*. In these circumstances Allied Ministers felt that it was impossible for them to suggest to their Governments that the troops should be recalled to Kazvin. They would, however, arrange that, so long as quiet reigned in Tehran, the force should advance no nearer than Karedj, twenty-six miles away.

In the course of the discussion the Persian Foreign Minister disclosed the terms on which his Government were willing to adopt a benevolent neutrality. These involved a complete revision of treaties with Russia and of the customs tariff, the cancellation of the Persian recognition of the Anglo-Russian Convention of 1907, a withdrawal from Persia at a later date of the Russian troops, a supply of arms etc. to form a Persian army, and the allocation to Persia of the same representation at the Peace Conference as other neutral countries.

During the next few days Persian Ministers, though they showed no signs of trying to carry out their promises to stop the German intrigues and agitation, continued to press for the recall of the Russian troops advancing towards Tehran. The German and Austrian Legations and Turkish Embassy hastily packing up many of their effects, moved them to houses adjoining the American and Spanish Legations, sent their arms and ammunition with many of their agents and adherents out of Tehran and in fact showed all the signs of a general exodus. There were also persistent rumours that the Shah and the Cabinet intended to move with the German Legation to Qum. The Germans and their Democrat sympathisers, realising that the Russian advance diminished the chance of their being able to bring off the *coup*, which they had hoped to start by an attack on the British Legation on the night 14th/15th, now bent all their energies on bringing about movements in various localities which would show the Persian Government that the Russian advance had roused the whole country against the Allies. On the 12th November Mr. Marling telegraphed that the Director of the Indo-European Telegraph Department had heard from his inspector on the Bushire-Shiraz line that the British consul and the manager of the Imperial Bank of Persia at Shiraz had been made prisoners and taken towards Bushire by the gendarmerie acting under orders from Tehran and that Qawam and Saulat had received instructions to attack Bushire. Mr. Marling also said that the leading clergy at Isfahan had telegraphed demanding that the Persian Government should break off relations with the Allies. This telegram was followed by two others sent by Mr. Marling on the same day. In the first he said that the Foreign Minister denied all knowledge of

General events and Allied policy; November 1915.

the alleged occurrence at Shiraz,* had suggested a change in the composition of the Persian Cabinet so as to gain the confidence of the Allies and declared that the Shah had no intention of leaving Tehran. But in the second telegram Mr. Marling showed that his suspicions that the Shah and the Cabinet did mean to accompany the Germans to Qum had been aroused by the way in which the Government were assisting the movement there of the principal German retainers.

On the 13th November Mr. Marling reported that the enemy representatives were insisting that they would demand their passports unless the Persian Government obtained the return of the Russian troops to Kazvin. He and the Russian Minister had asked for an audience next day with the Shah and he added that the German Minister was dejected, the Persian Foreign Minister very cordial and that our Persian friends expressed great confidence. On the 14th the audience with the Shah was inconclusive. Though assured that the advance of the Russian troops was prompted only by the necessity of ensuring the protection against German attacks and agitation which the Persian Government were clearly unable to afford, the Shah would only agree to the appointment of a new Minister of the Interior after the Russian troops had withdrawn. Though told that this was impossible and that if the Persian Government did not take steps against the Germans the Russian troops would do so, the Shah maintained his refusal.

Monday, the 15th November, was a critical day. In the morning two Persian Ministers came to the British Legation and announced that the Shah found it impossible to remain in his capital while Russian troops were at the gates and that His Majesty intended to remove the Court and Government. Mr. Marling again explained to them that the Russian advance was only precautionary and that as long as there were no disorders at Tehran the troops would remain at Karedj. The Russian Minister arrived a little later and gave the same assurances. Both Ministers were then invited to a meeting that afternoon of Persian Ministers and leading men to discuss the situation, when they were again informed that unless the Russian troops withdrew the Shah would leave Tehran at once. They repeated the assurances they had given and explained the reason why they had found it necessary to ask for the protection of Russian troops.

---

* This denial was accepted at Bushire as contradicting reports they also had received of British arrests at Shiraz and elsewhere.

After some three hours' discussion, in the course of which frequent messages came from the Shah indicating that he was in a nervous state of alarm and indecision, an arrangement was arrived at, which the two Allied Ministers agreed to recommend to their Governments. The Cabinet was to be reconstructed by the inclusion of Ain-ud-Daula and Farman Farma, whose presence and responsibility would be a guarantee to the Allies of a policy of benevolent neutrality ; and in return the Russian troops would not advance beyond Karedj, which they were expected to reach that night. When the Cabinet had been actually reformed and conversations had commenced concerning the measures to be taken to carry out the conditions on which the Russo-British subsidy had been offered, the troops would move half-way back to Kazvin and eventually to Kazvin itself.

The two Allied Ministers then went and personally informed the Shah, who was painfully agitated, of the proposed arrangement. Being reassured by their statement, he said that he would not leave Tehran till the British and Russian Governments sent their reply and that, if this were favourable, Persia would in future maintain intimate and cordial relations with the Allies. As regards the Germans, who had been persuading him to leave Tehran, he expressed himself in very strong terms.

The German, Austrian and Turkish representatives left Tehran that afternoon on the way towards Qum, and the exodus of their friends and sympathisers, including Democrat members of the *Majlis* and a large number of the gendarmerie, continued for the next day or two. But as the Shah failed to leave Tehran also, as up to the last moment they expected him to do, it was soon evident that the German plot had definitely failed. Enemy accounts of this episode, which fully confirm the German intention of utilising the Persian Democrats and gendarmerie to get the Shah away and to form, at Kermanshah, a Government favourably disposed to the Central Powers, also show that it was only the advent of Russian troops which saved the situation. They also say that the German negotiations with the Persian Cabinet, which despite the denials of Persian Ministers had been nearly completed, had been carried out without the knowledge or assistance of the Turks. Persia was to enter the war on the side of the Germanic alliance, Germany providing money and the necessary arms and munitions. The Germans also stipulated that the command of all forces operating in Persia was to be given to Field-Marshal von der Goltz, who was then, they said, on his way to Persia at the head of a Turco-German force.

Mr. Marling did not know what importance to attach to these statements of an approaching Turco-German force, but on the 16th November he telegraphed advocating an Allied assurance of support to Persia to repel any such aggression, or, as the best solution, the formation of a defensive alliance with her. It was impossible, he said, to predict what effect in the provinces the events of the 15th would have, but the German agents there—more resolute and reckless than those at Tehran—would probably try to start a revolution. If, on the other hand, in the next few days the Allies could definitely commit the Persian Government to their side, he thought it probable that the majority of their partisans would abandon the Germans.

On the 17th Mr. Marling reported matters to be improving. Farman Farma, as Minister of the Interior, was acting vigorously and felt confident that, so long as the Shah stayed at Tehran and Russian troops remained at Karedj, he could save the situation.

Seizure of British consul and colony at Shiraz; November 1915. Next day the Deputy Political Resident at Bushire (Major A. P. Trevor) telegraphed to Tehran, London and Delhi that he had just received a letter from Major O'Connor (British consul at Shiraz) from Borazjan, where he and Mr. Fergusson (Manager, Imperial Bank of Persia, Shiraz) and other British subjects were prisoners. Details of their capture were not given, but they appeared to have been escorted down by gendarmerie and were stated by Major O'Connor to be well treated and in no danger. The British ladies from Shiraz were expected to reach Bushire next day and would be able to give further details. On the 19th another telegram from Bushire reported the receipt, by the Persian Governor there, of a telegram from Qawam forwarded by the Governor of Kazerun,* which gave an account of the arrest on the second day of the *Moharram* (i.e., 10th November), of the British subjects at Shiraz. The gendarmerie had first seized the citadel, police quarters and other commanding points and then, after warning the British consul, bank manager, telegraph superintendent and other British subjects that they must leave for Bushire within an hour, had arrested and marched them off. To Qawam's enquiries and protests they had replied that they were acting under orders from the Government, which had declared war on the Allies; and, as the telegraph line was cut, Qawam could get neither denial nor confirmation of their statement, which

---

* The telegraph line had been cut some time previously.

was generally believed by the public. Major Trevor added that he had learnt from local sources that a detachment of about forty gendarmerie had escorted the British party to Borazjan, moving by a devious route to avoid Saulat who had tried to intercept them, and that the hostile Khans proposed to assure the better security of the male prisoners by sending them to Ahram (about thirty miles east of Bushire). At Bushire also there were so many reports of war that even the Persian Governor did not know what to believe.

On the afternoon of the 20th November Mrs. Fergusson, her two daughters and Mrs. Smith* arrived safely, under escort, at Bushire, bringing a letter from Major O'Connor which showed the above reports to be substantially correct. The responsibility for the outrage lay with a committee, composed of Persian gendarmerie officers but prompted by the German consul, which styled itself " National Committee for the protection of the independence of Persia." Major O'Connor, Messrs. Fergusson and Ayrton of the Imperial Bank, Mr. Smith and a clerk of the Telegraph Department, Mr. Livingstone a merchant, a Cingalese clerk and the escort sowars had been taken to the vicinity of Ahram, where they were apparently in charge of Wassmuss and the hostile Khans, who laid down the following conditions for their release :—The release of all German and Persian prisoners arrested by the British in Persia, the repayment of certain sums which had been attached at Bushire and which belonged to the Khans, and the withdrawal from Bushire of all the British troops.

Mr. Marling reported that on the 20th, when Persian Ministers learnt from him what had occurred, they were genuinely horrified and at once issued telegrams to Qawam and Saulat to use every effort to rectify matters. They and other leading officials in the provinces were also warned that the reports as to war were pure fabrications, as Persia was still neutral and on very friendly terms with Great Britain and Russia. In this respect, it is noteworthy that the change of attitude of the Persian Cabinet had just been indicated by an intimation to the British and Russian Ministers that they were prepared to enter into conversations for an alliance against Turkey. As the Germans were making lavish offers of arms, money and officers, which were being increased daily

Changed attitude of Persian Government; 20th November 1915.

---

* She subsequently died in England as a result of the hardships she had undergone.

in the hopes of winning Persia over to the Central Powers, Mr. Marling trusted that the Persian proposal to the Allies would be favourably considered.

<small>Russian military action; end of November 1915.</small> Russian forces, moving out from Urmia and Tabriz on the 8th November had recently occupied Ushnu and Sauj Bulag without difficulty and it was now learnt that the Russian expeditionary force under General Baratoff would police the triangle Hamadan-Qum-Tehran with a small cavalry force and would then operate against Kermanshah and Khaniqin. The composition of this force was reported to be fifty squadrons of cavalry, four batteries of artillery and six and a half battalions of infantry with an effective strength of about 10,000,* of whom about half had already reached, or advanced beyond, Kazvin. In the meantime, however, the Swedish commandant of gendarmerie at Tehran had been so sedulously playing on the nervous apprehensions of the Shah by stories of his imminent arrest by the advancing Russian troops that the Russian Minister had felt compelled to promise that they would at once withdraw to Yengi Imam. They commenced this withdrawal from Karedj on the 21st November.

On leaving Tehran the Austrian and Turkish representatives had gone no further than Shah Abdul Azim (ten miles south of Tehran), whence they continued to maintain touch with their sympathisers in the capital; but Prince Reuss, some fifty Democrat deputies of the *Majlis* and a large number of the gendarmerie with many of the German agents and levies had gone to Qum. Here they formed a body which styled itself the Committee of National Defence and which, with the assistance of several of the leading Persian officials and of the gendarmerie, not only flooded the country with official-looking telegrams announcing a revolution at Tehran and the flight of the Russian and British Ministers, but also stopped all Government messages. Another step taken to neutralise the depressing effects of the German failure at Tehran was the organisation of an attack on the Persian Cossacks at Hamadan by a force of gendarmerie under their Swedish officers. Since the arrival at the end of October of these Cossacks and the consequent desertion of the German levies, a reinforcement of the gendarmerie at Hamadan had encouraged many of these levies to return and had caused such a deterioration in the Allied position that the Russian Minister had recently arranged for a sotnia of Russian Cossacks to move there from

---

* Mr. Marling's telegrams of this period complain that the Russian Minister had practically no information of the strength or intentions of Baratoff's force.

Kazvin. On the 22nd November, however, long before they could arrive, the Persian Cossacks were attacked by the gendarmerie and, after a very slight show of resistance, surrendered. The British and Russian consuls found it necessary to leave Hamadan for Kazvin and the gendarmerie plundered the Imperial Bank. The news of these events caused a great sensation at Tehran, but the Persian Government, though they realised that the gendarmerie under their Swedish officers were in open rebellion, were afraid to take strong measures and even induced the Russian Minister to telegraph to General Baratoff requesting that the sotnia of Cossacks *en route* to Hamadan should be instructed to avoid a collision with the German forces in that vicinity, which were reported to number about 1,200 men including gendarmerie, levies and tribesmen advancing from the Kermanshah direction. As a result, this Russian Cossack detachment withdrew a few days later from the point it had reached, a movement which was exaggerated by the Germans into a victory.

In reporting this attack on the 22nd November, Mr. Marling attributed the hesitation to act of the Persian Government to their doubts whether we and the Russians would offer them an alliance and he expressed the opinion that if we did not do so at once they would go over to Germany. He therefore requested permission to open negotiations at once. Two days later (on the 24th), the Viceroy of India telegraphed to London also advocating such an alliance, which, if it were not concluded on political conditions of an unduly extravagant nature, would, he considered, be advantageous from an Indian point of view. On the 24th Mr. Marling further telegraphed that if negotiations were begun, the British subjects arrested at Shiraz would probably be released and that, as both he and the Persian Ministers considered that in the meantime these prisoners would be in no personal danger, we should refuse the demands of the Khans of the Bushire hinterland, many of which were, in any case, inadmissible.

On the 26th November Mr. Marling reported that the situation was developing somewhat unfavourably. There were some 3,000 gendarmerie and a larger number of German levies at Hamadan, where more were expected. Russian troops were moving in that direction from Kazvin, but he did not know in what force. The Turkish and Austrian representatives with a number of levies and Austrian ex-prisoners of war were returning to Tehran and it seemed possible that with the help of the gendarmerie an attempt

British policy; end of November 1915.

might be made on Farman Farma, who had already been threatened. A signal Russian success at Hamadan would reassure the Government, who were so overawed by German threats that they scarcely dared to talk of an alliance with us. Klein was still, said Mr. Marling, at Kermanshah.

On the 28th, Sir Edward Grey, who had by then heard that General Townshend was retiring to Aziziya after the battle of Ctesiphon, telegraphed to Sir George Buchanan at Petrograd that Mr. Marling's telegram of the 26th made it clear that we could only save the situation by meeting force with force. For this purpose a Russian defeat of the rebellious gendarmerie at Hamadan or elsewhere would be most effective. It was particularly important to make Farman Farma secure and also to prevent the gendarmerie and Germans from occupying and becoming masters of Tehran. An Allied occupation of the capital, however, unless it was essential to protect the Legations, might precipitate the departure of the Shah. Sir Edward Grey trusted that Russians might be ordered to take action accordingly.

Von der Goltz and Persia; November 1915. With reference to the reported advance to Persia of a Turco-German force under Field-Marshal von der Goltz, rumours of his advent had been current since the end of October. But they were not confirmed till about a fortnight later when reliable news was received that he was to leave Constantinople for Baghdad on the 10th November. Kiesling says that in Goltz's instructions of that date he was told that his task was to destroy Russian and British power in Persia, to ensure the future freedom and independence of that country and to assist in the organisation of a Persian army. The officers and expeditions sent from Germany and Turkey to Persia and Afghanistan, the German and Turkish military attachés in Persia and the officers appointed as vice-consuls or consular administrators there were all placed under his orders, while the diplomatic representatives of the two countries were to co-operate with, and support him, in every way. Kiesling and other German writers show, however, that, in spite of this semblance of concord, relations between Germans and Turks were never harmonious. The Turkish Government had formed the alliance to serve their own ends and not from love of Germany, for the sympathies of a great part of the Turkish nation, and particularly the educated portion, inclined rather to France and Great Britain. Goltz consequently experienced constant difficulties in his diplomatic relations with the Turks.

At Bushire, there were no special incidents of importance during November. At the beginning of the month, the naval squadron in the Persian Gulf was strengthened by the arrival of the *Philomel, Britomart* and *Bramble,* so that arrangements could be made for a blockade of the ports if Persia entered the war against us.

Bushire ; November 1915.

In East Persia Colonel Wikeley, receiving information early in November that Germans were concentrating at Yezd with the intention of advancing first to Naiband and then of breaking through the British cordon between Neh and Kain, disposed his forces to intercept them. But the movement never materialised. It was subsequently ascertained from captured German documents that a concentration had taken place at Yezd early in November and that on the 13th Becker and Winkelmann, who had gone back to Yezd from Tabas after recovering their treasure, had set out for Naiband with a small advanced party. But, as most of them were soon afterwards captured by robbers, who only released them on paying a ransom, and Becker was wounded, the project was abandoned.

East Persia ; November 1915.

The British also learnt early in November that a force of Baluchi tribesmen had collected in the Bam–Rigan area and were evidently acting in collusion with the Germans at Kerman. By the middle of the month it was reported on good authority that they intended to co-operate with Seiler, who for some time past had been mentioned as having the intention of advancing from Isfahan into Afghanistan with a force of some strength, composed of Germans, Austrians and Persian levies. As it appeared that the reported movement via Naiband had fallen through, Colonel Wikeley now adjusted his dispositions to intercept Seiler's advance, which now seemed likely to come via Kerman. One result of this section of Baluchis espousing the German cause was to induce other Baluchi chiefs to proffer their assistance against the Germans to Major Prideaux ; and, as he considered that German action and Persian supineness justified acceptance of their offer, he obtained sanction from India to enlist two hundred of their tribesmen. By employing these men to guard and escort convoys, etc., Colonel Wikeley would be able to release a number of his Indian troops for more important work.

Niedermayer in his book says that Seiler's party was composed of forty Germans and Austrians and fifteen Afghans (Afridis ?), apparently in addition to a number of Persian levies, and that he realised that, as he had little chance of being able to force his way through the East Persia Cordon, he must try to get past by skilful manœuvre. He considered that the route via Tabas was no longer possible and decided to go via Yezd and Kerman to a point within a few days' march of the frontier zone, whence the existence of several easterly routes afforded him a chance of deceiving the enemy. He left Isfahan on the 24th November with Dr. Niedermayer, three Germans, ten Austrians, five Afghans (Afridis?) and the whole of the Niedermayer expedition baggage, i.e., gold, silver, medicines, wireless station, explosives, arms, munitions, tents, etc. After beating off an attack by robbers near Nain, they arrived at Yezd on the 4th December.

The general situation in Persia and news of Seiler's intentions led the authorities in India to reinforce Colonel Wikeley with one section 25th Mountain Battery and the fourth squadron 28th Light Cavalry, both of which left Nushki to join him during the last week in November. On the arrival of these reinforcements Colonel Wikeley proposed to distribute his force as follows:—

Sehdeh and Birjand ..	One squadron of cavalry; Two machine guns; A few infantry.
Neh	One troop of cavalry; 72 infantry (with riding camels).
Nasratabad (Seistan) ..	Headquarters; Two squadrons of cavalry; Two mountain guns; 100 infantry.
Lutak	One squadron of cavalry, less one troop; Two machine guns.
Kacha-Robat	350 infantry; Two machine guns.

Colonel Wikeley had also by this time **150 Hazara ex-soldiers,** recruited at Meshed, at his disposal, to be increased gradually to a strength of 200. These he proposed to distribute in posts between Neh and Birjand.

CHAPTER IV.

DECEMBER 1915–MAY 1916:
SUCCESSFUL RESULTS OF ALLIED OPERATIONS.

(Maps 2, 4 and 5.)

It soon became evident that though the Persian Cabinet had been reconstructed to introduce a policy of actively benevolent neutrality towards the Allies, its composition rendered it unlikely to fulfil that purpose. Mustaufi-ul-Mamalik himself was too identified with the Russophobe Democrat party to view a Russian alliance with any real favour, while two Democrat Ministers whom he insisted on retaining in office had been among the most active of those assisting the Germans. Farman Farma, as Minister of the Interior, did what he could by vigorous instructions to the provinces to restrain German agitation, but his efforts were much hampered by the action of his colleagues. For instance, they attempted, by illusory suggestions that they could bring pressure to bear on the gendarmerie to cease their rebellious activities, to delay the Russian advance from Kazvin; the Minister of Telegraphs not only furnished the Germans with information of the Russian military movements, but also spread reports of Russian defeats; and, though the Prime Minister dismissed the Swedish officers who had openly acted with the Germans in West Persia, he refused to take similar action in the case of the Swedish commandant of gendarmerie and of another senior Swedish officer who had been implicated at Tehran.
Central and West Persia; December 1915.

Since it was the general impression in Persia that the Germanic alliance would emerge victorious from the world-war, the attitude of the Persian Government was not surprising. They were uncertain, moreover, whether, even in Persia, the Russians would be able to cope successfully with the strong position which the Germans had attained in the provinces. At Qum the Germans dominated the Committee of National Defence which was denouncing the Cabinet as traitors and calling on all true patriots to rise against British and Russians; the Turco-German emissaries were collecting considerable forces

Central and West Persia; December 1915.
of gendarmerie, levies and tribesmen at Qum, Hamadan, Kermanshah and Burujird ; Saulat-ud-Daula, the Vali of Pusht-i-Kuh and even the Shaikh of Mohammerah were said to have espoused the German cause ; a sudden change of attitude on the part of the Bakhtiaris seemed to show that they also were hostile to any arrangement with the Russians ; and the German asseverations of the imminent advance into Persia of a large Turkish force under Goltz were universally believed. Moreover, the British, having failed in their advance on Baghdad and in their attack on the Dardanelles, were apparently incapable of helping the Russians in Persia. Mr. Marling, however, still continued to work for a treaty of alliance, which the Shah also suddenly began to advocate.

On the 4th December, General Baratoff, who had been awaiting the arrival of his artillery, started his advance from Kazvin. His main column, composed of twelve squadrons of Russian Cossacks, one battalion of infantry* and six guns, moved towards Hamadan ; two columns, each of about half that strength, advanced towards Tehran and Qum respectively ; and he held in reserve a force of twelve squadrons, half a battalion and two guns. A mixed force of two or three thousand gendarmerie and levies, which had been barring the Hamadan road at a point about fifty-five miles south-west of Kazvin, retired hastily before the Russians, who on the 9th drove them with loss from the Sultan Bulag pass. On that day Mustaufi-ul-Mamalik informed the dragomans of the British and Russian Legations that the expressions of public opinion against an alliance and in favour of neutrality were so strong, both at Tehran and in the provinces, that he feared that he could not run counter to them. While inclining to the opinion that the Prime Minister, though anxious to conclude an alliance, was awaiting the result of the Russian operations, Mr. Marling reported that the chances of an alliance were growing very slender and would only be possible by making the largest concessions to Persian demands.

During the next week it became manifest that the Persian Cabinet was not prepared to conclude an alliance with the Allies, though the Shah, influenced apparently by Farman Farma, was anxious to do so. On the other hand, the Russian Government and the Government of India had both expressed a preference for mere neutrality, as the price demanded for an alliance seemed to them to be quite disproportionate to any advantages to be gained.

---

* At this stage none of his infantry were regulars.

By the 14th December Baratoff's main column had occupied Hamadan and his Qum column had reached Lalekhan, about sixty miles west-south-west of Tehran. The Persian Government, however, were still powerless, as the Germans controlled the telegraphs and all Persia south of the Kermanshah—Sultanabad—Qum—Yezd line, while even to the north of that line the pro-German Democrats were so active that the Government had little authority. The reports he had received of the strength of the local and tribal forces which the Germans were concentrating about Kermanshah—where Goltz apparently intended to join them shortly with a large Turkish force—made it most important, telegraphed Mr. Marling on the 15th December, that the Russians should crush the local forces before the Turks could arrive. He consequently urged that Baratoff's force should at once be considerably increased. Telegraphic communication with Yezd and Kerman had been cut, he said, and Mr. Marling assumed, correctly as it turned out, that the Germans had obliged our consuls and colonies to evacuate those places as they had recently done at Sultanabad.*

The Shah now informed the Russian and British Ministers of his intention to form a new Cabinet for the purpose of concluding an alliance, subject to the proviso that Baratoff's operations made good progress. This condition having been fulfilled by a Russian occupation of Qum on the 20th December, a Russian success against a force of gendarmerie and levies twenty-four miles south-west of Tehran on the 22nd and the practically unopposed advance of Baratoff's main column to the south-west of Hamadan, the Shah, on the 24th December, sanctioned the formation of a new Cabinet with Farman Farma as Prime Minister. In the belief that the British force in Mesopotamia would shortly resume its advance on Baghdad and that this in conjunction with Baratoff's advance in West Persia would cause the Persian Government to moderate their demands, Mr. Marling had recommended on the 22nd that we should still work for the alliance which the Shah and Farman Farma desired. It seemed, he said, essential to bind the Persian Government to us by some kind of formal agreement. A further indication that the tide had begun to turn in favour of the Allies was the fact that Dr. M. Y. Young of the Anglo-Persian Oil Company had just succeeded in obtaining from the Bakhtiari

---

* Sultanabad was evacuated on the 9th, Kerman on the 14th and Yezd on the 17th December. At all these places the Imperial Bank of Persia was pillaged by gendarmerie or the Germans.

Central and West Persia; December 1915.

chiefs a written guarantee of protection for the oil-fields and an undertaking that they would prevent enemy agents entering their country to agitate.

By the 26th December, Baratoff's main column had reached Asadabad, having detached a force which had arrived at Daulatabad on its way to Sultanabad, while the Qum Column had passed through Kashan in the direction of Isfahan. On the 22nd, Major Marsh, British liaison officer with Russian Caucasus Army Headquarters, had telegraphed that two frontier infantry regiments (i.e., eight battalions totalling some 6,000 rifles) were being sent to reinforce Baratoff; and on the 30th he further reported that four more cavalry regiments and twelve mountain guns would embark at Baku on the 7th January, for the same purpose. Russian reports said that a Turkish division had advanced to Qasr-i-Shirin between the 15th and 20th December and that Turkish reinforcements had also arrived at Ushnu. Though the former report was considered doubtful by our own Intelligence staff in Mesopotamia, the latter was confirmed by an attack before which the Russian troops at Sauj Bulag were forced to retire on the 29th December.

Various suggestions had been made both by British and Russians for some measure of co-operation between their respective forces in Mesopotamia and Persia. But the siege of Kut, on the one hand, and the difficult mountain country facing Baratoff on the other precluded any such idea for the time being.

Most German writers attribute the revival at this period of Turkish dreams of territorial expansion to their success in repelling the attacks on the Dardenelles. This, it is said, led Turkish statesmen and leaders to overestimate their military capacity and to disdain German military advice. Even though there may be some truth in these statements, the German General Staff at Berlin cannot be altogether absolved of blame in the matter. For, as Kiesling narrates, they had greatly overestimated the effect of the Turco-German propaganda and activities in Persia. He was shown a General Staff map on which 35,000 armed Persians were indicated as fighting for the Germans in various parts of Persia, whereas, when Goltz reached that country, he found that there were actually only 2,000-3,000 gendarmerie under Swedish officers and a few groups of armed, but undisciplined and unreliable, tribesmen, totalling perhaps 2,000.

Shortly after his arrival at Baghdad early in December, in reply to urgent requests from Persia for military assistance, Goltz sent there from the Tigris three infantry battalions, a mountain battery and a machine gun company. But he maintained that the Persian undertaking must be limited to operations to guard the flank of the Turkish army in Mesopotamia. His main object, he decided, must be to defend Baghdad and to operate against the British trying to relieve Kut, whither he at once proceeded to inspect the situation.

After returning from Kut to Baghdad, Goltz proceeded at the end of December, with Colonel Bopp and the Minister appointed to relieve Prince Reuss, to Kermanshah, to meet Kanitz, Klein and Persian representatives of the Democrat party who were in temporary revolt against the Cabinet. Winter rains and snow on the mountain tracks emphasised the difficulties attending the organisation of a line of communication and of the operations in Persia which Kanitz advocated so strongly. At Kermanshah Goltz found a most critical state of affairs, which many Germans ascribe to Kanitz's policy of openly disregarding Persian neutrality. Baratoff's force had reached the neighbourhood of Kangavar, while to oppose him the German-Persian parties of gendarmerie and partisans, none of them particularly reliable, were extended over a long stretch of country from Sultanabad via Kangavar to Sehneh. The country itself was in a state of political chaos, as the leading men were hopelessly divided in opinion and the Persian Cabinet was powerless outside Tehran. The Democrats, on whom Kanitz had placed reliance, proved to have neither the power nor the capacity to fulfil their pledges; and the great tribal chiefs, who exercised much of the power in the provinces, put personal interests before patriotism. Kanitz had attempted to win the latter over by gifts of arms and of large sums of money, with promises of still larger sums to follow. But so far at any rate he had not obtained much support from them; and they were negotiating also with Russians and British, evidently with the idea of taking the stronger side. Moreover, German and Turkish aims were fundamentally divergent and there was consequently a constant struggle between their representatives on the spot as to the measures to be taken. This had the further effect of dividing even the Persian party which favoured the Central Powers into pro-German and pro-Turkish sections.

Into the midst of this political turmoil came the few German officers of the Persian military mission, not knowing the language, with insufficient personal interpreters and without the necessary troops, resources, arms or the large sums of money which the Persian tribesmen had been led to expect. Goltz's arrival with empty hands, combined with his inability to fix any date for the advance of a Turco-German force, caused trouble and opposition. It is noteworthy that German accounts specially emphasise the fact that, at this stage, the only really useful force available was the advanced guard of the small Turkish force from the Tigris, consisting of a battalion of infantry, a mountain battery and a machine gun detachment under the command of Major Raith of Goltz's staff. Goltz had nominated him to this command with stringent orders to maintain strict discipline, in the hope of removing the bad impression which the previous excesses of Turkish troops had created among the Persians. This party arrived at Kermanshah early in January. In the meantime, Goltz, leaving Bopp to command and as his representative in Persia, had returned to Baghdad.

Bushire; December 1915. At Bushire, beyond a few ineffective night raids by the ever hostile tribesmen of the hinterland, little of importance occurred during December. On the 21st the Deputy Political Resident there received a very friendly letter from Qawam, acting Governor-General of Fars, saying that the *coup* of the 10th November had taken him by surprise but that he hoped soon to restore the situation by an attack on the gendarmerie with a tribal force, in which he had invited Saulat to co-operate. Two days later news was received that this attack had been carried out, but there was no confirmation of the initial success which it was said to have attained.

East Persia; December 1915. Early in December information was received by the British that the Germans at Yezd had been joined by Seiler and his party with a large caravan and a wireless station. Seiler's evident intention of establishing bases there and at Kerman, from which to move into Afghanistan and to foment disturbances on the Baluch and Makran borders, was further confirmed by reports from Yezd and Kerman of the German action which led in the middle of the month to the evacuation of both these places by the British and Russian consuls and colonies.

German accounts say that Seiler's first intention, after reaching Yezd, was to move eastward from there towards the Afghan border; and that he had made all arrangements to do so, including the severance of all telegraphic communication, when he heard from Isfahan of the Russian advance from Kazvin. He then decided to go to Kerman, which Zugmayer by himself would be scarcely strong enough to dominate. For the possession of Kerman was necessary for German schemes against India, Baluchistan and Afghanistan; and Seiler hoped to be able to hold it till communication with the west was reopened and till Goltz arrived in Persia with the expected force. Seiler left Yezd on the 16th December with his caravan of over two hundred animals and reached Kerman on the 27th to find that the Democrats had risen, had driven out the Allied consuls and had cut telegraphic communication.

Beyond various reports received by Colonel Wikeley, indicating German intentions to attempt to pass into Afghanistan, nothing of importance occurred in December in the frontier districts of East Persia. At Meshed two cipher messages to the German Minister at Tehran from the mission at Kabul were obtained by the Allies, and were sent to Petrograd where they were deciphered. From these it appeared that the Germans at Kabul had gained little satisfaction from their interview with the Amir on the 26th October and were not hopeful of success unless at least one thousand Turks with machine guns could reach there. They were, however, prepared to proceed to the extreme measure of organising a *coup d'état* if this proved necessary to achieve their object.

On becoming Premier, Farman Farma started at once to make attempts to reassert the authority of the Government. He dismissed the senior Swedish officers who had been assisting the Germans, redoubled his efforts to keep the great tribal chieftains from espousing the German cause and impressed on the Shah the advantages of an alliance with Russia and Great Britain. Further, when General Baratoff visited Tehran on the 6th January, the Persian Cabinet agreed to an arrangement by which the strength of the Persian Cossack Brigade was to be raised to 10,000 so as to replace the rebellious gendarmerie and was to be officered, equipped and maintained by Russia for the duration of the war.

Central and West Persia; January 1916.

German headquarters, both political and military, had by this time been concentrated at Kermanshah. But the 3,000–4,000 Persian gendarmerie and levies under their control in that area

West Persia; January 1916. showed little inclination for serious fighting. Consequently Baratoff's main column, reinforced by the 4,000 rifles of a frontier regiment, occupied Kangavar on the 13th January without much opposition, and prepared to advance on Kermanshah as soon as the cavalry division (3,600 sabres and 12 mountain guns), then on its way from Baku, had reached Hamadan. On the 15th, Kanitz, with a force composed of a Turkish battalion, some gendarmerie and tribal levies, attacked the Russian outposts. But the tribesmen would not fight and the attack miscarried, whereupon Kanitz, apparently realising the failure of his policy, disappeared and was reported to have committed suicide.

Information had been received by the British at the beginning of the month that though the Vali of Pusht-i-Kuh might appear to be siding with the enemy, neither he nor his son had any real intention of doing so. The news from West Persia, which since British consuls had left had been rather indefinite and unreliable, now seemed to show also that other tribal chiefs there were not really giving the Germans much effective assistance. That this supposition was correct is confirmed by the German accounts, which say that the Germans got little return for the vast sums of money they spent among the tribesmen and especially among the Lurs and Kurds. For instance, Nizames-Sultaneh (ex-Governor of Luristan), to whom they made a personal monthly allowance of £4,000 on the understanding that he would raise for them a force of at least 10,000 horsemen, never produced any noteworthy force beyond his own personal escort of one hundred men; while Klein, who had been organising a force at Kermanshah since September, found that the most reliable body under his command was that formed of fifty Pathan deserters from the Indian Army.

The main danger seemed to be the large Turkish force, which reports from Mesopotamia and elsewhere all agreed was about to invade Persia. Turkish troops had certainly begun to move across the Persian frontier and it seemed more than probable that they would ere long be joined by others released by our recent evacuation of Gallipoli.

South Persia; January 1916. The forced departure from Shiraz, and subsequently from Yezd and Kerman, of the British consuls had upset our intelligence arrangements in those areas also, while a new organisation based on the Persian Gulf ports, East Persia and Meshed had not yet begun to function properly. At this period, therefore,

THE SOUTH PERSIA RIFLES 139

our information of events in South Persia was generally scanty and indefinite. It was consequently not till Qawam's son-in-law arrived at Bandar Abbas on the 8th January that we learnt definitely that Qawam's attempt to hold his own against the gendarmerie had been unsuccessful and that he himself had been forced to retire to the vicinity of Lar. His failure had been due to the better armament and equipment of the gendarmerie and to the fact that Saulat had refused to come to his assistance. Qawam now sent word that, if the British would assist him with money, arms and ammunition, he was certain of success. On the 12th January Mr. Marling telegraphed that, unless the Government of India were able to send a military force or British officers to assist Qawam, the condition of Fars and South Persia would go from bad to worse. He also suggested that the British should organise a Persian force to restore and maintain order in South Persia in the same way as the Russians were doing in the north. This suggestion not only met with approval in London and Delhi but was agreed to by the Persian Cabinet and led to the organisation of the force subsequently known as the South Persia Rifles.

With the elimination from the situation of Qawam, the gendarmerie and partisans from Shiraz would be free to attack Bushire, and this they seemed likely to do with the acquiescence if not the assistance of Saulat. The only immediate remedy was to give Qawam the assistance in money and arms that he required and this we agreed to do, instructions to that effect being issued to the Deputy Political Resident at Bushire on the 18th January. Two days later the Viceroy of India recommended Lieutenant-Colonel Sir Percy Sykes, who from considerable past experience in Persia had an intimate knowledge of the country and its inhabitants, for charge of the mission to raise and organise a military police force in South Persia. His appointment with the rank of Brigadier-General was at once approved by H.M. Government.

In the meantime, on the 16th January the Persian Cabinet's terms for a Treaty of Alliance with Great Britain and Russia had been communicated to their respective Ministers at Tehran by Farman Farma. Though these terms were just as high as those of the preceding Cabinet, the three Governments concerned all understood that they were subject to considerable modification. The Russian Government, however, never

Central and West Persia; January 1916.

Central and West Persia; January 1916.
favoured a treaty, and in consequence the three-cornered conversations between Tehran, London and Petrograd dragged on for many months without result. But the fact that the negotiations were proceeding seems to have had an appreciable effect on Persian policy.

On the 21st January one of Baratoff's columns occupied Sultanabad, thus reducing still further the area under German control. But though the reinforcing cavalry division was due at Hamadan in the first week of February, heavy falls of snow in the area seemed likely to delay the main advance on Kermanshah.

Kiesling says that he arrived at Kermanshah on the 25th January. After a thorough discussion with Goltz it had been decided that their first aim must be to organise a more efficient line of communication from Constantinople to Baghdad and that they could then proceed to build up a national Persian army round the Persian gendarmerie. His experiences on his journey to Kermanshah showed Kiesling how difficult it would be to create a good line of communication through the Persian mountains, where, moreover, the country was more suitable to military operations by small detachments than by a large force. At Kermanshah itself he realised what little reliance could be placed on Persian tribal co-operation and that, in any case, little could be done till the promised money, personnel and material came from Germany. To meet only the obligations already incurred the German mission required a monthly sum of at least two million marks, and there was nothing like this amount of cash available, the paper money (printed in Persian characters) sent from Germany being quite unnegotiable. Though some officers allotted to the mission were on their way, none of the material was forthcoming; and the Germans had other difficulties to contend with. They found that their activities, based on an expressed desire to establish the independence of Persia, were constantly undermined and thwarted by the Chauvinistic policy of the Turks. Kiesling, who felt that the only result of German action had been to turn neutral Persia into a war area and to bring about a Russian advance which threatened the Turks in Mesopotamia, left Kermanshah again on the 6th February to return to Baghdad. He considered it essential to proceed there so as to explain to General Headquarters in Berlin how far they had been misled concerning conditions in Persia.

THE SYKES MISSION

In recommending that General Sykes should take charge of the mission to organise a Persian military police force, the Government of India had suggested that he should begin his work in Seistan and gradually extend his operations to Kerman and Bandar Abbas; also that an officer, under his orders, should at the same time start recruiting from the friendly tribes in the vicinity of Bushire. Mr. Marling and Farman Farma, however, impressed with the immediate necessity for supporting Qawam in Fars and for restoring Persian Government authority in Kerman, urged the despatch of a small military force—or failing this a mission with some guns—to Bandar Abbas. A few officers should also, they thought, be sent there to recruit a nucleus for the military police force from Qawam's following. But any attempt to recruit near Bushire was strongly deprecated by Farman Farma. On the 28th January the Government of India replied that they were not in a position to send a military force to Bandar Abbas, but they proposed that Sir Percy Sykes should start work there instead of in Seistan. The Foreign Office in London also made the same proposal and agreed that recruitment at Bushire was inexpedient, at any rate for the time being.

South Persia; January–February 1916.

On the 1st February Mr. Marling once more urged that a small force with guns should be sent to accompany General Sykes to Bandar Abbas. This led the Foreign Office in London, apprehensive of the reaction in neighbouring Moslem countries and eventually in India if the whole of South Persia were allowed to go over to the enemy, to ask the War Office on the 4th if they could see their way to sending any troops to Fars, if only by way of a demonstration. The War Office replied that they could spare from Egypt a force of two squadrons of Indian cavalry, two battalions of Indian infantry, a mountain battery and a British machine gun detachment, but that its sphere of action must be limited to the low country, as they were opposed to any operations of an extended nature in Fars. This proposal was telegraphed to India by the India Office on the 12th February.

In the meantime Qawam, who had got together a considerable number of Baharlu and Arab tribesmen and was in hopes of getting Saulat to assist him, intended, with the assistance he was obtaining from us in money, arms and ammunition, to start operations against the gendarmerie about the end of the month. By then the cold weather would be over and the nomad tribes on whom he relied for support would not have started their annual northerly migration. It was most desirable

South Persia; February 1916. that before he started he should be consulted regarding General Sykes's mission. But as the latter could not get to Persia in time, it was arranged that Qawam should at once go to Bushire and discuss matters with Sir Percy Cox.

As it was evident that the force from Egypt could not reach Bandar Abbas in time to assist Qawam and as its sphere of operations was to be limited to the low country, the authorities in India telegraphed on the 16th February to London deprecating its despatch as unnecessary and inexpedient. They also said that if it could be spared from Egypt they considered that it could be more usefully employed in Mesopotamia or India than in Persia. In replying to this next day, the Chief of the Imperial General Staff explained that the proposal had emanated from the Foreign Office and he went on to say that the Prime Minister had ordered the War, Foreign and India Offices to hold a conference on the political and military situation in India, Persia and Aden. The General Staff were then to give an opinion as to the adequacy of the military resources available in those areas and as to any additional military measures considered necessary. To assist him, Sir William Robertson asked for the views of the Commander-in-Chief in India.

These Sir Beauchamp Duff telegraphed on the 18th February. He proposed to hold Bandar Abbas with one hundred Indian infantry from Muscat till Sir Percy Sykes had time to secure his footing. The presence at Bandar Abbas of the force proposed by the War Office might, it was thought by the political authorities in India, imperil the success of the scheme for raising Persian military police, while from a military point of view he himself was afraid that it would lead to entanglements in the interior and would eventually necessitate the employment of larger forces there. He would be glad if any Indian battalions that could be spared from Egypt could be sent him to enable him to relieve tired units in Mesopotamia. In regard to the military situation in the East :—Our resources at Aden were sufficient until we assumed the offensive, which for the time being need not be undertaken. The proper base for operations against Shiraz, Qawam's objective, was Bushire, but Sir B. Duff did not suggest that we should do more than hold that place. The situation in Persia, he said, was governed by our success in Mesopotamia and by that of the Russians against Kermanshah and Khaniqin ; while to consolidate our position in East Persia, where our troops so far had fulfilled their object, he was taking steps to have the Nushki-Kacha road made fit for mechanical transport. The latest news from Kabul was reassuring and, though the strain on Indian resources would be considerable if the Amir disappeared or yielded to pressure, Sir Beauchamp Duff did not foresee a situation that India could not deal with.

Baratoff, delayed by the abnormal winter conditions, had not yet started to advance on Kermanshah, but on the 13th February the Russian Commander-in-Chief in the Caucasus, with a view to relieving the pressure on us in Mesopotamia, sent him orders to occupy Kermanshah without further delay and then to advance on Khaniqin. *[Central and West Persia; February 1916.]*

On the 15th February Mr. Marling signed an agreement with the Bakhtiari Khans by which they undertook, so long as amity existed between Great Britain and Persia, to maintain security and prevent agitation in their territory, to protect the oil-fields and generally to preserve an attitude of benevolent neutrality towards the Allies. This was a further indication of the improvement in the Allied situation in Persia. Unfortunately, however, local intrigues were beginning to undermine the position of Farman Farma, who had proved himself a strong and capable Minister and had rendered the Allies good service by his steadfast support of their interests for some months past. The former rivalries and jealousies in Persia between Russians and British and their respective local partisans had died down in face of the common danger and as a result of the personal friendship between Mr. Marling and M. de Etter, the Russian Minister. But, no sooner had the situation at Tehran been rendered secure by Baratoff's operations than the pro-Russian party set to work to oust " British " Farman Farma and replace him by " Russian " Sipahsalar. The chief rôle in these intrigues was played by a Russian official who succeeded in misleading the Russian Minister and in causing friction between him and Farman Farma, who, moreover, by his avaricious tendencies played into his enemies' hands. Mr. Marling realised what was happening and tried to warn Farman Farma, but without success ; and Mr. Marling did not like to endanger his relations with the Russian Minister by enlightening him in regard to his subordinate's intrigues.*

The weakness of the German position in Persia at this time appears to have been but imperfectly realised by the British.

---

* Mr. de Etter learnt of these subsequently, when it was too late.

Several German accounts show that Goltz saw little chance of success for his Persian mission. In an appreciation of the situation, which he sent to Constantinople and Berlin on the 16th February,* Goltz gave his opinion in unequivocal terms. The Germans, he said, had got no return for the vast sums of money they had spent and had promised to spend in Persia. The tribes were thoroughly unreliable, and the failure to produce the arms and munitions which the Germans had promised them had done much harm to the German cause. If Colonel Bopp, who, he said, described the Persian enterprise as already shattered, had to retire from Kermanshah, Goltz would try to make it possible for him to maintain himself at Qasr-i-Shirin. In conclusion, Goltz attributed the unsatisfactory situation of the Turkish forces in both the Eastern theatres of war to the excessive demands of the Dardanelles operations.

About this time Goltz diverted to Persia, in response to urgent appeals from Bopp, four more Turkish infantry battalions from the Tigris. These, however, were too late to save Kermanshah, which was captured by Baratoff on the 25th February. Bopp retired to the Pai Taq pass and Baratoff pushed his advanced troops towards Karind, his main body remaining at Kermanshah. Though by this time Baratoff's total force seems to have numbered about 9,000 sabres, 10,000 rifles and 36 guns, they were distributed over a wide area. His strength at Kermanshah did not exceed 1,400 sabres, 3,000 rifles and 20 guns, and supply and transport difficulties hampered his operations considerably.

South Persia; February 1916. In the latter half of February there was a difference of opinion between India and Tehran in regard to the rôle of the Sykes Mission. According to the Government of India its primary object should be to raise a force of military police, beginning at Bandar Abbas and gradually extending to Kerman and the rest of South Persia. Then, by linking up with the nucleus in Seistan, this force would provide the necessary instrument for the restoration and maintenance of order. On the other hand, Mr. Marling, realising that this would take time, considered that its immediate aim should be to assist Qawam. For this purpose Sir Percy Sykes, taking with him money, men, arms and ammunition, should get into touch with Qawam as soon as possible at whatever place was most convenient.

---

* Given in full in Appendix I.

Qawam himself, it may be noted, arrived by sea at Bushire from Lingeh on the 24th February, while Sir Percy Sykes could not hope to reach Bandar Abbas till early in March, by which time Qawam hoped to be well on his way towards Shiraz.

During January and February the British garrison at Bushire had a comparatively quiet time, though hostile tribesmen hovered round and took every opportunity to shoot and raid. In January news was received that Major O'Connor and the other British prisoners at Ahram were in good health and well treated. In fact, for a time communication with them was permitted and they were allowed to receive several mule loads of books, papers and provisions sent from Bushire. The possibility that the gendarmerie from Shiraz, accompanied by German levies and partisans, might attack Bushire and that no help could be expected from Saulat led General Edwardes at the beginning of February to ask for reinforcements. He pointed out that his force barely sufficed to defend the area concerned against tribal raids and would certainly be inadequate against an attack in force such as was possible, if not probable. On the 19th February General Edwardes proceeded to take over command of a brigade in Mesopotamia and was succeeded at Bushire by Brigadier-General J. A. Douglas. *Bushire; January and February 1916.*

At the beginning of January the British force in East Persia under Colonel Wikeley, consisting of the 28th Light Cavalry, section 25th Mountain Battery, 19th Punjabis (less one double company), machine gun section 12th Pioneers, twenty rifles 106th Hazara Pioneers, ten Sappers and Miners and two hundred Hazara levies, was distributed on the Birjand–Kacha line as follows:—At Birjand, 120 sabres, 130 rifles and 2 machine guns; at Neh 60 sabres and 80 rifles; at Nasratabad (Seistan) 275 sabres and 2 machine guns, 2 mountain guns and 135 rifles; at Robat 30 rifles; and at Kacha, 30 sabres, 280 rifles and 2 machine guns. The Hazara Levies were distributed in various small posts between Birjand and Seistan. In addition, Major Prideaux had enlisted a certain number of Seistani Levies for convoy and escort duty, etc., and early in January their increase up to a total of 400 was sanctioned by the Government of India. The whole force was experiencing some difficulty in purchasing fodder and grain locally, owing to the attitude of the owners who were trying to corner the market. *East Persia; January 1916.*

East Persia; January 1916.
(See Map 2.)

Information received by Colonel Wikeley in the first half of January indicated that the Germans at Kerman were likely to use either the Khabis-Neh line of advance or that via Naiband to Birjand. Owing to the lack of water, however, both these routes appeared to be unsuitable for the movement of large bodies of men. A party of three Germans with a number of Persian sowars was also reported to have reached Bam in the second week of January and to be instigating Sarhaddis and Baluchis in the neighbourhood to join in the *Jahad* and attack the British.

On the 18th January Colonel Wikeley learnt that Seiler, two Germans and sixteen armed followers had reached Deh Salm, a village on the borders of the Kain highlands and the Dasht-i-Lut; that they were being followed by a second party of some strength; and that two other parties intended to attack Birjand and move towards Robat respectively. The news of the German arrival at Deh Salm had been brought into Neh the previous day by one of the local British intelligence agents, who had been taken prisoner by the German party at Deh Salm on the 16th but had managed to escape the same evening. Lieutenant J. Brownlow (28th Light Cavalry) at once set out from Neh with fifty sabres and reached Deh Salm early on the 18th, while a party of infantry and levies followed him in support. On approaching Deh Salm his cavalry made a detour in the hope of cutting the enemy off, but found that they had left the village and had taken up a position on a ridge to the westward. Here Lieutenant Brownlow's men made attempts to surround them, but they retreated fighting further into the hills and maintained their hold of the commanding heights till dark with the loss of only one of their number, Lieutenant Winkelmann, who was taken prisoner. The remainder with their camels succeeded in effecting their escape after dark.

On the 18th Colonel Wikeley had also started off with the bulk of the force at Nasratabad to march to Neh. But his advance was delayed by difficulty in getting boats to cross the Hamun which was in flood; and his column did not reach Neh till the 24th, when he learnt that Seiler's party had returned to Khabis. As Seiler was unlikely to attempt another advance by the same route in the near future and as there was insufficient forage for animals at Neh, Colonel Wikeley left that place on the 27th and moved back with the greater part of his column to Seistan.

It appears from German accounts that over forty Germans and Austrians were at Kerman at the beginning of January.

Zugmayer, Griesinger, Dr. Biach (an Austrian) and Wedig formed what was known as the Baluchistan group, but the remainder under Seiler were to enter Afghanistan with the main caravan of the Niedermayer-Hentig mission. After careful enquiry Seiler decided that the Neh locality offered him the best facilities for a passage through the British cordon, and he made arrangements to move there at once. After some difficulty in obtaining the necessary animals and drivers, Seiler, giving out that his objective was Birjand, left Kerman on the 2nd January for Khabis, a village fifty miles off, which was close to the western edge of the Dasht-i-Lut. From Khabis routes led to Birjand, Bam and Neh, and Seiler was informed that on the last-named, which was a desert track, he would find sufficient water for his caravan.

After moving on one stage from Khabis, to Deh Saif, however, Seiler found that there was no water at all between Deh Saif and Deh Salm. He therefore halted; and, after starting to lay out a chain of food and water depots in advance of his caravan movement, he himself with two Germans (Winkelmann and Waldmann) and fifteen armed Persians on camels went on ahead to inspect the road and to reconnoitre the British dispositions on the east side of the desert. Versen was left in charge at Deh Saif with orders to follow with the main body as soon as the chain of depots was completed.

Seiler's party, reaching Deh Salm on the 16th January, captured a British agent, who escaped, however, in the evening. Realising that he could no longer hope to surprise the British, Seiler sent back two of his Persian following next morning to meet the main body, which would probably have started, and turn it off to the north. But as the need for drinking water might oblige it to come in to Deh Salm, Seiler decided to remain there for a couple of days. He left the village, however, and took up a position on a commanding ridge about a mile to the westward, with the camels in a ravine below him. After the fight on the 18th the party managed to escape in the dark, Seiler and Waldmann, who had made good their retreat on foot over the hills, being joined a few hours later by the Persians, who, to Seiler's surprise, had managed to get their camels out of the ravine and away in the dark. On the 22nd, when a day's march from Deh Saif, Seiler was met by a messenger from Versen reporting that just as the chain of depots had been completed they had been plundered and destroyed by a body of Baluchi tribesmen and that the main body had consequently been unable

East Persia; to advance. By the irony of fate, says Seiler in his account,*
January the German wireless set at Deh Saif picked up a message
1916. from Berlin on the 20th which made much of the friendly
relations between the Germans and Baluchis!

Seiler now realised that it was senseless to attempt with his small party to try to break through the British cordon, and he decided to increase his armed strength by enlisting Baharlu tribesmen. He left his main body at Khabis so as to mystify the British and returned with Dr. Becker to Kerman, whence, after preliminary negotiations, he sent him to Darab to enlist Baharlus.

As regards the Baluchistan group, Zugmayer, having received favourable news and an invitation from the tribes, sent Biach and Wedig to Bam and Bampur on the 12th January, with an intimation that he himself would shortly follow them. On the 17th he heard that they had been well received at Bam.

To return to the British in East Persia. The supply situation, which was not yet satisfactory, was rendered more difficult by several raids in the vicinity of Robat carried out at this period against our camel convoys by tribesmen acting apparently under German instigation. On the 28th January Major Prideaux telegraphed to Delhi, representing that the insufficient strength of the force under Colonel Wikeley did not ensure that Germans would not break through some part of the long line to be watched. Though the difficulties of supplying the existing force had nearly been surmounted, these would again become acute if reinforcements were sent and he suggested that the solution lay in despatching more mountain and machine guns. This telegram led the Chief of the General Staff in India to ask Colonel Wikeley for his views, informing him at the same time that no more machine guns could be sent and that, owing to more important demands elsewhere, it was most unlikely that any mountain guns or reinforcements could be spared. Colonel Wikeley replied on the 4th February to the effect that recent rainfall had made it feasible for strong German parties to cross the desert from Khabis and that his own force might not be able to block their advance. He emphasised the absolute necessity for getting early intelligence from Kerman and Khabis if his force was to stand any chance of effecting its purpose and he said that much depended on the attitude of the Afghans on the border.

---

* Given in Niedermayer's book "Unter der Glutsonne Irans."

During February Colonel Wikeley received various reports of German intentions and preparations, which generally referred to a movement towards Neh or Birjand. Seiler was reported to be at Kerman raising levies for an attack and Zugmayer was said to have gone early in the month to Narmashir, where it appeared that he and his companions were meeting with considerable success among the Baluchis and Sarhaddis. *[East Persia; February 1916.]*

In the meantime, the military authorities in India had initiated steps to make the Nushki-Robat road fit for mechanical transport and to obtain the necessary vehicles from England. It was also decided to appoint a more senior officer to command in East Persia and on the 17th February Brigadier-General R. E. H. Dyer received his instructions* at Delhi and at once left for Kacha.

At the end of December, the news of the German activities based on Kerman had caused H.M. Government to enquire what the position was in Makran and what measures the Government of India proposed for its defence if this became necessary. There was considerable unrest in Narmashir and Bampur, owing mainly to the lavish expenditure of the German emissaries. But on the 12th January the Government of India replied that there were no indications of any immediate hostile advance on Baluchistan and that, in any case, the distances involved and the desert nature of the country precluded any attack in strength. Raids were probable and, to deal with these, arrangements had been made to distribute more arms and ammunition to loyal tribesmen, to offer generous rewards for services rendered, to expend money freely in obtaining timely information and to increase the Makran Levy Corps by 200 men. Endeavours were also being made to secure the co-operation of friendly chiefs in Persian Makran, and the Political Agent in Kalat (Lieut.-Colonel A. B. Dew) was touring the border to see what further measures were necessary. As they did not consider the menace on the Baluchistan border to be serious, the Government of India did not consider it advisable to lock up troops there even if they were available. In February Major T. H. Keyes of the Political Department was sent with some Indian non-commissioned officers to assist Colonel Dew in organising the tribal forces on the Makran border; and by the end of the month Colonel Dew had succeeded in winning over, or arranging a truce with, many of the hitherto hostile chiefs of the Persian borderland. *[Makran; December 1915– February 1916.]*

---

* These instructions were a recapitulation of those issued to Colonel Wikeley.

East Persia; February 1916. From Zugmayer's diary we learn that he and Griesinger left Kerman for Bam on the 6th February with a total following of 71 men and 97 animals. Reaching that place six days later, they were making arrangements to follow Biach and Wedig to Bampur, when various disquieting rumours reached them, including a report that the British were about to advance on Bam and Kerman from Seistan. The British, it was said, had already begun to concentrate near Nasratabad Sipi. Zugmayer and Griesinger accordingly halted at Bam and sent out patrols and agents in that direction to gain definite information.

After Zugmayer's departure from Kerman, the situation there deteriorated from the German point of view, largely as a result of the news of the Russian advance in Central and West Persia. The Governor and those of the local officials with pro-British sympathies were emboldened to try to stand up against the German–Democrat activities, while Seiler found himself cut off from communication with West Persia, owing to the Russians having gained control of the Central Persian telegraph line. In regard to this, Kiesling says that, when telegraphic communication was cut, orders were sent to Zugmayer and Seiler, to Schönemann in Bakhtiari country, to Wustrow at Shiraz and to Wassmuss in the Bushire hinterland to withdraw with their parties to the west, but that these orders were cancelled by the Foreign Office in Berlin.

British policy; February–March 1916. On the 29th February the War Committee of the Cabinet in London considered a memorandum which they had had specially prepared for them by the Chief of the Imperial General Staff, after consultation with the Foreign and India Offices. This appreciation, reviewing the military situation in the various theatres in the East which affected the Moslem world, considered whether it was possible, by timely action with small forces, to avert dangers which might otherwise eventually call for the employment of much larger forces. After coming to the conclusion that the British forces in Aden and Mesopotamia sufficed to carry out the policy decided on and that Egypt—which it had been thought might be in danger owing to the evacuation of Gallipoli—was secure against any attack on a large scale, the memorandum went on to say that the situation in Persia and especially in South Persia was unsatisfactory, though it had recently improved as the result of Russian action. It was recognised that the British had considerable difficulties to face in South Persia, but it was considered that we ought to carry out a more active policy there and that we should take steps to defeat the enemy schemes by measures of a nature similar to those which the Germans had adopted. In regard to India, as the force there would be inadequate to cope with an Afghan invasion combined with a general rising on the frontier, it was recommended that two divisions in Egypt should be held available to reinforce India if necessary.

The War Committee accepted these conclusions in principle, and on the 2nd March the India Office telegraphed a summary of the views expressed in the appreciation and of the decisions of the War Committee to the Government of India. Sir Percy Sykes, they were told, was to discuss the situation with Qawam and report the result. H.M. Government, desiring to lend all possible support to enable Qawam to drive the Germans out of Fars and recover Shiraz, were prepared to supply him with arms, ammunition and money and also if necessary to send to Bandar Abbas the small force which the War Office had previously offered; though it was to be understood that this force was not intended to operate inland. For such work H.M. Government were prepared to lend a few British officers, who could recruit locally under Qawam's authority such force as it might be possible to find arms for. As the War Committee considered that the most effective way to meet German activity was by counter-activity of the same kind, they wished that an irregular force should also be recruited in Seistan at once. Such a force, stiffened by the regular cavalry already there and led by active and enterprising officers, could take the offensive in detachments and hunt down the German parties.

Sir Percy Cox, who arrived at Bushire on the 5th March to discuss matters with Qawam, was informed by him, however, that as he had to collect his tribesmen before they began their spring migration to the highlands, he could not afford to wait for Sir P. Sykes. Qawam wished to return to Lingeh in order to start his advance from there as soon as he could be given money and arms, but would send a representative to Bandar Abbas to meet Sir Percy Sykes. He also declined the offer of British officers to accompany him, as the Germans would, he said, make use of their presence to discredit him in Persian eyes as a mere instrument of the British. At the same time he pointed out that it had only been his lack of guns and his shortage of rifle ammunition that had obliged him to retire from Shiraz. As regards the suggested despatch of a British

South Persia; March 1916.

force to Bandar Abbas he did not see how it would help him in any way, though it might react favourably on the Kerman situation.

The Government of India having agreed, Qawam left Bushire for Lingeh on the 8th March, taking with him a large sum of money, four Turkish guns, four machine guns, 550 rifles and a considerable quantity of ammunition, all of which Sir Percy Cox had handed over to him. As ammunition was not available for the German rifles with which the majority of his men were armed, arrangements were made to send him from India 4,000 serviceable rifles and a million rounds of ammunition. The services of six Indian non-commissioned offiers were also lent him to assist in working the guns which he had been given.

It was now decided that Sir Percy Sykes was to go to Bandar Abbas and start there to recruit a military police force. When this had received sufficient training, he could either advance on Kerman or support Qawam in Fars as circumstances dictated. Sir P. Sykes was also of opinion, telegraphed the Government of India, that no useful purpose would be served for the time being by sending a British force to Bandar Abbas.

General situation; March 1916. In the meantime the intrigues against Farman Farma had effected their purpose, as on the 2nd March, feeling that he could no longer count on the necessary Russian support, he had resigned the Premiership. He was succeeded by Sipahsalar, an agreeable individual, whose proverbial carelessness and lack of knowledge, however, rendered him quite unfit for this position. But, avowedly pro-Russian with no discordant elements in his Cabinet, he enjoyed a more complete sense of security than any of his predecessors since the outbreak of war. For German propaganda was losing ground in the country owing to the disgust which many of the Persian populace felt at the anarchy resulting from the German activities. In fact, it seemed to Mr. Marling that, unless the Germans could manage to continue their system of lavish bribery or obtain a considerable military success, they had little chance of recovering their influence. In West Persia their main force had retired to the Pai Taq pass; Nizam-es-Sultaneh, their principal supporter, was said to be wavering in his adherence to their cause; and their small party at Isfahan, evidently in anticipation of a Russian occupation, was reported to be moving south to Shiraz. At Shiraz the rebel gendarmerie seemed to be bent on plunder rather than on active operations.

At Bushire, the British garrison had been reinforced from Mesopotamia by the 124th Baluchistan Infantry and by two squadrons 15th Lancers, which replaced the squadron 16th Cavalry. Qawam had expressed the opinion that a display of British military activity from Bushire would help him, and Sir Percy Cox and Mr. Marling both agreed that a raid against some of the hostile Khans of the hinterland would have an excellent political effect. But the authorities in India, with their hands already full with the Kut relief operations, were averse from entanglements in the Bushire hinterland and, after discussing the question with General Lake in Mesopotamia, decided to postpone the punishment of these hostile chiefs till we could carry it out with an adequate force at a time more convenient to ourselves.

Bushire; March 1916.

Soon after taking office, Sipahsalar expressed himself to the British and Russian Ministers as being entirely in favour of the proposals for the organisation of Persian military police forces in the north and south by Russian and British officers respectively and as ready to negotiate a triple alliance. For this the British Government were also prepared, but the Russian Government preferred to discuss a limited agreement only and even for this showed little desire. With the occupation of Isfahan on the 19th March, when a Russian force drove a small German party, supported by a number of local ruffians, out without difficulty, they seem to have felt that their position in Persia was already secured.

Central and West Persia; March 1916.

In West Persia on the 17th March an advanced detachment of two Russian Cossack squadrons was driven out of Karind, which it had occupied five days previously, by Turkish regular troops of which, by this time, there were eight battalions in Persia; and on the 20th Baratoff reported that his advance was much hampered by heavy snow, bad roads and lack of local supplies. On the 24th the War Office in London also telegraphed to India and Mesopotamia that the Grand Duke commanding in the Caucasus informed them that the climatic, transport and supply difficulties precluded further operations in the direction of Baghdad. It appears that the Kazvin–Hamadan road was almost impassable, that beyond Hamadan only pack animals could with difficulty be employed and that there were constant breakdowns in telephone and telegraphic communication, for which, moreover, the Russians were very short of equipment. One good result of the Russian occupation of Kermanshah was to elicit from the *Vali* of Pusht-i-Kuh a written assurance of his loyalty to the Persian Government.

South Persia; March 1916. Sir Percy Sykes landed at Bandar Abbas on the 16th March and met with a most gratifying reception from the Persian Governor of the Gulf Ports and other local notables. The Sykes Mission included four other British officers, three Indian officers, twenty Indian non-commissioned officers and a personal escort of twenty-five sabres of the Central India Horse. A company of the 94th Infantry had also reached Bandar Abbas from Muscat a few days previously to assist Sir Percy Sykes in securing his position. He at once started to enlist men for the military police force, recruiting 100 in the first five days and 180 by the end of the month. The prospects of further recruiting seemed to him to be good.

East Persia; March 1916. In the middle of March news reached Tehran that, as the result of fighting between the German party at Kerman and the local authorities, the Germans there under Seiler had gained the upper hand. Seiler says[*] that, finding opposition to him growing, he first brought back all his group from Khabis and then decided to drive the hostile elements out of Kerman by force. Fighting began on the 14th, when the anti-Germans were driven out, the Governor made preparations to leave and the Democrats assumed control. The Germans, however, did not remain masters of the situation for long. The Russian occupation of Isfahan, which completely cut the German communications, gave the pro-Ally Persians fresh confidence while correspondingly reducing that of the Germans' supporters. Rumours of a Russian advance on Yezd and of the arrival of a British force at Bandar Abbas followed; and Seiler came to the conclusion that his position at Kerman was no longer tenable. Deciding to retire on Shiraz via Saidabad, he sent off the bulk of his party towards the end of March, when the Persian Governor plucked up courage to reassert his authority by force. He attacked the German partisans, while he sent Seiler and the remainder of his party off on the 31st March, giving them an escort of Bakhtiaris to see them safely out of the province.

---

[*] In his account given in Niedermayer's book.

To face page 155.

Saindak Camp.

Robat.

GENERAL DYER'S ARRIVAL 155

On the 3rd March, having made the journey from Nushki to Robat in a motor car in six days (including one day's halt at Saindak), General Dyer took over command of the Seistan Force. He had, he reported, experienced no great difficulties, and from his book " The Raiders of the Sarhad,"* it appears that his main troubles arose from sand-dunes and shallow stretches of rain water which constantly obliterated the rough camel track and from which his car had on occasions to be towed out. That the route was, in his opinion, feasible for cars was shown by his request for others to be sent him for the use of his force.

On the 5th the Chief of the General Staff in India telegraphed for his views and proposals on the employment of irregulars with cavalry as suggested by the War Committee. On his journey from Nushki General Dyer had found supply convoys completely held up by the raids of Sarhaddi tribesmen, and on arrival at Robat had learnt that these raids were assuming such troublesome proportions as to render the supply situation critical. He had consequently decided that his first object must be to win over the chiefs of these tribes, who were evidently acting under German instigation ; and on the 6th, in a telegram which crossed that from the Chief of the General Staff, he said that he proposed to move some of his troops and levies towards Bam with the combined object of threatening the German party there and of gaining the confidence of the Sarhaddis. On the 8th he telegraphed that he agreed fully with the War Committee's suggestion and would proceed to carry it into practice. The Sarhad tribesmen, he said, offered good material for levies. He was not yet sufficiently acquainted with local conditions to define his proposals exactly, but a reserve at Seistan seemed to him to be too far away to be able to afford timely support to the flanks of the cordon, and he considered it preferable to make posts self-supporting and to furnish them with rapidly moving detachments of cavalry and levies.

Sarhad is the name given to the mountainous tract in Persian Baluchistan which lies between the Perso-British frontier and the districts of Narmashir and Bampur. It is an arid, barren and sandy region, in which there are several salt water lakes but which suffers generally from a lack of fresh water. Many of its mountains rise to considerable heights, the highest being the Kuh-i-Taftan, a volcanic peak over 13,000 feet high, which

---

* It is interesting to note that his car with its headlights was such a novelty in the area that it was mistaken one night by the tribesmen for a German airship.

East Persia; is situated in the centre of the tract and from whose spurs the
March 1916. drainage, passing through the Ladis valley to the north and
the Khwash (or Vasht) valley to the southward, renders those
districts less desolate than the rest of the area. Full advantage,
however, was not taken of the water available here or elsewhere,
and the sparse cultivation afforded insufficient grain for its
inhabitants, while grazing and fuel were also limited. Traversed
by difficult tracks and generally only passable by pack animals,
the country is possessed of a climate which is bitterly cold in
winter and unpleasantly hot in summer.*

The tribes of Sarhad—*Sunni* Mahomedans of Arab origin—
were nomads whose main occupation was raiding and whose
few villages usually took the form of mud forts. The chief
tribes were the Rekis, Ismailzais and Damanis, the last-named
at that time so dominating the first two as to control the whole
tract. The Damanis were divided into two distinct sections,
the Yar Muhammadzais under a chief called Jiand Khan and
the Gamshadzais under Halil Khan, each of them being able
to muster six or seven hundred fighting men, of whom over
half had modern rifles. Their headquarters were at Khwash†
and Jalq respectively. The Ismailzais under Juma Khan
inhabited the western part of Sarhad and could produce a
fighting strength of about eight hundred, while the Rekis,
of whom, however, only a portion inhabited the northern part
of the area, could muster about one thousand.

The reports received by General Dyer placed the fighting
strengths of these tribes at about double the above numbers.
Juma Khan certainly, and Jiand Khan—who was the most
important chief of all—probably, were in German pay and
were in constant communication with the German emissaries
at Bam and Bampur, where Bahram Khan (the leading chieftain
in that region) was also acting in collusion with them. It was
currently reported that the German parties in this area contemplated an advance into Afghanistan via Robat or Seistan
and that they hoped to raise the whole of Narmashir, Bampur
and Sarhad against the British.‡ It seemed clear to General
Dyer that the only way to stop the raids against the Nushki-
Robat line was to form a movable column and operate against

---

* See Map 4.

† Though Vasht is the more correct nomenclature, the place was generally
known at the time to our troops as Khwash.

‡ At the end of March Major Prideaux reported that a German accompanied
by six horsemen had just succeeded in entering Afghanistan from Persia.
But he appears to have mistaken this party for one under an Austrian, Bayerl,
sent by Niedermayer from Kabul to try to get news of the situation in Seistan.

PROJECTED OPERATIONS

the Sarhaddis. But he first sent out and invited the four tribal chiefs to meet him at Kacha to discuss the situation. As, however, only the chief of the Rekis—who had been consistently friendly to the British—accepted this invitation, General Dyer realised that he must regard the Ismailzais and Damanis as definitely hostile. He accordingly began to prepare to operate against them and about the middle of March went to Nasratabad (Seistan) to see how many men could be spared from there for a movable column.

He had already had to divert men from the cordon to try to stop the raiding against the convoys on the Nushki-Robat line and he found that he could only draw twelve sabres, twenty rifles and the two mountain guns from Nasratabad, while of 103 men of the 19th Punjabis at Kacha he discovered that 69 had never yet fired their rifles. His supply situation, however, was critical and on the 30th March he telegraphed to India saying that a quick method of diverting the raiders would be for him to advance with a small force of one troop of cavalry, two mountain guns and 50 rifles, accompanied by Kurd and Reki tribesmen who were willing to co-operate, to Khwash, to punish the Damanis. Though the raids against his line of communication were continuing, General Dyer learnt that a German party returning to Bam after visiting Bahram Khan at Bampur had been plundered by Bahram Khan's men. This was good news, as it showed that Colonel Dew's efforts to win over the hostile chiefs were meeting with success. On the 31st March the Chief of the General Staff in India telegraphed that the Commander-in-Chief approved General Dyer's proposal to move against Khwash.

By this time General Dyer had formulated proposals for a redistribution of his force as follows :—

	Mountain guns.	*Cavalry Squadns.*	*Infantry Coys.*	*Machine guns.*
Birjand	—	1	1½	2
Neh-Bandan	—	1	½	—
Nasratabad (Seistan)	—	—	1	1
Nasratabad Sipi	—	1*	1	2*
Robat	2	1	1	—
Kacha	—	—	1	1

The more southerly concentration of the force was due to the changed direction of the German menace. As regards the levies, the 200 Hazaras were at Neh and to its north, 200

---
* Part to be distributed between Robat and Kacha, as necessary.

Seistani horsemen were between Seistan and Bandan, 100 Seistani camel sowars were between Seistan and Robat, and 100 Seistani camel sowars were between Robat and Nasratabad Sipi. The Seistani levies were to be increased to a strength of 1,000 and Sarhad levies were also to be enlisted.*

In the northern part of the cordon the Russians had a force of about 1,600 Cossacks (1st and 2nd Semirechia Regiments). To improve our intelligence organisation there and also to maintain a military *liaison* with this Russian force, Major E. A. F. Redl was on his way from England via Russia to take up the appointment of military attaché at Meshed, which had been vacant for some months.

Zugmayer's diary shows that he and Griesinger at Bam, having ascertained that the news of a British advance from Nasratabad Sipi was incorrect, set out on the 10th March to join Biach and Wedig at Bampur; only to find, however, that these two had been forced to leave that place and had been plundered of all their belongings. The four Germans, deserted by many of their followers, then settled down near Bam for what they supposed would be a long stay, but, finding that communication with Kerman was cut, returned to Bam on the 30th March. Here Zugmayer heard that Kermanshah and Isfahan had been taken by the Russians, that Goltz had gone back to Baghdad and that, as a converging Anglo-Russian advance from all sides was being prepared, Seiler proposed to abandon the Afghan project and retire on Shiraz. Zugmayer decided that he also must follow the same course and give up all idea of a Baluchistan expedition.

South and East Persia; April 1916. The month of April saw practically a total collapse of German hostile activities in Persia and with it the discomfiture of their Persian dupes. Qawam, who was believed by his opponents to be accompanied by a strong British contingent, met with little or no opposition in his advance towards Shiraz. The revolting Khamseh tribesmen surrendered to him before he reached Lar at the end of March and the rebel gendarmerie evacuated that place and their other positions in Fars and on the Bushire road, being attacked in their retirement by tribesmen and gendarmerie who had hitherto been their comrades in rebellion. Saulat also joined Qawam with some 8,000 men and with Qawam's son pushed on, with the bulk of their combined

---

* The Seistanis were not considered to be such good material as the Sarhaddis, but were to be enlisted so as to deny their services to the Germans.

forces, from Lar to Shiraz, which they reached in the last week of April. Here a Persian gendarmerie officer had already taken over control on behalf of Qawam and had arrested many of the rebels who had fled there.* Qawam himself was unfortunately killed by a fall from his horse while proceeding from Lar, but his son was shortly afterwards promoted to all his father's offices by the Persian Government.

Seiler and his companions on leaving Kerman, unaware of the rapid change of events, made for Shiraz, but only to encounter disaster. After being attacked—and suffering several casualties—near Saidabad by followers of the pro-British Sardar Nasrat of Kerman, they were attacked and robbed on several other occasions before managing to reach Shiraz at the end of April. Here they were definitely imprisoned, and a large sum of gold and silver money in their possession was confiscated. Zugmayer, who heard on the 3rd April of Seiler's departure from Kerman, left Bam next day with his party, only to be attacked in his turn on the 9th near Baft. Biach and several of the party were taken prisoners; while Zugmayer, Wedig and Griesinger, who managed to make their escape with eight followers, wandered about for some days suffering some hardship and being again attacked and robbed before they reached Niriz on the 17th April. Here they also were made prisoners.

At the end of March the Persian Government decided to appoint Farman Farma as Governor of Kerman and to send him there at once to restore order. This appointment, which was an admirable one from the British point of view, was welcomed by Farman Farma himself as likely to lead to his subsequent accession to the Governor-Generalship of Fars. *South Persia; April 1916.*

On the 1st April the Government of India received a telegram from the India Office asking for Sir Percy Sykes' views and proposals, and enquiring what action had been taken or was contemplated to carry out the War Committee's suggestions regarding operations against German parties and Persian rebels. What the War Committee desired at the moment, said the telegram, was the earliest possible action in this respect rather than the organisation of a highly trained force for the eventual restoration of order. This telegram was passed on by India to Sir Percy Sykes on the 4th April

---

* One of the Swedish gendarmerie officers, Nystrom, assisted him and arrested two other Swedish officers.

South Persia; April 1916. for an expression of his views and crossed one from him, sent the same day, in which he said that the situation had been profoundly modified by Qawam's success and the appointment of Farman Farma. He recommended that the latter should be given arms and ammunition and that he himself with arms, ammunition and police should join forces with Farman Farma and act against the Germans. Soon after this, however, he received news of the German flight from Kerman; and he replied to the India Office telegram on the 6th April. He was recruiting as fast as he could handle the men, he said, and the prospects were good. He recommended that recruits should continue to be enlisted and trained at Bandar Abbas and that he himself, with his cavalry escort increased by a mounted machine gun section, a squadron of cavalry and a hundred infantry, should actively support Qawam or join Farman Farma as circumstances required. Mr. Marling concurred, and the Commander-in-Chief in India asked General Lake if he could send to Bandar Abbas from Bushire a squadron of cavalry, half a battalion of infantry and two mountain guns. On the 9th April Sir Percy Sykes telegraphed again suggesting that he should advance on Kerman with the small force he had asked for, as Qawam seemed unlikely to require further support. If this was to be done, however, the necessary arrangements should be made as quickly as possible, as after the end of April, owing to the intense heat, very few transport animals would be obtainable at Bandar Abbas. On the 17th April the Foreign Secretary in India informed him that H.M. Government approved his moving forward as early as possible and that the small force to accompany him would reach Bandar Abbas in a few days time. He at once began to make his arrangements for supply and transport, which he hoped to complete by the middle of May; and on the 24th April a squadron 15th Lancers, a section 23rd Mountain Battery and a half-battalion 124th Baluchistan Infantry, all from Bushire, with a section of a field ambulance from Basra, reached Bandar Abbas.

South Persia and Bushire; April 1916. At the beginning of April the question was again considered of endeavouring to secure the release of Major O'Connor and the other British prisoners at Ahram. As soon as they learnt that Qawam and Saulat had been successful in reasserting their authority, the Persian Government issued orders to Saulat to effect the prisoners' release. Wassmuss was said to have fled from Borazjan, and a few days later the two

RUSSIAN ADVANCE ORDERED

principal hostile Khans offered definite terms of release to Major O'Connor himself. As, however, there was a good prospect of securing the release without any terms and as the prisoners themselves appeared to be well treated and in no personal danger, it seemed unnecessary and inadvisable to continue negotiations with chiefs who had been outlawed and dismissed from their positions by the Persian Government. Major Trevor at Bushire suggested that a show of military activity might assist in bringing about the desired result, and on the 27th April a strong column from Bushire made a reconnaissance across the *mashileh*. The enemy's advanced post was found to be deserted and the column attacked a small force of the enemy which was strongly entrenched in the village of Chaghadak. Only slight resistance was encountered and, the village having been destroyed, the force returned to Bushire, having sustained only two casualties, including a British officer of the 15th Lancers killed. Motor lorries were utilised for transport of the machine gun detachment and to tow the guns, but they experienced considerable difficulty in the heavy ground on the eastern part of the *mashileh*.

As regards the Russians in West Persia, Major Marsh informed the War Office on the 1st April that orders had been issued to Baratoff from Caucasus Army Headquarters to make an immediate advance on Khaniqin with all his available forces, including reserves. At this time Colonel Bopp with his Persian forces and 6,000 Turkish infantry with 12 guns was holding the Pai Taq pass, with outposts about Karind, while Baratoff, with his force dispersed over a wide area, was faced with considerable difficulties of movement and maintenance. His main column, in strength 3,450 sabres, 4,000 rifles and 20 guns, was between Kermanshah and Karind; he had columns and detachments operating round Kangavar, Burujird and Kurdistan aggregating about 4,000 men and 10 guns; between Enzeli and Hamadan, there were some 1,000 sabres and 3,500 rifles including line of communication troops; 1,500 sabres, 500 rifles and 4 guns were distributed between Qum, Kashan and Isfahan; and there were 1,200 sabres and 2 guns near Tehran. But, in the last week of April news was received by the War Office that the General Officer Commanding the left flank of the Russian Caucasus armies would advance on the 28th towards Ruwandiz, with a view to co-operating with Baratoff who was to advance

West Persia; April 1916.

simultaneously against Khaniqin. This movement, which, as will be seen subsequently, had the effect of diverting Turkish troops from the Tigris in order to defend Baghdad, was unfortunately too late to have any effect on the Kut relief operations.

German accounts say that Field-Marshal von der Goltz died at Baghdad on the 19th April and was succeeded in command of the Sixth Army by Halil Pasha, who then also regarded the Tigris front as the decisive point. Colonel von Gleich, Chief of the General Staff to Goltz, who had arrived at Baghdad a few days previously, received a telegram from Bopp on the 20th, asking that the Persian group should be removed from Turkish control and should be allowed to act independently under direct orders from German General Headquarters. This proposal was opposed by Gleich, with the result that the German Persian mission was definitely placed under the orders of Halil, whose Chief of the General Staff Gleich now became. At the same time, Gleich, who considered an offensive in Persia impossible till the British on the Tigris had been driven back and was also of opinion that the military uselessness of the Persians had rendered the Persian project a failure, recommended to Falkenhayn that, as nothing further could be done in Persia without the assistance of Turkish troops, the German character of the Persian undertaking should be abandoned. This, however, was not agreed to.

East Persia; April 1916. To cover their retirement, Seiler and Zugmayer seem to have spread stories of an intended German advance. For, during the first week in April, news reached General Dyer from several sources that a German party, numbering about 1,000, had left Kerman for Bam. By the 8th, when he had concentrated his small column for the expedition against Khwash, he was still unaware that the Germans had fled from Kerman. He hoped to win over the Sarhaddi chiefs and thus check raiding, as well as counter German activities. But he realised that his column, composed of only one troop 28th Light Cavalry (about twenty-five sabres), a section 25th Mountain Battery, a machine gun section 12th Pioneers and seventy-five rifles 19th Punjabis, with the few Reki levies who had promised to co-operate, was too small to defeat the tribesmen in open fight, especially as most of his infantry were partly trained recruits. He consequently spread stories that he was advancing with a force of 5,000 men and intended first to march against Halil Khan at Jalq.

On the 9th April he marched with his column to Ladis, where he was joined by a band of about forty Rekis and where, hearing that Jiand Khan was coming in to surrender, he halted on the 10th. This report, however, proved to be untrue and next morning the column continued its southerly advance, having received a slight accession in strength by the arrival of sixty more Rekis, a handful of Chagai levies and a small tribal escort accompanying the local Persian official who was responsible for maintaining relations with the Sarhaddis. Most of the Rekis, however, were either badly armed or not armed at all.

The movement continued on the 12th, Sangun being reached without incident. Next morning, after advancing four miles or so, General Dyer's scouts reported Jiand Khan's men in position on a line of low hills about half a mile to the front. From a personal reconnaissance General Dyer estimated that the tribesmen numbered about 2,000, as had been previously reported, and he saw that they had a strong position. His own strength and dispositions were concealed by the hilly ground and, trusting that the enemy believed his strength to be much greater, he decided that his best course was to attack at once. He accordingly ordered his guns into position on some low hills to his left, his cavalry to move forward under cover on his right and his machine guns to a favourable position in his centre. His six hundred camels were brought up and placed under cover in charge of about sixty recruits of the 19th Punjabis, while the remaining handful of infantry and levies were detailed to carry out the assault.

As the troops were moving into position, two of the enemy bearing a flag of truce arrived with a message from Jiand Khan offering to meet General Dyer half-way between the forces to discuss the situation. General Dyer, however, could not afford to risk discovery of his weakness, especially as the flag of truce seemed to show that the enemy thought the British to be in strength; and he refused to negotiate, sending back word that he meant to attack at once. He then sent orders to his cavalry to demonstrate as if they intended to get round the enemy's left, and as soon as the messenger had had time to get back, i.e., at 7.50 a.m., General Dyer ordered fire to be opened. Jiand Khan, seeing his retreat threatened and believing that 5,000 men were attacking, mounted his camel and fled, followed by his men who scattered in such haste that by 9 a.m. they were all out of sight, seven of them, including Jiand

East Persia; April 1916.
Khan's son, having been killed. Only three of General Dyer's men had been wounded. Continuing its march, the British column reached Chah-i-Zar the same evening.

General Dyer felt that, if Jiand could be induced to surrender, the other tribes might be persuaded to follow his example and thus obviate the necessity for long and tiresome operations in Sarhad. It was, however, necessary to act at once before Jiand Khan discovered that he had been duped; and consequently General Dyer pushed on with his pursuit, marching over twenty miles eastward on the 14th April to the oasis of Kamalabad. But here he just missed Jiand Khan, who escaped into the mountains where it was hopeless to think of following him. Next day messengers were sent after him to say that, if he surrendered, his own life and that of his followers would be safe and that the considerable acreage of standing crops at Kamalabad, on which he and his tribe largely depended, would be spared. In the belief that the strength of General Dyer's force was overwhelming and that the losses of his own men on the 13th had been much greater than they actually were, Jiand Khan came in and made his submission on the 17th April, Halil Khan of the Gamshadzai tribe having surrendered on the previous day.

Jiand and Halil, both having sworn that neither they nor their tribes would raise a hand against the British in future, were told that with their small following they must accompany General Dyer in his advance to capture Khwash; and, although he realised the danger, General Dyer, wishing to show that he was not afraid of them, let them retain their arms. On the 18th the mud fort of Khwash surrendered to General Dyer without offering opposition, which was fortunate as he would have found it difficult to assault successfully with his small force. Though rather dilapidated, it was seventy yards square with thirty-foot walls and higher towers at the four corners. Situated on a high-lying plateau, with a good water supply and surrounded by a fair amount of cultivation and grazing, it afforded a good centre from which to dominate Sarhad; and General Dyer decided to retain it in his possession for the time being, informing the tribesmen that he would hold it as a pledge for their good behaviour.

In the meantime, a party of Ismailzais under Juma Khan had carried out a raid between the 6th and 11th April in the area between Nasratabad Sipi and Neh and had looted a large number of camels and sheep belonging to Seistanis. To intercept them as they returned with the booty to their homes at

FAILURE OF SEISTANI LEVIES

Galugan, Captain Wise (28th Light Cavalry) with one troop 28th Light Cavalry and some Seistani levies moved out westfrom the Robat–Seistan road and Captain Bennett (19th Punjabis) with the 100 rifles 19th Punjabis and 117 Seistani camelry levies garrisoning Nasratabad Sipi moved eastward.

On the 11th April, leaving fifteen rifles to hold Dehani Baghi, Captain Bennett marched twelve miles to the south-eastward to Garagheh and on the 12th, getting news of the raiders, to Lirudik. Here on the morning of the 13th the raiders were sighted, some seven miles to the north of the camp, moving in a south-westerly direction across a wide valley towards a range of hills to the east of Garagheh. Sending off the Seistani camelry, under command of Major Heron, I.M.S., to get between the raiders and the hills, Captain Bennett moved off westward after them with his infantry and the baggage. But as the raiders then made off in a north-easterly direction Captain Bennett also changed direction and followed them, sending a request to Major Heron for the levies to leave the hills and move directly against the raiders. The levies, however, evidently disliking the idea of coming to close quarters, refused to obey this order and made a wide detour to the west, losing touch with Captain Bennett.

Affair of Lirudik; 13th April 1916.

The raiders, about six hundred strong, now made for an isolated hill in the centre of the valley with the plundered animals, and, detaching about two hundred of their number to hold an advanced position rather over a mile to their front, awaited Captain Bennett's attack. This started at about 10.30 a.m. and the Punjabis gradually drove the enemy's advanced parties back for about a mile till, reinforced from the hill, they stood fast. Putting all his seventy available rifles* into the firing line, Captain Bennett advanced over the flat and open ground till he got within about two hundred yards of the enemy's position. The raiders still held fast, however, and Captain Bennett, whose men had suffered five casualties, decided to avoid further and heavier losses by delaying his assault till dusk. At the same time he sent another message asking Major Heron to bring the levies up behind the Punjabis. But the levies were scattered, out of control and in no mood to risk close fighting. In fact, about 5 p.m. they fled altogether, in the direction of Garagheh, before a demonstration by the raiders. About the same time the thin line of the Punjabis was suddenly and unexpectedly charged by about four hundred of the enemy

---

* Fifteen rifles had been posted to guard the baggage.

Affair of Lirudik; 13th April 1916. with the result that a good many of the very young Punjabi recruits were seized with panic and broke before they could be stopped. Most of them, however, were rallied in time to stop the enemy's charge when it got within about forty yards, though they could not stop some two hundred of the tribesmen sweeping past the flanks and attacking the transport. The fighting continued till dusk,* when the raiders made off with their looted herds, some twenty-two of our camels and five boxes of our ammunition, at an estimated loss, however, of 45 men killed, including three of their leaders. The British casualties totalled 27, including Second-Lieutenant W. H. Chalmers and ten of the 19th Punjabis killed. Captain Bennett withdrew after dark to Garagheh. He was subsequently commended by the G.O.C. Quetta Division for the conspicuous coolness and gallantry he had displayed.

Next day, Captain Wise encountered a part of the raiders about six miles to the south-west of Gorandi and attacked them with such success that they fled, leaving about 150 camels, most of their plunder and about 30 dead. The British casualties were only two.

The news of this affair strengthened General Dyer in his opinion that it would be necessary for him to march at once to Galugan and secure Juma Khan's submission. Leaving the head of the Reki tribe with a few of his men and five rifles of the 19th Punjabis—which was all the force he could spare—to hold Khwash fort, General Dyer with his column and accompanied by Jiand and Halil with their followers started off on the 19th April. Galugan was reached on the 24th April without opposition and Juma Khan made his submission, his readiness to do this being largely due to the losses he had sustained on the 13th and 14th.† Next day the column accompanied by the three chiefs started on its return march. Kacha was reached on the 28th April and on the 30th General Dyer held a darbar, when the chiefs signed an agreement and swore on the *Koran* to be friendly to the British Government and to give timely warning of the approach of any German agents or parties. They were then given presents of money and allowed to return to their homes.

Affair of Kundi; 17-18th April 1916. Although General Dyer's movement into Sarhad had brought about a diminution of raiding on his line of communication, a serious attack on a British convoy was carried out by a body of about two hundred tribesmen on the night 17th/18th April

---

* Sunset was about 6.25 p.m.
† These, it was ascertained later, had amounted to about 150.

DYER'S OPERATIONS

at Kundi, about one hundred miles to the south-east of Kacha. This attack was driven off by the escort of 28th Light Cavalry, with the loss of one man killed and two wounded in addition to three merchants accompanying the convoy killed. The raiders left two dead, but succeeded in carrying off some of our camels.

General Dyer's success had been mainly due to the way in which he had outwitted the Sarhaddi chiefs, and he was warned that Jiand Khan and Halil Khan had come to suspect this; and as, in any case, they could not be relied on to keep their oaths, their resentment would probably lead them to take the first opportunity of turning against him and attacking him, as soon as they discovered how weak in strength the British really were. On the other hand, Juma Khan, he was told, could be fully trusted to keep his word. Events seemed to prove the accuracy of these warnings, for no sooner had the Sarhaddi chiefs left Kacha than General Dyer received information that Jiand and Halil intended to collect their fighting men, retake Khwash and then attack General Dyer. Juma Khan, it was said, had refused to join them. *East Persia; May 1916.*

General Dyer decided that he must at once march on Khwash, moving as quickly as possible. His small column, therefore, started off again on the 4th May and General Dyer decided to precede it himself in his motor car, trusting to the moral effect of its novelty and unknown qualities to impress the tribesmen. Accompanied only by his English chauffeur and a Chagai levy sowar (a Reki named Idu), who had throughout been acting as his assistant and intermediary with the tribesmen, General Dyer reached Khwash early on the 9th May after overcoming considerable difficulties among the trackless hills. Here and there on the journey, says General Dyer in his book, he came across groups of human beings, mostly of a low type, who bolted in terror at sight of the car. Khwash fort had not been attacked, though Jiand Khan was reported in the vicinity with an armed gathering. On the 10th the column arrived, having covered the distance from Kacha in seven marches; and next day Jiand and Halil both came in to visit General Dyer and denied having had any hostile intentions. They agreed to return to us the plunder they had taken on our line of communications and General Dyer began to enlist levies from the Sarhaddi tribes. In fact on the 14th, reporting to India that he was making good progress in enlisting levies, he said that Sarhad was practically settled and that he proposed to hold Khwash. Work was at once put in hand on a defensible camp there and

East Persia;
May 1916.
by the end of the month it was garrisoned by one squadron 28th Light Cavalry, two mountain guns, about one hundred rifles 19th Punjabis, and four machine guns. Jiand and Halil began to return the plunder they had taken, and on the 30th May all the leading Sarhaddi chiefs assembled at Khwash to meet General Grover, commanding the Quetta Division, who was visiting the place on a tour of inspection.

General Dyer proposed to raise 400 levies from the Sarhad tribes and by the end of May had enlisted about half that number. Owing to this and the settlement with their chiefs, a general immunity from raids was experienced during May on the Nushki–Robat line of communication. Some loss and a few casualties, however, were caused on the line near Bandan, to the north-west of Seistan, by raids of robber tribesmen from across the Afghan border. In these raids they themselves only suffered a few casualties and escaped all real punishment as it was not permissible to pursue them across the border line.

Some misunderstanding had arisen in regard to the control of the various levies we had raised, and the Government of India found it necessary to define the relative positions in this respect of General Dyer and the political officers. For purposes of organisation and administration, they decided, the levies were to be entirely under the political authorities: i.e., the Hazara and Seistani Levies under Major Prideaux, who was to be General Dyer's political adviser for Seistan and Kain, and the Sarhad Levies under a political agent to be appointed for Sarhad. For operation purposes General Dyer would be the sole authority over the levies and he was also to supervise their training.

Work on the improvement of the Nushki–Robat route, in order to make it passable for mechanical transport, continued throughout May, part of the 106th Hazara Pioneers from Quetta being employed for the purpose; and a few motor lorries were sent to Nushki for work on the road. The results, however, were not satisfactory.

Makran;
April–May 1916.
In April, Colonel Dew, after a visit to the headquarters of the Government at Delhi, returned to Makran in the hope of coming to terms with Bahram Khan of Bampur and other tribal chiefs of Persian Baluchistan and Makran, to induce them to lay aside their tribal quarrels and to assist the British in opposing German influence and activities. He also hoped to raise, from among their tribesmen, levies who would co-operate with those in Sarhad and Seistan. In addition to a personal escort of fifty rifles 1/7th Gurkhas, he had with him a few

political officers to assist in raising these levies. Unfortunately on the 16th April two of his political assistants—Lieutenants Hughes and Horst—were assassinated by fanatics at Mand, instigated it was believed by some of the German agents. The murderers themselves were at once killed by levies who were in the vicinity. But the incident illustrated one of the effects of the German propaganda. In fact, at the end of the month Colonel Dew reported that it was the effect of the German propaganda and of the fanaticism which it had aroused that was to be feared rather than the danger of the Germans raising tribal chiefs against us. *Jahad* was being actively preached and, unless steps were soon taken to check the propaganda spread by German Moslem agents throughout the country, it would continue to spread and create fanaticism. Pamphlets announcing the conversion to Islam of Germany were, he said, having considerable effect. In view of the state of part of the population, he considered it advisable that the mission under Major Keyes, which was about to tour the Persian borderland, should have some military protection. For instance, his own personal escort of fifty Gurkhas might accompany Major Keyes. The Agent to the Governor-General in Baluchistan, on receiving Colonel Dew's report, recommended on the 5th May that, in addition to this escort, 200 Indian infantry should at once be sent to Mand to accompany Major Keyes; and this was at once agreed to by the Government of India, who asked for a further report on the matter after Colonel Dew had met Bahram Khan.

This chief came to Mand on the 8th May and next day Colonel Dew concluded an agreement by which Bahram Khan and other local chiefs promised to punish the instigators of the murders of the two political officers, to refuse the Germans assistance and to help us against them, and also to stop raiding into British territory. Colonel Dew, however, putting little faith in Bahram Khan's word, felt it necessary to refuse to allow Major Keyes to cross the frontier till the additional 200 rifles had arrived. They reached Mand (a double company 127th Baluchis) via Gwadur on the 24th May and on their arrival, Colonel Dew having left, Major Keyes was authorised by the Agent to the Governor-General in Baluchistan to proceed on his mission.

At this time, owing to the effect of the German propaganda emanating from Makran and Persia, there was a sudden recrudescence of unrest in Southern Jhallawan, in British territory. This led to an outbreak of serious raids on the Sind border and the British political agent at Kalat (Colonel Dew) had to be sent at once to tour Jhallawan with a strong military escort in order to restore order.*

German Mission to Afghanistan. (See Map 5.) On the 27th May the Chief of the General Staff in India telegraphed to General Dyer that the German mission was reported to have left Kabul on the 21st to return to Persia via Herat. This report proved to be correct. German accounts show that for some time past the patience of the mission had been sorely tried, in their many interviews with the Amir, at their failure to win him over from his neutral attitude and his loyalty to his word to the British. The Germans had managed after a time, by punctilious behaviour, to gain almost complete freedom of movement; and the Amir had gone so far as to utilise their services in helping to increase the efficiency of his arsenal and various factories and also, latterly, in carrying out other military preparations. But he would go no further. On their part they laid themselves out to cultivate friendly relations with the high officials, most of them anti-British, and they started a system of propaganda, not only in Afghanistan but in India and especially among the frontier tribesmen. Mahsuds, Mohmands and Afridis, says Niedermayer, responded well to German instructions and this, he boasts, in many cases fructified later.†

Very little reliable news had reached the mission from the outside world, but in mid-April Niedermayer says that he obtained reliable information from a friendly Indian who had come from Kerman. The news was bad. The German Minister at Tehran had fled to Baghdad; Russian columns were advancing on Isfahan and Kermanshah; Seiler's party had come into conflict with the British in East Persia,‡ Winkelmann having been captured; Seiler was at Kerman preparing for another advance; and Zugmayer was working in the Bam-Bampur area. Niedermayer, feeling that his own presence was required in Persia, decided to ascertain definitely if the

---

* To complete its task, this escort had to prolong its operations till the beginning of August.

† In the light of subsequent events, it seems evident that Niedermayer and his mission laid the seeds of the trouble which India experienced on the North-West Frontier, in India and with Afghanistan from the summer of 1916 to 1920.

‡ It is interesting to note that Niedermayer still believed that the British force in East Persia was 10,000 strong and that the Russians had a mixed brigade there.

Amir had any intention of abandoning his neutrality. The reply he received was most unsatisfactory and the Amir also said that if the Germans contemplated departure the whole mission must go. On the other hand, if they wished to remain at Kabul they must all stay. The Germans decided to go; and, being given every assistance by the Afghans, who displayed great friendliness, their departure took place on the 21st May.

Their plan of movement was as follows. Paschen (at Herat) was to cross the frontier to the westward and try to get across Persia. Voigt, with a few Indians, was to go to Taiwara in Western Afghanistan, via Ghazni and Kandahar, and there await further orders. Niedermayer, Hentig, Wagner and Röhr, with the main caravan, were to start northwards from Kabul. After a few days' marching, Hentig and Röhr were to turn off north-eastward and make for China, while Niedermayer and Wagner with the main body would move towards Herat. Wagner and the caravan were to remain at Herat, awaiting further orders, but Niedermayer himself would choose an opportunity to leave the party and cross the Russian or Persian frontier.

It will be convenient here to state very briefly what befel these various groups. Paschen succeeded in penetrating the Russian cordon to the south of Turbat-i-Haidari and reached Tabas, where, however, he was captured by Persians early in July 1916 and handed over to the Russians. Voigt, after reaching Taiwara and being told by Niedermayer to cross into Persia and join the German group at Kerman, was captured with two Indian revolutionaries by the British near Sehdeh at the beginning of August 1916. Hentig and Röhr, after an adventurous journey, succeeded in crossing Chinese Turkestan and China and eventually got back to Germany. Niedermayer, after accompanying Wagner and the main caravan to Sar-i-Pul, left them on the night 22nd June disguised as a Turkoman and accompanied by his Persian servant and six Turkomans. His further movements were full of adventure and privation. Proceeding westward, he crossed the Russian frontier into Turkestan and thence entered Persia south of Sarakhs. In various disguises he passed through Meshed and Tehran and finally reached Hamadan on the 31st August 1916. From there he at once continued to Kermanshah, where he stayed for several months. Wagner with the main caravan remained for a very long time at Herat, anxiously waiting for instructions, which never reached him. Finally in despair he crossed into

Persia, penetrating the Russian cordon to the south of Turbat-i-Haidari in November 1917. But he was surrounded by the Persians in a fort whence, in the ensuing fight, though most of his companions were captured, he succeeded in escaping; and after many adventures and much privation succeeded in reaching Turkey via Tehran and Kurdistan.

The courage, skill and tenacity displayed by Niedermayer and his companions in their enterprise are worthy of our highest admiration. That their mission to Afghanistan met with little or no success was due mainly to the fact that the late Amir Habibulla Khan realised that it was in the best interests of his country to remain neutral and that, having told us that he would do so, he would not allow himself to be persuaded or intimidated into breaking his word.

CHAPTER V.

MAY TO DECEMBER 1916:
TURKISH INVASION OF WESTERN PERSIA AND BRITISH MEASURES IN SOUTH AND EAST PERSIA.

(General Map and Map 4.)

The Russian advance, directed against Ruwandiz and Khaniqin, which commenced on the 28th April, met at first with complete success. Baratoff's main column, driving back the Turco-Persian force holding the Pai Taq pass, occupied Qasr-i-Shirin on the 7th May; and, on the 13th, part of the force under Chernozuboff captured Ruwandiz. Then for a while the Russian advance was stayed. Kut had fallen and the Turks, in addition to counter-attacking in the north, were able to reinforce the Persian frontier from both Baghdad and Kut. The Russians, and especially Baratoff, were faced with great supply and transport difficulties; while Baratoff, who had with him at Qasr-i-Shirin only about a third of the 20,000 Russian troops in Persia,* was apprehensive of a Turkish attack from the Kut direction which would cut his long line of communications. He reported on the 13th May that the Turkish position at Khaniqin was a formidable one and received orders three days later that he was not to attack it, but was to entrench himself in his position eight miles to the west of Qasr-i-Shirin.

West Persia; May 1916.

It appears from German accounts that Colonel Bopp, commanding the mixed force opposing Baratoff, gave way to panic when driven back from Pai Taq. The Russians were not pressing the pursuit; but Bopp, ignoring his orders to fall back slowly and to stand fast at Khaniqin or on the Jabal Hamrin and despite the fact that the Turkish 18th Infantry Regiment and a German machine gun company were on their way from Baghdad to reinforce him, gave orders for a retirement to Baquba. The Turkish portion of the force, under Shevket Bey, saw no reason to obey these orders and took up a good position to the east of Khaniqin, but Bopp and his Persians all retreated to Baquba. In the meantime, Bopp's alarmist reports had caused Halil Pasha, with Gleich as his Chief of Staff, to hurry back from Kut to Baghdad, which they

---

* i.e., troops south of Hamadan.

West Persia; May 1916. reached on the 6th May, to receive further alarmist and false reports that two Russian divisions were marching on Baghdad. Without consulting Gleich, Halil next day ordered the withdrawal from Kut, for transfer to the Persian frontier, of a Turkish cavalry brigade and the 2nd Division, an order which was confirmed on the 8th by Enver Pasha. In the meantime Bopp had been superseded and an order had been received by Gleich from Falkenhayn that the Duke of Mecklenberg (ex-Governor of Togoland) was to take over control of the Persian Mission. This, however, he does not appear to have done, owing to Halil's opposition.*

Gleich tried, but without success, to send the Persians at Baquba back to the front and then, realising their military uselessness, suggested their disarmament. But this, on political grounds, the Turks refused to agree to; and on the 15th May Halil decided to use the 400 Persian volunteers and 320 Persian gendarmerie, who were all that had not deserted, with their German and Swedish officers to carry out garrison duties at Mandali and Kifri. The German Minister from Tehran and Nizam-es-Sultaneh, with his escort of one hundred tribesmen, had already proceeded to Baghdad, where they started to agitate for an active Persian policy. To this Gleich was much opposed, for, although he considered that a local offensive might be necessary to throw back the Russians, he was convinced of the necessity for preparing for autumn operations against the British on the Tigris. In fact, he tried to get Falkenhayn to put a stop to the notion still prevalent that an undertaking through Persia and Afghanistan to India was feasible.

Halil was gradually won over to the idea of a Persian expedition and would not listen to Gleich's warnings of the danger of getting entangled in Persia. On the 16th May, Gleich learnt from Halil that Enver, who was also favourable to the idea of invading Persia, would arrive at Baghdad on the 19th and had already ordered more infantry and artillery to be withdrawn from the Tigris front and sent to Khaniqin. In fact, as Gleich says, the intended stroke against the Russians had gradually developed into a big expedition into Persia. Halil, who was of opinion that the British would, of their own accord, shortly retire from the vicinity of Kut, refused to pay any attention to Gleich's objections to the undue weakening of the Tigris front.

* It was only after much German pressure that Halil consented to the appointment of this Prince to the command on the 6th June of a small Turkish force known as the Sulaimaniya group. This he held for less than three weeks, when he was recalled to Germany.

Enver reached Baghdad on the 19th May with a large staff, including his German Chief of Staff, von Schellendorf, and members of the German and Austrian military missions; but none of them would support Gleich in his objections to an active Persian policy. In fact, he found his position so anomalous that he would have resigned but for Falkenhayn's request that he would remain and do what he could to assist in the forthcoming operations. After visiting Kut and Khaniqin, Enver decided that Persia was to be the main theatre of operations for the Sixth Army, its advance being co-ordinated with a great offensive in the north which the Second Army, supported by the Third, was to begin in July. Enver, impressed by the pleasant manners of Nizam-es-Sultaneh and the Persian consul at Baghdad, also came to a definite agreement with them before he left to return to Turkey on the 25th May. At this time German influence in Turkey was at a low ebb and, in consequence of this Turco-Persian agreement, Gleich found the arrogant attitude of Turks and Persians towards him and the other Germans almost unbearable. His own intense dislike of the Persian policy, in which he was obliged to acquiesce but which he really considered as both hopeless and dangerous, led more and more to a deterioration of his relations with the Persians and with Halil. It must have been, therefore, some relief when—the Turks, at the beginning of June, having arrogated to themselves complete control of the Persians in Mesopotamia—he sent orders for all the German and Swedish officers with these Persians to give up their appointments and return to Baghdad, thus putting an end to the German military character of the mission, a result he had been striving to achieve for several weeks. By this time practically the whole of the Turkish XIII Corps had been concentrated near Khaniqin, in readiness to advance on Kermanshah.

Owing to the general improvement in the situation in West and Central Persia, consequent on Baratoff's operations, the British Consul-General (Mr. Grahame) and British community were able to return to Isfahan from Ahwaz during May; and with them went Lieutenant-Colonel H. A. K. Gough to take up the appointment of British consul at Kermanshah.*

At Shiraz, though most of the German agents were prisoners with many of their partisans, the activity of a number of Democrats and rebellious gendarmerie gave some cause for anxiety till it became certain that Saulat was really assisting

Shiraz; May 1916.

---

* He was subsequently detailed to go instead to Shiraz and Lieut.-Colonel R. L. Kennion was sent to take up the Kermanshah appointment.

Qawam to restore order. Farman Farma was appointed Governor-General of Fars early in May, but it was to be several months before he actually arrived at Shiraz in person; and until he did so the Persian Government entrusted the young Qawam with the responsibility for the administration.

The Sykes Mission; May 1916. For the march of his small force from Bandar Abbas to Kerman, a distance of about 270 miles, Sir Percy Sykes was engaged till the middle of May in the necessary preparations. The Persian authorities agreed to lay out supplies at the various stages, but it was decided, as a precautionary measure, to carry with the force forty days' rations for men and seven days' forage for animals. The chief difficulty was transport, as at that time of year no caravan owner from the interior would risk his camels in the intense heat of the coastal region. The local camels were generally only used for the carriage of grain and neither they nor their owners were accustomed to other loads, to move in convoy or to march at fixed hours, while the carrying capacity of the slow-moving donkeys was limited.

In the meantime Mr. Marling had represented that British interests and the desirability of supporting Farman Farma required that Sir P. Sykes should proceed to Shiraz and start the organisation in Fars of the South Persia Rifles with the least possible delay. The British Minister, however, realised the necessity for proceeding with the movement to Kerman* for which the arrangements were almost complete. But when he learnt that the Government of India considered that the question of proceeding to Shiraz from Kerman should be left for decision according to subsequent developments, both he and Farman Farma urged that some other British officers should be sent direct to Shiraz from Bandar Abbas to start organising the South Persia Rifles. This suggestion was negatived in India, as it was felt that to send officers without an adequate escort—and this could not be provided—would be to run undesirable risks.

The British prisoners at Ahram; May 1916. A further reason for an early restoration of British influence in Fars was the desirability of obtaining the release of Major O'Connor and the other British prisoners at Ahram. There had been various suggestions for effecting this. The Deputy Political Resident at Bushire, the British Minister at Tehran and the Foreign Office in London had advocated offensive operations from Bushire against the rebellious Khans. But, after consideration in Mesopotamia and India, the idea was

---

* The route from Bandar Abbas to Shiraz via Kerman was also easier than the direct road.

definitely rejected owing to the approach of the hot season and the difficulty of providing the force required. Another suggestion arose from a proposal which Major O'Connor sent in, namely that he and his companions could probably seize the fort in which they were interned if they were certain of relief by a force from Bushire (twenty-six miles away). General Douglas, commanding at Bushire, was ready to move out with a force for this purpose. But General Lake in Mesopotamia considered that the difficulties of water supply *en route* and the lack of mountain guns with the force—a deficiency which he could not make good—rendered the project hazardous. The Government of India, also regarding the enterprise as too risky, decided against it. Apart from the questions of guns and water, they considered that a surprise movement would be practically impossible, and that it would be politically disastrous if the small force got seriously entangled or the prisoners were murdered. It appeared to the authorities in India that the best solution of the whole question was that Saulat should be delegated to do all that was possible to effect the prisoners' release, that Sir Percy Sykes with his escorting force should go to Shiraz as soon as possible and start organising the South Persia Rifles there, arranging if possible for the safe conduct from Bandar Abbas of British officers to assist him, and that the Bushire situation should be cleared up when the weather got cool and troops from Mesopotamia could be made available.

Sir Percy Sykes had started for Kerman on the 17th May, marching in two echelons owing to the scarcity of water at some of the stages. The composition of his force was as follows :—*

The Sykes Mission; May–June 1916.

Brig.-General Sir P. Sykes and part of his South Persia Rifles staff,
Personal escort of twenty-five sabres Central India Horse,
One squadron 15th Lancers (Major S. M. Bruce),
One section 23rd Mountain Battery (Major R. S. Rothwell),
Half-battalion 124th Baluchistan Infantry (Lieut.-Colonel E. F. Twigg),
One section No. 108 Indian Field Ambulance,
Supply and Transport details, and
Various members of the Imperial Bank of Persia and of the Indo-European Telegraph Department returning to Kerman.

---

* The total numbers comprised 27 British (all ranks), 611 Indians (all ranks), 180 followers, 134 horses, 88 mules, 800 hired camels and 477 hired donkeys.

The march fell naturally into two sections—the first over the hot coastal plain and the low hills to Daulatabad, 126 miles distant; and the second through the mountains, in which the climate though bracing was treacherous as, after the enervating heat of the coast, the cold nights were apt to bring out latent fever. In the first section had to be traversed the ill-famed Tang-i-Zindan, or "Prison Defile," in which wet weather was liable to cause sudden floods, which had in the past swept away many a caravan. No accident occurred, however, and even the robber tribes of the area offered no molestation. On arrival at Daulatabad, which is in the Kerman province, Sir P. Sykes was met by some old friends, who brought him a letter of welcome signed by the leading inhabitants of Kerman city. From this point Sir P. Sykes had no further anxieties, as friends joined him at every stage and his march became a triumphal progress. It was fortunate that the columns were not molested, as the small number of troops would have found it difficult to protect adequately their large convoys of donkeys and half-wild camels.*

Bushire; May–June 1916. At Bushire during May and June no military operations took place. The 14th Sikhs from Egypt arrived there on the 22nd May, when the 96th Infantry were sent to Mesopotamia. On the 12th June the Government of India informed the India Office of the reasons for their decision not to take the risks of offensive operations from Bushire, a military policy in which the Chief of the Imperial General Staff expressed his concurrence.

On the 17th June Mr. Marling telegraphed to Major Trevor at Bushire that the Foreign and India Offices had decided that he was to open negotiations, for the release of the British prisoners at Ahram, with the Khans on terms which it was understood they were likely to accept. These included the release by us of sixteen prisoners to be named by the Khans, the return to them of money and a consignment of tea which we had confiscated at Bushire, and the assurance that the Bushire-Borazjan-Shiraz road would be re-opened for traffic. Further, though the Khans had not put in a demand for a full pardon, if this was found to be essential Major Trevor might grant it with a warning that it would be cancelled if the Khans gave further trouble. In reply Major Trevor submitted

---

* In his report Sir Percy Sykes said that the last European column to traverse the Kerman province was that of Alexander the Great in B.C. 325 and that in the long interval of 2,241 years there had been no improvement in communications.

a long telegram of protest, especially against giving the Khans any assurances which would render them immune from punishment for their long list of offences against the British. The prisoners were, he said, comparatively well treated and were allowed exercise and to receive stores, books, papers and letters from Bushire. He considered—and local naval, military and friendly Persian opinion coincided—that to accept the Khans' terms would have a very bad effect on the British position in South Persia, having regard to the fact that the British force at Bushire had remained inactive for ten months in face of the opposition of three petty chiefs with a few hundred men. Sir Percy Cox also protested strongly, and the Government of India asked Mr. Marling to suspend his orders to Major Trevor pending a submission of their views to H.M. Government.

On the 30th June, Dr. Azzopardy—a Maltese and one of the prisoners at Ahram—arrived at Bushire, having been released on account of his ill-health. He reported that all but two of the prisoners were in good health, though they suffered from the heat and monotony. They were well treated and had received all the stores and most of the books and papers sent from Bushire. Wassmuss, he said, was short of money and had lost influence; while the Khans, who were short of men and had been hard hit by the closing of the road to trade, were distinctly apprehensive. The general population was friendly to the prisoners. On the 6th July, Mr. Marling telegraphed to India and Major Trevor that, in view of Major Trevor's protest and of the views expressed by the Government of India, H.M. Government had decided that a pardon could not be granted to the Khans. With this exception his previous orders to Major Trevor were to hold good. Mr. Marling also said that, although he did not place much hope in him, Saulat professed to be pressing the Khans to release the prisoners unconditionally.

With regard to the organisation by Great Britain and Russia of military police forces in Persia and to the granting to the Persian Government of a subsidy, both questions which had already been agreed to in principle by the two Powers, Mr. Marling telegraphed on the 2nd June that Persian Ministers were urging on him and the Russian Minister the pressing necessity for a definite settlement. The insecurity of the roads and the alarming increase of brigandage, consequent on the rebellion of a large part of the gendarmerie, proved the imperative need of an early understanding with the two Powers, said

General Situation; June 1916.

the Persians, while they trusted that their readiness to agree to a Mixed Commission to control finances would be accepted as an earnest of their sincere desire for real reform and a justification of the subsidy. The Russian Minister and Mr. Marling were strongly of opinion that a definite settlement should be at once concluded, and they asked that they should be authorised to negotiate it. They believed that the Persian Government would agree, (1) to an increase of the Persian Cossack Brigade to a strength of 10,000 men and to the organisation in the south of a British-officered force of similar strength, (2) to accept a monthly subsidy of 200,000 tomans for the period of the war, its expenditure being entrusted to a Mixed Commission, and (3) to the extension of the powers of this Mixed Commission to provide for effective control over the whole Persian financial administration. H.M. Government agreed to Mr. Marling's proposal, but the Russian Government, which, ever since Baratoff's successful advance, had been gradually cancelling the concessions to Persia which they in common with Great Britain had been previously ready to agree to, adopted a passively obstructive attitude.

West Persia; June 1916. This was all the more unfortunate as Baratoff — failing in an attack, on the 3rd June, on Khaniqin, where he found the Turks in superior strength—was forced to retreat and was followed up by Ali Ihsan Pasha with the greater part of the Turkish XIII Corps (2nd and 6th Divisions). On the 9th June, the Turks occupied Qasr-i-Shirin without opposition and, although on the 22nd they met with a reverse eight miles to the north-west of Karind, in a second advance they reached Karind on the 26th. That a Russian retirement in this area would be necessary had already been envisaged by the British General Staff in London, who realised that the Turks at Baghdad, acting on interior lines, might be able to contain the almost immobile British corps on the Tigris with a comparatively weak force while concentrating against Baratoff. The latter, moreover, was operating in most difficult country, was weak in strength and was hampered by a long line of communication and by serious maintenance difficulties. Information given at the time by the Chief of the Russian Staff in the Caucasus to the British liaison officer, that the attack on Khaniqin was intended to be pressed to a definite conclusion, seems to indicate that it had been ordered under a total misapprehension of the real situation. It is noteworthy that few, if any, German officers took part in this Turkish advance.*

---

* Gleich, having fallen sick at the beginning of June, resigned his appointment and left Baghdad for Germany on the 23rd.

SYKES REACHES KERMAN

At the beginning of June, the situation at Shiraz seemed to Mr. Marling to be still unsatisfactory. Saulat, who was jealous of Qawam, annoyed at Farman Farma's appointment and disappointed at not being subsidised by us, was causing trouble. Some eight hundred gendarmerie remaining at Shiraz were said to be loyal and Mr. Marling suggested that British officers should be sent there, via Ahwaz and Isfahan, to take over control of these men. The Foreign Office in London supported the proposal, and the despatch of five or six British officers by this route was arranged for by the Government of India. But they considered that, to avoid multiplying risks by further embarrassments, it would be best if these officers arrived at Shiraz simultaneously with Sir P. Sykes, who was almost due at Kerman and who, India suggested, should march from there to Shiraz at an early date, moving via Yezd.

Shiraz situation; June 1916.

Sir Percy Sykes reached Kerman on the 11th June, receiving a warm welcome from the Governor and leading notables, to many of whom he was well known personally from his previous residence there. On the 15th the Government of India asked him for a broad outline of his scheme of organisation for the South Persia Rifles* to enable them to restore order in South Persia generally and especially on the main trade routes. A strength of 10,000 men might, he was told, be regarded as the limit of the ultimate size of the force. On the 18th he replied that his policy would aim at reducing the tribes to submission rather than to stringing men along the roads. For the Bandar Abbas–Kerman road he considered the provision of a telegraph and telephone line, as well as its improvement to take wheeled traffic, to be essential; while for that area he estimated the strength of the police force required at 14 British officers, about 2,700 men, 6 guns and 8 machine guns. For the Bushire–Shiraz road and area the strength required would probably be a little greater, but he was not yet in a position to make an accurate estimate. He proposed to start the formation at Kerman of a cavalry regiment at once and of an infantry battalion as early as possible; and he asked for the services of more British officers and Indian instructors,† also of an Engineer officer for road making and the construction of posts. He also asked that two motor cars might be sent to him via Seistan, as they were urgently required.

The Sykes Mission at Kerman; June 1916.

---

* This title, it may be noted, was only settled later.
† Shortly after this he asked that he should be sent British instead of Indian instructors for the South Persia Rifles.

The Sykes Mission; June–July 1916. On the 22nd June the India Office, at the instance of the Foreign Office who were most anxious for the early arrival of British officers at Shiraz, asked India to ascertain when the situation at Kerman would permit Sir P. Sykes to start for Shiraz and whether he could safely proceed there direct instead of via Yezd. There were several reasons why Sir P. Sykes considered it preferable to move to Shiraz via Yezd instead of by the direct road, although the distance by the former was 459 miles against 334 miles by the latter. Along the Yezd road there was a telegraph line, and this would facilitate both the laying out of supplies required for his column and the maintenance of communication with the authorities. On the direct route supplies were reported to be scarce and, until Farman Farma reached Shiraz, it would be practically impossible to lay them out between Niriz and Shiraz, while the section of road from Saidabad to Niriz was known to be very difficult for troops. Moreover, this road ran through country inhabited by Baharlus and other Arab tribesmen who had been helping the Germans. So that, apart from the possibility of hostilities on their part, owners of hired transport would probably be easily intimidated into deserting. On learning, however, of the wishes of the Foreign Office, Sir P. Sykes at first agreed to go by the shorter route, for which, in view of possible hostilities, he started to obtain transport mules, as his column would be too small to safeguard a long line of hired camels with undisciplined drivers. Mules, however, were not obtainable locally and on the 30th June he reported that it would take two months to obtain them, whereas if he moved by Yezd he could use camels, which he could collect in one month. Owing to this and the delay there would be, in the absence of a telegraph line, in ascertaining if supplies had been laid out along the direct route, he estimated that he would gain a month by moving through Yezd, as well as running infinitely less risk of supplies failing. On the 3rd July the Government of India instructed him to arrange to start without delay and move via Yezd. It was desirable to take advantage of the collapse of the German propaganda to re-establish ourselves in Fars before the effect of the Russian check in Western Persia was fully felt there. Colonel Gough, the new British consul for Shiraz, would accompany Farman Farma there from Isfahan, as well as five British officers for the South Persia Rifles.

TROUBLE IN SARHAD

To turn to East Persia. On the 1st June the British Seistan Force was disposed as follows:—

	Sabres.	Rifles.	Mountain guns.	Machine guns.
Birjand	111	100	—	1
Neh	56	—	—	—
Bandan	53	51	—	—
Nasratabad (Seistan)	5	113	—	1
Dehani Baghi	27	97	—	—
Robat	—	69	—	—
Kacha	69	132	—	—
Khwash	148	125	2	4
Total	469	687	2	6

East Persia; June 1916.

The Hazara Levies—just under 200 strong—were distributed in posts to the north-west of Seistan as far as Neh; the Seistani Levies—400 camelry and 400 horsemen—were, with the exception of about 100 camelry in the Dehani Baghi vicinity, mostly in Seistan; and some two to three hundred Sarhaddi Levies had been enrolled at Khwash, though as yet they had not been called upon for duty.

At Khwash, where General Dyer had his headquarters for the time being, the troops were mainly occupied for the first half of June in improving the defences of their encampment. Jiand Khan had surrendered five hundred camels and much of the rest of the plunder he had taken in his raids on the British lines of communication. But his attitude was not satisfactory and he absolutely refused to sell any forage to General Dyer, whose horses and mules had to be put on half rations. He was also strongly suspected of having instigated the destruction by fire of a quantity of forage which another man had collected, for sale to the British, at Deh Bala, a village fifteen miles to the east of Khwash. On the 14th June, General Dyer marched thither with a force of two troops 28th Cavalry, the section 25th Mountain Battery, fifty of the 19th Punjabis, two machine guns and a few levies, to investigate the matter and to punish the offenders. On his way he learnt that Jiand Khan was at Deh Bala with an armed following and, as the column advanced, Jiand and his men were seen to have taken up a defensive position between the British and the village. Seeing the British strength, however, Jiand evidently thought better of it, closed his men and came forward personally to meet General Dyer.

Sarhad; June 1916. (See Map 4).

Sarhad; June 1916.

Deh Bala was reached about 2 p.m.; and the British column went into camp about three-quarters of a mile from the village, while General Dyer went on there to hold his enquiry, taking with him a troop of cavalry, about twenty infantry and ten levies. Jiand and a number of his men attended the enquiry and, in a heated controversy aroused by the obviously false evidence, assumed such a threatening attitude towards General Dyer that he felt compelled to order their immediate arrest. This was quickly effected by the escort, who seized and disarmed Jiand and thirty-seven of his men and marched them off as prisoners to the British camp.

Next day the column marched back to Khwash with the prisoners, whom General Dyer was warned that the Damanis would certainly attempt to rescue. He therefore decided to send them into Quetta, and, as he had not sufficient troops to escort them, asked that troops should be sent from Quetta to take over charge of them at Kacha. General Grover at Quetta immediately ordered three hundred rifles, of the half-battalion 106th Hazara Pioneers working on the road, to proceed at once from Dalbandin to Saindak. From there, 150 of them were to escort the prisoners to Quetta, while 150 remained at Saindak in order to reinforce General Dyer in case the removal of the prisoners caused disturbances in Sarhad.

On the 25th June, General Dyer sent the prisoners off from Khwash, with an escort of two troops 28th Light Cavalry, fifty rifles 19th Punjabis and a machine gun, under command of Captain F. James, 28th Light Cavalry, to move via Kalchat and the western spurs of the Kuh-i-Taftan to Kacha, so as to avoid the Sangun area where it was reported that Halil Khan meant to attempt a rescue. That night, however, at Kalchat, all the prisoners, with the exception of Jiand, his son and two others, managed to excape.* On news of this reaching General Dyer at Khwash at 4 a.m. on the 26th, he at once realised that a strong attempt to rescue Jiand and his son would certainly be made and also that a wireless detachment (two pack sets), which was on its way from Kacha via Sangun to join him at Khwash, would be in danger of attack. He immediately sent orders to Captain James to march to Chah-i-Zar, for which place he himself left at 8 a.m. with one troop 28th Light Cavalry and a machine gun. He also sent orders to Colonel Dale at Kacha to send half of the

---

* All of them, except Jiand and his son, had been put inside a barbed wire enclosure for the night. In the dark, however, managing to slip their ropes, they stripped off their clothing and, laying it across the barbed wire, escaped naked.

300 rifles of the 106th Pioneers, due at Saindak on the 1st July, to Khwash. At Chah-i-Zar, he ordered Captain James to start next day with the four prisoners, escorted by two troops of cavalry and fourteen infantry rifles, for Saindak via Sangun, where he was to pick up the wireless detachment and take it with him. He himself marched off the same night with a troop of cavalry, thirty-seven infantry rifles and two machine guns to Kamalabad, so as to engage and divert the attention of a tribal force under Halil Khan, the Gamshadzai chief, which it was said was on its way from Gusht to rescue Jiand.

Reaching Kamalabad very early on the 27th June, General Dyer found it deserted, Halil Khan with his following and the tribal families being reported to have retired into the hills to the eastward. On the 28th General Dyer moved off in that direction so as to drive them further into the hills. But he did not encounter them and returned the same evening to Kamalabad. On the 29th, on his way back to Khwash, he learnt that Captain James's party had been attacked north of Sangun on the previous day and that Jiand Khan and his son had escaped. It appears that on the morning of the 28th June the column had been ambushed by a party of tribesmen which included most of the prisoners who had escaped on the night 25th/26th. They were fortunate enough with their first shots to wound Captain James, as well as the only other British officer with the escort and the senior Indian officer. In the course of the fight, which went on till dark, the guard over the prisoners and their horses were all wounded, and in the confusion Jiand and his son managed to escape, though the other two prisoners were killed. The escort had eleven other Indian casualties, while twelve of their horses were killed and fourteen were missing, as well as thirty-seven camels.

On reaching Khwash the same evening (29th), General Dyer at once despatched Lieut.-Colonel P. S. D. Claridge with one troop 28th Light Cavalry and fifty of the 19th Punjabis to Sangun to collect both Captain James's party and the wireless detachment. This detachment had, in point of fact, been held up by a party of tribesmen at Siah Jangal on the 28th, when it had sent off a message to Colonel Dale (which he received on the 29th afternoon) asking for reinforcements. Colonel Dale at once sent out fifty of the 28th Light Cavalry to help them and at the same time instructed the three hundred men of the 106th Pioneers, then marching on Saindak, to proceed direct to Khwash. Colonel Claridge met with no opposition and, picking up first

Sarhad; Captain James's party and then the wireless detachment without
July 1916. difficulty, moved on to Ladis to await the arrival of the 106th
Pioneers. These, under command of Captain L. E. Lang,
reached Ladis on the 3rd July; and two days later Colonel
Claridge with the combined parties and accompanied by Major
W. G. Hutchinson, Political Agent of the Chagai district, who
had been appointed Political Agent for Sarhad also, moved
to Khwash, which was reached on the 10th July.

In the meantime Jiand Khan with an armed gathering had
appeared near Khwash, which he attacked on the night
8th/9th July. This attack was easily and quickly beaten off;
and, on the approach of the British reinforcements, Jiand and
his men retired to the tribal summer quarters in the Sar-i-
Drukan valley. General Dyer, who had only been awaiting the
arrival of the 106th Pioneers before taking the offensive
against Jiand, marched off from Khwash on the 12th July with
a column consisting of two troops 28th Light Cavalry, the
section 25th Mountain Battery, the 12th Pioneers' machine gun
section, three hundred rifles 106th Pioneers, a medical unit
and a transport train of seven hundred camels carrying a
months' rations and forage for men and animals.

The Sar-i-Drukan valley, which was General Dyer's objective,
is enclosed throughout its length of about forty-five miles by
rugged and precipitous hill ranges, which limit the practicable
entrances into the valley to the Dast Kird gorge at its northern
end and the Gusht defile to the south. The difficult nature of
both these entrances rendered them easy to defend, and
General Dyer decided, by feigning an advance on Dast Kird,
to try to draw Jiand in that direction so as to give his own
column a chance by rapid movement to seize the Gusht defile.
If he could forestall Jiand at Gusht, the possible point of
junction of the Yar Muhammadzais and the Gamshadzais, he
might also gain the co-operation of the free-lance chieftain of
that place, who was known as Gushti. Accordingly, on the 12th
July General Dyer marched to Kamalabad and from there sent
on his cavalry towards Dast Kird with orders to retrace their
steps after dark and rejoin him. This ruse was entirely successful[*]
and General Dyer learnt the same night that Jiand Khan was
on his way to hold the Dast Kird gorge.

Next morning (13th), the British column moved southward
and reached Gusht, fifty-five miles distant, on the 16th without
further opposition than a few shots fired at its advanced guard

---

[*] Before retiring, the cavalry lit camp fires and left them burning.

DYER IN THE GUSHT DEFILE

on the previous day*, but suffering a good deal from the intense heat. Gushti professed to be friendly, and General Dyer halted on the 17th to augment his meagre information of both the enemy and the country. It was only by bribing Gushti heavily, however, that he learnt that the tribesmen had collected in force to the north and that a move in that direction would probably draw an enemy attack. Accordingly, on the 18th July the column moved northward into the Sar-i-Drukan valley for about three miles, the high hills on both sides of the Gusht defile proving very difficult to piquet. Camp was pitched by a small *karez* about a mile above Kalag fort, (in the centre of the Gusht defile) the surrounding piquets coming under a good deal of spasmodic rifle fire during the evening and ensuing night.

On the 19th July an advance was made by part of the column up a defile to the north-east towards a position which Halil Khan was reported to be holding in strength. As, however, the guide at first took the wrong direction and the enemy threatened the camp piquets, the advance was much delayed. The defile, with its lofty, steep and precipitous hill sides, was then found to be very difficult to traverse and to piquet; and the enemy offered much opposition. The operation took so long, in fact, that after going about two miles General Dyer decided not to advance any further. The column, followed by the enemy, accordingly retired to camp, at one place having to halt for three hours to enable the rear guard to get a wounded man down from a piquet on a particularly steep hill. The total British casualties, however, were only three and it was believed that the enemy had suffered considerably. *Affair of the Gusht Defile; 19th–21st July 1916.*

The country was so much more difficult than he had anticipated that General Dyer decided, having regard to the heat, the scarcity of the water and the strength of the opposition, that it would be better to halt for a day or two in the hope that the enemy would come down to attack the column, or at any rate use up much of his ammunition in sniping and most of his supplies. Moreover, General Dyer desired rather to demonstrate to the Sarhaddis that it was useless waste of life for them to fight him than to engage himself in hard fighting, wherein severe casualties might render his task of winning them over more difficult. As water at the camp was getting scarce, General Dyer moved back on the 20th to Kalag fort, where there was an excellent water supply and where the camp could be more easily piquetted. Enemy opposition was encountered and the

---

* A detachment from the column pursued the small body of the enemy concerned, inflicting a few casualties and capturing 360 sheep.

British piquets were engaged throughout the day with tribesmen, who fired away much ammunition but only killed one sepoy and one battery mule.

At dawn on the 21st July, after opening a heavy fire on the piquets to the west of the camp, a body of about 150 tribesmen under the leadership of Halil Khan made a most determined attack and tried to break through between two piquets. These piquets had to be reinforced from camp by two successive half-companies, of which the first suffered six casualties before it succeeded in driving the enemy back at the point of the bayonet. After this, however, the enemy retired under the effective fire of the British, taking their wounded and many of their dead with them. In the captured position was found the dead body of Halil Khan, who had the reputation of being the finest fighter in Sarhad. Firing ceased altogether about 10 a.m. and after that, except for one small body sighted moving off in an easterly direction, nothing further was seen of the enemy. In the afternoon reports were received that Jiand and his men were retiring northward and the Gamshadzais to the south-eastward. The enemy had evidently lost so heavily that he had no stomach for further fighting. General Dyer's own casualties had been surprisingly small, only amounting to 5 killed and 6 wounded during the whole three days' fighting.

Sarhad ; July 1916. That day General Dyer heard that the Makran Mission under Major T. H. Keyes, with its escort of 250 rifles (1/7th Gurkhas and 127th Baluchis), which had left Mand on the 24th June to tour Persian Baluchistan, had arrived on the 18th July at Sib, forty miles south of Gusht. It would have to remain at Sib, to await the arrival of supplies, till the 23rd, when Major Keyes proposed to advance and meet General Dyer at Gusht. General Dyer, however, felt that it was advisable for him to follow up the retreating tribesmen at once. He decided therefore to march to Dast Kird and thence to Khwash to replenish his supplies before returning to Gusht.

On the 22nd July his column carried out a long and very trying march to Gaz. The piquetting duties were arduous, owing to the height and the broken nature of the surrounding hills, and there was scarcely any water. Of the retreating enemy the only signs were the numerous blood tracks of his wounded. At dawn on the 23rd the advance was resumed and, before reaching camp at Bandaran, about 10,000 sheep were captured. These apparently constituted the entire Damani stock ; and as, in Sarhad, success is gauged by the number of sheep captured rather than by human casualties, this showed how complete was the demoralisation of the enemy. The march was again a most arduous and trying one and the rear guard did not reach camp till 11.15 p.m. On the 24th advantage was taken of the existence of an excellent water supply, of good grazing and of plenty of fuel, to halt for the day, thus giving the tired men and exhausted transport animals a much needed rest. On the 25th the column crossed the Bandaran Pass to Sar-i-Drukan and again found the piquetting duties most arduous owing to the rugged and high hills on either flank. Next day the column left the valley, traversing the Dast Kird gorge to Gulas. This gorge, lying between precipitous and rugged heights, was in many places barely a hundred yards in width, affording a position which a few determined riflemen could defend easily against considerable numbers. Here again, an extraordinary number of piquets were required to secure the flanks. Khwash was reached on the 29th July, the last two marches proving so hot that about half the captured sheep died.

These operations between the 12th and 29th July had been a severe test for men and animals. Although after the 21st there was no fighting, the great heat, the lack of water and the extraordinary difficulty of the country made very great calls on the endurance of the troops. In testifying to the praiseworthy manner in which his men had responded, General Dyer especially commended the good work of Captain Lang, commanding the 106th Pioneers' detachment.

On reaching Khwash, General Dyer learnt that a party of twenty to thirty Damanis had attempted to raid the native population there the previous day, but that they had been driven off by a small party consisting of six sabres 28th Light Cavalry and twenty rifles 19th Punjabis and 106th Hazara Pioneers under 2nd Lieutenant A. B. Duncan. Seeing that the raiders were making off under the long range fire of the infantry, Lieutenant Duncan had gallantly charged into them with his six sowars, killing five of the enemy. In this charge Lieutenant Duncan himself and three of his men were wounded, but the infantry then came up and drove off the raiders, killing four more of them.

On the 2nd August, General Dyer left Khwash again, accompanied by Major Hutchinson and taking with him the same force as before (less one troop of cavalry), to meet Major Keyes at Gusht. The punishment inflicted on Jiand and the Yar Muhammadzais would probably suffice to keep them quiet for some time, but, as few of the Gamshadzais had been engaged in the Sar-i-Drukan operations, further action against them

Sarhad; August 1916.

Sarhad; August 1916. might be necessary. Gusht was reached on the 6th August and, after discussion of the situation with Majors Keyes and Hutchinson, General Dyer decided that he would move through the Gamshadzai country to Jalq, where the Gamshadzai chiefs were said to be ready to discuss terms of submission. Major Keyes and his mission would remain at Gusht to protect supplies and the sick.

Leaving Gusht on the 8th August, General Dyer with his column reached Jalq unopposed on the 13th after a trying and arduous march through difficult country. On the 15th his terms, namely the surrender of one hundred rifles and three hostages, as well as an agreement to sell General Dyer as many sheep as he might require for the winter rations of his force in Sarhad, were rejected by the Gamshadzai chiefs. These were then ordered to leave Jalq, as General Dyer proposed to move out and operate against the tribe till it submitted. But he heard that Major Keyes wished to return to Sib, both to secure supplies and to reassure the inhabitants of the country to the south of the Gusht-Jalq line, who were in a nervous and disturbed state owing to an influx of the Damanis who had evacuated Sarhad in consequence of General Dyer's operations. He also received instructions from India that though his operations in Sarhad should be continued till they ensured a reasonable prospect of peace, the Government of India desired to withdraw their troops from that area as soon as the Germans had been dealt with and political arrangements had been made to control the border. General Dyer himself was to locate his headquarters as soon as possible in the Robat-Saindak-Kacha area, where he would be in a better position to carry out his main object, which was the capture of German parties re-entering Persia from Afghanistan. General Dyer consequently started his return to Gusht on the afternoon of the 15th August, proceeding to Sinukan. There, however, hearing from Major Keyes that he had sufficient supplies to last him at Gusht till the 21st, General Dyer decided to return rapidly to Jalq, where some Gamshadzai fighting men were said to be harboured in a fort. With a portion of his force he made a night march and surrounded the fort before dawn on the 16th, capturing five Gamshadzais and some cattle. In the fort were also many Gamshadzai women and children, and these expressed great surprise when they learnt that General Dyer had no intention of holding them captive. General Dyer then marched back via Gusht to Khwash, where he arrived on the 24th August and was obliged a few days later to apply to

India to be relieved on account of ill-health. Major Keyes and his mission moved to Sib, where the Gamshadzais approached him for terms of submission but again rejected those offered.

While these events had been taking place in Sarhad, the troops holding the cordon in Seistan and Kain under Colonel Dale had maintained a vigilant watch for members of the German mission from Kabul re-entering Persia. Several reports, more or less reliable, were received during July, which indicated that different portions of the mission were making for Bokhara, Trans-Caspia, Yarkand, and Herat respectively.* But though Paschen succeeded in penetrating the Russian line to the north of Birjand, there were no attempts to pass through the British line till, early in August, Captain A. D. Wise with some levies captured Voigt and two Indians at Sehdeh.

<small>East Persia; July–August 1916.</small>

During July and August raids from across the Afghan border continued to be made against the Nushki–Robat line of communication, which was controlled by the General Officer Commanding the Quetta Division ; and these necessitated the reinforcement of the half squadron Gwalior Lancers and half battalion 126th Baluchis, guarding the line, by the other half battalion of the latter regiment.

Supplies for the forces in East Persia had always been a difficulty. As far as possible they were obtained locally, mainly from Seistan, but much had to be brought from Quetta. Their transport from Quetta, their collection from Seistan, and their distribution to the various detachments along the 400-mile line from Birjand to Khwash required a very large number of camels. But among these the lack of grazing and the desert nature of the country had caused very great wastage. On the 27th June General Dyer, in answer to a request from India, placed his total transport requirements, excluding animals required for the part of the line controlled by Quetta, at 4,600 camels. Of these, 2,000 were required to distribute supplies to the normal detachments, 1,000 for building up a supply reserve at Kacha and 1,600 for allotment to posts to give their garrisons the necessary mobility. General Dyer pointed out that, except at Birjand and Khwash, all the posts suffered in a varying degree from immobility, due to lack of reserve supplies or transport, or both. Measures were accordingly taken to increase the number of camels in East Persia, but, having regard to their transport requirements elsewhere, the military authorities in India found it impossible to provide

---

* The actual movements of the Mission members have already been given in Chapter IV.

and maintain the numbers which the situation required. This led them to apply to Government for the extension westwards of the Quetta–Nushki railway.

Nushki railway extension. They pointed out that the recent Turkish advance into West Persia might compel the increase of the force which Turco-German plans to bring Persia and Afghanistan into the war had made it necessary for us to employ in East Persia. The maintenance of this force by animal transport alone had always been a very difficult matter, and the recent demands could not be met without drawing on the camel transport reserved to meet the case of operations on the North-West Frontier of India. Therefore, if the existing force was not to be reduced, the communications must be improved. At one time it had been hoped that mechanical transport would meet the situation. But experience and further investigation had shown that the distances involved were too great and the improvement of the waterless road too difficult to make it a reliable communication, even if the 250 motor lorries required could be made available without interfering with more important demands elsewhere. As the maintenance of the existing force was dangerously near a breakdown and the feasibility of a steady and sufficient mechanical transport service was so doubtful, the provision of a light railway had been considered. But the railway authorities in India was of opinion that the extension of the broad gauge railway from Nushki, for which material was available, would be the most economical and satisfactory solution. The extension of the railway (120 miles) to Dalbandin, which was the most difficult section of the route for animals and lorries, then the employment of mechanical transport to Mushki Chah (130 miles), and thence animals to Robat was suggested as the most practical solution.

On the 26th July the Government of India addressed the Secretary of State for India on the subject. After giving the military reasons for the project as set out above, they also said that, if the strategical situation compelled us to strengthen our hold on South Persia, this railway extension would become essential. But they wished to make it clear that the scheme could not, for the time being, be supported on commercial or political grounds. They were uncertain of the cost and would experience some inconvenience in providing the material for the permanent way. In fact, it was only on cogent military grounds that the scheme could be justified and it was for H.M. Government to decide whether these existed. In any case they deprecated any limitation of the extension to Dalbandin as a half measure calculated neither to give speedy or adequate relief to the existing situation nor to meet the wider strategical considerations which they trusted might not arise.

During August the transport situation became critical, owing almost entirely to the strain caused by the requirements of the troops in Sarhad. General Dyer had increased his estimate of the number of camels required in his command to 5,600, as well as monthly drafts of at least 250 to replace wastage. At this period he had a total of about 1,800 camels in East Persia, while there were about 5,000 working between Nushki and Saindak; and the authorities, who were hard put to it to keep up even this number of animals, had to warn General Dyer of the imperative necessity for economy.

There had, in the meantime, been further telegraphic discussion between London and Simla regarding the Nushki railway extension. The Chief of the Imperial General Staff, whose opinion had been asked by the India Office for the information of the War Committee of the Cabinet, considered that the maintenance, and possibly the increase, of the force in Seistan was necessary. But, though he expressly qualified his opinion by the statement that his knowledge of the situation was limited, he did not consider the railway extension to be a cogent military necessity, as he favoured the use of mechanical transport and the improvement of the road for that purpose. The Commander-in-Chief in India then telegraphed direct to the Chief of the Imperial General Staff and informed him that owing to the lack of water it had been found impracticable to make a water-bound Macadam road and it was doubtful if the substitute being tried would stand wear. If it did, 250 motor lorries would be required and, as there was no reserve of vehicles or personnel in India, these would have to be supplied and renewed by the War Office. On the other hand, railway material and personnel could be made available at once from Indian resources and the number of lorries required for the Dalbandin-Mushki Chah section would be only 75, of which 33 were already available or in sight. A breakdown in the maintenance of the existing force by animal transport was dangerously near, and would be certain if the force had to be increased or to extend its radius of action. This explanation satisfied the Chief of the Imperial General Staff, and on his advice the War Committee of the Cabinet approved, on the 22nd August, the railway extension to Dalbandin as an urgent war measure.

West Persia and the general situation; July 1916. In West Persia, after several days' serious fighting in which both sides suffered considerable casualties, the Turks occupied Kermanshah on the 1st July, driving the Russians back towards Hamadan. At Tehran the news of this Turkish success created much alarm, which was not lessened by the information that the British community had been warned by the Russians to be ready to leave Hamadan. On the 5th July, Sir Charles Marling* reported to the Foreign Office that the Turks, who were in considerable numerical superiority, might possibly reach Hamadan in three or four days' time and that if they made Tehran their objective there would be no force to oppose them. To prevent Tehran from falling into Turkish hands it seemed, to him and the Russian Minister, essential to enlist the considerable moral influence which the Persian Government still possessed by means of an alliance. This would, he believed, secure the loyalty of the Bakhtiaris, which might enable us to retain some hold of South Persia and should also make it possible to harry the Turkish line of communication. Though this would not be a very great result, an alliance would also probably prevent the instalment of a Democrat Cabinet, under which almost all Persia would become actively hostile. The whole political situation, said Sir Charles Marling, had been turned upside down by the Russian retirement and it was imperative to take any and every step to hold Tehran and to save the situation until the British force on the Tigris could advance in the autumn or till the Russians were sufficiently reinforced.

The Foreign Office, however, replied at once that the situation was hardly favourable for pushing the treaty negotiations on satisfactory terms and it did not appear how these could materialise into active opposition to the Turks. Sir Charles Marling could, however, take such financial measures as he might think desirable to secure action on the part of the Persian Government, the Bakhtiaris or any tribal force that could be utilised. It is to be noted that the General Staff at the War Office, in their weekly military appreciation submitted on the 6th August for the information of the Government, concluded that there was as yet no reason to anticipate that the Turks, whose line of communication was lengthening, would reach Tehran. Their strength was estimated at about 16,000, while it was understood that Baratoff's force of about 11,000 would be reinforced in eight days' time by another 4,000. The Russians could hold a strong defensive position at Hamadan, and the

---
* He had just been made a K.C.M.G.

shortening of their line of communication would facilitate supply and lessen the difficulties recently caused by depredations of Kurds.

The alteration in the situation which Sir Charles Marling's telegram disclosed caused, however, considerable apprehension at Simla, as the opening of the road eastwards through Persia to even small enemy parties would render the position in Afghanistan very serious ; and the Commander-in-Chief in India telegraphed to the Chief of the Imperial General Staff on the 5th July suggesting that the situation in Persia called for a British offensive on the Tigris, where it was possible that the Turks had reduced their strength in order to concentrate against Baratoff. But General Lake in Mesopotamia telegraphed that he did not regard the situation, from a military point of view, as seriously as the Tehran telegram painted it. The Turks would have to halt to reorganise their line of communication before they could think of advancing to Tehran, even if they did occupy Hamadan, and Baratoff was believed to have over 12,000 men and 26 guns, excluding detachments on his communications, while at the most the Turkish strength could not be more than 18,700 men and 45 guns. Further, said General Lake, anything but a strictly limited British offensive on the Tigris was precluded by the intense heat and his supply difficulties. The Chief of the Imperial General Staff replied to India that he saw no reason to issue any further instructions to General Lake, who evidently did not consider an offensive feasible.*

A few days later the Russian Grand Duke Nicholas asked the Chief of the Imperial General Staff if the British in Mesopotamia could bring pressure to bear on the Persian tribes to the south of the Khaniqin–Kermanshah line to induce them to abandon their hostility to the Russians. The Russian Government were also invoking the assistance of the Persian Government, as, if the Kurds could be persuaded to assist the Allies, the Turks would find it impossible to maintain their long line of communication. The Chief of the Imperial General Staff consequently telegraphed on the 17th July to General Lake informing him of the Russian request, regarding which the Foreign Office was communicating with Sir Charles Marling. Sir William Robertson also asked General Lake whether it would be feasible and desirable to send, from Mesopotamia, a small mixed force to Isfahan through the Bakhtiari country, as its presence would

---

* For further details of this discussion see Official History of the War Mesopotamia Campaign, Vol. III., pp. 19–20.

West Persia; July 1916.

influence not only the Kurds through the Bakhtiaris but also the South Persian tribes. General Lake replied on the 22nd that the movement suggested was practicable though difficult. Apart, however, from the disadvantages of detaching this small force beyond support, it was unlikely to influence the Kurds or to have any useful effect in South Persia. Its maintenance would depend much on the Bakhtiaris, whose attitude towards us was only favourable as long as they thought that we stood between them and their domination by the Russians or others hostile to them. Consequently, if they thought that the force was being sent to assist the Russians in establishing Zil-es-Sultan,* they might prove hostile, with unfortunate results both to the detachment and to our cause. In view of these factors the project seemed to General Lake to be undesirable. Steps were being taken, he said, which would, he hoped, influence most of the tribes concerned except the Kalhurs, who were for the most part pro-Turkish. In view of this opinion the Chief of the Imperial General Staff dropped the proposal.

Baratoff's retreat from Kermanshah naturally encouraged the anti-Ally elements in Tehran, and the consequent intrigues did much to lessen the influence and authority of the Cabinet. On the other hand, these political results brought home to the Russian Government the necessity for a settlement of the outstanding questions of military police forces and of financial assistance to the Persian Government; and in the middle of July the Russian Minister received the necessary instructions to push the negotiations.

As the month progressed and the Turks made no attempt to advance beyond Kermanshah, the situation at Tehran improved somewhat. But in the Bakhtiari country an influx of enemy emissaries† and of fanatical volunteers, whose propaganda met with considerable success, combined with the Russian retreat to give the German cause a great impetus. In the third week

---

* This great-uncle of the Shah, who had previously great influence in Persia and had been banished at the time of the revolution, had recently been allowed to re-enter the country in the hope that he could help the Allied cause, especially among the Bakhtiaris. It appears, however, that his former stern and savage rule had caused him to be hated and feared by the Persians generally and especially by many of the Bakhtiari Khans; that the Shah regarded him as a possible rival to the throne; that his age and the deterioration of his mental faculties rendered him incapable of re-establishing his former influence and position; and that, in effect, his reappearance had given the enemy agents excellent material for anti-Ally propaganda.

† Some Germans who had remained there after Baratoff's successful advance were being forced by the Bakhtiari Khans to leave when news of the fall of Kermanshah arrived. They then stood fast and started recruiting a force to take Isfahan.

of July the situation had so deteriorated that a force, composed largely of Bakhtiaris, attacked a small Russian detachment near Isfahan, though, fortunately, without success.

Throughout July British information regarding the situation at Shiraz was rather indefinite. Farman Farma had sent his deputy* there to take over charge, but there appeared to be friction between him and Qawam. Saulat was discontented and was intriguing with the German prisoners; and though Sir C. Marling had faith in the Deputy Governor's ability to prevent German trouble, the latter had only the loyal gendarmerie to support him. Telegraphing on the 9th July, the British Minister said that there were as yet no indications of the effect in Fars of the Russian retreat, but he recommended that Colonel Gough should at once leave Isfahan without waiting for Farman Farma and proceed to Shiraz, where the hands of the Deputy Governor would be much strengthened by his presence. Farman Farma left Tehran on his way south on the 14th July, but it was arranged that Colonel Gough should not wait for him and should start from Isfahan on the 1st August; as his presence at Shiraz seemed urgently required to put an end to the many local intrigues there. Qawam and the Deputy Governor at Shiraz were, however, unable to provide the necessary escort in time; and at the end of July it was arranged that Colonel Gough and five British officers for the South Persia Rifles, who were due at Isfahan from Ahwaz on the 12th August, should leave Isfahan two days later, by which time an escort also would be available.

Shiraz;
July 1916.

Sir Percy Syke's supply and transport arrangements for his march from Kerman to Yezd took some time, and it was not till the 27th July that he was able to start. His column, consisting of one squadron 15th Lancers, one section 23rd Mountain Battery and a half-battalion 124th Baluchis, totalled some 500 fighting men with a transport train comprising 140 mules, 540 camels and nearly 200 donkeys. Four days previously the new British consul (Major D. G. R. Lorimer) had reached Kerman from Bandar Abbas, his caravan having been attacked and partially plundered near Daulatabad by a band of Baharlu

Kerman;
July 1916.

---

* Sir P. Sykes in his "History of Persia" says that this deputy was notoriously corrupt and began to "squeeze" when it was particularly unwise to do so.

tribesmen, whose constant raids in this vicinity were giving considerable cause for anxiety. Major G. L. Farran was left in military charge at Kerman, with the escort of twenty-five of the Central India Horse and about forty sick Indian details, to continue the enrolment and training of men in the South Persia Rifles. By this time about 250 men had been enrolled at Kerman, where Major Farran had only two British officers and a small number of Indian instructors to assist him. Sir Percy Sykes, however, reported that as soon as this instructional staff was increased the strength at Kerman could be rapidly raised to about 1,000. About 150 men had also been enrolled at Bandar Abbas, though for the time being no further increase there was to be expected. In addition to instructors for the South Persia Rifles, Sir Percy Sykes also asked for drafts to maintain his strength of regulars; and these were ordered by India to be sent from Mesopotamia to Bandar Abbas.

Anglo-Russian Agreement with the Persian Government; August 1916. After the Russian Government authorised their Minister at Tehran to conclude the agreement with Persia, there was little further delay in the matter. The Prime Minister, Sipahsalar, who owed his position to Russian support, placed no difficulties in the way; and on the 7th August his Government sent a satisfactory reply to the joint note presented two days previously by the British and Russian Ministers. The proposal for the gradual formation of forces of 22,000* military police under British and Russian instructors under the orders of the Persian Ministry of War was accepted. The Persian Government would, however, maintain another force at Tehran and also, until the new forces were formed, gendarmerie. The grant of extended powers over the national finances by the Mixed Commission was agreed to, subject to the proviso that they would not be retrospective; and the monthly subsidy of 200,000 tomans was gratefully accepted with the hope that the Mixed Commission would soon be able to secure payment of taxes by foreigners. In conclusion it was stated that these measures would be submitted for approval to the National Assembly and the Senate when those bodies met.

Sir Charles Marling was much surprised that the Cabinet had dared to accept terms which must obviously be most unpopular, especially as Baratoff's force, whose reinforcements had not yet reached it, had been obliged by Turkish pressure to fall back to a position at Asadabad, about fifteen miles to

---

*i.e., each force, 11,000.

the west of Hamadan. As Sir Charles Marling reported to the Foreign Office, a great opportunity had been lost in the last few months for concluding an agreement that would have set the future British and Russian relations with Persia on a new and practical basis. The Russian Minister also realised this, but the Russian Government had gradually withdrawn, one by one, the concessions to Persia which had been originally contemplated and which, as they affected Russian interests more than British, only concerned Sir C. Marling to the extent that he had to obtain for himself a repetition of the assurances given to his colleague that the Persian Government accepted these successive amputations without demur.

On the 9th August Baratoff's force at Asadabad was attacked by the Turks and driven back, with the result that the Turks occupied Hamadan on the 10th and the Russians, leaving the bulk of their cavalry and guns on the Kara Chai river (twenty miles to the north-east of Hamadan) to watch the Turks, withdrew their infantry to take up a position on the Sultan Bulag pass. On the 11th Sir Charles Marling reported that in view of the possibility of this position being forced, when Tehran would be virtually isolated by the threatened cutting of its communications at Kazvin, he would be glad of immediate instructions. The Legation and British colony might remain in Tehran, awaiting developments, or retire either to Meshed or to Resht, though the transport difficulties would be very great. This telegram drew a strong protest from the Viceroy of India, who, considering that the retirement of the Legations would have most disastrous effects, not only in Persia but in Afghanistan, trusted that they might be instructed to stand fast. Sir Charles Marling replied at once that the British Legation would of course stay till the last moment. But he did not think that its departure then would create any worse impression than its virtual capture two or three days later.* The Russian Legation would hardly be able to remain, owing to the fact that the Russians had previously captured and deported the Turkish Ambassador.

West and Central Persia; August 1916.

On the 12th August, Sipahsalar was informed by the Shah that he had selected Vossuk-ud-Daula to form a new Cabinet. Although it had taken office with better prospects than almost any recent Persian Government, Sipahsalar's Cabinet being

---
* Though British women and children left Tehran for Resht about the 16th August, no necessity arose for the men to leave.

labelled Russian had never been popular. This it might have outlived had it taken any steps to improve the state of the country or to lessen the corruption in the public administration. But its succession of stupid blunders in the conduct of domestic affairs and its complete subservience to Russia in the domain of foreign politics gave its numerous enemies the opportunities they desired to influence the mind of the Shah and public opinion. The climax came when, at the moment that the Russian military situation was becoming precarious, the Cabinet accepted terms from Great Britain and Russia which amounted to a virtual administrative partition of the country.

Sir Charles Marling was of opinion that he would find Vossuk-ud-Daula far easier to deal with and quite as friendly as Sipahsalar. Vossuk's political views were moderate, and the extremist advisers of the Shah put such difficulties in his way that it was not until the end of the month that he was able to form a Cabinet. During this delay the whole political situation was most uncertain. Colonel Kennion, the British consul-designate for Kermanshah, reported from Kazvin on the 14th August that Baratoff meant to hold the Sultan Bulag pass and that though, in Colonel Kennion's personal opinion, the Turks were strong enough to take it, he did not think they would risk a further advance so far from their base. They would trust, he thought, to the pro-German element in the country to bring about a revolution. He also said that Baratoff did not intend to withdraw the eight hundred Russian Cossacks and two guns then occupying Isfahan.

The Sykes Mission; August 1916. On the 14th August Sir Percy Sykes with his small column of Indian troops reached Yezd, where they were cordially received. Though the whole country was infested by robber bands, his march had been carried out without special incident. Learning of the Turkish occupation of Hamadan and the possible evacuation of Tehran by the Allied Legations and colonies before reaching Yezd, he had telegraphed (on the 12th) to India suggesting that the serious nature of the situation rendered it desirable to send reinforcements of Indian troops to Kerman, in which province the exaggerated reports of Turkish successes had caused much unrest, aggravated by the constant raids of the Baharlus.*

West and Central Persia; August 1916. On the 14th Sir Charles Marling reported, first that Baratoff had telegraphed to the Russian Minister advising partial

---

* This suggestion, which had originated from the British consul at Kerman on the 9th, had also been strongly urged by Sir Charles Marling on the 11th August.

evacuation of Tehran and Isfahan and describing the situation as serious; and, then, that the British military attaché who had just returned from the front agreed with Colonel Kennion that, though the Turks were strong enough to drive the Russians from Sultan Bulag, they were unlikely to advance beyond Hamadan. Sir Charles Marling, however, saw in this a Turkish intention of advancing on Tehran direct or by Qum. That day at Yezd, Sir Percy Sykes discussed the situation over the telephone with Mr. Grahame and Colonel Gough at Isfahan and with Sir Charles Marling at Tehran. As a result, he telegraphed next day to India that he considered that his march to Shiraz should be postponed, and that his column should protect Yezd and Kerman and be ready to help Isfahan. Farman Farma, it may be noted, had reached Isfahan on the 9th August and Colonel Gough proposed leaving with him for Shiraz on the 18th.

For the next fortnight a considerable telegraphic discussion between Tehran, Simla and London ensued regarding the immediate movements of the Sykes column. Sir Charles Marling was afraid that the German prisoners at Shiraz would effect their escape and the situation in Fars collapse unless Farman Farma and Colonel Gough proceeded there at once. But he considered that the risks of their doing so were immense unless they were accompanied by the column under Sir P. Sykes. On the other hand, Colonel Gough and the British consul at Isfahan, Sir Percy Sykes and the political and military authorities in India were all in favour of acceding to the request of the Russians at Isfahan that the column should proceed there. It appeared to them that, by securing Isfahan against any tribal ebullitions and against anything but a larger number of troops than the Turks seemed likely or able to divert from Hamadan, the situation in Fars as well as in Yezd and Kerman would be favourably influenced. Moreover, the shortest British line of communication with Isfahan would be from Mesopotamia via Ahwaz and the Lynch road, thus influencing the Bakhtiaris. Farman Farma was willing to accompany Colonel Gough at once to Shiraz, and the latter considered the advantage of their presence there to be well worth any risk to himself and the five Europeans who would accompany him. Sir Charles Marling, however, still held to his opinion, especially as the danger to Isfahan seemed to be lessening with the Turks showing no signs of advancing beyond Hamadan and Baratoff's position beginning to improve with the arrival of reinforcements. The question was finally solved by Colonel Gough leaving Isfahan for Shiraz with Farman Farma on the 24th August, during a period when an interruption of telegraphic communication with Tehran left him in ignorance of the British Minister's objections. On the 28th Sir Percy Sykes with his column also left Yezd for Isfahan, under orders from the India Office; and when—at the request of the Foreign Office—he was told to proceed instead direct to Shiraz, it was found that his supply arrangements made it quicker for him to go first to Isfahan.

The Sykes Column at Yezd; August 1916. On arrival at Yezd Sir P. Sykes had found that the depredations of locusts and the insecurity of the roads had brought about such a scarcity of supplies as to cause him much anxiety. Caravans had been held up by well-armed large robber bands on every side, till Yezd resembled a besieged city. Some of these bands stopped a caravan which was taking supplies for the Sykes column from Isfahan to Dehbid, and they attacked a detachment of fifteen Indian sowars (of the Isfahan consulate guard) and twenty Russian Cossacks escorting 350 mules purchased at Isfahan for the South Persia Rifles, first at Kuh Pa, about fifty miles east of Isfahan, and then at Aghda, about sixty miles north-west of Yezd. For his gallantry in beating off the first of these attacks Lieutenant Kolominski, commanding the Cossack detachment, was awarded the British Military Cross; while, to relieve the escort at Aghda, Major S. M. Bruce with his squadron of the 15th Lancers covered sixty-two miles from Yezd in about eighteen consecutive hours, i.e., travelling from about midnight till dark. On the 18th August Sir Percy Sykes recommended the location of a detachment of British troops at Yezd, both to render the British position at Kerman secure and to offer a rallying post to British refugees from Isfahan. But the Government of India did not approve.

Kerman; August 1916. Before leaving Kerman, Sir Percy Sykes had made arrangements for a party of twenty-three enemy prisoners,* who were at Saidabad in charge of a Persian official with a guard of fifty Persians, to be handed over at Daulatabad to a detachment of forty-two rifles, 108th Infantry, who had left Bandar Abbas for that place on the 22nd July.† But the threatening attitude of the Baharlus and the sickness of some of the prisoners prevented their start from Saidabad. On the 7th August a party of drafts for the Sykes column (3 British officers and 130 Indians under Lieutenant A. D. Fraser, 15th Lancers) also

---

* Germans, Austrians and Obeidulla, the Turkish Envoy to Kabul.
† They had been sent from Muscat to Bandar Abbas for this duty.

ENEMY PRISONERS ESCAPE

left Bandar Abbas with a large convoy for Kerman; and on the 8th and 10th orders were sent from India, in view of the reports received of the unrest in Kerman province, to despatch a further eighty rifles from Muscat to Bandar Abbas, whence forty of them were to proceed to Baft. Here all three parties were to concentrate and, after withdrawing the prisoners from Saidabad, the eighty odd rifles from Muscat were to escort them back to Bandar Abbas. All concerned were warned of the importance of not allowing the prisoners to escape.

Before these movements were completed, however, the situation in the Kerman province deteriorated so greatly that Major Farran was obliged, with the concurrence of Sir Percy Sykes, to cease work on the organisation of the South Persia Rifles and to concentrate upon raising tribal levies for immediate service and upon other precautionary arrangements to render his position secure. At Saidabad the state of unrest was so marked that, after trying unsuccessfully to get the prisoners sent to Baft, Major Farran on the 19th August sent Captain J. N. Merrill* with nine of the South Persia Rifles and twenty Persian horsemen to Saidabad to carry this out. On his arrival at Saidabad, however, most of the prisoners and their Persian escort fled. The prisoners had been allowed to mix freely with the populace, who had become so affected by the exaggerated reports of the Turkish successes that Captain Merrill could obtain no assistance locally to enable him to pursue the prisoners. In fact, he found his own position to be difficult and somewhat dangerous. Nevertheless, he managed to raise some levies locally.

News of the prisoners' escape reached Lieutenant Fraser on the 25th and Major Farran on the 27th August. On the latter date Lieutenant Fraser's party was at Baft, which it had reached the previous day; forty-two rifles of the 108th Infantry were at Daulatabad; and the third party (under Captain L. C. Wagstaff) was due there on or about the 29th. Major Farran at once sent instructions down the road that the three parties were to concentrate at Baft, ready to move on Saidabad if necessary. But, though preparations for its erection had started, there was as yet no telegraph line along the road and messages took some time to reach their destination. So that some days before receiving Major Farran's order, Lieutenant Fraser had already come to the conclusion that the sooner he got to Kerman—with his large convoy of some 600 camels

---

* An American, formerly employed with the gendarmerie, who had been engaged in Persia to serve with the South Persia Rifles.

carrying guns, arms and ammunition for the South Persia Rifles as well as specie—the better. Major Farran concurred in this decision as soon as he heard of it, and on the 2nd September Lieutenant Fraser marched into Kerman with his convoy.

Bushire; July-August, 1916. The negotiations for the release of the British prisoners from Ahram took some time, but, after some hitches, the last of them, Lieutenant-Colonel O'Connor, was brought into Bushire on the 20th August. Beyond this, no incidents of importance occurred at Bushire during July and August. The 2/22nd Punjabis relieved the 11th Rajputs early in July, and in August the half-battalion 124th Baluchis at Bushire was expanded into a full battalion as the 2/124th.*

West and Central Persia; September 1916. The absence of any indication that the Turks intended to advance eastward from Hamadan and the improvement in the condition of Baratoff's force—which had been rested and its ranks refilled—combined, with the better political outlook caused by the formation at the end of August of a Cabinet (under Vossuk-ud-Daula) generally well disposed to the Allies, to exercise a tranquillising effect at Tehran. In the Isfahan area, however, a disquieting number of Bakhtiaris had joined the force raised by Turco-German agents and, though on the 2nd September they were decisively defeated to the west of Isfahan by the Russian garrison of that place, there was the possibility that the Turks might detach regular troops to assist this revolutionary movement. On the other hand, Captain Noel of the Indian Political Department had succeeded, under Sir Charles Marling's orders, in raising several hundred loyal Bakhtiari tribesmen, and these had pursued the defeated rebels with a success that promised to upset the German plans. In consequence of this rebel attack Sir Percy Sykes, at the request of the British consul, accelerated his march and reached Isfahan on the 11th September. Though his force had been too strong to be itself molested, it had seen constant evidence, on its way from Yezd, of the many large robber bands which had brought about absolute insecurity on the roads.

Fars situation; September 1916. In the meantime, Saulat, having met Farman Farma and Colonel Gough at Qumisheh with apparently satisfactory

---

* In December 1916 the 2/22nd Punjabis became the 22nd, replacing the battalion captured in Kut; and the half-battalion 124th Baluchis with Sir P. Sykes became first the 1/124th (half of it remaining in India) and then early in 1917 the 3/124th (only two companies strong without battalion headquarters).

PERSIAN OBJECTIONS TO FARMAN FARMA 205

results, had returned to Shiraz, while Farman Farma and Colonel Gough continued their march and reached Dehbid on the 7th September, having picked up the German prisoner Paschen at Abadeh and despatched him to Isfahan.* At Dehbid, however, Colonel Gough received a message announcing that Saulat, Qawam and the Persian commanding the gendarmerie at Shiraz absolutely refused, on account of the exactions of his deputy and of his own rapacity, to accept Farman Farma as Governor. They had arrested the deputy and had taken possession of the telegraph office at Shiraz. On learning of this development, Sir Charles Marling at once sent instructions to Colonel Gough to stand fast at Dehbid and arrange to secure his retreat to Isfahan. Accordingly, on the 15th September, after a few days' fruitless telegraphic negotiations with Saulat and Qawam, Colonel Gough with Farman Farma withdrew to Abadeh. On the 14th September Sir C. Marling reported that he suspected the obstructive movement at Shiraz to be directed as much against the Sykes Mission as against Farman Farma. It looked, therefore, he said, as if we must, for the time being, abandon the idea of action in Fars and use the Sykes column in connection with the Bakhtiari and Isfahan problem, bearing in mind that Colonel Gough and Farman Farma might themselves have to be relieved. On the other hand, Colonel Gough, who urged that the Sykes column should move to Shiraz as soon as possible, reported on the 18th that he learnt from many sources that it was really Farman Farma and his deputy, and not the British, who were objected to. In fact Farman Farma, he said, had suggested that the question might be solved by his exchanging appointments with the Governor of Kerman. Colonel Gough agreed with him, but Sir Charles Marling considered that Farman Farma's appointment to Fars was essential to British success in organising the South Persia Rifles. An explanation of this incident, which does not appear to have been known at the time, is given by the statement in Sir P. Sykes' "History of Persia," that Saulat had been estranged by Farman Farma's refusal at Qumisheh to confirm him as Il-Khan of the Qashqais unless he made Farman Farma a present of £10,000. This Saulat declined to do.

Sir Charles Marling's suggestion that Sir P. Sykes should remain at Isfahan was in accordance with the wishes of the Russians there, with Sir P. Sykes's own views and with those of the The Sykes Mission; September 1916.

---

* Here he managed on the night 13th/14th October to effect his escape from a guard of Indian troops.

The Sykes Mission; September 1916. of Captain Noel, who considered that their anti-Russian views and their fear lest the Russians should force Zil-es-Sultan on them were the main grounds for Bakhtiari disaffection. On the 16th and 20th September the Government of India also recommended that the Sykes column should remain at Isfahan to support the Russians. For the time being, the greatest danger to us in Persia, they said, seemed to lie in the German-Bakhtiari-Turkish threat to Isfahan, as if this materialised it might not only embarrass us in Mesopotamia but would imperil the security of the oil-fields in Arabistan. So long as the Bakhtiaris were kept quiet, any trouble at Shiraz would probably be purely local and might be left to the responsibility of Saulat and Qawam. Sir Percy Sykes should, however, be warned to avoid the possibility of any reverse and the Russians should be disabused of the idea they had formed that Sir Percy Sykes's column was to form part of Baratoff's force. It should be clearly explained to them that Sir Percy Sykes's proper rôle was to raise the South Persia Rifles. These views met with general acceptance at Tehran and in London.

Hitherto Sir P. Sykes had received his orders from the Government of India, who were responsible for the provision and maintenance of his regular troops and for a moiety of the expenditure, personnel and material required in raising the South Persia Rifles; and who would also be most certainly called upon to provide any regular reinforcements he required.* Though, as will be evident from the preceding narrative, previous discussions had shown the difficulty in reconciling the views of the Indian authorities with those of the British Minister at Tehran and the delay involved by this difficulty, the question of a change of the controlling authority did not arise till the beginning of September, when Sir P. Sykes asked India if he was to accept orders regarding the movements of his column direct from the Minister. Without expressing any opinion the Government of India referred the question to London, instancing recent orders which the Foreign Office had sent direct to Sir P. Sykes through the Minister. In reply, the India Office telegraphed on the 22nd September saying that, after discussion, they had accepted the Foreign Office view that to ensure unity of action Sir P. Sykes should take his orders from the Minister. The Government of India, were, however, to keep the Minister and the India Office fully informed of their

---

* During September various recommendations were made by the Minister at Tehran and Sir P. Sykes that more troops should be sent to Persia from India.

views. Accepting this decision, the Government of India then also ascertained that, although they were to retain general supervision of the South Persia Rifles, they were to take no action without previous consultation with the Minister, who was primarily responsible to H.M. Government for all political questions in connection with Persia.

The only road leading to Isfahan which the Russians there were able at this time to keep even reasonably safe was the one from Tehran. That part of the Lynch road from Ahwaz which lay within their tribal limits was safeguarded by the Bakhtiaris, but the last fifty miles into Isfahan were so infested by brigands as to be most insecure. The result was that during September a large amount of British merchandise had accumulated on the Bakhtiari side unable to pass the dangerous zone. It was accordingly decided to send out 3,000 empty camels under an escort furnished by the Sykes column and bring this merchandise in. This was duly effected, though the convoy was attacked on its return journey near Kawaruk on the 4th October by a large band of robbers. These, however, were driven off with loss, while the escort under Major Bruce* only suffered one casualty. *Isfahan; September–October 1916.*

At Shiraz, Saulat and Qawam, finding their hands forced by the unwillingness of the gendarmerie to wait any longer for the several months' arrears of pay which Colonel Gough alone was in a position to provide, withdrew their opposition to Farman Farma on the understanding that they were to be confirmed in the headship of their respective tribes. Consequently, on the 30th September, Colonel Gough reported that it would be perfectly safe for Farman Farma and himself to proceed to Shiraz, provided they were quickly followed by Sir P. Sykes with his column. Instructions were accordingly issued for these movements. *Shiraz; September 1916.*

Major Farran at Kerman, at the beginning of September, decided to move both the party of drafts under Lieutenant Fraser and the eighty odd rifles of the 108th Infantry under Captain Wagstaff to Saidabad, in the hope that their converging movement, from Kerman and Baft respectively, would bring about not only the capture of the German prisoners and their Persian adherents, who were at Balward (east of Saidabad), but would also have a salutary effect on the inhabitants of the *Kerman; September 1916.*

---

* The escort was composed of forty of the 15th Lancers, the section 23rd Mountain Battery, 150 rifles 1/124th Baluchis with two machine guns, and ten Russian Cossacks.

district. These two detachments left Kerman and Baft on the 6th and 7th September respectively, but the Germans* and their Persian companions under one Hussain Khan managed to slip away, their escape being much facilitated by the anti-British attitude of the populace. It was then decided that the combined detachments—totalling 27 Indian cavalry, 200 Indian infantry, a mountain gun manned by South Persia Rifles gunners and some levies—should remain temporarily at Saidabad under the command of Captain Wagstaff to aid in the restoration of order. This force encamped in a garden outside the town.

Capture of Saidabad; 28th September 1916. During the night 27th/28th September Hussain Khan with a mounted following of twenty to thirty armed men managed to enter the town and to induce two to three hundred of its armed inhabitants to join him and occupy its walls and towers. Next morning Captain Wagstaff proceeded to attack them. His men surrounded the town, and by the evening his infantry had worked up close to the walls and his mountain gun opened fire at a range of 250 yards. Hussain Khan and his mounted following, however, making a sudden dash for freedom, managed to effect their escape in the dusk. Further opposition then ceased and in the morning Captain Wagstaff occupied the town, where his force remained throughout October, During the fighting, in which his levies had kept well in the background, Captain Wagstaff's casualties had totalled ten—eight Indians and two Persians—while those in the town were estimated to be slightly larger.

Kerman; October 1916. During October, Democrat intrigues in Kerman town and the anti-British attitude of the tribesmen in the Kerman province both militated against a satisfactory improvement in the general situation. Consequently recruitment for the South Persia Rifles made little progress.

Reserve of Indian troops at Muscat; October–November 1916. During September, Sir Charles Marling and Sir Percy Sykes had both on several occasions suggested that more troops might be sent from India to aid in the restoration of order in Persia. The Government of India, with practically no troops to spare and averse from further commitments in Persia, did not agree; but as a precautionary measure they took steps to form a small reserve at Muscat for use in Persia if the need should arise. For this purpose they sent a half-battalion 83rd Infantry from India to relieve the 94th Infantry detachments in the Persian

---

* There were also many Austrians in the party.

Gulf ports and thus during October concentrated the 94th at Muscat. Here were also the 108th Infantry, less the detachments at Saidabad and Bandar Abbas. Four mountain guns were also held ready in India to proceed to Persia if necessary and the Chief of the Imperial General Staff was asked if he could spare some Indian cavalry from Egypt for the purpose. As, however, the situation in South Persia improved, the project was dropped and the 94th Infantry were withdrawn to India in November.

Farman Farma and Colonel Gough arrived at Shiraz on the 15th October and were well received. Saulat had left before their arrival, but Qawam's attitude and the bearing of the gendarmerie gave no apparent cause for anxiety. Meanwhile, owing to the prevailing scarcity in Fars, Sir Percy Sykes had been obliged to delay his departure from Isfahan till he had purchased sufficient wheat to feed his column at Shiraz. He left on the 20th October, reaching Shiraz on the 12th November.

Shiraz; October–December 1916.

On arrival, Farman Farma had at once taken over charge of the sixty odd enemy prisoners* at Shiraz, but at the end of October Seiler and two others managed to effect their escape. As it appeared to Farman Farma and Colonel Gough that lawlessness and anti-British activity were decreasing, Sir Charles Marling proposed that Sir P. Sykes should escort the prisoners to Kazerun and hand them over to a British column to be sent for the purpose from Bushire. Although at the end of October General Maude in Mesopotamia had felt justified in withdrawing the 2/124th Baluchis from Bushire, neither the political nor military authorities there agreed that either the anti-British sentiments or the rebellious attitude to the Persian Government of the Khans of Borazjan, Chah Kutah and Tangistan had changed for the better; and they were consequently of opinion that a British force sent to escort the prisoners from Kazerun would have to be of some strength. General Maude, advised by Sir Percy Cox, held the same opinion and, as he did not consider the time propitious for an expedition to Kazerun, suggested that the prisoners should be sent to Basra via Isfahan and Ahwaz. The Chief of the Imperial General Staff also agreed that any military commitment in the Bushire area was, for the time being, undesirable; but he left the question of the prisoners for the Commander-in-Chief in India and General Maude to decide between them.

---
* 15 Germans, 31 Austrians, 2 Swedes, 8 Turks and about 12 Afghans or Pathans.

Shiraz; October–December 1916. The Government of India then intervened and on the 24th November informed the India Office that, as neither they nor General Maude could provide an adequate force to proceed from Bushire and as in view of the past numerous escapes it seemed undesirable to send the prisoners via Isfahan and Ahwaz, it was considered that they should remain for the time being at Shiraz under a guard of Indian regulars. The Viceroy also said that the proposal had led them to review the whole situation in the Bushire–Shiraz area and they had come to the conclusion that the hostile Khans might now be prepared to make such submission as we could honourably accept. The Government of India favoured a policy of clemency towards these chiefs which, though it might savour of weakness, might go further to effect a permanent peaceful settlement than isolated military operations in a difficult country. This telegram crossed one from Sir Percy Sykes saying that Farman Farma proposed that he, with some Persians and accompanied by Sir P. Sykes with his column, should in January 1917 march down the Bushire road so as to re-establish Persian authority and reopen the road. He felt confident of success. As both Sir Percy Cox and Sir Charles Marling deprecated any idea of negotiating with the recalcitrant Khans and thought it preferable to allow Farman Farma and Sir Percy Sykes to open the road in their own way, H.M. Government decided that the proposals from India could not be sanctioned.

South Persia Rifles; November–December 1916. On Sir Percy Sykes's arrival at Shiraz he at once took over, for incorporation in the South Persia Rifles, such of the gendarmerie as remained in Fars. This had been previously agreed to by the Persian authorities, and Farman Farma concurred in the arrangement, though so far the Persian Government had failed to take any steps to ratify the agreement made by their predecessors in August for the formation of a military police force by the British. Lacking this official recognition Sir Percy Sykes was in a difficult position, but fortunately Farman Farma was friendly and helpful and quite appreciated the realities of the situation. The majority of the gendarmerie also welcomed the idea of getting paid regularly, though a considerable minority resented the inauguration of an orderly era which promised to put an end to illegal perquisites. Sir Percy Sykes still continued to press for official recognition, and on the 11th December Sir Charles Marling telegraphed to him that there were the usual intrigues on foot at Tehran to overthrow the Government and that the Prime Minister was afraid to furnish further material for anti-Government agitation by taking any open step in execution of the August agreement. He had, however, promised the British Minister to find some formula to convey the necessary instructions to Farman Farma. In the meantime Sir Percy Sykes should continue to act as if the position had been regularised. The promised formula took the form some ten days later of a long telegram from the Government to Farman Farma which, while it ostensibly censured him for allowing Sir Percy Sykes to exercise greater powers than were admissible under the August agreement, was really intended, and accepted by everyone concerned, as official recognition of the South Persia Rifles.

The organisation which Sir Percy Sykes aimed at—and for which it was arranged to send him the necessary British officers, non-commissioned officers and material—was as follows :—

Fars Brigade : 800 cavalry, 1,600 infantry, 18 guns and 6 machine guns.
Kerman Brigade : 400 cavalry, 800 infantry and 12 guns.
Bandar Abbas Area : 400 cavalry, 800 infantry and 6 guns.

On the 1st December he reported that the strength of the force, including levies and ex-gendarmerie, was then :—

Fars area : 450 cavalry, 2,000 infantry, 2 guns and a machine gun.
Kerman area : 550 cavalry, 550 infantry and 4 guns.
Bandar Abbas : 50 cavalry and 100 infantry.

Since October there had been an increasingly noticeable revival of caravan traffic on the Bushire–Shiraz road, and one of Sir Percy Sykes's British officers visited Kazerun in November to make the necessary arrangements for incorporating the gendarmerie there in the South Persia Rifles. These appear to have been the main reasons why Farman Farma, Colonel Gough and Sir P. Sykes regarded the situation in that direction as favourable. It is true that Saulat's attitude was doubtful, but Farman Farma, who had every reason to suspect him, apparently did not do so and advised Colonel Gough to treat him in friendly fashion so long as he behaved correctly. In December, however, events occurred which showed that their optimism was premature and that, as subsequently ascertained, Saulat had been actively engaged in plotting against the Farman Farma régime. On the 17th December the South Persia Rifles detachment at Kazerun was treacherously attacked, stripped and turned out by Nasir Diwan, the Kalandar or headman of Kazerun, who also seized and imprisoned the local governor. Other posts on the Shiraz side were attacked

Shiraz; November–December 1916.

simultaneously and there was reason to believe that Wassmuss and the rebel Khans of the Bushire hinterland, if not Saulat and others, were involved in a well organised plot. Sir Percy Sykes telegraphed that he proposed to move out at once with a column to Kazerun and intimated that he might have to call for assistance from Bushire, which Sir Charles Marling also asked might be authorised at once. Colonel Gough then reported that the rising had been organised in Shiraz by Qawam's chief adviser (though probably without Qawam's knowledge) and some gendarmerie officers and that probably Saulat and Wassmuss were also both involved.*

On the 21st December, after some fighting, the rebels captured the South Persia Rifles post at Dasht-i-Arjan and took its garrison prisoners. Sir Percy Sykes then telegraphed to India that both Colonel Gough and he considered that the situation called for the movement of a strong column from Bushire. In the meantime, the military authorities had already asked General Maude for his views regarding a column from Bushire. He replied that he could of course send the necessary troops, but only at the expense of the operations he had just commenced on the Tigris, and, as it would take time to prepare a force, he asked for early instructions. It was to be regretted, he said, that at such a time Sir Percy Sykes should have sent out detachments in a partially unsettled country and so invite their capture.

Sir Percy Sykes had by this time decided that the possibility that Qawam might be involved rendered it advisable that he himself should remain with part of his column at Shiraz. The column which he sent out in the Kazerun direction met with considerable opposition and was not successful. Its operations will be narrated in the next chapter.

Kerman; November–December 1916. During November and December the situation in the Kerman province improved as tribal lawlessness decreased. Qawam intended in the near future to move with his Khamseh tribesmen against the Baharlu robber bands between Shiraz and the Bandar Abbas–Kerman road, and it was decided that in the meantime Captain Wagstaff's detachment should remain at Saidabad. A telegraph line was being laid between Bandar Abbas and Kerman via Daulatabad and Baft, and Major E. T. Rich, R.E., of the Survey of India arrived at Bandar Abbas in November with a small party to survey a route suitable for the

---

* Subsequently another explanation came to our knowledge; see Chapter VIII, pp. 297–8.

construction of a motor road. He reported in December that one through the Tang-i-Zindan defile would be prohibitive in cost and that he was seeking for an alternative route.

At the end of October a Turkish force from Hamadan of about ten battalions with sixteen guns had attempted to advance eastward, but after driving back the Russian outposts had been forced by the Russians to retire again.* Reports were current in November that there was much sickness among the Turkish troops and that they were very short of supplies owing to difficulties on their long line of communications and to something approaching famine conditions in the Hamadan area. It was also reported that owing to these factors the Turkish commander had broached the possibility of a Turkish retirement to the local Persian Democrats, who had objected strongly and had informed the Turks that if they attempted to do so they would be attacked by Persian tribesmen, between whom and the Turks relations were already strained. There were other persistent reports that the Turks had definite orders to retire from Hamadan, but these were not confirmed and General Maude's information showed that reinforcing drafts had been reaching Hamadan steadily for the last two months. General Baratoff had orders that as soon as he learnt that the British on the Tigris had commenced a really serious offensive he was to take steps to prevent the Turks withdrawing troops from the Kermanshah–Hamadan line to Baghdad. On the 15th/16th December, however, a Russian cavalry reconnaissance showed that the Turkish strength at Hamadan had not decreased. In the last week of December the Russians advanced and occupied the heights twenty miles to the north-west of Hamadan, thus cutting Turkish communications with Bijar.

West Persia; October–December 1916.

During November the Russian detachment at Sultanabad was engaged in frequent hostilities with irregular forces of Bakhtiaris and Lurs collected by Turco-German agents. At the end of the month a reinforcement enabled the Russians to take the offensive successfully, when the defeated tribesmen scattered to their homes and ceased to give further trouble.

In the southern Bakhtiari area a small British movable column marched from Ahwaz on the 17th November and

---

* The Turkish force on the Kermanshah–Hamadan line was estimated at some cavalry, twenty-one battalions of infantry and fifty guns, totalling about 18,000 fighting men. The Russian force under Baratoff was believed to be 23,000 strong, of whom rather over half were in the Hamadan area.

moving via Dizful and Shushtar returned to Ahwaz on the 7th December, having been well received everywhere by the local tribesmen.

East Persia; September 1916. In East Persia, during the last four months of 1916, there were few incidents of importance. Although by the beginning of September Damani opposition had practically ceased, the Yar Muhammadzais and the Gamshadzais had not yet accepted General Dyer's terms. He, therefore, still considered it necessary to maintain a fairly strong force at Khwash and also to locate small military posts at Gazu and Kamalabad in order to deny to the Damanis the fertile valley between those two places. But the great mortality among the British transport camels brought about a crisis in the supply situation which forced General Dyer, before the end of the month, to move sixty sabres, the mountain battery section and about a hundred rifles from Khwash to Saindak, Kacha and Robat. He also moved with his own headquarters to Saindak in readiness to hand over command to Brigadier-General C. O. O. Tanner, who was being sent from India to relieve him.

On the 29th September General Dyer reported that he had only 1,200 effective camels left, but that the 1,600 then on their way to join him from India would, with monthly replacements of 400 to meet wastage, suffice for the requirements of the force during the cold weather. Of this total of 2,800, he estimated that about 1,800 would be required to distribute supplies from the depots at Saindak and in Seistan and about 1,000 for allotment to posts to enable their movable columns to operate carrying fifteen days' supplies. It appears that out of 10,082 camels utilised on the Nushki line of communication and with the Seistan Force between the beginning of June and the end of September, 1916, no less than 4,775 had become casualties. Of these 331 had been due to raids, 764 had occurred on the Nushki line of communication and the remaining 3,680 had died on service with the Seistan Force, a large proportion of them in Sarhad.

Affair of Kalmas; 26th September 1916. On the 26th September an action took place at Kalmas, thirty miles north of Nasratabad Sipi, between a small British detachment and some gun-runners moving a convoy of arms towards Afghanistan. Second-Lieutenant B. W. Wahl, with twenty-three of the 28th Light Cavalry and thirty-six levies, surprised and attacked the gun-runners. The whole convoy was captured, four of its escort being killed and one taken

SETTLEMENT OF SARHAD

prisoner. Unfortunately Lieutenant Wahl and one sowar of the 28th Light Cavalry were killed in the cavalry charge with which this successful affair commenced.

The Makran Mission ; September 1916.
The Makran Mission under Major Keyes remained in the vicinity of Sib throughout September. Although, from a military point of view, its presence might no longer be necessary, it was considered that Major Keyes was well placed there for communication with Bahram Khan of Bampur, to receive overtures of submission from the Damanis and to exercise a steadying influence on Makran generally.

East Persia ; October–December 1916.
General Tanner took over command of the Seistan Force on the 5th October and a week later, as the Damanis showed signs of willingness to submit, the Government of India issued instructions that they should be summoned to a *durbar* to discuss terms of settlement. On the 4th November this was accordingly held at Khwash, and General Tanner, assisted by Majors Hutchinson and Keyes, arranged a satisfactory settlement with Jiand Khan and the Yar Muhammadzais. Ten days later at Gusht Major Keyes made a similarly satisfactory agreement with the Gamshadzais. From Gusht the Makran Mission then marched southward via Sib and Magas and in December Major Keyes had a satisfactory interview near Bampur with Bahram Khan. The mission then continued southward towards Chahbar and reached Qasrqand at the end of December, having been most successful in establishing friendly relations with the chiefs and tribesmen of the areas traversed.

After the *durbar* at Khwash General Tanner returned to Saindak, reporting on the 8th November that, pending compliance by the Damanis with the terms of settlement, it would be necessary to retain at Khwash a troop of cavalry, two platoons of infantry and a machine gun section. It was, however, found possible to send about one hundred and fifty of the 106th Hazara Pioneers back to Quetta and also the personnel of the 12th Pioneers' machine gun section.* On the 15th November, General Tanner started off with his brigade-major to carry out a thorough inspection of his command, travelling in two motor cars which had just reached Saindak from India.† Although he had to traverse some nine hundred miles of almost entirely unmade roads—in fact at times there

---

* The guns were handed over to the 19th Punjabis.
† Two other cars, which were to go across the desert and via Kerman to join Sir P. Sykes, also arrived at the same time. These were followed in December by two motor cars for the use of the medical staff and by two motor ambulances.

was not even a camel track—his tour was carried out most successfully during the next four weeks, only very slight repairs to the cars being required.

From September to December many reports were received, both by Major Redl at Meshed and by the British force in East Persia, regarding movements by German parties in Western and North-Western Afghanistan. From these a fairly accurate idea was formed of German movements. Wagner was still at Herat and many of the reported movements of his party were apparently reconnaissances made by members of his party with a view to attempting to break through the Allied cordon.

Work on the railway extension from Nushki began in September and, in spite of frequent engine breakdowns at first due to the scarcity of water, good and steady progress was made. The line was mainly a surface one and the rate of construction in the latter half of the period grew to an average of over a mile a day, so that by the end of the year it was anticipated that the line would reach Dalbandin about the end of January or beginning of February.

British troops in Persia; 31st December 1916. A statement showing the British troops in Persia at the end of 1916 is given in Appendix II.

CHAPTER VI.

DECEMBER 1916–AUGUST 1917:
EFFECTS OF BRITISH SUCCESS IN MESOPOTAMIA.

(Maps 6 and 7.)

In consequence of the attacks on the gendarmerie recently transferred to the South Persia Rifles in the Kazerun and Dasht-i-Arjan areas, Sir Percy Sykes on the 20th December despatched Major Bruce with about sixty of the 15th Lancers and two machine guns (South Persia Rifles) to support the Persian garrison of Khan-i-Zinian.; and on the 21st he ordered a further detachment under Lieut.-Colonel E. F. Twigg to pick up Major Bruce's party and proceed to Dasht-i-Arjan, whence he was to reconnoitre the Pir Zan (Pass of the Old Woman) and report by telegraph for orders to Sir P. Sykes. South Persia; The affair of Dasht-i-Arjan, December 1916. (See Map 6.)

Colonel Twigg's detachment, consisting of a section 23rd Mountain Battery and one hundred and fifty rifles 124th Baluchis in addition to ten sabres, two mountain guns and a company (118 rifles) South Persia Rifles under Lieutenant-Colonel F. F. Hunter,* joined Major Bruce's party at Khan-i-Zinian on the 23rd December and marched next day to Dasht-i-Arjan without seeing any signs of the rebels. That evening Colonel Twigg telegraphed to Sir Percy Sykes that it was almost impossible to feed his animals at Dasht-i-Arjan and that a 15th Lancers' patrol which had pushed on five miles to the foot of the Pir Zan had been fired on by the enemy, who were apparently in small numbers. His information and circumstances seemed to indicate, he said, that his proper course was to move to Kazerun where he could feed his column without difficulty; and he went on to say that, unless he received orders to the contrary, he would march next day (25th) to Miyan Kutal (on the far side of the Pir Zan). Sir Percy Sykes at once replied that Farman Farma hoped to induce Nasir Diwan† to submit and that until he refused it was not at all desirable for the column to proceed to Kazerun, which in case of a heavy snowfall or of a rising would be isolated from Shiraz. Colonel Twigg might, however, advance to Miyan Kutal if his supplies warranted it. Colonel Twigg, in the belief

---

* Colonel Hunter was also staff officer to the column.
† The headman of Kazerun who had started the rebellion.

The affair of Dasht-i-Arjan; December 1916. that the rebels' strength in front of him was only about forty —and in any case two hundred at the most—and that to delay would give them time to collect more men and make his task impossible, issued orders for the column to start at 9 a.m. next morning (25th) for Miyan Kutal, where he felt certain of obtaining supplies. At a later hour that night Colonel Hunter gave him further information regarding the natural strength of the Pir Zan position and told him of various current rumours of the rebel numbers and intentions. Colonel Twigg thereupon decided to commence his movement next day by effecting a lodgment on the Pir Zan range about two miles to the south-west of Dasht-i-Arjan.

The flat and open valley here, lying at a height of 6,600 feet above the sea, is about six miles long by three broad and is entirely surrounded by precipitous mountains which rise some two thousand feet above it, their slopes to within two or three hundred yards of the summits being heavily wooded, strewn with huge rocks and intersected by great clefts. The summits are for the most part sheer cliffs of bare rock, honeycombed with caves and holes and accessible between Dasht-i-Arjan and the Pir Zan by very few paths.

On the morning of the 25th December, after pushing on the 15th Lancers (at 8.30) towards the foot of the Pir Zan, Colonel Twigg detached a section 124th Baluchis and the South Persia Rifles infantry company under Captain G. H. Weldon at 9 a.m. to ascend the range to the west of the road and, moving along its top, to act as right flank guard to the main column, which then also started to advance slowly. At 10 a.m. both the cavalry in front and Captain Weldon's party were fired on; and half an hour later the 23rd Mountain Battery guns were ordered to fire a few shells at a small group of the enemy seen on the heights above where Captain Weldon's party was assumed to be. At 11.30 a.m., however, there were still no signs of this party, and Colonel Twigg halted the main body while Colonel Hunter, to assist Captain Weldon's party if possible, took the two South Persia Rifles guns into action on a low hill near an old caravanserai about five miles from Dasht-i-Arjan. The range of these old 7-pdrs. was, however, quite insufficient, while their ammunition proved defective; and at noon Captain Weldon rejoined the main column having failed in his task, owing to the treachery of his guides and his inability to get sufficient of the Persian infantry to advance in face of the opposition encountered in a most difficult piece of ground.

BRITISH TROOPS IN DIFFICULTIES

Half an hour later Captains Weldon and A. F. Wittkugel, having collected forty or fifty of the scattered Persian infantry, volunteered to make another attempt. This was supported by the South Persia Rifles machine guns under Colonel Hunter, by the 23rd Mountain Battery guns and by the rifle fire of the 124th Baluchis, of whom a section was also sent forward to assist the advance by taking a subsidiary ridge. This section, however, missing its direction and moving off to the right, got completely lost and out of touch with the rest of the force. Captain Weldon's and Wittkugel's parties also got separated and at 2.40 p.m., in answer to a request from Colonel Hunter, Colonel Twigg sent forward a platoon 124th Baluchis under Captain Hinde to support the Persian infantry, a small party of whom under Captain Weldon had made their way with the close support of the machine guns to within two hundred yards of the summit, where they were stopped by the enemy's fire. Captain Hinde's platoon, however, deserted by its guide, also lost direction and went off to the left, where, as soon as it emerged from the woods, it found itself under very heavy fire and confronted by a precipice which appeared to be inaccessible. Reporting this to Colonel Twigg, Captain Hinde received orders to retire.

Colonel Hunter and Captain Weldon, meanwhile, with only half a dozen Persian infantry left with them in addition to the machine gun crews, had started to make another attempt to reach the top, when news reached them that Captain Wittkugel had been wounded and several of the Persian infantry with him killed, at the same time that a heavy fire was opened on Captain Weldon's party and the machine guns. Colonel Hunter then realised that it would not be possible to take the summit before dark and he went off to bring Captain Wittkugel in. Two of three Persians with him and he himself were wounded in reaching Captain Wittkugel, whom they found it impossible to move from the open where he was lying within about a hundred yards of the enemy. Colonel Hunter's machine gun ammunition also gave out ; and he sent a message to Colonel Twigg asking for assistance by the 124th Baluchis and for more machine gun ammunition and sending information to correct the direction of the artillery fire. This message reached Colonel Twigg about 4.45 p.m. and he complied by sending forward his last platoon of the 124th Baluchis with a stretcher party and the machine gun ammunition. These all reached Colonel Hunter towards 6 p.m.,* by which time the guns had also got the

---

* Sunset was about 5 p.m.

exact target. With some difficulty, under cover of a heavy supporting fire, Captain Wittkugel and the wounded were got away, but it took two more difficult and toilsome hours to transport them down through the boulder-strewn forest in the dark.

The affair of Dasht-i-Arjan; December 1916. They reached the main body at the old caravanserai at 8.30 p.m., but an Indian officer and nineteen rifles 124th Baluchis, as well as a Persian officer and about twenty South Persia Rifles, who had all been missing since the morning, were still out; and although they could be heard firing in the distance it was impossible to locate or support them. At this stage Colonel Twigg received information that the enemy had been strongly reinforced and meant to cut Col. Twigg's line of retreat by blocking the passes in his rear; and several Persian officers warned Colonel Hunter to look out for treachery on the part of some of the South Persia Rifles, of whom many were said to have already deserted or to have gone over to the enemy. Meanwhile the fires of the enemy indicated an encircling movement. Colonel Twigg had just decided to avoid being cut off by starting immediately to march back to Khan-i-Zinian, when a party of the enemy made a bold attack from a point about 150 yards off to the south. This was beaten off, but nearly all the Persian muleteers immediately fled and many of the camels and mules made off.

Orders to evacuate the valley were issued about 10.30 p.m. and within a few minutes the whole of the South Persia Rifles went off, abandoning the remainder of the column, which, owing to the muleteers' desertion, did not start till 1 a.m. Thanks to the cool behaviour of the Indian troops, however, the retirement was most orderly, Dasht-i-Arjan being reached at 3.30 a.m. Here, the order for the Persian garrison to accompany the column to Khan-i-Zinian caused some confusion and the desertion of more muleteers; but by 6 a.m. the whole force with its wounded had got safely over the Sin-i-Safed pass immediately to the east of Dasht-i-Arjan. Khan-i-Zinian was reached at 9.30 a.m., and at 11 a.m. the Indian officer and section 124th Baluchis, which had been missing for twenty-four hours, also marched in, having had a most adventurous experience. That night (26/27th) the camp was attacked by a small enemy party, who were easily driven off by the piquets; and next day the march was resumed to Chenar-i-Rahdar and continued on the 28th to Shiraz.

The total casualties in Colonel Twigg's column had been only ten, seven of them being in the South Persia Rifles. The action

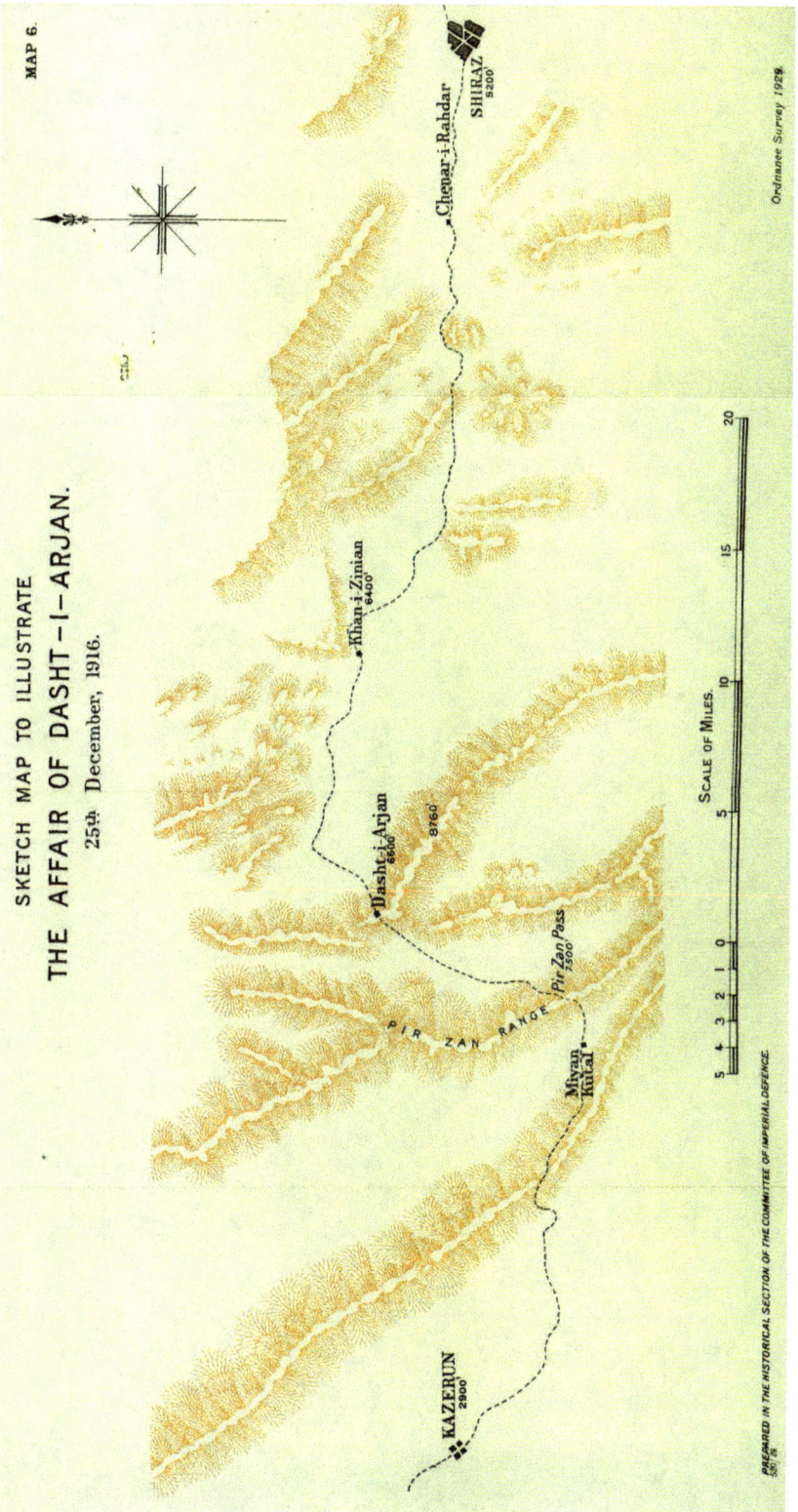

on the 25th December would have ended, says Colonel Twigg in his report, about 3 p.m., but the wounding of Captain Wittkugel* made it imperative to continue. All ranks of the Indian troops had behaved splendidly and, although two-thirds of the South Persia Rifles had shirked fighting, the remainder had shown considerable gallantry. Colonel Hunter was specially commended for his intrepid and gallant attempt to bring in Captain Wittkugel, and Colonel Twigg considered that there must have been other incidents of individual gallantry which had escaped notice in the intricacies of the ground.

The suggestion by Sir Percy Sykes and Sir Charles Marling that a British column should move from Bushire to relieve the situation on the Shiraz road was not regarded with favour in India or in Mesopotamia, where it was considered that for the time being all our efforts and resources should be devoted to the operations on the Tigris. But the Chief of the Imperial General Staff, being pressed on the matter by the Foreign Office, telegraphed on the 23rd December that if the Commander-in-Chief in India, after consultation with General Maude, considered that action from Bushire was practicable and would produce the desired effect, he could authorise it on the understanding that commitments entailing possible subsequent relief operations were to be be definitely avoided.

Bushire-Shiraz road; December 1916.

On being consulted, General Maude telegraphed his views in some detail. The force to be employed must be adequate if the risk of failure and of subsequent complications were to be avoided, he said, while owing to the nature of the country over which it would have to operate, its line of communication would be specially vulnerable and it would be faced with great supply and transport difficulties. The thorough organisation of this line, both from an administrative and a defence point of view, would, therefore, be essential before the expedition could start. Having regard to the difficult physical conditions and calculating that the enemy would number at least 1,500 to 2,000 rifles, General Maude considered that the striking force should consist of one infantry brigade; while he estimated that the total strength, excluding the necessary administrative units on the line of communications, should be one cavalry squadron, four mountain guns, two hundred mounted infantry and seven infantry battalions. He deprecated such a fresh commitment, however, at that stage of the operations in Mesopotamia and

---

* He subsequently died of his wounds.

recommended that, if it was undertaken, the expedition should be controlled and conducted from India, independently of Mesopotamia.

On the 27th December General Sir Charles Monro, in reporting the gist of General Maude's telegram to the Chief of the Imperial General Staff, said that he did not intend to authorise the expedition, from which in any case Sir Percy Sykes could not obtain any assistance for a period of at least six weeks. The operations of the Sykes Mission, observed General Monro, were controlled from Tehran, but it seemed to him that if the position of the Mission at Shiraz became precarious it could only withdraw to Isfahan.

Control of operations in South Persia; December 1916–January 1917.

The risk that the operations of the troops under Sir Percy Sykes might necessitate the despatch into South Persia of a British relief force led the War Cabinet in London to consider the question of the control of such operations. The Chief of the Imperial General Staff recommended that they should be regarded as military operations proper and should be controlled by a military officer, responsible to military authority but assisted by the advice of the local British political officers. On the other hand, the War Cabinet had to bear in mind that the force which Sir Percy Sykes was raising was for the Persian Government and was primarily a police force which it was proposed to maintain after the war. It was neither possible nor desirable, the War Cabinet agreed, to place military operations in South Persia under General Maude, but it seemed advisable that the preparations for any such operations and their control should be in the hands of the Government of India, who should keep the British Minister at Tehran fully informed of the measures proposed and taken. It was necessary that Sir Percy Sykes should maintain his hold on Shiraz, and reinforcements for him should go via Lingeh or Bandar Abbas, as it was undesirable that any force operating from Bushire should commit itself to operations in the mountains lying between there and Shiraz. Before they issued definite orders, however, the War Cabinet decided that the India Office should telegraph for the views of the Government of India.

This telegram, which issued on the 9th January and was repeated to Sir C. Marling, stated that as the War Cabinet held that the operations round Shiraz would probably make it necessary to replace the Sykes Mission and the South Persia Rifles under the Government of India, the command being exercised by a military officer, the War Cabinet desired an appreciation of the situation as it was likely to develop in the next few months and of the best means of dealing with it. The Government of India were asked if they advised:—(1) the reinforcement of Shiraz, Lingeh or Bandar Abbas and if so to what extent ; (2) the occupation from Bushire of the plain country up to Dalaki, for some months at any rate, on the understanding that the troops were not to commit themselves to an advance through the mountains. The Government of India were also asked to say if they could supply the troops and what effect their despatch would have on other Indian military commitments. They were further requested to give their views in regard to the functions and position of Sir Percy Sykes and whether, to ensure proper co-ordination between the forces at Bushire and Shiraz, they thought it desirable that they should have control of both. In conclusion they were reminded that it would be necessary for them to be guided in all questions of policy in regard to Persia by the British Minister at Tehran, whom, in addition to the Secretary of State for India, they would have to consult and keep fully informed.

Before the Government of India replied to this telegram, Sir Charles Marling telegraphed on the 15th January that if a military officer was appointed to supersede Sir Percy Sykes in command of operations in South Persia, the latter would, in the opinion of the British Minister, be so seriously prejudiced in the eyes of the Persians as to make it impossible for him to remain.

The reply of the Government of India was despatched on the 20th January. It appeared to them possible that the impending reinforcement of the Turkish Sixth Army,[*] taken in conjunction with the fact that the unrest in South Persia seemed to be due to Turco-German influence, indicated an enemy intention to revive the project of pushing troops towards Afghanistan. The Turks might intend either to try to overwhelm General Maude at Kut or to await the floods and hot weather to enable them to hold him to his ground with a containing force while they moved through Persia with the bulk of their troops. An attack on General Maude would be best carried out during the cold weather, but a movement through Persia would preferably be an operation for the hot weather. On the success or failure of these plans would depend the development of the Shiraz situation. But so long as we maintained our position on the Tigris the enemy

---

[*] i.e., the army based on Baghdad and operating in Mesopotamia and Persia.

Control of operations in South Persia; January 1917. plans would be impeded, his eastward move checked and the arrival in South Persia of his organised forces rendered improbable.

The Government of India had two recommendations to make to deal with the situation. The first was that the control of the South Persia Rifles, which should be raised and organised on the same lines as units of the Indian Army, should be placed under the Commander-in-Chief in India, who would nominate an experienced general officer to exercise command in South Persia up to the borders of Baluchistan and to have supreme control of operations in the area. He should receive his instructions from the Government of India, acting under the orders of H.M. Government and after consultation with the British Minister at Tehran; but he must have freedom to act according to the needs of the situation, in judging of which he would have the advice of the local political officers or, in matters beyond their competence, of the Minister at Tehran. Sir Percy Sykes should, it was suggested, be appointed as his chief political adviser. They pointed out that the Commander-in-Chief in India already received reports from General Maude; and, with reports also from the General in South Persia, he would be able to co-ordinate the military policy of these areas and India and advise the Chief of the Imperial General Staff and the Government of India accordingly. They emphasised the paramount importance of avoiding, in Persia, anything in the nature of dual control and any complication, which—without decided compensating advantages—was likely to result in further military commitment. The second recommendation was that trade should be encouraged on the Bushire–Shiraz road and that for this purpose the rebel Khans should be permitted quietly to re-establish relations with us without promise being made them of anything in the future.

The Government of India did not advise either the occupation of the Bushire–Dalaki plain or the reinforcement of Lingeh or Bandar Abbas. They proposed that they should reinforce Sir Percy Sykes by sending, with the party of ten British officers and fifty-three British instructors intended for the South Persia Rifles, an escort of one company of mounted infantry, one battalion of Indian infantry and cavalry and artillery drafts, with four 10-pdr. mountain guns and four machine guns; a force which they hoped to send via Bandar Abbas immediately so as to avert the risks of complications in Shiraz which the spring migration of the Qashqai and Khamseh tribes would otherwise increase.

On receipt of this telegram, Sir Charles Marling at once reported that he considered the recommendations excellent, but he thought that the idea of carrying out our policy in South Persia with a minimum of reference to Tehran was impracticable. This system was working well, he believed, in Kerman and East Persia, but, until the General Officer Commanding had an adequate force to compel respect, he did not think it would answer in Fars, which was in close touch with Tehran and whose tribal chiefs were very susceptible to Tehran influence. He consequently considered that the closest co-operation with the Tehran Legation would be necessary as regards the Fars question. Subject to this, however, he thought that the proposed appointment would have excellent results as calculated to co-ordinate our efforts. He presumed that the General Officer would be represented to the Persian Government as organiser of the South Persia Rifles and nominally in their service. He added that, in his opinion, the unrest in South Persia was due less to German influence than to the dislike of all the local chiefs, great and small, to a prospect of efficient authority which would curtail their own opportunities for brigandage and blackmail.

The question was considered by the War Cabinet on the 25th January and they decided to reserve the question for further consideration of its political aspects. They had learnt that the Russians intended to reinforce Baratoff in the near future with a view to an offensive which aimed at reaching the Upper Tigris; and they instructed the India Office to telegraph to India on the question. In this telegram, which issued on the 30th January, the Government of India were told that the War Cabinet did not consider that there was imminent or grave danger of a strong Turkish advance into the interior of Persia, but that to render the position at Shiraz more secure the Government of India were to send there immediately the reinforcements they had proposed. As regards the appointment of a General Officer, the War Cabinet felt great hesitation in superseding Sir Percy Sykes, who had an exceptional knowledge of the country and was very much liked by Persians generally and by Farman Farma in particular. It was also felt that such an appointment was likely to give the South Persia Rifles and the whole situation a military appearance which would justly excite the suspicions of the Persian Government and might, moreover, constitute an inconvenient precedent for similar action elsewhere. The Government of India and Sir Charles Marling were accordingly asked to review the question again in the light of these considerations.

South Persia; January 1917. The effect at Shiraz of the set-back to Colonel Twigg's detachment was not as serious as was at first feared, and a heavy snowfall in the mountains to the west early in January stopped the rebel activity in that direction and sent them back to Kazerun. Colonel Gough, who worked in harmonious co-operation with Farman Farma and was convinced that Qawam was trustworthy, was authorised to provide the latter with funds for an expedition into Laristan against the Baharlus. With this object, Qawam started to move to Darab on the 7th January, but, owing to the hostile activities of the Turco-German agents who had escaped from Saidabad in August, by the end of the month he had not been able to effect much improvement in the situation. The extent of Saulat's connection with the outbreak in Kazerun was not then known to the British, though he was suspected. Consequently when, during January, he professed his obedience to, and readiness to carry out, Farman Farma's orders to suppress the rising if he were given money for the purpose, Colonel Gough recommended that we should do this, as Saulat's action or inaction would then enable us to gauge his real attitude. It is noteworthy that at this period we were also supplying funds to Farman Farma and for the South Persia Rifles.

During January arrangements were made in India to send the reinforcing column, which has already been mentioned, so as to reach Shiraz in March. It was to consist of about 230 mounted infantry rifles (composed of Sikhs and Punjabis from the Burma Military Police), the 16th Rajputs and two sections of an Indian field ambulance; and it would take with it the instructors, material and administrative corps' personnel required for the South Persia Rifles, besides drafts for the Indian units already at Shiraz. It was to concentrate at Bandar Abbas by the 20th February and was to march to Shiraz via Saidabad and Niriz. Arrangements were also made during the month to relieve the Indian troops at Shiraz of the duty of guarding the German prisoners by handing the latter over to the Russians at Isfahan.

Bakhtiari territory; December 1916–January 1917. In Bakhtiari territory the situation was not altogether satisfactory, owing to Russo-Bakhtiari discord, and in December Captain Noel suggested raising a force of Bakhtiari levies under British officers, whose primary duty it would be to maintain order along the Lynch road. This project, which met with the approval of the various British authorities concerned, was finally approved by H.M. Government at the end of January. As will be seen, however, the scheme never materialised and was abandoned in May, 1917.

In West Persia General Baratoff started an offensive along his whole front on the 1st January in order to ascertain the Turks' intentions and to prevent their withdrawal. After three days' operations, during which the Russians incurred some 300 casualties, a heavy snowfall stopped further fighting, but Baratoff had definitely come to the conclusion that no Turkish withdrawal had taken place. In the last week of January the British *liaison* officer with the Caucasus Army Headquarters was informed by the Russian Chief of Staff that Baratoff was shortly to be reinforced to enable him to co-operate in an extended offensive aimed at Mosul and the flanks and rear of the Turkish Sixth Army. This would also clear up the position in Persia. Till the end of February, however, Baratoff took little action.

<small>West Persia ; January–February 1917.</small>

Towards the end of December there had been indications in East Persia that Jiand Khan and the Yar Muhammadzais did not intend to keep the agreement they had made with the British. General Tanner, who requested Major Hutchinson to impress on them that transgression on their part would bring swift and certain punishment, also considered it necessary to make preparations for punitive military measures. Among these preparations was the commencement of work on the camel track from Saindak to Khwash, via Ladis and Sangun, so as to make it passable for motor transport. This had the effect of indicating to the Yar Muhammadzais that the British intended to remain in Sarhad, with the result that, in February, Jiand and his men made complete submission and complied in full with the British terms.

<small>East Persia ; December 1916–February 1917.</small>

The railway extension from Nushki was completed to Dalbandin on the 23rd January, but otherwise there were no incidents of importance in East Persia at this period. In the northern part of the cordon the Russians had been obliged to withdraw one of their Cossack regiments to deal with some tribes who had risen in revolt in Russian Turkestan, while to the south the Makran Mission reached Chahbar on the 2nd February. Here it remained for nearly two months before the Mission was broken up and set sail for India.

West Persia; February–March 1917. In West Persia the Turks appeared, during February, to be drawing in their outlying detachments towards Hamadan, but there were no indications that they had withdrawn any considerable number of troops to Mesopotamia. The Russians, however, abstained from any forward movement as they wished to avoid possible infection from an epidemic resembling plague from which the Turkish troops were said to be suffering.

Shortly after General Maude's successful crossing of the Tigris at the Shumran bend, the Turkish force at Hamadan began to retire. As we now know, this was in accordance with orders sent by Halil Pasha from the Tigris on the 23rd and 26th February. On the 28th the Chief of the Imperial General Staff telegraphed to the Grand Duke Nicholas trusting that the Russians would make every effort to co-operate with General Maude by carrying out as early an offensive as the snow permitted, especially towards Mosul. Although neither Baratoff's reinforcement nor Chernozuboff's preparations had been completed and the latter's advance towards Mosul was blocked by snow, the Grand Duke responded at once by ordering them both to advance. Baratoff, who had already occupied Bijar (on February 28th) took Hamadan on the 2nd and Kermanshah on the 11th March. From there the deep snow and the Turkish action in destroying the road and clearing the country of inhabitants, animals and supplies, so increased the already great supply and transport difficulties that the Russians could only advance in reduced strength and with a limited equipment. Consequently, their shortage of both guns and ammunition enabled the Turks to hold the strong position they had previously entrenched at the Pai Taq pass for ten days; and it was not till the 31st March that Baratoff's advanced troops reached Qasr-i-Shirin.

South Persia; February–March 1917. During February the situation at Shiraz remained quiet. Though at the beginning of the month rebels captured a small South Persia Rifles post at Dasht-i-Arjan, they had withdrawn again to Kazerun by the 13th. On that date Sir Percy Sykes was joined by drafts of 100 Indian troops, who had moved via Ahwaz and Isfahan to Shiraz; and four days later 45 German and Austrian prisoners there were marched off under an Indian escort to be handed over to the Russians at Kumisheh. The reinforcing column from India, under Lieutenant-Colonel G. R. Vanrenen, after concentrating at Bandar Abbas, started for Shiraz on the 27th February, moving in two echelons at four days interval. By this time Qawam, who was making better progress in subjugating his robber tribesmen, had reached Lar. Saulat also was displaying a readiness to respond to Farman Farma's requests to suppress the Kazerun rebels. Our political officers at Shiraz and Bushire quite realised that he was unreliable and unlikely to deal firmly or effectively with the situation, but they considered that, as British operations from Bushire were inadmissible, it was best to furnish Saulat with the money he asked to pay his men in the hope that he would effect a temporary improvement which would last till the South Persia Rifles were sufficiently trained to take over the task. Saulat's tribesmen would start on their northerly migration in April and it was doubtful if he would or could undertake action as far as Dalaki or Borazjan. But it was thought that Darya Begi, the Persian Governor of Bushire, might be able, with the assistance of friendly Khans and of British arms and ammunition, to restore the situation in those areas if Saulat co-operated at Kazerun.

General Maude's success in driving the Turks up the Tigris at the end of February and in capturing Baghdad on the 11th March had as great an effect on the situation in the south as it had elsewhere in Persia. In fact, the Government of India, who had every reason to mistrust Saulat's intentions and consequently deprecated the idea of utilising his services, hoped that one effect would be to solve the problem of the Bushire-Shiraz road. But the local British political officers and the Minister at Tehran all considered that the best, if not the only, solution was to make terms with Saulat and try to win him over to our side, in which task they would be aided by the news of the British victories in Mesopotamia and of the arrival of the reinforcements coming from Bandar Abbas. Moreover, they proposed only to pay Saulat by results. This was approved by H.M. Government on the 14th March. They also agreed to the idea of action by Darya Begi; but neither guns, machine guns, nor regulars to work them could be spared from India, and the Government of India rather doubted the expediency and efficacy of this project. In any case, on the 26th March, Sir Charles Marling sent orders to Bushire that, as an entire change of the situation at Tehran might be produced by the Russian revolution, no further action was to be taken in the matter for the time being.

It may be mentioned here that arrangements had been made by the Government of India to relieve the famine conditions prevailing in Shiraz by the despatch of flour from India, the first consignment reaching Shiraz on the 12th March.

In the meantime Sir Percy Sykes was proceeding with schemes for the organisation and training of the South Persia Rifles. Those in the Fars province consisted, at the beginning of March, of about 2,000 ex-gendarmerie, whose reorganisation and training would take some time and all the efforts of the British officers and non-commissioned officers then on their way to assist him.

Kerman ; January–March 1917. During the first three months of 1917 the growing decrease in tribal restlessness and brigandage in the Kerman province brought about a great improvement in the local situation. Consequently recruitment for the South Persia Rifles, as well as organisation and training, made good progress. In the middle of February it was found possible to send a company of South Persia Rifles infantry under a British officer to Saidabad, and at the beginning of March the total numbers at Kerman and Saidabad amounted to about 400 sabres, 500 rifles and the nucleus of a mountain battery. Towards the end of February the four Austrian prisoners* were sent off to Bandar Abbas from Saidabad escorted by the detachment 108th Infantry, which then rejoined its battalion headquarters at Muscat. The telegraph line from Bandar Abbas, where about 400 men had been recruited for the South Persia Rifles, to Kerman was nearly complete by the end of March† and Major Rich, after a prolonged survey, had reported that the best alignment for a motor road lay through the Tang-i-Zagh and via Saidabad.

Control of operations in South Persia ; February–March 1917. The correspondence regarding the control of military operations continued in February and March. In reply to the War Cabinet's request for further consideration of the political aspect, Sir Charles Marling admitted that the situation required the presence of a prudent soldier of experience, but did not consider that the appointment of a General, with the large powers suggested, was necessary. The Government of India said that they realised the advisability of avoiding disturbance of Persian susceptibilities. But they doubted if Sir Percy Sykes, whose political qualifications they recognised, had sufficient military experience for a situation in which military necessities were paramount ; and they still considered that

---

* These Austrians, being sick or wounded, had remained in Saidabad when the remainder of the prisoners effected their escape in August 1916.

† It was not actually completed, however, till the 30th April.

command should be exercised by a military officer. They had already pointed out, they continued, that it was essential to avoid dual control; and they did not see how this could be done unless India, who was already responsible for reinforcements, munitions and supplies, was also made responsible for operations.

The Chief of the Imperial General Staff, who had originated the proposal for a unified military command in South Persia, was still of opinion that it was the only way to avoid confusion and delay and to ensure that hostile efforts were adequately dealt with. But the War Cabinet, who considered the question on the 13th February, were not convinced, either that a case had been made out for unified military control or that the local situation required it. They accordingly decided that, unless and until the Turks advanced into Persia in force, the existing arrangements should continue. Sir Percy Sykes should remain in command of the combined Indian and Persian force and India should send him, as adviser, a military field officer experienced in tribal warfare to whom Sir Percy Sykes would in practice delegate the charge of military operations and the executive command in the field. On receiving these orders, the Government of India, pointing out that it would be inequitable and unsound to make this officer responsible for operations without any power of direction, replied that they would not send him pending further orders. They considered it preferable to leave Sir P. Sykes in full charge of both organisation and operations, for which India should be relieved of all responsibility. They were in the meantime sending a qualified general staff officer and a highly experienced senior administrative staff officer to serve under Sir Percy Sykes.

Further correspondence ensued, and on the 19th March the Government of India were told that the War Cabinet considered that, in view of the retirement of the Turks in Persia and Mesopotamia, Sir Percy Sykes ought, with the assistance of this staff and of a good financial adviser, to be able to deal with the situation. He was to remain under the orders of Sir Charles Marling, and India would only be responsible for compliance with reasonable requisitions from him for personnel and material. The telegram also said that the War Cabinet had decided that, in view of General Maude's distance from Basra and his other pre-occupations, the control of the force of Bushire should revert to India. As Sir Charles Marling, however, doubted his own competency to supervise the organisation and finances of the South Persia Rifles, India agreed to audit the finances and on one or two occasions offered advice regarding organisation. In the meantime, actuated no doubt by our success in Mesopotamia, the Persian Government had sent Sir Charles Marling, on the 13th March, an official recognition of Sir Percy Sykes' appointment to organise the South Persia Rifles. They had also sent a satisfactory telegram notifying their recognition to Farman Farma ; and the Minister of War had sent his approval of the various appointments, etc., made by Sir P. Sykes.

Bushire ; February–March 1917. At Bushire, where the Indian infantry garrison had been reduced by General Maude early in February to one battalion (22nd Punjabis), there were no incidents of importance in February and March. On the 24th March General Douglas was informed by the Chief of the General Staff in India that our policy remained purely defensive, his rôle being the active defence of Bushire town and port, and that he was to keep in close touch with Sir Percy Sykes, the local political authorities and the Commodore commanding in the Persian Gulf.

General situation ; March–May 1917. For some months past the political situation at Tehran, reacting to the military domination of Russia, had given the Allies little cause for anxiety. On the 27th March, however, the British Minister reported that this state of affairs might be profoundly modified by the revolution in Russia.* The hostile elements, with whom the Shah was in full sympathy, were, he said, spreading the belief that the new régime in Russia was ready to reverse former Russian policy in Persia, to withdraw Russian troops, to refrain from insisting on the validity of the agreement made in August 1916 and to encourage the meeting of the *Majlis*. The extremists were also urging that demands in the above sense should be at once addressed to Russia and were trying to wreck the Cabinet on the ground that Russophile Vossuk-ud-Daula would not press such demands. As the Russian chargé d'affaires† had no instructions, the position of the Persian Cabinet was so difficult that it might be forced to resign, when it would be succeeded by an extremist Ministry with its accompanying intrigues and anarchy.

---

* In this connection it must be remembered that anarchists and revolutionaries from the Caucasus had had a great deal to do with the genesis of the Persian revolution a few years previously.

† The Minister was on leave in Russia.

EFFECT OF RUSSIAN REVOLUTION

On the 2nd April, Sir Charles Marling telegraphed that the position of the Cabinet had been restored by a declaration by the Russian chargé d'affaires that he had received instructions that Russia desired no political changes in Persia for the time being. But the relief proved to be only temporary. On the 21st and 25th April the British Minister reported the appearance from Russia of Workmen's and Soldiers' delegates, whose preposterous assurances had aroused a nationalist agitation which was likely to force the Cabinet to resign.

At the beginning of May it became evident that, fearing the institution of a republic, the Shah was giving way to the agitators and that only the apprehension that the Allies would cancel the moratorium prevented the formation of a hostile Cabinet. Then for a few days in the middle of the month it appeared as if Vossuk-ud-Daula would be able to remain in power. But orders on the 20th for fresh elections to the *Majlis*, followed by the assassination two days later, by anarchists from the Caucasus, of the editor of a pro-British Tehran newspaper and by further agitation, caused Vossuk-ud-Daula to resign on the 27th May.

During March there had been serious acts of insubordination among Russian troops at Kazvin and in Caucasia, and, though these had subsided, it became clear during April that the discipline, cohesion and fighting capacity of the Russian troops in Persia were deteriorating. Baratoff had been relieved of his command and had been replaced by Pavloff, whose advanced troops in Mesopotamia still remained in touch with the force under General Maude. But the British authorities, forced to the opinion that little in the way of a co-operating offensive could be hoped for from the Russians, decided that it was not feasible to withdraw British troops from Mesopotamia, as they had intended, for service elsewhere. For it seemed probable that, unless the Russian situation developed much more favourably, the Turks would be able to make a determined effort to recapture Baghdad.

West Persia; April–May 1917.

At this period also troops were being withdrawn from the Caucasus to reinforce the Russian main front, and among those remaining in the Caucasus there was great apathy and much peace talk. A Russian secession seemed possible; and early in May the General Staff in London, considering its possible effects, came to the conclusion that it might become necessary to reinforce General Maude in order to prevent a Turkish penetration into Persia. In Persia, as elsewhere, the *moral* and discipline of the Russian troops grew steadily worse during May, and at the end of the month General Maude was informed by the Russian commander in Mesopotamia that the total absence of local supplies, combined with Kurdish raids on his line of communications and sickness among his men, obliged him to withdraw the bulk of his force to Harunabad. By this time it was estimated that the number of desertions from the Russian armies since the revolution amounted to two million, while it was also reported, on reliable authority, that the Turks had decided on an offensive in Mesopotamia.

One result of the Russian situation was that on the 15th May Sir Charles Marling recommended that the scheme for a Bakhtiari levy corps under British officers should be abandoned. It had originally been intended mainly for co-operation with the Russians in the maintenance of order, so as to prevent collisions between the tribesmen and Russian troops. But, as the latter were unlikely in future to be used in their former high-handed fashion, the scheme no longer appeared to be necessary. H.M. Government at once agreed.

South Persia; The Turkish defeats and retirements, the removal of the
April–May German prisoners from Shiraz, the approach thither of the
1917. British reinforcements from Bandar Abbas, the increasing success of Qawam against the Baharlus and Saulat's improved attitude, all combined to improve the situation in Fars. By the end of April Saulat was approaching Kazerun to restore order ; and about three weeks later Colonel Gough, accompanied by Sir Percy Sykes, went out to meet him and came to a satisfactory arrangement by which Saulat assumed responsibility for security of the road from a few miles west of Kazerun to Dasht-i-Arjan. Both British officers were favourably impressed by Saulat and, believing that they had gained his confidence, considered that he could be trusted to carry out his promises.*

The bulk of the reinforcements from Bandar Abbas reached Shiraz in two echelons on the 14th and 18th April respectively, and with them came Lieutenant-Colonel E. F. Orton, the administrative staff officer previously mentioned by India, who took up the post of Chief of Staff to Sir Percy Sykes. A detachment of Indian troops had been left at Saidabad,

---

* In his " History of Persia " Sir P. Sykes says that they fully realised that the agreement was not a final settlement and that Saulat was thoroughly untrustworthy. But it kept Saulat and his tribe from open hostility for the time being and gave time for organisation of the South Persia Rifles.

S.P.R. ORGANISATION

in accordance with the policy which Sir Percy Sykes proposed to adopt of dividing up his Indian troops in practically equal portions between Saidabad, Shiraz and Dehbid, to take over part of the duties of restoring and maintaining order, so as to allow more of the South Persia Rifles to be concentrated at Shiraz and Kerman for the requisite training. Sir Percy Sykes considered the advisability of establishing an entrenched post at the summit of the Pir Zan pass, overlooking the Kazerun valley. But, after a full discussion with Colonel Orton, this idea was abandoned as objectless. Owing to the unpopularity at Kazerun of Indian troops, Sir Percy Sykes did not propose to send any there.

Sir Percy Sykes had not yet definitely formulated his scheme for the South Persia Rifles, but in the first half of April he addressed the authorities in India asking them if they approved the lines of policy which he proposed to follow and which he stated in general terms. In reply he was reminded that the British Minister at Tehran was reponsible for policy and distribution, but—evidently with reference to his previous proposal to form the force into brigades—he was told that there was no necessity for his organisation to be on the lines of a war division. Instead, it was suggested that South Persia should be divided into military districts, suitable garrisons being located at large towns and at posts on the main trade routes, with one or more well equipped movable columns of all arms in each district ready to suppress disorders in any direction. Sir Charles Marling does not appear to have offered any opinion on this suggestion, but he agreed generally with Sir P. Sykes' definition of the duties of the force, namely the maintenance of order, particularly on the main routes, the reduction to submission of refractory tribes and the restoration generally of the authority of the Persian Government. Since it was apparently beyond the strength of the South Persia Rifles as yet to open the Bushire road, Sir Charles Marling also agreed that the vital communications to be guarded were those from Bandar Abbas and Kerman to Saidabad and thence via Niriz to Shiraz, as well as the Isfahan road from Shiraz to Aminabad. He also approved of the proposed distribution of the Indian troops.

On the 26th May, a comprehensive memorandum on the duties and proposed organisation of the South Persia Rifles, which had been drawn up by Colonel Orton in consultation with Sir Percy Sykes, was forwarded by the latter to *Scheme for organisation of the South Persia Rifles; May 1917.*

Scheme for organisation of the South Persia Rifles; May 1917. Sir Charles Marling; a copy, which was sent to Army Headquarters in India, being received there on the 20th June. The following is a brief summary of its contents.

For the time being the scope of the duties of the force was confined to the provinces of Fars and Kerman; but the levies in Seistan and Bakhtiari territory would probably be embodied in the force in course of time and the question of controlling Arabistan, Laristan, Behbehan and Persian Baluchistan would also have to be taken up.

The political factors in Kerman and Fars affecting the question were then summarised, the relations of Qawam and Saulat to each other, to the Persian administration and to the British being especially referred to, as well as the difficulties caused by the Persian dislike to the British occupation of Bushire and by the German intrigues. The landowners in Fars had, it was stated, welcomed the arrival of the British from the first, but the religious class, the "democrats" and a large percentage of the townspeople were hostile, as also were most of the nomads. British influence and prestige were, however, steadily rising as reports spread of the good treatment accorded to the Persian troops by their British officers* and as the populace began to realise the advantages of law and order.

If the force were to be a success, heavy expenditure, both initial and annual, would have to be faced, but would be reproductive from the consequently increasing trade and prosperity. With a total strength limited to 11,000 men it was not possible to allot higher establishments than those noted below to meet existing requirements:—

To Divisional headquarters, Shiraz (including two troops of cavalry) 120

To the Kerman Brigade:—
Brigade headquarters, including one troop of cavalry .. .. ..
One regiment of cavalry .. .. ..
Three battalions of infantry .. .. } 4,480
One mountain battery (4 guns) .. ..
One section of field artillery (2 guns) ..
One machine gun company (6 maxims)..
One Engineer field company .. ..

---

* The system under which each man was personally paid by a British officer was especially appreciated by the Persians.

S.P.R. ORGANISATION

To the Fars Brigade :—
    Brigade headquarters including one troop ⎫
        of cavalry   ..   .. ⎪
    Wireless troop   ..   .. ⎪
    Two regiments of cavalry..   ..   .. ⎪
    Three battalions of infantry   ..   .. ⎬ 5,200
    One mountain battery (4 guns) ..   .. ⎪
    One section of field artillery (2 guns)   .. ⎪
    One machine gun company (6 maxims).. ⎪
    One Engineer field company   ..   .. ⎭
To the Bandar Abbas battalion (3 companies)   800

        Total   ..   ..   10,600 men

The Lar Brigade, which was not likely to be organised until after the end of 1918, could be constituted by expanding the Bandar Abbas battalion, by forming a mountain battery and by withdrawing a proportion of troops from the Fars and Kerman Brigades.

The cavalry establishment had been restricted to the bare minimum required, owing to its expensive maintenance and the difficulty of obtaining horses.

Political measures and the co-operation of local chiefs would have to be depended on in a large measure for the restoration of law and order, but, as important districts and tribes in the Kerman and Fars areas were dealt with, it should be possible to alter the force's disposition so as to utilise the available strength further afield.

Since serious fighting was most likely to occur in mountainous districts and off the main roads, a mountain battery had been allotted to each brigade, while the field artillery sections, armed with guns already with the gendarmerie, could be utilised in the large open valleys which were accessible by roads fit for wheels.

Medical, supply and transport personnel would be disposed on a station basis as being the most economical and efficient.

For the time being the best military policy for the force to follow was one of patience and caution, utilising the factor of safety afforded by the Indian troops until the South Persia Rifles were sufficiently trained.

The memorandum also contained a military analysis of existing conditions in the different areas, a statement of the military objects to be attained and an estimate of the accommodation required. It emphasised the necessity of an immediate improvement of certain roads, referred to the provision from India of equipment, clothing, stores, etc, went into the system of finance and gave tables of the proposed establishments for the different units.

Control of operations in South Persia ; May-June 1917. In the meantime, on the 14th May, the India Office had telegraphed to the Government of India that the Foreign Office proposed that, in addition to finding material and personnel and supervising the expenditure of the South Persia Rifles as recently arranged, India should control all technical questions relating to the distribution, organisation and handling of the force. The Tehran Legation would decide the purposes for which the force was to be used other than the ordinary duty of policing roads. It would also decide when and in what direction the force was to extend its sphere of work and generally all matters which involved political interests. Further, when any proposal which was made by one authority was likely to affect the sphere of the other, the two would mutually consult each other. The Government of India were asked if they agreed to the above.

The Government of India replied on the 19th saying that they had consulted the Commander-in-Chief in India who regretted that, for the following reasons, he could not agree. He still doubted Sir Percy Sykes' military qualifications, while the Foreign Office proposal, which apparently did not emanate from the War Cabinet, involved dual control, as it would make India responsible for the tactical and administrative efficiency of the force without the deciding voice in its employment. As he regarded the South Persia Rifles as practically a military organisation, it should, like other forces, be under one control. Mutual consultation with the Legation was apt to result in confusion and delay, and he still adhered to his previous recommendation. The Government of India agreed generally with the Commander-in-Chief, but they realised that, in existing circumstances, H.M. Government might be disinclined to place the proposed General Officer Commanding in supreme control, both political and military, of South Persia. If so, they themselves would prefer to adhere to the existing arrangement whereby they were merely responsible for personnel, material and audit. Unless they were invested with full authority to decide the purposes for which the force was to be used beyond mere police duties, subject always to the orders of H.M. Government and to consultation with the Minister, they could not accept responsibility for its organisation, distribution and handling.

Neither of the above telegrams had been repeated to Tehran, but at the request of the India Office the one from India was so repeated in June after Sir Charles Marling had telegraphed on the 13th to the Foreign Office regarding a discussion he had held with Sir P. Sykes and Colonel Hunter, who had been Sir P. Sykes' principal staff officer before Colonel Orton's arrival. In this telegram the British Minister urged that Sir P. Sykes should be given much greater latitude regarding organisation, conditions of service, appointment of officers and in financial matters, to all of which it seemed unnecessary and inadvisable to attempt to apply Indian ideas and regulations. Sir Percy Sykes' scheme of organisation was being sent home by the next bag and, if it was approved by H.M. Government, he should be at once empowered to act in general accordance with it, provided he remained within the limits of the approved budget estimate of three million tomans. On receiving a copy of India's telegram of the 19th May, which he gathered referred to the question of control of the South Persia Rifles, Sir Charles Marling sent a further wire, in which he disagreed entirely, on political grounds, with the proposal to appoint a General with full civil and military control in South Persia. This would arouse Persian suspicions in regard to our intentions, and he did not believe that such an officer would be able to rely in any way on the South Persia Rifles. Persian feeling was not with us, said the British Minister, and in the altered conditions due to the Russian revolution the only possible way of making the South Persia Rifles a success was to make it a truly Persian force, to be used by the Persian Government and not in a way which would make it appear an adjunct to British forces. Sir Percy Sykes thoroughly understood this, and for this reason Sir C. Marling trusted that there would be no question of replacing him. Moreover, the results he had hitherto achieved, for a long time with insufficient means, were said to reflect the greatest credit on him and his staff. On the 20th June the India Office informed the Government of India that H.M. Government had carefully considered the whole question in the light of the above telegrams from Tehran and would await the receipt of Sir P. Sykes' scheme before passing final orders.

**Bushire;
April–May
1917.** Early in April, after the Russian declaration at Tehran had effected an improvement in the political situation there, Sir Charles Marling had ordered Major Trevor at Bushire to proceed with the scheme for assisting Darya Begi to undertake an expedition against the rebel Khans of Chah Kutah, Tangistan and Borazjan. At Bushire both Major Trevor and General Douglas doubted whether it was not now too late, as Darya Begi had as yet made no preparations and the collection of the harvest in May might make it difficult to collect the necessary fighting men. General Douglas, who said that he could lend three guns and two maxims with ammunition and men to work them, thought that the expedition would be a mistake unless there was a good prospect of success, as failure would have a very bad effect locally. Two days later, however, Major Trevor, learning that, owing to a poor harvest, friendly Khans professed their ability to collect over 1,000 men and seemed confident that, with the support of our guns, they would meet with success, considered the chances of this to be reasonable; and he asked for authority to lend the guns, to advance Darya Begi money and to let him proceed with his preparations. The Government of India then referred the matter to H.M. Government, as they shared General Douglas' misgivings, especially as success would still leave the worst part of the road untouched and they saw little reason to suppose that Saulat would deal with that effectively. At first, Sir Charles Marling was still inclined to consider that the exploit was justifiable but, after discussion with Colonel Gough, he finally came to the conclusion at the beginning of May that the contemplated action was not worth undertaking. The idea was consequently abandoned.

It is to be noted that while this project was under discussion in April news was received at Bushire that three Germans, disguised as Persians, had arrived early in the month at Ahram, after having stayed for some time with Saulat. These men turned out to be Bruggmann, Oertel and Dettmar, who had been among those who had escaped from Saidabad in August 1916; and it was subsequently confirmed that Saulat's assistance had enabled them to join Wassmuss.

At the end of May the command known as the " O.C. Troops, Gulf of Oman " was abolished, when the various British detachments at Muscat and at the ports and islands in the Persian Gulf and Gulf of Oman, including the base for the South Persia Mission escort at Bandar Abbas, came under the orders of the General Officer Commanding Bushire. On the 29th May the 3rd Brahmans from Mesopotamia relieved the 108th Infantry at Muscat.

In East Persia, the complete submission of the Damanis in the middle of February led General Tanner to suggest a reduction in the Seistan Force. This being approved, the headquarters and two squadrons 28th Light Cavalry, the section 25th Mountain Battery, the Wireless section and the detachment 106th Hazara Pioneers were all withdrawn to India during March. The Seistan Force then consisted of two squadrons 28th Light Cavalry, a few Sappers and Miners, the 19th Punjabis (now 1/19th) and the Hazara, Seistani and Sarhaddi levies.

East Persia; February–May 1917.

On the 24th March a small British detachment under Captain J. A. C. Kreyer, 28th Light Cavalry, captured, at Nakhela near Dehani Baghi, a caravan containing 450 rifles and several thousand rounds of ammunition, which gun-runners were trying to take across the border. There were no casualties on either side.

At the end of March, the situation was so quiet and satisfactory that General Tanner reported that there was no longer any necessity for a General Officer and brigade-major, as the force could quite well be commanded by the commandant of the infantry battalion, assisted by a staff captain and a reduced administrative staff. Soon afterwards he recommended that another squadron of cavalry should be withdrawn to India, as he considered that the Seistani and Hazara levies* were fully competent to carry out the duties of the cordon north of the line Robat–Dehani Baghi; and later, in April, the Agent to the Governor-General in Baluchistan, after a visit to Sarhad and a satisfactory interview with the local chiefs, joined with General Tanner in recommending a still further reduction in the force.

The Government of India were at first inclined to approve these reductions, but during April disquieting reports were received of the situation in Russian Turkestan. General Kuropatkin and four other Generals had been removed from their appointments as the result of pressure by Workmen's and Soldiers' committees, and a serious mutiny of troops was said to have been brought about by German agents who had recently come from Mongolia and by others lately released from Siberia. These German agents, it was also said, were trying to stir up

---

* The Hazaras formed a company in the Seistan Levy Corps.

trouble in Afghanistan. The Chief of the Imperial General Staff also advised the Commander-in-Chief in India to consider fully the possible effect of the Turkestan revolt before deciding to weaken the cordon in East Persia. As a result, on the 9th May General Tanner was informed that it was considered undesirable, for the time being, to reduce the strength of the force. He himself and his brigade-major (Captain M. Saunders) were, however, recalled to India, the command of the force being taken over on the 13th May by Lieutenant-Colonel G. A. Dale, 1/19th Punjabis, Captain R. W. Hornsby of the same battalion remaining on as staff captain. At the end of May Lieutenant-Colonel Redl at Meshed reported that the committee appointed by the Russian provisional Government expressed its inability to administer Russian Turkestan in face of the difficulties created by the Soldiers' and Workmen's committees.

North-West Frontier, India; May 1917. In India itself conditions on the North-West Frontier became so disturbed that the Government of India found it necessary to undertake a military expedition into Waziristan. At the time it was considered that the disturbances were due partly to the effect of the Russian revolution in Persia and Russian Turkestan; but, in the light of the information given in Niedermayer's book, there is ground for the supposition that German propaganda was largely responsible.

Persian and British policy; June– August 1917. At the beginning of June a new Persian Government was formed with Ala-es-Sultaneh as Premier. He and two others of the Cabinet, belonging to the Moderate party, were friendly to the British but had insufficient strength of character to counterbalance the five other Democrat Ministers, from whom the Germans in 1915 had obtained great material and moral support. These men, realising that Russian influence was no longer a force to be reckoned with and that their own political opponents, the Moderates, relied mainly on British support, directed their unscrupulous activities to exploiting the Anglophobia which formed their main, if not their only, political capital. Declaring that they would free Persia of the British oppressors and would remove the friends of the British as traitors, they instigated a series of assassinations, whose victims' only apparent fault was that they were using their influence to bring about the election to the *Majlis* of moderate and intelligent deputies.

The Russian Government, afraid for internal political reasons to take an active part in Persian affairs, found it impossible to oppose the Democrats and in fact sent their representative at Tehran instructions to show sympathy with them. Though he only did this in a perfunctory manner, it placed Sir Charles Marling in a most difficult position, as, nominally at any rate, Russia was still our ally. The new Persian Cabinet refused to follow the policy of its predecessors by recognising the South Persia Rifles, while the Democrats, talking loudly of the immediate necessity for the abrogation of the Anglo-Russian Convention of 1907 and of the Russo-British-Persian Agreement of August, 1916, also boasted of an imminent Turkish military advance into Persia. The possibility that the Turks would take advantage of the situation to further their Pan-Turkish aims was enhanced by reports that Salar-ud-Daula was with the Turkish forces in Kurdistan and was intriguing with the Russians. As there seemed every chance that all moderate elements in the Persian Cabinet might soon be eliminated and a Government composed entirely of Democrats come into power, it appeared both to Sir Charles Marling and the Government of India that we might have to modify our immediate policy.

A telegraphic discussion ensued between Tehran, Simla and London regarding such modification. It was felt that we should endeavour to regain that confidence in British friendship that existed in Persia before the conclusion of the 1907 Convention and that, from our point of view, there was no objection to its abrogation or to re-opening the questions dealt with in the August 1916 agreement. The Russians, however, expressed a desire that the 1907 Convention should be allowed to stand, and the Persian Government showed no inclination at all to admit the possibility of allowing the South Persia Rifles to continue, even with a greater measure of Persian control. As our military position in South Persia, as well as the prevention of anarchy—from which the enemy might profit by enabling him to carry the war to the borders of India—depended on this force, the authorities in India were much concerned. In regard to possible developments in Persia, Sir Charles Marling was able to re-assure them to some extent. He did not consider that a Democrat Government would make any formidable effort, either against us or to assist our enemies, though they would probably combine, as in 1915, official passivity with unofficial assistance to the enemy. But the advance of a Turkish force through the country would, he said, be viewed with dismay in Persia.

The question of what concessions we could make to Persian nationalist sentiment was not an easy one. Any British endeavour to encourage reform would certainly be misrepresented by hostile elements as further evidence of our interference, and though the wave of democratic feeling might appear, on the surface, to be more genuine and widespread than any similar previous movement, there was really little hope of Persia's self-regeneration. The Democrat leaders seemed to desire power chiefly as affording them opportunities of self-aggrandisement, if not self-enrichment, and not as a means of promoting better government. Consequently the idea of conciliating them or of giving them financial assistance held out little prospect of improving the situation. On the other hand, any concessions we made in the way of modifying our control of their finances and of the South Persia Rifles would certainly weaken the Democrat party by removing the main source of its political propaganda. Russia, however, had still to be considered and the signs of a Russian recovery in July postponed further immediate consideration of the question.

General situation; June–August 1917.
The discipline of the Russian troops in the Caucasus and Persia had continued to deteriorate, owing partly to the depreciation of the rouble; and our military agent in the Caucasus was suggesting the formation of Armenian divisions to obviate a Russian evacuation of Armenia. In his "History of Persia" Sir Percy Sykes gives his personal experiences of the state of affairs at Isfahan in June. The Cossacks there had ceased to mount guard or to salute their officers, whom they had even turned out of their quarters. Some of them had taken to highway robbery, others got hopelessly drunk on all possible occasions, and their complete failure to patrol the area had, he says, enabled robber hordes to overrun the country roads.

On the western frontier by the third week in June a further Russian retirement had enabled the Turks to occupy Khaniqin and Qasr-i-Shirin and had necessitated a call on India for an early reinforcement of General Maude, who had been forced by the Russian retirement to extend his operations in order to cover his right flank. At the end of June, however, the influence of Kerenski and the appointment of Brusiloff as Commander-in-Chief held out hopes of a Russian recovery; and this, followed by a Russian offensive in Europe in July, produced a steadying effect on the political situation at Tehran. The offensive failed, however; the Russian troops in West Persia withdrew to Kermanshah; and, though Baratoff again took over command there from Pavloff, further demoralisation took place in August. In that month more Russian troops were transferred to Europe from the Caucasus front, whence the Turks were also said to have been recently withdrawing troops for Syria or Mesopotamia.

On the 29th July Sir Charles Marling reported that the Persian Cabinet could scarcely survive long. It had lost all credit and was openly flouted by the press for its failure to take any action to suppress political assassination and for its generally weak inefficiency. As there were strong dissensions among the Democrats, he said, the Cabinet would probably be succeeded by one of much the same complexion. In the middle of August, however, it displayed unexpected energy in arresting some of the persons implicated in the recent assassinations. But, ten days later, Sir Charles Marling telegraphed that the Democrat section of the Cabinet had apparently not only succeeded in preventing any further steps against the terrorists but were demanding the release of those already arrested. Most virulent threats against the British and Farman Farma were, he continued, being published daily and the worst characters in Persian politics were returning to Tehran, which was filled with rumours of revolution. As the Prime Minister was afraid to reconstruct his Ministry so as to allow of energetic steps against the terrorists, a complete change of Cabinet seemed the best hope of avoiding anarchy.

For some weeks there had been some talk of a Russian column re-advancing in the autumn to the line of the Diyala, so as to co-operate with the British in Mesopotamia, on the understanding that General Maude would maintain and supply it. But by the end of August the reports of our officers in the Caucasus made it clear that it was unlikely to materialise or to be effective. The effects of the revolution had greatly accentuated the Russian difficulties of supply, transport and finance, and the Russian staff had absolutely no confidence in the fighting efficiency of their troops. Moreover, Russian troops from Persia were being withdrawn to the Caucasus. By this time H.M. Government had decided to reinforce General Allenby for an offensive in Palestine. This would indirectly assist General Maude and was all the more necessary as it was reported that Turco-German plans were in progress to start a revolution in the Caucasus.

Operations of the Sykes Mission; June–July 1917.

On the 1st June, the Indian troops of the Sykes Mission were distributed as follows:—

	Sabres.	Rifles.	Guns.
Shiraz:—			
15th Lancers	146	—	—
23rd Mountain Battery	—	—	2
16th Rajputs	—	539	—
3/124th Baluchis	—	18	—
Saidabad:—			
16th Rajputs	—	78	—
Burma Mounted Infantry	—	110	—
On convoy duty between Saidabad and Shiraz or Bandar Abbas:—			
16th Rajputs	—	233	—
En route to Dehbid:—			
3/124th Baluchis	—	395	—
Burma Mounted Infantry	—	123	—

They reached Dehbid on the 5th June.

The South Persia Rifles totalled about 4,450 Persian combatant rank and file. Of this total, the 2,500 belonging to the Fars Brigade were now nearly all concentrated at Shiraz, with a detachment at Abadeh. Of the 1,300 belonging to the Kerman Brigade, the bulk were at Kerman with a detachment at Saidabad, and there were 650 in the Bandar Abbas battalion. During June, Sir Percy Sykes, travelling in the two motor cars which had successfuly crossed the desert from East Persia, visited Tehran and was received by the Shah.

Ever since Nasir-ud-Din's death brigandage had been prevalent and, by the insecurity to life and property which it caused, had brought about great misery and poverty in the land. Certain nomad tribes were by this time living mainly by robbery and their power had so increased that, unless checked, it must soon deprive the ordinary villagers of all their possessions in favour of the tribesmen, who also blackmailed the great landowners. Neither the central nor the provincial Governments had taken any adequate action to cope with this evil, which promised to ruin the peasantry and stifle trade; and even the Swedish-officered gendarmerie had never been sufficiently mobile to exercise effective control. Sir Percy Sykes proposed to mend matters by undertaking punitive operations against the offenders, in the first place against those in the vicinity of the main trade routes. For the time being, this work was to be carried out mainly by the Indian troops. Some of their activities and those of the South Persia Rifles in this direction, from the end of May till the end of August, are given in the following brief summary.

On the 28th May, Captain A. N. I. Lilly, commanding the South Persia Rifles detachment at Abadeh, learning that a band of Qashqai robbers had carried off some sheep and donkeys, promptly took out forty-five South Persia Rifles cavalry and surprised the robbers, numbering seventy to eighty, at a point about ten miles away. The robbers retired fighting into the hills till darkness enabled them to escape, though with a loss of at least ten casualties. The South Persia Rifles appear to have had no casualties and recovered all the stolen property.

On the 1st June, a squadron of the Burma Mounted Infantry, under Major V. P. B. Williams, on their way to Dehbid, came into collision with a band of robbers belonging to a Khamseh tribe and pursued them for some miles, inflicting casualties without loss to themselves.

On the 10th June a few South Persia Rifles, escorting a caravan on the Isfahan road north of Abadeh, beat off an attack by a band of Qashqai robbers, suffering one casualty.

On the 12th June a donkey caravan, carrying wheat for Shiraz and escorted by a few South Persia Rifles, was attacked and captured by Qashqai robbers not far from Abadeh, two of the South Persia Rifles being killed and two of the robbers wounded. Captain Lilly at Abadeh, on hearing of the occurrence, at once went in pursuit with sixty South Persia Rifles cavalry. He caught up the robbers and after a running fight forced them to abandon a number of laden donkeys and inflicted several casualties on them. The South Persia Rifles, who covered over fifty miles during the day, suffered no casualties, though one of their horses was wounded and two died of exhaustion.

On the 18th and 19th June part of the Burma Mounted Infantry detachment at Dehbid were engaged in that vicinity with a robber band who had looted a donkey caravan. The action was most effective, nine of the robbers being killed or wounded and eighteen captured, while part of the lost property was recovered. This affair had an excellent effect in the neighbourhood.

On the 4th July Major Williams moved out from Dehbid, in a south-westerly direction, with a column composed of the Burma Mounted Infantry squadron and 150 rifles and a machine gun section of the 124th Baluchis, to deal with a band of robbers belonging to a tribal section of the Qashqais. There was a long list of robberies against these particular men and they were held in greater dread than any other tribe in the area, which, as Major Williams said in his report, was saying a great deal. So little was known of their location and of the topography of the country that it had taken Major Williams many days to acquire sufficient information to enable him to form a plan of action. As it turned out, however, much of this information proved to be hopelessly inaccurate. With a view to effecting a surprise, every precaution had been taken to prevent news of the British intention becoming known. But, although Major Williams was unaware of it, one of the robber chief's spies had given him ample warning and the tribesmen had had plenty of time to plan a defence, by which they confidently expected to defeat the despised Indian troops.

Affair of Kafta; 5th July 1917. (See Map 7.) Starting at 3 p.m. on the 4th, the column did not reach the position of assembly till 1.40 a.m. on the 5th July, as the distance proved to be about 26 miles instead of the $21\frac{1}{2}$ which had been estimated. The robbers were said to be located in several camps in a position about two miles south-west of this point. But Major Williams was by this time in such doubt regarding the correctness of his information that he decided to strengthen the detachments he had previously allotted to surround and attack the enemy from the south and west.

At 2 a.m. Major O. A. Chaldecott with 75 of the Baluchis moved off in a south-westerly direction, and Lieutenant W. R. Morley with two troops Burma Mounted Infantry left in a west-north-westerly direction. Major Chaldecott had orders, first to surround the most southerly of the camps and capture the robber chief reported to be there* and, then, to form the southern attack on the main camp. Lieutenant Morley was to move round the various camps and attack from the west-south-west. The remaining 75 Baluchis (less baggage guard), the two machine guns and two troops Burma Mounted Infantry were reserved by Major Williams for a direct attack from the east. All three attacks were to hinge on that made by Major Chaldecott's party; and Major Williams had purposely left a northern line of retreat open to the enemy, as the country in that direction was an open plain extending for three miles. The Bassari tribe, which was said to be encamped to the east of the robber tribesmen, was not to be molested unless its members showed open hostility.

---

* This proved to be incorrect.

AFFAIR OF KAFTA

Major Williams, with the party for the direct attack from the east, left the position of assembly at 2.40 a.m., being led due west by his guides instead of south-west as he had been led to expect. The enemy's camps were not sighted till 4 a.m., when they could be discerned about a mile away to the west. The column then also came suddenly under long range fire, while there were still no signs of the two other attacking detachments. Moreover, an old fort near the main robber encampment, whose walls had previously been reported as having fallen to a height of only two or three feet from the ground, was now seen to be a much more formidable defence than had been reported. Perched on the top of a small steep isolated hill, rising two hundred feet above the plain, its high walls were intact on all but the eastern side and were well loopholed. Moreover, it was closely surrounded by the intact roofless walls of an old village, so located on the hill slopes that the enemy could fire in tiers from the loopholes in them. Deploying his men, Major Williams took up a position about one thousand yards east-south-east of the fort. Here, under a desultory but continuous fire from the enemy, he decided to wait till he got into communication with Major Chaldecott and Lieutenant Morley.

At about 4.30 a.m. Major Chaldecott's detachment appeared, a mile and a half away to the south-east, moving down the slope of a hill towards what was said to be the chief's camp. At the same time tribesmen could be seen running to and fro between the fort and a gap in the hills to its south-west, where Lieutenant Morley's attack should have been launched at dawn.*
Major Williams decided to isolate the fort from all communication with the hills—which were about two miles to the south-east, south and south-west of it—and then, if necessary, to assault the fort. In furtherance of this plan he sent a troop of Burma Mounted Infantry under Jemadar Partab Singh to clear a large camp just south of the fort and to cut in between the latter and the hills.

In the meantime, Lieutenant Morley's party, moving steadily at a fast pace to the west-north-west, had had to go about nine miles in order to keep clear of a continuous line of encampments, among which his guide professed his inability to distinguish between those belonging to the robbers and Bassaris. To settle the point before turning south-east, Lieutenant Morley surrounded the largest camp, whose inhabitants at once

---

* Sunrise was about 5 a.m.

Affair of Kafta; 5th July 1917. surrendered. But as they were Bassaris he left them alone.* Major Williams sighted Lieutenant Morley's party at about 5.30 a.m. as it was taking up a position on the hills west-south-west of the fort. From here, during the next hour or so, it completed the isolation of the fort by engaging and driving back some more Bassari tribesmen.

By this time Major Chaldecott had also effectively cleared several camps and had driven the tribesmen, including some belonging to another section of the Qashqais, well back into the hills to the south. Under orders from Major Williams, Jemadar Partab Singh's party, which had encountered heavy though inaccurate fire, had joined Major Chaldecott; and at 6.30 a.m. the combined parties, having driven the enemy back sufficiently, joined Major Williams, whose detachment was still engaged in a fire-fight with the fort.

The Indian troops, having been under arms for over fifteen hours and having marched distances varying from thirty-three to forty-six miles, were by this time all very tired and hungry. But they responded with spirit to the order to assault the fort starting at 7.30 a.m. An attack by tribesmen from the hills to the south had, however, to be dealt with first and the advance against the fort did not commence till 8 a.m., when it was carried out in fine order and with great spirit and dash. Some of the Qashqai and Bassari tribesmen made attempts to assist the fort garrison by advancing from the hills. But these were ineffectual, and the tribesmen in the fort, discouraged by the steady determination of the advancing Indian infantry, started to flee when these arrived within one hundred yards and fixed bayonets. Streaming away through the hills to the south-west, the discomfiture of the tribesmen was effectively completed by the British fire; and by 9.30 a.m. fighting had ceased. Many cattle in the fort and much property in the encampments were captured; and of the 500 tribesmen engaged, 23 were known to have been killed and many were wounded. The British only suffered three casualties (one killed), while the moral effect of the crushing defeat they had inflicted proved to be very great among all the other tribes in Fars.

Operations of the Sykes Mission; August 1917. On the 23rd August Lieutenant-Colonel Farran at Kerman received news by telegraph that a party of Persian officers of the South Persia Rifles, travelling from Tehran to Kerman, had been attacked near Anar by a large body of brigands, and,

---

* It was subsequently ascertained that this tribe had actually already sent men and ammunition to assist the robber tribesmen, but Lieutenant Morley's action stopped them sending any more.

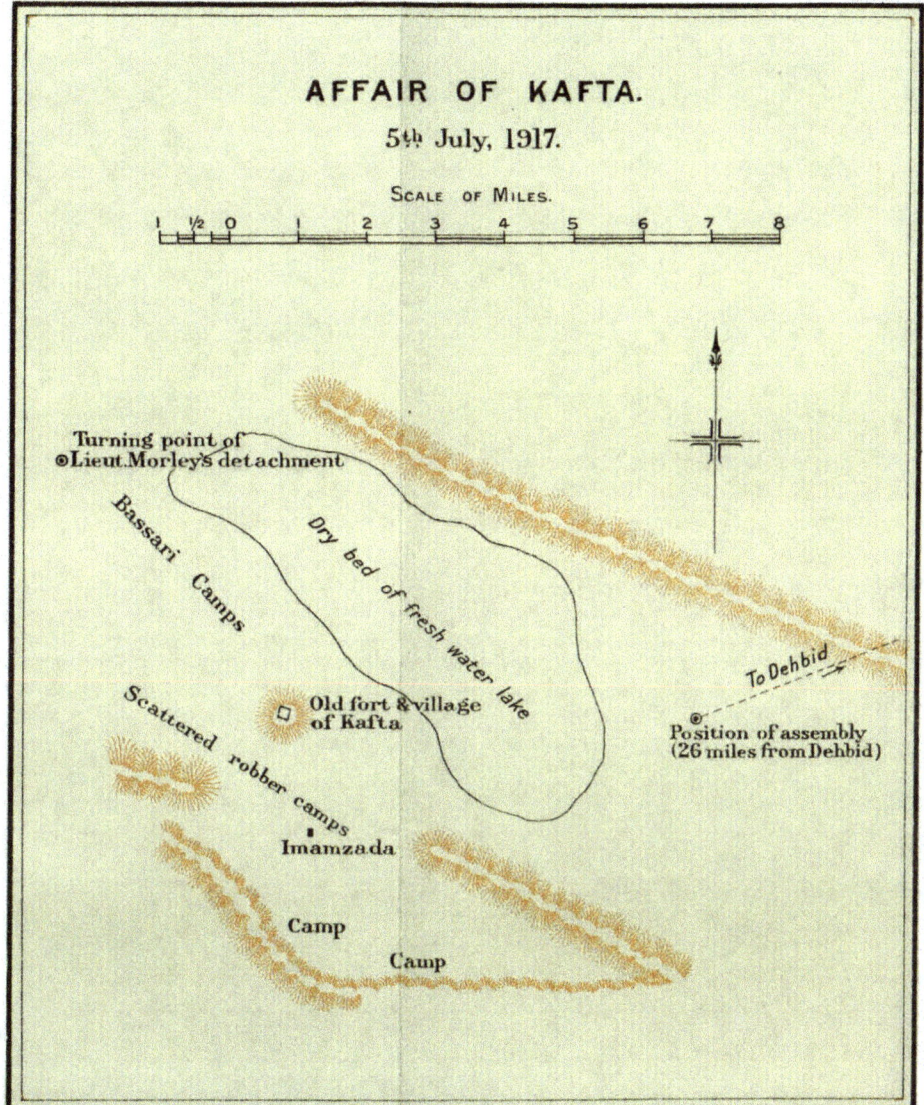

though the officers had escaped, the whole convoy with them had been captured. These brigands were reported to be then attacking another large caravan and to have the intention of raiding Anar. Colonel Farran at once sent off Captain D. N. Carr with a squadron South Persia Rifles cavalry and a mountain gun to proceed with all possible speed to Anar, 128 miles distant. Leaving Kerman at 4 p.m. on the 23rd, Captain Carr reached Anar at daybreak on the 27th August to find all well. But as the raiders were in the vicinity, he moved out again with some of his cavalry to round them up if possible. In this he was fairly successful, killing or capturing ten of the brigands and recovering four hundred of the plundered camels. Next day, another squadron South Persia Rifles, which had left Kerman on the 24th to follow and join Captain Carr, encountered a large body of the raiders and in the ensuing fight killed a number of them. The South Persia Rifles casualties in the two affairs totalled only two men and seven horses and the effect locally was excellent.

Besides carrying out these military police duties and continuous organisation and training, the troops under Sir P. Sykes did a considerable amount of work between June and August in improving the road communications. By the end of August the following had been made passable by motor vehicles:—

Shiraz to Aminabad	217 miles.
Saidabad to Kerman	112 ,,
Saidabad towards Tarum..	about 30 ,,

By the end of August the total strength of the South Persia Rifles had risen to nearly 6,000 Persian ranks, and there were about 70 British officers and 84 British non-commissioned officers * either serving with the force or on their way to join it. The rate of recruiting then became somewhat slow, as some eighty per cent. of the candidates offering for enlistment had to be rejected on medical grounds.

---

* The British N.C.O. instructors, from regular units in India, were attached to various South Persia Rifles units approximately as follows :—

7 infantry battalions, at 6 each	42
3 cavalry regiments, at 8 each	24
1 machine gun squadron	3
2 mountain batteries, at 3 each	6
2 companies, Sappers and Miners, at 2 each	4
5 transport units, at 1 each	5
	84

To increase their prestige, *vis-à-vis* the Persian officers, these instructors wore no badges of rank as sergeant or corporal and were addressed as Mister.

The recent successful operations had proved a strong deterrent to the habitual robbers and there was great improvement in the direction of the restoration of law and order. More rapid progress was, however, still hampered by the feeling of uncertainty in the country engendered by the so-called democratic, but really anarchical, movement in the north of Persia and by the unfriendly attitude of the central Government. On the Kazerun–Bushire road, which still remained closed to ordinary traffic,* the anti-British attitude of many of the chiefs and tribes showed that nothing but active military operations was likely to mend matters. On the other hand, it seemed probable that, if left alone, these chiefs and tribes were unlikely to force active intervention on us. The agreement with Saulat gave time to organise and train the South Persia Rifles, so that it was obviously the best policy for the moment to leave the Bushire road alone.

Bushire Force; June–July 1917. In June General Douglas from Bushire inspected Bandar Abbas and found it necessary to make various recommendations to improve the existing conditions for the detachment of Indian troops. In July the half-battalion 83rd Infantry, furnishing garrisons for various posts along the Gulf littoral, was relieved by men of the 3rd Brahmans from Muscat. For this purpose the latter battalion was increased from India to a strength of over 1,400 rifles and was organised in six companies, of which two provided the Gulf detachments.

East Persia; June–August 1917. In East Persia there were no incidents of importance from June to August. The Sarhad tribes, thanks to the lesson taught them by General Dyer, gave no trouble and the Indian troops were able to devote much of their attention to the improvement of the roads, on which they did much useful work. There were continued reports of unrest and disturbances in Russian Turkestan, including a serious rising in the Khanate of Khiva, but the Russians maintained their part of the cordon to the north of Birjand.

On the 29th June the Government of India telegraphed to the India Office that recent events in Russia had altered the whole political and strategical position in the East. Reports regarding the growing inefficiency of the Russian armies and the internal dissensions in Russia led the Government of India to apprehend a renewal of the Turco-German movement on

---

* During August a few caravans proceeded along the road by paying blackmail.

RAILWAY TO MIRJAWA SANCTIONED

Tehran, as well as the progress eastwards towards Afghanistan of organised hostile bodies. The unstable political condition of Persia, the military failure of Russia and the reported nomination of Mackensen and Falkenhayn to commands in Asia Minor and Mesopotamia would render this hostile project more formidable than the previous attempts by German emissaries, while we might on this occasion have to guard the Perso-Afghan frontier single handed. Further, the same factors would react to our disadvantage in South Persia.

Consequently, the Government of India recommended the extension westward of the Dalbandin railway, so that—
  (a) they might be in a position to develop and maintain military strength in, and northwards of, Seistan, thereby threatening the movement of enemy detachments towards Afghanistan and denying to them Seistan as a rendezvous and base;
  (b) from Seistan they could threaten the march of enemy detachments marching southwards in Afghanistan; and
  (c) they could afford better support to the South Persia Rifles in Kerman, thereby covering the Baluchistan frontier.

For the time being, these considerations could be met by extension to Mirjawa on the Persian frontier; and the Government of India accordingly requested sanction to commence work on it as soon as the weather became favourable.

The hopes that were held in England at this period of a Russian recovery appear to have delayed consideration of the question, for it was not till the third week in July that the India Office replied, asking what measures had been taken since February for the improvement of the Dalbandin—Seistan road and to what extent the difficulties in utilising motor transport there had been overcome. To this India replied that all attempts to provide a road westward from Dalbandin, fit even for light motor traffic, with light soling and shale, had failed and that the idea of using motor transport on this route had been abandoned as impracticable. Further expedients to obviate the necessity of a railway were then discussed, but were also finally discarded as impracticable in the circumstances; and on the 22nd August H.M. Government finally sanctioned the railway extension to the Persian frontier.

CHAPTER VII.

SEPTEMBER 1917–APRIL 1918:

THE FAILURE OF PERSIA TO MAINTAIN HER NEUTRALITY NECESSITATES FURTHER BRITISH INTERVENTION.

(Map 8.)

The Russian situation; Sept.–Nov. 1917. During the autumn of 1917 the Russian situation caused Great Britain and her Allies grave anxiety. Even before the revolution a great proportion of the Russian soldiers had not wanted to fight, and since that event the total abrogation of the usual bonds of discipline had combined with the lack of real patriotism in the country to bring about an almost universal desire to cease fighting. Moreover, the Russian workmen by their impossible demands forced many munition factories to close, and at the beginning of September a general lock-out appeared imminent. Stocks of military stores and munitions were also constantly being destroyed, apparently through German agency, while the confusion on the railways was so great that the supply of food was uncertain. At one time it looked as if General Korniloff, a strong character and an honest patriot, might succeed in effecting an improvement. But he failed to obtain the support of Kerenski to the measures necessary to restore army discipline, and, shortly after the capture of Riga by the Germans at the beginning of September, he started a revolt against the Provisional Government. This failed; and from that date the condition of the Russian armies grew steadily and continuously worse.

The proclamation of a Russian republic by the Provisional Government on the 15th September, though made without any popular mandate, seemed likely for a short time to stabilise the political situation. But it soon became apparent that the members of the moderate political party, with their oriental tendency to take the line of least resistance, were no match for the extremists, with their strong Jewish element and their command of German money and support. Early in November, Lenin and Trotski definitely gained the upper hand and issued a wireless message to the world demanding an immediate armistice as a prelude to peace negotiations. To maintain themselves in power, and incidentally to carry out the wishes of their German paymasters, they then set themselves deliberately to destroy the efficiency of the various Russian military forces.

The Russian troops in the Caucasus and in North-West and West Persia still retained their positions; but they were no longer receiving either pay or food regularly, and their consequent lack of discipline and loss of *moral* rendered them of such little fighting value that by the middle of October all that we could hope for was that they would not evacuate Persia nor leave the roads into that country open to the enemy.* The Caucasus; Sept.–Nov. 1917.

In Trans-Caucasia, where the disintegrating effects of the revolution appeared to have brought about no striking development, the Tartars, though really pro-Turk and antagonistic to the Armenians, agreed to act with them and the Georgians in proclaiming, on the 20th September, an independent *federal* republic. By thus avoiding the question of complete independence—which the uncertainty regarding the future also rendered advisable—the leaders of these three races managed for a time to preserve an outward form of unity. At the beginning of November, General Offley Shore, the British military agent in the Caucasus, reported that the Russians intended their forces to retain their line there for the winter. But, a few days later, he telegraphed that anarchy was spreading and that, owing to the Bolsheviks having obtained control of the railway at Baku, the supply difficulties, already great, had become much worse. On the 23rd November he further reported that the Russians could no longer be relied on in any way and that it was extremely doubtful if they could keep their army in position throughout the winter. Moreover, the soldiers' committees on the spot were selling arms, ammunition, clothing and military stores of all kinds to the local races and to Persians, Kurds and others, the Russian officers being powerless to prevent it. If Armenian and Georgian troops were to be formed to replace the Russians, he considered that the question ought to be seriously taken in hand at once.

In Mesopotamia, General Maude hoped to be ready by the end of September to meet the expected enemy offensive, which could hardly commence till well on in October. It was learnt that early in September the Persian Government received Enemy intentions; Sept.–Nov. 1917.

---

* H.M. Government did their best to obviate this by supplying Baratoff with considerable sums of money.

information from enemy sources that the Turco-German offensive would begin within a month and that the Turks, occupying Azerbaijan and invading Persia, would then move towards Turkestan in the north, and Afghanistan in the south. Also that they were sending 300,000 rifles to arm Persians.

To the Chief of the Imperial General Staff it appeared improbable that the enemy meant to attempt more than the recapture of Northern Mesopotamia and the despatch of small parties to stir up trouble in Persia, Afghanistan and Turkestan. But the Government of India were not convinced that he was right. News had just been received of the Turkish intention to send back to Persia the gendarmerie and levies—who had accompanied the Turkish XIII Corps in its retirement in March—evidently with a view to furthering enemy aims; and it was also suspected that the unrest in Russian Turkestan was a manifestation of the pan-Turkish movement, which aimed at linking up the Turks of Anatolia, through the Caucasus and Turkestan, with the Turks of Bokhara.

On the 19th September the Government of India addressed the India Office on the subject. Russia, they assumed, would be unable to hinder effectively the enemy plan, which seemed to imply a movement on a broad front via Azerbaijan, Urmia and Qasr-i-Shirin into the Tehran–Hamadan area, followed by an advance into Afghanistan by two or three lines, either in small parties or in force. To counter this plan they suggested political action as follows. The only prospect of obtaining the co-operation of the Persian Government appeared, they said, to lie in our ability to demonstrate that we harboured no designs on Persian independence and desired sincerely, in our own interests, to see that country strong and self-sufficient. They, therefore, again advocated, though they admitted that the idea might seem Utopian, that we should conciliate the Democrats as a possible means of influencing, through subsidies and other inducements, the tribal chiefs and other Persian leaders to support us. The military precautions they advocated were:—
A development of our intelligence system throughout Western Persia, in which the support of local notables suggested above would assist greatly; the effective recognition by the Persian Government of the South Persia Rifles, whose command we might agree to hand over to a Persian general advised by a British staff; and the improvement of communications as recommended separately, i.e., the extension of the railway from Dalbandin to the Persian frontier and the improvement of the Bandar Abbas–Saidabad–Kerman road.

Although by the capture of Ramadi at the end of September General Maude obtained much information indicating the enemy's plans for an advance, it became clear soon afterwards that General Allenby's preparations for operations in Palestine were seriously delaying any considerable enemy offensive in Mesopotamia.* On the other hand there was evidence that Turco-German agents were being constantly sent into Persia ; and for a time it was said that Niedermayer, then in Upper Mesopotamia, was about to move into Persia with the returning gendarmerie. On the 29th September General Maude occupied Mandali, and this so affected the Turkish supply situation as to oblige them to withdraw a considerable portion of their forces from the left to the right bank of the Diyala. Three weeks later, by occupying the Jabal Hamrin, General Maude still further lessened the chances of a Turkish advance into Persia via Qasr-i-Shirin. In Armenia and Trans-Caucasia, however, the increasing demoralisation of the Russian troops improved Turkish prospects, while Germany was evidently contemplating intervention in Georgia. Towards the end of October news was received that Niedermayer had been summoned to Aleppo ; and early in November the gendarmerie returning to Persia, to the number of about twelve hundred, surrendered at Qasr-i-Shirin to a Russian detachment sent to intercept them, at our request, by Baratoff. For the time being, therefore, the chances of enemy penetration into Persia had appreciably lessened.

In the meantime, Sir Charles Marling had telegraphed on the 4th October that, if military considerations necessitated the policy of conciliation towards Democrat leaders advocated by the Government of India, it would be preferable to effect our change of attitude when a stronger and more friendly Cabinet relieved the existing one, which was tottering. As, however, Persia would always prefer to remain neutral, he must warn H.M. Government that they could expect very little, if any, active assistance from any Persian Cabinet, though naturally if it were friendly it would hamper us less than if it were hostile.

On the 13th October, the Government of India, when informing the India Office that they had received from Sir Percy Sykes a revised scheme for the South Persia Rifles,† pointed out that our policy of creating an expensive and

---

* In point of fact, although we did not know it, the enemy had already abandoned the idea of this offensive.

† This differed only in details from the one which has previously been referred to.

highly organised force under British officers was apparently intensely distasteful to the Persian Government and people. While, they continued, they realised that the only hope for the permanent tranquillisation of South Persia lay in the presence of a really efficient force under British officers such as was contemplated, they queried whether this warranted us in straining our relations with Persia at a critical time. They accordingly suggested some form of compromise admitting of such increased Persianisation of the force as would render it tolerable and even acceptable in Persia.

On the 25th October the Foreign Office informed Sir Charles Marling that H.M. Government had carefully considered the recent telegrams from Tehran and India regarding the general situation in Persia and the question of the South Persia Rifles. It seemed improbable, although possible, that the enemy would attempt to invade North Persia. At the same time it was likely that small raiding parties might make their way across the country as they had done in 1915. There seemed to be no Persian Government with whom it would be worth our while to negotiate, in view of the doubtful value of their goodwill; and in any case during the war H.M. Government could not contemplate loss of control over, or the lowering of the prestige of, the South Persia Rifles. If, however, a satisfactory Government were formed, a modification of our policy could be considered; and authority was given to Sir Charles Marling to afford such a Government material support. In the same telegram the Foreign Office said that there was a fear of the Russian cordon in East Persia melting away, and Sir Charles Marling was asked if he considered that the Russians would have any objection to British troops forming, or helping to form, the cordon from Birjand to Sarakhs.

Sir Charles Marling replied next day that the formation of a friendly Cabinet seemed daily more probable, and he asked for further details regarding the financial assistance which he might give such a Cabinet and which it was certain to ask for.

On the 16th November the Foreign Office answered that, before making any definite promises, H.M. Government were anxious to arrive at a clear understanding of their future Persian policy. They accordingly invited the views of the British Minister and of the Government of India on the objects which they then proceeded to define as being desirable for us to keep in view for the time being and on the price we should be prepared to pay to secure these objects. They were three in number :—The appointment of a Government actuated by general friendliness to British intersets and paying due regard to British representations; the security of Persia against Turco-German intrigues and more especially against the entry of roving bands; and the recognition of the South Persia Rifles in their existing form and organisation until the end of the war. The War Office were impressed, said the Foreign Office, with the danger of penetration by roving bands through the depleted lines of Russian defences between Isfahan and the Caspian; and a friendly Persian Government should be prepared to undertake and guarantee its security. If invited, H.M. Government would endeavour to aid Persia in this task by lending her, for the duration of the war, a fleet of armoured cars with the necessary personnel. Further current expenditure in Persia on a large scale, however, continued the Foreign Office, would have to be most carefully examined, owing both to the great difficulty of providing *krans* and to the heavy liability already incurred in advancing Persian currency for the maintenance of the Russian forces remaining in Persia. As a subsidiary point, Sir Charles Marling would be authorised to offer inducements to local tribes or chieftains to arrest and hand over the European leaders of enemy bands; though this would not apply to the Bushire–Shiraz road, which H.M. Government would rather allow to remain closed than concede blackmail to the rebel Khans, whose notorious evil doings called for condign punishment.

On the 20th November Sir Charles Marling reported that, owing to the general and bitter attacks on the Persian Cabinet, the Shah had decided on another attempt to reconstruct it. But, as he insisted on including Ministers committed to an anti-British policy, there was little chance of a Cabinet being formed which would justify our financial support.

On the 22nd Sir C. Marling telegraphed that he concurred generally in the views expressed in the Foreign Office telegram of the 16th. He considered that the danger from roving bands lay in the use that they might make of disaffected tribes in the west and north-west—such as the Jangalis of Gilan, who were practically masters of Resht and of some fifty miles of the Kazvin road—to threaten, with the help of the local revolutionary element, the existing regime at Tehran, where the situation was none too stable, owing to the general discontent with the Shah and to the fear of famine. If the Russian troops could not be relied upon, armoured cars would be a guarantee against such a danger, but, as it would be useless to place them at the disposal of the existing Persian Government, they should be sent in the first instance to support the Russian troops. If these proved untrustworthy or were withdrawn, the Persian Government could do nothing to oppose Turkish or German military action, though they might act against a tribal subversive movement fostered by enemy agents. We could then offer them the assistance of the armoured cars to support the Persian Cossacks, which was the only organised force they possessed, with the exception of 2,000 gendarmerie under Swedish officers. As, however, the Russian troops were of such very doubtful value, it would appear prudent to employ part of the large sum paid to Baratoff to finance the Persian Cossacks. After going on to discuss the details of the subsidy to be given to a friendly Government, Sir Charles Marling said that another factor to be considered was the disposition on the part of the Persian Government and Persians generally to speculate on the local effect of the conclusion of a separate peace by Russia— a contingency which was locally deemed probable. Finally, he observed that, so long as the issues of the war remained uncertain in Persian eyes, no Cabinet would do anything but temporise.

Persian policy; Oct.–Nov. 1917. On the 24th November a new Cabinet was formed, with Ain-ud-Daula as Premier and with several of its members so anti-British as to render improbable any change of policy.

The Cabinet of Ala-es-Sultaneh had proved to be one of the most feeble and impotent that Persian democracy had yet seen. It had certainly come into office at a time when prospects throughout the country were most gloomy. For Tehran was not only in the throes of a campaign of political assassination, but was afraid of famine; the Treasury was empty and a large portion of the grain-producing areas were occupied by Russian troops, whose necessities practically forced them to pillage, while the province of Resht was in the hands of the Jangalis; and many of the roads were infested by brigands. But Ministers, who had come into power on a wave of journalistic patriotism—preaching the elimination of foreign interference— and of an artificially created Anglophobia, preferred the risk of famine to acceptance of financial assistance at our hands; and in many other ways proved that they were actuated only by self-interest. The result was that everywhere but in the south their authority became negligible, while lawlessness and misery increased. In the south, owing to the South Persia Rifles and the assistance we gave by means of flour from India and large money grants, there was an unusual degree of peace as well as considerable relief from famine. But this was entirely due to our action, taken in face of the intrigues and defamatory press campaign set on foot against us by Ministers and their followers. Their foreign policy appears to have been governed by the idea that the new-found Russian democracy would make great concessions to Persia and that, with the Russian power in the country broken, we should be obliged to ensure Persian neutrality by granting great concessions and a heavy money subsidy. When Russia let it be known that she was not prepared to discuss concessions till the end of the war, the blame for her action was cast on us and, when we would not allow ourselves to be blackmailed, Ministers used every defamatory weapon in their power against us. But all their efforts could not save them from the clamour of a hungry population, and, after a few ineffectual changes in the Ministry in September, they were forced to resign. It was particularly unfortunate for the country that the young Shah had neither the experience nor the courage to deal effectively with the situation. In point of fact he feared so greatly for his own throne that during this period he was steadily remitting his personal savings to Europe.

On the 18th September, Bruggmann, one of the Germans who had escaped from Saidabad thirteen months previously, was captured at Bushire, where he had come in disguise for medical treatment. One of his companions, Dettmar, had just died at Ahram, where, according to Bruggmann, Wassmuss was in constant communication with Germany and with many of the Persian and tribal leaders, including Saulat and Qawam. One of Wassmuss' main objects was to keep the Bushire–Shiraz road closed, and it was probably owing to this that Farman Farma was unsuccessful in the negotiations he carried out during the autumn months with the rebel Khans. A certain amount of traffic, however, managed to proceed between Bushire and Shiraz by avoiding the rebel districts and by the payment of blackmail. The Government of India thought that we might assist Farman Farma by intervening as peacemakers. But Sir Charles Marling, Sir Percy Cox and Colonel Gough all agreed that little benefit would result and that our intervention would be ascribed by the Persians to weakness rather than to magnanimity. It appeared certain that nothing short of direct British military action would clear up the situation, and after some discussion the matter was allowed to drop.

Bushire; Sept.–Nov. 1917.

OPERATIONS IN PERSIA

Punitive operations by the Sykes Mission; Sept.–Oct. 1917. (See Map 8.)

The hostility of the Democrats to the South Persia Rifles had been evidenced for some time past by the constant attempts they made to excite disaffection in the Persian ranks; and their efforts, backed up by the active support of some fanatical *mullahs* and the continued refusal of the Persian Government to recognise the force, were the reasons which Farman Farma gave for deprecating any great activity against robber tribes by the forces under Sir Percy Sykes. There was ground for supposing, however, that Farman Farma's real reasons were of a more personal nature. It was also felt by Sir Percy Sykes that both Saulat and Qawam, realising that the establishment of law and order was bound to lessen their own power and influence, were at heart hostile to the Sykes Mission. They recognised, however, that for the time being it was in their own interests to maintain friendship with us, while we, on our part, realised that they would be unlikely to help us out of any difficulty. Nevertheless, on the 26th August Sir Percy Sykes telegraphed to Sir Charles Marling and urged the necessity for punishing the robber tribes who had been guilty of a long series of depredations on the Kerman–Yezd, Shiraz–Isfahan and Shiraz–Saidabad roads. For this purpose he proposed to despatch mixed columns of Indian and South Persia Rifles troops into the area which extended for about one hundred miles north of the line Saidabad–Niraz–Shiraz. This proposal was sanctioned by the British Minister.

The first tribe to be dealt with was the Lashanis, who inhabited the country between Niriz and Arsinjan, immediately to the north of Lake Niriz. Farman Farma had received orders in the spring from the Minister of the Interior to punish this tribe, but, for a variety of reasons, had postponed doing so. In July and August 1917, however, the Lashanis started a fresh raiding campaign which they seemed determined to continue.

The available information concerning them and their country was meagre, but, by means of agents sent out in August, Sir Percy Sykes' staff managed to collect a good deal of valuable intelligence. Supply depots were formed at Qawwamabad and Niriz; and by the 19th September a small column was concentrated at each of these places. That at Qawwamabad, termed the Dehbid Column, was commanded by Major R. S. Rothwell and consisted of one squadron Burma Mounted Infantry, the section 23rd Mountain Battery, 250 rifles and machine gun section 3/124th Baluchis, an improvised pioneer section, one troop South Persia Rifles cavalry, one section No. 162 Indian Field Ambulance, and transport details. The Niriz Column was commanded by Major S. M. Bruce and consisted of one squadron 15th Lancers, two platoons 16th Rajputs, a mountain gun section and a machine gun section South Persia Rifles, an improvised pioneer section and some medical and transport details.

The distance between Qawwamabad and Niriz by the route through the Lashani country was about 120 miles, and the columns from those two places were instructed to advance south-eastward and north-westward respectively, carrying out punitive measures as they went and dealing severely with any professional robbers they encountered. They were to meet at Kushkak, forty-three miles north-west of Niriz, and were to return together to Niriz by about the 1st October. From Niriz they were told that, after refitting, further operations were intended.

The Dehbid Column, marching off from Qawwamabad on the 20th September, reached Abadeh Kaleh on the 24th. It encountered no opposition, as the Lashanis, having (it was said) received warning from Tehran, had fled from their homes taking with them most of their possessions. The column, having destroyed several forts and having captured or destroyed a considerable amount of forage, halted at Abadeh Kaleh on the 25th to destroy several more forts. Here at 1.15 a.m. on the 26th it was attacked by a small party of tribesmen, who were easily and rapidly driven off.

Starting off on its march again at 6.15 a.m. the same day, the column found its way blocked at about 9 a.m. by a body of some five or six hundred Lashanis who were holding a position round the village of Khwaja Jamali. Situated at the northern edge of the stony plain, this village lies immediately under and between the steep slopes which run up to the Kuh Vali, over 10,000 feet high, to the north. There was a strong, well-built fort in the village, as well as six separate loopholed towers, several thickly wooded gardens and a number of fields surrounded by stone walls and separated from the plain by broken and stony ground. The position which the tribesmen had taken up round the village extended from the summit of a rocky spur to the west, past the gardens and fort (which was held) in front of the village, to a *nala* and tower to its south-east.

About 9.15 a.m. when the British column had formed up about three thousand yards to the south of this position and had come under long-range fire from the enemy, Major Rothwell issued his orders for the attack. Two troops Burma Mounted Infantry were sent to attack and turn the enemy's

Punitive operations by the Sykes Mission; Sept.–Oct. 1917. left, and two platoons and the machine gun section of the Baluchis were directed to capture the rocky spur to the west. Their advance, covered by the fire of the mountain guns, commenced at 9.40 a.m. Twenty minutes later another platoon of the Baluchis was ordered to advance directly against the village and the guns moved forward to give closer support. The tribal riflemen had good cover and kept up a heavy fire, but by 10.15 a.m. the Baluchis had gained a footing on the lower slopes of the western spur and had begun, under cover of their machine-gun fire, to fight their way upward. By 10.30 a.m. the Burma Mounted Infantry had turned the enemy's left flank, and, ten minutes later, the tribesmen in this part of the position were seen to be fleeing northward. By 11 a.m. the fort, which had been evacuated, was in our hands; and immediately afterwards the Baluchis reported that they held the western spur and were working round to the north of the village. By 11.30 a.m. all fighting had ceased, as the enemy, leaving eight dead and one wounded behind him, had fled at a great pace, and the nature of the country prohibited pursuit. Our own casualties only amounted to two. This rapid success owed much to the skilful handling of their men by officers and non-commissioned officers and to the dash and enterprise displayed by all ranks.

Next day, after destroying the village and fort at Khwaja Jamali, the column marched off southward to Kushkak, where it met the Niriz Column, which had encountered no opposition. The combined columns then marched to Niriz, which they reached on the 2nd October.

For the second phase of the operations, it was arranged to visit an area still farther north, one column advancing northward from Niriz and another south-westward from Anar. The two columns were to meet at Marvas, whence one column would work westward and eventually return to Shiraz whilst the other was to move south-eastward to Saidabad.

The column formed at Niriz was termed the Shiraz Column and was commanded by Lieutenant-Colonel E. F. Orton. It consisted of one squadron 15th Lancers, one squadron Burma Mounted Infantry, the section 23rd Mountain Battery, one troop South Persia Rifles cavalry, one company 3/124th Baluchis, one section No. 162 Indian Field Ambulance, a demolition party of Persian labourers trained in the use of explosives, and a supply column carrying twenty days' rations for men and two days' for animals. The Kerman Column,

CHEHAR RAH ROBBERS SURPRISED

which concentrated at Anar, was under command of Lieutenant-Colonel G. L. Farran and consisted of one squadron Burma Mounted Infantry, one section South Persia Rifles mountain battery, one platoon South Persia Rifles infantry, a small medical unit and a three days' supply column.

Leaving Niriz and Anar, respectively, on the 5th October, the two columns met at Marvas on the 14th, neither of them having encountered opposition. Lieutenant-Colonel Orton had made settlements with various local chieftains for their future good behaviour and had imposed certain punishments; while Lieutenant-Colonel Farran had had to inflict summary justice at Javazin, a robber stronghold, on a number of men who had murdered three of the South Persia Rifles who had gone, unarmed, to buy food in the village. He had also destroyed the stone fort and several towers at Javazin.

At Marvas, the 15th Lancers' squadron, one hundred rifles of the 3/124th Baluchis and 150 transport camels, with the supplies they carried, were transferred from the Shiraz to the Kerman Column, from which the Burma Mounted Infantry squadron was transferred to join the other squadron of the same unit in the Shiraz Column.

On the 15th October Colonel Orton with the Shiraz Column marched off from Marvas westward. On the 17th he made an early start and turned off to the south-east, moving across country to surprise the robber stronghold of Chehar Rah. After following a mountain track for some ten miles, Colonel Orton sent on his mounted troops under Major Williams to act independently, and these succeeded in completely surprising the tribesmen living in the Chehar Rah plain some eight miles farther on. This plain was several miles in extent and there was not time that day to capture more than two of the forts in it. These surrendered, as the tribesmen had no time to organise resistance, but there was constant skirmishing between them and the mounted troops who were occupied most of the afternoon in rounding up livestock. On the 18th, the third fort was captured and two of the three were destroyed, the other, where the column camped, being prepared for demolition next day. It was estimated that the enemy had suffered over thirty casualties, but though they had fired away a lot of ammunition they had succeeded in wounding only one of our men. On the 19th the column marched off to the north-west, and by the 28th had arrived back at Shiraz without further incident. In his report Colonel Orton says that the Persian inhabitants of the area traversed were much impressed by the admirable behaviour of the Indian troops, which illustrated a standard of discipline and good conduct never witnessed before in the country.

The Kerman Column, having destroyed some robber forts in the vicinity of Marvas, left there on the 17th October and marched southward to Herat-i-Khurreh and thence eastward to Shahr-i-Babak. At this small town, where it arrived on the 20th, it met with an enthusiastic reception from the inhabitants, who had suffered severely in the past from the robbers. On the 22nd the column moved against Maimand, hoping to surprise the robber tribesmen who inhabited its cave dwellings. The appearance of the column was apparently a surprise to the tribesmen, but they had removed their possessions some time previously and, after firing for a short time on the column as it approached, they rapidly dispersed into the hills. The column started next day for Saidabad, which it reached on the 25th.

In forwarding the reports on these operations, Sir Percy Sykes said that by their success a great step forward had been made in the direction of the restoration of law and order on the main caravan routes. The excellent work of the Indian troops had enhanced their prestige locally and had afforded not only a fine example to the South Persia Rifles, but had increased their *moral* and their faith in their British officer and non-commissioned officer instructors.

The Sykes Mission; October 1917. At the end of October the Indian troops* with Sir Percy Sykes, totalling about 1,700 combatants, were located at Shiraz and Saidabad, the detachment at Abadeh having been relieved in September by the South Persia Rifles.

Of the South Persia Rifles, the Fars Brigade, some 3,500 strong, had its headquarters at Shiraz and provided detachments at Dehbid, Abadeh and Niriz, as well as smaller detachments along the Shiraz–Abadeh and Shiraz–Niriz roads. The Kerman Brigade, about 1,900 strong, was mainly at Kerman, with a strong detachment at Saidabad. The Bandar Abbas battalion was about 650 strong. Of the 76 British officers employed with the South Persia Rifles, 12 were with the Headquarters Staff, 9 were medical or veterinary officers and 6 were supply and transport officers. General Sykes had with him five motor cars and two Ford vans, and during September and October

---

* Squadron 15th Lancers. Two squadrons Burma Mounted Infantry. Section 23rd Mountain Battery. 16th Rajputs. 3/124th Baluchis (half-battalion). Portions of Nos. 108 and 162 Indian Field Ambulances. Portions of 47th Mule Corps and 10th Camel Corps.

continuous work on the improvement of the road communications had been carried out. At the beginning of October H.M. Government sanctioned the project for improving the road from Bandar Abbas via Saidabad to Kerman to a standard sufficient to take continuous light motor traffic at a slow pace ; and to assist Sir Percy Sykes in carrying this out additional technical officers were to be sent from India.

On the 10th November Sir Percy Sykes left Shiraz for a visit to India, where he wished to discuss with the authorities certain questions concerning the South Persia Rifles. He travelled by motor car via Saidabad and embarked at Bandar Abbas on the 27th. During his absence Colonel Orton officiated as Inspector-General of the South Persia Rifles.

In East Persia during the autumn there were no incidents of importance. Considerable chaos prevailed in Russian Turkestan, where mutinous outbreaks were reported at Tashkend and Askabad, followed by fighting between the different political factions. Owing to the general disorder, there was a widespread feeling of insecurity and uncertainty in regard to the future ; and this feeling spread to the Russian troops holding the northern portion of the East Persia Cordon. It was difficult to obtain information of what was happening in Turkestan ; and at the beginning of November, in accordance with instructions from London, the British representative at Meshed was instructed to expand his intelligence organisation so as to keep well in touch with developments. *East Persia; Sept.–Nov. 1917.*

At the beginning of November, news was received at Meshed that Wagner, and the members of the German Mission to Kabul who had remained at Herat, intended to move westward into Persia in disguise. Soon afterwards Wagner and his companions did manage to pass through the Russian cordon. But they came into conflict with the Persian authorities at Turshiz, to the west of Turbat-i-Haidari, when, though Wagner himself managed to escape, Bayerl was killed and the remaining Europeans of the party were captured and handed over to the Russians.*

On the 2nd December hostilities were suspended between Russia and the Central Powers as a preliminary to negotiations for peace. This portended a greatly increased burden for the *General situation; December 1917.*

---

* It is noteworthy that subsequently messages to Wagner were captured. sending him instructions to remain at Herat. His departure appears, therefore, to have been unauthorised and unintended by the German authorities.

General situation; December 1917. Allies, as it would allow Germany to transfer a considerable number of troops from her eastern to her western front ; and, by enabling her to obtain from Russia much of the food and raw material of which she was so urgently in need, would undo much of the advantage we had gained by our blockade. Further, both we and France had recently been obliged each to send six divisions to support the defeated Italians ; France was war-weary and was breaking up divisions ; America was not yet in a position to give material assistance ; and our own infantry was much below establishment and likely to become more so. An early concentration of effort in Europe on our part was clearly necessary, and fortunately this was rendered feasible by the fact that our recent successes in Palestine and Mesopotamia had, for the time being, upset the Turco-German plans. It was consequently decided early in December that an Indian division should at once go to Palestine from Mesopotamia and that a considerable number of British troops in Palestine should be transferred to France and be replaced by Indian troops from Mesopotamia and India.

As regards the Caucasus and Persia, it was realised that Russian troops could not be relied upon much longer to provide an effective barrier to a hostile penetration, which would enable the enemy to carry the war into Persia and Afghanistan and to threaten the flanks of our force in Mesopotamia. The danger of this was, of course, not immediate ; but, to support the remnant of the Rumanian army and to prevent Germany obtaining food and raw material, H.M. Government, in agreement with their Allies, decided to assist and support any responsible body in Russia which was prepared to help the Allied cause. In furtherance of this policy H.M. Government agreed at the beginning of December to finance the Persian Cossack Division and to meet any reasonable demands for money, etc., for the national forces it was proposed to raise in Trans-Caucasia. At this period, it may be noted, the total strength of the Persian Cossack Division was reported by the British military attaché at Tehran to be 5,000, with about 100 Russian officers. It was distributed in various detachments in Northern Persia and, though not as efficient a force as the South Persia Rifles, was said to be better than the gendarmerie.

Persian politics and British policy; December 1917. The Government of Ain-ud-Daula proved from the outset to be incapable of dealing with the difficult national situation, while the Shah displayed such pusillanimity that it was said that his deposition was mooted. Among other indications of the loss of authority by the central Government was an extension of the revolt of the Jangalis, which was said to be gaining support from the Bolsheviks, who were by this time extending their activities to the Caucasus and North Persia. Turco-German agents were also said to be instigating the Jangalis, who were buying arms and ammunition from the Russian soldiery. Kuchik Khan, who appears to have originally formed this band of outlaws in January 1915 under Turkish instigation, had gained the sympathy of the poorer classes by confining his depredations to the wealthy, of the peasantry by his declared intention of distributing among them the land of the great landowners, and of the general public by his vigorous opposition to the maladministration and corruption of the Tehran Government. Two Russian and two Persian military expeditions had been sent against him in the last three years, but they had all failed, mainly owing to the thickly-wooded and intricate nature of the Jangali country.

On the 7th December Sir Charles Marling telegraphed that it seemed probable that Vossuk-ud-Daula would be asked to form a Cabinet, and, as this seemed the best chance of averting anarchy in the country, he requested definite instructions as to the support H.M. Government would be prepared to give this Cabinet. Two days later the Shah informed the British Minister that he had decided to make Vossuk Prime Minister, with a free hand to deal with the situation, provided that H.M. Government would guarantee the Shah himself a safe departure and a pension if he was forced to abdicate. Vossuk himself on the 15th December told Sir Charles Marling (with the Shah's approval) that he was prepared to take office, put matters right with a strong hand and co-operate closely with the British, on the understanding that H.M. Government would afford him financial assistance and give him the following assurances —genuine assistance and support for Persia's regeneration; the embodiment at the end of the war of the South Persia Rifles in a uniform force under neutral officers and our good offices to bring about a similar change in the Persian Cossack Division; cancellation of the Anglo-Russian Convention of 1907 and cognate agreements; and representation of Persia at the international peace conference at the end of the war. Sir Charles Marling was in favour of giving these assurances and of guaranteeing the Shah a pension.

On the night 16th/17th December, the head of the detective service at Tehran was assassinated. This was so clearly a political murder indicating a recrudescence of the extremist

Persian politics and British policy; December 1917. campaign of assassination that Sir Charles Marling at once urged that he should be given immediate authority to give the assurances asked for by Vossuk and the Shah, as the latter was so terrified as to be likely, otherwise, to throw himself into the arms of the Democrats and appoint an extremist Cabinet. In another telegram, also sent on the 17th, the British Minister suggested that, in view of the demoralisation of Baratoff's troops, our force in Mesopotamia should take over the protection of the Kermanshah–Hamadan road. Such action was calculated, he said, to stabilise the situation at Tehran. On the 18th the Government of India once more advocated a policy of winning over the Democrat leaders, but Sir Charles Marling, though he considered that we might win over the moderate men among the Democrats, thought it useless to attempt to conciliate the whole party. To win them over, he said, we should have to yield to their every demand till they were our masters, and even then their friendship would only be superficial.

On the 20th December the Foreign Office authorised Sir Charles Marling to give the Shah and Vossuk-ud-Daula the assurances they demanded, practically in full. But these no longer sufficed in face of the greatly increased influence of the extreme section of the Democrats. They were in communication with the Germans, who expected the early re-arrival of their Legation at Tehran with a large staff; they were negotiating with the Bolsheviks, who had recently arrived and who promised support against the British; and they were intriguing with the Jangalis, who had also adopted an anti-British attitude. As an indication of the changed situation, the Persian Government on the 19th had presented a note to the British Minister which argued from a case of pillaging by Russian soldiers that the occupation of Persian territory by foreign soldiers had brought about lamentable results and difficulties in Persia's foreign relations. It went on to request the withdrawal of all the British troops and forwarded the copy of a note from the German Foreign Minister to the Persian Minister in Berlin, dated 15th October, which promised that Germany would give every assistance to ensure Persian neutrality if Great Britain and Russia withdrew their troops which threatened the Turkish frontier and that Germany would approach her own allies on the subject of withdrawing their troops also.

The Shah and Vossuk-ud-Daula, apparently through fear of the Democrats, saw fit to increase their terms to a preposterous extent, and on the 22nd the Shah refused to accept the

KERMANSHAH-HAMADAN AREA

resignation of Ain-ud-Daula. H.M. Government were thus forced to the conclusion, based on this refusal coming after their experience of the past two years, that force was the only thing which Persians would respect and that, beyond financing the South Persia Rifles and the Persian Cossack Division, there seemed little else worth spending British money on.

On the 20th December, General Marshall telegraphed from Baghdad that, besides being beyond the scope of the mission laid down for his force, to take over the protection of the Kermanshah–Hamadan road would involve the employment of more men than he could spare and, in view of the indifferent condition of the road itself, would entail considerable supply difficulties. In this view he was supported by the Chief of the Imperial General Staff, who referred to the arrangements being made for the despatch to Trans-Caucasia of the Dunsterville Mission* and also possibly of some armoured cars to support or take the place of Baratoff's force.

Some of the most demoralised units of Baratoff's force had already been moved out of Persia in the hope of improving the situation. But a mutinous outbreak at Hamadan amongst those remaining at this period tended to show that there was really little hope of improvement.† Sir Charles Marling consequently persisted in his recommendation that British troops should take over the protection of the Kermanshah–Hamadan road. They would soon in any case, he said on the 25th December, be required to open the way for the Dunsterville Mission. Two days later, the news that the enemy was trying to obtain a safe passage through the Caucasus for the return of the German Legation and Turkish Embassy to Tehran—where their presence might easily lead to a British rupture with Persia—afforded a further reason for the presence of British troops in North-West Persia.

On the 31st December, Lieutenant-Colonel Kennion, the British consul at Kermanshah, reported that the prospect of the early Russian departure had induced the Democrats there to cease their anti-British agitation and to approach him with an offer of co-operation on the understanding that we did not send British troops into the area. Colonel Kennion was of opinion that the offer represented genuinely the views of all

British policy; January 1918.

---

* For further details regarding this Mission see "The Campaign in Mesopotamia," Volume IV.

† It is relevant to note that, although the Germans and Turks were trying to arrange for the withdrawal of Russian troops from Persia in accordance with the armistice terms, German agents in the Diyala region received instructions at this time to incite the Kurds to attack these troops as they withdrew.

British policy; January 1918. but a pro-German minority and that it deserved encouragement. Sir Charles Marling, who was at this time himself making special efforts to win over the moderate section of the Democrat party, at once instructed Colonel Kennion to cultivate good relations with the Democrats as far as possible. The Government of India went further and suggested to H.M. Government that, in view of this Kermanshah offer, they should reconsider their policy of sending troops from Mesopotamia, whence a really adequate force could not be made available for the time being. But—H.M. Government having decided that it was necessary to prevent the German and Turkish Missions and other enemy parties from reaching Tehran and to ensure the safe passage through Persia of the Dunsterville Mission, as well as to rally the loyalists among the Russian troops at Kermanshah—the Chief of the Imperial General Staff had already requested General Marshall to despatch into Persia some British mounted troops and armoured cars. The Government of India were accordingly informed by the India Office that the Foreign Office had every reason to question the grounds for the apparent change of policy of the Kermanshah Democrats, and that in all the circumstances a negative policy could scarcely be justified.

Sir Charles Marling's efforts to win over the moderate section of the Democrats made good progress. On the 8th January he reported the formation of a new Cabinet under one of that section, Mustaufi-ul-Mamalik, as a step in the right direction; especially as Mustaufi-ul-Mamalik appeared to be prepared to co-operate with us on terms which were well within the limits H.M. Government had already agreed to. In reply, on the 15th January, the Foreign Office said that H.M. Government would give this Cabinet the same assurances they had been ready to give Vossuk-ud-Daula, it being clearly understood that the South Persia Rifles under British officers should be maintained till the end of war and that British financial assistance would automatically cease in case of any unfriendliness on the part of the Persian Government.

Mustaufi-ul-Mamalik, however, experienced great difficulty in forming a Ministry, and the Cabinet with which he took over office on the 19th January was of such a weak composition that it seemed unlikely to last long. Three days previously Sir Charles Marling had reported his views on the situation. Although he had frankly pointed out to them, he said, that Persia's failure to protect herself or us against enemy efforts might oblige us in future to take self-defensive measures such as in the past had been stigmatised as unfriendly and aggressive, he had succeeded in winning over no inconsiderable portion of the Democrat party. Though there was little hope of their being able to put an end to German activities, we might succeed in creating a body of public opinion strong enough to steady the situation and to act as a check upon the reckless party with which the Germans worked. It was evident, he concluded, that in the long run we should have to rely on force, which, used unhesitatingly, would not only have no ill-consequences but would reassure our friends and be a relief to the general public as putting an end to the existing uncertainty and apprehension.

On the 25th January the British Minister telegraphed that Bravin, the Bolshevik representative, was expected to reach Tehran next day and that, though the Persian Government were unlikely to recognise him, unofficial relations would certainly be established, when Bravin would probably agree to cancel the 1907 Convention and any other instruments objectionable to Persia.

Various attempts were made at this period to organise a Russian force to prevent hostile penetration into Persia. Untrustworthy troops were moved out of the country and Baratoff, assisted by British money, was trying to form a corps composed of the loyal elements. To help him, Bicharakoff— a Russian officer who with a detachment had been fighting alongside the British in Mesopotamia—moved to Kermanshah at the beginning of January. A small mixed British detachment also on the 8th January occupied Qasr-i-Shirin, where it was joined by another small mounted detachment ten days later. But it was decided that none of these troops should go farther than Harunabad until informed by Bicharakoff that their presence farther east was desirable ; and in the meantime they made arrangements to carry out an immediate improvement of the road over the Pai Taq pass, which was in a very bad state. Their advent, however, was reported by our consular officers in West Persia as having exercised a tranquillising effect on the local tribes and a check on German propaganda. *[North-West Persia and British policy; January 1918.]*

By the end of January practically all the Russian troops had left Kermanshah and the chances of forming a corps of Russian volunteers strong enough to provide a protective cordon in that area were evidently very remote. Realising this, Sir Charles Marling submitted that H.M. Government should consider whether we should not take the necessary measures ourselves. He was of opinion that a comparatively small number of British troops would suffice and that their presence would actually strengthen our political position at Tehran. He also pointed out that, owing to the strength of Bolshevik influence on the Caspian and at Baku and to the fact that the local government at Tiflis had no military force at their command, the Dunsterville Mission would have to occupy itself as much with politics as with military matters unless it had a backing of British troops.

It had also been hoped to obtain Russian volunteers for service in Persia from Trans-Caucasia. But our efforts had met with very little success, as the general feeling there, both in the Russian forces and among the local population, was strongly in favour of peace. The Georgians were evidently most unwilling to fight and, though some Armenian units had been formed, our support of them had alienated the Tartars. For this, Armenian action was largely to blame, as they started to kill Tartars and by their indiscreet doings and sayings had so confirmed suspicions aroused by the Turkish propaganda that the Tartars began to regard the British policy in Trans-Caucasia as anti-Islamic. Consequently they were becoming hostile to us, a singularly unfortunate result, as the potential military reserve they afforded—due to their past exemption from Russian military service—was a valuable asset. The Armenian action also lent force to the Turkish incitements to the Tartars to retaliate by killing Armenians.

A further complication was the fact that the Jangalis, in co-operation with the Bolsheviks, had gained complete control of the port of Enzeli. The Bolsheviks and Turco-German agents, in communication with the extremist Democrats at Tehran, were also instigating the Jangalis to oppose by force all British action in Persia and to extend their own authority to Mazanderan, Kazvin and Zenjan as a preliminary to moving on Tehran and establishing there a new government under German influence. This, it was said, the Jangalis had agreed to do.

East Persia; December 1917–January 1918. In Russian Turkestan revolutionary organisations had taken advantage of the general chaos and increasing insecurity to gain control at Tashkend and Askabad. Pan-Turkish emissaries, assisted by itinerant *mullahs*, were very active and were reported to be moving into Bokhara and Afghanistan. It was said that local Moslem opinion was divided, but the local tribesmen were arming themselves, ostensibly for self-defence against Bolshevik excesses. It was estimated that at Tashkend alone there were about 12,000 Austro-German prisoners of war enjoying complete liberty, some of them actively assisting the Bolsheviks or engaged in anti-British propaganda. The War Office had received information that the German General Staff, advised by the Indian Committee at Berlin, had considered several plans for designs against India, but had come to the conclusion that the only hope of success lay in organising an attack from Afghanistan; and during December it became known that there was much current talk in Turkey of a project to send German officers, released from Russian internment camps, to Afghanistan, where it was believed that the Amir's attitude towards the British had completely altered owing to the Russian revolution.

Although we had no reason to believe this or to doubt the Amir's loyalty, there was no doubt that the released prisoners of war in Turkestan were a potential source of danger. Consequently, on the 20th December the Government of India asked H.M. Government if there was any likelihood of the northward extension of the British cordon in East Persia which had been mooted in October. If so, they would like early intimation and also sanction to begin preliminary preparations for the considerable arrangements which would be necessary to ensure the proper maintenance of any force sent north of Birjand. Two days later news was received in India that the Russian Cossacks holding the northern portion of the cordon had been ordered to concentrate at Meshed in readiness to leave Persia. Lieutenant-Colonel W. H. Grey, the Consul-General at Meshed, also represented that when the Russian troops left Khurasan it would be desirable to replace them by British troops in order to check the anti-British activities of Persian extremists, to secure escaped enemy prisoners of war and to ensure the safety of the roads.

In accordance with orders from H.M. Government, instructions were sent to Colonel Dale at the beginning of January that the troops under his command were to extend northward to take over the cordon from Birjand to Sarakhs, which the Russians were evacuating. He was at the same time informed that he would be reinforced forthwith by headquarters and two squadrons 28th Light Cavalry and headquarters and two sections 24th Company, Sappers and Miners. For road-testing purposes he was also being sent as soon as possible a motor van unit of eleven vans and a workshop lorry. He was instructed to improve the road between Robat and Birjand to a light-motor-traffic standard, to sink wells and to take other necessary measures for the improvement of communications. As it was

East Persia; January 1918. estimated that he might require further reinforcement, the military authorities in India got ready four more squadrons of cavalry and some administrative units to send him if necessary. At the same time the British consul in Seistan was directed to enlist 700 more men in the local Levy Corps.*

On the 4th January, 1918, the India Office, at the instance of the War Office, asked if the Government of India considered it practicable to despatch a mission to Turkestan similar to the Dunsterville Mission to the Caucasus. At this time it appeared to H.M. Government that, owing to loss of effective Russian control and to the Bolsheviks' policy, the enemy's determined efforts to arouse the fanaticism of the Moslem population of Turkestan and to excite anti-British hostility were meeting with considerable success. A Turco-German mission was believed to be either in Turkestan or on its way there and the anti-British Moslem movement was spreading to Persia, where it would greatly encourage and strengthen the extremists' influence. There was a serious danger that Turkestan, falling under Turco-German influence, would be made a base for the despatch of large numbers of enemy emissaries, or even organised armed bodies, into Persia and Afghanistan. It was consequently as much in Afghan interests as in our own to prevent such action.

A few days later Colonel Redl reported from Meshed that for the moment the Turkestan Moslems seemed to be mainly concerned for their own lives and property and that, though the local Moslem press was undoubtedly anti-British, he had received no definite information regarding a Turco-German mission. On receipt of this report, the Government of India informed the India Office that they deprecated the despatch of a mission to Turkestan for the moment, though preliminary preparations to send one seemed advisable. Their information regarding the situation there was incomplete, but there appeared to be no kind of Government to which a mission would be helpful as well as useful to us. It would also seem desirable that the mission should be sent in answer to a definite request, and even then the difficult communications would preclude effective military support to it or its proper maintenance.

By the 8th January Colonel Dale had extended his line northward as far as Kain, by the 13th up to Rui Khaf, and on

---

* This brought the total to 1,700. Composed of Seistanis, Baluchis, Kainis and Hazaras, they were in future to be organised in three wings with their headquarters at Seistan, Kain and Meshed (or Turbat-i-Haidari) respectively. In addition to a British commandant, adjutant and quartermaster for the whole corps, there were to be two British officers with each wing.

the 15th he moved his headquarters to Birjand. There was, however, some delay in the Russian evacuation owing to the desire of the Russian officers to remain and to the conflicting nature of the orders they received. The rank and file, on the other hand, were anxious to return to their homes and on the 30th January, taking the law into their own hands, they decided that they would leave for Askabad early in February. By this time the reinforcing Indian units had reached East Persia and, as Colonel Dale preferred infantry to further cavalry reinforcements, one company 98th Infantry (to be followed later by a second company) from India was placed under orders to join him forthwith.

The Persian Government considered it expedient to protest privately against this extension of the cordon. On the other hand, there were few, if any, objections to our action locally, where the uniformly excellent behaviour of the Indian troops and the increased security to person and property which their presence afforded were generally appreciated. Moreover, H.M. Government, on the recommendation of Colonel Grey, sanctioned expenditure of British money on famine relief work in Khurasan and thus alleviated much local distress.

In the second and third weeks of January information was received in India of an autonomous movement among the Turkestan Moslems. This was said to be anti-Bolshevik and seemed to be part of a scheme—obviously of pan-Turkish origin—for forming a Moslem state embracing Turkestan and Trans-Caucasia, independent of Russia and prepared eventually under the aegis of Constantinople to form an alliance with Turkey, Persia and Afghanistan. Reports were also again received that another Turco-German mission was being sent to Afghanistan to exhort the Amir to support Islam by an attack on India and to develop propaganda in India with a view to bringing about a rising there simultaneously with the attack from Afghanistan. Our Consul-General at Meshed, it may be noted, was of opinion that the autonomous movement in Turkestan was not anti-British.

On the 25th January the India Office telegraphed to the Viceroy that the War Office considered that the despatch of a suitable mission to Turkestan, to exploit anti-Bolshevism and the pro-autonomous elements, should be undertaken without delay. The absence there of a regular government seemed an argument for, rather than against, such a mission, and its effective military support was not considered essential. The Government of India were to submit their proposals and make preliminary arrangements at once. Information having been received during the month that pan-Turkish emissaries had proceeded as far east as Khokand, Ferghana and Kashgar, the Government of India came to the conclusion that the mission should be based on two centres, i.e., Meshed and Kashgar. The difficulty was, however, to find officers who were qualified and immediately available for such work.

South Persia; December 1917– January 1918. Comparative tranquillity reigned in South Persia during December. A detachment under a British officer, of a troop of cavalry and a company of infantry of the South Persia Rifles, was sent at Qawam's special request to accompany him on his winter tour in the *Garmsir* among his Arab tribes, some of whose chiefs were rather recalcitrant owing to intrigues by Saulat. At the beginning of the month the British Consul-General at Isfahan suggested the advisability, in view of the imminent Russian military withdrawal from there, of sending a detachment of the South Persia Rifles to safeguard the scattered British community in that town and to maintain general order. Colonel Orton accordingly concentrated a force of South Persia Rifles at Abadeh in readiness to move to Isfahan. He also considered it advisable and an administrative improvement to abolish a number of small posts on the Shiraz–Isfahan road and to concentrate larger numbers at the remaining posts. Attacks by robbers had sensibly diminished, the only one of importance occurring on the 23rd December between Shiraz and Dehbid, when a party of South Persia Rifles, suffering only one casualty themselves, drove off a robber band which attacked the convoy they were escorting with a loss of about eight men.

This affair, however, proved to be the first of a series of raids in that area by Arab tribesmen, which the South Persia Rifles, whose conduct was most disappointing, proved to be unable to deal with effectively. In fact, on the 18th January, fifty South Persia Rifles cavalry, encountering some 200 raiders near Saadatabad, broke and fled as soon as one of their number was killed; their British officer and non-commissioned officer, left in the lurch, being lucky to escape. On receiving news of this affair and learning that many caravans were afraid to leave Saadatabad, Colonel Orton at once sent off a squadron of Burma Mounted Infantry under Major H. R. Dyer to re-open the road and deal with the robbers.

PUNITIVE OPERATIONS 279

There had recently been several indications that a systematic campaign of anti-British propaganda was being carried out in Fars, under instigation from Tehran. Persian officers of the South Persia Rifles, on detachment duties between Shiraz and Abadeh, were making frivolous complaints and giving trouble in a way they had never done before; captured raiding tribesmen declared that they had been instigated by influential persons in Tehran to attack South Persia Rifles escorts along the Shiraz-Isfahan road; and camels of merchants had in some of the raids been allowed to go free, only the South Persia Rifles baggage animals being taken off by the raiders. Moreover, it was unusual for Khamseh tribesmen to be in camp during December and January in the highlands east of Saadatabad, as they normally moved for the winter to the Niriz Valley or farther south.

Reaching Qawwamabad on the 21st January and learning that the robber band was in the hills to the north-east of Saadatabad, Major Dyer moved out at 2 a.m. on the 22nd with his Burma Mounted Infantry and two troops South Persia Rifles cavalry to try to get round them. But the robbers had moved off the previous day; and, after covering about thirty-five miles without encountering them, Major Dyer camped that night at Saadatabad. Here he received information that the robbers had moved to the south-east via Arsinjan; and on the 23rd he marched to that place, where he received further information that they were encamped in the vicinity of Gumun, about twelve miles to the south-east. He encountered them there on the 24th, killed or wounded about 25 of them, destroyed two of their camps, and recovered a considerable number of plundered animals, his own casualties totalling only 3 men and 7 horses. The weather was intensely cold* and his men had covered from twenty-four to forty miles during the day. But as the robbers had followed up his withdrawal to camp, he decided to move out again next morning in the Gumun direction to inflict further punishment. A heavy snowfall on the 25th, however, and the necessity for carrying out a foraging expedition on the 26th delayed further operations till the 27th. On that day he encountered considerable opposition, but the Burma Mounted Infantry, well handled and displaying considerable dash and spirit, completely routed the robbers, killing or wounding about 80 of them, burning their remaining camp and recovering many more of the animals they had plundered, the cost in casualties to the Burma Mounted Infantry squadron amounting to 3 killed

Affair of Gumun; January 1918. (See Map 8.)

---

* Arsinjan stands at an altitude of over 9,000 feet.

and 15 wounded. After an uncomfortable return march in intensely cold and snowy weather, the squadron reached Shiraz on the 3rd February. The complete success of the expedition and the well-deserved severe punishment inflicted on the robbers had an immediate and excellent effect.

<small>British policy; January 1918.</small> At the end of January Sir Charles Marling informed the new Persian Cabinet that, with a view to meeting Persian objections, H.M. Government were prepared to negotiate with them on certain outstanding questions, including the incorporation of the South Persia Rifles in the uniform force under European officers which the Persian Government desired to organise. Though at first the Persian Government showed little inclination to negotiate, on the 4th February they suggested that if we withdrew all British troops from Persian territory they would officially recognise the South Persia Rifles and would use every means to prevent the entry and activity of enemy agents. In a verbal discussion over this suggestion Sir Charles Marling gathered from the Persian Foreign Minister that his Government would not object to the retention of British consular guards nor of the levies, etc., holding the East Persia Cordon and that they proposed to utilise the Persian Cossack Division to carry out their part of the bargain. The British Minister pointed out, however, that the utility of this division depended entirely on the presence of its Russian officers and that they might disappear at any moment, either as the result of circumstances or of action by the Persian Government who were credited with a desire to get rid of them. Although it seemed doubtful if the Persian proposal was a sincere one, it appeared to be worth consideration if we could ensure that the Persian Cossack Division were maintained on a satisfactory footing.

At this time the Jangalis were reported to be trying to enter into an alliance with the Shah Sawan tribe in Azerbaijan, with the Kurds and other tribes in the Kermanshah area, and to be corresponding with the Austrian Legation at Tehran and the gendarmerie there as well as with the Germans and Turks —all indicating an increasing danger from this direction.

<small>British policy; February 1918.</small> H.M. Government decided that the Persian offer constituted a fair basis for negotiation and on the 9th February they telegraphed to India and Tehran that, as it was essential on general military grounds to maintain communication with the Caucasus by the Kermanshah–Enzeli road, they were disposed to agree to the withdrawal of the Indian troops with

Sir Percy Sykes, on the understanding that the Persian Government would officially recognise the South Persia Rifles and would accept British officers for the Persian Cossack Division for the duration of the war.

General Marshall in Mesopotamia, in reply to a query by the Chief of the Imperial General Staff, had telegraphed on the same day that he estimated that a cavalry brigade and a division would be required to replace the Russian troops in North-West Persia and that to maintain them in that area would take all the transport he possessed. He himself was against locking troops up in Persia, where their presence would be resented by the Persians; and he considered that a steady advance on Mosul was more likely to achieve the object in view. At the time this telegram was sent our information was that the Turks were withdrawing troops from their Caucasus front to concentrate in Palestine or Syria. Further, our Consul-General at Isfahan had just requested that, as the Persian Cossack detachment there was proving quite incapable of maintaining order, a force of South Persia Rifles should be moved to that town, while the British liaison officer with Baratoff at Hamadan reported about the same time that it would be at least a year before the Persian Cossacks, under British officers, could be trusted to hold the road and that even then he did not think that they could be relied on without a backing of British troops.

On the 12th February the Government of India telegraphed welcoming the proposal from London. But Sir Charles Marling on that day also telegraphed that it was impracticable. The Cossack Division, he pointed out, was distributed all over North Persia in detachments which could not be withdrawn without imperilling the local situation; and in any case the Persian Government would never agree to the replacement of Russian by British officers. If the road to the Caucasus was to be kept open it must, he said, be done by British troops.

In another telegram sent the same day he said that the Persian Government showed no inclination to conclude the negotiations and would, in the meantime, do nothing to secure the road. He did not believe that they would, in any case, do anything really effective in that direction or that they would ever venture to interfere with the German emissaries. We must therefore seriously consider undertaking both tasks ourselves. For this it would be sufficient, he thought, if we held the road to Kazvin in sufficient strength to show both Tehran and the Jangalis that we were not to be trifled with. The Jangali movement had

British policy; February 1918.
only attained its existing proportions from lack of opposition, and with British troops in Persia it would be easy, he said, for neighbouring chiefs to destroy its power. If H.M. Government decided to take this step, he advocated a declaration of the concessions they were prepared to make to meet Persian wishes and also an explanation that our action was necessary as a measure of self-defence. Unless we adopted half measures he did not anticipate anything but a certain amount of protest from Persians, while, on the other hand, the majority of the intelligent part of the population would be relieved at our forcing the country out of the vacillating policy which they recognised as fatal to her. We had already had to disregard Persia's professed neutrality in the east, south and south-west and, as circumstances were likely to compel us sooner or later to use troops in the north-west also, it seemed better to act at once than to drag on negotiations which entailed ever-increasing concessions.

Four days later, Sir Charles Marling again urged H.M. Government to despatch troops into North-West Persia. The Jangali movement, the German peace with the Ukraine and the immobility of the British force in Mesopotamia all combined to cause the Persian Government to procrastinate, and he considered further negotiations with them to be waste of time. Additional concessions would bring us no more converts from the Democrat party; and the extremists, who would always be irreconcilable, would collapse before an exhibition of force.

The Government of India, however, did not agree with Sir Charles Marling and still advocated a policy of conciliation to win over the Persian Government and people and induce them to maintain the South Persia Rifles and the Persian Cossacks in an efficient state. The Indian authorities said that they saw no immediate likelihood of a Turco-German thrust into North Persia and they thought that the Persian Cossacks should suffice to avert the immediate danger from enemy emissaries and acts of brigandage. On the other hand, if we were to employ force it would have to be on a scale sufficient to overawe the country completely, and there were military and political objections to such a course. In default of serious provocation, it would finally discredit us in Persian eyes and it would be so misrepresented elsewhere as to bring on us the odium of the whole Moslem world.

Sir Charles Marling considered that these views from India were largely based on erroneous premises. The immediate German object, he said, was to bring Persia into the war against

A CHANGE FOR THE WORSE

us by the use of agents and emissaries without employing troops. This danger could not be met by Persian Cossacks and the South Persia Rifles. Even if the South Persia Rifles could be spared from South Persia, which was improbable, the extension of their sphere northwards would provoke as great an outcry as the despatch of British troops, while the Persian Cossacks would not act without an order from the Persian Government, which the latter would be afraid to give if German influence became formidable. To effect the replacement of Russian by British officers in the Persian Cossack force would also require the presence of British troops. Moreover, said Sir Charles Marling, only a small British force was required to overawe the handful of reckless factions whose political capital was a spurious patriotism inspired by Germany. The despatch of such a force would be welcomed by our friends and the whole peaceful community and would facilitate real government, as it would remove the fear of the extremists which every Persian Cabinet experienced. In conclusion, Sir Charles Marling said that the Government of India had overlooked the necessity for keeping open communication with the Caucasus.

In the meantime, various incidents indicated a change for the worse in the general situation. The forced resignation—due to Russian intrigues and Persian action—of various Russian officers of the Persian Cossack Division showed that its discipline, never too good, was deteriorating. General Dunsterville had been stopped at Enzeli by Bolsheviks and Jangalis and had been forced to retire to Hamadan. The Jangalis, joined by German agents and working in co-operation with the Bolsheviks, were displaying uncompromising hostility to the British and were meditating an advance on Hamadan, where the Turk Obeidulla, from the Turkish Embassy at Tehran, had promised that they would soon be joined by Turkish troops. The Bolshevik Government had been forced unwillingly to agree to the terms of the Brest-Litovsk peace treaty. The pan-Turkish movement was reliably reported to have gained a great impetus from recent events in Russia. The Turks had broken off negotiations with the Federal Republic of Trans-Caucasia, where the pro-Turk Tartars were fighting the Bolsheviks ; and there was evidence that Turkey looked to obtain territorial compensation in Trans-Caucasia for the probable loss of her Arab provinces. Finally, the Persian extremists were in active communication with the enemy powers, the Jangalis and the Bolsheviks.

On the 21st February the Foreign Office telegraphed to Sir Charles Marling that, as the despatch of a small force might

British policy; February 1918. develop into a military occupation of parts of North Persia—or might call for the despatch of reinforcements which could not be spared—such a policy was likely, as pointed out by India, to arouse the suspicions of the Moslem world. They consequently desired to know if any alternative proposal in return for the withdrawal of British troops would have any chance of success. The main British desire was to secure the immunity of Persia from the inroads of enemy agents or forces which might subsequently constitute a threat to Afghanistan. H.M. Government had hitherto attached much importance to keeping open the Hamadan–Enzeli road as a means of helping the loyal elements in Trans-Caucasia and, though reports as to this were not hopeful, they increased the desirability of maintaining a cordon on the western frontiers of Persia. For this purpose it might be possible to supply a considerable number of armoured cars, officers and non-commissioned officers for employment in the Persian service if acceptable to Tehran and the Cabinet; and from a British point of view this would provide a reasonable *quid pro quo* for the withdrawal of British troops.

Sir Charles Marling replied on the 23rd that he had no alternative to suggest. He warned H.M. Government that if they decided against a military occupation of the Kermanshah–Kazvin road in favour of a policy of conciliation, there would be no end to Persian demands and that, as the Persian Government had no reliable force to prevent inroads and could not use it if they had, concessions made by us would not bring us anything whatever in exchange. The real trouble was that the extremists, who were in league with the Jangalis, had terrorised the Cabinet into subservience. If H.M. Government were willing to give an undertaking to send troops to protect the Cabinet if necessary against the Jangalis, it would be advisable to try that course.

On the 26th February the Persian Government resigned. Though their resignation was really due to the discontent in the country which their incapacity had aroused, they cast the blame on us. In point of fact Sir Charles Marling had been trying to come to terms with them for the past three weeks, but without success owing to their fear of the extremists. The latter had established relations with the Germans, Turks, Bolsheviks and Jangalis, all of whose assistance against us they counted on; and, when the Cabinet resigned, they saw in the situation caused by recent events in Asia Minor* and the

---

* The Turks, starting to advance eastward again, recaptured Trebizond on the 24th February.

SERIOUS SITUATION

Caucasus an opportunity of getting rid of British interference by an early rupture of relations. As a preliminary they proceeded to organise a great anti-British demonstration in Tehran so as to intimidate the Shah and prevent him appointing a new Cabinet with moderate tendencies. In describing the situation in a telegram on the 26th, Sir Charles Marling said that it was necessary for us to use force so as to check the extremists and forestall an early rupture of relations. He advocated a military occupation of Kermanshah, Hamadan and, if necessary, Kazvin, as soon as the Russians left.

General Dunsterville at Hamadan had also come to the same conclusions. On the 26th he telegraphed to the Chief of the Imperial General Staff that it seemed necessary for us to occupy the Qasr-i-Shirin–Enzeli road and that such action would, he was convinced, be welcomed by the inhabitants, whatever the Persian politicians might say.

From these and other reports H.M. Government realised that the position was very serious. The combination of Bolsheviks, Austro-German prisoners of war,* Jangalis, Moslem fanatics and Persian extremists meant a coalition of forces to produce a world revolution, a holy war and a pan-Turkish rising. They were probably incapable of organised or prolonged hostilities, but the anarchy they would produce in Persia meant potential danger to Afghanistan and India. The main factor in our favour was the strength of our position in Mesopotamia. On the other hand, the news that the Turks had been withdrawing several divisions from their Caucasus to their Palestine front was now found to be exaggerated. They had only transferred two divisions.

On the 27th February the Foreign Office, referring to Sir Charles Marling's telegram of the previous day and to other past telegrams from him and India,† explained that H.M. Government were not in favour of a policy of unlimited concessions. If the Persian Government rejected those already offered, there was no advantage in further discussions. It might consequently become necessary to move British troops (i) from Khaniqin to Hamadan to protect the road and prevent enemy incursions and (ii) from Shiraz to Isfahan, or even near Tehran, either to safeguard the British Legation or to protect a friendly Persian Cabinet. Their military advisers were examining the question.

---

* Numbers of these were constantly moving from Trans-Caspia into Persia, where they joined the Jangalis and assisted the extremists.
† The Government of India, it may be noted, were still advocating strongly a policy of conciliation, and they continued to do so.

British policy; March 1918. In accordance with instructions from H.M. Government, the Chief of the Imperial General Staff telegraphed on the 1st March to both Mesopotamia and India. General Dunsterville was for the time being to remain in Persia and General Marshall was to keep open the road from Qasr-i-Shirin to Kermanshah and possibly later to Hamadan ; while the Commander-in-Chief in India was asked for his views in regard to a move of British troops from Shiraz to Isfahan and possibly to the vicinity of Tehran. On the 3rd March the Chief of the Imperial General Staff telegraphed that, owing to the uncertain situation on the Persian frontier, the War Cabinet had decided to reduce the size of the force which it had been proposed to transfer from Mesopotamia to Palestine ; and on the 6th he enquired how long it would take General Marshall to get troops to Hamadan if this became necessary.

On the 8th March General Monro, after consulting Sir Percy Sykes, informed the Chief of the Imperial General Staff that, for a move on Isfahan, Indian troops with a detachment of South Persia Rifles should be utilised. As Indian troops must be retained at Shiraz and on the line of communication from Bandar Abbas, he considered that it would be necessary to reinforce Sir Percy Sykes with three squadrons, four guns and one battalion.

By this time the Turkish forces were advancing along their whole front from the Black Sea to Lake Van and it was evident that they were on their way to occupy Ardahan, Kars and Batum, ceded to them by the treaty of Brest-Litovsk, and that the only opposition they would encounter would be from the Armenians, who were also in conflict with all the Moslem tribes in the area to be traversed. Information had also been received that the Persian extremists were raising a military force at Kazvin for action against the British.

On the 7th March the Secretary of State for Foreign Affairs sent the following telegram to the British Minister at Tehran :

" Present situation has been engaging earnest consideration of H.M. Government, who have desired nothing so much as a Cabinet at Tehran capable of preserving Persia's neutrality and maintaining order throughout country and who have recently re-affirmed publicly their unqualified adhesion to principle of Persian independence.

I have accordingly instructed you on many recent occasions to enter into friendly discussions with Persian Government. All that was asked of them was that they should manifest a spirit of general friendliness to British

To face page 286.

Summit of Asadabad Pass in March.

THE BRITISH CONCLUSION

interests and due regard to our representations; that they should take measures to secure Persia against a recurrence of the situation brought about by enemy activities in autumn and early winter of 1915, when country was overrun by enemy agents and marauding bands; and, lastly, in view of predominant interests of Great Britain in South Persia and chaos which would result from absence of any organised force, that they should formally recognise South Persia Rifles, for which H.M. Government have continued to bear charge, as at present constituted until end of war.

On their side H.M. Government have been prepared to offer financial assistance to Persian Government on an enhanced and liberal scale; to favour creation after war of a uniform military force for whole country in which South Persia Rifles should be eventually incorporated under foreign officers of a nationality to be determined hereafter; to treat Anglo-Russian Convention of 1907 as in suspense pending creation of a duly constituted Government in Russia with whom its abrogation could be formally discussed; to accede to withdrawal by Persia of her recognition of Convention; to agree to revision of customs tariff with Persia; and in accordance with expressed wishes of Persian Government to welcome presence of Persian representatives at any international conference to which non-belligerents might be invited.

These offers, which are still open, have not so far met with acceptance from Persian Government. On the other hand, lawlessness is rife. Turks have entered Western Azerbaijan at various points. Jangalis have practically severed connection between capital and Enzeli; and H.M. Consul at Resht is in personal danger.* In fact, North-West Persia from the Caspian to the Turkish border is either in a state of active disorder or is exposed to hostile movements which dominate northern approaches to capital, effectively threaten neutrality of Persian Government and constitute a serious menace to interests which H.M. Government are endeavouring to defend within Persia.

In view of this situation, daily growing worse, H.M. Government have been reluctantly forced to conclude that they must make themselves responsible for measures of protection against a common danger which Persian Government are either unable or unwilling to adopt.

---

* Actually he and the British bank manager at Resht had been arrested the previous day by the Jangalis.

British policy; March 1918. They have decided to despatch a sufficient force of British troops from Turkish frontier to north-west. Point to which they will advance will depend upon steadying influence which presence of this detachment will be found to exert and upon the degree of authority exercised by Persian Government themselves. . . ."

At the same time Sir Charles Marling was asked for his opinion regarding the move of Indian troops to Isfahan. He replied on the 10th March doubting the utility of such a move. Further discussion on the point ensued between London, Tehran and India, and this continued till the 30th, when it was decided to abandon the idea for the time being. In the meantime, steps had been taken to send from India the reinforcements required for the move; and it was decided that, on their arrival at Bandar Abbas at the beginning of April, they were to be sent to join Sir Percy Sykes.

On the 11th March, the day on which Mustaufi-ul-Mamalik resumed office as Prime Minister, Sir Charles Marling presented the note announcing and explaining British intentions. It at once became apparent that the extremists—expecting, it was said, an event in about five weeks time which would enable them to defy us—were urging a policy of stubbornness. To this end they were resorting to force to crush all opposition, their methods being well illustrated by the assassination on the evening of the 14th of the editor of a pro-British newspaper. The difficulties of the road and of transport were causing delay in the despatch of troops from Mesopotamia; and on the 16th March Sir Charles Marling telegraphed urging speed in sending even a very small force to join General Dunsterville at Hamadan, in view of a possible Jangali advance on Kazvin. The only Russian troops left at Hamadan were Bicharakoff's partisans, who had agreed to co-operate with the Dunsterville Mission and who, it was hoped, would shortly move to Enzeli to prevent the Caspian falling under the control of a hostile combination.

The reply of the Persian Government to the British note was presented on the 18th March and was somewhat uncompromising in tone. They stigmatised the British action as incompatible with past British assurances of respect for Persian independence and they requested the withdrawal of British troops. Further, though they expressed gratification at the concessions tendered, they put forward pretensions to others which were clearly inadmissible. The resignation of two of the moderate members of the Cabinet showed, however, that

To face page 288.

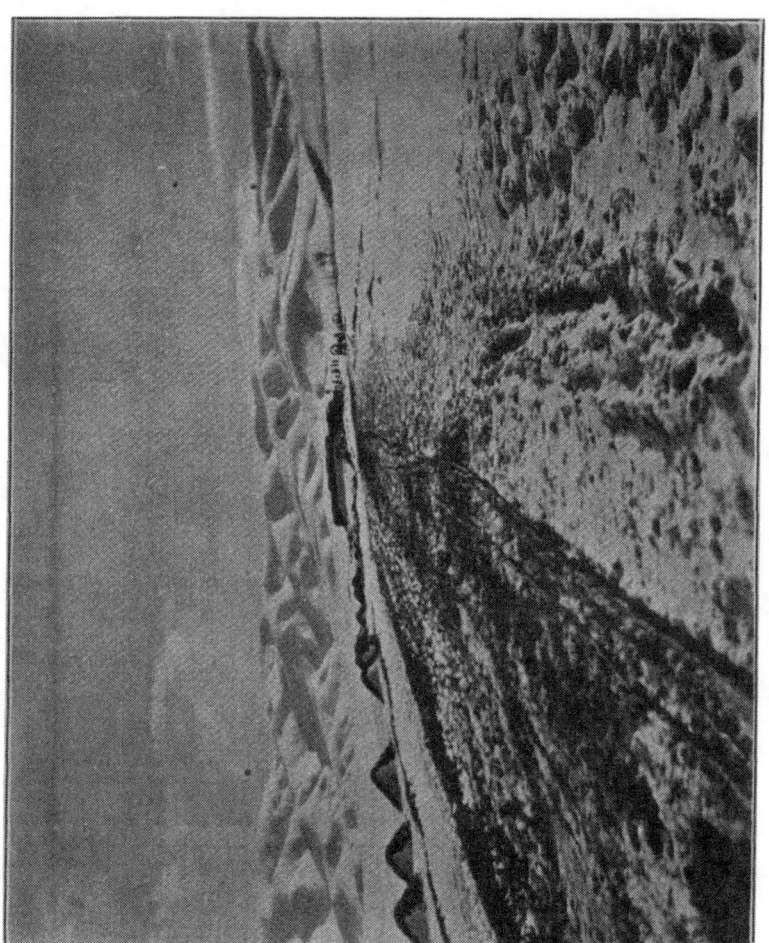

Road between Kazvin and Hamadan in March.

the desire for opposition to the British action was by no means universal; and this was further confirmed when the Shah sent word to the British Minister that he was prepared to dismiss the Cabinet and appoint a new one under Ain-ud-Daula. Sir Charles Marling considered, however, that such a Cabinet was unlikely to be very different in complexion to the existing one, whose imminent fall appeared to be responsible for the extremists' efforts to induce a Jangali *coup*, first at Kazvin and then at Tehran.

On the 18th March the Jangalis arrested Captain Noel of the Indian Political Department, who had just returned to Enzeli from a mission to Trans-Caucasia on which Sir Charles Marling had sent him. But the British Minister had reliable information that the Jangalis were not disposed to commit themselves to an advance southwards until the Turkish troops whose assistance they had been promised had actually arrived on the scene. Moreover, they had recently quarrelled with and been worsted by the Shah Sawan tribe, who inhabited the area east of Tabriz; and the financial crisis brought about by their arrest of the British bank manager at Resht had caused serious trouble between them and the Bolsheviks.

The Persian Government's attitude was further explained by information from a reliable source that neither they nor the Shah believed that we were in earnest about sending troops from Mesopotamia.

In the last week of March the Jangali menace to Kazvin was dispelled by the arrival there of Bicharakoff's detachment. At the same time a small advanced party of the 1/4th Hampshire Regiment from Mesopotamia reached Hamadan, where anti-British sentiment had decreased owing to the tactful and conciliatory methods of General Dunsterville and to the initiation by him of famine relief measures.

By the beginning of April, information from various sources made it clear that the Turks were actively working for the formation under Turkish control of the new Moslem state, which should include not only Russian and Persian Azerbaijan but also part of Gilan. Enver's brother, Nuri, was on his way to Tabriz to organise a Moslem army, another Turkish notable had been sent to Urmia to invoke Kurdish assistance, and the Tartars were clearly ready to help the Turks. Turkish agents were negotiating with the Persian extremists and the Jangalis, but, finding that they objected strongly to any cession of Persian territory, were concealing their real aims under the guise of an intention to resist British attempts to intervene in Persia

British policy; April 1918.

British policy; April 1918.
and Trans-Caucasia. The Germans had occupied Odessa in the middle of March, were likely to obtain control of the Black Sea and obviously meant to move into Georgia if not farther east; while their agents were skilfully playing on the motives of all the anti-British factions and hoped to bring about a revolution in Persia, where their chances of success had been enhanced by the news of the recent German victories in France. On the other hand these Turco-German actions and movements had alarmed the Bolsheviks, who, to save Trans-Caucasia, where the terms of the Brest-Litovsk treaty had intensified the racial conflict of interests, had begun to co-operate actively with the Armenians. This Armenian-Bolshevik alliance, coupled with the Armenian co-operation with the loyalist Russians against the Turkish Caucasus armies, completed the alienation of Russophobe Georgia. The whole situation in Trans-Caucasia was, therefore, chaotic and the Federal Government had practically no control.

The hostility to Great Britain which the Persian Government continued to display throughout April was only kept in some sort of check by the Shah's refusal to sanction more vigorous action. The Shah, it appears, was still prepared to dismiss the Cabinet and replace it by one of more moderate complexion. But he doubted if the force we were sending from Mesopotamia would be of sufficient size to ensure his own position and to defend the Government against a threatened Jangali *coup*, which, it was reported, was to be carried out by an advance avoiding Bicharakoff and his men at Kazvin.

During April the only British troops to reach Hamadan were one squadron 14th Hussars, three armoured cars and some officers and non-commissioned officers for special duty. But the position had so far improved that General Dunsterville had begun to raise levies locally, and by the end of the month the situation in the Kermanshah-Hamadan area showed a still greater improvement owing to the check to hostile propaganda and activities caused by the defeat inflicted on the pro-German Sinjabis and the occupation of Kifri by General Marshall's troops. The advent of a more moderate regime—calling themselves Social Revolutionaries—at Baku was also of advantage, especially as they had control of the Russian Caspian fleet.*
But elsewhere in Trans-Caucasia the situation was still chaotic. The Turks had made sure of the territory assigned to them,

---

* On learning that the Trans-Caucasian authorities had recently tried to sell this fleet, H.M. Government had instructed the British Mission to buy it if possible.

having occupied Batum, Ardahan and Kars, and later in the month started a converging movement through Persian Azerbaijan towards Tabriz, which called forth a strong protest to Constantinople from the Persian Government. The Germans had entered the Crimea and, as a means of preventing their seizure of the Russian Black Sea fleet, the Bolsheviks had in desperation suggested that we should re-organise it. There were also reliable reports that Turco-German relations were considerably strained owing to their divergence of views regarding the Caucasus.

On the 29th April the War Office telegraphed to General Marshall in Mesopotamia that it was certain (i) that the Turks intended to occupy Azerbaijan, (ii) that German agents in collusion with members of the Persian Government were preparing for a general rising against us when Turkish troops appeared in Persia, and (iii) that the Turks would shortly dominate the whole of Trans-Caucasia. In these circumstances —though it was necessary to maintain a small British force on the Hamadan road in order to stabilise the situation at Tehran, occupy Enzeli if possible and perhaps gain control of the Caspian in co-operation with the Bolsheviks and Armenians —the maximum force which General Marshall could maintain on the Persian plateau would only eat up all his transport and do nothing to frustrate the immediate Turkish designs.

The War Office accordingly advocated a hard and immediate stroke by General Marshall in the Kirkuk–Sulaimaniya direction, so as to force the Turks to divert troops destined for Azerbaijan, and possibly some from Armenia, to oppose him. In the meantime the British troops allotted to the Hamadan road and the Persian plateau were to be limited to a cavalry regiment, an infantry battalion and as many armoured cars and aeroplanes as could be spared, while the organisation of local levies was to be pushed forward.

During February and March, beyond the fact that Saulat was trying to stir up trouble in the area under Qawam, the situation in South Persia was comparatively peaceful. A considerable amount of work in improving road and telephonic communications and in training the South Persia Rifles was, therefore, possible. The Persian rank and file appeared to be well contented and, though inclined to over-estimate their own attainments, were gradually acquiring better discipline and confidence in their British instructors. The Persian officers

South Persia; Feb.-April 1918.

South Persia; Feb.–April 1918. were the weak spot. A small force of South Persia Rifles behaved well in some fighting with robbers which occurred between the 24th and 28th February to the north of Abadeh.

The reinforcements despatched from India at the end of March consisted of drafts to form a third squadron for the Burma Mounted Infantry,* two sections 33rd Mountain Battery, half-battalion 120th Infantry, headquarters and half-battalion 3/124th Baluchis, a brigade supply section and two sections 161st Indian Field Ambulance. These arrived at Bandar Abbas at the beginning of April and then marched up country towards Shiraz.

On the 6th April, Sir Percy Sykes, who on return from India three weeks previously had re-assumed command at Shiraz, reported to Sir Charles Marling that the constant attempts to excite disaffection among the Persian officers and men of the South Persia Rifles were placing a severe strain on their loyalty to their British officers. The Germanophile Persian Minister of the Interior, Mukhbar-es-Sultaneh, who was responsible for much of this, was also displaying open hostility to the British by his telegraphic orders and letters and was inciting the Qashqais and other tribes to cause disorders and to attack caravans. Landowners and other leading men appreciated the benefits accruing from our presence; and Farman Farma was, generally speaking, pro-British. But he was timid and frightened at the state of affairs. Sir Percy Sykes was afraid of desertions, possibly on a large scale, unless the Persian Government withdrew their repudiation of the South Persia Rifles.

Sir Charles Marling at once asked for details, and on the 13th April Sir Percy Sykes sent a long report giving several instances in proof of his statement. In December 1917, he said, the Persian Government had instructed their officials in South Persia, not only not to recognise the South Persia Rifles but to obstruct the force actively in every way. Since then, Farman Farma, Persians friendly to the British, and the public generally in South Persia had been intimidated and incited to anti-British and anti-South Persia Rifles action by telegrams, pamphlets, circulars, newspaper articles and other means, all emanating from Tehran, the implication of Mukhbar-es-Sultaneh being clear in many instances. Further, in addition to other clear evidence that the tribes were being incited to oppose and attack the British and the South Persia Rifles,

---

* It was proposed to send also two cavalry squadrons from India.

To face page 293.

Floods (between Duzdab and Robat); 27th March, 1918.

ATTITUDE OF SOUTH PERSIA RIFLES

letters had been received by his friends at Shiraz from Saulat professing perplexity at receiving orders from Tehran to harry the South Persia Rifles.

The fears of Sir Percy Sykes proved well-founded. On the 18th April a number of South Persia Rifles deserted from Abadeh leaving a letter indicating political reasons for their action; and on the 21st, when he reported further desertions, Sir Percy Sykes said that Farman Farma's attitude had become unsatisfactory. On the 24th he further reported that many Persian friends warned him that he could no longer place any reliance on the loyalty to their British officers of the Fars Brigade of the South Persia Rifles.

Early in April the position at Abadeh and Dehbid had been considered unsatisfactory and insecure, and during the month a company of the 16th Rajputs was sent as a reinforcement. One platoon remained at Dehbid and the remainder of the company proceeded to Abadeh. Major W. A. K. Fraser (commanding at Abadeh) was instructed to form an inner perimeter of defence which the Indian troops could hold as a last resort.

With effect from the 1st April, 1918, Colonel Orton was appointed Deputy Inspector-General of the South Persia Rifles, and in addition was given executive command in the field over all the Indian troops with the Sykes Mission.

The strength and distribution at the end of April of the South Persia Rifles, as well as the distribution of the Indian troops with the Sykes Mission, are given in Appendix III.

Owing to the increase of the force in East Persia and the extension of its sphere northwards, its official designation was altered to East Persia Cordon Field Force and Lieutenant-Colonel Dale, with the temporary rank of Brigadier-General, was appointed to command it with an increased staff. By the 16th February, the day after the last Russian troops left Meshed, the British cordon had reached Turbat-i-Haidari, but, owing to difficulty in procuring transport, it did not reach Meshed till the 14th March.

East Persia; Feb.–April 1918.

By the end of March General Dale's force consisted of the 28th Light Cavalry, half 24th Company Sappers and Miners, 1/19th Punjabis, two companies 98th Infantry and 1,700 Levies.* Their distribution on that date is given in

---

* One company 98th Infantry was still *en route* from Quetta and the levy establishment was not quite complete.

Appendix IV. The necessary administrative units included a Ford van section and some motor ambulances; and the sappers, with some of the troops, were employed in improving the road.

On the 1st February the Government of India telegraphed to London recommending that the proposed mission to Russian Turkestan should be based on two centres, i.e., Meshed and Kashgar, from which emissaries could be sent out as opportunity offered. The centre at Meshed would be concerned with the country west of the Oxus and the Bokhara plain, while Kashgar would deal with Ferghana and Samarkand, where for the moment the autonomous movement seemed to be strongest.

This movement, which aimed at eliminating the Russian element and making Russian Turkestan autonomous, was being resisted by the Bolsheviks, who desired to retain Turkestan within the Russian federation. The consequent armed struggle was being carried out with varying fortune amid the chaos resulting from the collapse of the Russian central Government, while, to complicate matters further, enemy agents were said to be active all through the country, their capacity for danger being greatly enhanced by the presence of over 30,000 Austro-Hungarian and German prisoners of war, who were scattered all over the area in complete freedom and trying to earn a living as best they could.

As the objective of a British mission seemed very vague and its chances of success very problematical, the Government of India telegraphed to London on the 12th February advocating caution and further consideration before its despatch was finally decided upon. They also wished first to receive a reply from the Amir of Afghanistan, whom they had addressed on the subject. At the beginning of March H.M. Government expressed their concurrence in this view.

The news received in India by the middle of March indicated that, after severe fighting, both with Cossack forces and with the Moslem elements striving for independence, the Bolsheviks had gained the supremacy in Turkestan and were maintaining their position by a reign of ruthless terrorism. The activity of enemy agents seemed to have died down, while the chaotic conditions appeared to have paralysed all pan-Turkish or similar political ideas. On the 21st March, after consulting the British consuls at Meshed and Kashgar, the Government of India informed the India Office that the Amir of Afghanistan had not yet replied, but that they proposed to send selected officers to these two places to acquaint themselves with local conditions. They would then be ready and available to take advantage of any favourable opportunity, though there was as yet no evidence of any pro-Ally elements with which they could co-operate.

In the meantime, the ruler of Bokhara, attempting to gain independence for his country, had come into bitter and heavy conflict with the Bolsheviks.

On the 9th April the Chief of the General Staff in India informed Colonel Redl that, in accordance with instructions from the Chief of the Imperial General Staff, certain officers were being sent to Meshed to investigate the possibility of sending a military mission to anticipate German propaganda in Russian Turkestan. Under the orders of Colonel Redl, who was to act in close consultation with the British Consul-General at Meshed, these officers were to collect all possible information regarding the situation and were to get into touch with notables and other elements who could assist a mission. But they were not to carry out active propaganda nor were they to enter Turkestan without orders from India. Should the mission be subsequently despatched, a senior officer would be sent from India to command it. A similar party of officers was proceeding to Kashgar to work there under the British consul. In reply to a request for further information concerning the lines on which a military mission would work, Colonel Redl was informed that its main object would be to combat Turco-German propaganda and attempts to organise the country's inhabitants and resources towards assisting hostile enterprises, aggression or even active operations against us. As a general principle it would afford support to elements ready to help the Allies. But beyond this, until something more definite was ascertained concerning existing conditions, it was not possible to lay down the lines for the mission to work on.

By this time, the Bokharans had been defeated and had made a fruitless appeal for assistance to Afghanistan, with the result that the Bolsheviks were masters of the country. It seemed clear that all the Moslem races of Turkestan, with the possible exception of the pro-Turk Caucasians, were ready to accept help from anyone who would free them from Bolshevik tyranny.

On the 29th April the Chief of the Imperial General Staff telegraphed to the Commander-in-Chief in India approving the action taken and expressing the opinion that Major-General W. Malleson, the officer selected to command the Turkestan Mission, should be sent to Meshed as soon as possible.

Till April, the Persian Government, with their customary lack of interest in East Persia, had offered practically no

East Persia; objections to British action there. But in that month they
April 1918. protested against our road-making operations in Seistan and
Kain and our railway extension towards the Persian frontier,
while in Meshed itself extremist Democrats gave us considerable
trouble by their propaganda, their attempts to prevent us
obtaining supplies, and their active obstruction to our famine
relief measures. The situation was further complicated to our
disadvantage by the intrigues of Russian reactionaries and
Bolsheviks, both of whom regarded our presence in North
Persia with disfavour. As the situation held out danger from
the threat, and possible use, of force, General Dale reported
that he found it necessary to reinforce his garrison at Meshed.
His request that the remaining half-battalion 98th Infantry
should be sent from India to join him was accordingly
sanctioned.

By the end of March, the Nushki railway extension had
reached to within fifty miles of Mirjawa on the Persian frontier;
and early in April the Government of India proposed to the
India Office that, in view of the general situation, it would be
advisable to carry out reconnaissance surveys, northwards
towards Birjand and westwards towards Rigan, in case further
railway extension became imperative.

H.M. Government deprecated the proposal as raising questions
of a far-reaching character, and suggested that an extension
in British territory from Mirjawa to Robat would answer
requirements. To this the Government of India replied on
the 26th April that, in view of the probable increase of enemy
activity in Persia and of a possible enemy movement along the
Russian railways towards Afghanistan, they regarded a railway
extension towards Neh as a precautionary measure of great
importance. It would enable us to counteract enemy action
in East Persia, would exercise a steadying influence on
Afghanistan without appearing to menace her and, by
threatening a hostile advance towards western Afghanistan,
would compel the enemy to dispersion or detachment of forces.
The suggested extension to Robat, they continued, was open to
topographical objections and might be construed as a direct
menace to Afghanistan. They, therefore, proposed that the
railway should run from Mirjawa, via Duzdab and west of the
Hamun, to some point in Persia within striking distance of
Farah in western Afghanistan. They realised the objections to
extending the railway into Persia, but the necessity for defending
our own and Afghan interests and for preventing enemy activity
in East Persia seemed to them to justify us, in all the
circumstances of the case, in taking this action.

CHAPTER VIII.

MAY TO JULY, 1918:
THE EFFECT IN PERSIA OF THE GERMAN SUCCESSES IN FRANCE; AND THE ANTI-BRITISH OUTBREAK IN FARS.

(Maps 8, 9 and 10.)

In considering the causes underlying the anti-British outbreak in Fars in May 1918, it is necessary to refer to apparently correct information regarding previous events, which only came to our knowledge at a later date and which implied that one of the most important factors was the enmity between Farman Farma and Saulat. It appears that Saulat's instigation of the Kazeruni revolt in December 1916 had been a measure of retaliation for intrigues set on foot against him in his own territory by Farman Farma, rather than an act of hostility towards the Sykes Mission; though British acceptance, in April 1917, of an offer of active assistance against the Kazerunis by Muhammad Ali Khan, a chief of the Kashquli section of the Qashqais and an enemy of Saulat's, caused the latter to suspect British intentions. Saulat's meeting with Colonel Gough and Sir Percy Sykes in May 1917, however, resulted in a friendly agreement which promised to improve matters. But Farman Farma declined to acknowledge this agreement, denounced Saulat to the Democrats as a servant of the British and protested to the Persian Government against Saulat's usurpation of power. Being remonstrated with by Colonel Gough, Farman Farma reconsidered his attitude and, paying a friendly visit in July 1917 to Saulat, came to an arrangement with him for the maintenance of security on the Kazerun–Shiraz road, in return for a very large British subsidy, from which both of them hoped to benefit. The refusal of the British to fall in with this arrangement was, to say the least, a disappointment.

Following this, in the summer and autumn of 1917 the punishment which Indian troops and the South Persia Rifles dealt out to various robber tribes can hardly have been welcome to Saulat and apparently led him to pay attention to the

Causes of Fars outbreak in May 1918.

anti-British emanations from Tehran and the machinations of Wassmuss. The British note of the 11th March 1918 and the tenour of the Persian Government reply, implying that they regarded it as an empty threat, followed by news from France indicating that Germany was winning the war, had an immediate and great anti-British effect in South Persia. Saulat, evidently seeing in the situation an opportunity both to prevail over his enemies and to gain in power and influence, decided to fall in with the instructions from Tehran to destroy the South Persia Rifles and to drive the British out of Persia. The constant assurances by Wassmuss of the inevitability of German success and of the consequent immunity of their Persian friends from British reprisals contributed, no doubt, to this decision.

In a report written in July 1918, Sir Percy Sykes expressed the opinion that the Persians had planned to undermine the loyalty of the South Persia Rifles so as to induce them to desert, or to murder their British instructors, and to co-operate with simultaneous tribal attacks against Shiraz, Abadeh, Dehbid, Niriz and Saidabad, while other tribes closed the road inland from Bandar Abbas.

Inception of anti-tribal operations; May 1918. On the 26th April and 1st May Sir Percy Sykes received information that Mukhbar-es-Sultaneh was still inciting the Democrats in Fars to anti-British action and the tribes to attack the South Persia Rifles and the Indian troops. The Kazerunis and Dashtis were said to be ready to do so, while the Chah Haqis and Labu Muhammadis were reported to have made a plan to capture Niriz, with, it was hoped, the assistance of the Lashanis. The accuracy of this information was uncertain, but it was significant that recently, on the plea of protecting caravans, a force of Kazerunis had occupied Dasht-i-Arjan and that several senior officers of the South Persia Rifles had resigned their appointments without giving any adequate reason. To anticipate a hostile combination of the tribes, which was not likely to materialise till late May when there would be better grazing for their animals, Sir Percy Sykes decided to take immediate military action against the Chah Haqis and the Labu Muhammadis, who inhabited the area to the north of Niriz and whose record of past robberies, in any case, justified such action completely. Lieutenant-Colonel G. P. Grant of the General Staff was accordingly sent at once to Niriz, where the leading portion of the reinforcements from India was expected on the 3rd May, to take command of the column and carry out the required operations. Before describing these, however, it is necessary to turn to events elsewhere.

THE ENEMY IN TRANS-CAUCASIA

By their occupation of Sevastopol on the 1st May and their seizure of a portion of the Russian Black Sea fleet, the Germans had gained a route to Trans-Caucasia on which they would be quite independent of Turkey—a factor of considerable advantage having regard to the divergent aims of the two countries. Georgia was entirely pro-German and a German military detachment* had already reached Tiflis, which the British military mission, finding itself in a dangerous and impossible position, was forced to leave on the 3rd May for Vladikavkas. On the other hand, the Bolsheviks, alarmed by Turco-German action, were fighting the Tartars and were less inclined to resent the idea of British assistance in Trans-Caucasia. But the War Office decided on the 4th May that the situation in the Caucasus did not permit of General Dunsterville's acceptance of the Armenian invitation to Baku, though it was hoped that he might be able to reach Enzeli and gain control of the Caspian fleet. The sympathies of the Tartars were all with the Turks, whose advance in Trans-Caucasia was now directed towards Russian as well as towards Persian Azerbaijan and whose intentions, according to Nuri Pasha, who arrived at Tabriz with a Turkish staff on the 6th May, were to take over the Moslem areas in the Caucasus and to fight the Armenians.

The Caucasus and North-West Persia; 1st–11th May 1918.

The converging advance of Turkish troops on Tabriz seemed to be hanging fire, owing apparently in part to the resistance they encountered from the Jelus and Armenians in the Urmia region, and also, possibly, to a slight extent to the British operations towards Kirkuk which had just started. But, as pointed out by the Commander-in-Chief in India on the 3rd May, these operations provided neither an effective counter to the Turkish penetration of Persian Azerbaijan nor the military demonstration in West Persia which Sir Charles Marling at Tehran required and expected. General Monro accordingly recommended that we should utilise all the available transport in Mesopotamia to carry out original intention of moving troops along the Hamadan road. On the 11th May General Dunsterville reported that a good opportunity had occurred for Bicharakoff to proceed to Baku and gain control of the Caspian, but that, as there were no British troops in the Hamadan area to relieve his men, Bicharakoff could not be spared from Kazvin. At this time also, owing to the Turkish threat to Tabriz, which perturbed them greatly, the Persian Government and Persians generally were more likely to welcome a display of force by the

---

* A regiment formed locally of German colonists and ex-prisoners of war and 800 Ukraine troops under German officers.

British in this area. On the 12th May General Dunsterville left Hamadan for Kazvin and Tehran, where he discussed the situation with Sir Charles Marling.

Persian politics and British policy; May 1918. The distress in the famine-stricken capital, as in the surrounding country, was still very great, though a good deal had been done by British and Americans to alleviate matters. Tehran was still terrorised by the extremists—though a counter-assassination of one of their most prominent writers had caused them somewhat to abate their activities—and money could scarcely be found, even for the most urgent Government requirements.

The Cabinet of Mustaufi-ul-Mamalik, forced by public disapproval of its incapacity to resign on the 25th April, had been succeeded on the 3rd May by one under Samsam-es-Sultaneh, a senior Bakhtiari Khan. But any hopes that we held of a consequent improvement in administration were soon dispelled. On the 14th May, in reply to a request from the Foreign Office, Sir Charles Marling telegraphed his views on the situation. He said that, though the Premier himself was well disposed towards us, neither he nor his supporters were strong enough to oppose the anti-British element in the Cabinet. It seemed probable, however, that it would soon be replaced by an Anglophile Ministry under Vossuk-ud-Daula. The anti-British propaganda promoted by successive Persian Governments during the past eleven months had undoubtedly affected the small proportion of the populace interested in politics, but the British Minister did not consider that German propaganda was making much headway, in spite of the multiplication of German agents and their extensive bribes. The real pro-German and pro-Turkish parties were, he thought, very small. The Jangali movement seemed to be losing ground at Resht,* though extending its activities further east.† It was, however, difficult to gauge and the Persian Government had no means of dealing with it.

After General Dunsterville's departure from Tehran, but apparently as a result of the discussion with him, Sir Charles Marling, who did not consider that the Persian levies being raised in North-West Persia would be of any military value, telegraphed to the Foreign Office on the 18th May protesting

---

* A party of about forty Turkish officers who arrived at Resht about this period appeared to be quite unsuccessful in their attempt to gain assistance from the Jangalis, who strongly disapproved the Turkish invasion of Persian territory.

† This Jangali attempt to gain co-operation from the Turkomans was a failure.

against the unimportance that was apparently being attached to the despatch of British troops into North-West Persia. He pointed out that the political situation at Tehran hinged entirely on the military action in North-West Persia which he had informed the Persian Government we were about to take, and that Vossuk-ud-Daula and our friends, who were already uneasy at the delay, would be dismayed if they knew the real facts. In another telegram of the same date Sir Charles Marling said that two Persian Ministers had resigned and the fall of the Cabinet seemed imminent. His own policy had been to aim at delaying Vossuk-ud-Daula's assumption of office until the situation had changed with the arrival of our troops at Hamadan and the approach of the new harvest. But Vossuk-ud-Daula professed his readiness to take office at once with a strongly Anglophile policy, though his demands in return, both as regards concessions and financial assistance, as well as demands from the Shah for a large personal allowance, were extravagant. As, however, our troops had not arrived and Vossuk was almost the only string to our bow, there was nothing for it but to give money freely.

By this time H.M. Government recognised that they had misunderstood the situation; and on the 18th May the War Office telegraphed orders that General Dunsterville was to be supported from Mesopotamia to the utmost extent of the available transport. Again, on the 21st, learning from Tehran that a prompt display of force might gain for us the active support of the Persian Government, they instructed General Marshall to make every effort to maintain a larger force than had been previously intended—up to the strength of a cavalry regiment, an infantry brigade, armoured cars and aeroplanes—at Hamadan and towards the Caspian. On the 24th General Marshall replied that the movement of troops into Persia, which had been delayed by the Kirkuk operations, would proceed; and he hoped to have the maximum force he could maintain at Hamadan by the middle of June.*

In the meantime Bicharakoff had expressed his desire to go to the Caucasus before it was too late, and General Dunsterville proposed to collect all the British troops in his vicinity and, severing his connection with Persia to the south of Enzeli, to accompany Bicharakoff. Sir Charles Marling, however, protested strongly against Persia being denuded of British troops; and learning from other sources that the capture of Baku by

---

* There was considerable discussion over the force to be sent. For details see " Mesopotamia Campaign," Volume IV.

Persian politics and British policy; May 1918. the Turks, who had just occupied Alexandropol and Erivan, seemed inevitable, H.M. Government decided that General Dunsterville was not to go to the Caucasus. His duties were to be confined to assisting to secure the Hamadan–Enzeli road and, eventually, to obtain naval control of the Caspian. Bicharakoff should be persuaded to stay where he was or not to go beyond Enzeli.

In his telegrams of the 20th and 25th May, Sir Charles Marling had referred to the possibility of trouble in Fars and the increasing difficulty of the position there as being further reasons for forming an alliance with a Persian Government under Vossuk-ud-Daula and for not allowing General Dunsterville to denude Persia of British troops. In addition, Sir Charles Marling had repeated telegrams from Shiraz describing the situation, and on the 28th May he informed the Government of India, on whom he urged the importance of hastening the despatch of British troops to Hamadan, that we could not expect Vossuk-ud-Daula, whom he still hoped to see in power, to pursue as friendly a policy towards us as he would like with this Shiraz trouble on his hands. On the same day Sir Charles Marling transmitted a message from the British consul at Tabriz saying that, as the Turks were close at hand and the Persians would do nothing to oppose their progress, all but four other British subjects and himself had left the town.

On the 29th the British Minister reported that four of the Persian Cabinet had resigned, that the Premier's intentions were unknown and that Vossuk—a popular candidate—was confident of being able to overcome the pressure being brought on the Shah to appoint someone else. Sir Charles Marling sent another telegram on the same day to the Foreign Office enquiring if H.M. Government contemplated any other means than the despatch of British troops for establishing the Tehran situation, preventing the ingress of enemy agents and for keeping open communication with the Caucasus. Though he had understood early in March that sufficient troops would be sent to North-West Persia and had pointed out the necessity of doing so quickly, there had been much delay owing to the Kirkuk operations; and the force now proposed was inadequate and was to be eked out by local levies whose value was problematical. He also deprecated the countermanding of General Dunsterville's mission just when it had a better chance of achieving something and when it seemed most necessary to take any risk to secure Baku. Should Baku—and later Krasnovodsk—fall to the enemy, only the British occupation of Tehran, or an effective resumption of the war by Russia, could prevent Persia falling completely under the influence of the enemy. A Persian alliance, which would cover the Shiraz situation also, was the only effective alternative means he could see.

On the 30th May Sir Charles Marling again telegraphed that Vossuk, the keynote of whose policy would be close relations with us, was quite confident of securing office. But the South Persia Rifles question was a great stumbling block and public opinion would probably demand some concession from us in that as well as in other directions, such as territorial acquisition in Kurdistan, to pave the way to an alliance.

On the 31st May, Samsam-es-Sultaneh resigned, and on the 1st June the War Office telegraphed that H.M. Government had decided that General Dunsterville, or one or more of his officers, might at General Marshall's discretion be sent to Baku ; but that the first military necessity was to occupy effectively the road to Kazvin and the Caspian.

To return to South Persia. Lieutenant-Colonel Grant's column, for operations against the Chah Haqis and the Labu Muhammadis, was composed of one squadron 15th Lancers, two squadrons Burma Mounted Infantry, one section 33rd Mountain Battery, the half battalion 3/124th Baluchis from Shiraz, bombing and demolition sections 16th Rajputs, an Indian field ambulance section and a supply column, i.e., a total effective fighting strength of about 100 sabres, 2 guns and 600 rifles (200 mounted). Part of the column started northward from Niriz at 4.30 a.m. on the 8th May and at 9.30 a.m. reached Hasanabad (thirteen miles), the concentration centre, where it picked up the 15th Lancers, the Indian field ambulance and a Persian demolition section. Colonel Grant, learning during the morning that news of the British advance was already on its way to Chah Haq, and hoping to forestall its arrival, gave orders for the whole column to leave Hasanabad for Chah Haq at 1.30 p.m.

The Lancers and Burma Mounted Infantry, pushing on ahead independently under Major S. M. Bruce, covered the thirty-eight miles to Chah Haq by 9.30 p.m., when Major Bruce at once surrounded its group of three forts with a cordon of piquets. During the night some shots were fired at the piquets and a few of the enemy, trying to break through, were killed or captured.

Early on the 9th May Major Bruce occupied two of the forts,

Operations in Northern Fars; May 1918. (See Map 8.)

Operations in Northern Fars; May 1918.

which had been evacuated the previous evening when Haji Baba had arrived.* But the third fort was still occupied by thirty riflemen, who refused to surrender till fire had been opened on their loopholes and till an attempt on their part to break out had been beaten back. Some of them, however, managed to escape through a covered water channel with the greater part of the arms and ammunition. The tribesmen's total losses were 5 killed or wounded and 27 captured. All three forts were demolished the next day.

At midday on the 9th, the remainder of the column arrived after a long march That evening Colonel Grant learnt that Haji Baba and the Labu Muhammadis were evacuating their forts at Herat-i-Khurreh and were moving their possessions into the mountainous country to the west, but that they had a large camp at Buru-i-Herat. Deciding to move against this camp at once, Colonel Grant started off soon after midnight (9th/10th) with the Burma Mounted Infantry and a Persian guide. The remainder of the column was to remain at Chah Haq on the 10th and move direct to Herat-i-Khurreh so as to reach there by 4 a.m. on the 11th.

Reaching and surrounding the camp at Buru-i-Herat early on the 10th May without difficulty, Colonel Grant found that the bulk of the tribe had already moved off to a camp at Chenar-i-Naz, to the north-west, in which vicinity a large band of Chehar Rahi robbers, returning from the Yezd road, were also said to be encamped. Colonel Grant decided to move to Chenar-i-Naz, guided by one of the few men he had just captured.

From a point about a mile to the north-east of Chenar-i-Naz, the Labu Muhammadi camp was seen, at 10.45 a.m., lying about $2\frac{1}{2}$ miles to the south-east of the village ; and Major Dyer with five troops Burma Mounted Infantry and four Lewis guns† was at once detached to move against it. A deputation of villagers, coming out to meet Colonel Grant, then pointed out the Chehar Rahi camp, lying about three miles beyond the village to the south-west, and said that it was occupied by about 300 riflemen, some thirty of them being mounted. Captain W. C. H. Thacker with the remaining two troops‡ Burma Mounted Infantry was then directed to push on and engage these Chehar Rahis.

Major Dyer encountered some opposition from the Labu Muhammadis, but two of the troops with him, advancing boldly

---

* Haji Baba, a chief of the Labu Muhammadis, had escaped from Niriz with the news of the British advance.
† Two of these belonged to the Baluchis.
‡ The eighth troop was escorting the transport and had lost its way.

and led by scouts who charged mounted with bayonets fixed, drove the tribesmen into the high hills to the west and pursued them for some distance.

In the meantime, Captain Thacker had been engaged with the Chehar Rahis, who had started about 10 a.m.—when they saw the dust of the British column—to remove their animals and possessions. At first it looked as if they might succeed in getting these away, but Colonel Grant, realising this, ordered Captain Thacker to detach half his small force to get round the enemy's right flank and at the same time sent mounted messengers to Major Dyer requesting him to reinforce Captain Thacker. The two parties were operating about three miles apart, and, separated from one another by difficult mountainous country, had lost touch; so that it was not till 2.15 p.m. that Major Dyer arrived with two troops and two Lewis guns. In the meantime Captain Thacker had detached another half-troop to a commanding position towards the enemy's left flank and thus prevented him driving off his animals in that direction also. Menaced thus from both flanks, the Chehar Rahis were forced to abandon the bulk of the animals and plunder they had recently taken from caravans on the Yezd road. Retiring in small groups on a front of two miles in a general south-westerly direction towards the Chehar Rah plain, they made a stand on a pass about nine miles south-westward of Chenar-i-Naz. But Major Dyer's two troops drove them from here in a final attack, which, coming after sixteen hours' fighting and marching, was a fine effort.

It was estimated that the tribesmen, whose numbers had amounted to about 350,* had sustained over 60 casualties, while the Burma Mounted Infantry, who recovered a large number of animals and much plundered property, had only two men wounded. They had been nineteen hours on the move and had covered about fifty miles. They bivouacked for the night at Chenar-i-Naz, where the villagers made bitter complaint of the robbers' depredations.

On the 11th May Colonel Grant marched eastward to Herat-i-Khurreh, moving by a route to the north of the one normally used owing to his anticipations that the robbers would attempt to recover their lost plunder. After crossing the Pir Zad pass a right flank patrol was fired on, and Major Dyer, moving out with five troops and two Lewis guns, attacked and drove the enemy off a high ridge of hills to the south. In the meantime the enemy had tried to cut off the animals crossing the Pir

---
* 150 Labu Muhammadis, 200 Chehar Rahis.

Zad pass, but the rear guard (two troops and two Lewis guns) succeeded in foiling his attempts. Fighting ceased by 7 p.m. and the rear guard, which had been reinforced, reached camp two hours later. The enemy, with a strength of about 200, is said to have suffered heavy casualties, while those of the Burma Mounted Infantry only amounted to two.

Major Bruce with the remainder of the column from Chah Haq had also reached Herat-i-Khurreh that day and the combined parties halted there during the 12th. Colonel Grant, receiving information that a well-known robber chief, Mullah Qurban, with a strong following, was near Ziarat, a village on the Arsinjan road some thirty-five miles to the westward, decided to take action against him. After taking various measures to deceive the enemy, the column marched off in two echelons during the night and concentrated at Khunsar (about twenty miles off in a south-westerly direction) at 7.30 a.m. on the 13th May. At 11.15 a.m., Colonel Grant with the mounted troops moved off again in the hope of surprising Mullah Qurban and left orders for the remainder of the column, with whom he maintained communication by heliograph, to be ready to move in support at short notice.

Affair of Ziarat; 13th May 1918. On approaching Ziarat at about 1.15 p.m., two troops 15th Lancers under Captain N. S. De Brath were sent forward to cut off the village and forts from the mountains which rose behind, and to the south of them, to a height of over 10,000 feet But it was too late, as the enemy was evidently prepared and was holding two steep and precipitous hills immediately behind the village to cover the removal of his animals and possessions.

The remaining troops of the 15th Lancers with two Hotchkiss guns were then sent to reinforce Captain De Brath, and Major Dyer with one squadron Burma Mounted Infantry was sent round the enemy's right to try to cut his line of retreat. The heavy fire which Major Dyer encountered and a report from Captain De Brath that his advance was checked showed Colonel Grant that the enemy was in some force; and at 2 p.m. he signalled orders for the infantry and guns at Khunsar to advance in support. Hearing in reply, however, that one company 3/124th Baluchis and the mountain guns would start for Ziarat at 3.30 p.m., Colonel Grant realised that they could not arrive before nightfall* and he decided to limit his operations accordingly.

During the afternoon the squadron of Burma Mounted Infantry under Major Dyer, reinforced by another half-squadron,

---
* Sunset was about 6.40 p.m.

gradually worked south driving the enemy, who fought hard, first off the hill immediately behind Ziarat and then up the rocky slopes as far as the snow-line. At 6.15 p.m. in accordance with orders from Colonel Grant, Major Dyer started his retirement to camp at Ziarat, which he reached, after leaving piquets on the hills, at 8 p.m. The enemy followed up the retirement, but the heavy loss he was believed to have sustained* evidently had had its effect and during the night he made no attempt to attack. Our own casualties during the day amounted to three killed and six wounded in the Burma Mounted Infantry, and two wounded in the 15th Lancers. The greater part of the Indian infantry with the guns from Khunsar reached Ziarat at 8.30 p.m.

Next morning (14th May) parties of infantry, covered by the fire of the guns, searched the mountain slopes, securing some abandoned animals and a few more rifles. During the day Colonel Grant received information that many of the Chehar Rahis, abandoning their forts and taking their possessions with them, had betaken themselves to the main tribal stronghold on the Kuh-i-Khan, which was about twelve miles west of Ziarat. Here, in a position which they deemed impregnable, they were said to be prepared to fight. Colonel Grant took steps to verify this information, and also on the 15th May carried out a personal reconnaissance of the position which enabled him to frame orders for an attack on the 16th.

A peak in the mountain range lying to the south of the road to Arsinjan and rising nearly 4,000 feet above the valley, the Kuh-i-Khan fell steeply to the north in slopes which were intersected by several narrow and precipitous ravines and which terminated in cliffs several hundred feet high. Astride the Tang-i-Zard, the largest of the ravines, the enemy's position lay along the top edge of the cliffs, his main body holding a line of sangars about six hundred yards long on the western side of the Tang-i-Zard. The cliffs here were about seven hundred feet high and everywhere the steep hill slopes were strewn with great boulders and were partly covered with bushes, while the ravines and foot hills were generally thickly wooded with dwarf oak and wild olive. Altogether a very strong position against a direct attack. *Affair of Kuh-i-Khan; 16th May 1918.*

Colonel Grant's plan was to move the mounted troops under cover of darkness so as to get round both flanks of the enemy's

---

* It is not known how Colonel Grant arrived at his estimates of enemy losses, but the figures given in all his reports on the fights of this period seem to be unduly high. For instance, on this occasion he estimated the enemy's losses to have been 185 killed and wounded out of 400 engaged.

position and prevent him breaking away before the frontal attack of the infantry. To ensure secrecy, news was spread that the column was about to march back to Khunsar and Chah Haq. But at 12.30 a.m. on the 16th May the column slipped away quietly in the darkness and moved off in the opposite direction for seven miles. A halt was then made and the baggage, captured animals, etc., were left under a guard. At 3.30 a.m. the Burma Mounted Infantry branched off from the column to the southward to get round the enemy's right and at 4 a.m. the 15th Lancers' squadron trotted off to get round the other flank, managing apparently to pass the mouth of the Tang-i-Zard without being observed by the enemy. The head of the infantry column arrived opposite this mouth at 4.30 a.m., and at a point about 1,600 yards from it one and a half companies 3/124th Baluchis* formed up for the frontal attack, with the two mountain guns in action a little further back.

Starting their attack at 5 a.m. under cover of the fire from the mountain, Maxim and Lewis guns, the infantry captured the enemy's main position in a little over half an hour and then pursued up the further slopes. About 6 a.m. the Lewis guns of the Burma Mounted Infantry could be heard in action on the slopes on the enemy's right and Colonel Grant ordered the mountain guns forward to a second position above the cliffs.

By 8 a.m. all three converging units, the 15th Lancers, the 3/124th Baluchis and the Burma Mounted Infantry, had gained touch with one another and had reached the snow line, with the result that very few of the enemy escaped. Thirty of them were taken prisoner and a very large number of them had been killed. The British casualties amounted to only three wounded, all among the Baluchis.

Operations in Northern Fars; May 1918. After withdrawing, and as there was insufficient water at Tang-i-Zard, the column moved off along the Arsinjan road; but, finding no water, the mounted portion of the column pushed on the same night to Arsinjan, which they reached at 12.30 a.m. on the 17th May, having covered some fifty-two miles in the twenty-four hours. From Arsinjan the column moved back by the Isfahan road to Shiraz, where the rear portion arrived on the 23rd May.

In these operations, whose success pleased Farman Farma greatly as adding to the security of the districts traversed and as enabling the revenue to be collected, the Chah Haqis, Labu Muhammadis and Chehar Rahis had all received severe punishment at a total cost to the British of 18 casualties. In a report

---
* A half-company was held in general reserve.

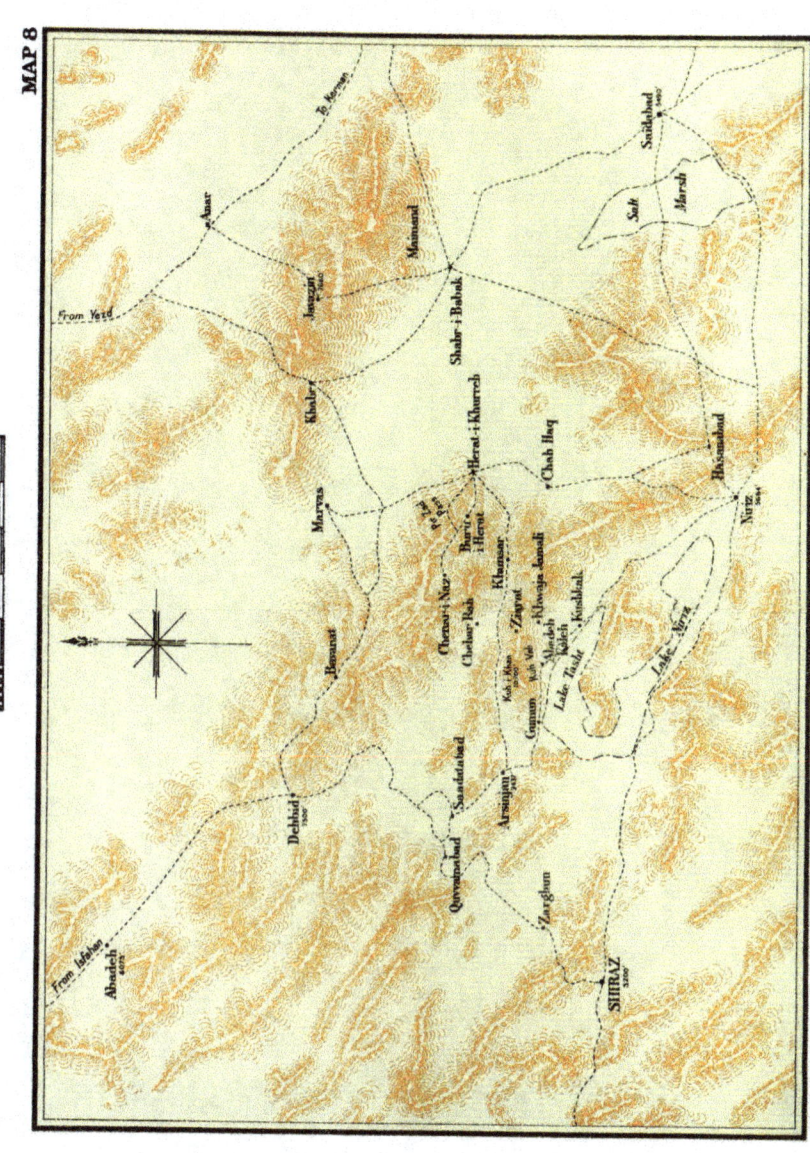

CRITICAL SITUATION IN FARS

written in July 1918, Sir Percy Sykes expressed the opinion that but for this expedition the number of our enemies would have been much greater. For it helped to keep these tribes quiet and Niriz safe at a time when strong inducements were held out to them to attack the British lines of communication.

Colonel Grant attributed his success to the accuracy of his intelligence, the rapidity of the column's movements and its long night marches, the fitness and marching powers of all the units engaged, the brilliant tactics of the Burma Mounted Infantry, and the presence of the Lewis guns.

While these operations were in progress the situation to the west of Shiraz had become critical. On the 7th May Sir Percy Sykes telegraphed that Saulat was reported to be trying to induce Qawam to join him in attacking the British and that there were further signs of disaffection among the South Persia Rifles. On the 10th May some two hundred Darashuris—a section of the Qashqais—attacked Khan-i-Zinian post, ostensibly in retaliation for the arrest of three of their men caught stealing South Persia Rifles' donkeys. Captain A. W. Will, who commanded the company of the South Persia Rifles holding the post, counter-attacked with fifty of his men, who behaved well and drove the Darashuris off with the loss of two casualties.   *South Persia; May 1918.*

Owing to the presence at Dasht-i-Arjan of several hundred Kazerunis, who had been boasting for some time that they would attack Khan-i-Zinian, and to the general hostile attitude of the Qashqais and of Saulat, who was encamped about two marches south of Shiraz,* Sir Percy Sykes considered it advisable to despatch a column from Shiraz under Lieutenant-Colonel V. P. B. Williams to deal with the situation and punish the Darashuris. This column, consisting, in addition to a troop of Burma Mounted Infantry, of one squadron, two guns, one company and two machine guns of the South Persia Rifles, marched from Shiraz to Khan-i-Zinian on the 11th May, covering the twenty-seven miles in one day.

Encountering the Darashuris in some strength to the north of Khan-i-Zinian on the 12th, Colonel Williams drove them off several successive positions. By 9 a.m. the country appeared clear of the enemy, but Colonel Williams had no sooner

---

* The spring migration of the tribe had commenced and would, in normal circumstances, have accounted for the presence here of Saulat and his tribesmen.

South Persia; May 1918. commenced his retirement than the Darashuris started a counter-offensive which was, however, soon effectively broken up. The South Persia Rifles, who only sustained one casualty, behaved well, killing or wounding 15 and capturing 36 of the enemy besides taking possession of many of his animals. That evening the chief of the Darashuris sent Colonel Williams an insolent ultimatum demanding the return of all men and animals captured, failing which the tribe, who had been reinforced and had again occupied the positions from which they had been driven, would attack. Colonel Williams thought it advisable to ask for a reinforcement of Indian troops from Shiraz and these arrived at 4.30 p.m. on the 13th May. The chief of the Darashuris, who had sent Colonel Williams another insolent letter on the 13th, was evidently not prepared for this, as on the 14th Colonel Williams, on advancing, found that all the tribesmen had gone. On the 15th he returned with his combined force to Shiraz without further incident.

On the 16th May Captain Will reported that the outpost at Timouri, about eight miles west of Khan-i-Zinian, held by twenty men of the South Persia Rifles, was surrounded by robbers and cut off from its water supply. As there were no signs of any general rising, Captain Will received orders to proceed, with as many men as could be spared from Khan-i-Zinian, to relieve Timouri. This he effected after some fighting, when he supplied the Timouri garrison with reserve ammunition and three days' water supply in skins. But on the 18th when Captain Will reported that this outpost was again surrounded and cut off from its water supply, orders were sent to withdraw the garrison. That night the telephone wire between Shiraz and Khan-i-Zinian was cut, and it was subsequently ascertained that only twelve of the Timouri garrison got back to Khan-i-Zinian, the other eight being captured.

On the 19th May Farman Farma received a letter from Saulat intimating that, unless they received orders from the Persian Government to the contrary, all the tribes of South Persia and the Qashqais in particular would fight the Indian troops and the South Persia Rifles, which he stigmatised as a foreign force repudiated by the Persian Government. He had written similarly to the Persian Government and to the local priests and others in terms which amounted to a call to *Jahad.* Colonel Gough, who regarded the situation as the direct result of intrigues of the late Persian Cabinet and of Wassmuss, considered, he said, that the action at Khan-i-Zinian had provided a spark to inflame the tribesmen already rendered nervous by recent punitive measures. There was a danger of Qawam and other tribes joining Saulat; but as Colonel Gough and Farman Farma hoped to reduce the size of possible hostile combinations by diplomatic and political measures, they advocated the avoidance of any immediate provocative military action beyond measures called for by actual tribal attacks. Colonel Gough did not consider that there was any chance of the Qashqais attacking Shiraz.

Sir Percy Sykes, who agreed to this policy, reported on the 21st that the mounted portion of Colonel Grant's column had just returned to Shiraz and that the infantry and guns were due on the 23rd. The Qashqais had cut off Khan-i-Zinian, where the garrison had two months' supplies and plenty of ammunition.

Next day Sir Percy Sykes sent a further report saying that Saulat with a force of 3,000 to 4,000 tribesmen was moving into a camp at Khan-i-Khabis, about sixteen miles to the south-west of Chenar-i-Rahdar. Captain Will's Persian servant had come in the previous evening from Khan-i-Zinian with a note saying that the post was closely invested, that the well in the fort had run dry and that there was a danger of the outside water supply being cut. It was estimated that there were 3,000 Qashqais round Khan-i-Zinian and possibly 6,000 at Dasht-i-Arjan. Saulat's priests were preaching a *Jahad* and all the Qashqais were united and aggressive. Colonel Gough was trying to detach Muhammad Ali Khan, the Kashquli chief. It was reported that the Boir Ahmadi tribe would attack Abadeh and that the Kuhistanis and Lashanis would attack Niriz, while men from Dashtistan were also said to be joining Saulat. Sir Percy Sykes strongly advocated a threat of action from Bushire and the despatch of aeroplanes to Shiraz.*

On the same day Colonel Gough telegraphed that Saulat was afraid to act openly without Government instructions and promises of help from the townspeople and the Arab tribes, but that the hotheads and women of the Qashqais were urging him on. Colonel Gough hoped to stave off further action for a few days, by which time the new Persian Cabinet might influence the situation favourably.

Farman Farma appears to have risen well to the occasion and had written very strong letters to Saulat in addition to taking various precautions to maintain order in Shiraz city. He had also telegraphed to the Persian Government, with the

---

* As Sir Percy Sykes was told in reply, the lack of proper facilities locally prohibited the use of aeroplanes.

result that on the 22nd May they replied telling him to order Saulat to keep the peace. But the effect of this telegram, which Farman Farma sent on to Saulat, appears to have been considerably minimised by private telegrams couched in friendly and sympathetic terms sent to the latter direct by Samsam-es-Sultaneh. In the meantime, raids by Qashqais on the 19th and 21st May had brought about encounters between them and detachments of Indian troops and South Persia Rifles.

On the evening of the 23rd May Farman Farma received a letter from Saulat, amounting to a declaration of war against the South Persia Rifles and the Indian troops, which there was little doubt he would not have sent unless he had considered that he had the support of Tehran and the Persian Government. There had been further desertions from the South Persia Rifles, and Sir Percy Sykes telegraphed to Tehran and India that night saying that the time for inaction was past and that the only way of preventing things getting worse was to attack Saulat at once. The Commander-in-Chief in India and the British Minister at Tehran both agreed, as they had already come to the conclusion that the situation demanded immediate action and that Sir Percy Sykes must be given freedom to act as the military situation required.

Qashqai operations; May 1918. On the 23rd May, in anticipation of this sanction, he had issued orders for the organisation of a column of 1,600 Indian troops under the command of Colonel Orton to move out and attack Saulat. It was composed of one squadron 15th Lancers (three troops only), three squadrons Burma Mounted Rifles,* two sections 36th Mountain Battery, 3/124th Baluchistan Infantry (eight hundred of the best trained men in the four companies, plus fifty recruits),† one company and a machine gun section 16th Rajputs, and administrative units. The remainder of the troops at Shiraz were concentrated in a previously arranged defensive perimeter—which included the British consulate and the telegraph office—a short distance outside the north-west corner of the city.

In the afternoon of the 24th May the column marched out and bivouacked near the post at Chenar-i-Rahdar, which was held, as was the post at Deh Shaikh, by a small detachment of South Persia Rifles. Colonel Orton's object was to defeat the tribesmen besieging Khan-i-Zinian and relieve its garrison,

---

* This change of title came into force on the 21st May when the third squadron was organised with the help of drafts from India.
† The wing just arrived from India was composed mainly of recruits. The fifty recruits taken out with the column were to assist with the mule transport, whose Persian drivers were quite unreliable.

ACTION OF DEH SHAIKH

who, according to a message from Captain Will dated the 23rd, could hold out as long as was necessary, as they had stored ample water in the fort.

On the 25th May the column started westward at 4.15 a.m., with an advanced guard, under Major Bruce, of his 15th Lancers' squadron, one squadron (less a troop) Burma Mounted Rifles and one platoon 16th Rajputs, and a left flank guard, under Lieut.-Colonel Dyer, of two squadrons Burma Mounted Rifles. Saulat, who was in camp near Khan-i-Khabis with about 4,000 of his tribesmen, was known to have given orders to his men to oppose any British column advancing towards Khan-i-Zinian. *Action of Deh Shaik 25th May 1918. (See Map 9.)*

At 6.45 a.m. the advanced guard came under rifle fire from a hill (christened Sangar Hill) about 1½ miles to the west of Deh Shaikh post; and a considerable number of mounted and dismounted men were seen on another hill (christened Kotal Hill), about a mile beyond Sangar Hill, and on the Kuh-i-Phan. It was obvious to Colonel Orton that Saulat's plan was to induce the British to commit themselves to an attack westward, when he himself would attack from the col called Gardan-i-Sagari in the hope of cutting them off from Chenar-i-Rahdar and eventually surrounding them.

After studying the ground, Colonel Orton decided, first to capture Sangar Hill and Kotal Hill and to work up the northern end of the Kuh-i-Phan; and, having achieved this, to attack with the bulk of his force towards Saulat's camp across the Gardan-i-Sagari, in which direction the left flank guard under Colonel Dyer was already moving.

A company of the Baluchis under Captain J. M. S. Gardner was detached to assist Major Bruce and was given Sangar Hill as its first objective, a section of the mountain battery under Lieutenant O. R. Pender-Smith being sent forward to support its advance from the vicinity of Deh Shaikh post. As this attack developed, considerable mounted enemy reinforcements appeared at the northern end of the Kuh-i-Phan. These were shelled by the rear section of the mountain battery, under Captain C. R. Willis, firing from the east of Deh Shaikh post; and a second company of the Baluchis under Major A. E. Stewart was detached to attack the northern end of the Kuh-i-Phan. By 9 a.m. Sangar Hill had been captured.

At 8.30 a.m. Colonel Dyer, having captured the Gardan-i-Sagari and an outstanding ridge above it to the eastward christened B.M.R. Ridge, reported that the enemy numbers opposite him were increasing rapidly. He was then sent

Action of Deh Shaikh; 25th May 1918.
reinforcements of the remaining half-battalion of the Baluchis and Captain Willis' section of mountain guns under Lieutenant-Colonel B. F. R. Holbrooke (124th Baluchis), who was instructed to make good the Gardan-i-Sagari but not to advance farther than half a mile south of it without further orders; as Colonel Orton wished to make a personal visit to the western flank and issue fresh orders there before returning to resume control at Gardan-i-Sagari. Colonel Holbrooke's column moved off at about 9.45 a.m.

Colonel Orton reached Sangar Hill about 10 a.m., just as Captain Gardner's company was taking Kotal Hill, Major Stewart's company was getting a footing on the northern end of the Kuh-i-Phan and Major Bruce's mounted troops were reforming from the low hills to the north of Sangar Hill. Colonel Orton made arrangements as follows:—One troop Burma Mounted Rifles was to hold Sangar Hill, falling back at nightfall to Deh Shaikh post; Major Stewart's company was to hold the summit of the Kuh-i-Phan; Major Bruce with his mounted troops was to advance south-eastward down the valley beyond the Kuh-i-Phan towards Khan-i-Khabis; and Captain Gardner's company with Lieutenant Pender-Smith's section of guns were to work their way up the Kuh-i-Phan, giving Major Bruce all the artillery support they could.

Returning eastward, Colonel Orton at about 11 a.m. moved the baggage, dressing station, etc., under its escort of one company 16th Rajputs,* to a point about 2¼ miles south-eastward of Deh Shaikh post. He found that Colonel Holbrooke with one of his Baluchi companies (Captain H. C. Dobbs) was holding the Gardan-i-Sagari and that Colonel Dyer, after some close fighting,† was holding B.M.R. Ridge, where his left flank was threatened by enemy from the main range to the eastward. Leaving Colonel Holbrooke to hold the Gardan-i-Sagari, Colonel Orton took Captain F. C. B. Wetherall's company of Baluchis and Captain Willis's section of guns (with an escort of one platoon 16th Rajputs) up to B.M.R. Ridge, where they arrived about 12.25 p.m. to find Colonel Dyer somewhat hard pressed by the enemy's outflanking attack. A fire-fight ensued at ranges varying from 400 to 1,100 yards, but the enemy, whose fire was heavy and continuous, gradually fell back to the longer ranges where the greater accuracy of our

---

* The platoon which had started out with the advanced guard had rejoined this company some time previously on return from piquetting heights.

† On one occasion Colonel Dyer had personally led a bayonet charge in which 36 of the enemy had been killed.

ACTION OF DEH SHAIKH

fire gave us an advantage. At 1 p.m. Colonel Dyer's two squadrons were sent down to the Gardan-i-Sagari to reform and refill with ammunition.

Meanwhile, to the west, the summit of the Kuh-i-Phan had been gained and Major Bruce's mounted troops had advanced down the valley on its west and south, meeting a growing opposition from scattered bodies of mounted tribesmen. About 12.30 p.m. his advanced troop captured the ruins of Chenar Fariab. By this time Major Bruce had lost all communication with our infantry on the Kuh-i-Phan and had failed in his attempts to re-establish it. At about 1.30 p.m., therefore, his right flank and rear being threatened by outflanking enemy movements, he started to retire on to the western slopes of the Kuh-i-Phan. The enemy at once began to press the retirement boldly and at about 2.30 p.m., as the result of a close attack, Major Bruce was shot and four of his men wounded, all in a few seconds. As he was dying Major Bruce said to his senior Indian officer: "I shall be dead soon. Hold on to this position and beat them off with fire". The attack was beaten off and, Captain De Brath was able to retire without further molestation with his dead and wounded up the Kuh-i-Phan, where he reported to Major Stewart on the summit at about 3.15 p.m.

At 1.30 p.m. Colonel Orton had come to the conclusion that he must attack and beat the enemy decisively and that for this purpose his best objective was Saulat's camp, which could be seen from the Kuh-i-Phan five or six miles to the south on the banks of the Qara Aghach river, where water would also be obtainable. Lieutenant-Colonel Grant was sent to the Gardan-i-Sagari to organise the attack which was to advance from there. It was to be carried out by two squadrons Burma Mounted Rifles under Colonel Dyer, three companies (less one platoon) 3/124th Baluchis under Colonel Holbrooke, and Lieutenant Pender-Smith's section of mountain guns. These guns and one of Major Stewart's two companies* were ordered down to the Gardan-i-Sagari from the Kuh-i-Phan, and Captain Wetherall's company (less a platoon) was also sent there from B.M.R. Ridge. Here there remained, with Colonel Orton, Captain Willis's section of guns, one platoon and a Lewis gun of the Baluchis and one platoon of the Rajputs, so as to bring a heavy fire to bear on Double-Headed Hill, whence the enemy would otherwise be able to enfilade the main advance.

---

* Captain Gardner's company was sent.

Action of Deh Shaikh; 25th May 1918. About 2.15 p.m. Colonel Orton received a message from Major Stewart saying that he could see Major Bruce's detachment in the valley to the south; and half an hour later a messenger he had sent to Sangar Hill returned reporting all well there. Colonel Orton had felt apprehensive lest enemy reinforcements should arrive from the Khan-i-Zinian direction.

The advance from Gardan-i-Sagari started at about 3 p.m. At 3.30 p.m. a few of the enemy on the main range, to the east of and above B.M.R. Ridge, attempted to outflank the party with Colonel Orton, but were driven back by Lewis gun fire, and Colonel Orton then ordered up the baggage column to Gardan-i-Sagari, both to obtain better cover and to show the enemy's flankers on the main ridge that we were advancing, i.e., winning the day. In the meantime the main advance had made good progress and the enemy could be seen retreating south-eastward. Colonel Orton consequently at 4 p.m. sent a message to Major Stewart to work his way south-eastward half-way down the Kuh-i-Phan, and he himself left for the Gardan-i-Sagari with the party from B.M.R. Ridge so as to follow the main attack with the baggage column and its escort.

The day's action closed at about 7.30 p.m., by which time Colonel Holbrooke's infantry had driven the enemy across the Qara Aghach river, near which the British made their camp. The rear guard arrived at 8.15 p.m., but Major Stewart's company, which had been out of signalling communication with Colonel Orton since leaving the summit of Kuh-i-Phan, did not march in till 9.50 p.m., after picking up and collecting many exhausted men left behind by the main attack. The mounted troops under Captain De Brath had lost their way and had made for Deh Shaikh post. But, again missing their road in the darkness, they reached Chenar-i-Rahdar about midnight and moved back to Deh Shaikh next morning.

It was calculated that the enemy strength in action had been about 4,500 Qashqais and 300 Khamseh men of the Baharlu tribe, of whom nearly half had been mounted on ponies extremely nimble in getting about even on the highest hills. They had been well armed with two machine guns, rifles and plenty of ammunition; and they had fought bravely, pressing in quickly to attack or outflank wherever they saw an opportunity. They were estimated to have sustained between 600 and 700 casualties.

The British casualties totalled 18 killed and 33 wounded.*

---

* In addition to Major S. M. Bruce, 15th Lancers, Captain H. C. Dobbs, 3/124th Baluchis, was killed.

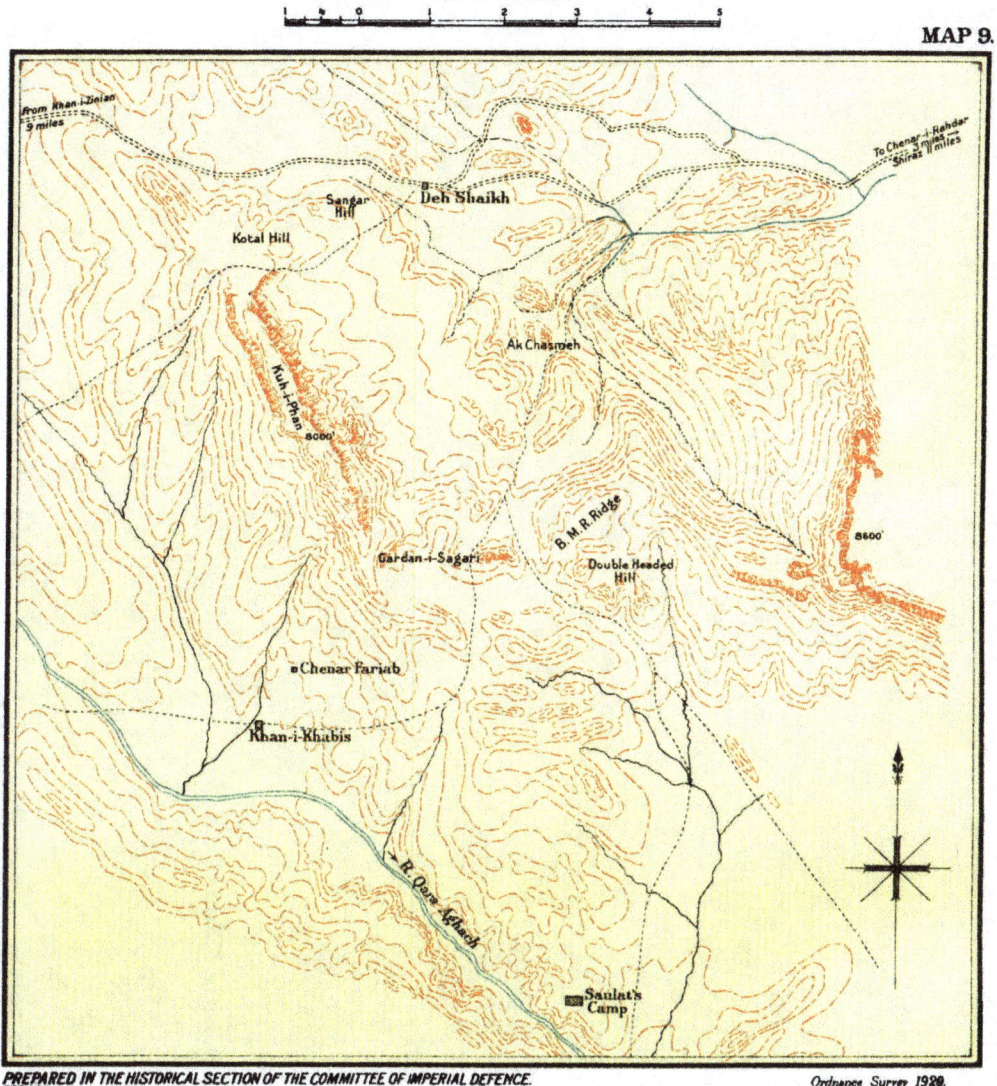

TREACHERY AT KHAN-I-ZINIAN

The long day's operations were a stiff trial for the young Indian soldiers who formed a great proportion of the column; but they stood the test well.*

In the early morning of the 26th May the Burma Mounted Rifles and a section of mountain guns advanced south-east from the camp for about three miles, many groups of mounted Qashqais emerging in flight from the various villages before them. No other signs of the enemy being seen, they then returned to camp and the whole column moved to Deh Shaikh, where it arrived about 2 p.m.

Here it was learned from a group of refugee South Persia Rifles that Captain Will and Sergeant Coomber had been treacherously murdered the previous day by the South Persia Rifles garrison of the Khan-i-Zinian post, which had then been surrendered to Qashqais and Kazerunis. Colonel Orton issued orders for an advance next day to Khan-i-Zinian and sent Colonel Grant in to Shiraz for explosives which might be required to blow in the gate of the post. *Mutiny at Khan-i-Zinian; 25th May 1918.*

Returning the same evening, Colonel Grant reported that the situation at Shiraz was bad. The Democrats were exploiting the Khan-i-Zinian disaster as a Qashqai victory and, as no one believed that Saulat had been defeated, were giving out that he had really surrounded the British column and prevented its return to Shiraz. The South Persia Rifles at Shiraz were in a nervous state. Colonel Orton, although he realised the desirability of striking a blow against the enemy at and around Khan-i-Zinian, finally decided that, in view of the danger constituted by the continued absence from Shiraz of the column of Indian troops, he must leave Khan-i-Zinian alone for the time being. The column consequently returned to Shiraz on the 27th May, taking with it the South Persia Rifles garrison of the Deh Shaikh post.

On that and the previous day, in telegrams to India describing the situation as serious, Sir Percy Sykes said that there was a widespread plot against us and that strong fanatical feeling had been aroused. Saulat was definitely committed, and in spite of his defeat would be so encouraged by the Khan-i-Zinian affair that he might soon assemble another force. The South *Shiraz; 26th–31st May 1918.*

---

* In these and the subsequent operations the mobility of the Indian troops at Shiraz gained greatly by the employment of the Shiraz South Persia Rifles Mule Corps, whose fifteen-hand mules each carried a load of 240lbs. At first its expert Persian muleteers were a source of some anxiety owing to their nervousness. But they were given extra pay and special escorts were detailed to watch them, with the result that they gave no further trouble and displayed faithfulness and gallantry in the field.

318 OPERATIONS IN PERSIA

Shiraz;
26th–31st
May 1918.
Persia Rifles were either disaffected or frightened, and it would at the moment be risky to send out any offensive column composed of the bulk of the Indian troops more than five or six miles from Shiraz. Sir Percy Sykes considered that in the near future the Indian troops might be invested and that it might be necessary for a strong column to march inland from Bushire. The news of the arrival of reinforcements at Bushire would, in any case, he said, improve the position at Shiraz.

As the quickest method of affording assistance, General Marshall in Mesopotamia was at once asked by the Chief of the General Staff in India if he could spare two infantry brigades with pack transport to move inland from Bushire, and General Douglas at Bushire was requested to report at once what administrative preparations there would be required for such a movement. General Marshall replied the same day (27th May) deprecating any further dissipation of the force under his command and saying that in any case he had not got anything like the number of pack mules that would be required. The Commander-in-Chief in India thereupon arranged to divert to Bushire immediately the 81st Pioneers, 2/113th Infantry and No. 169 Indian Field Ambulance, then under despatch to Egypt, as well as two sections of an improvised Indian machine gun company; and he further ordered that two companies 3rd Brahmans should move from Muscat to Bandar Abbas to secure the base there.

In the meantime, however, Sir Percy Sykes—after consultation with Colonel Orton on his return from Deh Shaikh—had telegraphed that, on reconsideration, he thought that an advance from Bushire would take too long to organise; and he recommended instead that a force of two squadrons of cavalry, a mountain battery and two infantry battalions should be sent to advance on Shiraz from Bandar Abbas. In a previous telegram he had estimated that Saulat might be able to collect 10,000 well-armed Qashqais* and 1,000 Kazerunis, whom he might be able to hold together for a month. They had a plentiful supply of rifle ammunition and had, besides, captured 60,000 rounds at Khan-i-Zinian. Farman Farma, he said, was working well with us and Qawam was also on our side. But though the latter had provided 700 of his Khamseh tribesmen to protect Shiraz, his character was so weak that he could only be relied on as long as things went well. In fact, a contingent of the Baharlu, one of the Khamseh tribes, was fighting with Saulat.

---

* The total fighting strength of the Qashqais was calculated at 30,000.

At Shiraz there were at this time a squadron (less one troop) 15th Lancers, three squadrons Burma Mounted Rifles, the 36th Indian Mountain Battery,* 3/124th Baluchis and 16th Rajputs (less five platoons); at Dehbid there was one platoon 16th Rajputs; at Abadeh one company 16th Rajputs (less a platoon); at Niriz there was a platoon of the same battalion; and at Saidabad there were one troop 15th Lancers and a half-battalion 120th Rajputana Infantry.

It transpired subsequently that, after the action of Deh Shaikh, Ali Khan, the younger half-brother of Saulat and acting as Ilbegi (second in command) of the Qashqai tribes, wrote to Farman Farma offering to desert from Saulat with his own personal following of tribesmen. Farman Farma did not disclose the receipt of this offer to the British, apparently owing to his fear of those personages in Tehran who had engineered the rising.

After the return of Colonel Orton's column to Shiraz, steps were taken to improve the defences of the perimeter, to dig more wells and to get in more supplies. Sir Percy Sykes was anxious that Saulat should be attacked again at any favourable opportunity. But the increase of disaffection among the South Persia Rifles, especially among the former gendarmerie who composed the greater part of the Fars Brigade, caused him considerable apprehension. In fact it seemed possible that this brigade might have to be disbanded.† Qawam's Arabs in the city would also probably join in against us in the event of any reverse, however slight. For the time being the city was quiet, but the people were frightened. The retention of a strong Indian garrison at Shiraz was, therefore, essential and this left little margin for a striking force.

British ranks with the South Persia Rifles were recalled from all the outposts furnished by the Fars Brigade except Abadeh, Dehbid and Niriz, where there were Indian detachments; and at those places precautions were taken for their safety. Even at Shiraz, the guns, machine guns and ammunition of the South Persia Rifles were kept in the hands of the British officers.

On the 28th May it appeared that the return of Colonel Orton's column to Shiraz must have much encouraged Saulat, for he was reported to have returned full of fight to the vicinity of Khan-i-Khabis with a following and to be inciting the tribesmen to close the roads and attack outposts. Strong tribal forces were said to be in the vicinity of the roads to the north and west of Shiraz.

---

* Composed of one section 23rd and two sections 33rd Batteries.
† The Kerman Brigade appeared to be quite loyal.

On the 29th the Commander-in-Chief in India reported the measures he had taken to the War Office. Sir Percy Sykes should be able, he hoped, to hold out at Shiraz till October, when it was proposed if necessary to despatch a brigade group to Kazerun from Bushire, as this was in every way the best route for a relieving force to use. In the meantime, the necessary administrative preparations, including the improvement of the road from Bushire to Dalaki, would be taken in hand.

On the same day the Government of India pointed out to the India Office the gravity of the situation and asked if H.M. Government contemplated any change in their policy regarding Persia generally or the retention of the South Persia Rifles on existing lines. The Government of India considered it unsound that the purely military situation should be controlled by the British Minister at Tehran.

The serious state of affairs had hitherto not been realised in London, and these two telegrams crossed one from the War Office to the Commander-in-Chief in India which queried the necessity for sending any troops to reinforce Sir Percy Sykes. A telegram in reply explaining matters further, however, brought a reply from the War Office of the 1st June, saying that H.M. Government had decided that henceforward Sir P. Sykes was to be under the orders of the Commander-in-Chief in India, who would be responsible for the control of operations in Sykes's area, including if necessary the disbandment of the Fars Brigade of the South Persia Rifles.

East Persia; May 1918. The situation in East Persia remained quiet during May, General Dale's force being strengthened by the arrival from India of the headquarters and remaining two companies 1/98th Infantry. At Meshed, where the detachment of Indian troops amounted to 130 sabres and 300 rifles, famine conditions prevailed, six thousand people daily being fed there by the British Consul-General.

In regard to the proposed extension of the railway beyond Mirjawa, the India Office replied to the Government of India on the 6th May that a committee of the War Cabinet after careful consideration had come to the conclusion that the strong political objections to the project could only be outweighed by paramount military necessity. But the War Office could not recommend the extension on strategic grounds and they also regarded the prospect of an enemy advance in strength

CHAOS IN TURKESTAN

through Afghanistan as too remote to justify a costly and questionable enterprise. The authorities in India still persisted, however, and at the end of May H.M. Government, though not satisfied of the need for the extension, sanctioned a preliminary reconnaissance for it.

Reports from Turkestan, where the Bolsheviks were apparently still in power, continued to depict the situation as chaotic. Famine was widespread and the European prisoners of war seemed to be suffering much from semi-starvation, against which the German agents, who were said to be very active, were apparently impotent to help them. The Bolsheviks, assisted by Austro-Hungarian prisoners of war, had, it was reported, defeated Dutoff and his Cossacks near Tashkend, but appeared to be having trouble in Bokhara, feared Afghan aggression and were so perturbed at Turkish progress in Trans-Caucasia that they had sent some assistance there.

At the beginning of May the Commander-in-Chief in India had deprecated, as premature, the despatch of General Malleson to Meshed, which the War Office had suggested, and the point had consequently been left to his discretion. In the meantime, under instructions from India to explore the possibilities of blocking a Turco-German advance along the Trans-Caspian railway, Colonel Redl had got into touch with an Armenian committee at Askabad, who met his advance with cordiality.

Throughout June the situation in Persia reflected generally the opinion held by many of the country's leading men that, pending the issue of the German military effort in France, inaction was their best policy. It is not surprising that, on the 11th June, Samsam-es-Sultaneh was called on to form a new Cabinet by the Shah, who may, as was alleged, have been influenced by bribes and by our refusal to subsidise him. For, even a much stronger man than he was might well have hesitated to appoint the Anglophile Vossuk-ud-Daula in face of the existing circumstances. The Germans, having gained control of the Black Sea, had opened the road to the Caucasus, where, with the sole exception of the Armenians, the inhabitants were either pro-German or pro-Turkish; and the Turks appeared to have both Persian and Russian Azerbaijan at their mercy. On the other hand, the British, in spite of their declared intention to use military force, had not only sent very few troops into North-West Persia but had started to raise Persian levies, whose military value no Persian believed in. Moreover,

Persian politics and British policy; 1st–20th June 1918.

Persian politics and British policy; June 1918. demands from the Bakhtiaris at Isfahan for the withdrawal of the British-paid Persian Cossacks and the rising of the tribesmen against the Sykes Mission and the South Persia Rifles showed the existence in the country of a strong and widespread anti-British movement.

On the 11th June, after hearing of the invitation to Samsam, Sir Charles Marling, who still hoped that the Shah might be induced to appoint Vossuk, appealed to London for increased forces to be sent from Mesopotamia to Hamadan. On the 14th he reported that the feeling in Tehran against Samsam was strong and that, as Vossuk might still be brought into office through pressure exercised by his supporters on the Shah, it would be more than ever necessary for us to support Vossuk by strengthening our force at Kazvin, so that we could if necessary bring troops nearer to Tehran. On the 19th June Sir Charles Marling again telegraphed that the efforts of Vossuk's supporters seemed likely to succeed and, after recapitulating the reasons for the Shah's persistent opposition to Vossuk, urged most strongly that a much stronger force should be despatched immediately into North-West Persia. Besides keeping the Enzeli road open or meeting the improbable case of a Turkish advance from Azerbaijan, the force should garrison Hamadan and Kazvin in sufficient strength to permit the despatch of say 1,000 men towards Tehran and another column to Isfahan if necessary.

On the 6th June H.M. Government had expressed the opinion that until General Dunsterville had consolidated his position on the Kazvin–Enzeli road there should be no question of British troops or of Bicharakoff and his Russians going to Baku. But General Marshall was asked for his appreciation of the situation, which he telegraphed on the 9th. This estimated that the Turco-German strength in Trans-Caucasia and on the borders of North-West Persia was very much greater than the forces likely to oppose them, and it pointed out that, owing to the length and nature of General Dunsterville's communications, it would be impossible to maintain a British force north of Hamadan of sufficient strength to withstand a Turkish south-easterly advance from Tabriz. Such an advance would, however, probably raise Persian national feeling against the Turks. General Marshall considered that the mobile motor column* then on its way should experience no difficulty in holding the Kazvin–Enzeli road and in thus opening communication with Baku, which place General Dunsterville considered

---

* 1,000 rifles, 2 mountain guns and a few machine guns, all carried in 500 Ford vans.

he could hold if he got there in time. It seemed desirable, continued General Marshall, to allow Bicharakoff to go to Baku and to send with him a British mission to ascertain the chances of holding the place, of purchasing the Caspian Fleet and of getting control of the oil-fields. Three days later General Marshall reported that Bicharakoff was determined to go to Baku, which place the Bolshevik Government, refusing to allow any British mission to set foot in Russian territory, had promised to reinforce.

The Chief of the Imperial General Staff, who concurred generally in General Marshall's appreciation, though he considered that it underestimated* the enemy strength, expressed the opinion on the 13th June that there was little likelihood of saving Baku and that, though there was no objection to a few of General Dunsterville's officers going there to report on the situation, it was inexpedient and dangerous either to send British troops there or to give its defenders any assurance of armed help. This telegram crossed one sent on the 14th June —the day on which Bicharakoff on his way to Enzeli reached Resht after brushing away Jangali resistance—by General Dunsterville asking for reinforcement by a brigade each of artillery and infantry to enable him to send assistance to Baku if opportunity offered. A day or two afterwards, the Turks' occupation of Tabriz on the 14th June led General Dunsterville to despatch a small detachment to watch for any southerly advance from there and to ask General Marshall if he could send any more troops to support the local tribes, who, though they hated the Turks, would be otherwise unlikely to oppose their advance. General Marshall at once replied that General Dunsterville must not count on any reinforcements, as it was difficult to maintain the troops already in North-West Persia with stores, oil, petrol and ammunition.

On the 20th June Samsam-es-Sultaneh formed a new Cabinet, but, though he promised to send a strong telegram to Saulat, his attitude appeared to Sir Charles Marling to be anything but satisfactory. By this time, however, the general situation had somewhat improved. A recent German offensive in France had failed, Turkish progress in Trans-Caucasia was evidently hampered by German opposition to Turkish schemes, an excellent harvest in the Hamadan region and the amount of rice available from the Enzeli district might enable us to place a larger force in North-West Persia, the cordial relations

---

*He had learnt that the 217th German Division had landed at Poti and was advancing on Tiflis.

between General Marshall and the Bakhtiaris in Arabistan promised to counteract the hostility towards us of the Bakhtiari regime at Isfahan, and the outlook at Shiraz, where Saulat was having difficulty in keeping his forces together, was better.

Shiraz; 1st–16th June 1918. By the beginning of June it seemed evident that German money was being spent freely among the Qashqais and at Shiraz; and Wassmuss with three or four other Germans was said to be on his way to join Saulat, who was trying to start a *Jahad*. Qawam, who would have welcomed his rival Saulat's defeat, was likely to be deterred for the time being from committing himself to us by religious and other local influence and by the attitude of some of his Arab tribes. Farman Farma, however, was working to win him over; and Colonel Gough was subsidising Sirdar Ehtesham—Saulat's elder brother and a useful candidate for Saulat's position—and was negotiating with Muhammad Ali Khan of the Kashqulis, whose enmity to Saulat had so far kept him out of the conflict.

Letters to Farman Farma and Qawam from Saulat, as well as a telegram he sent in for despatch to the Persian Government at the beginning of June, tended to show that he was not too anxious to try conclusions with us. For in all of these he denied that he had been the aggressor in the recent fighting, and he promised that he would keep his tribes in order and safeguard the roads in his territory, provided he received assurances that neither British troops nor South Persia Rifles would in future interfere with his tribes, whose robberies, he contended, did not concern the British.

On the 4th June the Chief of the General Staff in India acquainted Sir Percy Sykes with the order placing him and the operations in South Persia under the Commander-in-Chief in India and at the same time informed him that it was proposed (i) to reinforce him at once via Bandar Abbas with two squadrons of cavalry and about 500 infantry drafts, and (ii) to start preparations for an advance on Kazerun from Bushire in the early autumn, till which time Sir Percy Sykes should be able to maintain his position at Shiraz. The news of the arrival of reinforcements and of the preparations at Bushire would, it was thought, not only make Saulat apprehensive but would deter tribesmen of the Bushire hinterland from joining him. Sir Percy Sykes was asked to telegraph his appreciation of the situation, which he did next day.

Saulat, he said, was near Khan-i-Khabis with 9,000 Qashqais; there was a body of Kazerunis about Khan-i-Zinian; and most of Fars province had turned hostile as the result of anti-British propaganda. Most of the Arab tribes would probably join Saulat; and, though the Fars Brigade of the South Persia Rifles would probably desert or revolt, its disbandment was at the moment undesirable as likely to precipitate matters and to have untoward results at Abadeh, Dehbid, Niriz and in Kerman. In the last-named province there was only the half-battalion Indian infantry at Saidabad, and it was possible that the Kerman Brigade, South Persia Rifles, might become disaffected. Sir Percy Sykes accordingly recommended that at least two squadrons of cavalry, one mountain battery and an infantry battalion should be sent from India to move to Saidabad from Bandar Abbas.

In consequence, it was decided to send to Bandar Abbas from India a squadron each of the 26th and 27th Light Cavalry, one section 35th Mountain Battery, headquarters and the remaining half-battalion 120th Infantry, 200 men as drafts for the 16th Rajputs and three sections of an Indian field ambulance. This was in addition to two companies 3rd Brahmans sent from Muscat to garrison Bandar Abbas.

On the 5th June the Government of India addressed the India Office on the situation in Fars. They regarded Saulat's rising as a definite expression of Persian nationalist resentment at our interference. We were powerless to deal with it till the autumn, when we were being forced into a serious military diversion such as the Germans had been trying to lure us into for the past two years. We would experience great difficulty in carrying out these operations, whose limits it was difficult to foresee and whose effect on other Moslem tribes and nations was likely to be unfavourable. The Government of India consequently urged earnest consideration of some other alternative. They themselves advocated an attempt to effect a peaceful settlement through the Persian Government—whenever a stable one was established, and after our troops had reached the coast—by conciliatory measures. We should, they considered, be prepared to hand over or disband the South Persia Rifles and to withdraw the Indian troops in Fars on assurances that our consuls and colonies would be protected. The original reasons for the inception of the South Persia Rifles had ceased, they said, and our position in Mesopotamia and on the Perso-Baluch border was much stronger than it was in 1916, while for the time being our only vital interests lay in North-West and East Persia.

On the 7th June Sir Charles Marling, who does not appear to have known of this telegram from India, submitted to the Foreign Office his views on the future of the South Persia Rifles. He discussed the disadvantages and advantages of their maintenance or disbandment and advocated the latter, either wholly or in great part. If we decided on disbandment we could explain, he said, to the Persian Government that we no longer intended to spend money on what would have been a valuable force had not Persian intrigue ruined it and that we should, during the war, keep a sufficient force of our own in Persia as long as the defence of our interests required it.

Qashqai operations; June 1918. (See Map 10.) Shiraz city, lying close to mountains which rise to its north and north-west some 1,500 to 2,000 feet above the plain, is situated at the northern end of a large valley which divides there into two branches, leading to the north-west and west respectively. The former, or Masjid-i-Bardi, valley is a mass of large walled gardens or orchards, with a few scattered hamlets and better class houses; while the western, or Chenar-i-Rahdar, valley is comparatively open, covered in June with ripening crops of barley or wheat and interspersed by a few small fortified villages. The most outstanding tactical features in the plain westward of the city were the walled and turreted serai of Afifabad, the block of walled gardens and dense vineyards connecting Kushan with Bagh-i-Janat, and the chain of fortified mud villages along the road to Ahmadabad.

On the 3rd June, owing to the increasing number of tribesmen in the vicinity, the South Persia Rifles detachment was withdrawn from Chenar-i-Rahdar post, and, at the instance of Farman Farma and Colonel Gough, one company 16th Rajputs was stationed at Bagh-i-Janat. Two days later, however, when the enemy threatened to enter the valley, Colonel Orton came to the conclusion that the Bagh-i-Janat would be difficult to defend and he withdrew this company. But Farman Farma considered that the withdrawal of all our outposts in this direction was having an unfavourable effect in the city; and on the 7th June Colonel Orton placed a garrison of fifty rifles of the 16th Rajputs in Afifabad, which also afforded a good *point d'appui* for operations westward.

On the 3rd and 9th June convoys of hired transport were sent from Shiraz to march to Saidabad for the use of the Indian reinforcements coming from Bandar Abbas; and it was not till the latter date that hostile tribesmen (Kazerunis) occupied Chenar-i-Rahdar and Bagh-i-Janat. By the 11th a few hundred of them had also occupied Kushan and Masjid-i-Bardi. On

OPERATIONS ROUND SHIRAZ

learning this, Colonel Orton, who was carrying out a tactical exercise that morning with the Indian troops, decided to give his young officers and men a practical lesson by driving the enemy out of Bagh-i-Janat and Kushan and thus possibly also causing him to evacuate Masjid-i-Bardi. A few shells and some long-range machine gun fire drove some 300 Kazerunis out of Bagh-i-Janat and Kushan, which places were then occupied after a little skirmishing. A few more shells were then fired from near Bagh-i-Janat into Chenar-i-Rahdar post and these had the effect of causing about 200 more tribesmen to vacate the gardens towards Masjid-i-Bardi. Colonel Orton's force broke off the action at noon and retired to Shiraz without being pressed by the enemy, having learnt some useful lessons at the cost of one man wounded. The enemy's casualties were subsequently ascertained to have totalled 20.

On the 13th June the enemy cut the stream which provided the main water supply for the city and the motive power for most of the local flour mills. But as the British had good wells within their defensive perimeter, the townspeople were the main sufferers. Muhammad Ali Khan, Kashquli, having by this time informed Colonel Gough that he was ready to assist the British by trying to get men away from Saulat, was sent ammunition and money, but was told to refrain from active opposition to the enemy.

During the night 14th/15th June the Rajput post at Afifabad beat off a heavy attack by Kazerunis, killing and wounding about 18, at a loss to themselves of only 3 casualties. Next morning some of the enemy were shelled out of the gardens about a mile west of the main British position, and twenty rifles of the Rajputs were sent to reinforce the Afifabad garrison. In the city, *mullahs* started to incite the population against the British and against all Persians who served or helped them. This agitation was evidently intended to bring about a rising to coincide with the attack which Saulat had written to say that he would shortly make on the British, and which, it was understood, would be carried out on the 17th or 18th.

Learning that evening (15th) that there were about thirteen hundred tribesmen, mainly Kazerunis, along the Ahmadabad–Kushan–Masjid-i-Bardi line, another three or four hundred under Nasir Diwan at Chenar-i-Rahdar and between two and three thousand Qashqais under Saulat at Deh Shaikh, Colonel Orton decided to take the offensive next day, so as to upset Saulat's plans by inflicting a large number of casualties on the tribesmen.

Action of Ahmadabad; 16th June 1918. (See Map 10.)

Accordingly, early on the 16th June, Colonel Orton, leaving a small garrison to hold the defensive perimeter, moved out with the greater part of the Indian troops and a few of the South Persia Rifles. His intention was to hold the enemy along the Masjid-i-Bardi–Bagh-i-Janat line, while he moved with the bulk of his force on Ahmadabad—where the Kazerunis were strongest—and secured a footing on the low hills to the south of it. He would then advance north-westward towards Chenar-i-Rahdar and, after inflicting as many casualties on the tribesmen as seemed necessary, he would return to Shiraz.

For the holding force under Lieutenant-Colonel G. R. Vanrenen (16th Rajputs), which was to take up a position immediately west of Afifabad, Colonel Orton detailed one troop 15th Lancers, one section 36th Mountain Battery and a company and machine gun section of the 16th Rajputs; to guard his left flank, he sent a platoon 3/124th Baluchis and a squadron and machine gun section South Persia Rifles cavalry, under Major C. Chapman, to observe some low hills which lie about three miles to the south; and he detailed one troop 15th Lancers and one company 3/124th Baluchis for the occupation of various tactical points within three miles of the city. This left him with one troop 15th Lancers, three squadrons Burma Mounted Rifles, 36th Mountain Battery (less one section) and the 3/124th Baluchis (less 1¼ companies), i.e., a total of about 25 sabres, 4 guns and 750 rifles, for the main attack.

To divert the enemy's attention from the Ahmadabad direction, a South Persia Rifles field gun (manned by British instructors) started the operations by firing a few rounds from the defensive perimeter into the gardens round Masjid-i-Bardi at about 5 a.m., just as Colonel Orton's troops were starting on their way to their respective destinations. By 7.15 a.m. Lieutenant-Colonel Dyer, with his Burma Mounted Rifles, after slight opposition had secured a low ridge about a mile to the south-east of Ahmadabad, and the main body had reached that place. A company of the Baluchis was then sent forward, supported by the guns and by enfilade fire by the Burma Mounted Rifles, to take Mottled Hill; a task which they carried out with such dash that the Kazerunis fled headlong before them. At 8.30 a.m. another Baluchi company was sent, supported by the guns and by enfilade fire from Mottled Hill, to take Brown Hill. This operation also was well carried out and caused the enemy considerable casualties. Large enemy mounted reinforcements then appeared, having come from the

ACTION OF AHMADABAD

Chenar-i-Rahdar direction; but by 10 a.m. they had suffered so heavily that most of them were in flight up the steep mountain slopes to the west.

In the meantime, Colonel Vanrenen's force, which had been firing occasional shells and machine gun shots into Kushan and on to the mountain slopes beyond, had been surprised by an attack against its right rear, carried out by a body of the enemy which had managed to evade the troop of Lancers. But the mountain guns and the Rajputs, swinging round to meet these tribesmen attacking at close range,* inflicted on them so many casualties that they made no further attacks in that quarter.

About 10 a.m., Colonel Orton ordered Colonel Dyer with his Burma Mounted Rifles to move up the valley, half-way to Chenar-i-Rahdar, and the Baluchi company on Brown Hill to capture End Hill. Then he himself followed the Burma Mounted Rifles with one troop 15th Lancers, the four mountain guns and a half-company of Baluchis, the remaining half-company being left to hold Ahmadabad. By 11 a.m. End Hill had been captured, the enemy was retiring in all directions and the Burma Mounted Rifles, with two mountain guns whose support they had asked for, were causing considerable casualties to tribesmen retreating along the northern slopes of the valley.

The two guns with Colonel Orton had been shelling Chenar-i-Rahdar fort, to the west of which he could see considerable bodies of mounted tribesmen, whose increasing numbers betokened Qashqai reinforcements. By this time the 2,000 tribesmen, for the most part Kazerunis, who had been in the valley, had all retired with a loss, in Colonel Orton's opinion, of about 250 casualties. His gun ammunition was running short and he felt certain that the Qashqai reinforcements would attack him as soon as he began to withdraw. He accordingly decided to start a withdrawal at once and had issued his orders for it by 11.30 a.m.

The retirement on Ahmadabad was delayed by the rather slow withdrawal of the Baluchi company from End Hill, caused by two men in the last section on the hill top being wounded; and the Qashqai horsemen, kept back for a time near Chenar-i-Rahdar by gun fire, began to advance before the Burma Mounted Rifles had started to fall back. The tribesmen came forward boldly, but their direct advance was checked by rapid gun fire and many of them swerved off towards Kushan and Bagh-i-Janat where they dismounted and enfiladed the rear guard.

---

* The guns fired seventeen rounds with fuzes at zero.

At 12.15 p.m., when the advanced section of mountain guns was in action about half a mile east of Ahmadabad and all but a half-company of the Baluchis were clear of that village, the Burma Mounted Rifles, retiring in line of squadron columns about seven hundred yards south of West Janat, were suddenly charged from the westward by a body of three or four hundred Qashqais; and at the same time they came under a sudden fire from West Janat which caused a number of casualties, including Lieutenant-Colonel Dyer and Captain M. J. Murray wounded. Behaving with great coolness, the Burma Mounted Rifles halted and dismounted to turn and face the enemy. A fire-fight continued for half an hour. The four guns with Colonel Orton at once began to fire rapidly over the heads of the Burma Mounted Rifles, the headquarter troop of 15th Lancers was sent forward to reinforce them, a message was sent to Colonel Vanrenen to open rapid gun fire against the southern edges of the Bagh-i-Janat, and most of the Baluchis from near Ahmadabad were sent up in support. The Qashqais displayed great bravery and in places got within two hundred yards of the Burma Mounted Rifles, but the increasing volume of fire they encountered was too much for them and by 1.15 p.m. they had fallen back, having sustained heavy losses.

This was practically the end of the fight, as the tribesmen soon all withdrew out of action and Colonel Orton's rear guard arrived back at Shiraz about 3.30 p.m. without further trouble.

Colonel Orton had achieved his object most successfully, it being estimated that of about 3,200 tribesmen engaged, 200 had been killed and 300 wounded; the total British losses being 5 killed and 24 wounded. Next day Sir Percy Sykes telegraphed to India expressing his high appreciation of the discipline, gallantry and soldierly spirit of the Burma Mounted Rifles.

Shiraz; In spite of this success, anti-British agitation increased in the city, where *mullahs* were openly preaching a *Jahad* and were inciting the mob to take action against all who helped the British. This had already resulted in loss and injury to some of the South Persia Rifles, and Sir Percy Sykes telegraphed on the morning of the 17th June that the strain on the Fars Brigade was so great that if it continued they were likely soon to leave the British side. Farman Farma and Qawam, he continued, did not seem to be doing their best to restore order, apparently hoping thereby to force H.M. Government to concede the large demands they had both already made for pensions and pecuniary compensation for losses they might suffer by siding openly with the British.

Next day, however, Sir Percy Sykes telegraphed that orders, issued the previous day in the city by *mullahs* and Democrats to plunder the houses and property of the South Persia Rifles and of all civilians who had worked for the British, had in several cases been carried out, with the result that Persian ranks of the South Persia Rifles had become infuriated with the populace and that Farman Farma had concurred in the necessity for military measures in the city. Consequently, during the night, key positions there had been occupied by detachments of the South Persia Rifles ; and early on the 18th, a company of Indian infantry had occupied the south-west gate—the eastern portion of the city having been already occupied by Qawam's Arabs—and about twelve of the most prominent Democrat agitators had been arrested.

The tranquillising effect of these measures was immediate and, although the telegraph line was cut on the 19th and was not restored for some weeks, this did not matter much as the crisis was really over. The losses suffered by the tribesmen in the fight on the 16th had not only upset Saulat's plan to attack on the 17th June, but had so discouraged him that he was afraid to think of another attack. In the city a sudden reaction set in and, recalling their sufferings from the loss of their water supply, the populace began freely to revile Saulat and the tribesmen.

To obviate the chance of the enemy obtaining even a slight success at a time when the tide was turning against him, the garrison was withdrawn from Afifabad on the 20th June ; and though it was occupied by Kazerunis on the 21st, they were promptly shelled out of it next day.

The tasks for which British troops in North-West Persia had been asked for by Sir Charles Marling and General Dunsterville had recently so multiplied that the War Office found it necessary on the 22nd June to instruct the British military attaché at Tehran to explain, to Sir Charles Marling, the technical difficulties of maintaining and supplying forces there. *British policy; 21st–30th June 1918.*

On the 24th June the Eastern Committee of the War Cabinet had a long discussion on the situation in Persia. A policy of conciliation, as advocated by India, and of giving up the South Persia Rifles was tempting. But it had obvious disadvantages. For it was impossible for Persia to pay the force if we handed it over or to guarantee its good conduct if we relinquished control. The possibility of forming an alliance with Persia

British policy;
21st–30th
June 1918.
was also discussed. But as she was helpless and incapable of defending herself or of assisting us materially, such a course would certainly commit us to keeping Turks and Germans out of Persia with British bayonets and to recovering Persian Azerbaijan; and as reports from General Marshall implied that he would find it impossible to send much stronger forces into Persia, it was clear that the dangers of an alliance outweighed its advantages.

The decision of the Committee to inform Sir Charles Marling that it was impossible to meet his demands was not, however, carried out. He had telegraphed that day saying that the political situation at Tehran would be seriously jeopardised if, as it appeared, it was not intended to reinforce General Dunsterville. There was every prospect, he explained, of a friendly Cabinet under Vossuk-ud-Daula being soon brought in. But, unless we gave it visible support, it would not retain office for long and would be succeeded by the enemy faction, who were under no illusions regarding the inadequacy of the force with General Dunsterville. Further, he again insisted on the great imprudence of relying upon native levies.*

But more important than the critical situation in Persia was the danger to Afghanistan from invasion via Russian Turkestan, though this was not immediate. As the Chief of the Imperial General Staff pointed out, the German advance through Ukraine and over the Don basin to the Volga was moving with incredible rapidity; the German troops at Tiflis were only waiting for reinforcements to advance on Baku; and in Turkestan there were 40,000 Austrian and German prisoners of war. The Turkomans and Sarts were all looking, it was said, to a British advent to save them from Bolshevism and they had sent representatives to our military agent in the Caucasus and to Meshed. If, however, we refused to go to their assistance they would certainly turn to the Germans. Bicharakoff was on his way to Baku with 1,500 men and four British armoured cars, and we ourselves had secured six ships in the Caspian. It consequently seemed well worth sending some officers and men from Enzeli to Krasnovodsk to get into touch with the friendly elements in that area and to prevent German agents exporting cotton. The General Staff at the War Office were not quite satisfied that General Marshall fully appreciated the situation and the necessity for interrupting the Trans-Caspian

---

* Our subsequent experiences in North-West Persia justified this warning completely.

railway.* This, it was considered, could be most effectively secured by closing the sea route from Baku to Krasnovodsk.

The Chairman of the Eastern Committee accordingly authorised the War Office to telegraph on the 28th June to General Marshall in the following terms. H.M. Government were not satisfied either that full advantage was being taken of our opportunity to make a maximum effort in North-West Persia and towards obtaining control of the Caspian, or that General Marshall appreciated the importance they attached to success in that sphere. The enemy's evident lack of offensive intention in Mesopotamia should enable General Marshall to free transport for use in Persia, and additional motor transport was also being sent him from England. He was instructed to take certain steps to improve communications between Mesopotamia and the Caspian and was to provide sufficient force at Kazvin to support Sir Charles Marling's policy at Tehran. In addition, control of the Caspian shipping and destruction of the oil stored at Baku and of the plant for obtaining more were aimed at. His own difficulties and the rather uncertain British policy of the past were, he was told, recognised, but he was to realise that in future his main attention must be directed to a supreme effort to accomplish our objects at Tehran, at Baku and on the Caspian.

General Marshall, thereupon, took immediate steps to comply with these instructions. By orders issued from London on the 25th he was to be responsible for a sphere of control embracing North-West Persia, the Bakhtiari country and Arabistan, while the Government of India would control activities and operations in South and East Persia, Trans-Caspia and Turkestan.

For the troops of the East Persia Cordon, the month of June was comparatively uneventful. No. 5 Ford Van Company arrived from India and road improvement was continued, the stretches from Kain to Turbat-i-Haidari and from Ladis to Khwash being completed to a " light motor traffic " standard. Also, Colonel Grey at Meshed was authorised to recruit 200 more Hazaras.

East Persia; June 1918.

---

* General Marshall did not consider that there was any real danger to India and was much against the despatch of troops into Persia. The considerable distances involved made it impossible, in his opinion, for us to carry out any effective action there, while the presence of our troops only antagonised the Persians. Consequently, as he himself admitted, he had hitherto delayed the movement of troops there.

East Persia; June 1918. In the early part of June reports indicated that the Bolsheviks dominated Russian Turkestan, though the whole country was famine-stricken and in a chaotic state. Turco-German agents appeared to be numerous and active in propaganda, but the Bolsheviks were evidently alarmed at Turco-German progress and activities in the Caucasus and Trans-Caspia and were said to be genuinely afraid of an Anglo-Afghan invasion. The Amir of Afghanistan was still most friendly towards us and about this period put forward a rather embarrassing request to the Viceroy for four million rifles, four hundred guns, ammunition and four crores of rupees, promising that, if he were supplied with these, no foreign enemy would ever pass through Afghanistan towards India.

As the Bolshevik attitude made it likely that they would welcome a British mission and as the activity of enemy agents rendered counter-action by us advisable, Colonel Redl, on the 8th June, recommended the depatch (i) of a British officer into Turkestan to enquire direct into the Bolshevik views and (ii) of General Malleson to Meshed. The Government of India, though inclined to favour the proposal to negotiate with the Bolsheviks, were in some doubt and referred the question on the 17th June for the views of H.M. Government. This crossed a telegram from the War Office (who had already received a copy of Colonel Redl's telegram) to the Commander-in-Chief in India, saying that the War Cabinet advocated the interruption of the Trans-Caspian railway* and asking for the Government of India's views regarding the despatch of a British officer to Tashkend, an indispensable preliminary to Bolshevik co-operation.

General Monro replied on the 18th June that he had ordered General Malleson to come to Simla, on his way to Meshed, to receive his instructions, which the Commander-in-Chief repeated for the approval of the War Office. The gist of these was :—

(i) The object of the Malleson Mission was to combat German and Turkish propaganda and attempts to organise men, railways and resources towards assisting hostile enterprises, aggression or active operations against us or our Allies.

(ii) The area in which it would work would extend from the Caspian to the Oxus at Charjui and thence to Tashkend and along the railway towards Orenburg.

---

* Arrangements were made to do this if it became necessary.

(iii) General Malleson would have under him Colonel Redl's organisation, but would not control the East Persia Cordon Force.

On the 21st June Colonel Redl reported that a delegate from the Armenian Committee of Askabad* asked for assistance, in arms and money, to enable them to organise a force of two to three thousand Armenians in Trans-Caspia to oppose a Turkish advance. According to the delegate, the Armenians controlled Trans-Caspia with the consent of the Bolsheviks and were also on friendly terms with the Turkomans, who were well disposed to the British but who might, unless they were approached soon, in self-defence side with invading Turks. Colonel Redl advocated tangible encouragement of these Armenians. But on the 22nd and 23rd he telegraphed that news had just been received of fighting near Askabad in which Turkomans, Armenians, Bolsheviks and Mensheviks† were all said to have participated, though how they had been grouped was not clear. On the 25th June he was instructed from Simla to send a British officer to Askabad to ascertain the real facts, and this telegram crossed one sent the previous day by Colonel Redl saying that the Bolsheviks had been defeated near Askabad by the Mensheviks.

On the 28th June General Malleson left Simla for Meshed.

Between the 21st and 27th June news was received at Shiraz of the surrender to Arab tribesmen of some small South Persia Rifles posts on the Isfahan road. The hostile tribesmen still remained in the vicinity of Shiraz and on morning of the 27th Colonel Orton moved out with an Indian detachment and dispersed a body of them near Bulvardi, two miles to the north-west, inflicting over thirty casualties at a loss to his own force of two slightly wounded. *South Persia; 21st June– 7th July 1918.*

Quarrels and desertions among Saulat's adherents were by this time reducing his following. A number of Baharlus reverted to Qawam and considerable sections of Qashqais joined either Muhammad Ali Khan, Kashquli, or Ali Khan, a younger brother of Ehtesham, who had also joined the anti-Saulat confederacy. A request, made on the 6th June by Colonel Gough to Sir Charles Marling to obtain Persian Government sanction to the deposition of Saulat in favour of Ehtesham

---
* A branch of the Armenian Association whose headquarters were in the Caucasus.
† Though anti-Bolshevik, this new faction was nearly as extreme in its political views.

had, in the absence of a Cabinet, elicited no reply by the time telegraphic communication was cut. But on the 30th June Colonel Gough took the responsibility of assuring Ehtesham in writing that he would be appointed; and though Farman Farma hesitated, lacking sanction from his Government to issue the necessary *sanad*, he was induced to do so on the 5th July on being informed by Sir Percy Sykes that it was an urgent military necessity. The result of this was that the anti-Saulat confederacy at once agreed to co-operate with a column of Indian troops in a decisive attack on Saulat.

Saulat's armed following had fallen in numbers to about 800,* of whom a quarter were about Chenar-i-Rahdar and the remainder some seven miles to its south-west, in camp at Ak Chasmeh. It was decided that the Indian troops under Colonel Orton should move directly against Saulat, while the tribesmen under Qawam, Ehtesham and Muhammad Ali Khan would move widely to the left in readiness to fall on Saulat as he retreated. (See Map 10.)

Affair of Chenar-i-Rahdar; 7th–8th July 1918. (See Maps 9 and 10.)

Colonel Orton's column—composed of three squadrons Burma Mounted Rifles, 36th Mountain Battery (less one section) 3/124th Baluchis, half-battalion 16th Rajputs and a squadron South Persia Rifles cavalry—started off from Shiraz at 6 p.m. on the 7th July. As the sun was setting, at about 7 p.m., opposition was encountered at the Kushan–Bagh-i-Janat gardens. But this was overcome with no great difficulty and by 8,15 p.m., when the vicinity of Chenar-i-Rahdar was reached, the enemy, about 150 strong, had all retired and firing had ceased.

An attack on the British bivouac at about 2.30 a.m. on the 8th only lasted a few minutes and at 4.20 a.m., just after the column had stood to arms, it was sufficiently light to see that Chenar-i-Rahdar fort, eight hundred yards distant,† was unoccupied. The hills which ran down into the valley close to the north and south of the fort were, however, occupied. Learning just then that his Persian allies had been delayed in leaving Shiraz, Colonel Orton decided to give them the good start they would require by postponing his attack for an hour or two if possible. But as, at 4.40 a.m., the enemy began to snipe and cause casualties in the camp, Colonel Orton decided that he must start the attack at once.

---

* Wassmuss had also quarrelled with and had left Saulat.

† In the darkness the bivouac had been taken to be 1,500 yards from the fort.

Lieutenant-Colonel Holbrooke with his battalion (3/124th Baluchis) was sent to attack the main ridge to the south of the fort, which was about 3,400 yards from the camp; and two squadrons Burma Mounted Rifles with one troop South Persia Rifles cavalry were detailed to seize the spur to the north of the fort. This the leading squadron of Burma Mounted Rifles did rapidly and without much difficulty. Colonel Holbrooke's attack, starting at 5 a.m., also made rapid progress, although the enemy opposing him, about 150 strong, were soon reinforced by a strong mounted contingent. This, it was subsequently ascertained, consisted of 450 men sent by Saulat from Ak Chasmeh with orders to check the Indian troops till Saulat had time to pack up and retreat. By 5.30 a.m., however, the Baluchis, by a dashing and continuous advance carried out under the cover of gun and machine gun fire, had seized the main ridge at a cost of 13 casualties. By this time our tribal allies were beginning to make their appearance on the main mountain ridge on Colonel Orton's left front, and as he desired their co-operation, for political as well as for military reasons, he decided not to push on too rapidly. At 6.25 a.m. he ordered first two guns up to support the Baluchis and then two squadrons of Burma Mounted Rifles to push on beyond the fort and prolong the Baluchi's right.

The advance continued, but Saulat's men were all retreating and Ak Chasmeh was reached at 9.30 a.m. without opposition, the Rajputs with four guns in a further advance towards Khan-i-Khabis seeing no signs of the enemy.

The column rested during the heat of the day till 4.15 p.m. when it marched back to Shiraz, having incurred a total of 19 casualties. It was estimated that the enemy had lost about 28 killed and wounded. Saulat had fled to Firuzabad (seventy miles south of Shiraz) and, in preparation to pursue him, Ehtesham encamped with the tribal forces near Khan-i-Khabis.

At 9 p.m. on the 8th July one of the South Persia Rifles detachment at Abadeh arrived at Shiraz, bringing a message dated 2nd July from Major W. A. K. Fraser, who was commanding at Abadeh, asking for assistance. This Sir Percy Sykes arranged to send off as soon as possible.

Defence and relief of Abadeh; 28th June–17th July 1918.

The garrison of Abadeh consisted originally of three platoons 16th Rajputs with two Lewis guns (about 150 rifles), and 2¾ squadrons of cavalry and three infantry companies of the South Persia Rifles. With the South Persia Rifles were six British officers and eight non-commissioned officers. The attitude of

Defence and relief of Abadeh; June–July 1918. the South Persia Rifles was fairly satisfactory, and on the 6th and 7th June the Persian officers swore to be loyal to their British officers and all but twenty of the Persian ranks declined to avail themselves of an offer of discharge, expressing an enthusiastic desire to remain. Major Fraser, however, considered it wise to keep the spare arms and the bulk of the ammunition in charge of the Rajputs.

It had from the first been anticipated that a local Qashqai notable, Muhammad Ali Khan, would give trouble, though he would probably wait upon events at Shiraz.* On the 8th June, however, he moved with his heterogeneous armed following of about 500 to a camp about twelve miles from Abadeh, apparently intending to attack next day. But, instead, he moved off to a camp twenty miles to the south-west of Abadeh. His constant anti-British agitation, however, combined with the inaction of the Persian Deputy-Governor to win over the passive, if not the active, sympathy of the populace; and, after communication with Shiraz was cut, a number of the South Persia Rifles deserted and their attitude generally deteriorated. By the 27th June, when Muhammad Ali Khan again approached the town, his following had increased to about 800 and he evidently meant to attack.

The area held by Major Fraser's force lay immediately west of the town and included, in a space measuring about nine hundred by five hundred yards, a number of buildings, walled gardens, orchards and vineyards. The perimeter was protected by a number of self-contained posts prepared for all-round defence and there were in addition about half-a-dozen small outposts covering various roads. All the posts, except two which commanded the Rajput's barracks at close range, were garrisoned by South Persia Rifles; and Major Fraser still hoped that, though probably incapable of any offensive action, they would defend their own quarters against attack.

The expected attack began at midnight 28th/29th June with a demonstration against the south-east corner of the perimeter, whence the attack spread northward. Several of the posts occupied by the South Persia Rifles surrendered at once; others held out for a time or as long as a British officer happened

---

* At the end of May a treasure convoy, escorted by a detachment of South Persia Rifles, reached Abadeh from Isfahan. The treasure consisted of two million krans, belonging to the Imperial Bank of Persia, in transit to the Shiraz branch of the bank. Major Fraser was ordered by telegram to detain this treasure at Abadeh, owing to the unsafe condition of the roads in Fars. Muhammed Ali Khan of Abadeh was very desirous of getting possession of this large sum of money.

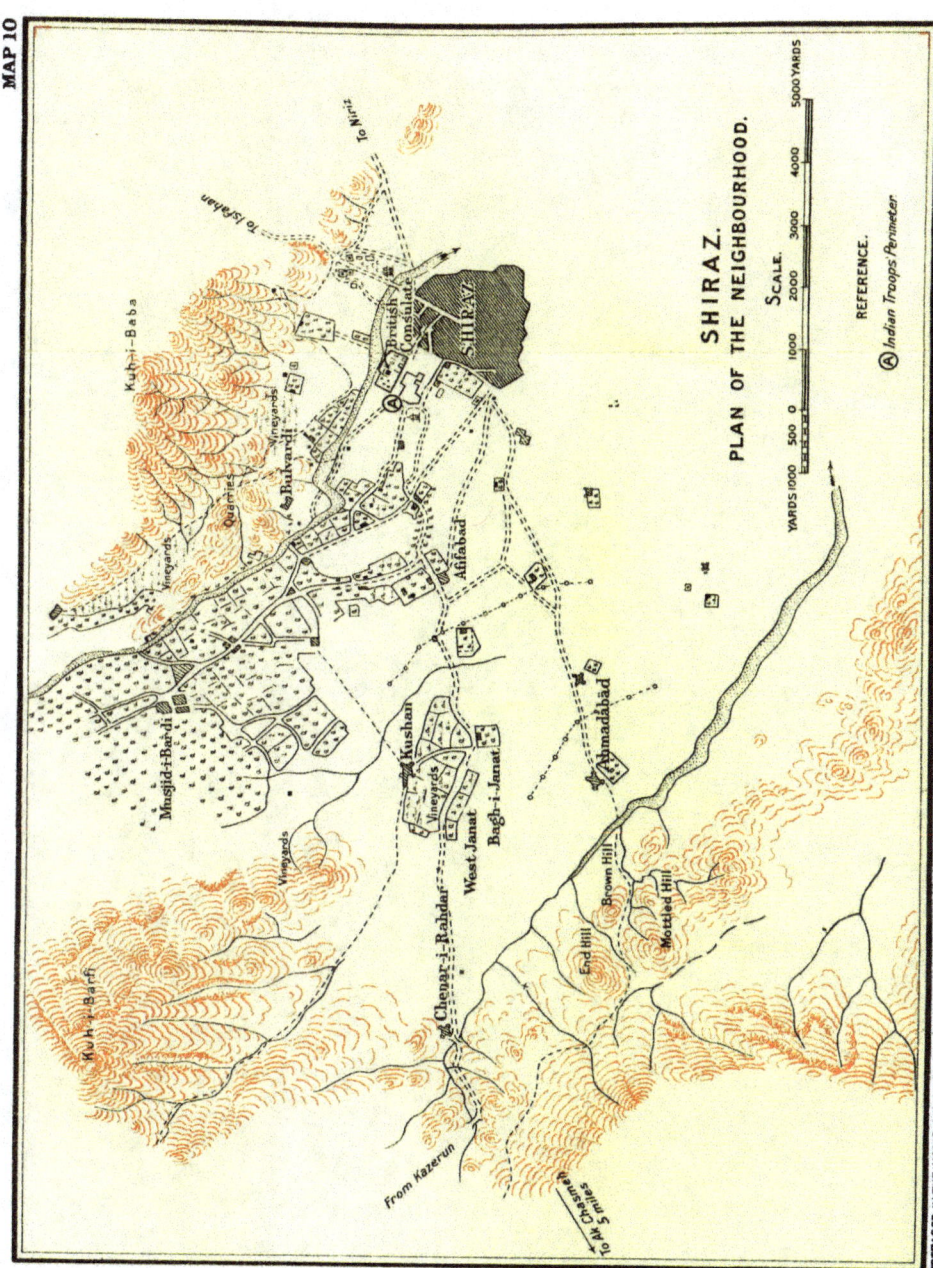

to be present and then also surrendered; the garrisons, having in some cases first murdered any loyal comrades, all going over to the enemy. By the morning all that remained in British hands was a small group of five buildings—the Rajputs' barracks, the officers' and sergeants' messes, the South Persia Rifles infantry barracks and the South Persia Rifles hospital—at the northern end of the perimeter; and all but about 200 of the South Persia Rifles had gone. Those remaining were now disarmed and were used only for non-combatant duties.

In accordance with a pre-arranged plan, Major Fraser carried out the evacuation, during the 29th, of the Rajput's barracks and the hospital, without much opposition from the enemy. The block of the three remaining buildings was fairly well suited for defence. But two notably weak points were the covered approach afforded by the proximity of the Rajputs' barracks and the fact that the water supply consisted of only two small wells and an underground stream of water.

The enemy occupied the hospital that had been evacuated and kept up a constant fire during the night 29th/30th, and on the 30th June he attacked boldly through the Rajputs' barracks. But he was repulsed with such heavy punishment that he never attempted another attack in this quarter. He again attacked the next night (30th/1st), advancing through the dense vineyards to the south-west. But he was repulsed, with the help of flares, without much difficulty and apparently with some loss, though he again attempted to attack along this line after dark on the 1st July but was once more beaten back.

On the 2nd July the enemy cut an irrigation channel to the north-west with a view to flooding, and thereby undermining the mud walls of the post buildings. When the consequent increasing inundation was observed, Captain G. D. M. Gwynne Griffith, R.E., sallied out with Sergeant Barnes, under the enemy's fire, to remedy matters. They found the cut in the channel, but in trying to mend it Captain Gwynne Griffith was mortally wounded. Major Fraser then went out himself and with Sergeant Barnes succeeded in mending the cut and in bringing in Captain Gwynne Griffith, who, however, died a few hours later. That night a bank and channels were dug by the garrison as a protection against a further similar attempt.

At this period cholera made its appearance, but fortunately was kept within bounds among the garrison.* The enemy

---

* Only eight cases occurred, of which three proved fatal.

leader, Muhammad Ali Khan, died from it on or about the 2nd July, and after this the enemy's action lacked vigour and boldness. He cut the underground stream of water, however, on the 3rd and so made it necessary to put all in the garrison on a strict water ration.

A rather half-hearted attack, though on a somewhat large scale, on the night 7th/8th July was the last really serious hostile attempt to assault the post, and thereafter the enemy confined himself mainly to mining operations, sapping close up to the perimeter walls. On the night 16th/17th July he retreated altogether, the garrison's belief that he had gone being confirmed during the night by a messenger from the town who also announced the approach of the relief force from Shiraz.

This force—consisting of two squadrons Burma Mounted Rifles, one section 36th Mountain Battery, two companies 3/124th Baluchis, one squadron South Persia Rifles cavalry, two platoons South Persia Rifles infantry and some administrative details—under the command of Lieutenant-Colonel V. P. B. Williams, had left Shiraz early on the 10th July and had covered the 170 miles in seven days, in spite of the intense heat. On the 12th Colonel Williams had managed to hire 278 mules, on which to mount most of his infantry, and he had left 43 sick men at Dehbid, taking on in their place 39 of the 16th Rajputs. On the evening of the 16th July, on reaching a point sixteen miles from Abadeh, Colonel Williams heard that the tribesmen investing that place were unaware of his approach; and, hoping to surprise them, he called on his troops, who had just finished a 24-mile march, for a final effort. He started off again at midnight, but the enemy had already been warned and he was too late to intercept them.

The actual battle casualties at Abadeh between the 28th June and the 17th July were not heavy, as they only totalled 12 (four killed and eight wounded).

South Persia; June–July 1918. When communication with Shiraz became interrupted, the Commander-in-Chief in India instructed Colonel Farran, commanding the Kerman Brigade of the South Persia Rifles, to assume command of troops and operations which could no longer be controlled by Sir Percy Sykes. The situation in Kerman province fortunately remained quiet, there were no signs of disaffection among the South Persia Rifles there, and

ASSISTANCE FROM ISFAHAN

the leading portion of the reinforcements from India landed at Bandar Abbas on the 27th June, leaving three days later for Saidabad, where they arrived on the 19th July.

On the 22nd June the India Office telegraphed instructions to the Government of India to send at once, if they saw no objection, an officer of the rank of Brigadier-General to take command of all British troops in South Persia, but not of the South Persia Rifles who were to remain under Sir Percy Sykes. But the authorities in India considered that it would be better to defer such an appointment till the Shiraz situation had been cleared up, and this was agreed to by H.M. Government. The Government of India, moreover, being of the opinion that one authority in South Persia should exercise both military and political control, did not approve of the proposal.

Colonel Farran was in telegraphic communication with Abadeh till the 29th June, when all communication was severed. Anxiety was, thereafter, felt for the safety of the detachments there and at Dehbid ; and, among other projects considered for their relief, assistance was requested from Isfahan. The local situation there was not too secure but, eventually, a small detachment of Persian Cossacks under a Russian officer was sent off and reached Abadeh on the 23rd July. News of the situation at Shiraz was received from various independent sources and, although its accuracy was of course uncertain, its nature never gave much cause for anxiety ; and in the early part of July messengers began to get through and brought reassuring information.

CHAPTER IX.

JULY–SEPTEMBER 1918:
THE TIDE TURNS IN FAVOUR OF THE ALLIES.

(General Map and Map 11).

British policy; July 1918. The Foreign Office had telegraphed on the 29th June to Sir Charles Marling that the Eastern Committee, much impressed by our accumulating difficulties in Persia, wished to know if it were not possible, by an adjustment of our policy, to secure Persia's active friendliness. The two main obstacles to this were apparently the Anglo-Russian Convention and the existence of the South Persia Rifles. H.M. Government had already declared the Convention to be in suspense and they were, said the Foreign Office, prepared to press for its abrogation as soon as assent was obtained from a Russian Government which they could acknowledge. As regards the South Persia Rifles, H.M. Government were prepared to abolish that title and to treat the force as a portion of a uniform Persian army, which they desired to assist the Persian Government to raise and of which the British officers, though they must be retained during the war, could be withdrawn later by mutual agreement. In return the Persian Government would be required to co-operate with the British in South Persia.

On the 1st July the Government of India telegraphed that it seemed as if the only hope of averting a serious catastrophe in South Persia* and war with Persia was to get the Persian Government to intervene energetically with instructions to the tribal rebels to cease hostilities pending a settlement. The effective co-operation of the Persian Government could only, however, be secured, they considered, by real conciliation of a more genuine character than the Foreign Office telegram contemplated.

Next day Sir Charles Marling replied to the Foreign Office that the concessions mentioned would make no appeal to the Shah, nor would they induce him to instal a friendly Cabinet.

---

* They feared disasters at Abadeh and Dehbid.

For he seemed to be entirely under German influence and was sceptical regarding our ability to despatch sufficient troops to carry out our declared intention of securing Persian neutrality by military means. The advent to power of a friendly Persian Cabinet would, continued the British Minister, undoubtedly counteract the danger arising from the serious situation in Central and South Persia. But, as the consciousness of this danger militated against that advent, the only solution was the despatch of a strong military force to Kazvin to reinforce General Dunsterville. It was, moreover, the only way of keeping Vossuk-ud-Daula in office, once he had been appointed, and of thus obviating the increased danger which would result if he again fell from power. This telegram crossed one from the Foreign Office sent on the 1st July authorising Sir Charles Marling—if the situation was as serious as the Government of India depicted it—to make any conciliatory offers which he thought desirable or necessary, though he would, of course, weigh well the dangers of yielding to Persian violence what we had refused to their arguments.

The discussion continued. As their orders to General Marshall showed, H.M. Government recognised the great importance of increasing as far as possible our forces in North-West Persia, and they also still considered that it was desirable to supplement these forces by local levies. The concessions they were prepared to offer were to facilitate the advent of a friendly Cabinet and to enable it to restore order in Fars, where British military measures which would affect the situation immediately were not possible.

Sir Charles Marling considered that the offer of concessions was useless and that the only practical policy was to bring about a change of Cabinet by a very early display of effective military strength. The Government of India, on the other hand, still advocated a policy of conciliation, as they were afraid of further serious and indefinite military commitments in Persia, which—apart from purely military disadvantages—were, in their opinion, calculated to react unfavourably on Moslem opinion in neighbouring countries and also on future Indo-Persian relations. They felt that our policy in Persia was being dictated without sufficient regard to our military resources—a condition due, they considered, to the divorce between political and military control, which they had previously, and still, wished to obviate by the appointment of a senior military officer combining both functions in Southern Persia. To enable them to exercise effectively the military control in that area—which had just been transferred to them—they considered that they should also have a voice in the direction of Tehran policy. For Tehran was Persia's political centre, and the Persian Government, in spite of their material weakness, exercised a surprising authority throughout the country. H.M. Government were not prepared to delegate political control of Tehran to the Government of India. But by the 19th July it had been decided to summon Sir Charles Marling to a consultation in London; and on that date the Government of India were asked if, during his absence, Sir Percy Cox, who was an officer of the Indian Political Department, could be spared from Mesopotamia to act temporarily in charge of the British Legation at Tehran.

The Caucasus and North-West Persia; July 1918.
At this time there was little danger of any serious enemy offensive either in Palestine or in Mesopotamia. A German offensive in Champagne had just failed; a recent change in the Bulgarian Government had altered the situation in the Balkans to Allied advantage; and unless the Turks abandoned their ambitions in the Caucasus they had few troops to spare for operations elsewhere. Their progress towards Baku continued, though it was evidently being hampered by German opposition to their plans. This was fortunate, as the only effective military opposition they encountered was from Bicharakoff's men, who had sailed from Enzeli on the 3rd July. All reports seemed to show that the Bolshevik power was waning, that the various separatist movements in Russia were gaining ground, and that the Bolshevik leaders were in open alliance with the Germans.

The reinforcements from Mesopotamia had begun to reach Hamadan, small British detachments had occupied thinly the road to Enzeli, and preparations were in hand to send naval detachments with guns to gain a footing on the Caspian. But the absolute refusal of the Bolsheviks at Enzeli and Baku to accept British assistance stood in the way of our sending even a small force to Baku or of obtaining possession of Caspian shipping.

We had recently opened communication with the Jelus at Urmia, and had made arrangements to supply them with ammunition and to send a few officers and non-commissioned officers to assist them in their fine resistance to the Turks. To attempt more was neither easy nor considered advisable, as it might precipitate an attack on them by the two or more Turkish divisions in the Tabriz area.

British occupation of Baku: 4th August 1918.
On the 19th July, owing to news that Baku might shortly request British assistance, General Dunsterville (who was paying a short visit to Baghdad) was authorised to send there one or two British infantry battalions, a field battery and some

armoured cars; on the 20th–22nd July the British detachment at Resht inflicted on a large body of Jangalis a defeat which practically put an end to Jangali opposition; and a *coup d'état* on the 25th placed in power at Baku a Government, free of Bolshevik influence, which asked for immediate British assistance. As the Turks, continuing their advance in spite of German protests, almost captured the town on the 31st July, it looked as if we should be too late. But the Turks suddenly retired and this gave General Dunsterville the time he required to send a succession of small British detachments which began to reach Baku on the 4th August.

By the 24th July, when Sir Charles Marling telegraphed that Vossuk-ud-Daula considered that it could not be long before he was appointed Prime Minister, several events had combined to bring about an improvement in the Tehran situation. The rebellion in Fars had collapsed and Saulat was in flight; the relief of Abadeh had put a stop to a plot to attack the British at Isfahan; our preparations for an advance from Bushire were having a tranquillising effect; British reinforcements were steadily arriving at Hamadan; the Jangalis had been put out of action; and the Allied counter-offensive in Champagne was making good progress. Tehran situation; end of July 1918.

In Fars, Qawam and Ehtesham, having completed their preparations, left the Shiraz neighbourhood on the 15th July with their tribal following and a small detachment of South Persia Rifles troops under a Persian officer to pursue Saulat, who had fled to Firuzabad. In this they were so far successful that, after some fighting, they occupied Firuzabad on the 24th, only to find, however, that Saulat had escaped. Fars and Kerman; end of July 1918.

At Abadeh, the relief force under Lieutenant-Colonel Williams halted for a week to rest, re-establish some sort of order, restore telegraphic communication and prepare for the return journey. Sir Percy Sykes had decided that both Abadeh and Dehbid were to be evacuated, and on the 24th July the troops left Abadeh for Shiraz, withdrawing the Dehbid garrison as they went.

On the 22nd July Sir Percy Sykes telegraphed to India recommending that the Indian troops at Shiraz should be formed into a mixed brigade under the command of Colonel Orton, who would at the same time retain his appointment as Deputy Inspector-General of the South Persia Rifles. The Commander-in-Chief approved this arrangement as a step towards compliance with the proposal, which H.M. Government had made a month previously, to place all the British troops in South Persia under a British brigadier-general, as a separate command from the South Persia Rifles. He also asked for Sir Percy Sykes' views on this proposal and learnt in reply that, in the latter's opinion, it would not only cause complications and duplication in administration but would involve additional staffs and extra expense.

Affairs in Kerman remained quiet. The reinforcements from India which reached Saidabad from Bandar Abbas in the third week of July had met with no opposition, though they had experienced a most trying and difficult march owing to the extreme heat.

Bushire; June and July 1918. At Bushire, during June and July, the preparations for an autumn offensive proceeded continuously and methodically. The combatant troops at Bushire consisted of a squadron and machine gun section 15th Lancers, 35th Mountain Battery (less one section), 71st Punjabis, 81st Pioneers, 2/113th Infantry, and headquarters with two sections No. 3 Indian Machine Gun Company. In India, orders were issued for the mobilisation of the following troops, to be ready for embarkation in the second week of September: an Indian cavalry regiment (less two squadrons), four Indian infantry battalions, two sections 3-inch trench howitzers, a section of mountain artillery, a machine gun company and two companies of Sappers and Miners. Among the administrative units were an unusually large number of hospitals.

The general plan of operations was :—
    (i) The pacification of the coast tract near Bushire and the establishment at Dalaki of an advanced base, including the construction to that point of a light railway and the improvement of such roads as were necessary ; and
    (ii) A deliberate advance to Kazerun and the establishment there of a force capable of operating in the direction of Shiraz, probably in co-operation with the force under Sir Percy Sykes.

On the 25th July, H.M. Government enquired whether, having regard to the favourable change in the military situation in Fars, the Government of India considered that an advance from Bushire was necessary on military grounds, as it seemed undesirable on political grounds. In reply, the Government of India referred to the uncertainties of the situation in Persia and said that they would continue their preparations at Bushire so as to be in a position to advance in October if necessary or desirable.

At the beginning of July the position in Russian Turkestan and Trans-Caspia was somewhat obscure, but Bolshevik dominance appeared to be on the wane. On the 6th Colonel Redl at Meshed was visited by a representative of a new anti-Bolshevik faction, terming themselves " The Turkestan Union." Their objects were to reinstate the Russian Governor-General, restore order and prevent a Turco-German invasion ; and they asked for British financial assistance, and also, as an indication of moral support, the despatch of a British detachment of two to four hundred men to the Russo-Persian frontier. Colonel Redl was at once instructed from India to advance this movement up to two million roubles and to tell General Dale to hold two hundred men in readiness to move to the frontier from Meshed.

East Persia ; July 1918.

On the 7th July Captain E. D. Jarvis returned to Meshed from his visit to Trans-Caspia with the opinion that the Bolshevik leaders there were in Turco-German pay and that they meant to evacuate the country so as to leave the road to Afghanistan open. Though Captain Jarvis had heard nothing of the plans of the Turkestan Union, he considered that such a movement afforded the only chance of keeping out the enemy ; but our assistance would be indispensable. He had heard, it may be noted, from all classes in Trans-Caspia, that we were too late to counter the German plans.

A few days later, on Colonel Redl reporting that the plans of the Turkestan Union were less advanced than he had been led to believe, he was told to postpone the departure of the detachment to the frontier till the arrival of General Malleson. As regards the rôle of this detachment, the India Office telegraphed on the 15th July that it was generally to form a rallying point for pro-Entente parties in Russian territory and to render them all possible support and assistance. Its commander must be guided as to detail by circumstances and by the instructions of the Government of India.

On the 17th July General Malleson, who had arrived at Meshed the previous day, telegraphed summarising the situation as follows :—

The Bolsheviks, whose power was on the wane, were disliked by all other classes and, being indifferent to British interests,

East Persia; were ready to facilitate German entry into Trans-Caspia in July 1918. return for assistance against their own domestic enemies. The Mensheviks, who were mainly anti-Bolshevik railway employés, were ill-organised, ignorant and unlikely to oppose actively the German plans. The Turkestan Union, which included officers and all the more respectable and stable elements, had monarchial designs. Their representative considered their prospects promising. Among the natives, there was a pro-Turk party in Bokhara which was not likely to take aggressive action except against the Bolsheviks. The Turkomans had made no response to pan-Islamic propaganda and, being anxious for settled conditions, were likely to support any party trying to secure these. The Bolsheviks had just been defeated by the Mensheviks and driven eastward from Askabad. It seemed an opportune moment to support the Turkestan Union.

On the same day (17th) the India Office telegraphed instructions to expedite the despatch of the detachment to the frontier and to despatch British officers or parties across the frontier if they saw an opportunity of rallying pro-Entente forces or of organising resistance to the enemy. On the 19th July the Government of India replied that orders had been sent on the 17th to General Malleson to send from Meshed 25 sabres and 175 rifles to Muhammadabad and an infantry platoon to Kuchan. The East Persia Cordon was being reinforced to bring it up to a strength of six cavalry squadrons, ten infantry companies and a half-company of Sappers and Miners. It had also about 1,600 levies. This increase would strain available transport to the utmost and, as the latest reports showed that the roads could not be improved sufficiently to take continuous motor transport, the Government of India were taking steps, in anticipation of sanction from London, to collect material for a north-westerly extension of the railway from Mirjawa.*

The detachment for Muhammadabad (25 sabres 28th Light Cavalry and 175 rifles and two machine guns 1/19th Punjabis) left Meshed on the 19th July, and the platoon 1/19th Punjabis for Kuchan left on the 24th, after General Malleson had received assurances from the Persian Governor-General of Khurasan that these movements would not meet with any local opposition. In the meantime the Bolsheviks had been driven back to the Oxus by the Mensheviks. But the latter were by no means pro-Entente and in any case General Malleson was unwilling

---

* The railway, which was making very good progress, had not yet reached Mirjawa.

to open negotiations with any other faction than the Turkestan Union, to whom he had already begun to advance money,* unless and until their *coup* failed.

On the 24th July in a telegram to the Commander-in-Chief in India the War Office recapitulated the instructions issued by H.M. Government for the guidance of the Malleson Mission. The guiding factor was to afford the maximum possible support to anti-German elements in Turkestan and Trans-Caspia, and the Commander-in-Chief in India was given discretion to move officers and troops to and across the frontier as required for this purpose. The sphere of control of General Marshall (Mesopotamia) was extended to cover the whole of the Caspian littoral, including Krasnovodsk, whither he had been recently instructed to send a small mission to get into touch with friendly elements. But all officers and parties east of that were to come under General Malleson's orders.

During the last week of July heavy fighting was reported to be in progress between Mensheviks and Bolsheviks in the vicinity of Charjui.

At the end of July it looked as if Turkish and German interests in the East were too divergent to admit of an early reconciliation. The German plan of dominating a Trans-Caucasian federation to secure for herself Baku, the Caspian and the road to Bokhara so completely blocked pan-Turkish ambitions that the Turks were hardly likely to accept, as sufficient, territorial compensation in North and North-West Persia, whence they could threaten the British position in Mesopotamia and co-operate with the German plans against the Indian borderland.

Summary of the general situation at the end of July 1918.

Turco-German friction had delayed the Turkish attack on Baku and we had taken the risk of attempting to assist in its defence with a view to denying its oil resources to the enemy, to obtaining control of the Caspian and also to gaining time to organise a defence of Trans-Caspia. These risks, already considerable owing to the Turkish advances towards Baku and eastward from Tabriz in the Enzeli direction, would be much enhanced if a Turco-German reconciliation enabled the Turks to use the railways through Georgia towards Baku and Tabriz.

The outlook in France was better and the situation in Persia had improved. But it was very necessary to consider the future, and particularly possible enemy action in the East in 1919.

---
* He had advanced 200,000 roubles.

The War Office had just arranged for a future increase of the force in Mesopotamia and had also ordered the construction there of new railways, one of which was to be extended into Persia from Khaniqin. But the enemy communications via the Black Sea and Trans-Caucasia would still give them the advantage in operations in North-West Persia and on and across the Caspian. To the General Staff in India, therefore, it seemed essential that we should develop our communications into and through South and East Persia in every possible way, i.e., open up the Shiraz road from Bushire, improve the port at Bandar Abbas and the road we were making northward from there, and extend our railway from Mirjawa to Neh.

Persian policy; August 1918. On the 3rd August Sir Charles Marling reported that the Persian Government had suddenly and without warning denounced all treaties concluded with Russia as well as concessions granted to Russians during the last hundred years, on the grounds that they had been brought about by force or fraud and also that they were incompatible with recent declarations of policy by Russia and the other Great Powers. This denunciation, said the British Minister, was considered generally to be intended as a patriotic demonstration by a moribund Cabinet calculated to embarrass its successors; and the Shah had declared, not only that he knew nothing of the measure, but that he intended to express his displeasure by dismissing the Cabinet.* This he promptly proceeded to do and, although there was a two days crisis owing to the refusal of the Prime Minister, Samsam-es-Sultaneh, and of the Cabinet to accept dismissal, Vossuk informed Sir Charles Marling on the 5th August that he had accepted office and would himself take over the Ministry of the Interior. Among the other new Ministers there were no eminent or particularly influential men, but they had all been selected with a view to ensuring harmonious support within the Cabinet to Vossuk's policy of repairing the errors and omissions of his predecessors and of inaugurating a pro-British policy.

British and Persian policy regarding the South Persia Rifles; August 1918. His opinion that the recent anti-British tribal risings had been engendered from Tehran and that the insurgents had good grounds for declaring that their action had the support and

---
* It is noteworthy that the Russian commandant of the Persian Cossack Division, which was to a great extent a royal bodyguard, explained to the Shah that this recognition of the Bolsheviks and repudiation of former agreements would make it almost impossible for Russian officers to remain with the force.

authority of the Persian Government was apparently Sir Percy Sykes's main reason for ordering the evacuation of Abadeh and Dehbid. He considered that, as long as the Persian Government refused to recognise, and adopt a friendly attitude towards, the South Persia Rifles and to punish the leaders and instigators of the revolt, it would not be safe to utilise South Persia Rifles troops towards Abadeh ; that it was too great a risk to send the six or seven hundred Indian troops he could spare from Shiraz to carry out the military operations which he considered necessary to restore order in the Abadeh–Dehbid districts ; and that until these had been carried out it was undesirable to re-establish military garrisons there. In the meantime, to safeguard the Isfahan road north of Shiraz, Lieutenant-Colonel Williams had under Sir P. Sykes's orders engaged local armed guards. At the end of July, Farman Farma, considering that the evacuation of Abadeh and Dehbid would make a very bad impression, suggested that, until order was restored, the safeguarding of this road should be left in his hands without intervention by the troops under Sir Percy Sykes. But the latter objected strongly. He attributed the suggestion to Farman Farma's desire for personal gain and antipathy to the South Persia Rifles. Sir Percy Sykes recognised that during the past eighteen months no other Persian Governor-General could have done as much for the British, and that as a Persian grandee it was perfectly natural for Farman Farma to intrigue and to look mainly after his own safety, his own pocket and his own interests. But as this want of principle had proved in the past, and was still, in Sir Percy's opinion, a source of danger to the British, he considered that Farman Farma should be controlled to an extent that Lieutenant-Colonel Gough considered neither politic nor necessary.

The relative positions of these two officers in regard to certain political questions had been impossible to define exactly, and friction had consequently arisen at times. Sir Percy Sykes now asked that as commander of a military force in the field he should be given general political control. This, however, the Government of India at once negatived, in a telegram of the 5th August, and said that, as a military situation no longer existed at Shiraz, exclusive political control must once more be assumed by Lieutenant-Colonel Gough. Farman Farma with all his faults was, they said, a valuable asset and, as he seemed to be the only person capable of restoring and maintaining anything like order on the Isfahan and Kazerun roads, he should be left to deal with them. It would be a serious error,

British and Persian policy regarding the South Persian Rifles; August 1918.

they continued, to risk estranging him or impairing his authority, on which we were bound to rely, as well as on his advice, so long as Persia remained neutral. On the same day, however, the Government of India telegraphed to the India Office, quoting this correspondence as evidence of the impossibility of separating military from political control, and recommending that, as the retention in their hands of military control was essential, the political control of Fars should also be vested in them until the situation cleared. H.M. Government, however, merely replied, on the 12th August, that they agreed that Farman Farma must be supported.

Vossuk himself was so anxious for an immediate settlement of the South Persia Rifles question that, two days after his advent to office, he suggested to the British Minister that a few selected Swedish officers should be substituted for all or most of the British officers, to whose presence he attributed the recent trouble in Fars. During the ensuing discussion he said that he doubted if even the most formal recognition of the South Persia Rifles by his Government would restore the loyalty of the force for some time to come, and it seemed to him that, unless we agreed to a control by neutral officers, we should find it necessary continually to increase our forces in the country, however much we disliked that course.

Sir Charles Marling, in reporting this discussion to London, said that as neither the Indian troops nor the South Persia Rifles were able to carry out their intended functions, the old pernicious system of arrangements with tribal chiefs for the maintenance of order was again being resorted to. He therefore considered that the Indian troops should be reinforced sufficiently to enable them to deal with any probable tribal combination. As regards the South Persia Rifles, he thought that the only alternatives were to agree to Vossuk's suggestion or to place a Persian officer in command with a British staff. Even if a suitable Persian could be found, however, he would be generally regarded as having been sold to us; whereas even Persians would regard a Swedish chief as a guarantee that the force would no longer be used for British, as opposed to Persian, purposes. Moreover, though we should have to continue to bear the cost in either case, under a Swedish officer the expenses could be cut down. Sir Charles Marling was well aware of the numberless difficulties attending Vossuk's proposal, but he thought that we should take advantage of the opportunity presented by the advent of a friendly Cabinet to come to some arrangement.

VIEWS OF GOVERNMENT OF INDIA 353

H.M. Government felt, however, that the situation was too critical to admit of the utilisation of Swedish officers, in view not only of their past behaviour in Persia, but also of recent reliable information that members of the Swedish Brigade in Finland were applying for military service in Persia and that one of the former Swedish commandants of Persian gendarmerie intended to collect Swedish officers for service in Persia under German auspices. Appreciating, nevertheless, the desirability of supporting Vossuk in his need to impress the Persian public, they desired Sir Charles Marling to suggest that American officers should be employed. Vossuk, however, would not accept either American or French officers.

The Government of India, in a long telegram reviewing the whole situation which they sent to the India Office on the 16th August, also objected to the re-introduction of Swedish officers. If the Persian Government in a really friendly spirit were prepared to accept the various military measures in North-West, South-West, South and East Persia, which were rendered essential by our military and political needs of the time, the Government of India considered that we on our part should be prepared to discuss the abandonment of the South Persia Rifles in their existing form and the withdrawal of our troops from Central Persia. This would remove the main cause of anti-British feeling in Fars, where the position had become impossible and where Sir Percy Sykes's policy seemed to them so unintelligible that they advocated his recall. They recommended that the reliable portion of the South Persia Rifles should be temporarily handed over to the Governor-General of Fars to be maintained at our expense, but on much more economical lines, under the general supervision of our consul. They realised that the policy they recommended would have to be carried out by degrees, necessary preliminaries being the solution of the Bushire hinterland question and the obtaining of reasonable guarantees for the safety of our consuls and colonies and also that trade routes would remain open.

By the 18th August the Foreign Office had learnt that Sir Percy Cox had agreed, at the instance of the Viceroy of India and of General Marshall, to act as British Minister at Tehran during Sir Charles Marling's absence; and on the 22nd they informed Sir Charles Marling that H.M. Government desired to postpone a decision on the subject of the South Persia Rifles. If, however, Vossuk's need of support rendered it undesirable to leave the question in abeyance, he should be asked to suggest another alternative such as the employment of Swiss officers or making the South Persia Rifles a purely Persian force.

Vossuk, who said that he could not understand how matters in Fars could have come to so serious a pass, considering the number of Indian troops there, agreed to accept Swiss officers and urged that a formal agreement should be come to as soon as possible. It seemed to him, however, that Sir Percy Sykes, between whom and Farman Farma there must have been serious friction, had failed in his mission and that the South Persia Rifles, judging from the number of desertions reported, seemed hardly worth keeping.

On the 22nd August Sir Charles Marling explained that Vossuk had come into power in radically different circumstances from those in which he had formerly expressed the opinion that he could settle the question of the South Persia Rifles in return for our assistance; and that his Government was much embarrassed by considerable financial difficulties. He was already assisting us by purchasing supplies, by replacing unfriendly officials and in services generally of a quiet unofficial character, and Sir Charles Marling considered that, until we had restored the situation in South Persia to something resembling what it had been six months previously, it would be imprudent for us to insist on Vossuk's fulfilment of his promises.

Two other events in August contributed to improve the situation in Persia; namely the friendly agreement come to between General Dunsterville and the Jangalis, on the 15th, and an arrangement for a British subsidy to Sirdar Zafar, Il-Khan of the Bakhtiaris, to maintain a tribal force which would enable him to stabilise the situation at Isfahan.

Fars;
August 1918. Lieutenant Colonel Williams with his column and the garrisons of Abadeh and Dehbid returned to Shiraz at the beginning of August, and Qawam also arrived back there with his Arab following from Firuzabad, where Ehtesham remained to keep a watch on Saulat. During the first half of the month there were signs of a further tribal outbreak in the Abadeh district, but the gatherings dispersed and everything remained quiet. At the end of August, however, information was received that Saulat had succeeded in collecting another following over a thousand strong and was bent on hostilities.

On the 20th August, one squadron 27th Light Cavalry and a draft of 200 men for the 16th Rajputs, being part of the reinforcements sent from India via Bandar Abbas, reached Shiraz. The half-battalion 120th Infantry and section 35th Mountain Battery had remained to garrison Saidabad, where the squadron 26th Light Cavalry also remained temporarily to rest its horses.

Military preparations at Bushire for an autumn offensive continued steadily throughout August. On the 20th Sir Charles Marling reported that, though Vossuk would not invite us to undertake these operations on the Bushire–Shiraz road, he would be glad to see us carry them out and had pointed out that, having once opened the road, we could not afford to see it again closed. *Bushire; August 1918.*

On the 26th August the Government of India informed the India Office of the progress of the preparations. Measures for improvement of the base were in hand and a light railway was in course of construction across the *mashileh*. The garrison of Bushire already included a squadron of cavalry, four guns of a mountain battery, half a machine gun company and three infantry battalions, besides a number of administrative units; another battalion of infantry, two Sapper and Miner companies, a section of trench howitzers, half a machine gun company, a labour corps, transport and more administrative units were under orders to sail from India in September; and additional units of troops and transport, including two squadrons of cavalry, two mountain guns and three more infantry battalions were under orders to follow them, though their shipping programme had not yet been arranged. Though the actual method of carrying out the operations would depend on current political conditions, the Government of India considered that the construction of the light railway as far as Dalaki would be necessary in any case, so as to give us the power of military action in South Persia if circumstances should render this necessary.

There had been some discussion regarding the political control after the force advanced from Bushire, and on the 28th August the Government of India issued their decision that the General in command would be vested with political as well as with military control, the Deputy Political Resident at Bushire being attached to his staff as Chief Political Officer to advise him on political matters.

North-West and North Persia; August 1918. On the 3rd August, taking advantage of the absence of 2,000 of the Jelus who had gone towards Bijar to take over a convoy of ammunition from us, the Turks captured Urmia ; and the whole of the Jelu population fled via Bijar to Hamadan for safety and protection. This was most unfortunate, as the advent of these 59,000 refugees so increased our supply and transport difficulties as to stop for a time the movement of British reinforcements towards the Caspian. The possession of Urmia, moreover, by covering their right flank, facilitated an advance by the Turks from Tabriz against our long and vulnerable line of communication with Enzeli, at the very moment that we were trying to prolong the defence of Baku by sending it military assistance. Such a Turkish advance would be also assisted by the active help which certain Persian extremists were affording them at Tabriz and would be in no way hindered by the useless and unreliable Persian Cossacks in the area. On the other hand, some bodies of Armenians were still holding out against the Turks in the Erivan and Julfa areas, there was growing Turco-Bulgarian friction and the Turks had reason for apprehension in Palestine. It was, therefore, doubtful if they could carry out operations simultaneously against Baku and to the southward of Tabriz, though it was reliably reported that they had formed a new Ninth Army for this purpose and had just overcome German opposition to their occupation of Baku by an agreement to give the Germans control of the oil supply. In the third and fourth weeks of August, however, Turkish troops did begin to advance southward from Tabriz, with the result that we had to divert troops towards Mianeh to oppose them and to withhold reinforcements which General Dunsterville required urgently to meet a Turkish attack on Baku.*

The Malleson Mission and Trans-Caspia ; August 1918. The detachment from Meshed, consisting of 25 sabres 28th Light Cavalry and 175 rifles and two machine guns 19th Punjabis, reached Muhammadabad (near the Perso-Russian frontier) on the 2nd August. But the Turkestan Union movement had failed to materialise and it looked as if the Mensheviks, who controlled Trans-Caspia for the time, would hardly be able to continue for long to oppose the better armed and equipped Bolsheviks. Foreseeing an appeal from the Trans-Caspian leaders for assistance, General Malleson telegraphed to India on the 1st August reviewing the advantages and disadvantages

---

* For details *see* " The Campaign in Mesopotamia," Vol. IV.

of acceding to their request and pointing out that, if we postponed action awaiting events, we should probably alienate all parties. The Commander-in-Chief in India repeated this telegram to London and at the same time wired to General Malleson giving him discretion to act as he considered fit if the delay involved in the reference to London would be prejudicial. On the 3rd August, however, H.M. Government telegraphed their decision to support the Menshevik leaders of the Trans-Caspian movement, as well as their sanction to the despatch to the Oxus, if considered advisable, of the machine gun section on the frontier. At the same time, they requested the Government of India to report the measures of military assistance which they could carry out from East Persia and added that General Marshall had been authorised to send, from Persia, a force with guns to Krasnovodsk, where they were likely to arrive within the next few days.

During the first week of August the news that General Malleson received of the fighting on the Oxus was somewhat conflicting. On the 7th, in a long interview at Meshed with a representative of the Trans-Caspian Government, General Malleson explained that while we had no desire to interfere with their internal affairs we must stipulate for certain facilities to enable us to organise the defences of Trans-Caspia.* The delegate said that he had no authority to conclude an agreement but that he had no doubt that all these points would be agreed to. On his part he urged that, as tangible evidence of our co-operation to the Turkomans and others in Trans-Caspia who held that we would not perform though we might promise, and as a definite check to pan-Turkish propaganda, we should at once despatch two machine guns to the Oxus front. General Malleson agreed to do this, to send the Trans-Caspian Government some machine guns, rifles and rifle ammunition, and to explain to H.M. Government that the Trans-Caspian Government also required sufficient financial assistance to enable them to pay their officials, railway employés and army. The delegate was also informed that we had sent troops to help in the defence

---

* These were briefly: Access to Krasnovodsk and permission to put it into a defensible state; a free hand to deal, as military necessity dictated, with the Trans-Caspian railway; permission to raise and train forces in Trans-Caspia to oppose any enemy advance; all possible assistance from the Trans-Caspian Government in seizing enemy spies and agents, some of whom were disguised in British uniforms; the securing of all the cotton in the area; the use of the Askabad--Meshed telegraph line; the improvement to a motor transport standard of the Askabad--Meshed road; and immediate facilities for a British officer to report on the military situation on the Merv front.

The Malleson Mission and Trans-Caspia; August 1918.

of Baku and were also shortly sending a force with guns for the defence of Krasnovodsk, for the safety of which the Trans-Caspian Government were very anxious.

Next day General Malleson learnt that the Trans-Caspian force had been driven back by the Bolsheviks to Bairam Ali, on the eastern edge of the Merv oasis, on which the Trans-Caspian Government were largely dependent for Turkoman man-power and supplies. Its loss, moreover, would probably also induce the garrison of Kushk, with its large amount of war material, to declare definitely for the Bolsheviks.

Telegraphing on the 10th August, General Malleson considered that it would be too great a risk to send the 175 Indian infantry from Muhammadabad to Merv. But he might save Merv, he said, if he made up this detachment to 500 rifles, as he could do by denuding Meshed of most of its garrison. On the other hand, the 175 infantry could be sent to Krasnovodsk, being joined there by guns sent from Enzeli, and he personally favoured that alternative. In a second telegram sent on the same day General Malleson reported the receipt of two telegraphic appeals from the Turkestan Union for guns and military assistance for Krasnovodsk, where they said the situation was very critical. From these General Malleson assumed that information had been received at Askabad of the imminent departure from Astrakhan of Bolshevik troops for Krasnovodsk.

In repeating these telegrams to the War Office, the Commander-in-Chief in India said that to secure Merv seemed less important than to block the enemy road eastward of the Caspian. He added that he was pushing 500 men up to Meshed as fast as the backward state of the railway communications permitted and that Colonel R. St. C. Battine, who had reached Krasnovodsk on the 6th August from Enzeli, should be asked for his views regarding the urgent necessity of troops for Krasnovodsk. This telegram was repeated to General Malleson for his guidance, as it was assumed that he was in constant communication with Colonel Battine. General Malleson, however, replied that he did not know what cipher Colonel Battine held and that it was most undesirable to mention the Turkestan Union in any telegram, as the Trans-Caspian Government, who were unaware of our negotiations with that movement, regarded it as a treasonable conspiracy to be ruthlessly rooted out.

On the 12th August the Chief of the General Staff in India wired an appreciation of the situation on the Caspian to General Malleson showing that, as long as Baku held out, Krasnovodsk was of minor importance and that a Bolshevik movement against it from Astrakhan seemed unlikely. On the same day General Marshall, in telegraphing a report on the Caspian situation, enquired whether he was to send a small infantry detachment to Krasnovodsk or whether General Malleson would do so.

On the 14th the War Office telegraphed to India and Baghdad saying that, as the situation was kaleidoscopic in its nature and not too clear, they could not lay down a detailed policy for General Malleson, who was directly controlled by India. Our three principal objects were to obtain control of the Caspian shipping, to occupy Baku so long as there was any hope of holding it and to occupy Krasnovodsk permanently. The main consideration at Krasnovodsk was guns, and General Marshall was to send there a battalion of infantry and at least two guns. Though it was as yet too early to lay down the strength of the garrison at Krasnovodsk, Generals Marshall and Malleson were to make every effort to build up a force there and to arrange for a satisfactory defence seaward. They were both expected to do their utmost to achieve the main objects and neither of them should be prevented from taking any necessary action by the definition of the spheres of control which had been laid down. Further, the War Office trusted them, as the men on the spot, to take energetic and rapid action when necessary without reference to India or the War Office.

The two machine guns of the 19th Punjabis left Muhammadabad on the 11th August and, moving by railway from Artik, reached Bairam Ali on the 12th. With them went Major W. H. Bingham to report on the military situation on the Merv front. Next day the Bolsheviks attacked. The Trans-Caspian force consisting of about 1,000 men—largely Turkomans—was lacking in organisation and discipline, had only one gun (on an armoured train) and five machine guns and, though commanded by an efficient enough officer—a Turkoman—had a useless Russian staff. The Bolshevik attacking force was composed of about 1,000 men, nearly all of them Austro-Hungarian prisoners of war, with a number of field and machine guns; and with another 2,000 men held in reserve. The Trans-Caspian force, making only a half-hearted resistance, was defeated; and its retirement would—as their official account admitted—have resulted in a decisive disaster, but for the gallant behaviour of the Indian machine gun detachment. These men fired their guns till they became too hot to handle

Trans-Caspian defeat at Bairam Ali; 13th August 1918.

and, according to the Trans-Caspian account, inflicted 350 casualties on the enemy. Two of the Indian detachment were wounded and one of its machine guns had to be abandoned after two men had been burnt in trying to carry it out of action. The Trans-Caspian force, thoroughly demoralised, fell back to Merv and on the 14th August, after damaging the bridge over the Murghab river, retired before a Bolshevik advance without attempting resistance past Tejend to Dushak. The Indian machine gun detachment, every man being ill with influenza, returned to Muhammadabad.

The Malleson Mission and Trans-Caspia; August 1918. On learning of this defeat, General Malleson arranged to send from Meshed the headquarters and two companies (325 rifles) 19th Punjabis, under Lieut.-Colonel D. E. Knollys, to join the detachment at Muhammadabad, with a view to assisting the Trans-Caspian force. This detachment,* with a section of a field ambulance, left Meshed on the 16th August and arrived at Muhammadabad on the 25th. In the meantime, on the 19th, owing to the appeals of the Trans-Caspian Government and the necessity of checking the Bolshevik advance, General Malleson, after ascertaining from India that such a course was not considered too risky, had ordered the 175 Punjabi rifles at Muhammadabad to join the Trans-Caspian force at Dushak. They arrived there on the 20th August by a train which also brought two Russian field guns from Krasnovodsk. But, as the position at Dushak proved to be unsuitable, the combined force moved back to Kaahka, where it was joined by Colonel Knollys' detachment on the evening of the 26th. The enemy, whose trains were twelve miles away, had that day made a reconnaissance in force.

The country was mainly flat, sandy desert with occasional low sand hills, though in the few places where water was available the soil was extremely fertile, as in the two main oases of Merv and Tejend. The climate was one of extremes with practically no rainfall, and most of the stations had to be supplied with water by train, for which oil was the principal fuel. The railway was a broad-gauge single line, on which both sides were entirely dependent for transportation. In fact, the two opposing forces lived and moved in long processions of trains covered by one or more armoured trains in which they protected themselves at night by removing some of the rails on the side nearest the enemy. Having a large element of expert railwaymen among

---

* Its equipment was deficient in several respects owing to the long time it took to get stores from India.

them, either side could repair the line more quickly than it could be destroyed ; and that force had the advantage whose armoured train guns had the longest range.

Lieutenant-Colonel Knollys found that, except for about a hundred Russian ex-officers and soldiers, the thousand or so Trans-Caspian infantry—mainly Armenians—were of little fighting value and that the few hundred Turkomans, mounted on ponies, were undisciplined and unreliable ; while the authority of the Turkoman commander of the force—an ex-officer—was nominal. By this time the force had four modern field guns, one on the armoured train being very efficiently manned by Russian ex-officers. The Bolshevik force had much better arms and equipment and its large element of Austro-Hungarian prisoners of war had the special incentive to fight that they had been promised release on reaching the Caspian.*

The village of Kaahka was grouped round the railway station and was surrounded by orchards and vineyards. About a mile to the east of it, the Trans-Caspian commander had taken up a position astride the railway line, the bulk of his troops being located on a low ridge running north and south on the southern side of the line. The combined Trans-Caspian and British force was too small to hold this position, which had the further disadvantage of being commanded by an extensive plateau one thousand yards away to the north-east. Ignoring this fact, the Trans-Caspian commander posted only a small Turkoman detachment to hold his left. Further, he placed his reserves too far forward to the east of the railway station.

On the evening of the 27th August the enemy were reported to be detraining, evidently meaning to attack next day ; and at about 7 a.m. on the 28th this attack opened with an artillery bombardment by guns which had been placed on the plateau to the north-east during the night. This bombardment did little damage. But the enemy infantry, turning the Trans-Caspian left flank, advanced towards the railway station and, meeting with only slight resistance from the Turkoman detachment, pressed forward till they reached the orchards immediately north of the station. Here they were checked for some time by the gallant resistance offered by a few Punjabis, who, left in camp on various fatigue duties, had been hastily collected by Lieutenant F. W. Stewart (Indian Army Reserve of Officers).

Meanwhile, in reply to urgent messages for assistance, Colonel Knollys had moved back from the eastward with a company

---

* An Austro-Hungarian Commission to assist them was at Tiflis.

of his Punjabis; and he now advanced so as to strike diagonally into the orchards with his left flank directed on the station. Arriving here almost simultaneously with the enemy, the Punjabis charged with the bayonet and drove him back, eventually putting him to flight and capturing five of his machine guns. This ended the fighting—which had been confined to the area north of the station—for the Bolshevik force all withdrew.

The British losses were 4 British officers wounded (one mortally), 4 Punjabis killed and 24 wounded. Several of them, it appears, had been shot from behind, evidently by Bolsheviks in the Trans-Caspian force. Next day (29th August) a company (120 rifles) 1/4th Hampshire Regiment reached Kaahka from Krasnovodsk, where they had arrived from Enzeli on the 27th and had been sent on by Colonel Battine.

East Persia; August 1918. During August the troops of the East Persia Cordon Force were reinforced by two squadrons of cavalry (one squadron each 15th and 37th Lancers) and by two companies 1/98th Infantry (bringing this battalion to a strength of six companies). General Dale still commanded the force, which included the troops as far north as Meshed (inclusive); but troops which moved north of Meshed came under General Malleson's orders. The latter was also authorised to raise for service in that area a Khurasan Levy Corps composed of 500 Hazaras.

Supply and maintenance difficulties had always been very great; and although, with the transfer in July of the railhead supply depot from Dalbandin to Juzzak (ten miles east of Mirjawa), matters had improved a little, the movement of troops to the Russian frontier and the despatch of reinforcements from India increased requirements to the maximum limit that could be provided. As, moreover, there was every indication that Meshed would become a locality of increasing strategic importance, the Government of India found it necessary on the 8th August to request sanction to an extension of the railway from Mirjawa to Neh via Duzdab, which they estimated it would take about eight months to complete. General Dale had already been instructed to concentrate on improving road communications with Meshed, and the vital necessity of making the road fit for motor transport throughout was again impressed on him.* As he pointed out, however, the difficulties of making

---

* The distance by road from railhead at Juzzak to Neh was said by General Dale to be 210 miles and from Neh to Meshed 416 miles, but by the alignment which was eventually followed the total distance was 670 miles.

SUGGESTED UNITY OF COMMAND

a road fit for motors were very great indeed, and to assist him it was arranged to send him half a labour corps (600 men) from India.

The recent rapid change in the strategical situation, both in France and in the Caucasus and Caspian areas, led the Commander-in-Chief in India on the 21st August to telegraph his views to the War Office at some length. Some six weeks previously the Chief of the Imperial General Staff had anticipated that Germany would make no serious military effort in Asia until her main effort in Europe either collapsed or was suspended; and it seemed to Sir Charles Monro that these conditions might soon be realised. On the assumption that the war would continue in 1919 and that the strategical centre of gravity might swing eastward, he gave his opinion on possible developments and measures to meet them. He considered that the existing diffusion of responsibility and duality of control in the eastern theatres of operations militated gravely against swift decision and effective action, and he advocated the adoption in the East of the principle of unity of control and command by forming the forces in theatres east of Suez into one group for military command and political control, which he suggested should be centralised in India. Apart from the question of an Eastern command, he also advocated the creation of one North Persia command to include the missions and forces under Generals Dunsterville and Malleson.

Suggestion for unifying the command of all British forces east of Suez; August 1918.

Sir Charles Monro then went on to discuss the various immediate objectives open to Germany in the East, and he emphasised the ample railway communications at her disposal as compared with our own very backward conditions in this respect. Though, he said, the best method of checking a German advance towards Afghanistan and the Indian frontier would be to obtain control of North-West Persia and the Caspian, we might fail to do this. It therefore seemed essential that we should be in a position to exercise strong military pressure from Meshed; and for this the extension northward of the railway from Mirjawa was imperative.

This telegram crossed one from the India Office conveying the sanction of H.M. Government to the extension of the railway as far as Duzdab and to the completion of the survey to Neh. The extension to this place could be considered later in the light of the situation when railhead approached Duzdab.

The suggestion for a separate Eastern command, including a North Persia command, was considered by the Eastern Committee of the Cabinet in London and caused considerable discussion, as, though all authorities agreed on the desirability of a North Persia command, several objections were raised to an Eastern command. On the approach of the Armistice, however, the question was dropped before a decision had been reached.

North Persia and adjacent territory; September 1918. During the first half of September it became apparent that both Persia and Turkey were beginning to realise, from the continued success of the Allied operations in France and Flanders, that Germany was likely to lose the war. In Persia public opinion became consequently attracted by the material advantages to be gained by a British alliance, while at Constantinople the pan-Turkish party were encouraged to insist that their aspirations in the East should no longer be sacrificed to German interests. The pan-Turks, professing to have no regrets for the loss of their Arabian provinces, looked to recoup themselves by territorial acquisition in the Caucasus, North-West Persia and Trans-Caspia.

By the 15th September the Turks had captured Baku, occupied practically the whole of Persian Azerbaijan and were moving towards Ardebil and Astara. They had also, it was said, sent a note to Persia demanding that she should choose which side she would join, as her neutrality could no longer be recognised.

The great gallantry of the small British force at Baku, lacking adequate or efficient local support, had failed to save that town. But the final British stand on the 14th September had caused the enemy such heavy casualties that General Dunsterville was able to extricate his men and guns and had withdrawn, without further molestation by the Turks, to Enzeli. The small British detachment which had pushed out along the Mianeh road from Kazvin had been forced to retire from the Kuflan Kuh by a numerically superior Turkish force of 1,500 men, and the situation in North-West Persia appeared to General Marshall at Baghdad to be so serious that on the 17th September he telegraphed to the War Office that our chances of controlling the Caspian were very small and that to meet the threat of a Turkish advance from Tabriz he advocated withdrawal from Krasnovodsk and Enzeli.

Commodore D. T. Norris, R.N., however, protested strongly against the order to evacuate Enzeli. He could, he said, man three or four ships with British personnel (using Russians for the engine-room) and, as fuel oil in sufficient quantities was available at Enzeli and Krasnovodsk, he would be able to carry out his orders in the Caspian provided Enzeli was held. General Dunsterville also reported that there was no reason to fear the Caspian fleet, which he had hopes of inducing to join us. General Marshall at once cancelled his orders for the evacuation of Enzeli and his action was confirmed by an order from the War Office, emphasising the importance of British control of the Caspian and saying that Enzeli was only to be evacuated in the direst military necessity. The General Staff at the War Office, it may be noted, did not consider that the enemy threat from Tabriz was as serious as it might seem to be, as the Turks were faced with great supply and transport difficulties at Tabriz and their railway was only working intermittently owing to the shortage of fuel oil. Consequently they could not, it was considered, send reinforcements to Tabriz—where they only had one division about 4,000 strong—before the end of the month.

During the next few days Commodore Norris reported that, as the fall of Baku had removed the Centro-Caspian Government, i.e., the main obstruction to his progress, the number of ships he could arm was limited only by the material, labour, personnel and time available. In the meantime Major-General W. M. Thomson had taken over command of all the British troops in North Persia,* General Dunsterville having been recalled on the break-up of his mission, whose officers and personnel were to be mainly employed with the Urmia Brigade of the Jelu refugees which General Marshall was organising.

Soon after the capture of Baku reliable information was received that Enver Pasha had ordered Nuri Pasha to detach one portion of the Turkish force at Baku to secure the country as far north as the Terek river and another portion to clear the south-western shores of the Caspian and occupy Enzeli. It was clearly the Turkish intention to consolidate the new State of Azerbaijan, which was to include the province of Tabriz and

---

* The troops of the North Persia Force comprised the 14th Hussars, one section 15th Machine Gun Squadron, 13th Brigade R.F.A., 21st Mountain Battery, one section 72nd Field Company, R.E., 36th Infantry Brigade (1/4th Hampshire, 36th Sikhs, 1/2nd and 1/6th Gurkhas), 39th Infantry Brigade (9th Royal Warwickshire, 7th Gloucestershire, 9th Worcestershire, 7th North Staffordshire), 6th Light Armoured Motor Battery (less one section) and Dunsterforce Armoured Car Brigade.

In addition to holding the road from Hamadan (inclusive) to Enzeli, the force provided detachments in Trans-Caspia and on the Zenjan, Bijar and Sehneh lines.

probably also Lenkoran and part of Gilan. A Turkish detachment of about 500 men from Tabriz on its way to Astara had also occupied Ardebil, which the Persian Cossacks evacuated after a feeble resistance.* But by the 21st September news was received that a Turkish division, which had been under orders to move from Trans-Caucasia to Tabriz, had been ordered instead to proceed forthwith to Constantinople.

Trans-Caspia; September 1918. In Trans-Caspia, where a serious epidemic of influenza had incapacitated a large proportion of the small British force, a section 44th Battery, Royal Field Artillery, reached the front at Kaahka on the 5th September from Krasnovodsk, where it had just arrived from Enzeli. The Bolshevik force based on Tashkend, disheartened by its defeat on the 28th August and pre-occupied also by operations towards Orenburg, was inactive; and advantage was taken of this to strengthen the Kaahka position, especially its vulnerable left flank, which had been taken over by the British.

On the morning of the 11th September, the Bolsheviks again attacked, moving against this left flank and opening the fight with a heavy bombardment by ten guns. This, however, proved quite ineffective, and the Bolshevik infantry attack broke down completely under the accurate fire of the two British field guns. The enemy in his subsequent flight abandoned three of his guns and, if the Turkoman cavalry could have been induced to pursue, he must have lost heavily before he could have entrained. There were no British casualties.

On the 18th September the Bolsheviks made another attack, much on the same lines, and although some of their mounted troops succeeded in outflanking the Trans-Caspian position and in destroying a small portion of the railway line—thereby creating a temporary panic among the Trans-Caspian troops— the British troops again put the whole Bolshevik force to flight, at a loss to themselves of only two wounded. The Turkoman cavalry again failed to pursue, thus tending to confirm reports received by the British that the Turkoman tribes generally could not be relied on against the Bolsheviks. This lack of efficient cavalry was, however, being remedied by the despatch

---

* H.M. Government were still paying the Persian Cossack Division and earlier in the month had favoured acceptance of an offer by Colonel Starosselski, its commandant, to raise its strength from 6,000 to 12,000 so as to help in opposing the Turks. But General Marshall had replied that he looked on the Persian Cossacks as unreliable, that he preferred to do without them and that in fact their presence could only be an embarrassment.

from Meshed (on the 16th September) of two squadrons 28th Light Cavalry (under Major J. A. C. Kreyer), which reached Kaahka on the 28th.

After the fight on the 18th, Lieutenant-Colonel Knollys reported to General Malleson that an advance eastward by the Trans-Caspian force was out of the question for the time being, as the British artillery had very little ammunition, the Russian staff of the force were quite incapable of organising an advance, the Russian and Turkoman elements of the force were unreliable and there was a large number of Bolshevik agents among them.

At this period we received reliable information that the Germans had formed a plan for military action in Turkestan but that Kress, who was commanding the German forces in Trans-Caucasia, had been warned to exercise care in his arrangements owing to German pledges to the Bolshevik Government of non-intervention in Turkestan and to the strained relations regarding Turkestan between Germans and Turks. What the German plan may have been is unknown, but that they had some material at their disposal was clear from a telegram sent at this time by the Swedish Red Cross Commissioner at Tashkend saying that there were 29,000 German and 26,000 Austrian prisoners of war in Turkestan.

At Tehran, Sir Percy Cox took over charge of the British Legation on the 16th September, and on the 23rd he sent the Foreign Office a long telegram reporting the result of two or three very frank and full discussions which he had carried out with Vossuk-ud-Daula and his principal supporter in the Cabinet (Nasrat-ud-Daula). The fall of Baku and our retirement from Kuflan Kuh had given hostile elements a pretext for reviving violent anti-British propaganda, he said, and this had resulted in weakening the position of the Cabinet and in a considerable run on the Imperial Bank of Persia. Though it was difficult to conceive that any intelligent Persian could dream, at this juncture, of entering the war on the enemy's side, said Sir Percy Cox, he had learnt from reliable sources that, if we suffered any further set-back in North-West Persia, there was a real danger that hostile elements would turn out the Cabinet and would replace it by one of extremists, by whom the country would certainly be dragged into war against us. After previous consultation with General Marshall, Sir Percy Cox had informed the Persian Cabinet in strict confidence of

British policy and Persian politics; September 1918.

British policy and Persian politics; September 1918. the strength of the British force which would reach North Persia by the time winter set in ; and Persian Ministers had come to the conclusion that it would be dangerous, unless we had at least two divisions there, for Persia to do more than maintain a form of neutrality. But even to do this, displaying moderation and secret benevolence towards us, the Cabinet did not consider that it could maintain its position, in the existing critical circumstances, unless it was able to create a favourable atmosphere and attract moderate democratic opinion by a public announcement of concessions which it had been able to secure from us. The terms of the announcement they wished to make were that :—

(i) We had reiterated categorically our determination to respect Persian independence ;

(ii) We had undertaken to press for the abrogation of the Anglo-Russian Convention as soon as a Russian Government existed which we could recognise ; and that

(iii) We had agreed to transfer the South Persia Rifles to the direct control of the Persian Government and to send a Commission of neutral officers—not Swedes, but preferably Scandinavians—to draw up a scheme for the formation of a uniform military force for the country, into which the South Persia Rifles would be merged. In the meantime the South Persia Rifles at Shiraz would be transferred to Farman Farma's control on the private understanding that he would retain an adequate number of *junior* British officers to administer the force. There would also be a private understanding that the South Persia Rifles at Kerman should subsequently also be handed over if the Fars arrangement succeeded and that, as soon as the Bushire–Shiraz road had been opened and tranquillity restored, the British troops in Fars should be withdrawn gradually.

In view of the run on the bank* and the possibility, in the near future, of a Turkish advance on Enzeli or Kazvin, Sir Percy Cox emphasised the necessity of avoiding delay in the publication of the above announcement if the existing Cabinet was to be maintained in office.

---

* The importance of this was all the greater in that we were experiencing, at this time, very great difficulty indeed in finding currency with which to finance our increasing commitments in the different parts of the country.

On the same day, it may be noted, Sir Percy Cox reported that Vossuk had agreed to telegraph the next day to the Persian Governor of Bushire informing him that it had been decided to open the Bushire–Shiraz road and that he was to take all necessary steps to co-operate with the British.

When these telegrams reached London, the danger of a further Turkish advance southward from Tabriz had been so much reduced by recent events elsewhere that the War Office sent the following telegram on the 25th September to the military attaché at Tehran for the information of Sir Percy Cox :—

"The complete destruction of the whole Turkish army in Palestine leaves Syria open to invasion. Every anti-Turkish element in the country will support the advancing British. The communications of the Turkish force in Mesopotamia are thus seriously threatened, and in all probability it will be forced to abandon Mesopotamia altogether. Arabia is completely lost to them and the fall of Medina is now imminent. Turkey, in addition to being faced with the loss of three-quarters of her Asiatic territory, is gravely threatened in Europe by the Allied advance in the Balkans, which, since 15th September, has continued uninterruptedly. The Bulgarian army is in a critical situation and a slight further advance by the Allies will sever it in two. To meet all these dangers on so many fronts, the Turks have only one army left, which is now in the Caucasus and Persia. General Allenby's victory has already compelled them to transfer to Constantinople a division which was destined for Tabriz; and the situation in the Balkans and Palestine will completely paralyse Turkish operations in the Middle East and in all probability will lead very soon to the evacuation of Persia. Thus the whole situation has been transformed in the last few days and the Turks must now think only of protecting their own territory and not of further aggression."

On the 24th September the War Office and the Admiralty had issued orders to General Marshall and Commodore Norris that steps must be taken immediately to gain control ot the Caspian, by drastic measures if necessary.

As the result of consideration on the 26th by the Eastern Committee of the Cabinet of Sir Percy Cox's telegram of the 23rd, the Foreign Office telegraphed on the 27th September asking Sir Percy Cox how the situation at Tehran had been affected by the recent victories in Palestine and Bulgaria. H.M. Government were disposed, they said, to concur in the greater part of the proposed public announcement. But they would first like to know if Sir Percy Cox and the local political officers were satisfied that the maintenance of order in Fars would not suffer if the South Persia Rifles were handed over to Farman Farma, and H.M. Government would prefer—if Vossuk would agree—to drop for the time being the question of a commission of neutral officers.

North Persia; end of September 1918. In the meantime the Turks had made no attempt to advance south of Kuflan Kuh, and their envoys, despatched to arrange co-operation with the Jangalis, had been turned back with a warning that a Turkish advance into Gilan would be opposed by the Jangalis, who had also informed General Thomson that, provided they could come to a complete understanding with the Persian Government, they would help us to oppose a Turkish advance. General Marshall had also received information that the Turks, in the expectation of an imminent British offensive up the Tigris, had ordered back there at once a division and some corps troops from the Urmia region.

Both Germans and Turks were reported to be endeavouring to purchase the Caspian fleet, which, according to a telegram sent on the 27th September by Commodore Norris, was under Bicharakoff's* complete control and was, in any case, much disorganised. Commodore Norris consequently proposed to ignore it as long as it was inactive and to push on with arming merchant vessels, of which he controlled thirty-seven at Enzeli and two at Krasnovodsk.

On the 29th September, in accordance with orders from the War Office to complete the detachment in Trans-Caspia to a battery and a battalion, the 9th Royal Warwickshire and a section 39th Brigade Machine Gun Company left Enzeli for Krasnovodsk. The remaining section of the 44th Field Battery was also to have gone, but the epidemic of influenza, which caused a very high sick rate among our troops in North Persia at this time, prevented their departure.

General W. Gillman, General Marshall's Chief of Staff, was then paying a visit of inspection to North Persia and, after he had met Commodore Norris, General Marshall reported (on the 30th September) to the War Office that the Commodore was preparing an armed flotilla of six large and six small ships. The first vessel would be ready on the 6th October, work on the second vessel had begun, and the completion of the remainder would depend on the arrival of the guns from Mesopotamia. When the ships were ready, the Commodore proposed

---

* Bicharakoff was at Petrovsk.

to watch Baku, capture all shipping entering or leaving that port and, if necessary, harass the railway. The Russian fleet, owing to lack of fuel, would either have to go to Baku or to join us or Bicharakoff, and in the last named case it would be advisable to continue our subsidy to that officer. The Commodore would keep Krasnovodsk and Enzeli open, seize shipping at the mouth of the Volga and would show the flag round the Caspian littoral. It was estimated that the cost of all this would total about £26,000 a month and General Marshall considered that the Commodore's proposals were the best that could be devised to carry out the War Cabinet's policy.

On the 30th September General Gillman, visiting Tehran, accompanied Sir Percy Cox to an interview with Vossuk and was able to reassure him completely regarding our ability to stop any further Turkish advance into Persia and to maintain Persian security at Enzeli and on the Caspian.

The general war situation continued to improve, as is shown by the following extracts from a telegram sent on the 30th September by the War Office to the Commander-in-Chief in India :—

> "During the past week the Allies in the Western theatre have been driving the enemy back along practically the whole front of 200 miles between the sea and the Meuse. The British have broken through the famous Hindenburg line, over 50,000 prisoners and several hundred guns have been taken and the number of captures is constantly increasing. . . . In the Balkans the Allied success has been turned into a decisive victory and an armistice has been concluded. Bulgaria by this action has separated herself from her Allies; and communications between Germany and Austria on the one hand and Turkey on the other hand will shortly be cut. In Palestine the Fourth Turkish Army east of the Jordan is surrounded. . . . Over 50,000 prisoners and 325 guns have been captured. These events remove all danger of Turkish aggression in Persia and Trans-Caspia. The whole situation in all theatres of war has been transformed. . . . and the situation of Austria and Germany will shortly be desperate."

The imminence of the fall of Baku led the India Office to telegraph on the 9th September to the Government of India emphasising the importance of strengthening our position at Meshed and our capacity for action in Trans-Caspia; and they

East Persia; September 1918.

asked what was the maximum force that we should be able to maintain north of Meshed by the spring of 1919. The Government of India replied on the 13th that this was entirely a question of communications and was difficult to estimate exactly. When railhead reached Neh, provided that a number of Ford vans from England previously asked for had arrived,* we should probably be able to maintain a force of at least a division north of Neh, of which a brigade group should be able to operate beyond Meshed. The Government of India realised thoroughly, they said, the importance of improving communications. But the extent of these and their bad state, the lack of water and of local supplies, and the scarcity of animal transport rendered it impossible to accomplish what was necessary until the railway had been extended and the Ford vans had been supplied.

A further difficulty, it may be noted, was the large amount of local transport being utilised by a recent sudden increase in the imports into East Persia and Khurasan of Indian trade goods, such as sugar and textiles, which had formerly come from Russia, but for which by this time the country had become entirely dependent on India. It was estimated that during the past two months these goods had been coming in at the rate of over 100 tons a month and the demand was such that private traders were proving serious competitors for the use of the available local transport. Consequently the Government of India were proposing to restrict the trade by a system of consular certificates. But this course presented so many difficulties and disadvantages that it might not be feasible.

On the 21st September the Commander-in-Chief in India issued orders placing under the command of the General Officer Commanding 4th (Quetta) Division (Lieutenant-General R. Wapshare) the whole of the East Persia Cordon up to and including Meshed, but exclusive of troops under General Malleson's orders. The functions hitherto vested in the General Officer Commanding the East Persia Cordon were in future to be divided between an Inspector-General of Communications, East Persia, and a General Officer Commanding Line of Communication Defences, East Persia, who would be responsible to the General Officer Commanding Quetta Division for the administration and defence, respectively, of the line of communication from railhead (exclusive). Brigadier-General W. E. R. Dickson was appointed Inspector-General of

---

* Some difficulty was being experienced at this period in England owing to American objections to providing Ford vans for operations in the East.

Communications, and on his arrival in East Persia General Dale was to become General Officer Commanding Line of Communication Defences.

General Wapshare was to be responsible not only for the supply and maintenance of General Malleson's troops, but for the development of the Line of Communications to meet the possibility of an increase, by the spring of 1919, of the force at and beyond Birjand to a cavalry brigade and a division, including a brigade in advance of Meshed.

At Shiraz the situation remained quiet. Ehtesham, who left Firuzabad at the beginning of September to continue his operations, attacked Saulat to the south of Qir about the 15th and put him to flight. But at the end of the month the situation altered somewhat in Saulat's favour owing to the migratory movements of various tribal elements and to the intervention of Wassmuss; and, in accordance with a request by Farman Farma, Sir Percy Sykes arranged to send twenty-five cavalry and a hundred infantry of the South Persia Rifles, under Persian officers, to reinforce the South Persia Rifles detachment already with Ehtesham at Firuzabad. Fars; September 1918.

On the 20th September Sir Percy Sykes reported that the Fars Brigade had been reduced* by one cavalry regiment and an infantry battalion and that the machine gun squadron had been absorbed temporarily into a cavalry regiment. This left in existence one cavalry regiment, a battery of artillery, an engineer company, two infantry battalions and a mule corps, amounting to a total strength of ten British officers and 1,640 Persian ranks. Sir Percy Sykes had been informed of the general plan for the advance from Bushire; and the extent of the co-operation with this advance by troops from Shiraz had been settled after discussion with him.

Even before the War and the events recorded in this history, the protection of British subjects and the maintenance of British interests in Fars and the Bushire hinterland had been, for several years, a source of great embarrassment to the British and Indian Governments. All the roads had been unsafe, merchandise had been plundered and unauthorised exactions had been levied. Moreover, numerous attacks on foreigners, including two British and two Russian consuls, and the murder Bushire; September 1918. (See Map 11.)

---

* i.e., by desertions and dismissals due to the revolt.

**Bushire;
September
1918.
(See Map 11.)** of Captain Eckford of the Indian Army had remained entirely unpunished. It is possible, therefore, as Mr. J. H. H. Bill (Deputy Political Resident at Bushire and Chief Political Officer, Bushire Field Force) said in his report of April 1919, that, even if the war had not broken out, a British expedition from Bushire would have been necessary.

Though the districts to the north and west of the Bushire-Shiraz road were generally friendly to the British, or neutral, those lying along it and to the south and east were for the most part in the hands of tribal leaders who were hostile to us. They were generally described as Khans, although few of them had any hereditary right to that title, being merely revenue collectors and headmen, nominees of the Persian Government, by which they had all, at various times, been dismissed.

Nearest to Bushire was the district of Tangistan, dominated by Zair Khidar, a petty headman who, by force of character and bribery, had ousted the hereditary Khan. His anti-British sentiments were not due to fanaticism but to his realisation that British influence in Persia, standing for law and order, tended to prevent his misappropriation of revenue and his illegal exactions. With a great reputation for bravery and competent leadership, he enjoyed considerable popularity locally.

Adjoining Tangistan lay Chah Kutah under Shaikh Husain, whose previous friendly attitude to the British, affected apparently by fanaticism and the influence of Wassmuss, had been changed into intense hostility when his favourite son was killed in an attack on Bushire. His exactions on passing trade had been very heavy and his cruelty had caused him to be generally detested by his people.

Next to Chah Kutah came Borazjan, whose Khan, Ghazanfar-es-Sultaneh, an educated man, was one of the most rapacious of the roadside chiefs. His consistent anti-British attitude was due to his fear of losing his privileged position of practical independence.

The Khan of Dalaki was outwardly friendly and the Khisht chiefs were really so, while Nasir Diwan, the headman of Kazerun, had always been hostile to any force directed towards the establishment of order, whether under Swedish or British officers. Between Kazerun and Shiraz there were no leaders of note, the country being dominated during their migrations by the Qashqais.

In dealing with these various leaders the principal complication was the certainty that, after one defeat in the field, they would decamp and take refuge in the inaccessible hills which border the road on the east and south unless terms could be found which they could accept and which would afford a real guarantee that matters would not revert to their former unsatisfactory state on the departure of the British force. Such terms, in the absence of a reliable Persian force to enforce their due performance, were difficult to find. After much discussion, it was decided that all that could be offered was exile in Mesopotamia till the end of the European war, after which their cases would be reconsidered.

As a base for operations Bushire had many drawbacks. The port consisted of an open roadstead with inner and outer anchorages, lying three and seven miles out respectively. The inner anchorage could only accommodate six or seven vessels of a maximum draught of twenty-one feet, and in the boat channel between it and the wharves there were only five feet of water at low tide. The outer anchorage became unusable in certain winds, and with any fresh breeze a sufficient sea arose to make disembarkation very difficult. On shore, wharves, jetties, roads, stores and other buildings were generally quite insufficient and the supply of good water was so meagre that arrangements had to be made to bring water from Bombay. Much preliminary work was, therefore, necessary. But by the middle of September considerable progress had been made in the administrative preparations, pending the approximate completion of which the additional troops required for the operations were not to be sent to Bushire.

On the 21st September the Government of India telegraphed to the India Office that the force at Bushire was sufficiently strong[*] to cover the construction of the light railway beyond the *mashileh*, and that it was desirable that operations should be over by the middle of December, when the passes were liable to be covered by snow. They were accordingly instructing General Douglas, commanding at Bushire, to begin this construction on the 25th so as to bring railhead to Dalaki by the beginning of November, by which time the striking force should be complete and ready to advance.

On the same day information was received at Simla from Bushire that Ghazanfar had arrived at Chah Kutah with about 400 riflemen and that it was said that he intended to make

---

[*] The combatant troops then at Bushire consisted of one squadron 15th Lancers, 35th Mountain Battery (less one section), a locally improvised section of two 15-pounder field guns, No. 3 Indian Machine Gun Company (less two sections), a local machine gun section, 54th Company Sappers and Miners, 81st Pioneers, 71st Punjabis and 2/113th Infantry.

Bushire; overtures so as to ascertain our intentions. Mr. Bill considered
September that the Governor of Bushire would have to call on Ghazanfar
1918.
(See Map 11.) to disperse his armed following and that if he refused it would
be necessary for British troops to occupy Chah Kutah. On
the 22nd September Mr. Bill further reported that Zair Khidar
with thirty men had joined Shaikh Husain and Ghazanfar at
Chah Kutah and, as overtures were expected at any moment,
he asked for immediate instructions.

The Government of India sent these instructions on the 23rd.
As they considered it obvious that the object of the outlaw
Khans was to surrender and come to terms and that the presence
of their armed following was only a customary precaution,
everything calculated to lead them to foolish action was to be
avoided and every opportunity should be given to them to
surrender. The Government of India, considering that a campaign of Khan hunting was to be avoided at all costs, deprecated
any demand for immediate disbandment of the armed following
and said that negotiations were to be carried out in a sensible
way unless the overtures were contumacious or otherwise really
unacceptable.

On the 24th September the Chief of the General Staff in
India telegraphed instructions to General Douglas, of which
the following is the gist. He was to command the field force
operating in the Bushire hinterland and Fars, in co-operation
with a column from Shiraz, which would come under his orders
for operations west of Khan-i-Zinian. He would be in full
political control of the areas, outside the Bushire peninsula,
directly affected by the operations, and Mr. Bill would be the
Chief Political Officer on his staff. General Douglas was to keep
the Government of India and Sir Percy Cox at Tehran fully
informed of all political developments and was to refer to these
authorities all questions of permanent policy. Should any
question, even indirectly affecting permanent policy, arise, in
which Mr. Bill's advice to him was not acceptable, a reference
to the Government of India would be necessary, except in
such an extremely urgent case that there was no time for
reference and, in that contingency, the Government of India
should receive an immediate report of the decision taken.

General Douglas was told that his objectives were (i) the
establishment of an advanced base at Dalaki, including the
construction to that place of the light railway, and (ii) a
deliberate advance therefrom to Kazerun with the object, in
co-operation with the Shiraz column, of opening up the Bushire
–Kazerun–Shiraz trade route. If his advance was opposed, he

was to take such military action as was necessary, bearing in mind that Persia was a neutral country, that any military action taken must be justified by military necessity, that it was to be carried out with the greatest possible forbearance and that it should inflict the minimum possible damage to Persian property. In this connection he was to give full consideration to all relevant political factors.

The strength of his field force would be :—

Bushire force.—Headquarters and two squadrons Indian cavalry.
                One Indian mountain battery.
                Two companies Sappers and Miners.
                One Indian machine gun company.
                Two sections of trench howitzers.
                Five battalions of Indian infantry.
                One battalion of pioneers.
                One brigade section, divisional signal company, and
                A proportion of an ammunition column.

Shiraz column.—One squadron of Indian cavalry.
(under Colonel Orton) One Indian mountain battery.
                Three squadrons of mounted rifles.
                One and three-quarter battalions Indian infantry.
                One squadron of South Persia Rifles cavalry, and
                One company of South Persia Rifles infantry.

The Shiraz column was to establish an advanced base at Khan-i-Zinian and to concentrate there preparatory to advancing at a date to be decided by General Douglas, towards Miyan Kutal in co-operation with the advance from Dalaki.

During the early stages of the operations the Inspector of Communications of the Bushire force would also be responsible to General Douglas for the tactical security of the line.

On the 25th September a proclamation was issued by the British at Bushire saying that, with the concurrence of the Persian Government,[*] British troops were being sent to open the road to Shiraz and to construct a railway to Dalaki, and that they would not interfere with peaceful inhabitants, though they would deal severely with any attempt at opposition.

---

[*] Vossuk-ud-Daula had sent the Persian Governor of Bushire the telegram which he had promised Sir Percy Cox to send, see *ante*.

Bushire;
September 1918.
At the same time the Persian Governor wrote to the outlaw Khans pointing out the futility of resistance and suggesting a meeting with a view to coming to terms.

It soon became evident, however, after an attempt to start negotiations, that the Khans were not convinced that they would have to come to terms ; and with a following of about 600 men they started to entrench a position at Chaghadak. A demand to evacuate Chaghadak was consequently sent to them on the 28th September.

Early next morning, by General Douglas's orders, a small column under Major J. S. Corlett (15th Lancers)—consisting of a squadron 15th Lancers, the field gun section, the 2/113th Infantry, a section machine gun company and a water party from the 54th Company Sappers and Miners—moved out from Bushire across the *mashileh*. At 6.15 a.m. the cavalry patrols came into contact with the enemy, who was holding a line of about 1,200 yards of trench in front of Chaghadak, with small bodies of riflemen scattered among the palm groves between that village and Ali Changi, some two miles to the south-east.

A heavy fire was opened by the advancing British, and the enemy at Chaghadak fled precipitately as soon as the 113th began to deploy and before the 15th Lancers had time to get round the enemy's rear. Chaghadak was occupied at 8.30 a.m. and, leaving two companies to hold that village, the remainder of the column advanced to Ali Changi, driving small parties of the enemy before them.

British casualties amounted to three killed and two wounded ; those of the enemy, which were not great, being subsequently estimated at thirty. The state of his demoralisation was, however, clear by the fact that he had abandoned in the trenches nearly 30,000 rounds of ammunition, a few animals and a good deal of other property.

CHAPTER X.

OCTOBER–11th NOVEMBER 1918: THE EFFECT OF OUR VICTORIES.

(Maps 11, 12, 13.)

On the 1st October Sir Percy Cox, replying to the Foreign Office telegram of the 27th September, said that the main effect of our victories in Palestine had been to remove Persian official fears of a further Turkish advance into Persia, but that it was not yet clear what their effect was on the Persian public. With regard to the South Persia Rifles he recommended that we should agree to an announcement that the force would be transferred to Farman Farma's control as soon as the two Governments had satisfied themselves as to the safety and security of foreign representatives and foreign interests, and also after the Bushire–Shiraz road had been reopened. Persian Ministers, he said, had no objection to French-Swiss officers for the force and were less concerned for an actual early assembly of a neutral Commission than for an immediate public announcement that it would be assembled. *British and Persian policy; October 1918.*

In another telegram sent the same day referring to an opinion favourable to a Persian alliance which the War Office had expressed in a recent telegram to General Marshall, Sir Percy Cox thought that there would be no difficulty in bringing Persia into the war on our side provided that we could demonstrate our ability to stop any further Turkish invasion and that we could furnish Persia with the necessary funds, material and armament. The moral effect of such an alliance would, he said, be considerable in Afghanistan and India, it would ensure Persia not coming in against us and it would in many ways place us in a more favourable position in the country. But Persia herself would be actuated solely by a desire to appear at the Peace Conference as a belligerent, in the hope of obtaining international guarantees of her independence and of acquiring Turkish territory as compensation for injury she had received; she was incapable of giving us material assistance; and it appeared to Sir Percy Cox that the elements in the country

British and Persian policy; October 1918.
who would gain in strength from an alliance were those who would be least likely to be friendly to us after peace was declared. He, therefore, considered that the disadvantages predominated.

The latter of these two telegrams was considered at the meeting of the Eastern Committee of the British Cabinet on the 23rd October, when it was decided that, in spite of the advantages of an alliance, the extravagant price Persia might demand for declaring war against Turkey rendered it wiser for the time being to wait on events. Next day, reliable information was received in London that the Turkish Government had announced to Germany their intention of asking for peace, that they were withdrawing four divisions from Trans-Caucasia and that, with only three divisions left there, they had abandoned their idea of moving on Enzeli. Reports also tended to show that Georgia realised her mistake in seeking German assistance, that Alexeieff and Bicharakoff were making progress in their fight against Bolshevism and that certain of the Moslem tribes, the Terek Cossacks and the Armenians in the Erivan–Julfa area were desirous of co-operating with us.

On the 3rd October Sir Percy Cox telegraphed to London enquiring whether the military situation permitted a British assurance to the Persian Government that the restoration of Persian Azerbaijan by Turkey would be insisted on. Reconnaissances by the North Persia Force at this period showed that the Turkish strength in the Mianeh area had decreased. But during the next few days it was learnt from a reliable source that Enver, in anticipation of peace and hoping that Great Britain and the United States of America would recognise a separate State of Azerbaijan, was building up there a dominating military organisation under his relatives and personal supporters.

In the meantime, Bicharakoff, realising that we were not prepared to assist him to an unlimited extent in his efforts to regenerate Russia, had practically broken off relations with us; and both General Thomson and General Marshall recommended that we should cease to subsidise him. This action would probably have the advantage that if he could no longer pay the Caspian fleet it would come over to us, as the progress Commodore Norris was making in subsidising and arming merchant vessels would make it afraid to join the Turks.

On the 7th October Sir Percy Cox was authorised to give the Persian Government the increased financial assistance which Sir Charles Marling had advocated a month previously. British

PERSIAN POLITICS

Ministers in England were pre-occupied by the German proposal for an armistice, and on the 11th October the Foreign Office informed Sir Percy Cox that the suggestions he had made on the 1st had been much debated but that nothing had been settled owing to the absence of Ministers in Paris.

On the 13th Sir Percy Cox telegraphed that the Turks were spreading reports that the Allies were prepared, in return for a separate Turkish peace, to recognise the inclusion of Persian Azerbaijan in the Turkish Empire; and he followed this up next day by telegraphing a summary of the Tehran situation. He had been unable to see the Shah, as both he and the Prime Minister had been among the victims of a serious influenza epidemic, but hoped to obtain an audience at the end of the week. It was by this time generally recognised, he said, that the war was going well for the Allies and that in Persian interests British friendship was desirable. But this did not tend to make Vossuk's position any easier, and the position of his Cabinet was daily becoming weaker. The Foreign Secretary was working for his own hand against Vossuk, the remaining Ministers carried little or no weight in the country, many of the moderate Democrats desired a share in the power and profits of office, and Starosselski (the Russian commander of the Persian Cossack Division), who had a good deal of influence with the Shah, was also intriguing against Vossuk. The latter would have to strengthen the personnel of his Cabinet and Sir Percy Cox thought that we should, if possible, expedite the issue of the friendly announcement of policy. In conclusion, he said that attempts were being made to oust Farman Farma.

Next day (14th October) the President of the United States of America received a communication from the Turkish Government asking him to take steps to establish peace. This, it was said, was due to action taken by the Sultan of Turkey, after the armistice with Bulgaria, which led to the resignation of Enver and Talaat and to the formation of a new Turkish Government.

On the 15th October Sir Percy Cox enquired whether H.M. Government wished to represent Persia's interests at the Peace Conference, in the event of her not being admitted as she hoped; and he suggested that it would seem desirable, in any case, to ascertain what requests she contemplated making. On that day Mr. Balfour informed the Persian Minister in London, in reply to a query on the subject, that the Turks had made no suggestion of a separate peace in return for the cession of Persian Azerbaijan and that if such a suggestion were made

British and Persian policy; October 1918.

H.M. Government would not entertain it. Sir Percy Cox was told of this and was authorised to give the Persian Government a similar assurance.

The Eastern Committee of the British War Cabinet, which had not met since the 3rd, considered several questions concerning Persia and adjacent territory on the 17th October. It was decided to discontinue the subsidy to Bicharakoff, whose assistance had been rendered of little value by enemy withdrawals from the Caucasus, and to defer a decision on Persian policy pending the preparation of a statement and of a draft telegraphic reply to Sir Percy Cox by the Foreign Office. There was evidently a general feeling that it was desirable to avoid undue haste over a question which had passed the dangerous stage.

On the 20th October General Townshend arrived at Mitylene with a direct offer of peace from the Turkish Government, and this led to the meeting between British and Turkish representatives which concluded the conditions of the armistice.

The Eastern Committee considered the Foreign Office paper and draft telegram on the 24th October; and the latter, being approved with some slight amendment, was sent to Sir Percy Cox the same day. It said that the guiding principle of future relations must be the permanent maintenance of British influence in a country bordering on India and not any temporary expedient to meet a sudden and passing emergency. H.M. Government, anxious to see a friendly and competent Government in Persia, regarded Vossuk as a suitable Minister. But it was no longer as imperative as it had been to secure his services in that position, though they would decidedly regret his disappearance from office. In these circumstances H.M. Government were not convinced that they were justified in accepting the proposed agreement regarding the South Persia Rifles, which might not be in the best interests either of Persia or of Great Britain. There were obvious objections to a gendarmerie paid by us being officered by another nation, especially as our experience of foreigners in Persia had not been reassuring. H.M. Government were, therefore, reluctant to decide on the employment of foreign officers at a moment when a definite commitment on the point did not seem to be absolutely necessary.

On the other hand, in order to strengthen Vossuk's Cabinet or any Government actively friendly to us, H.M. Government were ready to make such other proposals for the permanent improvement of Perso-British relations as might safely be done.

To this end Sir Percy Cox was authorised to inform the Prime Minister that Great Britain reiterated categorically her determination to respect Persia's independence and undertook, as soon as a Russian Government existed which she could recognise, to press for the abrogation of the Anglo-Russian Convention, which in the meantime she regarded as being in suspense and which she had no intention of renewing.

The transfer to the Governor-General of Fars of the South Persia Rifles, though attractive, was rendered more difficult of acceptance by the report that Farman Farma might be dismissed. But if some guarantee could be given that Great Britain should be consulted before any future appointment to that office, H.M. Government would gladly consider the transfer of the force.

It would be impossible for the Allies to make in Persia's favour an exception to the principle that non-belligerents would not be represented at the Peace Conference, and the suggestion that Great Britain should represent Persia there seemed open to the misinterpretation that she was assuming the rôle of a protecting Power. H.M. Government desired to act at the Conference as a friend of Persia and would be ready in every possible way to safeguard her political and territorial independence. It the Persian Government desired to place before H.M. Government their views as to the way in which these objects might best be attained, these would be gladly received. In conclusion, Sir Percy Cox's observations on the above points were invited.

This telegram, repeated as usual to India, crossed one from the Viceroy despatched on the 26th* referring to Sir Percy Cox's telegram of the 14th October and to a report which Colonel Gough, then in India, had written without any knowledge of the recommendations of either Sir Percy Cox or the Government of India. In it Colonel Gough urged the abolition of the South Persia Rifles as untrustworthy, useless, expensive, dangerous and involving a permanent escort of British troops to control them. The Government of India trusted that the announcement of policy desired by Sir Percy Cox to strengthen the hands of the Persian Cabinet would be sanctioned forthwith.

Sir Percy Cox replied on the 29th October to the Foreign Office telegram. While he agreed with the Foreign Office estimate of Vossuk's material value, he found him a serious and capable man to work with and thought that he had a reasonable

---

*The Viceroy was away from Government headquarters, which explains the date discrepancy.

<small>British and Persian policy; October 1918.</small> hope of remaining some time in office and of making progress in our joint interests, once we had given him what he desired to strengthen his position. Sir Percy Cox also agreed that we could afford to defer the question of foreign officers and felt that he might be able to persuade the Cabinet to drop the proposal for the time being if he could convince them of our friendly intentions regarding the South Persia Rifles. But, in order to dispel public mistrust, there should be no hesitation in meeting their wishes regarding the Fars Brigade of the South Persia Rifles, whose very name was anathema among Persians. In fact, for them the crucial test of our friendly intentions was our attitude towards the force, for which, according to Sir Percy Cox, no one among our own officers had a good word to say. He, therefore, urged strongly that he should be authorised to agree to the announcement regarding its transfer to Farman Farman, subject to the safeguards mentioned in his telegram of the 1st October and to the desired formal assurances regarding the appointment of future Governors-General of Fars. He anticipated little difficulty in obtaining this, and he said that an excellent impression had been caused by the prompt and explicit British assurances regarding Persian Azerbaijan.

In the meantime, reliable information which had been obtained regarding German and Turkish intentions in the Caucasus showed that it would be necessary for the Allies to retain some form of control there after peace was declared. Germany, desiring to placate American sentiment, was apparently agreeing to evacuate the country, but was actually intriguing for a protest by the Georgian authorities against a total German withdrawal. Enver, foreseeing that the Turks would be forced to withdraw from Azerbaijan, was arranging for his father, Nuri, Halil,* many Turkish officers and a Turkish division to remain on there, after peace was declared, in the guise of subjects of the new State. Germany objected to this plan and wished to abide by the terms of the Brest-Litovsk treaty, but, in spite of reports to the contrary, she had no real power to prevent it, and the Committee of Union and Progress still dominated the situation at Constantinople.

<small>Situation in North-West Persia and Caspian; end of October 1918.</small> In Persian Azerbaijan by the end of October the advanced Turkish detachments which had pushed south-eastward from Tabriz were all retiring; Ardebil had been evacuated soon after the Turkish project of an advance on Enzeli had been abandoned; and a Turkish evacuation of Persia had, it was understood,

---

* Nuri and Halil were near relatives of Enver.

been ordered from Constantinople. Beyond, however, a few reconnaissances and some aeroplane attacks, General Thomson's troops had taken no steps to advance in pursuit. There was no particular advantage to be gained by doing so ; supply and maintenance would be difficult ; and a great part of the British force was ineffective owing to the influenza epidemic. On the Caspian, Commodore Norris had made good progress. He had established fitting-out and repairing naval bases at Enzeli and Krasnovodsk and had practically completed the arming and manning of five small merchant vessels. He himself had been incapacitated by an accident, but Captain B. G. Washington, R.N., who succeeded him, reported that by the beginning of November he would be in a position to secure complete control of the sea. On the 29th October the Admiralty sent him telegraphic instructions that our object was to retain such control of the Caspian as would enable us to prevent any communication by water between its shores by forces hostile to us and to help any forces friendly to us.

The hopes that had been entertained at Baghdad that the Urmia Brigade, now called the Assyrian contingent, would be able to fight its way back to Urmia via Bijar had turned out to be impracticable, and the force had been transferred to be trained and equipped in Mesopotamia with a view to regaining Urmia via Kifri and Kirkuk.

On Thursday, the 31st October, Sir Percy Cox telegraphed in continuation of his report of the 29th to the Foreign Office that the Persian Cabinet had decided to form a representative Committee, including various groups of political opinion and not confined to members of the Government, to consider what Persia should seek from the Peace Conference. The next Sunday had been fixed for the Committee's first meeting and Vossuk asked urgently that he should, if possible, be placed in a position when opening the proceedings to clear the ground by making the contemplated announcement. Sir Percy Cox recommended strongly that this request should be acceded to and asked that he might have the Foreign Office reply regarding the South Persia Rifles by Saturday morning.

British and Persian policy ; October-November 1918.

The Government of India also telegraphed to the India Office on this question on the 1st November. They regarded it as better to effect the permanent maintenance of British influence by regaining the confidence and friendliness of the Persian people than by measures Persians would construe as interference with their national independence. Existing circumstances offered a golden opportunity for a liberal policy and for removing causes of irritation; and the best practical proof of our sincerity, said the Government of India, would be the immediate announcement of our intention to give up the South Persia Rifles, whose existence rankled deeply. Besides proving useless, untrustworthy and expensive, this force had involved us in the most undesirable commitments, and its continuance on existing lines, in the face of Persian opinion, would be regarded as a proof of the insincerity of our protestations.

While the question of neutral officers might, they considered, well stand over for subsequent discussion, the Government of India urged an immediate declaration of our willingness to hand over the South Persia Rifles in Fars to the Persian Government when the Bushire–Shiraz road was opened. The Governor-General might retain or disband part as he thought fit, and the Indian troops would be withdrawn. We should also agree to give him arms and a subsidy for the maintenance of a force; and this, Colonel Gough considered, would enable him to safeguard our interests and maintain reasonable order. If we could regain the confidence of the Persian Government and people and could convince them of our desire to co-operate rather than to dominate, it seemed unnecessary to embarrass the Persian Government by stipulations regarding the selection of future Governors, as there should be no difficulty in securing satisfactory nominees. Moreover, a Governor subsidised by us would be inclined to serve our interests, while the Persian Government would be averse from the breakdown of an arrangement so convenient to themselves and so considerate of their aspirations and withal so economical for ourselves.

The Foreign Office had, however, already on the 31st October authorised Sir Percy Cox to proceed with the assurances proposed, subject to the safeguards suggested in his telegram of the 1st and to additional reservation regarding the Governor-General of Fars.

Armistice with Turkey; 31st October 1918. On the 31st also the armistice with Turkey had come into force. Under its terms the Allies obtained free access to the Black Sea. Turkish troops were to withdraw immediately from North-West Persia and from part of Trans-Caucasia. The remaining troops in Trans-Caucasia were to be withdrawn if required by the Allies after they had studied the situation. The portions of the Trans-Caucasian railways under Turkish control were to be placed at the free and complete disposal of the Allies, who would also occupy Batum; and the Turks were to raise no objection to an Allied occupation of Baku.

The War Office at once informed General Marshall that importance was attached to an early occupation of Baku and they asked if he could arrange for it to be carried out from Enzeli.   *Preparations to occupy Baku.*

Our previous information and suspicions regarding Turkish intentions were further confirmed by the announcement, by Nuri at Baku on the 1st November, that all ranks of the Turkish forces in Azerbaijan would be regarded in future as in the service of that republic and not of Turkey; and he himself assumed the title of Commander-in-Chief of the Azerbaijan army. Under this pretext of serving a separate State the Turkish forces continued their operations against the Russians and Armenians at Petrovsk, which Bicharakoff consequently prepared to evacuate. On the 3rd November General Marshall informed the War Office that four armed ships were leaving Enzeli that day for Petrovsk to explain our intentions to Bicharakoff, to come to an arrangement with him regarding control of the Caspian and to invite him to come to Baku with his Cossacks; as his arrival there with us would, it was considered, help to dispel any distrust which the local inhabitants might feel regarding our intentions. In the meantime, General Marshall would concentrate troops of the 39th Infantry Brigade at Enzeli in anticipation of the move to Baku.

The Germans were reported to have a small mission at Baku and some seven battalions with a few batteries in Georgia, where they desired, for economic reasons, to remain as long as possible. But, as their communications were endangered by recent events, it was obvious that they would soon have to retire.

On learning the terms of the Armistice, the Persian Government requested Sir Percy Cox to express to H.M. Government their high appreciation of Great Britain's friendly action in making the evacuation of Azerbaijan one of the conditions of peace. This he did on the 6th November.   *British and Persian policy; 1st-11th November 1918.*

Three days previously he had reported to the Foreign Office that Persia's claim to be directly represented at the Peace Conference would be the first question to be mooted. She based this claim, (i) on the fact that her soil had been used as a field of warlike operations by four of the belligerents, a factor which was not present in the case of any other neutral, and (ii) on the point that the damage which Persia had suffered from the presence of foreign troops, and especially from the depredations by Russians and Turks, had been very severe and probably heavier than that which any other neutral had suffered. Sir Percy suggested that it might be expedient for us to act as her adviser if not as her representative. It was probable, he said, that Persian politicians had very exaggerated ideas of what Persia could reasonably ask for or hope to obtain; and he asked if it would not be better for us, if it was in any way possible, to support their claim to be represented. In that case any extravagant demands would be rejected by the Peace Conference. On the other hand, if we said that we were unable to support their claim to a special dispensation and refused also to be associated with any extravagant pretensions, we should incur permanent resentment on both accounts.

On the 7th November the Foreign Office replied that H.M. Government could not, by themselves, decide the question of the representation of neutrals at a peace congress, which was a matter for the whole body of the Allies. But, as far as H.M. Government were concerned, a duly authorised Persian representative would be welcomed if and when questions directly affecting Persian rights should come up.

Situation at Baku; 1st–11th November 1918. On the 6th November, General Marshall had reported that the Turkish commander at Baku, in reply to a communication sending him the terms of the Armistice, had notified his receipt of orders to move all Turkish troops out of the Caucasus within six weeks. But he had no special instructions, he said, regarding a British occupation of Baku, concerning which point he intimated that the British should address the Azerbaijan Government. General Marshall proposed to make it clear in reply that the Allies did not recognise the Azerbaijan Government and that the Turkish commander would be held personally responsible for the evacuation of every Turkish soldier. He had already been warned, said General Marshall, that he would be held responsible if the Turks continued their offensive against Bicharakoff. As his reference to the Azerbaijan Government was considered a typical Turkish attempt to confuse the issue, General Marshall recommended that the Turkish Government should be requested to send him clear instructions.

On the 7th November the War Office issued orders to General Marshall to occupy Baku as soon as possible and on the 8th the Admiralty instructed the Naval Commander-in-Chief in the Mediterranean* to insist that the Turkish Government should issue instructions for all Turkish elements, including those despatched for service in any capacity with the so-called Islam Army, to withdraw from the Caucasus behind the pre-war frontier.

---

* Admiral the Hon. S. A. Gough-Calthorpe conducted the armistice and subsequent negotiations.

On the 9th November General Marshall reported that, in addition to officers sent there previously, he was sending to Baku a senior staff officer accompanied by the former vice-consul and Colonel Chardigny of the French Mission, to inform the Turkish commander and Nuri that, unless the terms of the armistice were immediately complied with, they and those acting with them would be treated as outlaws.

The Turks were still attacking the Russian–Armenian force at Petrovsk under Bicharakoff, who had already evacuated 3,000 refugees to Enzeli; and on the 10th November General Marshall reported that Bicharakoff was expected to reach Enzeli that day with 500 Cossacks, 8,000 armed Armenians, 3,000 refugees and the Caspian fleet. Bicharakoff had intimated that he no longer opposed British control of the Caspian.

On the same day General Marshall reported the receipt of a telegram from Nuri, sent on the 8th, saying that the movement of Turkish troops to Batum from Azerbaijan had commenced and that he had sent a private message to the commander of the North Caucasus Force, who was not under his orders, advising a cessation of hostilities against Petrovsk and a withdrawal of troops. He also said that the Turkish evacuation was being hampered by transportation difficulties and that the British must refer the question of an occupation of Baku to the Azerbaijan Government, as Nuri had no authority in the matter. General Marshall then went on to say that the Azerbaijan Government, with the assistance of Turkish troops, controlled Baku, where order existed and business had been resumed. The leaders of this Government, while considering a Russian restoration by the Allies desirable, were doubtful of their success and, in the meanwhile, wished to be recognised as a State with an autonomous government. Turkish soldiers were being transferred to their service and they aimed at raising a force of 25,000 men. General Thomson had been instructed, continued General Marshall, that he might receive a Tartar deputation, but that he was not to give them any promise regarding recognition or assistance and was not to hold out any likelihood that the transfer of Turkish troops would be permitted. General Marshall was also sending officers that day from Enzeli to Baku with a demand that the Turkish commander should hand over the town to our troops at 10 a.m. on the 17th November, when there would be 1,300 British infantry available to land there. These officers would also investigate the situation at Baku and the likelihood of armed resistance;

and would report the feasibility of forming a satisfactory local Government, composed of Tartar, Armenian and Russian representatives, after British troops had landed.

On the 11th November came the Armistice with Germany.

Trans-Caspia; October 1918. At the beginning of October the general war situation made it clear that no German or Turkish military movements into Trans-Caspia were at all probable, though the hostile activities of enemy agents would still have to be guarded against.

The Trans-Caspian force at Kaahka consisted of, approximately, the following numbers: 50 Russian cavalry and 1,000 Russian infantry, mostly Armenians and, except for about 100 Russian ex-officers and soldiers, of very poor quality; seven field guns (three of obsolete pattern) fairly efficiently manned; 300 Turkoman cavalry and 150 Turkoman infantry, undisciplined and of little fighting value; and two small armoured trains, inferior in gun power to those of the Bolshevik force. General Malleson's efforts to assist in the defence of Trans-Caspia by organising, arming, equipping and paying a Russian unit, 1,000 strong, had met with no success owing to the impossibility of obtaining reliable recruits. The Trans-Caspian Government had also failed to avail themselves of his offer of machine guns to be manned by Russians trained by British instructors at Meshed.

The British detachment at Kaahka was composed of about 180 sabres, 28th Light Cavalry, two guns of the 44th Field Battery, 120 rifles 1/4th Hampshire Regiment and 330 rifles 1/19th Punjabis.

The Bolsheviks' force was at Dushak, some twenty-five miles to the east. But they usually had an armoured train and one or two other trains at Arman Sagad, about half-way between Dushak and Kaahka.

The Trans-Caspian Government were anxious to take advantage of the recent Bolskevik loss of *moral* to advance and regain the Tejend and Merv oases. This would not only secure them against famine, but would prevent the gradual disintegration of their armed force which would certainly ensue in the event of prolonged inaction. General Malleson, however, had insisted that, before an advance was attempted, certain changes in the staff and organisation of the Trans-Caspian force must be carried out to the satisfaction of British officers on the spot. This had been done; and when a new Chief of

Staff to the Trans-Caspian commander (Oraz Sirdar—a Turkoman) took up his duties on the 1st October, preparations were begun for an advance.

On the 7th October General Malleson asked that he might be given some indication of H.M. Government's intentions in regard to future operations in Turkestan. The Trans-Caspian Government, for the most part a collection of insignificant adventurers, maintained, by a liberal distribution of blackmail, a precarious and partial control over the armed mob for the time being. There was a distinct danger of a pan-Islamic Turkoman rising to seize power and to kill or eject all Russians, such as had already occurred in areas adjoining the Persian frontier; and the Bolsheviks would be at liberty—when winter conditions prevented extensive operations on their Orenburg and Semirechia fronts—to concentrate against Askabad, where our own detachment was the only reliable force. In fact, Turkestan would, in General Malleson's opinion, continue in a state of anarchy unless a compact British force were there.

In repeating this telegram to the War Office the Commander-in-Chief in India said that he proposed to instruct General Malleson to aim at keeping the railway from Krasnovodsk to Kaahka in the hands of friendly elements. General Malleson, he continued, had urged the necessity for driving the Bolsheviks beyond Tejend and Merv, so as to gain access to the corn districts. But General Monro considered that any advance should be limited to an occupation of the Merv oasis and that even this should not be undertaken until there were sufficient reliable troops in Trans-Caspia and the political situation had been fully reviewed. He was considering the possibility of sending another Indian cavalry regiment to join General Malleson and this, when the troops from Force D* had all arrived, would bring the total at Krasnovodsk and on the Trans-Caspian railway up to six squadrons of Indian cavalry, a field battery, a battalion of British infantry, a section of a machine gun company, 500 rifles Indian infantry and 50 Persian levies. It might be possible, said General Monro, to send also another Indian infantry battalion.

The Trans-Caspian force had already completed its plan for an advance to Dushak. Accompanied by the British detachment under the command of Lieutenant-Colonel Knollys (less the company 1/4th Hampshire, which remained at Kaahka) the force advanced during the night 9th/10th October to a previously

---

* i.e., the Expeditionary Force under General Marshall in Mesopotamia.

Trans-Caspia; October 1918. reconnoitred position within artillery range of Arman Sagad. The intention was to attack at dawn any enemy trains there or, if they were not present, to destroy the armoured train which generally came up daily. But Arman Sagad proved to be empty and no hostile armoured train appeared.

Having reported the enemy's absence, the two squadrons 28th Light Cavalry, under Major J. A. C. Kreyer, moved forward during the 10th along a previously reconnoitred concealed route south of the railway to a small village six miles south of Dushak; and here they waited so as to co-operate in an attack which the main force, after a further advance during the night 10th/11th, was to make on Dushak, from the north of the railway, at dawn on the 11th. The main force, apparently undetected by the enemy, halted during the daylight hours of the 10th in a ruined village three miles north of Arman Sagad; the railway between Kaahka and Arman Sagad was repaired; and an armoured train moved up. But, when the time came to start the night advance, it had to be abandoned, as the Trans-Caspian troops declined to move on the ground that they had no food. The 28th Light Cavalry were consequently recalled and it was finally decided to postpone the attack on Dushak till dawn on the 14th October.

On the 9th October, General Malleson telegraphed saying that the news of the Allied successes had brought about an immediate and striking improvement and that British prestige, which had been rather shaken by the fall of Baku, now stood very high.

On the 11th October General Malleson sent a long telegram, summarising a report on the situation at Tashkend which a Russian ex-officer and agent of the Turkestan Union had just given him on return from a visit to that place. German influence there was very strong, he said, and was working to prevent the British obtaining a footing in Turkestan. The Bolsheviks, disheartened at their failure to gain Askabad, hoped to open up the Orenburg line, when the Germans promised two divisions from Russia to settle affairs. But the hatred towards the Bolsheviks was general and intense, their power was tottering, and if the Trans-Caspian force could drive them back to the Oxus all Bokhara would rise against them. The Turkestan Union had a strong party in Tashkend, though their greatest asset was 4,000 good men in Trans-Caspia, who possesesd arms and were ready to rise, when, if they gained any preliminary success, crowds would join them. General Malleson's informant was convinced that a successful rising could be brought about by an expenditure of two million roubles, and General Malleson himself thought that the chances might warrant risking this sum.

On the same day as this telegram was received at Simla another telegram arrived from the Kashgar Mission giving a *resumé* of the situation in Turkestan, derived from reports from Sir George Macartney, Colonel Bailey and Major Blacker, who had all reached Tashkend from Kashgar in August. This Mission had left Kashgar before our troops had intervened in Trans-Caspia and it had been impossible to stop it. The Turkestan Soviet had naturally regarded it with great suspicion, but Sir George Macartney had been able to convince the Bolshevik leaders that it had come from the British and Indian Governments and was entitled to some consideration. Sir George Macartney and Major Blacker had managed, not without difficulty, to leave Tashkend again on the 14th September and return to Kashgar. But Colonel Bailey had remained, as his position seemed fairly secure.* Their report confirmed the general and intense hatred towards the Bolsheviks and also the possibility of their being turned out of power by the Left Social Revolutionary party, who without being pro-British favoured the continuance of the war against Germany; and it also said that there was a constant and universal cry for British intervention and British occupation. The native population, desiring tranquillity and security, would welcome any party or foreign intervention affording this. Nine thousand of the thirty thousand or so Austrian and German prisoners of war had been forced to join the Red Army, in which they exceeded the number of real Russians. They could control the whole country if they could obtain arms and ammunition and they might become masters any day, in which case Germany could have Turkestan. They had instructions, it was said, from their own Governments not to leave Turkestan, as they might be required to play an important part later. But actually most of them wished only to be repatriated and had no desire to fight against the Allies or to remain in Turkestan.

The War Office were asked by the Commander-in-Chief in India if they considered that the expenditure of the two million roubles was justified by the general Russian situation. But they replied that, as their experience during the past year had shown that financial assistance to anti-Bolshevik Russian

---

* There was subsequently considerable anxiety about him, as he was obviously in danger. But he eventually succeeded in escaping safely.

elements was useless without material assistance and direction by British personnel, they could not recommend this expenditure.

<small>Action of Dushak; 14th October 1918.</small> The Trans-Caspian and British force at Arman Sagad started again on the 13th October to attack Dushak. During the day the 28th Light Cavalry squadrons moved once more to the village six miles south of Dushak, and during the following night the remainder of the force on the north of the railway line marched eastward. But, as surprise was no longer probable, a reserve of Russians moved on the right rear of the main force to guard against a counter-attack.

The march met with considerable delays and dawn* on the 14th found the main body some distance to the north of Dushak. The intervening ground was flat and almost devoid of cover. But the enemy, though not surprised, appears to have made his dispositions very hurriedly. His guns were on the higher ground immediately east of Dushak station, to the west of which he had a line, composed mainly of machine guns—at least thirty being in action—posted along a fringe of trees, and to the north he had thrown out a line of skirmishers.

The infantry, deploying at once, advanced to the attack, Russians and Armenians on the right, the three Punjabi companies under Captain G. E. F. Shute in the centre and the Turkomans on the left. The British and Russian guns, taking up positions in the open, started to fire just before 7 a.m.; and about the same time Major Kreyer's cavalry, who on the previous evening had occupied a position a mile to the south of Dushak, started a dismounted attack against the enemy to the west of the station. But, after a while, perceiving an opportunity, Major Kreyer broke off the action and, mounting his men, charged a body of the enemy with great effect, killing or wounding about 25 of them with the lance and dispersing the remainder into the scrub and broken ground south of the station. He then proceeded, after clearing this area, to take up a position to the east of the station so as to meet a possible attack from that direction.

When the infantry attack arrived within about one thousand yards of the Bolsheviks' position, it was met by a heavy gun and machine gun fire, and all the Russians and Armenians—except the small body of ex-regulars—and the Turkomans ceased to advance. The Punjabis pushed on with speed and determination, but incurred heavy casualties. The British guns, firing with great accuracy, did much damage to the enemy

---

* Sunrise was about 6.15 a.m.

ACTION OF DUSHAK

trains and to the station, which, just as the Punjabis reached it at about 10 a.m., was totally wrecked by an explosion of some trucks full of munitions. The Bolshevik losses had evidently been considerable and the Russian, Armenian and Turkoman infantry now came on and indulged in an orgy of massacre and plunder, which the Punjabis, with their British officers all casualties, were quite unable to stop or restrain. Hearing of the Punjabi losses, Major Kreyer at once sent one of his own British officers to take command of them and to occupy a position to the west of the station.

The enemy had lost the station, but some of his trains under cover of an armoured train had moved to the west of it and at about 11.30 a.m. the occupants of these trains started a counter attack, at the same time as enemy reinforcements from the Tejend direction commenced an attack from the east. By this time all the Trans-Caspian soldiery, except about 80 of the ex-regulars (who had remained with the Punjabis) and the men with the field guns, had gone off with their plunder. So that the enemy attacks had to be met by about 150 Punjabis, 80 Russian ex-regulars and four Russian guns to the west of the station, two British guns to the north of the station and 120 dismounted Indian cavalry to the east. A retirement became necessary and withdrawal in a north-westerly direction was ordered. This was carried out coolly and in excellent order, being well covered by the 28th Light Cavalry and the British and Russian guns. The enemy did not press his attack and all the British wounded were evacuated safely, Arman Sagad being reached by dusk. Here a halt was made for the night, when most of the Trans-Caspian soldiery again disappeared. Next day the remainder of the force fell back to Kaahka.

The British casualties had been considerable. Those in the 28th Light Cavalry amounted to 6 killed and 12 wounded, while the 19th Punjabis with 47 killed and 139 wounded had lost about 50 per cent. of their strength. The Trans-Caspian casualties only totalled about 30, practically all among the small body of ex-regulars. The enemy's casualties are unknown, but prisoners' and subsequent reports estimated that at least 1,000 of them had been killed or wounded.

As the Trans-Caspian Chief of Staff said in his official report, only the disgraceful action of their own troops had prevented them from obtaining a decisive victory, and only the heroic conduct of the Indian troops and of a few of their own men had saved them from complete disaster. General Malleson also reported that Russian circles were filled with the greatest admiration for the part played by the British and Indian troops, whom they regarded as being equal to ten times their own number of any of the other combatants.

<small>Trans-Caspia;
October 1918.</small>
As the first reports that reached General Malleson at Meshed of the fighting at Dushak were of rather an alarming character, he suggested on the 15th October to Army Headquarters in India that if it were proposed to send him any additional troops it would be as well to despatch them at an early date. He had no troops at Meshed available either to reinforce Trans-Caspia or to replace casualties there. On the 16th he gave the total estimated casualties as 178 and asked urgently for their replacement. He also suggested that a cavalry regiment should be sent from India forthwith as a first reinforcement. In consequence of these telegrams, orders were sent from Simla to General Wapshare at Quetta on the 17th October to despatch to Meshed as early as possible the headquarters and two remaining squadrons of the 41st Cavalry—a newly raised unit, in which the squadrons 15th and 37th Lancers already sent to East Persia had been embodied ; and at the same time arrangements were made to mobilise the 42nd Cavalry as a further reinforcement.

These orders crossed a telegram from General Malleson submitting further considerations affecting the question of future British intentions in Turkestan. The whole country was in a state of anarchy and he did not think that an armistice in Europe would have any effect on it. The Trans-Caspian Government was incompetent and powerless, and a Turkoman bid for power was possible. This would mean a pan-Islamic rising and continued anarchy, possibly spreading to Khurasan and Herat. Our very small force could hardly stop a Bolshevik advance in strength into Trans-Caspia, which we were pledged to defend against all enemies, an expression interpreted everywhere in Trans-Caspia as including the Bolsheviks. British troops were urgently required, as the Russians could not be depended upon. In conclusion, General Malleson expressed the opinion that the whole of Trans-Caspia could be quickly recovered by a force of three cavalry regiments, three batteries, an infantry brigade and a few armoured cars and aeroplanes.

On the 18th October the Government of India received a telegram sent the previous day by the India Office regarding the difficulty of obtaining currency in Persia, in which they requested that General Malleson should be warned not to commit H.M. Government to any financial assistance to the Trans-Caspian Government beyond what had already been promised. The change in the general military situation and the confused position in Central Asia raised doubts, continued the India Office, as to the value of the Trans-Caspian Government and the desirability of committing ourselves too closely to their support or maintenance. In conclusion, the Government of India were requested to send their appreciation of the situation as affected by recent events and also to state the policy they desired to pursue.

On the same day a telegram of the 17th October from General Malleson was received at Simla saying that the news from Trans-Caspia was better. The Bolsheviks, it appeared, in order to counter-attack at Dushak, had removed there the greater part of the troops from Tejend, which had, thereupon, been promptly attacked by Turkoman bands friendly to us, who had slaughtered the garrison and wrecked the station. This had so alarmed the Bolsheviks that they had hurriedly evacuated Dushak and retired eastward to Tejend, or even beyond, destroying the railway behind them.

Next day (19th October) General Malleson was informed by the Chief of the General Staff in India that, in view of the impending addition to his force, Brigadier-General G. A. H. Beatty had been ordered to Meshed, accompanied by a brigade headquarters, to take executive command of the troops under General Malleson's orders.

The Trans-Caspian force, less the British detachment which remained for a few days at Kaahka to recover and refit, advanced along the railway behind the retiring Bolsheviks without, however, attempting to accelerate their retreat; and, on the 20th October, occupied Tejend without opposition. Here they were rejoined by the British detachment.

On the 23rd October the Government of India telegraphed their views on the situation to the India Office. Though the menace of a Turco-German thrust towards Afghanistan—which had resulted in our assisting the Trans-Caspian Government and fighting the Bolsheviks—had been materially reduced, they were of opinion that the following considerations required the continued maintenance of General Malleson's Mission :—the necessity for a close watch on political movements in Trans-Caspia and Turkestan, more especially in view of their possible effect on Afghanistan and the frontier tribes; the importance to us of a friendly Government to which we could lend support; and the desirability, having regard to British policy on the Caspian, of maintaining communication between Meshed and Krasnovodsk. At the moment the Trans-Caspian

Trans-Caspia; October 1918. Government were the only body with whom we could deal, but, unless H.M. Government required their co-operation with other Allied movements against the Bolsheviks, General Malleson's support should be limited to what was required by the considerations outlined above. In any case, the difficulties of communication with Meshed and the shortage of transport made it impossible to despatch any considerable force there from India. The Government of India considered that for the time being we should continue to support the Trans-Caspian Government, subject to their undertaking to reorganise and control their forces satisfactorily, to their acceptance of the military measures considered necessary by our military representatives, to their ceasing to treat barbarously their military-political prisoners and to their according equitable and proper treatment to the Turkomans. We should have to give the Trans-Caspian Government some financial assistance and also military support to the extent possible, so as to prevent a Bolshevik advance west of Kaahka, to keep the Turkomans in order and to maintain communication between Meshed and Krasnovodsk. Without express orders from H.M. Government, however, the Government of India proposed to make it clear that our troops were not on any account to engage in enterprises east of Kaahka.

The Bolshevik force, retiring eastward of Tejend, was reported a few days later to have been reinforced and to have the intention of taking the offensive from a point to the westward of Merv, where it had stayed its retrograde movement. But a threat to its communications by a party of Indian cavalry and Turkomans sent to move wide of its flanks caused it to retreat hurriedly, abandoning Merv and evacuating Kushk; and on the 1st November the Trans-Caspian force occupied Merv.

Trans-Caspia; November 1918. This rapid Bolshevik retirement appears to have been rather unexpected by General Malleson, though he had reported to India on the 31st October that, if the Allied leaders in Siberia could prevent reinforcements reaching the Bolsheviks via Orenburg, their early evacuation of the Merv–Kushk line was quite likely and that their next line on the Oxus could be taken by us in the spring if they had not collapsed by then. On the 1st November he sent a further telegram announcing the occupation of Merv. But neither this nor the telegram of the 31st October reached India till the 4th November, though a clear-line message which he sent on the 2nd had arrived the same day. In this he said that, if the Orenburg door was kept closed, the small British force which had been arranged would suffice to clear up Turkestan, a result which would very greatly enhance British prestige in Central Asia.

On the 3rd November the Government of India received a telegram sent on the 31st October by the India Office saying that the War Cabinet were considering the general question of their attitude towards Bolshevism and that, pending their decision, no definite line of policy could be laid down. In the meantime, they continued, there was no objection in principle to supporting anti-Bolshevik movements, but great caution should be exercised and each case must be judged on its merits.

It was not quite certain from General Malleson's telegram whether British troops had accompanied the Trans-Caspian force to Merv. But the authorities in India regarded the advance which General Malleson seemed to contemplate with disfavour, as it appeared to them to be an unnecessary risk, having regard to the unreliability of the Trans-Caspian force. It would, moreover, be going beyond the extent to which they had recommended, in their telegram of the 23rd October to the India Office, that General Malleson's support to the Trans-Caspian Government should be limited. Consequently, on the 4th November instructions were sent to General Malleson that our troops were not to be employed eastward of Tejend, pending the receipt of clear indications of H.M. Government's policy, and that in no circumstances were British troops to proceed towards Kushk, for fear of arousing Afghan susceptibilities.

General Malleson at once asked that these instructions—other than those referring to Kushk—should be reconsidered. In the first place the bitterly cold weather made it essential to house the troops and, as both Tejend and Dushak were in ruins, this could only be done in Merv. Secondly, there were good grounds for believing that we had a unique opportunity of securing the Charjui bridge, which was of great strategical importance, either for offensive or defensive operations. The Trans-Caspian Government without our active support were not only unlikely to make the best use of such an opportunity, but would regard our withdrawal as a preliminary to our abandoning them. Moreover, the presence of our troops deterred Turkomans and Russians from the outrages and reprisals on one another which were so harmful.

In reply, General Malleson was informed on the 6th November that the Government of India had no orders from H.M. Government which would justify them in authorising him to support the Trans-Caspian Government in hostilities against the

Trans-Caspia; November 1918.

Bolsheviks to the extent he suggested and that they were not prepared to approve the occupation of the Charjui bridge or the retention of Merv by British or Indian troops. His difficulties with the Trans-Caspian Government were realised, but they should be made to understand that they must be prepared to hold their own against the Bolsheviks by their own unaided efforts and that he had not been authorised to give them more assistance than that which he had originally been told to afford them. His instructions not to advance eastward of Tejend must, therefore, hold good and it was left to his discretion to distribute and house his troops as he thought fit.

Other telegrams from General Malleson received at this period showed that anti-Bolshevik risings seemed to be gaining ground in Turkestan, that the Bolshevik force had retired to Ravnina, 65 miles east of Merv, and that the Central Bolshevik Government were organising a great effort to enlist all the Austro-Hungarian prisoners of war to fight for them. With regard to the last named report General Malleson suggested that we should forestall the Bolsheviks by intimating to the prisoners of war in Turkestan that we were prepared to repatriate them as soon as the Baku–Batum route was open, provided they laid down their arms and came over to us. This would greatly simplify our task in Turkestan, but to ensure success would have to be done at once. In reply, he was told that the question had been referred to London, but that in the meantime he could make all his arrangements for the necessary propaganda, though he would have to be cautious, as considerable difficulties would be involved in accommodating, feeding and transporting large numbers.

On the 6th November the Government of India asked the India Office for an early indication of H.M. Government's policy in Trans-Caspia and also suggested that full weight should be given to the disturbing effect, on the war party in Afghanistan, of the presence of British troops at Merv and the rumours of their future possible advance, at a time when fanatical feeling over the Turkish armistice would be running high.

On the same day General Malleson sent a long telegram to India urging strongly that an early decision should be given regarding our policy in Central Asia. The allied operations against the Bolsheviks in North Russia, Siberia and Turkestan, following the British declaration to the Russian peoples, had, he said, been interpreted by everyone in Turkestan as pledging the Allies to suppress Bolshevism so as to allow of Russian self-determination. If this was not the Allied intention, it ought to be made clear at once. At the moment the Trans-Caspian Government could probably make terms, but if, relying on our support, they continued to fight and were subsequently abandoned by us, they would receive no mercy from the Bolsheviks. In Trans-Caspia, continued General Malleson, Bolshevism was latent and its adherents openly urged the folly of relying on our promises and the desirability before we abandoned them of making terms with the Tashkend Bolsheviks. Their greatest lever was the desperate financial situation, and if the Trans-Caspian Government failed to pay their way the Bolsheviks in their midst would call in the mob, fraternise with the Tashkend men and combine with them in wholesale murder and in creating anarchy, in which the Turkomans would seize the opportunity to kill both parties indiscriminately. There was great need of immediate financial assistance, and in this respect H.M. Government had already recognised some obligation. The Trans-Caspian Government had given us real help in time of need and in essentials had followed our advice ; so that, although we could now afford to dispense with their help, we were morally bound to support them. We might not intend to abandon them, but this impression was gaining ground owing to our delay in assisting them financially and in announcing our policy. In conclusion, General Malleson said that the situation was serious, requiring a firm and unequivocal declaration of policy, coupled with prompt and practical steps for financial assistance. We should thus enable the sane and sober elements among Russians and Turkomans to restore law, order, commerce and settled government ; while, if we failed, the existing Government would fall, with resultant anarchy and the disappearance of our reputation for good faith. A summary of this telegram was sent to the India Office by the Government of India on the 9th November.

On the 7th November General Malleson asked for more precise instructions than those sent him the previous day, as he pointed out that the aid both originally and subsequently given the Trans-Caspian Government had been solely against the Bolsheviks and he was now not sure to what extent this was to be continued. In reply, on the 8th, he was informed that the difficulties of his position were realised but that the assistance he could give to the Trans-Caspian Government had been now limited for the following reasons :—the changed situation and the removal of the Turco-German menace ; the lack of instructions from London ; the size of his available force ; the unreliable character of the Trans-Caspian troops ;

Trans-Caspia; November 1918.

and the political objections to action calculated to disturb Afghanistan and to embarrass the Amir. The telegram then went on to point out that the authority given him in the past to support the Trans-Caspian Government had been issued as the best means of closing the Trans-Caspian railway to enemy elements, i.e., one of the main objects of his Mission; and that, although the support he could give the Trans-Caspian Government in future was limited, it should suffice to free them, during their operations beyond Merv, from anxiety in regard to their base and communications.

On the 8th November General Wapshare at Quetta was told by the Chief of the General Staff in India that owing to the altered military situation it had been decided to stop the movement of the six squadrons of cavalry *en route* or under orders to Meshed and to maintain the force at and beyond that place at a strength of a field battery, a British infantry battalion and machine gun section, an Indian cavalry regiment and an Indian infantry battalion. He was also requested to consider the possibility of reducing the strength of the cavalry, infantry and levies in East Persia. Next day he was informed that, if circumstances permitted, it was intended eventually to withdraw from Trans-Caspia, leaving the Mission in Meshed with an escort of two squadrons of cavalry and an infantry company.

General Malleson on the 9th November again urged a reconsideration of the order to withdraw from Merv. The agreement which he had been authorised to make with the Trans-Caspian Government was, he said, regarded by them as one of mutual advantages and responsibilities entailing a combination for defence against the enemies of both parties. Consequently, if we cried off our bargain now that the fortunes of war had disposed of Turks and Germans while the Bolsheviks remained, we should be accused of the grossest ill-faith. He asked if it was not permissible for him to continue to act on the authorisation and policy of H.M. Government communicated to him at the beginning of August. As housing facilities elsewhere were inadequate, he continued, withdrawal from Merv entailed withdrawal to Askabad, which would be regarded as proof of our intention—already widely ascribed to us by our enemies—to seize Trans-Caspia. Before announcing our withdrawal it would be essential to evacuate our wounded from Askabad to save them from the mob, and, if H.M. Government desired to retain it, to complete the garrison of Krasnovodsk and stock it fully. The moment was particularly unfavourable for such an announcement. The Trans-Caspian Government money was coming to an end and the extremist opposition had gained great strength by our failure to give them financial assistance; all the Bolsheviks were exploiting the revolution in Austria-Hungary as a triumph for their ideas; the situation on the Orenburg front was inclining the waverers to embrace Bolshevism; and anything pointing to a withdrawal by us would bring about the fall of the Trans-Caspian Government. He considered the whole situation so serious that he suggested the suspension of further action till he had been himself to Trans-Caspia to examine the situation and see if it was possible to devise some means of giving effect to the orders he had received without precipitating a definite rupture.* He did not think that anything had happened to offend Afghan susceptibilities.

On the 12th November the Chief of the General Staff in India telegraphed to General Malleson that summaries of his telegrams urging reconsideration of the order sent him had been repeated to the India Office with a request for instructions as to the policy of H.M. Government. His presentation of the situation from the Trans-Caspian point of view was not accepted as quite correct, and the Government of India did not regard the support sanctioned by H.M. Government in August as applicable to the extensive operations undertaken. Should the Trans-Caspian Government cavil at General Malleson's action he could point this out to them, as well as the fact that only the presence of our troops had saved them from annihilation by the Bolsheviks. However, in the meantime, pending instructions from London, General Malleson might proceed himself to Askabad as he wished to do and need take no steps to withdraw our troops from Merv, though an advance beyond that place was not to be made.

General Dickson arrived at Juzzak, the railhead of the Nushki–Mirjawa railway, on the 4th October and took up the duties of Inspector-General of Communications in East Persia. He had an arduous task before him. The maintenance of the force already at and beyond Meshed and of the troops and services on the line of communication beyond railhead was sufficiently difficult. But he had in addition to make preparations for maintaining the much larger force which it might

East Persia; October-November 1918.

---

* Next day General Malleson made certain proposals as possibly likely to enable us to cancel our agreement with the Trans-Caspian Government. But, as the narrative will show, the need to consider them did not arise.

East Persia;
October-
November
1918.

become necessary in the spring of 1919 to send beyond Meshed and to locate on the lines of communication; and for these preparations there was little time available, having regard to the great distances and difficulties involved.

Road improvement or construction, calculation of the additional transport required with its distribution, and the administrative organisation of the line of communication were the three most urgent problems.

Extension of the railway beyond Mirjawa was in progress, and it was anticipated that a new railhead at Duzdab would be open for use by Christmas and that the line to Neh would be completed by May 1919. The length of road from the temporary railhead at Juzzak to Meshed was 670 miles. To work on it the only technical personnel in East Persia had hitherto consisted of the Seistan detachment of the 3rd Sappers and Miners and half No. 104 Labour Corps; and, though a great deal of road work had been done by the Indian infantry* under General Dale, the general condition of the existing tracks left much to be desired. They were unmetalled and their roughness was very hard on motor transport, while the scarcity of water hindered the use of large numbers of transport animals.

The following brief and necessarily incomplete summary gives some idea of the state of the different portions of the road at this period. The section from Juzzak to Hurmuk, approximately 100 miles in length, was fit, though not good, for motor transport. But, as it would no longer be required after the railway reached Duzdab, it was unnecessary to spend much labour on it. An entirely new road, however, 36 miles long, was required to link Duzdab with Hurmuk and General Dickson at once gave orders that the 107th Pioneers, then under orders from Quetta to East Persia, were to undertake this work on arrival.

From Hurmuk to Shusp, 150 miles, the track, which lay over the open plain skirting the east of the Palangan range, had been somewhat improved by the Sappers and Miners, had a hard surface and coincided for some distance with the route to Seistan, whence considerable supplies were drawn. But there was very little water along it. On the other hand, the alignment for the railway to Neh followed a route on the west of the Palangan range, on which there was more water and apparently no great engineering difficulties. There were other advantages to be gained by constructing the road along this alignment, the most important being that it would shorten

---

* In "East Persia" General Dickson pays a well-deserved tribute to the work done by the 19th Punjabis and 98th Infantry.

Birjand, from the north-east.

Dehani Sulaiman Pass (north-west of Kain).

road communication by utilisation of the railway as it advanced. But General Dickson, who had to come to an immediate decision, came to the conclusion that, considering the work already done and the important factor of time, it was best to continue to use the existing road. In his book, it may be noted, he implies that his subsequent experience showed that he would have done better to choose the alternative route.

From Shusp to Birjand, 102 miles, the road followed the old caravan track and a good deal of work had been done on it. It was passable by motor vans, but in one place there was a bad stretch of sand which could not be avoided and, though specially treated*, gave constant trouble.

In the 78 miles from Birjand to Kain the road had to cross three mountain ranges and, though the old track existed and a good deal of work had been done on it, much heavy work was necessary. In the meantime motor vans could only get along with difficulty, man-handling being necessary in many places.

From Kain to Meshed, a distance of 240 miles, the road was impassable for motor transport.† As far as Turbat-i-Haidari there were alternative routes, via Rui Khaf and Gunabad respectively, and though the former had advantages General Dickson decided on the latter as being two marches shorter. A stretch of desert in this section also gave continuous trouble owing to its drifting sand and creeping sand-hills. Between Turbat-i-Haidari and Meshed the three rocky and precipitous mountain ranges which had to be crossed made this stretch the most difficult of all to cope with; and, as the road here would have to carry a considerable amount of local Persian iron-tyred wheeled traffic, it would require metalling.

The metalled carriage road which the Russians had made from Meshed to Askabad was passable for motor transport as far as Kuchan, and beyond that place arrangements had been made to repair it in places so as to enable light motor traffic to get through.

The necessity for immediate road improvement was well exemplified by the large number of derelict Ford vans which General Dickson encountered along the road. Their breakdown had been caused by the attempt to meet the recent heavy and urgent demands from the force in Trans-Caspia for such things as hospital stores.

---

* Experiments with wire netting laid on the surface, as was done with success by the Egyptian Expeditionary Force in Sinai, were not satisfactory, as the netting broke and caused tyre troubles.

† General Malleson had taken a motor car over it, but only with difficulty and by man-handling.

East Persia; October–November 1918. Major W. P. Pakenham-Walsh, the senior R.E. officer in East Persia, was appointed Assistant Director of Works, and General Dickson was able to obtain local labour, supervised by British officers and personnel of the Seistan Levy Corps, for most of the work north of Shusp. But the desert stretch south of there to Hurmuk was uninhabited and No. 104 Labour Corps, the remaining half of which had just arrived from India, was allotted to this section. Attempts made to import labour from Seistan were not very successful, and when the Duzdab–Hurmuk road had been completed the 107th Pioneers were moved up to the desert section, where, owing to the bad and scanty water, the climatic extremes and the desert conditions, all the men employed had a very trying time.

Within a few days of his arrival, General Dickson was requested to telegraph his estimate of the transport he would require. The local situation in this respect was, he found, in a somewhat chaotic condition owing to the recent rapid development of events in Trans-Caspia. The different organised camel corps had got mixed up and were distributed all over the line; hired transport was working on two or three different systems; and a great proportion of the motor vans had broken down. Finding that Colonel M. Synge, his Assistant Director of Supply and Transport, was consequently experiencing great difficulty in arriving at a satisfactory estimate of what would be required, General Dickson hit on the idea of finding a simple formula, giving the producing capacity of the various forms of transport, which could be readily applied to the problem. In " East Persia "* he describes how, by taking the unit of transportation energy as the moving of one ton once a week over a distance of one mile, he obtained a figure giving the average weekly ton-mile capacity of each form of transport; and, by expressing consumption in a similar manner, tables were obtained from which it was possible to calculate transport requirements with a minimum of trouble.

On the 14th October, after a necessarily rapid examination of the existing situation and of local resources, General Dickson telegraphed his preliminary estimate of his additional transport requirements. Without allowing for any additional animals which he might be able to procure locally—of which he could not yet give an estimate—he considered that he would require 11,680 Government camels *or* 14,600 hired camels *or* 1,450 Ford

---

* Readers interested in the administrative problems of this desert line of communications will find in this book much of interest which cannot be included here for lack of space.

vans. This was calculated to enable him to provide for the requirements of the existing force and, by the 1st April, 1919, for the requirements of the force increased to a cavalry brigade, an artillery brigade and a division at Meshed and a cavalry and an infantry brigade on the line of communication, including in all cases a month's reserve.

In organising his line General Dickson was influenced by the fact that Army Headquarters in India had included four administrative commandants in his staff. He accordingly divided it into the following four sections, which corresponded to General Dale's division for defence purposes :—

South section	Juzzak–Hurmuk	100 miles
South-central section ..	Hurmuk–Shusp	150 ,,
North-central section ..	Shusp–Kain	180 ,,
North section	Kain–Meshed	240 ,,

From the first two and the last of the above sections branches ran out to Khwash, Dehani Baghi and Seistan, and Rui Khaf respectively.

The Line of Communication Headquarters, both for defence and administration, were established at Birjand.

In the instructions issued to General Dickson it had been laid down that the line of communication should end at Meshed. But General Malleson subsequently requested that it should continue to Askabad, when General Dickson obtained sanction to increase the number of sections to seven, as follows (See Map 12) :—

1st section	Meshed to Askabad	170 miles		
2nd ,,	Turbat-i-Haidari to Meshed	90 ,,		
3rd ,,	Kain to Turbat-i-Haidari	160 ,,		In each case the headquarters of the section was at the southern end.
4th ,,	Birjand to Kain	67 ,,		
5th ,,	Shusp to Birjand	102 ,,		
6th ,,	Hurmuk to Shusp	150 ,,		
7th ,,	Juzzak to Hurmuk	100* ,,		

Having regard to the length of the line and to other special conditions, General Dickson considered it essential to institute a much greater measure of decentralisation and decontrol than is normally the case. He accordingly deputed to his administrative commandants complete control of all the administrative services in their respective sections, an arrangement which appears to have had most satisfactory results. The influenza

---

* When railhead reached Duzdab, from there to Hurmuk—36 miles.

epidemic spread to East Persia and there also caused a very high rate of sickness during the autumn months, a curious feature about it being the comparative immunity enjoyed by the cavalry as compared with the infantry.

Operations from Bushire; October 1918. (See Map 11.)
In view of the instructions he had received, General Douglas considered that, having occupied Chaghadak and Ali Changi, it would be advisable to give the hostile chiefs an opportunity of accepting terms before he made a further advance. Ghazanfar, the whole of whose men had fled straight back to Borazjan, was reported to have retreated into the hills; Shaikh Husain was said to have left Chah Kutah and Zair Khidar wrote in excusing himself for having fought and began to negotiate.

As many of the local inhabitants were coming in to submit, it seemed unlikely that Zair Khidar would, in any case, be able to raise any serious following. But on the nights of the 5th/6th and 6th/7th October his men fired heavily into our camp at Ali Changi, though only wounding two men, and on the 7th they attacked a company of the 2/113th Infantry, reconnoitring in broken ground, and inflicted nine casualties on them. It appears that Zair Khidar's personal inclination to accept our terms was overcome by the persuasion of some of his followers, who dreaded the treatment they would receive at the hands of his successor. On the 9th October General Douglas reported that the negotiations with Zair Khidar had failed, that the latter was entrenching himself in the hills to the south-east of Ali Changi and that Shaikh Husain and Ghazanfar had reappeared at Chah Kutah and Borazjan respectively, with small followings.

In the meantime the 63rd Company Sappers and Miners, the remaining two sections No. 3 Machine Gun Company and the 1/117th Mahrattas had arrived at Bushire from India, and the last named regiment with three sections of the Machine Gun Company and two sections of the 35th Mountain Battery were sent on the 8th and 9th October to reinforce the column at Ali Changi. The 81st Pioneers had previously been sent out for railway work to Chaghadak, to which place the railway was completed on the 9th October. Chah Kutah was occupied that day without opposition, and on the 10th a small garrison was put into the fort at Ahmadi, which had been deserted. At both these places water was scarce and bad, and the bulk of the column remained at Ali Changi, where water was fairly plentiful though of indifferent quality.

BUSHIRE OPERATIONS

On the 11th General Douglas reported that everything possible had been done to induce the chiefs to negotiate, but without success. They had become fugitives with a petty following incapable of serious opposition and were, moreover, being attacked by their private enemies. General Douglas intended to make every effort to detach the remainder of their following. He would maintain a small mobile force in the plains both to protect his line of communication and to support the nominees of the Persian Governor who would be installed at each rebel's home.

On the 14th October Brigadier-General A. M. S. Elsmie took over command of all troops east of the *mashileh*. By this time military operations and work of every kind were seriously hindered by the large numbers incapacitated by influenza; and on that date General Douglas asked India to postpone the despatch of further troops to Bushire till the epidemic subsided. It was too late, however, to stop the 2/94th infantry and two sections of a trench mortar battery, which both arrived at Bushire before the end of the month. The local inhabitants, it may be noted, suffered even more severely than the troops, and the mortality among them from influenza was very much higher.

On the 15th October a brother of the former Khan was installed at Chah Kutah and the British garrison was withdrawn. On the night 18th/19th a small column of all arms marched to Ahram, whither Zair Khidar had retreated a few days previously and where Wassmuss was also reported to be. After a long march, the column entered Ahram, practically unopposed, on the morning of the 19th, only to find, however, that both Zair Khidar and Wassmuss had fled. After demolishing part of the fort, the column returned the same afternoon to Ali Changi.

Next day (20th) Ghazanfar came in and tendered his submission to the Governor and the Chief Political Officer. He was given time to arrange his private affairs (before being deported to Mesopotamia) and was permitted to return to Borazjan to do this, on his promising to meet General Elsmie and personally conduct him and his troops into the town. This promise he fulfilled on the 23rd October, when General Elsmie occupied Borazjan. But during the ensuing night, at the instigation of his following, Ghazanfar absconded and fled to the hills.

The influenza epidemic had now about reached its height, there being 1,453 sick in hospital on that day, including half the medical personnel in the force.

The 2/94th Infantry joined the column at Borazjan on the 27th October and two days later half that battalion with a detachment 54th Company Sappers and Miners occupied Dalaki. The railway had been completed to Ahmadi, and a temporary advanced base formed there, on the 25th; and work was now commenced on a motor road between Borazjan and Dalaki, though progress was much hampered by the influenza epidemic.

Ghazanfar refused to return from Lardeh, a place in the mountains east of Borazjan where he had collected another armed following. General Elsmie consequently decided to break up this following before it grew in size and to prevent it harassing our line of communication. Lardeh, which lay at an altitude of some 4,000 feet higher than Borazjan, was only eight miles in a direct line from that place. But it was considerably farther by the mountain tracks leading to it. These lay over very difficult and precipitous country, in which a few well posted men could cause considerable delay to any column.

Affair of Lardeh; 31st October 1918. From information he acquired and from a night reconnaissance by Captain Wallace (G.S.O. III), General Elsmie came to the conclusion that, to ensure success, any operation must come as a complete surprise to the enemy. He consequently decided to move by night, operating in two columns. He himself took command of the Right Column, consisting of the 35th Mountain Battery (less one section), a section of trench mortars, the 3rd Machine Gun Company (less three sections), 150 rifles and two Lewis guns 1/117th Mahrattas, 150 rifles and two Lewis guns 2/94th Infantry and a detachment 169th Indian Field Ambulance. The Left Column, under Major K. Franks 1/117th Mahrattas, consisted of 150 rifles and two Lewis guns 1/117th Mahrattas and one section 3rd Machine Gun Company. The composition of both columns had been arranged with due regard to the possibility that they would not succeed in cooperating with each other.

The two columns, each accompanied by a Persian guide, marched off from Borazjan at 11 p.m. on the 30th October. The march of the Right Column proceeded according to plan and its leading infantry reached the summit of a hill overlooking the Lardeh valley at 3 a.m. on the 31st, where, being very tired, they halted to rest. As no hostile piquets had been encountered the enemy appeared to have been surprised. The mountain battery reached the summit at 3.30 a.m. and, the advance being resumed at 4.15 a.m., a commanding position was

AFFAIR OF LARDEH

occupied about 5 a.m. By this time it was light.* Nothing had been seen or heard of the Left Column, and, as its point of debouchment into the valley was clearly visible, it was assumed to have lost its way. The 117th Mahrattas then advanced into the valley to deal with the enemy and at once encountered fire from three sides. But, pressing on, they drove the enemy first out of his *sangars* across the low ground and then out of two encampments on this low ground, inflicting considerable loss on him and forcing him back into the higher hills.

The retirement of the column was ordered at 8.45 a.m. and, except for some slight amount of firing, was not interfered with by the enemy. The rear guard reached Borazjan at 4 p.m., by which time the column had covered since 11 p.m. on the 30th about 24 miles including an ascent and descent of 4,000 feet. As the foot of the hills had been reached on the return march, a column, taken to be Major Franks's, had been observed issuing from the hills on a parallel alignment two or three miles to the north. But after arrival at Borazjan it was found to consist only of the machine guns, Lewis guns and transport mules of that column with an escort.

The Left Column, which was accompanied by Captain Wallace, had found its route a great deal longer and more difficult than had been expected and was also delayed for three quarters of an hour through the guide losing his way. Moreover, the last portion of the track proved quite impassable for mules. But Major Franks decided to push on with his leading infantry (about 100 rifles) so as to co-operate with the Right Column. These infantry reached the crest over the valley at 7.30 a.m., just as they heard the guns of the Right Column open fire, and then pushed on, sweeping up the valley, but failing, in spite of several attempts, to gain touch with, or sight of, the Right Column; and it was not till 10 a.m. that the ground on which the Right Column should have been was sighted.

In the meantime these 100 infantry had cleared the valley against a certain amount of opposition, which steadily increased; they had taken about 30 prisoners and many animals; had burnt Lardeh village and an encampment; and had blown up a magazine containing about 70,000 rounds of rifle ammunition and 150 bombs and shell. Their own casualties totalled 8 and they had killed at least three times that number of the enemy.

At 7.30 a.m. Major Franks had sent his Persian guide back to lead the rest of his column up by another track which the

---
* Sunrise was about 6.15 a.m.

Affair of Lardeh; 31st October 1918.

guide said he knew. When they did not arrive, Major Franks sent back an N.C.O., who returned saying that he could not find them.* Major Franks then sent another man back and, as the men with him had no water, ammunition or support, he went forward himself to extricate them. It took him a considerable time to collect the various detached parties with their captures. But he effected it soon after 1.30 p.m. and was superintending the withdrawal of his rear party under a considerable and accurate enemy fire, when he heard firing break out at the head of his column. Going forward there to ascertain the situation, he discovered that the tribesmen had made their way round and, holding positions commanding his line of retreat, had surrounded him. His men, very tired and short of water, had suffered over twenty more casualties and he realised that, with these, it would be disastrous to attempt to continue his retirement along the narrow homeward track, which could only be traversed in single file and which the unclimbable mountain sides made it impossible to protect with piquets.

He, therefore, decided to collect his men and hold a position till relieved; and this he did, finding a position surrounded on three sides by hills which he could piquet and on the fourth by a precipice. His main difficulties were lack of water and shortage of ammunition, only 25 to 30 rounds a man being left. Captain Wallace then volunteered to try to get back to camp and started off about 3.30 p.m. taking one man with him.†

Major Franks had had to leave some of his wounded men lying out, and during the night Jemadar Nanajirao Palande made two attempts to bring them in. But, being fired on at close range, he failed, though he succeeded in getting in three in the morning. The enemy kept on firing all night, though without much effect, but about 8 a.m. on the 1st November began to retire on the approach of the relief column.

This column General Elsmie had made arrangements to send out early on the 1st as soon as he discovered that Major Franks's column had not returned; and at 10 p.m. on the 31st October Captain Wallace reached camp and reported that Major Franks's position was in little danger of assault, though it was considerably harassed by fire. The relief column, commanded by Lieutenant-Colonel W. J. H. Hunter, 1/117th Mahrattas, and

---

* It transpired that the Persian guide had invented a message ordering them to return to Borazjan.
† He subsequently picked up five men who had been cut off from the vanguard.

DISTRIBUTION OF BUSHIRE FORCE 413

accompanied by Lieutenant-Colonel Gregson, the political officer who had previously gone out with the Right Column and who volunteered to go out again, set out at 5 a.m. on the 1st November. It consisted of two troops 15th Lancers, 200 rifles 1/117th Mahrattas and 20 rifles 2/94th Infantry and, in addition to food, water and riding mules, took with it all available stretchers and 60 unarmed man of the 2/94th as a carrying party. It effected its task successfully without encountering opposition.

The total casualties among the 100 men or so composing Major Frank's detachment were 13 killed and 22 wounded. In his report of the affair General Elsmie specially commended their gallantry and endurance and he also brought to notice the special services of Major Franks, Captain Wallace and Jemadar Nanajirao Palande.

At the end of October the combatant troops of the Bushire Force were distributed as follows :— *Operations from Bushire; October 1918.*

Dalaki—One section No. 3 Indian Machine Gun Company.
    One section 54th Company Sappers and Miners.
    2/94th Infantry (less two companies).
Borazjan—Headquarters Striking Force (General Elsmie).
    One squadron, 15th Lancers.
    35th Mountain Battery (less one section).
    No. 3 Indian Machine Gun Company (less one section).
    54th Company Sappers and Miners (less one section).
    1/117th Mahrattas.
    Two companies, 2/94th Infantry.
    Two sections, Trench mortar battery.
Khushab—One company, 2/113th Infantry.
Ahmadi—One section, 63rd Company Sappers and Miners.
    2/113th Infantry (less two companies).
    81st Pioneers.
    Bushire section of field guns.
Chaghadak—One company 2/113th Infantry.
Bushire—63rd Company Sappers and Miners (less one section).
    71st Punjabis.
    Bushire machine gun section.

The sphere of control and command of the Inspector of Communications, which Colonel H. C. Tytler had taken over on the 12th October, extended from the base at Bushire to Khushab.

Operations from Bushire; November 1918.

On the 2nd November, as the influenza epidemic was subsiding, General Douglas asked India to send the additional troops so as to arrive by the 15th November. The reinforcing units consequently began to reach Bushire on the 12th.

In the meantime, thanks to the work done by the troops, the fourteen mile stretch of road between Borazjan and Dalaki had been made practicable for motor traffic by the 6th November. General Elsmie then moved his headquarters and the bulk of his troops to Dalaki and work was begun on improving the rough mule track, beyond that locality, into a camel road.

Zair Khidar had again resumed negotiations, but refused to accept the terms offered, and on the 9th November a small British column visited Ahram without opposition, installed a new Khan and rejoined headquarters three days later.

Operations based on Shiraz; October-11th November 1918. (See Map 13.)

To enable a column from Shiraz to co-operate with the Bushire force, as had been arranged, Colonel Orton started on the 9th October and established, without incident, a series of posts along the road to Khan-i-Zinian, where he formed an advanced base. This was to be stocked by the end of the month with eighteen days' supplies for Colonel Orton's column, which would then be ready to move direct from Shiraz through Khan-i-Zinian any time it was required after the 7th November.

Saulat had been reported to be in the hills to the west of Firuzabad, which was occupied by Ehtesham with a tribal following and about 200 of the South Persia Rifles under Persian officers. The size of Saulat's following and his intentions were uncertain till the 14th October, when a request for reinforcements reached Shiraz from Ehtesham, who feared attack by Saulat and some 500 Qashqais. It appears, from information subsequently obtained, that Saulat, hearing of the British movement to Khan-i-Zinian and assuming that they were committed to operations on that line, thought that he could attack Ehtesham without interference. On the 17th October, on news reaching Shiraz that Saulat's men had surrounded Ehtesham at Firuzabad, Farman Farma, the British Consul* and Sir Percy Sykes all came to the conclusion that immediate action was necessary to save Ehtesham and to prevent another Qashqai rising. Next day, orders were sent from India, to Sir Percy Sykes to take immediate action, and to General Douglas to readjust his plans to suit the temporary diversion of the troops from Shiraz.

Colonel Orton accordingly left Shiraz on the 20th October with a column composed of three squadrons Burma Mounted Rifles, two sections 36th Mountain Battery, the 3/124th Baluchis

---

* Mr. J. E. B. Hotson had succeeded Lieutenant-Colonel Gough.

RELIEF OF FIRUZABAD

and 700 baggage mules*. On the 22nd, when he crossed the Muk pass unopposed, Colonel Orton received information that Saulat's following had increased to about 2,000 and that Ehtesham, most of whose Qashqai following had deserted him, was practically besieged at Firuzabad.

Next day, when traversing a defile, Colonel Orton's column encountered some opposition; and he decided to cut short his march and camp that night at Ismailabad, about fifteen miles short of Firuzabad, so as to endeavour by skirmishing during the afternoon to discover the enemy's numbers and dispositions. As a result of the day's operations he cleared the vicinity of Ismailabad of the enemy, whose numbers he estimated at five or six hundred and on whom he inflicted a loss of about 40, at a cost of 11 casualties among his own men.

During the night 23rd/24th October the enemy fired constantly into his camp, hitting a few animals, and made an attack which was easily repulsed.

Colonel Orton hoped that the Qashqais, emboldened by the idea that they had stopped his advance, would stand and fight early on the 24th October, thus enabling him to defeat them on his side of the high ridge of tangled hills which separated Ismailabad from the Firuzabad valley. The main route across this ridge lay through the Tangab defile, which was about four miles long with precipitous cliffs on either side and which Colonel Orton intended to avoid by using a track over the ridge to the westward.

On Colonel Orton resuming his advance on the 24th October, it was at once evident that the enemy intended to stand and fight; and about 250 of his men—the bulk of his force—were seen in occupation of a ridge, about 4,000 yards to the south-south-west and about 2,600 yards westward of Ibrahimabad village. By 8 a.m. Lieutenant-Colonel Dyer with two squadrons Burma Mounted Rifles, their advance supported by the fire of the mountain guns, had secured a minor ridge some 1,200 yards north of the enemy's main position. Lieutenant-Colonel Holbrooke with the 3/124th Baluchis (less one company) was then sent forward to secure the left flank about Ibrahimabad and to attack this position. The remaining Burma squadron and a Baluchi company were retained by Colonel Orton as a reserve.

Relief of Firuzabad; 24th October 1918. (See Map 13.)

Two of the Baluchi companies gained a knoll about 1,000 yards north-west of the enemy's position without difficulty; the third company, securing the left flank about Ibrahimabad,

---
* No tents were taken and baggage was on a reduced scale.

went on and drove the enemy off a ridge about 700 yards to the south of that village; and two of the mountain guns pushed forward to give closer support. These movements had brought the enemy's main position under accurate gun fire and a cross fire from the Lewis guns and rifles of the Burma Mounted Rifles and the Baluchis; with the result that when Colonel Holbrooke launched his attack at 9.30 a.m. it attained complete success within twenty minutes. Having gained the enemy's main position, Colonel Holbrooke pushed on, and by 11 a.m. had occupied a ridge a mile further to the south, where a halt was made and the whole column (including the transport) concentrated. So far, the British casualties had been only seven, all among the Baluchis, but the enemy, according to subsequent reports, had lost about eighty men killed and wounded.

Colonel Orton resumed his advance just before noon and, moving by the track to the westward of the Tangab, reached the crest of the main ridge about 3 p.m. without encountering further opposition. Colonel Dyer, who with two squadrons Burma Mounted Rifles was working along about half a mile to the west of the main column, then reported that he could see Saulat's camp, near Firuzabad, being struck and numerous parties of mounted Qashqais moving about; and he obtained permission to advance straight down the ridge towards Deh-i-Barm. Colonel Orton himself with the main column moved down the track bending eastward towards Gilak, which place he reached, practically without opposition, at 4.45 p.m., the rear guard marching in an hour and a half later. Between 5 and 6 p.m. Colonel Orton, hearing from Colonel Dyer that the Qashqais had fallen back to the south-west, had sent him the third squadron Burma Mounted Rifles with instructions to join the camp at Gilak before dark.

In the meantime Colonel Dyer had inflicted severe loss on the Qashqais. He had reached Deh-i-Barm just after 4 p.m., evidently unobserved by the enemy (whose attention had been concentrated on the main column) and had taken up a concealed position in front of and in the village, while sending some of his scouts southward towards Saulat's camp. These scouts shortly afterwards came galloping back to the village pursued by some five or six hundred Qashqai horsemen, who were allowed by Colonel Dyer to approach within 400 yards. The Burma Mounted Rifles then opened fire with their Lewis guns and rifles with devastating effect before the Qashqai could wheel off and get out of range. Nevertheless, and in face of this heavy fire,

the tribesmen made two or three very gallant attempts to gallop in again so as to recover their wounded men and rifles. But, as they only sustained further casualties without succeeding, they finally abstained, and at dusk Colonel Dyer withdrew to Gilak without molestation. After dark the Qashqais returned and carried off their wounded, subsequently estimated at 100, leaving 103 dead where they had fallen. Beyond one pony wounded, the Burma Mounted Rifles had sustained no casualties.

At 8 p.m. a messenger from Ehtesham reached Gilak with the news that the force besieging him had all fled ; and next morning Colonel Orton's column marched into Firuzabad. Then, here and throughout Fars generally, troops and inhabitants alike were prostrated by influenza in its most virulent form. Within a week so many of Colonel Orton's men were affected that men and animals could only be fed with the greatest difficulty.

A list of the British troops in Persia and their general distribution on the 15th November 1918 is given in Appendix V. *British troops in Persia; 15th November 1918.*

CHAPTER XI.

CONCLUSION.

(General Map and Map 11.)

General Situation. Though the war was over, it very soon became apparent to H.M. Government that, in Persia's own interests, British troops should not all be at once withdrawn from that country. As it happened, in fact, some of them remained there till 1921. It would, however, be beyond the scope of this history to carry on the narrative till then, and it will consequently be brought to a close at the earliest definite phase in the situation of each of the different forces.

The question of the retention of British troops was also affected by the situation in Russia and by the decision arrived at, on the 14th November, 1918, by the War Cabinet in London, regarding future British military policy in that country. On the general principle of assisting those Russian elements which had stood by us during the last period of the war, H.M. Government decided, amongst other action, to recognise the Omsk Directorate as a *de facto* Government,* to establish touch with General Denikin at Novorossisk† (so as to assist him as far as possible with military material) and to occupy the line Batum–Baku. This involved participation to some extent in hostilities against the Bolsheviks, whom, it may be noted, the Germans were known to be using for their own purposes in other countries as well as in Russia. But H.M. Government particularly and emphatically disclaimed any intention of conducting an anti-Bolshevik crusade, a declaration that was all the more necessary

---

* Such recognition was actually never accorded. On the 18th November 1918, the Omsk Directorate overthrew the so-called Omsk Government, and on the 27th Admiral Koltchak became head of the Directorate as "Dictator of all Russia." Professing itself pro-Ally and anti-German, this Directorate aimed at governing all Russia and undertook to accept all national obligations and treaties which M. Kerenski's Government had accepted on behalf of Russia in the autumn of 1917. Although H.M. Government and the Allied Powers did not give *de facto* recognition to the Omsk Directorate, they did give practical support to Admiral Koltchak on certain conditions till the last hope of his Government disappeared with the failure of General Denikin's operations in 1919.

† On the coast of the Black Sea, about 275 miles north-west of Batum.

BAKU AND THE CASPIAN

and advisable since many of their advisers on the spot, faced with the violent outrages and the pitiful and disastrous effects of Bolshevism, were inclined to take a contrary line.

Under the terms of the Armistice with Germany, all German troops, instructors, prisoners and agents were to evacuate Russian territory or to be recalled to Germany. German troops were to cease all requisitions, seizures and other undertakings with a view to obtaining supplies, intended for Germany, in Russia. Germany was also to abandon the Brest-Litovsk Treaty and all supplementary treaties; she was to evacuate all Black Sea ports, hand over or release all Russian and neutral ships she had taken or detained; and to return all warlike and other material she had taken.* {Terms of the Armistice with Germany; November 1918.}

As a result of the interview between Captain Washington, R.N., who had proceeded with his five armed ships to Petrovsk, and Bicharakoff on the 6th November, the Russian flotilla, whose lack of discipline and Bolshevik tendencies had recently been very marked, agreed to co-operate with the British; and three of the Russian gunboats arrived at Enzeli with Bicharakoff and his troops on the 12th November. {Trans-Caucasia, the Caspian and North-West Persia; November 1918.}

On the previous day General Marshall had suggested to the War Office that, as difficulties connected with shipping in which to send supplies, etc., to the garrison no longer existed, Krasnovodsk should again come under his orders; as this would obviate conflicting orders arising from a dual control in the port, which was essential to naval command of the Caspian. This was agreed to.

On the 15th November representative delegates from Baku arrived at Enzeli and came to a satisfactory arrangement with General Thomson. Baku was to be evacuated by the Turks, local troops were to be withdrawn and the town was to be occupied by a combined force of British and Russians on the 17th.

On the 16th November the War Office telegraphed to General Milne, commanding the British Expeditionary Force at Salonika, informing him that H.M. Government could not embark on an anti-Bolshevik crusade, but desired to help, with the least military commitments, Russian elements, making for internal security and stable administration, to stand by themselves; and to ensure by military action compliance in Trans-Caucasia with the Armistice conditions. General Milne was to establish

---

* For Terms of Armistice with Turkey, see page 386.

Trans-Caucasia, the Caspian and North-West Persia; November 1918. touch with General Denikin and afford him all possible assistance in military material but was not to send him troops ; while as regards Trans-Caucasia it was intended that General Milne should occupy Batum and proceed with the occupation of the Batum–Baku railway to enforce compliance with the Armistice conditions. This would give us better communications to ensure our control of the Caspian and, if necessary, enable us to support operations up the Volga from Astrakhan. In view of the Turks' attitude it looked as if we might require a force of one or more divisions in Trans-Caucasia. But General Milne's views were requested on this and also as to the ultimate division of responsibility between himself and General Marshall, to whom the telegram was repeated with a request for his views also on the latter point.

The occupation of Baku was duly effected on the 17th November, the British[*] and Russian troops being transported from Enzeli in thirty ships, escorted by the British armed vessels and Russian gunboats. Bicharakoff, who accompanied the force, had previously stated that he had no desire to take any part in the government of Baku and that he was about to disband his Cossacks. To meet his wishes the British armed vessels flew both the British and the Russian flags.

The British met with a good reception at Baku, especially from the poorer classes. The first impression that the Turks had withdrawn as ordered was, however, soon found to be incorrect. A considerable number of their troops remained in the vicinity till compelled to withdraw ; and they had broken up one of their divisions and had distributed its personnel among formations of the so-called Azerbaijan army. Moreover, before leaving the town and in contravention of the Armistice conditions, they had plundered its inhabitants, dismantled the wireless installation, damaged government buildings and removed a large quantity of supplies. At this time, it may be noted, the enemy rifle strength in Trans-Caucasia was estimated at : Germans 8,000, Turks 17,000, and irregulars 13,700.

On the 18th November General Marshall recommended that the Caspian, including Krasnovodsk, should come under the General Officer Commanding in the Caucasus and that his own responsibilities should be confined to North-West Persia.

---

[*] Advanced Headquarters, North Persia Force ; 39th Infantry Brigade (less 9th Royal Warwickshire, one and a half companies 7th Gloucestershire and one section machine gun company) ; 8th Battery, R.F.A. (less one section), one section 44th Battery R.F.A. ; 15th Light Armoured Motor Battery (less two sections) and 22nd Lorry Wireless Station.

These views were based, not only on political and tactical considerations, but mainly on the difficulty that had always been experienced, even during the dry summer months, in maintaining troops on the Caspian from Mesopotamia. On the 20th he further reported that, owing to his food reserves having been consumed by the Jelu refugees, his shortage of motor transport, the revival of trade and peace conditions and the damage caused to the road by early and heavy rains, he would only be able to supply at most the infantry brigade and attached troops then in the Hamadan–Enzeli area ; and he could only do this by stopping all but maintenance work on the road, by withdrawing a cavalry regiment and a battery and by withholding all reinforcing drafts. He would be unable to maintain the troops at Baku, who would have to depend on local resources until the railway from Batum could supply them. In his opinion, the Batum–Baku railway would also be the best line of supply for the troops between the Caspian and Hamadan.

Sir Percy Cox, in telegrams to the Foreign Office sent on the 14th November, had expressed the opinion that, if the British troops withdrew from Persia, a great part of the country would be plunged into complete disorder and that the Persian Government would have neither the money nor the force to cope with it. The ignorant and democrat elements in the country would doubtless, he continued, begin agitating at the first opportunity for the withdrawal of our troops. But he himself strongly urged that they should remain in North-West Persia and maintain order, so as to give the Persian Government time to endeavour to reform the administration and forces of the country. Consequently, on the 23rd November, when the War Office informed General Marshall that his proposals for a reduced force were agreed to, they also told him that his continued control of the main road via Hamadan to Enzeli was still considered of great importance, both for political reasons and as a means of communication with the Caspian. His proposals that troops between the Caspian and Hamadan should be supplied via Baku had been referred to General Milne, who had been ordered to occupy Batum with a division—another division being held ready in support—as soon as the naval situation permitted, with a view to securing the railway to Baku. A few days later the War Office intimated that both Baku and Krasnovodsk would come under General Milne's orders after he had established connection between Batum and Baku.

On the 19th November, General Thomson telegraphed describing the political situation in Trans-Caucasia. The

Mahomedan Government of Azerbaijan (installed by the Turks) and the Georgian Government were tyrannical and anti-Russian, the result of years of corrupt, oppressive and incompetent Russian military administration; and any attempt to restore these old methods would probably bring all parties together into an intense opposition. An occupation by the Allies and the restoration of order would not be difficult; and moderate men of all parties accepted gladly the idea he suggested of a temporary coalition government for Azerbaijan, to replace the existing Turkish-made Cabinet, which the Allies had not recognised and with which he could not work. It seemed advisable, he said, that Allied representatives should assume early control at Tiflis of railways, telegraphs, posts, customs and other civil services and accelerate the withdrawal of the Germans.

By the end of November, the evacuation of the Turks was on the whole proceeding satisfactorily, though the Armenians were taking advantage of their departure to massacre Tartars, and the Turkish troops were taking with them much plundered material and food stuffs which we had to take steps to detain at Tiflis or Batum.

As soon as Baku had been occupied, arrangements were made by Captain Washington to control and organise trade on the Caspian under a shipping controller; and the coasting trade in the southern portion of that sea at once began to revive. To the north, however, it remained limited. Towards the end of November four of the British armed ships started on a sweep to the north, from which they returned to Krasnovodsk early in December, their cruise having asserted British control and put heart into the pro-Ally Ural Cossacks. It was reported that the Astrakhan Bolsheviks were arming ships and, with torpedo-boat destroyers and submarines which had arrived from the Baltic via the Volga, intended to establish an ice-free base at Chechen with a view to operations against the British flotilla and to the capture of Baku.

Trans-Caucasia, the Caspian and North-West Persia; December 1918.

On the 8th December, two of the British armed vessels, at anchor in a fog off Chechen, being attacked by three Bolshevik armed ships which were convoying three transports carrying Bolshevik troops, immediately weighed and accepted battle. A running fight ensued which lasted two hours and resulted in the Bolshevik ships fleeing northward and escaping under cover of the fog, one of them having apparently sustained serious damage. This defeat by a force inferior both in ships and guns*

---

* The armament of all the British ships was weak and they were all very short of British personnel.

had a great moral effect. Next day a Bolshevik destroyer was sighted, but retreated at full speed without attempting to fight ; and till the end of the month, when the Bolshevik fleet at Astrakhan was frozen in, no further encounters occurred.

By the end of November, three more ships had been armed, which brought the total number in the British squadron up to eight and Captain Washington had requested the Admiralty to reinforce it, by sending via Batum and Baku from eight to twelve coastal motor boats. On the 1st January, 1919, the control of the British Caspian flotilla was transferred to the Mediterranean Command.

On the 14th December General Thomson reported that the Tartar leaders, being convinced that they could not stand alone and having no desire to return to government by Russia, had expressed a desire to send a delegation to the Peace Conference to request that Azerbaijan should be put under British protection. Two days later the War Office repeated to General Marshall a telegram sent to General Milne on the 11th December informing him that, for the time being, Allied policy in the Caucasus was to ensure compliance by the Turks with the Armistice terms and to re-open the railway and oil-pipe line between the Black Sea and the Caspian. The Allies desired to see strong independent states in Georgia, Daghestan and Russian Azerbaijan. The question of Armenia and of its and the other States' protection had not yet been settled. But H.M. Government had no intention of converting them into a British protectorate or of undertaking commitments involving the permanent maintenance of large forces in those districts. Whatever steps were taken should, therefore, be such as would not involve us in any long-continued obligations to the inhabitants and as would be consistent with the complete independence of these States.

General Milne's troops did not occupy Batum till the 27th December and up to that time General Thomson, with only a small force (which General Marshall was unable to reinforce) at his command, had a very difficult task in attempting to restore order. Germans under Kress remained at Tiflis, where they retained control of the wireless installation and intrigued with the Georgians and Bolsheviks, whose possible advance into Trans-Caucasia the Georgians regarded with great apprehension. The Turks took every opportunity to try to delay the evacuation of their troops, which was in any case rendered difficult by the state of the railways ; and they continued to plunder and destroy property and commit outrages in the

Armenian districts. The Armenians fought with the Tartars and at one period with the Georgians, while in Baku Russians and Bolsheviks succeeded in bringing about a labour strike, which though it did not cause actual disorder, kept the town in darkness and disorganised railways and shipping. British officers were sent by General Thomson to Elizabetopol, Tiflis and Batum to exercise a steadying influence and to accelerate the movement of Turkish troops; and he also sent small British Missions to the south-west of Shusha, to stop the Armenians fighting the Tartars, and to Petrovsk which was threatened by the Bolsheviks. Bicharakoff received orders from a Russian General, who was with Admiral Kolchak in Siberia, to take command in the Caucasus and restore Russian domination; and, although Bicharakoff agreed that the Bolsheviks must be his first objective, it seemed to General Thomson that it would not be long before he attacked the Georgians and the Azerbaijan Government. In Lenkoran also trouble seemed probable owing to Bolshevik activities.

On the 1st January 1919, General Milne assumed responsibility for supplying and maintaining the British force on the Hamadan–Enzeli line and on the 15th January he took over complete control of all the British forces in Trans-Caucasia. General Marshall suggested that General Milne should also assume tactical control of the force in North-West Persia. But the latter would not agree, and in February it was arranged that his tactical control should extend southward to the line Enzeli–Zenjan–Bijar–Sehneh. In that month also H.M. Government decided, after some discussion*, that, for political reasons, the British force on the Hamadan–Enzeli line should be maintained at its existing strength until the results of the Peace Conference were known.

By this time the road from Mesopotamia to Hamadan had been made fit for motor transport. In dry weather it was passable by light lorries but, if rain occurred, it was only passable, twenty-four hours after, by light lorries for the first 100 miles and by Ford vans for the remainder of the distance.

Trans-Caspia; November 1918. After evacuating Merv the Bolshevik troops withdrew to Ravnina, a railway station 65 miles to the north-eastward, while the Trans-Caspian troops, distributed for the most part

---

* H.M. Government were anxious, on the grounds of economy, to withdraw British troops from Persia at the earliest opportunity. But they acceded to Sir Percy Cox's representations that they should remain, pending the conclusion of negotiations for an Anglo-Persian agreement.

between Merv and Bairam Ali (on the eastern edge of the Merv oasis) held an advanced post at Annenkovo, a station about 19 miles short of Ravnina.

On the 11th November General Malleson telegraphed from Meshed that he had just received a most urgent appeal for immediate financial assistance from the Trans-Caspian Government, who had come to an end of their money and complained of having borne the whole cost of the campaign for our joint aims without any British financial aid. General Malleson's *liaison* officer at Askabad, in confirming their urgent need of money, emphasised the serious results if they were unable to pay their railway workmen. Next day General Malleson reported a danger of a Turkoman rising and proposed that he should warn both the Trans-Caspian Government and the Turkomans that if a rupture occurred no further British support would be forthcoming. The Government of India thereupon requested and obtained H.M. Government's approval to instructions to General Malleson to inform both sides that he would withdraw the British detachment from Trans-Caspia at the first signs of a rupture.

In intimating this approval on the 15th November, the India Office enquired why the movement from Quetta to Meshed of six reinforcing squadrons of Indian cavalry had been cancelled by the Government of India ; and on the same day the India Office informed India of H.M. Government's future policy in Trans-Caspia. Though, they said, it was not intended to embark on an anti-Bolshevik crusade in Russia, considerations of interest and honour demanded that we should keep the region east of the Black Sea clear of Bolshevism. Our object was to help the Russians to stand by themselves by supporting and strengthening existing organisations which offered a hope of maintaining law and order and which were working in our interests. Generally speaking, this support would be limited to financial aid and assistance in war materials ; but, as the Trans-Caspian Government could evidently only be protected by an occupation of Merv, General Malleson was authorised to retain his force there as long as the military situation demanded it, though British troops were not to be employed east or south of the Merv area. As General Malleson was to use all means in his power to prevent a Trans-Caspian–Turkoman conflict, it might be necessary to send him the reinforcements whose move had been cancelled.

General Malleson had just gone to Askabad, where he received assurances from the Trans-Caspian leaders that they would do

Trans-Caspia; November 1918.

their utmost to settle their differences with the Turkomans amicably ; and he answered this telegram (which was repeated to him) on the 18th November. If the position was to be saved, he said, financial assistance was essential; but war material would be useless and dangerous, as the Trans-Caspians lacked reliable men to use it. The only way to defeat the Bolsheviks was to support the local contingents with a small compact British force and to secure the line of the Oxus, the only natural line of defence. This could be done without difficulty; it would produce an immense moral effect on the Trans-Oxus population; and it would enable us to treat with the Bolsheviks. He considered that the reinforcements from Quetta should continue their move. On the same day he also telegraphed a summary of a formal memorandum to H.M. Government from the Trans-Caspian Government. They viewed with dismay the order limiting British troops to Merv, as the Oxus was the sole line of defence, to which a British advance was anticipated with eagerness by the whole of the population in Turkestan, Russian and Mahomedan, and in Bokhara. All regarded it as an urgent political and military necessity, and, if it was not carried out, the Trans-Caspian Government disclaimed any responsibility for the serious results.

On receipt of this telegram the Government of India telegraphed their views to the India Office on the 19th November. They had cancelled the movement of the reinforcements for the following reasons :—the removal of the Turco-German menace ; the proved adequacy of the existing British detachment to save the Trans-Caspian Government when their own troops had failed both them and us; the great difficulty in maintaining an increased force, especially in regard to animal transport and medical equipment and staff ; and the economy compelled by the serious trouble we were experiencing in finding currency to meet our various obligations in Persia. Their aim generally, they continued, had been to take the earliest opportunity of withdrawing altogether from Trans-Caspia and of confining themselves to assistance in money and war material. Consequently, before ordering the reinforcements to proceed, they ventured to enquire if the above factors had been fully considered and to indicate that a British occupation of Merv might aggravate the difficulties of the Amir of Afghanistan in dealing with the fanatical sections of his people at a time when their susceptibilities had been considerably disturbed, and might also induce him to lay a claim to former Afghan territory which would be embarrassing. If H.M. Government considered it essential that British troops should remain at Merv, and therefore inferentially increased in strength, it would be necessary to extend the railway as far as Neh (instead of only to Duzdab as had been recently proposed). In conclusion, the Government of India presumed that they would receive an early decision as to the extent to which General Malleson might promise the Trans-Caspian Government financial assistance.

On the 20th November the Government of India sent the India Office a summary of a report of the 17th from General Malleson detailing the sums of money asked for by the Trans-Caspian Government*. On the same day General Malleson reported that, as money had to be provided and as he owed the Trans-Caspian Government several million roubles for rations supplied to our troops, he had felt justified in starting to raise money locally to repay them.

The Trans-Caspian situation was considered by the Eastern Committee of the War Cabinet in London on the 21st November. In the ensuing discussion it became clear that our policy of supporting the all-Russia Government at Omsk—which hoped to establish communication with Tashkend via the Orenburg railway—and our apprehensions lest anarchy in Trans-Caspia should react on the Persian and Afghan borders required the retention of British troops in Trans-Caspia for the time being. We had accepted in principle a financial liability to the Trans-Caspian Government. But our various financial obligations in Persia—whence the money would have to come—had so outstripped the available supply of silver that, if further expenditure were incurred, there was a danger of financial dislocation with a resulting disturbance of our policy. It was decided, however, to give the Trans-Caspian Government a lump sum in liquidation of all our liabilities, the amount being left to the Government of India to suggest.

But before they were requested to do this, other important telegrams on the subject were received. On the 21st November the Government of India repeated to London with their own comments General Malleson's two telegrams of the 18th advocating an advance to the Oxus. The cost of maintaining the force suggested and the consequent strain on our resources seemed to them to be disproportionate to the advantages to be gained. They considered that the time had come to disabuse the Trans-Caspian Government of the hopes they appeared to entertain that we would fight their battles and gain territory for them, as well as supply them with money to dominate

---
* These totalled about £1,000,000 down and £130,000 a month in future.

Trans-Caspia; November 1918.

Turkestan. They should, considered the Government of India, be informed that, while we were prepared to give aid financially to some extent in the establishment of an orderly and friendly government, we did not regard ourselves as bound to maintain them indefinitely with men and money, and that our financial assistance would depend on the energy they themselves displayed in realising stability. Further, they should be made to understand that they must rely on their own troops for any extended operations and that we would not go further than afford them support at Askabad. In conclusion, the Government of India requested an early declaration of British financial and military policy.

On the same day, the Government of India telegraphed a suggestion made by General Malleson to liquidate our obligations by inducing a conference, under our auspices, between the conflicting elements with a view to arranging a referendum by the whole population on the future form of government. The desperate condition of the Tashkend Bolsheviks, the chance of depriving them of the military assistance of the Austro-Hungarian prisoners of war by offers of repatriation and the readiness of the Trans-Caspian Government to agree, were the grounds given by General Malleson for believing that this course might be successful. The Trans-Caspian Government had already projected a scheme on similar lines and the Government of India recommended that they should be informed that they should carry out the negotiations on these lines, though they would, as they had told General Malleson, prefer his intervention. It may be noted here that on the 26th November the Trans-Caspian Government issued a wireless appeal to all forces opposing them calling for the cessation of internecine strife with a view to the formation of a stable and representative government. But, as it had no effect, no further action on these lines was taken.

In two telegrams sent from Merv on the 20th November, General Malleson pointed out the utter and disadvantageous instability of the Trans-Caspian front and again urged the political and military advantages of securing the line of the Oxus, which the Turkoman Commander-in-Chief of the Trans-Caspian forces also advocated. The latter assured General Malleson that Mahomedan feeling everywhere in Central Asia was so entirely and markedly pro-British that the declaration of a British protectorate would be received with the greatest enthusiasm*. On the other hand, the Bolsheviks were finding

---

* It must be remembered that the Allied defeat of the Central Powers had very greatly increased British prestige at this time, and that in Persia and Turkestan it was generally held at this period that there was no limit to what we could do if we desired.

it increasingly difficult to get fighting men. The Turkoman Commander-in-Chief had also assured General Malleson that he would do his best to prevent a rupture between his fellow-countrymen and the Trans-Caspian Government. In further telegrams sent in the next few days General Malleson reported the Trans-Caspian financial position as very grave. He himself was finding his own position increasingly difficult owing to the rather conflicting and indefinite instructions he had received.

The India Office, in a telegram sent on the 26th November, said that the sudden urgent demand for money for the Trans-Caspian Government had taken them by surprise and that, while it was desired to keep this government in existence, H.M. Government could not meet the large recurrent payments mentioned in the telegram of the 20th from India. Actual liabilities incurred, and any definite promises of financial support given, by General Malleson would of course be met and for this they proposed to pay a lump sum in Persian currency to the Trans-Caspian Government. They asked the Government of India to advise what this amount should be. The latter repeated the telegram to General Malleson asking him to state the amount due under the two heads mentioned.

Shortly before this, they had sent General Malleson five lakhs of rupees towards meeting the expenditure of his Mission, and on the 28th November, after he had failed to raise sufficient money locally to pay the amount due for rations, he asked if he could pledge this sum or give any other guarantee, as the Trans-Caspian Government, faced with bankruptcy and unwilling to face the chaos that would ensue, had just intimated that they were going to resign at once. Later in the same day he replied to the telegram asking for the amount of his liabilities. In his original agreement with the Trans-Caspian Government in August he had, he said, included a clause promising them financial assistance, but had soon afterwards learnt that they had money sufficient in their estimation to last them for five or six months. This estimate of theirs had proved optimistic owing, partly, to their inexperience, to the fall in value of the rouble and to the rise in prices. But the amount had been in any case a comparatively small sum* on which to govern the country, maintain an army and a railway, and assist in feeding thousands of refugees. He had pointed out to them, however, that their miscalculation had involved delay in procuring financial assistance for them. He himself had never named any sum to them and he had as yet been unable to ascertain what

---

* It was 72,000,000 roubles.

Trans-Caspia; November 1918.

was due to them for rations, etc. But he urged that on all grounds very substantial financial assistance should be promptly guaranteed. If we held on a little longer, he said, the fight against the Tashkend Bolsheviks was likely to succeed very shortly. In reply he was authorised to hypothecate the five lakhs of rupees and was reminded of H.M. Government's intention to limit their expenditure, regarding which a reference had been made to Tehran to ascertain what money there could be made available.

Reports from General Malleson on the 28th and 29th November depicted the situation of the Trans-Caspian Government as desperate, owing to the financial crisis and to Turkoman intrigues with the Bolsheviks. He had, however, induced the Government to hold on for another day or two, though they were convinced that their inability to pay workmen and soldiers would bring about an immediate collapse at the front and a sanguinary outbreak at Askabad. They had urged him to bring British troops immediately to maintain order and control the mob at Askabad, which was full of women, children and refugees from all parts. He consequently asked leave to move at once a squadron of Indian cavalry and a company of Indian infantry from Meshed to Askabad, as he could not withdraw any troops from the Merv front and the only British troops available were those at Krasnovodsk, whose strength had been recently reduced by two companies of the 9th Royal Warwickshire ordered by General Marshall to Baku.*

On the 29th November the India Office telegraphed asking if the financial decision conveyed in their telegram of the 26th was likely to bring about the early collapse of the Trans-Caspian Government, and if so, how it would effect the future of General Malleson's force. His telegrams seemed to imply that he required reinforcements, and the India Office asked if the Government of India agreed, and if they could send him at once what he required. Further, the views of the Government on India were requested on the War Office proposal to place General Malleson's force under General Milne, to be supplied via Batum, Baku and Krasnovodsk. In this case, they concluded that the extension of the railway from Mirjawa to Neh would no longer be of military importance.

On the 30th November the War Office, who had already warned General Milne that as soon as he had occupied Baku he should be prepared to support General Malleson, sent orders

---

* General Marshall had also replaced the section 44th Field Battery there by a section of the 8th Field Battery which was immobile, i.e., without horses.

to General Marshall to reinforce General Malleson immediately ; and orders were consequently issued for two companies of the Warwicks to return at once from Baku to Krasnovodsk, whence General Malleson was authorised to despatch up to three companies to Askabad. A report from General Malleson of the 30th November showed that apprehensions felt in India regarding the security of the Merv front, owing to the reported Turkoman intrigues, were groundless, as the difficulties of the Tashkend Bolsheviks were too great to enable them to attack effectively ; but that the grave danger of local disturbances at Askabad had obliged him to order there immediately the squadron and company from Meshed. He also said that he was issuing local bills to repay the Trans-Caspian Government five million roubles, which was approximately what he estimated was due to them for rations supplied.* On the 1st December he reported that, as a result of a week's hard endeavour, he hoped he had saved the local Government for the time being ; while other telegrams sent that day, by Sir Percy Cox at Tehran holding out hopes of the Imperial Bank there being able to buy ten million roubles and by General Marshall reporting that General Thomson had been able to send two million roubles from Baku to Askabad, promised to relieve temporarily the financial stringency. The chance of local disturbances at Askabad was also removed by the arrival there of two companies of Warwicks on the 3rd and 4th December and by the impending arrival of the squadron 28th Light Cavalry from Meshed.

On the 2nd December General Malleson expressed his inability to suggest what amount beyond the five million roubles for rations should be given the Trans-Caspian Government, owing to the important questions of higher policy involved. He read H.M. Government's declaration of their desire to keep Bolshevism out of the region to the east of the Black Sea as intended to include Turkestan, but apparently the Government of India thought otherwise ; and he consequently asked for an authoritative decision. He pointed out that the Trans-Caspian troops were unable to stand alone and then went on, after discussing the alternative policies before us, to urge a precise indication of British policy for the immediate future. No satisfactory results, he concluded, were likely to accrue from half measures and we should either see the business through or withdraw. The Government of India accordingly asked the India Office on the 5th December whether Turkestan was included " in the

Trans-Caspia; December 1918.

---

* He could not get a figure from the Trans-Caspian Government, but they accepted his estimate.

Trans-Caspia; December 1918.

region east of the Black Sea." Their interpretation, based on the limitation of the British military operations to the Merv area, had been that it was not, and General Malleson had been hitherto instructed accordingly.

On the same day in London the Eastern Committee discussed the situation in Trans-Caspia, which was evidently critical. The Government of India had not yet expressed their views either as to the amount of the lump sum to be given the Trans-Caspian Government or whether it was worth while bolstering up that Government. The Committee decided that £100,000 should be given to meet immediate necessities, but without necessarily implying that a further sum would be given, and also that the Government of India should be requested to reply to the above questions. This decision was notified to India by the India Office in a telegram sent on the 7th December, which said that, in addition to the five million roubles for rations and two million roubles sent from Baku, H.M. Government were prepared to give the Trans-Caspian Government £100,000 in Persian currency, but could not undertake to go beyond that sum. At the same time the Government of India were requested to give their views regarding the importance, from the Indian standpoint, of maintaining General Malleson's force in Trans-Caspia and also regarding the tenability of his position if the Trans-Caspian Government collapsed.

This telegram crossed one sent by the Government of India on the same day replying to the India Office questions of the 29th November and elicited a further reply sent by the Government of India on the 10th December. In these two telegrams the situation was reviewed fully and the Government of India, pointing out that they were without necessary knowledge of the future policy towards Russia which H.M. Government proposed to follow, tendered such advice as their available information permitted. The British Government's financial decision as intimated in the telegram of 7th December might certainly, in the opinion of the Government of India, cause the collapse of the Trans-Caspian Goverment, as their only hope of paying their way was to obtain revenue by the sale of raw materials and to attract the support of the orderly and well-to-do elements in the country. For this they desired to gain Tashkend, but it seemed doubtful if they could succeed. The Government of India agreed with General Malleson that with a limited increase of force he could disregard popular disturbances and also that a withdrawal from Merv might lead to a Bolshevik advance or to fraternisation between Trans-Caspians and Bolsheviks and a Turkoman withdrawal. All elements of the situation, however, were so unreliable and uncertain as to render it unsafe to make any forecast. There was no longer a danger of a Pan-Islamic Turkoman rising, but if our troops left Trans-Caspia, a Bolshevik–Turkoman conflict might ensue with results which it was difficult to foresee. The greatest difficulty, in the case of a Trans-Caspian Government collapse, would be the extrication of the British detachment from Merv, though, once it had concentrated at Askabad, the Meshed portion could withdraw southward or south-eastward to the Persian frontier, where it would menace a Bolshevik advance on Askabad or Krasnovodsk and would prevent hostile incursions into Persia. If the detachment was to remain at Merv, or even if it had to withdraw in the above circumstances, it might require reinforcements. These could be sent from Quetta, but would take at least six to eight weeks to arrive, and the increased force would be difficult to maintain from India. The Government of India agreed that the Batum–Krasnovodsk route was the natural line of supply and that the force in Trans-Caspia should come under General Milne's orders. The value of the Mirjawa–Neh railway lay in its practical immunity from danger, and its military importance would, therefore, remain unaltered if we desired to influence events in Trans-Caspia independently of the Black Sea route.

The alternatives before H.M. Government, said the Government of India, were, either to assume responsibility for financing the Trans-Caspian Government till they were self-supporting—an indefinite period—or to withdraw altogether, after giving them the lump sum suggested and ignoring possible accusations of bad faith. For the former course, the Trans-Caspian Government would apparently require about 118 million roubles down to clear them of debt and about 16 million roubles* a month thereafter. India could not find the currency for this and Tehran evidently could not supply more than a few million roubles. The Government of India preferred withdrawal and agreed that the lump sum to be paid should be the amount suggested by the India Office. For they considered that the objects and results of remaining in Trans-Caspia did not justify either the heavy and indefinite financial liability or financial dislocation and disturbance of our policy in Persia. From the Indian point of view, we could do all that was likely to be required if we had access to, and could maintain sufficient troops to operate

---

* At this period the rate of exchange was about 133 roubles to the English pound.

Trans-Caspia; December 1918. from, the Birjand area. General Malleson should, however, be safe enough at Meshed if the Trans-Caspian Government collapsed. The only danger might be via Orenburg, but the Government of India had not sufficient information to estimate its significance.

In the meantime the situation in Trans-Caspia appeared to have improved in several respects. On the 2nd December a Bolshevik attack on the Trans-Caspian armoured trains and advanced posts was repulsed. On the 5th and 6th Bolshevik agitators at Askabad and Krasnovodsk were arrested, and though there was some trouble in consequence, all was quiet by the 8th, when the 28th Light Cavalry squadron from Meshed reached Askabad. On that day the Trans-Caspian force carried out a successful raid, in the course of which they captured Ravnina though they did not hold it. The Turkomans continued to give trouble, but General Malleson intervened with some success.

On the 9th December General Malleson reported that he had found it necessary to give the Trans-Caspian Government another five million roubles and he requested to be informed as soon as possible of the extent to which further financial assistance would be authorised. In reply he was told that, pending orders from London, he was to give no further financial assistance. On the 10th December the Trans-Caspian Commander-in-Chief informed General Malleson that the gradual exhaustion of his ammunition and the declining discipline among his troops, caused by inaction, rendered it essential to make a serious effort to gain the Oxus line. He had formulated a plan for his mounted troops, acting in concert with the Turkomans and the Amir of Bokhara* (who held the Charjui bridge), to cut the Bolsheviks off from the Oxus, and he asked that a portion of our troops should be sent forward in trains, not to take part in the operations but to afford moral support to the movement. He considered that this would bring about a Bolshevik surrender and, as the moral, political and military advantages of gaining the Oxus line were so great, he hoped that this relaxation of the order prohibiting an eastward movement of our troops would be permitted. General Malleson also urged the advantages of such a course and asked if the movement of British troops asked for could be sanctioned. In reply, on the 11th December, the Chief of the General Staff in India telegraphed that it was not approved. The small cutting out expedition proposed should, he said, be well within the powers

---
* He was keeping in the closest touch with this ruler.

of the Trans-Caspian force. Copies of both General Malleson's telegram and the reply were at the same time repeated to the War Office. On the 10th December the Trans-Caspian Commander-in-Chief had also asked General Malleson for certain war material and the latter had sent him what he could, including a Russian detachment with six Lewis guns recently trained at Meshed, and had informed him that guns and other war material were being sent him as soon as possible via Baku.

On the 12th December the India Office telegraphed their reply to the query whether Turkestan was included in the region east of the Black Sea which was to be kept clear of Bolshevism. General Malleson's objects should be two, they said : firstly, to keep the Bolsheviks from overrunning Trans-Caspia from the north and so overturning the Trans-Caspian Government and penetrating Khurasan and, secondly, to hold on to the railway till the presence of our troops was no longer necessary. The difficulty of maintaining our troops would diminish, the telegram continued, when the Batum–Baku line opened, but we should never be in a position to undertake extensive anti-Bolshevik operations even if it was desirable politically. General Malleson was to limit himself to what was necessary to effect these two objects and his rôle was to support the efforts which the Trans-Caspian Government were able to make to strengthen their position eastwards. In this way H.M. Government hoped that the Trans-Caspian Government would shortly be able to stand and act by themselves. The telegram concluded by saying that the Austro-Hungarian prisoners of war in Turkestan should be repatriated as soon as General Milne could receive them.

The orders conveyed in this telegram, it may be noted, appeared to the General Staff in India to be too vague, as they could be construed as authority to advance to the Oxus.

On the 15th December General Malleson returned to Meshed, where General Beatty had arrived on the 8th November to take over executive command of all the troops at Meshed and beyond. On the 20th December, with General Malleson's concurrence, a company of the Warwicks returned to Krasnovodsk from Askabad.*

The Trans-Caspian situation was considered by the Eastern Committee in London on the 18th and 23rd December with the result that the India Office telegraphed on the 24th to the Government of India saying that H.M. Government were anxious to get rid as soon as possible of military commitments

---

* General Marshall was very anxious to move two companies to Baku to enable General Thomson to send a small force to Petrovsk.

Trans-Caspia; December 1918. in Russia and particularly in Trans-Caspia. On the other hand, they realised that the loss of the Trans-Caspian railway would enable the Bolsheviks to threaten Krasnovodsk and would prevent repatriation of the Austro-Hungarian prisoners of war*. The Bolsheviks might also penetrate into Persia, as with the withdrawal of the British detachments no reliable troops would be available in Trans-Caspia. But there were insuperable objections to further British financial assistance to the Trans-Caspian Government. After pointing out that the advent of General Milne's troops to the Caspian would help us in attaining the objects given in their telegram of the 12th December, the India Office asked for the views, both of the Government of India and of General Malleson regarding the probable result if the latter did not give any further financial assistance for the time being. The views of the Government of India on the general situation also were requested.

This telegram was repeated to General Malleson on the 30th December and crossed one from that officer, which said that at the front the Bolsheviks were very weak and despondent but the Trans-Caspian force was in even worse case and their Russians were deserting. Plenty of Turkomans were available and willing to serve in the Trans-Caspian force, but the Russians who were jealous or afraid of them, would not agree. The Trans-Caspian Commander-in-Chief urged that a stronger Trans-Caspian Government should be formed or that the British should take control. The Trans-Caspian Government, said General Malleson, were without power, prestige, money or credit. They would almost certainly collapse within the next three days and, unless we were prepared with a programme, would be succeeded by extremists who would join the Bolsheviks, while the Trans-Caspian front would break up unless we intervened. The uncertainty regarding future British policy prevented respectable people from taking part in the Government. General Malleson said that he could rely on the Turkomans, who with our troops largely commanded the situation; and he urged the necessity for, at least, preserving order till the allied policy had been decided. He recommended that, when the existing Government resigned, he should put in an emergency Government of five members, including two prominent Turkomans, who would proclaim martial law, punish all

---

* A German Red Cross Mission had recently arrived at Askabad with a view to repatriating prisoners of war, and General Malleson was endeavouring to negotiate with the Bolsheviks for leave to allow this Mission to proceed to Tashkend.

disturbers of the peace, carry out a partial disarmament of the people, arrest and deport Bolshevik agitators, guard railway stations, telegraph offices, banks, etc., threaten to try deserters, and pay the railway workers. As events were moving fast, he said in conclusion, a very early reply was essential.

In repeating this telegram to London on the 31st December, the Government of India pointed out that the twofold objects desired could not be achieved without either a definite offer of larger financial support than H.M. Government contemplated or the intervention of armed force. Such intervention would make us morally responsible for the maintenance of law and order and would involve us in much heavier financial and military commitments than those which we already experienced difficulty in meeting. If financial support still presented insuperable difficulties and unless we were prepared to let General Malleson take the action he proposed, we should, considered the Government of India, instruct him to concentrate his troops on the Persian border so as to protect Khurasan and to be in a position to advance on the railway if necessary.

At this time, when General Beatty and his staff were on the way to Askabad, the troops of the Malleson Mission were distributed as follows :—

Merv Area
- Headquarters and one section 44th Battery, R.F.A.
- One company 1/4th Hampshire Regiment.
- Two squadrons 28th Light Cavalry.
- 1/19th Punjabis (less one company).

Askabad
- One company 9th Royal Warwickshire Regiment.
- One squadron 28th Light Cavalry.
- One company 1/19th Punjabis.

Meshed
- One squadron 28th Light Cavalry.
- Details 1/19th Punjabis.

Replying to the India Office telegram of the 24th December on the 31st, General Malleson amplified his report of the 30th. Instability at the front, a perpetual Bolshevik menace in the rear and lack of money to pay workmen and soldiers were the main evils. Turkomans formed 75 per cent. of the population but could not be armed owing to Russian jealousy ; the Russians themselves were generally lazy, worthless and cowardly ; and the Armenians, thousands of whom were armed, were treacherous, unreliable and constantly intriguing. On the other hand, the situation of the Taskhend Bolsheviks was precarious. The first thing to do in his opinion was to restore military and political stability ; and the only real way to do this was to drive the Bolsheviks across the Oxus. This he considered to be perfectly feasible with the active assistance of the British troops in the Merv area. Having achieved this he would disarm most of the Russian and Armenian soldiers, holding the Oxus with Turkomans and picked Russians. With the cessation of the heavy military cost of the Russian and Armenian soldiery, he saw no reason why Trans-Caspia should not be able to pay its way. For trade with Europe would follow the opening of the Batum–Baku route; with increased stability, revenue would accrue from customs duties, taxes and railway earnings; and the Government had great assets in cotton stocks. Any British reinforcements—up to 1,000 men in all and particularly guns, machine guns and one or two aeroplanes—that could be made available from Trans-Caucasia would, he continued, be very welcome. If H.M. Government were not disposed to sanction an advance to the Oxus and at the same time did not wish to see Trans-Caspia overrun by the Bolsheviks, the only alternative was to defend the eastern edge of the Merv oasis, though of the two courses this would require the larger number of troops. If it was decided to evacuate Trans-Caspia the result would, he thought, be serious. A large force would be required to defend the Persian border and the inevitable Turkoman-Bolshevik conflict would probably develop into a prolonged *Jahad*, which might react on neighbouring Moslem nations.

Trans-Caspia; January 1919. On the 1st January he telegraphed that notices which had been published prohibiting riots and the presence of Indian cavalry patrols had succeeded in allaying a danger that had recently been manifesting itself, both at Askabad and Krasnovodsk, of an anti-Government rising by Bolsheviks and railway workmen. He had material for an emergency Government, but, in view of the undecided character of British policy, he hesitated to give it the assurance of British support which it would require.

On the 2nd January, he further reported that, as it was dangerous to allow matters to drift, workmen's houses at Askabad had been searched, arms, ammunition and bombs found there had been confiscated and several workmen and prominent Bolshevik agitators had been arrested. The results had been markedly satisfactory, and, besides continuing the search for arms and the arrest of agitators, all public meetings were being prohibited. The enemy at the front had made another unsuccessful attack.

On the 3rd January General Malleson reported that the Trans-Caspian Government had resigned and had been replaced by a fresh body, composed of four Russians and two Turkomans. Askabad was quiet and the great bulk of the population appreciated the British action in suppressing disorder without bloodshed. On the front all was quiet.

As his telegram had not given a direct reply to the specific question from London regarding the situation that would result if his Mission was retained without further financial assistance being afforded to the Trans-Caspian Government, General Malleson was requested on the 4th January to send this. He replied the same day that an accurate forecast was impossible, but that, with no wages forthcoming, the workpeople and the Russian troops at the front would probably give trouble. He thought that, as the Bolsheviks were so weak, he could effect the two-fold objects desired by H.M. Government with the existing British force and could certainly do so with the reinforcements previously suggested. He had reliable confirmation of the suppression by the Tashkend Bolsheviks of all news of the Armistice and also reliable information that if the Austro-Hungarian prisoners of war, who were all anti-Bolshevik, knew the truth they would take strong measures to free themselves. He was endeavouring by all means to get news across the line to them.

On the 5th January he represented the urgent necessity of paying the wages of the railwaymen and he pressed for a very early decision regarding British policy. He had done everything possible, he said, to keep things going pending this decision, but it would be most difficult to stave off trouble much longer. If the existing Government went, he continued, the only possible alternatives were Bolshevism, anarchy, or British control. In reply the Chief of the General Staff in India telegraphed, on the presumption that General Malleson had made arrangements to concentrate his force at Askabad if necessary, that, if the situation took an unfavourable turn, he could expend money to secure the co-operation of the railwaymen in providing the necessary train service for this concentration, though this payment should not include arrears of wages.

On the 6th January General Malleson telegraphed that the Government would resign that night unless money was forthcoming. His telegram of the 4th had not given the direct reply which the Government of India required and on the 7th the Chief of the General Staff in India asked him to send this in full without qualifications. In the meantime, on the 6th, the Government of India repeated his telegram of the 31st December to the India Office and said that, though his direct reply had

Trans-Caspia; January 1919.

not yet been received, he evidently considered it necessary to establish stability by advancing to the Oxus. Though they no longer felt that this would arouse Afghan susceptibilities, they advocated the withdrawal of the British force from Trans-Caspia to the Persian border, from where it could deny the use of the Trans-Caspian railway to any force moving from the eastward to threaten Krasnovodsk and could prevent a hostile penetration of Persia. Should H.M. Government decide to retain the force in Trans-Caspia, financial assistance to the Government there should at once be given to pay outstanding debts, while any further assistance required in troops, supplies or money should be provided via the Batum–Baku line.

On the same day General Malleson repeated a telegram he had just received from General Beatty in Trans-Caspia pointing out how extremely precarious the situation of the British troops east of Askabad would be if the railway strike eventuated, as seemed probable. Immediately on receipt of this the Government of India authorised General Malleson to make payments to secure the railway service essential for supplying our troops at Merv and between Askabad and Merv.

On the 8th January the India Office telegraphed to India that, as a matter of policy, H.M. Government desired to withdraw the Malleson Mission to Meshed and were not prepared to continue indefinitely the financial assistance without which the local Government could not stand. There were, however, the following military reasons for the retention of the Mission in Trans-Caspia :—To prevent a Bolshevik advance into Persia and also against the rear of the Orenburg Cossacks ; the repatriation of the Austro-Hungarian prisoners of war ; and the protection of Krasnovodsk from the east, including a hold on the Trans-Caspian railway. It was accordingly considered desirable to await a full report which General Milne had been ordered to submit. He was on his way to confer with General Malleson, but might not arrive for two or three weeks.

On the 8th January also, General Malleson telegraphed his reply to the question asked. The Government would collapse, he said, and we should have to take control, or see anarchy. If we took control, money would be required and we should find it difficult to govern without administrative machinery. Financially, the fall of the Government would mean that all revenue would cease and that there would be a railway strike. From the military point of view, our withdrawal from Merv would cause a collapse at the front, an irruption of the Bolsheviks with Bolshevik risings elsewhere and a possible Bolshevik penetration of Persia. The Turkomans would start guerilla warfare and brigandage and possibly a *Jahad*. Morally, our prestige would suffer greatly. Already, said General Malleson our indecision, delay and varied instructions had given rise to reports that we intended to betray our friends. He was not a pro-Russian, he continued, as he had found the Russians inefficient, unstable, dishonest and highly emotional and their troops undisciplined, cowardly and, for the most part, treacherous. The Turkomans, on the other hand, appeared to be kindly, simple and well-disposed towards us. Mahomedan opinion in Central Asia was, he considered, of great value to us and he considered it would be deplorable and disastrous if we withdrew military and financial aid from Trans-Caspia. If the provision of money was the stumbling block, he was convinced that he could raise ample for immediate needs by means of promissory notes, payable at six or even twelve months date and bearing no interest.

This telegram reached Delhi on the 9th, when another telegram, sent by the War Office on the 7th January to Vladivostok and repeated to Constantinople, Baghdad and India, was also received there. The question of Allied policy towards the Russian problem, it said, was to be considered early at Paris and the discussion might be prolonged. In the meantime no active measures could be taken by our troops in North Russia or in Turkestan. Public feeling in Great Britain and the Allied countries disliked the presence of small Allied detachments in Russia, though there was as yet little objection to sending material assistance. The War Office considered it imperative to hold the Orenburg front, however, so as to maintain a possible link between South Russia and Siberia, and to retain a force between Krasnovodsk and Merv, thus preventing the enhancement of the strength and material power of the Bolsheviks.

On the 9th also, the Chief of the General Staff in India, in repeating to General Malleson the India Office telegram of the 8th, authorised him to afford such temporary financial assistance as was absolutely necessary to the Trans-Caspian Government, so as to give time for the meeting between General Milne and himself.

On the 14th January General Milne reported that except for maintenance of the troops south of the Askabad–Merv line, he would assume command next day of General Malleson's force.

General Malleson telegraphed on the 15th January that General Beatty had just requested permission to move his detachment from Bairam Ali towards the Oxus in support of a Trans-Caspian advance in co-operation with the Amir of Bokhara, which had been planned to commence on the 19th. General Malleson, who had informed him that orders from India prohibited such an advance and that the internal situation in Trans-Caspia was too critical for our troops to risk involvement in a reverse, asked for confirmation of his orders.

Action of Annenkovo; 16th January 1919. Next day (i.e., 16th January) a Bolshevik force, subsequently estimated at several squadrons of cavalry, eight guns and four thousand infantry (a considerable portion of whom were German or Austro-Hungarian prisoners of war), made a sudden attack on the Trans-Caspian position at Annenkovo. This position was not a good one, but a few sand-hills beside the railway line afforded better facilities for defence than any other position between there and Merv. Besides the Trans-Caspian force, consisting of two small armoured trains, 70 Russian mounted infantry—trained at Meshed under General Malleson's orders and known as the Meshed detachment—400 Turkoman horse and 100 Armenian infantry, there were at Annenkovo a half-squadron 28th Light Cavalry and a company (150 rifles) 1/19th Punjabis. Owing to the intense cold and the lack of any suitable location closer, the nearest British supports were at Bairam Ali, some thirty odd miles away. Here were a squadron 28th Light Cavalry, a section 44th Battery, R.F.A. and headquarters and two companies (300 rifles) 1/19th Punjabis. At Merv there were a half-squadron 28th Light Cavalry and a company, only 80 strong, of the 1/4th Hampshire Regiment.

The line of low sandhills, which formed the Annenkovo position, lay to the north-west of, and parallel to, the railway (which at this spot curved to the northward) and afforded some protection from view and fire from the better armed Bolshevik armoured trains usually stationed about three miles off. Both sides lived and moved about in their trains, and news of an impending enemy attack had been generally obtainable by patrols observing a forward movement by enemy trains.

For some days past there had been indications that the Bolsheviks had received reinforcements and were contemplating an attack. This morning there was a thick fog, but by 8.30 a.m. the usual mounted patrols had returned without having seen any signs of the enemy. Twenty minutes later, however, loud explosions in the rear of the position were heard and mounted patrols were sent out in all directions. They soon reported that the railway line and telegraph wires in rear had been cut and that they had sighted four Bolshevik cavalry

ACTION OF ANNENKOVO 443

squadrons about three miles to the north-west. A little later a prisoner was brought in who stated that the Bolsheviks were advancing to attack the Trans-Caspian left.

By 10 a.m. the broken railway had been repaired and communication restored with Bairam Ali, where a company of the Punjabis at once entrained and started for the front, being followed by most of the other troops there and by the half-squadron 28th Light Cavalry from Merv.

Fog continued to obscure the view and it was not till about noon that Trans-Caspian mounted patrols reported an enemy concentration about three miles north-west of the position. In the meantime the following dispositions had been made to meet the plan of attack which the enemy was said, by the captured prisoner, to be following. The right flank, where the railway curved northward, was covered by the half-squadron 28th Light Cavalry and the Turkoman horse, with the two armoured trains drawn up in their rear. In the centre, to the north-west of these trains, the Punjabi company (Captain G. Pigot) was deployed parallel to the railway with the Meshed detachment on its left; and to the left again, and a little in advance, were the Armenian infantry.

At 12.30 p.m. the last named were ordered to advance and soon encountered advancing enemy infantry. At the same time eight hostile guns opened fire but, owing to the poor visibility, their continuous fire had little effect.

The Punjabis experienced little difficulty in maintaining their position, but the Armenians, who were unexpectedly fighting very well, were greatly outnumbered and had to be reinforced by a Punjabi platoon. The enemy, however, continued to push in fresh troops and, under a heavy enfilading machine gun fire, the Armenians broke and fled. The Meshed Detachment then took their place, but by 3 p.m. the enemy had brought up so many men that he threatened to outflank completely the whole position. Fortunately, at this critical juncture, the train carrying Major J. G. P. Drummond's company of Punjabis from Bairam Ali steamed up and came on right into the hail of bullets. The men jumped out of the carriages, formed into line and advanced straight against the enemy's right flank. The Bolsheviks held their ground till the Punjabis were within 50 yards and then broke and fled in disorder, losing heavily as they crossed the front of the other Punjabi company.

In the meantime about three squadrons of Bolshevik cavalry and 1,500 Bolshevik infantry had started to attack the

Trans-Caspian right and by about 5 p.m., when the Bolshevik attack against the Trans-Caspian left was beginning to break up, the 28th Light Cavalry and the Turkomans had been driven back and one of the armoured trains had been surrounded. Its crew of Russian ex-officers, however, jumped out and, charging the enemy with gallantry and vigour, just as a platoon of Punjabis came up to their assistance, brought him to a standstill. By this time the main Bolshevik force was in full flight across the desert and, seeing this, those attacking the Trans-Caspian right also broke and fled. The Meshed Detachment and some of the Turkoman horse pursued, but the 28th Light Cavalry from Bairam Ali had not yet arrived and the enemy managed to save his guns, although he lost seven machine guns. His casualties had been severe, nearly 200 corpses being found next morning, his total losses being subsequently estimated at 600. In addition, it was said, the bitter cold had caused him about 500 cases of frost-bite.

The Trans-Caspian casualties totalled about 70 and those among the Punjabis 46.

It was subsequently ascertained that the Bolshevik plan had been to cut the railway and telegraph communications and then immediately surprise and overwhelm the Annenkovo detachment by simultaneous attacks against both flanks, that against the left being carried out by 2,500 infantry and the one against the other flank by 1,500 infantry.

This affair enhanced greatly the already high reputation locally of the Indian troops.

Trans-Caspia; January 1919. General Milne met General Malleson at Askabad on the 27th January and, after visiting Merv and the front, ordered certain alterations in the distribution of the British troops. The whole of the 28th Light Cavalry were to be concentrated at the front; the weak company 1/4th Hampshire was to return to Mesopotamia, being replaced at Merv by a company of the 9th Royal Warwickshire; and Askabad was to be garrisoned by infantry only, i.e., a company 9th Royal Warwickshire and a company 1/19th Punjabis.

He also arranged that Kizil Arvat, where danger threatened from the Yamut country, was to be occupied by a detachment from Baku.

Trans-Caspia; February 1919. On the 1st February General Milne telegraphed to the War Office at some length, giving his views on the situation which, he considered, called for an immediate decision as to our future policy. The recent telegraphic reports to India from General Malleson, he said, presented very fairly the political, economic and financial situation, as well as the probable results of a British withdrawal. He recapitulated briefly the sequence of events which had led to the British agreement with the Trans-Caspian Government, to their subsequent resignation owing to financial difficulties, and to the hurried formation of a Committee of Public Safety to administer the country; and he pointed out that the presence of British troops had been the only obstacle to a Bolshevik domination and was the sole security for the position and safety of the existing administration. The majority of the Russian element in the country inclined towards Bolshevism and would adopt it if it gained ascendancy; and the feeling between them and the Turkomans, who claimed the country, was strong. But the unfitness of the Turkomans to govern and the helplessness of the Russians had led to a temporary bond between the two. The President of the Administration had informed him, he continued, that the Russians had lost heart and had begged that the British should remain. The railway workers were complying with British demands only as long as they received wages, but the non-payment of money due for January might lead to a stoppage of traffic. The attempt of the Trans-Caspian Government to raise troops by a general mobilisation having proved unsatisfactory, the existing administration had annulled the order and had instituted the formation of volunteer detachments. But as they had no money to pay these, the scheme had met with no success and the whole Russian, as opposed to the Turkoman, force apparently only consisted of about 200 infantry and three armoured trains. The country was bankrupt, a financial crisis was rapidly approaching and no great improvement could be expected till a strong Government was placed in power and trade was re-opened with areas in the hands of the Bolsheviks. Sixteen or seventeen million roubles monthly would be required to maintain the Government, and of this amount General Malleson estimated that we should have to supply £100,000 a month.

The military situation, which he described, would, he continued, be ludicrous if it were not so unsound. The presence of the British detachment maintained our Allies in position and prevented a revolution at Askabad with paralysis of rail and telegraphic communications. The exisitng triple responsibility of command—between British, Russians and Turkomans—was unsatisfactory, but was the best in the circumstances. The Turkoman Commander-in-Chief was anxious to obtain a better covering position by an occupation of Charjui and the Oxus

Trans-Caspia; February 1919. line, but lacking the support of a strong British contingent had neither the men nor the ammunition to carry it out. Moreover the recent Bolshevik capture of Orenburg* had considerably altered the situation to our disadvantage, as they would now be able to obtain support from Moscow. The small number of British troops, who were the only real obstacle to a Bolshevik advance, the military inefficiency of our allies and the scarcity of arms and ammunition rendered the situation so unsatisfactory that it could not be allowed to continue, and in this General Malleson agreed with him. We must either, he concluded, help the local Government financially and with troops, arms and ammunition, or we must withdraw altogether.

The first of these alternatives would mean bringing up more Indian troops so as to render the position secure, the minimum force required in Trans-Caspia, in his opinion, being a cavalry regiment, a battery of artillery, four infantry battalions, and some aeroplanes and heavy guns. The conditions were unsuitable for British infantry and they should be replaced by Indian infantry. In addition, the armament and organisation of Turkomans would have to be considered and, though this would stir up prejudices, they might well be ignored. In this connection he thought that the formation of a Turkoman State merited consideration, though their treatment of Russians was difficult to foresee. The necessity of holding the Merv oasis was obvious, but strikes at Baku, other difficulties and the maintenance of shipping on the Caspian added to possible mischances on the requisite long line of communications.

In regard to the second alternative General Malleson considered that we were in honour bound to support the local administration. But General Milne failed to see how we could do so except as he had stated above. They had done little to maintain an army, and General Malleson himself admitted that we were bolstering up a lot of effete Russians. General Malleson considered that, before we withdrew, we should make the front safe by advancing to the Oxus. But General Milne did not believe that we could do this with the means at our disposal in view of the latest change in the situation, and he considered that a withdrawal should not be difficult from a military point of view, though it might be so politically if the inhabitants turned against us or a railway strike occurred. It would be necessary to give the local administration money, arms and ammunition if we withdrew. General Milne would also prefer to abandon Krasnovodsk, as it would not be easy to hold and

---

* This had occurred on the 22nd January.

we should have to feed its inhabitants. That question, however, was chiefly a naval one. He saw no reason for us to trouble about the repatriation of the Austro-Hungarian prisoners of war. He then referred to the possible results of our withdrawal as depicted by General Malleson in his telegram of the 7th January and said that the question was whether we were to continue the necessary assistance to maintain order in the country for what might be an indefinite period. The only apparent advantage to ourselves was one concerning our national prestige.

If we decided to remain, he advocated organising the Turkomans to take over the country, while if we were to withdraw, warning of our intentions would have to be given to allow better-class Russians an opportunity of leaving, though this would be difficult. In conclusion, he said that he wished to make it clear that we could not allow the existing situation to continue and that half measures were impossible. We should either assume the burden of complete control and of support, involving time, money and labour in an almost hopeless task, or we should leave the country to its fate with the accompanying anarchy and bloodshed.

On the 9th February the India Office telegraphed to the Government of India that General Milne's report made it quite clear to H.M. Government that the Askabad Government were as helpless as ever and that, owing to the fall of Orenburg, the military situation had changed for the worse. H.M. Government were not prepared to send military reinforcements and considered it undesirable to prolong a situation in which General Malleson appeared to be virtually in charge of the Government. They had consequently decided, unless the Government of India saw grave reasons against it, to order a withdrawal, which, though it must be deliberate enough to give our friends an opportunity to get away, should commence as soon as possible. This withdrawal should be to Meshed, where General Malleson's Mission would revert to control by India and from where he could protect North-East Persia from Bolshevik incursions. They had also decided to pay the Trans-Caspian railway workers their arrears of pay and wages till the withdrawal was complete and to allow General Milne to hand over arms and ammunition to the Turkomans. The Government of India replied on the 11th February concurring in these decisions.

In the meantime General Malleson had reported an improvement in the Bolshevik situation at Tashkend (where they had

Trans-Caspia; February 1919. suppressed a rising) owing to the capture of Orenburg, though the railway through that town had apparently not yet been opened. The Amir of Bokhara had sent an envoy to Askabad to ask for 4,000 rifles to arm his men against the Bolsheviks, and General Malleson himself had begun to issue rifles and ammunition to the Turkomans.* The local administration, he reported, had begun to issue their own notes, so that further financial assistance by us was undesirable.

On the 15th February, in issuing orders to General Milne for the withdrawal of General Malleson's force, the War Office said that Krasnovodsk was to be retained. On the 17th General Malleson informed General Milne that supply arrangements, necessary precautions and action to create a suitable atmosphere would take a little time; and he asked for discretion to announce the withdrawal at his own time and that in the meantime its advent should be treated as secret. He saw no reason why his force should not be back in Persia before the end of March and, though the movement might be carried out more quickly, he did not think it desirable to attempt this. As General Milne agreed with him and thought that he would do very well if he achieved the withdrawal by the end of March, his proposals were approved by H.M. Government.

Between the 18th and 23rd February, General Malleson reported a growing disinclination to fight among the Tashkend Bolshevik troops on the front as well as further anti-Bolshevik risings along their communications. He had begun his arrangements for withdrawal which he hoped would be facilitated by the early arrival of some Russian reinforcements, which were coming from Baku. Internally the situation was quiet, though some of Bicharakoff's Cossacks, who had reached Askabad, had given trouble and had been confined as a preliminary to sending them back to Daghestan, and the Russian ex-officers and the workmen in Trans-Caspia were mutually suspicious of one another. The Turkomans betrayed anxiety regarding the future.

General Malleson telegraphed on the 26th February, on hearing of the assassination a few days previously of the Amir Habibulla of Afghanistan, that this might possibly have an important bearing on the situation. General Malleson had learnt, he said, that the decision to kill Habibulla had been due to his failure to seize the opportunity which had occurred in the spring of 1918 for declaring a *Jahad*. At that period and during the ensuing summer the Turkomans had been induced

---

* General Malleson's headquarters had been established at Askabad by General Milne's orders.

by Bolshevik outrages to listen to the Turkish and German agents who were flooding the country. But they had finally decided to combine with the Mensheviks in appealing for British assistance, a step they had never regretted. They were not fanatical, continued General Malleson, and, realising that they could not govern the country by themselves on modern lines, did not desire absolute independence but only equal rights and just treatment. The main danger for the future was that, coming into conflict with Russian reactionaries or with Bolsheviks, they might declare a *Jahad* and call on their Moslem neighbours for assistance. In this case, if Nasrulla became Amir of Afghanistan, as was reported, he would be a danger.

On the 1st March General Malleson reported that a confidential announcement he had made to the members of the local Government of our coming withdrawal had caused considerable consternation. They would certainly resign, some of them would leave the country before us and General Malleson was trying to find a new Government to replace them, though it would be difficult. The public announcement would be deferred till the Russian reinforcements, then landing at Krasnovodsk, had reached the Merv front, where, though the enemy was demoralised he might recover if he had an inkling of our departure. In the meantime British surplus stores were being disposed of, and arrangements were being made for the 28th Light Cavalry to retire by the Dushak–Meshed route and the 19th Punjabis by the Askabad–Kuchan road, while the Warwicks would remain at Askabad till the day the Indian troops marched out and would then rail to Krasnovodsk. On the 4th March General Malleson reported that with the arrival of the Russian reinforcements, which included a large number of officers, the political situation had become unsettled and lively, owing to their asserting that they had been assured of Allied support in their efforts to restore the monarchy. The railway workmen and Turkomans openly stated their intention of opposing these efforts, by civil war and a railway strike if necessary, and though General Malleson had repeatedly informed the representatives of all parties that the Allies would not support reactionary or monarchial designs, his assurances had been misrepresented and had done little to ease the situation. He suggested that action should at once be taken to prevent this misrepresentation of Allied intentions.

By the 6th March the Russian reinforcements from the Caucasus, about 900 in number, had passed through Askabad; on the 9th General Malleson gave the local administration formal

Trans-Caspia; March 1919.

Trans-Caspia; March 1919. notice that they must be prepared to take over the British positions at the front by the 15th March; and on the 11th the impending British withdrawal was publicly announced. This caused considerable and general concern, and during the next few days all elements in the country sent representatives to appeal to us to remain. On the 15th March the 28th Light Cavalry were withdrawn from Annenkovo to Bairam Ali; on the 24th General Malleson reported that the elections for a new Government had been carried through without incident; and on the 29th he telegraphed that the 28th Light Cavalry were on their way to Dushak, whence they would march into Persia on the 30th, and that the 19th Punjabis would leave Merv on the 30th and 31st for Askabad, which they were due to leave for Kuchan on the 1st April.

All these moves were carried out without incident and the Indian troops evacuated Trans-Caspia, leaving behind them a reputation for discipline and gallantry which any troops might be proud of and which they well deserved. One of their last exploits at the beginning of March, though of little material importance, is worthy of narration as exemplifying the fighting spirit with which they were imbued. A reconnoitring patrol of the 28th Light Cavalry, fourteen strong, finding itself cut off by a body of about 150 Bolshevik cavalry, had charged through them and had then turned and charged through them again, killing or wounding 21 of the Bolsheviks, at a loss to itself of one wounded and two made prisoner.

General Malleson himself left Askabad for Meshed on the 2nd April and on the 16th, when the 19th Punjabis reached that place, the control of the force and Mission reverted to India.

The intervention of this British Mission in Trans-Caspia at a critical period had achieved most important results. In addition to saving the country for many months from the horrors of Bolshevism, it had suppressed enemy influence there and had deterred the Turkomans from acceding to the self-interested enemy advocacy of a *Jahad*, which, irrespective of its danger to our Indian Empire, must have caused misery to thousands by its extension, and possible prolongation, of the war. Though the courage and endurance displayed by the British and Indian troops contributed largely to these results, much of the credit for them was due to General Malleson himself. Faced throughout by an unusually difficult task and frequently without clear-cut orders to guide him, he had used his discretionary powers with discernment, ability and energy. That the country itself did not benefit more was due to its own inhabitants, who failed

EAST PERSIA

to take proper advantage of our assistance; and though up to the last General Malleson, impelled by generous motives, urged their claims for further assistance, subsequent events serve to confirm the wisdom of the British decision to withdraw.

In the meantime, under General Dickson's able and energetic administration, work on the line of communication through East Persia had been making good progress. It was not, however, till a month after the armistice with Germany that the Indian military authorities were in a position to instruct General Wapshare in Quetta that the standard of preparation on the line of communication was to be based on the maintenance of a force, at and beyond Meshed, consisting of a regiment of cavalry, a battery of artillery and a brigade of infantry with the necessary administrative troops. During the next two months the uncertainty regarding our future policy in Trans-Caspia, as well as the possibility that the increasing public demand in Great Britain for acceleration of demobilisation might necessitate the despatch of Indian to relieve British troops in the Caspian region, pointed to the undesirability of relaxing our efforts till it was quite certain that we should not have to re-expand our arrangements. On the 18th February General Wapshare was informed confidentially of the impending withdrawal from Trans-Caspia to Meshed, and he at once enquired if he was to limit the standard of preparation to allow for the maintenance of only the 28th Light Cavalry and the 1/19th Punjabis at Meshed. But, as the instructions from London intimated that the force to be maintained at Meshed was to prevent Bolshevik incursions into North-East Persia and it was as yet uncertain what this would involve, he was directed in reply to continue his arrangements for the force mentioned in December.

It is impossible in the space available here to describe all the work that had to be done, but an indication of its magnitude is afforded by the ration strength in East Persia at this period (middle of February). In personnel this totalled over 800 British, nearly 11,000 Indians and 639 levies, of which only 840 Indians were there for purely combatant duties. There were about 3,300 horses, mules, ponies and donkeys and 15,600 camels drawing rations, besides 5,500 hired camels and 1,900 hired mules and donkeys. The motor transport consisted of a company and a section of Ford vans, a light lorry section and a motor ambulance section.

East Persia Line of Communication.

By this time about three-quarters of the road from Duzdab to Meshed had been made fit for motor transport and, in fact, a long convoy of motor ambulances actually conveyed the sick and wounded (from Trans-Caspia) to railhead from Meshed in February. By the end of March the whole road was practically complete.

On the 20th January the India Office queried the necessity of continuing the railway extension from Mirjawa. In reply the Government of India pointed out that the railway had already reached within eleven miles of Duzdab, where the water supply and climate were better than at Mirjawa; that the railway material, to complete to Duzdab, was already on the spot; that there was no intermediate site suitable for a railhead; and that the road from Duzdab to Hurmuk, which saved 67 miles of difficult road from Juzzak and more from Mirjawa, was already complete. In these circumstances extension to Duzdab was sanctioned and the railway reached there on the 2nd February.

Bushire Field Force; November 1918. (See Map 11.) The reinforcements from India, withheld during the influenza epidemic, began to reach Bushire on the 12th November and had all arrived by the 23rd. Two days later the light railway reached Borazjan, which then became the advanced base of supply. Thereafter the striking force under General Elsmie—with headquarters then at Dalaki—consisted of one squadron 15th Lancers, 35th Mountain Battery, 54th Company Sappers and Miners, 1/55th Rifles, 1/117th Mahrattas, 1/127th Baluchis, a trench mortar battery and No. 3 Indian Machine Gun Company; the remaining troops in the force being detailed for duty on the line of communication and at Bushire.

Owing to the severity of the influenza epidemic at Shiraz, the advance of Colonel Orton's column from Khan-i-Zinian had been countermanded; and General Elsmie's troops were mainly occupied in road construction, covered by small detachments of troops which were gradually pushed forward from Dalaki. There was no serious enemy opposition, though at times our troops suffered casualties from the fire of small bodies of raiders. Nasir Diwan, who had recently been joined by the Khans of Khisht,* was said to intend to oppose our advance on Kazerun. But he had only about 500 men; the heavy mortality from

---

* These Khans had hitherto been supposed to be friendly and they had ostensibly welcomed and escorted General Elsmie's troops moving from Dalaki to Khisht on the 13th November.

influenza had stopped the usual southerly migration of the Qashqais; and Wassmuss had been informed that he and his German companions would be repatriated if they came in, but would otherwise be treated as prisoners of war if captured. It was, in fact, clear that the difficult country, bad roads and difficulties of supply and transport would be greater obstacles to our advance than enemy opposition.

General Elsmie's troops occupied the summit of the Mallu pass on the 18th November; and on the 23rd General Douglas who had already intimated that the railway was unlikely to reach Dalaki before the end of January, reported the road up the Mallu pass to be so bad that, with the means at his disposal and unless he interfered seriously with the railway construction, it would take a month to make it passable for camels. As the improvement of the road over the Kamarij pass would probably take just as long, he estimated that, if road and railway were to be completed before the final advance to Kazerun, this could hardly take place till February. He saw no political objections to such delay, which would ease the transport situation by enabling him to collect more supplies in advance of the base and would allow time for the January snow on the passes east of Kazerun to melt and for the troops at Shiraz to regain their health. In these circumstances the Commander-in-Chief in India sanctioned the postponement of the advance.

The total absence of local supplies (including fodder and firewood) between Bushire and Dalaki increased greatly the transport difficulties; and General Douglas, who had already had to ask for more transport, reported at the end of November that, for a variety of reasons, the railway situation was most unsatisfactory and that he was experiencing great difficulty in supplying his troops. He, therefore, asked for the services of an experienced railway officer and for the despatch of additional railway material. Steps were at once taken in India to supply his requirements.

At the beginning of December the hostilities of enemy raiding parties in the neighbourhood of Dalaki necessitated the despatch from there into the surrounding country of four small punitive columns. Only one of them, however—a company 1/55th Rifles under Major D. B. Mein which proceeded to Jamileh—achieved any results. But its success and the defeat, at the same period, of a small enemy body which made a vigorous attack on a road piquet near Mallu caused the raiders to cease hostilities. *Bushire Field Force; December 1918.*

454 OPERATIONS IN PERSIA

Bushire Field Force; December 1918. After the new camel road over the Mallu pass had been completed, the striking force (less the cavalry squadron and a section of the machine gun company) concentrated on the 19th December at Charum, five miles from the Kamarij pass, to the summit of which the track ascended steeply through a rocky and precipitous defile. That afternoon, from a high hill which commanded the summit of the pass from the west at a range of 4,500 yards, General Elsmie could see some 100 or 150 of the enemy building *sangars* along the main ridges; and he decided to attack next morning. A direct attack was to be made by the 1/55th Rifles, advancing under cover of fire from the mountain guns on this high hill and of rifle and machine gun fire provided by the 1/117th Mahrattas and a section of the machine gun company posted on a ridge to the south-west of the pass; and the 1/127th Baluchis were to advance up the main range well to the left, so as to gain the crest about a mile to the north of the pass and cut off the enemy's retreat to Rahdar.

The attack took place as arranged. Under an accurate and effective covering fire the 1/55th Rifles, under Lieutenant-Colonel H. E. Herdon, went forward without a check and cleared the summit at the cost of only three casualties. They then pressed on and occupied Kamarij village. The casualties of the enemy, who had fought well, are unknown; but they do not appear to have been heavy, the 127th Baluchis not having reached the crest in time to take part in the action.

Kazerun, which was only about twenty miles from Kamarij, could have been occupied without difficulty. But as the transport and supply arrangements were incomplete, a pause was made in the British advance; and General Elsmie's troops were employed in carrying out reconnaissances and in improving the routes leading from Charum into the Kazerun valley. At first the enemy strove to interfere with the working parties by long range fire, but after the 27th December, when he was attacked and driven off the neighbouring hills, he attempted no further hostilities.

On the 23rd December General Douglas reported that Wassmuss and Oertel, saying that they had received no orders from their own Government and could not recognise our authority, declined to come in. It is noteworthy, in this connection, that the armistice terms with Germany did not specifically apply to Persia.

During December, the sphere of control of the Inspector of Communications was extended to the Mallu Pass. Camels were generally working from railhead at Borazjan to Dalaki, whence onwards for the most part pack mules only were employed.

About Christmas heavy rains caused such serious damage to the railway that all traffic on it had to be suspended for several days. The railway had only reached about four miles beyond Borazjan* and the Commander-in-Chief in India agreed with General Douglas that construction beyond Borazjan should be discontinued and that more Ford vans should be despatched to Bushire to be utilised instead. It was also arranged, about this period, that the Royal Air Force in Mesopotamia should send a flight of aeroplanes to join the Bushire force. Of these the first arrived on the 9th January 1919.

At the end of December 1918, in order to escort the Deputy Political Resident to the installation of a new Persian representative at Khurmuj (the principal village of Dashti) and to afford moral support to a Persian force under Darya Begi operating against Zair Khidar, two squadrons 15th Lancers and the Bushire field artillery section moved to Ahram, whence on the 31st they proceeded to Khurmuj, returning next day to Ahram without incident. Darya Begi, however, finding himself unable to make headway against Zair Khidar, then appealed for British military assistance; and the detachment at Ahram, reinforced by a company 71st Punjabis and the Bushire machine gun section, sent a small column to join Darya Begi on the 8th January. Zair Khidar fled immediately and the British troops were then withdrawn.

The epidemic of influenza, which had started in October, spread throughout South Persia and lasted till the middle of December, causing the deaths of hundreds of the troops and thousands of the inhabitants. In Fars, where it assumed its most virulent form, the rate of mortality varied from about twenty per cent. among the Indian troops to about eighty per cent. among some of the tribesmen and villagers. It effectively put a stop, for the time being, to all military operations and it was only by degrees and by marching by easy stages that Colonel Orton got his enfeebled troops back from Firuzabad to Shiraz by the 1st December. *Fars; November 18th to January 1919.*

Saulat's following had dwindled to very small proportions, but he still remained to the south of Firuzabad; and in order to assist Ehtesham to maintain his position as head of the Qashqais by undertaking further operations against Saulat, it was found necessary, in the second and third weeks of December to despatch from Shiraz reinforcements of South Persia Rifles troops and a body of Qashqais to Firuzabad.

---

* Up to Borazjan the country is easy, but beyond it is hilly, very broken and intersected by ravines.

On the 25th November the India Office, referring to the recent decision to hand over the Fars Brigade of the South Persia Rifles to Farman Farma, telegraphed to India that, as the presence of so senior an officer was no longer necessary at Shiraz, Sir Percy Sykes should be instructed to proceed at once to London, where his advice regarding the future maintenance of order in South Persia would be welcomed. Accordingly, Sir Percy Sykes, handing over his duties to Colonel Orton, left Shiraz for India on the 15th December.

On the 5th January 1919, Mr. Hotson reported from Shiraz that Farman Farma had received a letter from Saulat, in which he disclaimed all desire to be Il-Khani and requested permission to live quietly in his village. In reply, after consulting Mr. Hotson, Farman Farma had held out hopes of a settlement if Saulat abstained from giving further trouble. Since Ehtesham had proved useless, and laborious operations by British troops would be necessary to crush Saulat, who was the only Il-Khani the Qashqais would follow, Mr. Hotson advocated offering Saulat light terms as well as hopes of restoration as Il-Khani. Both Mr. Hotson and Colonel Orton were convinced that Saulat had been the dupe of Tehran politicians and of his own perverted patriotism. Ehtesham himself, said Mr. Hotson, would gladly give up the position of Il-Khani if assured of personal safety and security; and as regards any future danger from Saulat, if made Il-Khani, Farman Farma hoped to break up the Qashqai confederacy by bringing certain tribal sections under his own influence and by increasing the power of their headmen. General Douglas and Mr. Bill concurred generally in Mr. Hotson's views and suggested terms which should be offered to Saulat.

Bushire Field Force; January 1919. On the 10th January the Government of India telegraphed at some length to the India Office reviewing the situation. From a military point of view the operations had proceeded satisfactorily. Opposition had been dispersed, the rebel Khans had been put to flight and the road had been opened. But the future outlook was unsatisfactory; as evidently the only way of ensuring a permanent improvement was by prolonged military occupation of salient points, a prospect which, if only on financial grounds,* H.M. Government were presumably not prepared to contemplate. There seemed no other alternative but to come to a settlement with our enemies, and the Government of India considered that, as we had demonstrated our

---

* At this period we were spending in Persia at the rate of £30,000,000 a year.

strength, we could now do this with good grace. They accordingly outlined the terms they suggested for such a settlement and enquired whether, subject to any objections by Sir Percy Cox, H.M. Government approved. A very early decision seemed to them to be desirable.

In reply, on the 19th January, Sir Percy Cox pointed out that the problem of Fars and the Bushire–Shiraz road had been prejudicial to our commercial and political interests and a constant source of worry to us for nearly ten years and that, as an opportunity had at last been found for regulating the situation effectively with the concurrence of a friendly Persian Cabinet, it would be a great pity not to pursue the task to a point which would obviate a relapse when the troops were withdrawn. Any such relapse would react prejudicially on the position of the Cabinet and on the general negotiations regarding our future policy in Persia which he was then engaged in. It would seem advantageous, continued Sir Percy Cox, to bring the Persian Government into the question of terms. He had gathered from individual members of the Cabinet that while they regarded the question of the lesser Khans as immaterial, they looked on Saulat as a public character to whom terms must be dictated rather than negotiated and must not be such as would reflect on us and on the Persian Government. Those suggested seemed to be too light, and Sir Percy Cox recommended that we should be in no hurry to initiate negotiations with Saulat and should be prepared, if necessary, to keep our troops on the Bushire–Shiraz line until early spring, when the general situation should have cleared and we should be in a better position to decide on the best solution of the Saulet question.

Dasht-i-Arjan had been occupied, without opposition, by a detachment of the 16th Rajputs on the 3rd January; and next day General Douglas telegraphed to Colonel Orton that, as he anticipated no difficulty in the occupation of Kazerun by the troops of the Bushire force, the only co-operation he was likely to require from the Shiraz column was the despatch of a detachment to Miyan Kutal, to open up communication with Kazerun as soon as it had been occupied. *Occupation of Kazerun and opening up of through communication; January 1919.*

By the 25th January progress in road improvement and in the collection of the necessary transport permitted an advance to Kazerun; and this was carried out without opposition by General Elsmie's troops on the 27th. Nasir Diwan had left Kazerun some days previously with a small following for a village about twenty miles to the south-east, but fled from there

into the hills on being attacked on the 27th by aeroplanes.*
That day also a detachment from the Shiraz troops† at Dasht-i-Arjan occupied Miyan Kutal without opposition, after a very trying march over the Pir Zan pass in a snow storm. On the 28th communication was established between Miyan Kutal and Kazerun.

With the reopening of the Bushire–Shiraz road the main object of the military operations had been attained. The authorities in England and India were anxious to withdraw the British troops as soon as the situation permitted. But, as Sir Percy Cox pointed out, it was only their presence and backing that enabled the Persian authorities to maintain order, a condition which it was most desirable for the time being to uphold so as to strengthen the position of the friendly Persian Cabinet, which was doing good work. On the 22nd January the Government of India pressed for an early decision, as, if troops were to remain on the road during the hot weather, the question of their accommodation must be taken in hand at once; and on the 23rd General Douglas also asked for instructions as to his future procedure. The lack of a Persian force to maintain order necessitated, he said, an early solution of the Saulat question and he asked on what lines he was to negotiate. He explained the great difficulty of crushing Saulat by military measures and expressed the opinion that, if a stiffening of terms caused a breakdown in negotiations, we must be prepared, either to face fresh outbreaks of disorder with which the South Persia Rifles would be unable to cope, or to keep our troops in the country for an indefinite period.

Bushire Field Force; February–March 1919. On the 7th February, Lord Curzon, telegraphing to Sir Percy Cox that H.M. Government would like to commence the withdrawal of troops and to carry it out gradually before the hot weather, asked for his views and those of Mr. Hotson on various points connected with the solution of the problem. This gave rise to a telegraphic discussion between London, India and Persia which continued for several weeks.

At the beginning of March Mr. Bill had an interview with Saulat, at which, after pleading that his action had been authorised by Persian Ministers and *mullahs*, he asked leave to submit at Tehran to his Government, subject to the proviso that his life should be spared and that his estates should be secured to his son.

---

* He finally took " *bast* " at Shiraz in April.
† A part of the 16th Rajputs under Lieut.-Col. Vanrenen.

On the 7th March the Government of India telegraphed to the India Office that General Douglas proposed a settlement on the following lines : acceptance of Saulat's offer to submit at Tehran under guarantee of life and property ; the reduction, as soon as Saulat left for Tehran, of the British force to two squadrons of cavalry, a mountain battery, three infantry battalions and a flight of aeroplanes ; and the issue of a proclamation that these troops would also withdraw as soon as the rebel Khans surrendered unconditionally. As these terms seemed to them unlikely to afford us an escape from an expensive entanglement, the Government of India did not approve of them and recommended that we should " cut our losses " and lay down a definite date for the withdrawal of our forces.*
This would, they considered, force the local authorities to devise a policy which would stand on its merits without an indefinite backing of military force and which would probably centre round a thorough-going settlement with Saulat as the one possible Il-Khani of the Qashqais. They pointed out that we were not in a position to crush Saulat and that, as all parties to the contest were anxious for peace, it would have to be made with " face-saving " all round. They suggested that Saulat should be made to submit to Farman Farma, who was reported to be nervous of any settlement with Saulat and especially of his being allowed scope to intrigue at Tehran† ; and that Farman Farma, who was the man who would have to see the arrangements through, should be left to settle matters, in his own Persian way, with Saulat.

Sir Percy Cox, however, considering that there were strong objections to this complete reversal of our attitude towards Saulat, supported strongly the proposals made by General Douglas. Sir P. Cox explained that he had hitherto hoped that the result of our military operations and the development of the general political situation would have rendered it possible for our troops to withdraw before the hot weather, and he did not even now contemplate their retention beyond the end of that period. But until Farman Farma's arrangements were in working order, the conclusion of the Peace Conference and the effective inauguration of our future policy in regard to Persia, he considered that the proportion of the force recommended by General Douglas should remain. For, having due regard to

---

* They recommended that the bulk of the force should be withdrawn at once and the remainder by the 1st May.

† It seems possible, they said, that these feelings arose from a guilty conscience, as there was good reason to believe Farman Farma to have been directly or indirectly concerned in Saulat's original defection.

our interests in Fars and to the larger question of future British interests in Persia, he did not think that a complete evacuation was immediately possible. It was most important, he continued, that Saulat should be kept out of Fars for at least six months and, as there was no guarantee that Farman Farma would remain in Fars, it was inadvisable to give him a free hand to make his own terms with Saulat. These terms should be settled in consultation with us and the Persian Government.

On the 21st March the India Office informed the Government of India that, pending the final decision of H.M. Government, the withdrawal of troops, within the limits proposed by General Douglas, might be proceeded with at once. Instructions to that effect were accordingly issued from India to General Douglas on the 28th March and were carried into effect during the next six weeks.

After the occupation of Kazerun, orders had been issued for General Douglas to take command, as opportunity offered, of all the Indian troops in Fars and to assume responsibility for the maintenance and protection of the whole of the Bushire–Shiraz road. The South Persia Rifles would remain as a separate command under Colonel Orton. For administrative reasons, General Douglas did not assume entire control till the 10th March, and in April most of the Indian troops which had been with Sir Percy Sykes in Fars were withdrawn to India.

By the end of March, thanks to the work carried out entirely by the troops of the Bushire force, the former difficult mule track between Bushire and the summit of the Pir Zan pass had been replaced by a good road, nowhere less than ten feet wide; the motor road from Shiraz to Dasht-i-Arjan, made by the South Persia Rifles in 1917, had been recently extended by them to the top of the same pass; and at the beginning of April a Ford van was able to go from Kazerun to Shiraz in a little over seven hours. By this time camel caravans were moving regularly between Bushire and Shiraz.

Bushire situation; April 1919. The situation in the middle of April was summed up by Mr. Bill in the concluding paragraph of his report on the political aspect of the operations as follows:—

" Thus, with the close of the active phase of the operations, the situation resolves itself politically into a matter of securing the road from raids by insisting on village responsibility for giving warning of, and resisting, robber gangs; of securing the present state of things by holding the principal centres, Shiraz, Kazerun and Bushire, with regular troops and gradually, in close communication with the Persian authorities, creating a position for our nominees all along the road which may be reasonably expected to survive the complete evacuation of the province by British troops. It must not, however, be supposed that Southern Persia, any more than any other country, will ever remain orderly without organised force to coerce it. The Fars Brigade of the South Persia Rifles are now recruiting to complete their strength and should, unhampered for the first time in their history by foreign intrigue and Persian opposition at headquarters, develop into a really useful force; while the village *tufangchis*, enlisted mainly as a means of justifying the punishment of a village for offences committed within its limits, should suffice to deal with petty gangs of marauders. The position will, however, be immensely simplified if it is found possible to maintain a small detachment of the Air Force in the country. In any case, the people of Fars have had a very wholesome and mush needed lesson; any legend which may have existed that Indian troops could not fight has been finally disproved; the conceit of their own power and importance with which the hostile chiefs were filled has been dispelled; and last, but by no means least, the presence of our troops in the country has resulted in a general movement of goods and reduction of prices, which has brought home the solid advantages of peace to every household in the land. The same lesson had been driven home by their first sight of a disciplined force, enormous according to Persian ideas, whose presence is a benefit to the country instead of a disaster to all in its neighbourhood, and by the revolution effected in the conditions of commercial transport by the construction of a good graded road."

Wassmuss and Oertel, who had left Fars in disguise, were apprehended at Qum at the end of March by Persian gendarmerie and, being handed over to us, were sent back to Germany via Baku. The discussion over the terms to be made with Saulat continued until, early in May, he of his own accord surrendered to the Persian Government.

Throughout the period under review in this chapter the situation in Kerman remained satisfactory. On the 19th December 1918, the Government of India, reporting to the India Office that 230 of the 322 miles of the Bandar Abbas–Kerman road had been made passable by motors at a cost of about 16 lakhs of rupees, recommended its completion to a light-motor traffic standard. This, it was estimated, could be

Kerman; November 1918– March 1919.

practically finished by the end of the cold weather at a further cost of about 20 lakhs. But in February 1919, owing to the urgent necessity for financial economy, orders were issued from India to stop all further work.

Policy; November 1918. Though the downfall of Germany and Turkey and the suspension of government in Russia had the effect of enhancing Persian respect for Great Britain, the Persian Government considered it advisable to try to gain the active sympathy and support of some of the other Great Powers. At the time of the Armistice we learnt that, at the end of October, the Persian Government had instructed their Minister at Washington to invoke the assistance of the United States Government in obtaining the evacuation of Persian territory by foreign troops, Persian representation at the Peace Conference, the preservation of Persian independence and the cancellation of treaties bearing no relation to existing Persian needs. Further, on the 14th November, Sir Percy Cox reported that the Persian Prime Minister said that Persian public opinion would not accept a British financial adviser instead of the American or Frenchman proposed.

In another telegram of the same date Sir Percy Cox, influenced by the coming Peace Conference and the unparalleled importance of the juncture in the world's history, ventilated ideas which he admitted might appear visionary. He understood that, while H.M. Government and especially the Government of India desired to avoid large commitments in Persia, the guiding principle of our future policy was to be the permanent maintenance of British influence there. This principle, however, could, he said, only be made good in a country where chaos reigned supreme by constructive means. The members of the recently arrived American Relief Commission, who had assured him that their Government had no intention of political or financial intervention in Persia, had spontaneously asked him why Great Britain, who had done such splendid work in Mesopotamia, could not do the same for Persia; as if left to her own devices, she would go from bad to worse. Great Britain was, they said, the obvious and only instrument capable of making a good job of it. These remarks had suggested to him the following thoughts. Persian public opinion, though realising the danger and detriment attending hostility to us, was by no means prepared to contemplate a future under our tutelage. But, though not knowing what they wanted nor what was best for their future, most Persians favoured international assistance. Sir Percy Cox then went on to ask if it would not be possible to discuss frankly with America the necessity for reforms in Persia and the desirability of an international mandate to us to carry them out. It would, he said, seem quite logical for the Peace Conference or the subsequent League of Nations to inform Persia that, as the last ten years had demonstrated her inability to govern herself and had resulted in a perpetual state of chaos and famine with a danger of Bolshevism, it was necessary in the interests of humanity and civilisation for some competent Power to take her in hand. In conclusion, Sir Percy Cox pointed out that Persian interests demanded that she should start the creation of a force and reform her administration before our troops, war subsidy and special arrangements were withdrawn. Otherwise, most of her provinces would be left in a state of complete disorder, which she would have neither the money nor the force to cope with.

On the 19th November, the Foreign Office informed Sir Percy Cox that, as Great Britain was providing the money to maintain the Persian administration, it was not too much to suggest that if they considered a foreign financial adviser necessary he must be a British subject. In reply on the 21st Sir Percy Cox said that, with the Persian mind full of the Peace Conference and of what Persia hoped to obtain from it, any attempt on his part to secure the appointment of a British financial adviser was doomed to failure. He, therefore, proposed to shelve the question for a few weeks, till Persians were better able to gauge their real position and to advise a suitable permanent policy.

The Eastern Committee in London discussed on the 21st November a number of recent telegrams regarding Persia's wish to be represented at the Peace Conference. Her motives were not clear, but it seemed likely that she desired to raise the whole question of her independence, especially regarding the Persian Gulf, and that, after obtaining admission under the *ægis* of Great Britain, she might endeavour to play off the various nations against one another. It would, it was felt, be preferable if Persian matters were not raised at the Conference at all, but as her admission did not rest with us, we must be prepared to meet her there.

The need for a public announcement in Persia of the assurances regarding British intentions, which the Foreign Office had agreed to on the 31st October, had, in the meantime, lost its urgency ; and the letter notifying these to the Persian Government was only issued, after some discussion over the precise terms of the

Policy; draft, on the 23rd November. At the same time an understanding was recorded, by an exchange of confidential notes, that we should be consulted before any change was made in the Governorship of Fars and that the services of an adequate number of British officers would be retained with the South Persia Rifles when handed over, till the Persian Government arranged to establish a permanent force.

Policy; November 1918.

The Government of India, on the 26th November, expressed their emphatic dissent from the solution of the Persian problem which Sir Percy Cox had suggested on the 14th. A mandate to us by the Peace Conference, unless coupled with a mandate from Persia herself, would in their opinion be a flagrant breach of our repeated guarantees of Persian integrity. To be successful, it would require an extended military domination involving an unwarranted drain on Indian resources. Its cost would be prohibitive, unjustifiable as far as Indian interests were concerned, and would provoke strong Indian protests. It would be difficult, if not impossible, to provide the requisite civil staff, while the expedient would not only render our eventual withdrawal the more impossible, but would further emasculate Persia and involve far-reaching consequences. In any case, at a time when our responsibilities—and consequent financial and military obligations—showed signs of increase in many different quarters in Asia, the Government of India would have felt bound to oppose the proposals even if they did not dissent from them on general grounds. Their view was that we should maintain out influence by regaining Persian confidence through a liberal policy and the removal of causes of irritation ; that we should continue to give Persia some assistance in arms and money ; that a British, American or other financial adviser should be provided ; and that for the rest we should give Persia the real chance of putting her house in order and of administering her provinces herself, which she had not had since Russian domination commenced. The Persian Prime Minister seemed anxious to make a start and the Governors-General of Khurasan, Kerman and Fars appeared competent, if helped and not hampered, to establish reasonable order. In this distressful country, concluded the telegram, we must not expect counsels of perfection.

In referring to this telegram next day, Sir Percy Cox said that the views expressed by the Government of India were those he had held himself on his arrival at Tehran two months previously and that, as a last resort, he still held them. The whole face of the situation had, however, been changed by our victories and by the alarming spread of Bolshevism and of revolutionary ideas. Though agreeing that his suggestions were a counsel of perfection, he queried whether they were not justified by existing portents. He felt convinced that, whether it suited us or not, the Powers assembling, literally to reconstruct the world and see justice established, would interest themselves collectively in Persia, where the condition of the peasantry was deplorable owing to the inveterate extortion, corruption and injustice on the part of the ruling classes from the Shah downwards and to famine due to dearth of communications. If our troops and our financial help—the only safeguards against active disorder and bankruptcy—were withdrawn on the signing of peace, Northern Persia must become a prey to complete chaos if not violent revolution. We could not, in our own interests, contemplate such a disquieting neighbour. Except for a few ignorant demagogues, all Persians now seemed to realise that without foreign personnel and foreign money Persia could not right herself. The extremists, disappointed in their hopes of substituting an anti-British element in America for Germany, wished to employ as few Europeans as possible and those of different nationalities; the moderates would welcome disinterested American advisers and financial assistance; and a considerable proportion, recognising that a very wide measure of foreign control would be necessary, realised that, to avoid friction and rivalry, the task must be entrusted to a single Power enjoying the good will and support of Great Britain. Sir Percy Cox was convinced that if the assembled Powers decided to grasp the problem, the only completely satisfactory solution would be to have a trained administrator in control of every provincial government and of every department of state for a specified term of years, during which Persians would be associated with them and trained to take their place. It was certain that articulate Persian public opinion would not accept spontaneously such a measure of control. But if it was imposed by the assembled Powers for a specific period with adequate safeguards against unscrupulous exploitation and with full guarantees of independence and integrity, he believed that Persia would resign herself to it. As a European administration must have a backing of force, the presence of our troops and existing circumstances indicated that we were the Power to undertake the mandate. But if we decided against acceptance, it could only be carried through successfully by a nation having our diplomatic and military support, who would recognise our predominant interests.

Sir Percy Cox then went on to say that, for the amelioration of conditions, the first essential was improvement of communications by the construction of motor roads and railways and he advocated an early completion of the Baghdad–Tehran line.

Policy; December 1918. During December the Shah's interference with the appointment by the Cabinet of the delegates to the Peace Conference and of other officials led to considerable friction. The Shah himself, leading a secluded life, guided in his actions by the intrigues of an undesirable following and afraid of a revolution, appears to have been generally regarded at this time by his subjects with contempt and resentment. Therefore, in the event of an acute rupture involving the resignation of the Cabinet, the latter would have most of the public sympathy. The Shah refused to allow Vossuk to go at the head of the delegation to the Peace Conference and insisted, instead, on the appointment of Mushaver-ul-Mamalik, the Foreign Minister, who was trusted neither by the Cabinet nor by the Allies.

On the 19th December, at a Meeting at which the Government of India were represented by their Foreign Secretary* as well as by the Secretary of State for India and at which Sir Charles Marling was also present, the Eastern Committee in London discussed the Persian question. In an opening statement the Chairman†, who alluded to the problem as one of the most puzzling and discouraging with which we had had to deal, described how the existing unsatisfactory and precarious situation had come about, and how our interests had been so magnified by the events of the war that it was impossible for us to leave Persia altogether alone. Though both we and France regarded the matters which Persia desired to raise as quite outside the scope of the Peace Conference, we might have to meet her there. As regards a mandate, neither France nor America were likely to accept it; no small neutral state would be able to do the work efficiently; a joint mandate would be a perilous experiment; and although we had no desire to do so we were naturally and inevitably the country who would be called upon to accept a mandate. We were not popular in Persia, but Lord Curzon said that he had been told by Nasir-ul-Mulk—the late Regent of Persia, who was resident in England and a personal friend of Lord Curzon's—that he advocated British assistance to bring about Persian regeneration. Further, that in reply to a question he had said that what the Persians really desired was that our

---

* Sir Hamilton Grant.
† Lord Curzon.

troops should remain so as to save the country from absolute ruin; that they would prefer any foreign neutral officers to British for their permanent force; and that they wanted a share in the control of the Holy Places in Mesopotamia.

In the ensuing discussion in the Committee it was recognised that, since the establishment of a constitution in Persia, no real leaders had arisen; that no Government had succeeded in restoring the authority which the Shah had previously wielded; that there was still no apparent possibility of an efficient government being formed, largely owing to the corruption and avarice prevailing everywhere; that if we left, there would be chaos; and that one or other of Persia's neighbours would inevitably take advantage of it. There was general unanimity, however, that if we were called upon to assume a mandate we should say that we were most reluctant to do so. But, when the meeting adjourned, no agreement had been come to regarding the alternative action we should take.

The discussion was resumed on the 30th December, when it was decided that we could not leave Persia alone to go to ruin and that, as the question of a mandate might not arise for months if at all, we should in the meantime discuss with the Persian Government and Persian delegates a future settlement, based on our readiness to meet them on the following points: a renewal of our definite assurances of Persian integrity and independence; the abrogation in a suitable manner of the Anglo-Russian Convention of 1907; our support and assistance in the establishment of a regular national Persian force, whose first commander must be British* though his assistants might belong to other nations; continued financial assistance, with at any rate a British chief financial adviser; and the withdrawal of British troops as soon as Persia was secure, from invasion in the north and from disorder in the south. In carrying out the negotiations we should be friendly and conciliatory, but firm.

The Eastern Committee was dissolved on the 7th January, but on the 11th Lord Curzon acquainted Sir Percy Cox, for his own guidance, with this decision and told him to defer action on it for the time being. This telegram practically crossed two† sent by Sir Percy Cox on the 13th, in which he said that the Persian Cabinet, strengthened by our support, were anxious to proceed with the measures of constructive reform desired by the public, who had generally come to realise how much they

Policy; January 1919.

---

* On this point the Government of India representatives disagreed.
† i.e., they had been drafted but not despatched and Sir Percy decided to send them on.

Policy;
January
1919.

must depend on us for the future. Vossuk and two other Ministers had told him that, as they had arrived at the conviction that we were the only nation who could successfully work her reform, the only sound course was for Persia to place herself in our hands, provided we were prepared to help her more seriously and constructively than in the past. If we agreed and came to a satisfactory understanding with them, they considered themselves strong enough to carry it through. They were anxious, however, that the negotiations should be proceeded with as promptly as possible, as they were apprehensive lest their delegates to the Peace Conference, who had already left for Paris, should mar matters by their intervention.

The Shah's obstructive action was making the position of the Cabinet insupportable; but on the 15th January Sir Percy Cox telegraphed that his warning to the Shah, that our financial and moral support would be withdrawn and our sympathy alienated if he did not stop his persistent intrigues against the Cabinet,* had produced the desired effect. In addition to informing Princes and Democrats, whose intrigues he had been encouraging, that their activities must cease, the Shah had openly announced his hearty support of the Cabinet. Also Starosselski, who had been an important factor in these intrigues, had, said Sir Percy Cox, lost his importance by the announcement that the subsidy we were providing for the Persian Cossack Division would in future be paid through the Cabinet instead of direct to him. Further, Salar-ud-Daula, who had recently re-entered the country to stir up rebellion, had been captured by our troops. Consequently the Cabinet were greatly beholden to us and found themselves in a much stronger position. The moment seemed to Sir Percy Cox to be favourable for initiating negotiations on the lines laid down, though in regard to a creation of a permanent force and of a financial department he considered that more comprehensive proposals were possible. He was accordingly authorised by Lord Curzon on the 23rd January to proceed with the preliminary discussions.

On the 27th January the Government of India telegraphed deprecating as comprehensive a programme of reform as Sir Percy Cox suggested, as they did not believe that it would be accepted by the successors of the existing Persian Cabinet on the grounds that we were aiming at a protectorate. For instance, rigid insistence by us on British officers for the permanent force seemed undesirable.

---

* This action had been approved by H.M. Government.

One of the difficulties foreseen—and proved to some extent to be correct—in carrying out the negotiations which then commenced was the danger that the Persian delegates to the Peace Conference would submit proposals or ask for decisions which were inconsistent with those we were ourselves discussing with the Persian Government. These delegates, on their arrival in Paris, issued a statement of the Persian case, but as the Peace Conference, realising that parts of this statement were obviously no concern of theirs, showed no inclination to admit them, the Persian representatives gradually realised that they must have recourse to Great Britain.

For some weeks the negotiations at Tehran were interrupted by the request of the Shah to H.M. Government to afford him facilities and assistance for an immediate visit to Europe, his apparent object being to secure there his personal savings estimated at about a million. To objections that he ought not to leave his country at such a vital juncture, the Shah replied that, while he personally agreed that Great Britain was the only Power Persia could rely on to give her much help and was consequently entitled in return to expect privileges, he could not as a constitutional monarch give formal consent to an agreement with Great Britain without the support of the *Majlis* or the general approval of his people. Neither of these could be expected, he said, till the Peace Conference was concluded. He suggested, however, that in the meantime the Persian Cabinet should cultivate public opinion in the desired direction and that he himself, when he reached Paris, should telegraph to the Cabinet after he had seen the British representative that, as the other Powers were not strongly interested, Persia's best policy was to rely on Great Britain. In an interview which he gave Sir Percy Cox the Shah undertook that, during his absence, he would make no change in the Cabinet or in his own views. Vossuk believed the Shah to be sincere, and Sir Percy Cox accordingly recommended that H.M. Government should grant his request. Lord Curzon, however, deprecated the suggestion as, apart from the great danger of intrigues, the abnormal conditions still prevailing along the route of travel rendered the physical difficulties of the proposed journey considerable. The Shah, however, persisted and showed himself to be so ready to meet the views of H.M. Government that both Vossuk and Sir Percy Cox continued to press the question, if only on the grounds of expediency. H.M. Government finally agreed, but then the Shah suddenly decided that he would not go, for the time being at any rate.

It also became necessary, at this period, to support the Persian Cabinet by disabusing the Jangalis of the idea that they could exploit their agreement of August 1918 with General Dunsterville to further their intrigues for obtaining independence. A British military occupation of Resht combined with other action had the desired effect, though it did not entirely crush the Jangali revolt.

Policy; April 1919. On the 9th April Sir Percy Cox telegraphed the draft terms of an agreement which the Persian Cabinet, with the approval of the Shah, were prepared to accept and which may be briefly summarised as follows : (1) a categorical reiteration of Great Britain's undertaking to respect Persian independence and integrity; (2) Great Britain to supply expert advisers for the several departments of the Persian administration, to be engaged on contracts and endowed with adequate powers by the Persian Government ; (3) Great Britain to supply the officers, munitions and equipment adjudged necessary by a joint Anglo-Persian Military Commission for the uniform force which Persia proposed to create ; (4) Great Britain in consultation with the Persian Government to arrange for a British loan to finance the reforms indicated in (2) and (3) above ; (5) Mutual co-operation by the two countries for the encouragement of Anglo-Persian enterprise in the improvement of communications in Persia ; (6) Great Britain to agree in principal to an examination of existing treaties with a view to their revision ; (7) Both governments to agree to the appointment forthwith of a Joint Anglo-Persian Committee of experts to examine and revise the customs tariff, and (8) Great Britain to support the admission of Persia into the League of Nations. In a subsidiary agreement, (*a*) it was to be mutually agreed that neither of the two Governments would make any claims against the other for war losses, while Great Britain was to agree to undertake to support Persian claims against other belligerents, and (*b*) Great Britain was to agree to endeavour to assist Persia to obtain such rectification of her frontiers as seemed just or expedient. The Shah, in return for his co-operation, asked for assurances of personal support to himself and his dynasty and for a personal subsidy for life, while the three members of the Persian Cabinet, who had carried out the negotiations, asked, in addition to personal guarantees for themselves, for a large sum of Secret Service money with which to win over the remainder of the Cabinet, newspapers, members of *Majlis*, etc. The Cabinet hoped by their efforts to bring about the assembly in the autumn of a friendly *Majlis*, who would accept the position.

On the 17th April Lord Curzon telegraphed to Sir Percy Cox, accepting generally, with a few reservations, the proposed agreement and expressing his appreciation of the manner in which Sir Percy had conducted the negotiations. The Government of India, however, on the 24th, while expressing their admiration of Sir Percy's skill, regretted that, as their views were still the same as those they had expressed on January 27th, they regarded the proposed agreement with considerable misgivings. For they doubted if the three members of the Persian Cabinet, who had conducted the negotiations, were true representatives of Persian opinion. The Government of India continued that it would be their duty to resist strenuously any extension of India's financial commitments. They considered that the scheme would not only dissolve our chances of ever being able to withdraw from Persia, but would increase enormously the likelihood of our having to use force, based on India, against a wave of Persian nationalism. Further, the anti-British feeling then prevalent in the Moslem world rendered it, in their opinion, a highly dangerous time for initiating so hazardous an experiment.

We are not concerned here with the subsequent course of the negotiations. But it may be noted that on the 9th August, 1919, an Agreement on the lines of the draft above-mentioned was signed—on behalf of H.M. Government by Sir Percy Cox and on behalf of Persia by the Prime Minister (Vossuk-ud-Daula) and the two members of his Cabinet who had participated in the negotiations. Almost immediately after its signature the Shah proceeded on his long-planned visit to Europe, and while in England made more than one public reference to the Agreement in appreciative terms. Unfortunately, circumstances combined to make its life a short and chequered one. Thus, the British troops on the Baghdad–Kazvin line, whose presence had been a great source of strength, were withdrawn ; Sir Percy Cox was transferred in June 1920 to Iraq as High Commissioner ; Vossuk's Cabinet fell and was replaced by one less Anglophile and containing Ministers who had espoused the German cause during the war ; and the new Cabinet decided to hold the Agreement in suspense pending submission to an assembled *Majlis* (there being none in session at the time). In suspense it remained until finally repudiated by the Government which ensued on the *coup d'état* of Riza Khan in February 1921.

APPENDIX I.

VIEWS OF FIELD-MARSHAL VON DER GOLTZ ON THE SITUATION IN PERSIA, AS STATED IN A MEMORANDUM DATED 16TH FEBRUARY, 1916, ADDRESSED TO CONSTANTINOPLE AND TO GREAT GENERAL HEADQUARTERS AT BERLIN.*

In Persia the situation is one of anarchy. It is therefore surprising that certain branches of the administration, such as the posts and telegraphs and the gendarmerie, are still in good order. For there is little trace of any real government. The impression prevailing in Europe of a nation strongly antagonistic to Russia and England is incorrect. The prevailing disorder has led to the disruption of the country and to the appropriation of governing powers by a number of local leaders, rendering united action very difficult. The numerous tribes dwelling in Persia, under their great feudal leaders, lead an independent life, each tribe having to be handled separately and at heart wishing to make itself as independent as possible. Since the best means to that end is money, they all expect, in return for their readiness to assist in rescuing the fatherland, a very high price—such as indeed they have already demanded and obtained. The whole Perso-Arab world is material-minded. Everything that the European touches becomes unclean, according to the tenets of the strictly religious Persian; but not so the gold that he lets slip through his fingers. Wholly absurd sums of money have been sacrificed in this way.

It is sufficient to cite the case of how Nizam-es-Sultaneh—regarded at the moment as the forthcoming national leader—was promised by treaty with our former military attaché, Count Kanitz, in addition to many other advantages such as the maintenance of his tribal cavalry at a cost of 350,000 marks, a personal monthly allowance of 80,000 marks, or nearly 1,000,000 gold marks per annum!

Persian patriotism has become an industry which seems to look for its gains to extortion. Thus our officers working in Persia, half leaders though they be, have also become half hostages. Examples are infectious. So Nizam's westerly neighbour on the Turkish frontier, the Vali of Pusht-i-Kuh, now demands 60,000 marks monthly; and Nizam himself advises us to at least negotiate with him, because he is in a position to cut the line of communications of the Germans with Turkey. The tribes along the line of communications from Kermanshah to Baghdad are likewise subsidised in order to guarantee its security; though they would certainly fail us if the flow of gold to them were to cease.

What we get for this extraordinarily high expenditure is practically very little. The traveller of importance is accompanied by a brisk horseman of good appearance, surrounded by a swarm of avaricious servants; but serious assistance in a fight is wanting. Only for their own selfish ends are the tribal warriors wont to fight well. There are very few exceptions to this. The Persian Nationalists now gathered in Kermanshah are extremely vain and secretive, and one cannot get out of them what their next intentions are. Quite openly they too, with every demand, indicate that they could get better prices from the English and Russians.

The reliable fighting strength on which Colonel Bopp can count is, in these circumstances, still very small. It is limited to the weak Turkish supporting-detachment, which does its duty bravely, and the Swedish-officered gendarmes —altogether about 2,000 men, with a few guns and machine guns. Beyond these, there are in existence a few local militia companies and then several thousand tribal horsemen, who however must be looked upon more as followers of their chiefs than as troops.

---

* "Mit Feldmarschall von der Goltz Pascha in Mesopotamien und Persien," by Lieut.-Colonel Hans von Kiesling, pp. 149–152.

APPENDIX I.

Our interests have been seriously damaged by the non-arrival of arms and munitions, promised by us prematurely and liberally to the Persians. These munitions are a long time on their way, because the line over the Taurus and Amanus is blocked by transport urgently required for the Suez Canal expedition and for the retreating Turkish Third Army. Only just now have the first consignments from Germany started onward from Aleppo. The difficulties to be surmounted and the length of time necessary in order to traverse the line of communications—2,500 kilometres long—from Constantinople to Kermanshah have been insufficiently taken into account.

The incessant queries of the Persians as to the promised arms have still to be answered in temporising fashion. The Persians reproach the German officers for not keeping their word, without understanding the causes. The present condition of affairs cannot be altered until we dispose of greater military strength, i.e., in regular troops. As soon as I can manage it, I will send Colonel Bopp an additional Turkish infantry regiment with a battery of artillery. Besides this, a frontier battalion has already been pushed forward from Khaniqin to Karind, in order to form there a base depot.

As soon as arms arrive, the formation of a training camp is to be begun at the frontier town of Qasr-i-Shirin. Perhaps the arrival of Duke Adolph of Mecklenburg with his equipment will facilitate this. Could we afford the necessary infantry, he would have in hand a first mixed Persian division. To make this possible we must at the least maintain our present position. I hope to do so, but naturally cannot foretell this with certainty.

I am not pessimistic, but am only giving a true and faithful picture of the actual situation. In a telegram received here to-day, Colonel Bopp describes our Persian enterprises as already shattered. It remains to be seen whether he is right. If he has to retire from Kermanshah, I will try to check his retreat at Qasr-i-Shirin on the Turkish frontier and attempt to make it possible for him to maintain himself there. He may then, with the remnant of those loyal to him, be able to protect the projected training camp, from which later on a conquest of Persia would have to begin.

The present situation in both the eastern theatres of war is due to the excessive former massing of troops at the Dardanelles, at the expense of which the other armies have been weakened and neglected.

As events at Erzerum* show, it was no longer possible to prevent the mischief engendered thereby elsewhere. Whether we shall still succeed here appears to be questionable. In any case we are still far distant from the time when we can start an administration in South and West Persia after the pattern of that instituted by us in Poland, such as they contemplate in Constantinople. Gentlemen in Constantinople would do well to come here so as to see things as they are.

---

* The Russians captured Erzerum on 15th February 1916.

APPENDIX II.

BRITISH TROOPS IN PERSIA; 31ST DECEMBER, 1916.

The British troops in Persia (excluding those in Arabistan under the command of the Mesopotamia Force), the Persian Gulf and on the shores of the Gulf of Oman were as follows:—

Bushire (Brig.-General J. A. Douglas (a)).

(a) Under the control of General Maude, commanding the Mesopotamia Force.
- One squadron, 15th Lancers.
- 14th Sikhs.
- 22nd Punjabis.
- Four captured Turkish guns.
- One 7-pr. Mountain gun.
- Four naval 12-pr. guns.
- Searchlight detachment.
- No. 51 Indian Stationary Hospital.

Muscat.

(b) Under the control of the C-in-C. in India.
- Headquarters, O.C. troops, Gulf of Oman.(b)
- 108th Infantry (less about one hundred rifles detached on duty in the Bandar Abbas–Kerman area).
- *Distributed between Jask, Chagbar, Bandar Abbas, Henjam, Kishm Island, Lingeh and Bahrein.*
- Half-battalion, 83rd Infantry.

Shiraz (Brig.-General Sir P. Sykes (c)).

(c) Controlled for administration by C-in-C. India; but taking his orders for policy and operations from the British Minister at Tehran.
- One squadron, 15th Lancers.
- One section, 23rd Mountain Battery.
- 1/124th Baluchistan Infantry (less half-battalion).
- One section, Indian field ambulance.

Kerman–Saidabad area (Major G. L. Farran, under Sir P. Sykes).
- About one hundred drafts for Sir P. Sykes's column at Shiraz.
- About one hundred rifles, 108th Infantry (from Muscat).

Seistan Force (Brig.-Gen. C. O. O. Tanner (d)).

(d) Controlled by the C-in-C. in India.
- 28th Light Cavalry.
- One section, 25th Mountain Battery.
- Nine rifles, Sappers and Miners.
- 19th Punjabis.
- One hundred and fifty rifles, 106th Hazara Pioneers.
- Two pack wireless stations.
- There were also about 1,100 locally-raised levies.

Makran Mission Escort (Captain C. H. Harvey-Kelly (e)).

(e) Controlled by the C-in-C. in India.
- In Persian Baluchistan, en route to Chahbar.
- Fifty rifles, 1/7th Gurkhas.
- One company, 127th Baluchis.
- One section, No. 118 Indian field ambulance.
- One troop, Mule Corps.

APPENDIX III.

DISTRIBUTION AND STRENGTH OF THE TROOPS WITH THE SYKES MISSION. 30TH APRIL, 1918.

INDIAN ARMY.

Shiraz	Mission Headquarters.
	Section, 23rd Mountain Battery.
	Headquarters and two companies, 16th Rajputs.
	One squadron, Burma Mounted Infantry.
	Portions of 108th and 162nd Indian Field Ambulances and of 21st Mule Corps.
	Supply and Transport details.
Escorts and Outposts ..	One company 16th Rajputs (approximate).
Abadeh	One company 16th Rajputs.
En route to Shiraz from Saidabad.	One squadron 15th Lancers.
	Half-battalion 3/124th Baluchis.
En route to Shiraz from Bandar Abbas.	Two sections 33rd Mountain Battery.
	Headquarters and half-battalion 3/124th Baluchis.
	Draft for Burma Mounted Infantry.
	Two sections 161st Indian Field Ambulance.
	101st Brigade Supply Section.
Saidabad	Portion of 162nd Indian Field Ambulance.
	Supply and Transport details.
En route to Saidabad from Bandar Abbas.	Half-battalion 120th Infantry.
Bandar Abbas ..	23rd Sanitary Section.
	Base Hospital.
	" D " Company, Basra Camel Corps.
	Part of 10th Camel Corps.
	Jat Bullock Corps.
	100th and 101st Labour Corps.

Total strength, excluding Mission Headquarters, was :—
60 British officers.
13 British other ranks.
74 Indian officers.
10 Indian sub.-asst. surgeons.
3,187 Indian other ranks.
2,753 Indian followers.
69 Persian followers.

SOUTH PERSIA RIFLES.

		Officers.			Other ranks.		
		British.	Indian.	Persian.	British.	Indian.	Persian.
SHIRAZ	Inspector-General's Headquarters	11	1	6	14	62	90
	Fars Brigade:—						
	Headquarters	8	—	4	5	2	110
	2nd Cavalry	2	—	12	7	—	282
	1st Machine Gun Squadron	1	—	4	3	—	103
	1st Battery Artillery	1	—	4	4	1	157
	1st Coy. Engineers	—	1	2	—	—	101
	4th Infantry	2	—	15	4	—	485
	5th Infantry	4	—	10	2	4	366
	Signalling School	1	—	—	4	—	13
	Band	—	—	2	1	—	61
	Field Ambulance	6	—	12	1	2	123
	Veterinary Hospital	—	—	1	2	—	30
	1st Mule Corps	1	—	1	1	—	287
	Wagon Establishment	—	—	—	—	—	47
	Ordnance Depot	—	1	4	2	4	8
	Miscellaneous	—	—	—	—	—	61
ABADEH	3rd Cavalry	3	—	13	3	—	277
	3rd Infantry	2	—	13	3	—	405
	Miscellaneous	—	—	—	—	—	3
DEHBID	2nd Cavalry	—	—	1	1	—	27
	5th Infantry	—	—	1	1	—	52
NIRIZ	2nd Cavalry	—	—	—	—	—	4
SAIDABAD	4th Infantry	1	1	1	1	—	111
	1st Artillery Battery	—	—	2	1	—	94
QAWAMABAD	2nd Cavalry	1	—	4	2	—	88
KHAN-I-ZINIAN	5th Infantry	1	—	5	1	—	168
On escort and detachment duties	From above units	1	—	3	1	2	130
	Total Fars Brigade	35	3	114	50	15	3,583

APPENDIX III.

SOUTH PERSIA RIFLES.

		Officers.			Other ranks.		
		British.	Indian.	Persian.	British.	Indian.	Persian.
KERMAN	*Kerman Brigade :—*						
	Headquarters	5	1	6	5	4	14
	Headquarters Troop	—	—	1	—	—	52
	1st Cavalry	2	—	15	2	8	327
	2nd Machine Squadron	1	—	4	2	—	78
	2nd Battery Artillery	2	—	5	3	3	161
	2nd Coy. Engineers	1	—	2	—	—	100
	2nd Infantry	2	—	10	4	3	289
	Signalling School	1	—	1	4	—	6
	Band	—	—	1	1	—	30
	Field Ambulance	4	1	8	1	1	124
	Veterinary Hospital	1	—	1	2	—	29
	Pack Mule Corps	1	—	—	1	—	196
	Ordnance Depot	—	—	—	2	—	—
SAIDABAD	1st Cavalry	1	1	3	—	6	83
	6th Infantry	2	3	13	—	—	406
	Field Ambulance	1	1	2	—	—	27
	Camel and Donkey Corps	—	—	—	—	—	34
ANAR	1st Cavalry	—	—	3	1	—	51
	2nd Infantry	—	—	2	1	—	78
On escort and detachment duties	From above units, including 100 men in Bam Camel Corps	1	1	11	—	—	617
	Total Kerman Brigade	25	8	88	28	25	2,702
BANDAR ABBAS and TARUM	1st Infantry	4	2	21	—	5	818
BANDAR ABBAS AREA	Base offices, Military Works office, etc.	13	3	3	12	65	276

Also 582 Indian and 1,000 Persian followers.

APPENDIX IV.

EAST PERSIA CORDON FIELD FORCE.
DISTRIBUTION OF TROOPS .. 31st MARCH. 1918.

Meshed	99 sabres, 28th Light Cavalry.
	77 rifles and two machine guns, 1/19th Punjabis.
Turbat-i-Haidari ..	99 sabres, 28th Light Cavalry.
Rui Khaf	35 sabres, 28th Light Cavalry.
Kain	35 sabres, 28th Light Cavalry.
Birjand	Force Headquarters.
	19 sabres, 28th Light Cavalry.
	26 rifles, 1/19th Punjabis.
En route to Birjand ..	153 rifles, 1/19th Punjabis.
Nasratabad (Seistan) ..	128 rifles and two machine guns, 1/19th Punjabis.
Dehani Baghi	22 sabres, 28th Light Cavalry.
	61 rifles, 1/19th Punjabis.
Hurmuk	10 rifles, 1/19th Punjabis.
	112 rifles, 24th Company Sappers and Miners.
Robat	53 sabres, 28th Light Cavalry.
	88 rifles, 1/19th Punjabis.
Kacha	56 rifles, 1/19th Punjabis.
Khwash	30 sabres, 28th Light Cavalry.
	193 rifles, 1/98th Infantry.
Road-making Party ..	16 sabres, 28th Light Cavalry.
	73 rifles, 1/19th Punjabis.
En route to various posts	86 sabres, 28th Light Cavalry.
	43 rifles, 1/19th Punjabis.

Of the levies, the Seistanis, Baluchis and Kainas (297 cavalry and 578 camelry) were distributed in various posts on the line Kain–Birjand–Neh–Seistan and Seistan–Dehani Baghi. The Hazaras (299 infantry) were on the line Meshed–Seistan, the largest groups being at Kain and Birjand. The Sarhaddi Levies (300) were at Khwash and other posts in the Sarhad.

APPENDIX V.

BRITISH TROOPS IN PERSIA, PERSIAN GULF AND TRANS-CASPIA;

15th NOVEMBER 1918.

(Exclusive of administrative units.)

MESHED and TRANS-CASPIA (Major-General W. Malleson)*—
    Two squadrons, 28th Light Cavalry
    44th Battery R.F.A. (less two sections) = 2 guns
    1/19th Punjabis (less one company)
    One company, 1/4th Hampshire Regiment
    } at Merv.

    Hazara levies (40 riflemen)—at Askabad.

    28th Light Cavalry (less 2½ squadrons)
    One Company, 1/19th Punjabis
    } at Meshed.

EAST PERSIA LINE OF COMMUNICATION†—
    Half-squadron, 28th Light Cavalry.
    Two squadrons, 41st Cavalry
    1/98th Infantry (with two additional companies, i.e., six companies strong).
    107th Pioneers.
    Seistan detachment, 3rd Sappers and Miners.
    Seistan Levy Corps (1,450 strong).
    Sarhad Levy Corps (250 strong).

SYKES MISSION (Brig.-General Sir P. Sykes)‡—
    Burma Mounted Rifles (three squadrons)
    One squadron, 15th Lancers
    One squadron, 26th Light Cavalry
    One squadron, 27th Light Cavalry
    36th (Reserve) Mountain Battery = 6 guns
    16th Rajputs
    3/124th Baluchis
    } Shiraz and Firuzabad,

    One section, 35th Mountain Battery = 2 guns
    120th Rajputana Infantry
    } at Saidabad.

    Two companies, 3rd Brahmans—at Bandar Abbas.

(The South Persia Rifles, of which Sir P. Sykes was Inspector-General, totalled about 6,000 Persian ranks with some 120 British officer and non-commissioned officer instructors: they were mainly located at Shiraz and Kerman.)

---

    * Under the direct orders of the Commander-in-Chief in India.

    † Under the orders of Lieut.-General R. Wapshare (G.O.C. Quetta Division), with Brig.-General G. A. Dale as G.O.C., Line of Communication Defences, and Brig.-General W. E. R. Dickson as Inspector-General of Communications.

    ‡ Under the orders of the Commander-in-Chief in India.

OPERATIONS IN PERSIA

BUSHIRE COMMAND (Major-General J. A. Douglas)*—
  3rd Brahmans (less two companies)†—Muscat and Persian Gulf detachments.

    One squadron, 15th Lancers‡
    35th Mountain Battery = 6 guns
    Local section R.F.A. = 2 guns
    No. 3 Indian Machine Gun Company
    Local machine gun section
    Two sections of trench howitzers
    1/55th Rifles
    71st Punjabis
    2/94th Infantry
    2/113th Infantry
    1/117th Mahrattas
    1/127th Baluchis
    1/81st Pioneers
    54th Field Company, 1st Sappers and Miners
    63rd Field Company, 2nd Sappers and Miners
      } at Bushire and in the Bushire hinterland.

IN ARABISTAN**—
    5th Cavalry
    31st Mountain Battery (less one section) = 4 guns
    8th Rajputs
    One section, No. 1 Indian Machine Gun Company
    Section of Sappers and Miners
      } Bulk at Ahwaz.

NORTH PERSIA FORCE (Major-General W. M. Thomson)**—
    One section, 44th Battery R.F.A.
    9th Royal Warwickshire Regiment (39th Brigade),
    One section, 39th Brigade machine gun company
      } at Krasnovodsk (Trans-Caspia).

    Advanced Hd. Qrs. North Persia Force
    39th Infantry Brigade (less 7th Gloucestershire, 9th Royal Warwickshire and one section, brigade machine gun company)
    8th Battery R.F.A. = 6 guns
    One section, 44th Battery R.F.A. = 2 guns
    15th Light Armoured Motor Battery (less two sections)
      } at Enzeli.

    7th Gloucestershire Regiment (39th Brigade)—*en route* for Enzeli
    Three platoons, 1/6th Gurkhas (36th Brigade)
    One platoon, 36th Sikhs (36th Brigade)
      } between Enzeli and Kazvin.

    Hd. Qrs., North Persia Force
    Two squadrons, 14th Hussars
    One troop, Machine Gun Squadron
    2½ flights, Royal Air Force
      } at Kazvin.

---

* Under the direct orders of the Commander-in-Chief in India.

† The 3rd Brahmans were six companies strong. Excluding the two companies at Bandar Abbas, the battalion was distributed thus :—Hd. Qrs. and 640 rifles at Muscat, 120 rifles at Jask, 115 rifles at Chahbar, 60 rifles at Qishm island, 25 rifles at Henjam, 30 rifles at Lingeh, and 20 rifles at Bahrein.

‡ The Hd. Qrs. and two more squadrons 15th Lancers arrived at Bushire from India on the 23rd November 1918.

** Under the orders of the G.O.C. Mesopotamia Force.

APPENDIX IV.

NORTH PERSIA FORCE**—*continued.*

36th Infantry Brigade (less 1/6th Gurkhas, 36th Sikhs, and one company 1/4th Hampshire), viz., 1/4th Hampshire, less one company, 1/2nd Gurkhas and brigade machine gun company
One section, 2nd Battery R.F.A. = 2 guns
One section, 21st Mountain Battery = 2 guns
One section, 72nd Company R.E.
One section, 15th Light Armoured Motor Battery
} at Zenjan.

2nd Battery, R.F.A. (less one section) = 4 guns
C/69th Battery, R.F.A. (howitzers) = 4 guns
1/6th Gurkhas (36th Brigade), less 3 platoons
36th Sikhs (36th Brigade), less one platoon
72nd Company R.E. (less one section)
One section, 15th Light Armoured Motor Battery
21st Mountain Battery (less two sections) = 2 guns
14th Hussars (less three squadrons)
One troop, Machine Gun Squadron
} at Hamadan.

One squadron, 14th Hussars
One section, 21st Mountain Battery = 2 guns
} at Sehneh.

LINE OF COMMUNICATION, NORTH PERSIA FORCE**—
(From Hamadan to the Perso-Mesopotamian frontier.)
" D " Squadron, 1/1st Hertfordshire Yeomanry.
26th Mountain Battery = 6 guns.
26th Punjabis.
62nd Punjabis.
5th, 12th, 15th and 61st Companies, Sappers and Miners.
48th Pioneers.
128th Pioneers.

** Under the orders of the G.O.C., Mesopotamia Force.

INDEX.

Abadeh, defence and relief of, 337–40
Afghanistan, Persian designs on, 25–6, German, 71–3, 85, 91; German agents enter, 96, treatment in, 116–17
Afghanistan, Amir Habibulla of, 72, 74–5, 77, 86, 88–9, 91, 93, neutrality of, 96; 114, 116–17, 137, 143, loyalty of, 170–2; 275, 294, request of, 334; 426, assassination of, 448
Afifabad, attack on post at, 326–7
Agreements, Anglo-Russian with Persia, 198–9, 243; Anglo-Persian (1919), 424, 470–1
Ahmadabad, action of, 328–30
Ahmadi, fort occupied, 408; railway at, 410
Ahram, British prisoners at, 125, 145, 160, 176, 178–9, release of, 204; fort destroyed, 409
Ain-ud-Daula, 63–4, 68–9, 71, 86–7, 123, 260, 268, 271, 289
Ala-es-Sultaneh, 242, 260
Alexeieff, Gen., 380
Ali Changi, occupation of, 408
Ali Ishan Pasha, 180
Ali Khan, 319, 335
Ali Quli Khan Nawab, mortally wounded, 107
Allenby, Gen. Sir E. H. H., 245, 257
Amanulla, (of Afghanistan), 116, 117
Annenkovo, action of, 442–4
Ardebil, Turks occupy, 336, evacuate, 384
Ayrton, Mr. (of Shiraz), taken prisoner, 125
Azzopardy, Dr. 179

Baghdad, 106, 113; effect of capture of, 229
Bahram Khan of Bampur, 113, 156, 157, 168, agreement with, 169; 215
Bailey, Col.. 393
Bairam Ali, Trans-Caspian defeat at, 359–60
Bakhtiaris, protection of oil-pipe line, 53, 70, 133–4, 143, to be subsidised, 98, 354; 112, attitude of, 132, 206
Baku, British occupy, 344–5; loss of, 364, effect of, 367; preparations to re-occupy, 387–9; occupation of, 420

Balfour, The Rt. Hon. A. J., 381
Bandaran, British at, 188–9
Baratoff, Gen. 126–7, 132–5, visits Tehran, 137–9, 143, 144, 153, strength of force under (April, 1916), 161, (July), 194, 195; 173, retreat of, 180; 194, 196, 199, 200, 213, 227–8, replaced by Gen. Pavloff, 233; succeeds Gen. Pavloff, 244–5; 257, 273
Barkatullah, Professor Moulvi, 84
Barnes, Sergeant, 339
Barrett, Gen. Sir A. A., 55
Battine, Col. R. St. C., 358, 362
Batum, occupation of, 423
Bayerl, (enemy agent), 156, killed, 267
Beatty, Gen. G. A. H., 397, 435, 437, 440–1
Becker, Dr. (enemy agent), 84, 94–5, 113, 129, 148
Bennett, Capt. A. D., 165, 166
Biach, Dr. (enemy agent), 147, 148, 150, 158, taken prisoner, 159
Bicharakoff, Gen., 273, 288–90, 299, 301–2, 322–3, 332, 370–1, 380, subsidy discontinued, 382; 387–9, 419–20, 424, 448
Bijar, Russians occupy, 228
Bill, Mr. J. H. H., 374, 376, 456, 458, 460
Bingham, Major W. H., 359
Blacker, Major, 393
Black Sea, Germans control, 321
Blomefield, Commr. T. C. A., R.N., killed, 101
Bohnstorff, H. (enemy agent), 56, 79
Bokhara, Amir of, 434, 442, 448
Bolsheviks, activity of, 270, 274 294–5, 321, 334, power waning, 344, 347–8. 392–3; 349, 356, 359–60, 366–7, 400–3, 419–20, 422–6, 430, 434, 436, 442–4, 446–8, 450. See also "Russia"
Bopp, Col. 135–6, 144, 161–2, 173–4
Borazjan, occupation of, 409
Bravin, M., 273
Brest-Litovsk Treaty, 283, 384, 419
Brooking, Brig.-Gen. H. T., Bushire, 102, defence of, 108–11 leaves, 111
Brownlow, Lt. J., 146
Bruce, Major S. M., 177, 202, 207, 217, 263, 303, 306, 313–14, mortally wounded, 315

INDEX. 483

Bruggmann, (enemy agent), 240, captured, 261
Brusiloff, Gen., 244
Buchanan, Sir George, 128
Bulgaria, effect of victory in, 369; armistice with, 381
Bulvardi, affair near, 335
Bushire, 56, 58, 64, affair near, 67; 73, British attacked at, 87; decision to hold, 89, 142; British occupy, 98, effect in Shiraz, 111; raids on, 102; strength of force at, 102; terms for restoration of, 107; defence of, 108–11; port facilities at, 375; operations from, 408–14, 452–4, 455–60 See also " Communications;" " Railways "; " Roads "

Carpenter, Capt. G., R.N., Dilbar, 99
Caspian Sea, naval measures to control, 370–1, 385, 422
Carr, Capt. D. N., 251
Casualties, defence of Muscat, 52; Chahbar, 66; Bushire, 67, 87, defence of, 102, 110, 111; Dilbar, 99, 100, 101; Chaghadak, 161, 378; Gen. Dyer's force, 164, 185, 187, 188; Lirudik, 165–6; Kundi, 167; Khwash, 189; Saidabad, 208; Kalmas, 215; Dasht-i-Arjan, 219, 220; Sykes's Mission, 247, 250, 251, 264, 278, 310; Kafta, 250; Gumun, 279–80; Chenar-i-Naz, 305–6; Ziarat, 307; Kuh-i-Khan, 308; Deh Shaikh, 315, 316; Afifabad, 327; Ahmadabad, 330; Chenar-i-Rahdar, 337; Abadeh, 340; Kaahka, 362, 366; Dushak, 394, 395; Lardeh, 411, 412, 413; Shiraz operations, 415, Firuzabad, 416; Annenkovo, 444
Chaghadak, attack on, 161; affair at, 378; occupation of, 408
Chahbar, 51–2; attack on 66; Makran Mission at, 227
Chah Kutah, occupation, of 408
Chalmers, 2nd Lieut.W. H., killed, 166
Chaldecott, Major O. A., 248–50
Chapman, Major C., 328
Chardigny, Col., 389
Chechen, naval affair off, 422–3
Chenar-i-Naz, affair at, 304–5
Chenar-i-Rhadah, affair of, 336–7
Chernozuboff, Gen., 173, 228
Claridge, Lt.-Col. P. S. D., 185, 186.
Committee of National Defence, 126; Germans dominate, 131

Communications, telegraphic, Chahbar-Jask wrecked, 66; Bushire and interior cut, 89; Shiraz cut, 124; Yezd and Kerman cut, 133; Bandar Abbas-Kerman, 212, 230 See also " Railways "; " Roads."
Concessions, commencement of, 29; 30–1; Russian, denounced, 350. See also " Agreements "; " Conventions "; " Treaties."
Conferences, Inter-Departmental on provision of troops, 142
Consten, (enemy agent), 75, 76
Control of Operations, 206–7, 222–5, 230–2, 238–9
Consuls, Allied, plots against, 105, 106, 107, 118
Conventions, Anglo-Persian, (1903), 31; Anglo-Russian, (1907), 34–6, 44, 243, 269, 273, 287, 342, 383, 467. See also " Agreements "; " Concessions "; " Treaties "
Coomber, Sergeant, death of, 317
Corlett, Major J. S., 378
Cox, Sir Percy, 55–6, 70, 142, 151–3, 179, 209–10, 261, 344, at Tehran, 353, 367–71, 376, 379–87, 421, 424, 431, 457–59, views on future policy, 462–71.
Curzon, Lord, " History of Persia " cited, 10, 19, 31, 32; 458, future policy, 466–71

Dalaki, occupation of, 410
Dale, Brig.-Gen. G. A., 85, 93–4, 97, 114–15, 184–5, 191, succeeds Gen. Tanner, 242; 275–7, 293, 296, 320, 347, 362, 373, 404, 407. See also " East Persia Cordon."
Darya Begi, 114, 229, 240, 455
Dasht-i-Arjan, South Persia Rifles post captured, 212–228; affair of, 217–21; occupied by Kazerunis, 298; British occupy, 457
De Brath, Capt. N. S., 306, 315–17
de Etter, M., 143
Deh Shaikh, action of, 313–17
Denikin, Gen., 418, 420
Dettmar, (enemy agent), 240, death of, 261
Dew, Lt.-Col. A. B., 149, 157, 168–70
Dickson, Brig.-Gen. W. E. R., 92, 372, 403–7, 451
Dilbar, 56, expedition to, 98–101
Dilman, enemy driven from, 59
Dobbs, Capt. H. C., 314–16, killed, 316
Dorman, Lt.-Com. T. S. L., R.N., Bushire, 111

Douglas, Brig.-Gen. J. A., in command at Bushire, 145, 177, 232, 240, 252, 318, 375–8; instructions to, 376–7; strength of force under, 377; operations from Bushire, 408–14, 453–4, 455–60

Drummond, Major J. G. P., 443

Duff, Sir Beauchamp, 74, and provision of troops, 142; 143, 148, 157, 160; and Nushki railway extension, 193

Duncan, 2nd Lt. A. B., wounded, 189

Dunsterville, Gen. L. C., 271–2, 274, 276, 283, 285–6, 288–90, 299–303, 322–3, 331–2, 343–5, 354, 356, 364–5, 470

Dushak, the advance to, 391–2; action of, 394–6

Dutoff, Gen., 321

Dyer, Lieut.-Col. H. R., 278–9, 304–7, 313–19, 328–30, wounded, 330; 415–17

Dyer, Brig.-Gen. R. E. H., appointed to command in East Persia, 149; "The Raiders of the Sarhad" quoted, 155, 167; 156, distribution of force under, 157, 183; advance of, 162–4, 166–8, 170; operations (June–August 1916), 184–91; junction with Major Keyes, 190; asks to be relieved, 190–1; transport requirements, 191, 193; strength of force under, 214; relieved by Gen. Tanner, 215; 252

Eastern Committee, 331–3, 342, 364, 369, 380, 382, 427, 432, 463, 466, dissolved, 467

East Persia Cordon, inception of, 85–6; 114, 130, 157–8, 191, extension of, 275, reaches Meshed, 293; strength and distribution of field force, 293–4, App. IV; reinforced, 320, 348, 362; 372

Eckford, Capt., 374

Edwards, Gen. S. M., Muscat, 52; in command at Bushire, 111, vacates, 145

Egypt, troops from, 141, 142

Ehtesham, Sirdar, subsidised, 324; 335–7, 345, 354, defeats Saulat, 373; 414–15, 417, 455–6

"Ekbatana" (German s.s.), 76

Elsmie, Gen. A. M. S., 409–14, 452–4, 457

Enver Pasha, 74–5, 174–5, 365, 380–1, 384

Enzeli, 59, 69; Russian force at, 106, 108, 118; Jangalis and Bolsheviks control, 274

Falkenhayn, Gen. von, 162, 174, 175, 253

Famine, relief work, 229, 260, 277, 300, 320; fear of, 259, 260; 321, 334

Farman Farma, 123–4, 128, 131–3, 137, 139, 141, intrigues against, 143; resigns, 152; 159–60, 176, 181–2, 197, 201, 204–5, (Shiraz) 207, 209, 210–11, 217, 225–6, 229, 232, 245, 261–2, 292–3, 297, 308, 310–12; loyalty of, 318; 319, 324, 326, 330–1, 336, 351–2, 354, 368, 370, 373, 379, 381, 383–4, 414, 456, 459–60

Farran, Lt.-Col. G. L., 198, 203–4, 207, 250–1, 265, 340–1

Fergusson, Mr. and Mrs. (of Shiraz), taken prisoner, 124, 125

Finance, 9, 38–41, 47, 61, 63, 65, 68, mixed commission to control, 180; 259, difficulties of, 368, 396; 456. *See also* " Subsidies."

Firuzabad, relief of, 415–17

Folke, Col., 57

France, aims of in Persia, 14, 22–3

Franks, Major K., 410–13

Fraser, Lt. A. D., 202-4, 207

Frazer, Major W. A. K., 293, 337–40

Gallipoli, hopes from success in, 106; effect of evacuation of, 138; drain on Turkish forces, 144

Gardner, Capt. J. M. S., 313–17

Gendarmerie, 207, 246, 260; strength of in 1914, 16; pro-German attitude of, 47, 51, 55–9, 70–1, 98, 103, 120; with Germans at Tehran, 118, 120; in open rebellion, 126–7; Swedish officers dismissed, 131, 137

Georgia, activity of German agents in, 49; Republic proclaimed, 255

Germany aims of, in Persian Gulf, 32; activity of agents of, 66, 69–73, 85, 103, 112, 117, 119, 226, 241–2, 269, 271, 274, 334; failure of, 123, 158; in Bakhtiari, 196; own account of agents' activities, 74–84, 94–6, 104, 119, 123, 138, 146–8, 150, 154, 158, 170–5; treatment of agents in Afghanistan, 116–117; relations with Turks, 128, and Persians, 175; reports of agents' movements, 216, 240. *See also* " Peace "

Ghazanfar-es-Sultaneh, 87, 374-6, 408–10

Gillman, Gen. W., 370, 371

Gleich, Col. von, 162, 173–5; resigns, 180

INDEX

Goltz, Field-Marshal von der, 119, 123, 128, 132–7, 140 ; appreciation of situation (16 Feb. 1916), 144, Appendix I ; 158, death of, 162
Gough, Lt.-Col. H. A. K., 175, 182, 197, 201, 204–5, 209, 211–12, 226, 234, 240, 261, 297, 310–11, 324, 326, 335–6, 351, 383, 386, succeeded by Mr. Hotson, 414
Gough-Calthorpe, Ad. The Hon. S.A., 388
Grahame, Mr. T. G., attempted murder of, 105 ; 106 ; returns to Isfahan, 175 ; 201, 207
Grant, Lt.-Col. G. P., 298, 303-9, 311
Grant, Sir Hamilton, 466
Gregson, Lt.-Col. E. G., 413
Grey, Lord, " Twenty-five Years " cited, 34, 36 ; 51, 63, 67, 70, 86, 105, 107, 117–18, 128
Grey, Lt.-Col. W. H., 275, 277, 333
Griesinger, Capt., (enemy agent), 61, 71, 75–84, 90, 147, 150, 158 ; taken prisoner, 159
Griffith, Capt. G. D. M. Gwynne, mortally wounded, 339
Grover, Lt.-Gen. Sir M. H. S., 168, 184, 191
Gumun, affair of, 279–80
Gusht, Gen. Dyer at, 186, 190
Gusht, Defile, affair of, 187–8
Gushti, free-lance chieftain, 186–7

Haidar Khan of Bandar Rig, 64
Haig, Lt.-Col. T. W., 85, 90
Haji Baba, 304
Halil Bey, 76
Halil Khan, 156, 162, surrenders, 164 ; 166–8, 184–5, 187, killed, 188
Halil Pasha, succeeds F.M.v.d. Goltz, 162, 173–5, 228, 384
Hamadan, 107, 112, strength of enemy at, 127, 213 ; Russians occupy, 133 ; Turks occupy, 199 ; Russians re-occupy, 228
Hardinge, Lord, 64–5, 72, 86, 91, 93, 96, 114, 127, 139
Hassan Raouf Bey, 62, 66, 74, 77–8, 80–2, 113
Hentig, Dr. W. O. von (enemy agent), account of activities, 74–84, 94–6, 90, 116, 119, 171
Herdon, Lt.-Col. H. E., 454
Heron, Major D., 165
Hinde, Capt. R. G., 219
History, summary to 1914, 17–41
Hjalmarsen, Col., 16
Holbrooke, Lt.-Col. B. F. R., 314–17, 337, 415–17
Hornsby, Capt. R. W., 242

Horst, Lt., assassinated, 169
Hotson, Mr. J. E. B., 414, 456, 458
Hughes, Lt., assassinated, 169
Hunter, Lt.-Col. F. F., 217–21, wounded, 219 ; 239
Hunter, Lt.-Col. W. J. H., 412
Hussain Khan, 208
Hutchinson, Major W. G., 186, 189–90, 215, 227

Idu, a Reki tribesman, with Gen. Dyer, 167
Inayatulla, 116
Isfahan, 61, 69, 71, 85, 97, 103, German activities in, 104 ; 105–6, British leave, 112, return, 175 ; Russians occupy, 153 ; Sykes's mission reaches, 204
Islam, Holy Places of, 51

Jalq, British at, 190
James, Capt. F., 184, wounded, 185
Jarvis, Capt. E. D., 347
Javazin, fort destroyed, 265
Jemadar Nanajiras Palande, 412–13
Jemadar Partab Singh, 249–50
Jiand Khan, 156 163, surrenders, 164, 166–8, 183, arrested, 184, escapes, 185 ; attacks near Khwash, 186, retires, 188 ; agreement with, 215, 227
Juma Khan, 156, 164, surrenders, 166 ; 167

Kaahka, affairs of, 361–2, 366–7
Kacha, British force at, 85
Kabul, German agents reach, 116 ; 137, 143 ; Germans leave, 170
Kafta, affair of, 248–50
Kalag fort, Gen. Dyer's force at, 187
Kalhur tribe, 196
Kalmas, affair of, 214–15
Kamarij, occupation of, 454
Kangavar, Russians occupy, 138
Kanitz, Count, 119, 136, 138
Karind, Turks reach, 180
Kashgar Mission, 393
Kashquli, 335
Kazerun, attack on South Persia Rifles at, 211 ; occupation of, 457–8
Kelburn, Commr. Viscount, Dilbar, 99
Kennion, Lt.-Col. R. L., 175, 200–1, 271–2
Kerenski, M., 244, 254, 418
Kerman, British Consuls leave, 133, 137, 150, Germans leave, 154
Kermanshah, 61–2, 112–13, 137 ; Russians occupy, 144 ; Turks occupy, 194 ;. Russians re-occupy, 228, leave, 273

Keyes, Major T. H., Makran Mission under, 149, 169, 189, junction with Gen. Dyer, 190; at Sib, 188, 191, 215
Khaniqin, failure of Russian attack on, 180; Turks occupy, 244
Khan-i-Zinian, attack on South Persia Rifles post at, 309, effect of, 310; invested, 311; mutiny at, 317
Khan of Bampur, 73
Khan of Dalaki, 374
Khisht, Khans of 452
Khwaja Jamali, village and fort destroyed, 264
Khwash, fort surrenders, 164; attack near, 186; raid on, 189; *Durbar* at, 215
Kiesling, Lt.-Col. H. von, account of German activities, 119, 128, 134, 140, 150
Kitchener, Lord, 35, 74
Klein, Capt., (enemy agent), 76, 79, 83, 112, 119, 128, 135, 138
Knollys, Lt.-Col. D. E., 360–1, 367, 391
Kolominski, Lt., 202
Koltchak, Ad., 418, 424
Korniloff, Gen., 254
Krasnovodsk, British occupy, 370; 449
Kress, Gen., 367, 423
Kreyer, Major J. A. C., 241, 367, 392, 394–6
Kuchik Khan, 269
Kuh-i-Khan, affair of, 307–8
Kundi, affair of, 166–7
Kuropatkin, Gen., 241

Lake, Lt.-Gen. Sir Percy, 153, 160, 177, 195–6
Lane, Lt.-Col. H. P., 109, 110
Lang, Capt. L. E., 186, 189
Lardeh, affair of, 410–13
League of Nations, 463
Lenders, Dr. (enemy agent), 56, 79
Lenin, M., 254
Liakhoff, Col. 37
Lilly, Capt. A. N. I., 247
Lirudik, affair of, 165–6
Listermann, Dr. (German Consul, Bushire), arrested, 55–6
Livingstone, Mr. (of Shiraz), taken prisoner, 125
Lorimer, Major D. G. R., 197

Macartney, Sir George, 393
Mackensen, Gen., 253
Mahendra Partap, 84
Makran, unrest in, 66. *See also* " Missions, Military "

Malleson, Major-Gen. W., 295, 321, instructions for mission of, 334–5, 349; report of 17 July 1918, 347–8; 356–60, 362, 367, 390–3, 395–402, 405, 407, 425, 427–32, 434–42, 445–51
Mallu Pass, occupation of, 453
Malty, Lt. C. M., 66
Marling, Sir Charles, succeeds Sir Walter Townley, 63; 67–72, 74, 83, 86–89, 93, 97–8, 105–8' 112–13, 117–18, 120–2, 124–8, 132–3, 139, 141, 143–4, 152–3, 160, 176, 178–81, 194–5, 197–201, 204–5, 208–10, 212, 221–3, 225, 229–36, 239–40, 243, 245, 257–62, 269, 270–3, 280–5; F.O. tel. of 7 March 1918, 286–8; 289, 292, 299–303, 322–3, 326, 331–3, 335, 342–5, 350, 352–5, relieved by Sir P. Cox, 367, 380, 466
Marsh, Major F. G., 134, 161
Marshall, Gen. W. R., 271–2, 281, 286, 290–1, 301, 303, 318, views of, 322–3, 364; 324, 332; instructions to, 333; sphere of control of, 349; 353, 357, 359, 365–7, 369–70, 379–80, 387–9, 391, 419–21, 423–4, 430–1, 435
Maude, Gen. F. S., 209, 212, 221–3, 228–9, 232, 255, 257
Mecklenberg, Duke of, 174
Mein, Major D. B., 453
Mensheviks, 335, 348, 349, 356, 357, 499
Merrill, Capt. J. N., 203
Merv, occupation of, 398; 424
Mesopotamia, correlation of operations in Persia and in, 106, 112, 117, 133, 134, 142, 143, 162, 195, 223–4, 228, 244–5, 255–7, 268, 271, 291, 301, effect of success in, 217, 229, 232
Milne, Gen. Sir G. F., 419, 420, 421, 423, commanding in Trans-Caucasia, 424, 430, 433, 435, 436, 440, 441, 444, 446, 447, 448
Mirage, defence of Bushire, 110
Missions, diplomatic, British, (1809), 23; Turco-German to Afghanistan, 46
Missions, financial, American, 1911, 38–9
Missions, military, 1810 to 1879, 14; French (1807), 23; German (1915), 135, 140, 144, 162, 174; British (Makran), 149, 169, 188, 215, 227. *See also* " Dunsterville "; " Kashgar "; " Malleson "; " Sykes, Sir P."
Miyan Kutal, occupation of, 458
Moharram, Persian festival, 120, 124

INDEX

Monro, Gen. Sir Charles, 222, 286, 299, 334, views of, 363, 391
Morley, Lt. W. R., 248–50
Muhammad Ali Khan, 297, 311, 324, subsidised, 327 ; 335–6
Muhammad Ali Khan of Abadeh, 338, death of, 340
Mukhbar-es-Sultaneh, 292, 298
Mullah Qurban, 306
Murray, Capt., M. J., wounded, 330
Muscat, 51–2 ; defence of, 52–3 ; 66, reserve at, 208–9
Mushaver-ul-Mamalik, 466
Mushir-ud-Daula, 58, 63, 65
Mustaufi-ul-Mamalik, 57, 102–3, 105, 119, 131–2, 272, 288, 300

Nasir Diwan, 211, 217, 374, 452, 457
Nasir-ud-Din Shah, accession of, (1848), 27 ; 246
Nasrat-ud-Daula, 367
Nasr-ul-Mulk, 466
Nasrulla, (of Afghanistan), 116, 117, 449
Navy, British, co-operation of, 56, 115, Bushire, 89, 108–11, Dilbar, 98–110, Persian Gulf (Nov. 1915), 129
Near East, appreciation of general situation in, 150–1
Nicholas, Grand Duke, 113, 153, 195, 228
Niedermayer, Dr., (enemy agent), 75–84, 130
Niedermayer, Oskar von, (enemy agent), account of activities, 74–84, 94–6, 104, 129–30, 170 ; 90, 112, 114, 116, 119, 156, 171, 172, 257
Nixon, Gen. Sir J. E., 64–5, 73, 87, 89, 101–2, 111, 117
Nizam-es-Sultaneh, subsidised by Germans, 138 ; 152, 174–5
Noel, Capt. E. W. C., 204, 206, 226, arrested, 287, 289
Norris, Comdre. D. T., 264–5, 379–70, 380, 385
North-West Frontier of India, unrest on, 91, 170, 191, 242
Nuri Pasha, 289, 299, 365, 384, 387, 389
Nystrom, (Swedish officer), 159

Obeidulla Effendi, 76, 202, 283
O'Connor, Lt.-Col. W. F. T., 58, 67, 69, 118, taken prisoner, 124 ; 125, 145, 160–1, 176–7, released, 204
Odessa, Germans occupy, 290
Oertel, (enemy agent), 240, 454, 461

Oil-field ; oil-pipe line, protection of, 53, 70, 98, 133–4, 206 ; Baku, 333, 423
Oliphant, Major E. H., killed, 87
Oppenheim, Baron, (enemy agent), 73
Oraz Sirdar, 391
Orenburg, Bolsheviks occupy, 446, effect of, 447, 448
Orton, Lt.-Col. E. F., 234–5, 239, 264–5, 267, 278, 293, in command against Saulat, 312–19, 326–30, 336–7, 414–17 ; 335, 345, 377, 452, 445–7, 460

Pahlevi, new name for Enzeli, q.v.
Pakenham-Walsh, Major W. P., 406
Palestine, correlation of operations in Persia and in, 245, 257, 268 ; effect of victory in, 369, 379
Paschen, P., (enemy agent), 80, 83
Paschen, W., (enemy agent), 71–2, 75–84, 90, 95–6, 114, captured, 171 ; 191 ; escapes, 205
Pavloff, Gen. 233, 245
Peace, Central Powers and Russia, 283, 384 ; Allies and Turkey, 386, and Central Powers, 390, terms of Armistice, 419, 454
Peace Conference, Persia and the, 379, 381–2, 383, 385, 387–8, 462–3, 368–9
Pender-Smith, Lt. O. R., 313–17
Pennington, Major W. H., killed, 110 ; 111
Persian Gulf, description of coast line, 3 ; suppression of piracy in, 24–5 ; British influence in, 29 ; German aims in, 32 ; naval squadron in, 98–101, 108–11, strengthened, 129
Pigot, Capt. G., 443
Policy, summary of Russian, British and Turkish, 42–3
Population, 8 ; distribution of, 11 ; races, 11–13
Prideaux, Major F. B., 85, 87, 90–4, 97, 129, 145, 148, 156, 168
Prisoners of war, escape from Trans-Caspia to Isfahan, 97 ; organised, 103, 104, 118, 120 ; 127, 202 ; at Shiraz, 209 ; Tashkend, 274–5 ; 285, 294, 332, at Bairam Ali, 359 ; 361, 367, 393, 400, 428, 435–6, 439, 442, 447 ; captured by British, Bushire, 111
Propaganda, 45, 49, 50–2, 54–6, 61–2, 66, 69, 71–3, 96, 152, 169, 196, 300, 334 ; German account of, 74–84, 242
Pugin, (enemy agent), 50, 57
Pusht-i-Kuh Vali of, joins enemy, 57

Qajar dynasty, foundation of, 22
Qashqai, operations, 312–12, 326–30
Qasr-i-Shirin, Turks occupy, 62; Russians take, 173; Turks reoccupy, 180; 244, Russians reach, 228; British occupy, 273
Qawam-ul-Mulk, Head of Khamseh tribes, 47, 67, 69, 70, 107, 111, 114, 118, 121, 124–5, 136, 139, 141–2, 144–5, 151–3, 158, killed and succeeded by son of same name, 159, 160, 176, 181, 197, 205–7, 209, 212, 226, 229, 234, 236, 261–2, 278, 291, 309, 311, loyalty of, 318; 324, 330–1, 335–6, 345, 354
Qum, Russians occupy, 133

Railways, 7; Quetta-Nushki extension of, 192–3, 216, 227, beyond Dalbandin, 253, 256, 296, 320–1, 348, 350, 362, 363, 404, 407, 427, 430, 433, reaches Duzdab, 452, Trans-Caspian, 334; new lines proposed, 350; from Bushire, 355, 375, 377, 410, 452, 453, 455; Batum-Baku, 421; Baghdad-Tehran, 466
Rais Ali of Dilbar, 87, killed, 109
Raith, Major, 136
Ramazan, religious fast, 87, 89
Ranking, Capt. J. G., killed, 87
Ravnina, 434
Recruiting, local, 90, 92, 97, 130, 141, 145, 152, 154, 158, 168–9, 183, 198, 203, 208, 230, 251, 276, 351
Redl, Lt.-Col. E. A. F., 158, 216, 242, 276, 295, 321, 334–5, 347
Reinforcements, British, 67, 85, 90, 114, 153, 228, 234, 292, 312, 320, 341, 355, 409, 452
Resht, occupation of, 470
Reuss, Prince, 62, 64, 81, 119, 126, 135
Rich, Major E. T., 212–13, 230
Riza Khan, 471
Roads, 5–7; Nushki-Robat, 149, 168; Bandar Abbas-Kerman, 181, 461–2; security of, 207; Bushire-Shiraz, 211, 457, 458, 460; lack of, 215–16; Saindak-Khwash, 227; improved, 251, 256, 267, 275, 333, 424, 460; condition of, 404–5; Borazjan-Kazerun, 410, 453, 454; Duzdab-Meshed, 452
Robertson, Gen. Sir William, 195–6, and provision of troops, 142; appreciation on Near East, 150–1 and Nushki railway extension, 193
Rohr, (enemy agent), 84, 171
Rothwell, Major R. S., 177, 266
Royal Air Force, 455, 458
Royal Indian Marine, 73, 98, 108–11

Royal Marines, Dilbar, 98–101
Russia, aims of, in Persia, 23–4, 29, 40–1; and German agents, 86, 87, 88, 90, 171, effect of revolution in, 229, 232–3, 239, 241–2, 245, 254–5, 267–8; activity of agents, 233; Republic proclaimed, 254; peace with Germany, 283. *See also* " Baratoff "; " Bicharakoff "; " Bolsheviks "; " Chernozuboff "; " Mensheviks "; " Pavloff "; " Policy "
Ruwandiz, captured, 173

Saidabad, British occupy, 208
Salar-ud-Daula, 243, 468
Samsam-es-Sultaneh, 300, 303, 312, 321–3, 350
Sardar Nasrat of Kerman, 159
Sarhad, location, topography and tribes of, 155–6
Sari Kamish, action of, 50
Sauj Bulag, Russians occupy, 126, retire from, 134
Saulat-ud-Daula, Head of Qashqai tribes, 47, 67, 70, 104, 111, 118, 121, 125, 132, 136, 139, 141, 145, 158, 160, 175, 177, 179, 181, 197, 204–5, 207, 209, 211–12, 226, 229, 234, 236, entertains enemy agents, 240; 252, 261–2, 278, 291, 293, 297–8, 309, threat by, 310–11; ordered to keep the peace, 312; declaration against South Persia Rifles and Indian troops, 312; operations against, 313–19, 326–30, 336–7, 414–17; strength of force with, 313, 318, 325, 336, 414, 415; 323–4, 331, 335, 345, 354, 373, 455–60, surrenders, 461
Saunders, Capt. M., 242
Schellendorf, Gen. von., 175
Schönemann, (enemy agent), 57, 75–84, 103, 150
Seiler, (enemy agent), 81, 104, 116, 129, 130, 136, reaches Kerman, 137; 146–50, leaves Kerman, 154; abandons Afghan project, 158; taken prisoner, 159; 162, escapes, 209
Seistan Force, strength and distribution of, 130, 145, 157, 183, reduction of, 215, 241
Sevastopol, Germans occupy, 299
Shah Sultan Ahmad, succeeds to throne, 37, 44; 69, 81, 83, 105, 120–4, 126, 132–3, 137, 200, 232–3, receives Sir Percy Sykes, 246; 259, 261, 268–70, 285, 289–90, 301–2, 321–2, 342, 350, 381, 466–70, visits Europe, 471
Shaikh Husain of Chah Kutah, 87, 374, 376, 408

INDEX

Shaikh of Mohammerah, support of, 49, 53 ; 132
Shedd, Dr., 59
Shevket Bey, 173
Shiraz, intrigues in, 56 ; 58, 66, 107, 118, 181, 197, effect in, of occupation of Bushire, 111 ; seizure of British at, 124, terms for release of, 125 ; operations based on, 414–17
Shuja-ud-Daula, 49, 50
Shore, Gen. Offley, 255
Shute, Capt. G. E. F., 394–6
Sib, British at, 188, 191
Sipahsalar, 143, succeeds Farman Farma, 152 ; 153, 198–200
Smith, Mr. (of Shiraz), taken prisoner, 125
Smith, Mrs. (of Shiraz), taken prisoner, and death of, 125
South Persia Rifles, inception of, 139 ; 142, 176, 177, limit of strength of, 181 ; officially recognised, 210–11 ; organisation, 211, 230, 235–8 ; desertions from, 220, 293, 338–9, 373 ; duties of, 235 ; new Government refuse recognition, 243, 262 ; strength and distribution of, 246, 251, 293, App. III ; disaffection in, 319 ; question of transfer to Farman Farma, 368, 370, 379, 383, 384, 386, 456
Staples, Lt. E. C., 111
Starosselski, Col. 366, 381, 468
Stewart, Major A. E., 313–17
Stewart, Lt. F. W., 361
Subsidies to Bakhtiaris, 98, 354 ; to Persian Government 108, 112, 119, 179, 198, 260, 380 ; German, to Nizam-es-Sultaneh, 138 ; to Qawam, 139, 141, 151, 226 ; Gushti, 187 ; Farman Farma, 266 ; Saulat, 229 ; Gen. Baratoff, 255, 260, 273 ; Persian Cossack Division, 268 ; Sirdar Ehtesham, 324 ; Muhammad Ali Khan, 327 ; "The Turkestan Union," 347, 349 ; Trans-Caspian Government, 401, 402–3, 427, 429, 431–4
Sulaiman Askari, 77–80
Sultanabad, Consuls leave, 133 ; Russians occupy, 140
Sultan of Turkey, 381
Supplies, internal, 9, 202 ; for East Persia, 191 ; depots formed, 262
Sweden, Government of, and Swedes in Persia, 47, 59, 70
Swedish officers. See " Gendarmerie"; " Folke, col. "; " Hjalmarsen, Col. "; " Nystrom "

Sykes, Brig.-Gen. Sir Percy, South Persia Rifles, 139–40, 142, role of mission under, 144, 206 ; 145, 151–2, strength of mission under, 154, 197, 246, 266, 293, App. III ; 159, 160, 176, composition of force under, 177 ; 178, reaches Kerman, 181, leaves, 197 ; 182 ; reaches Yezd, 200, leaves, 202 ; 201, 203, reaches Isfahan, 204 ; 205–6, under orders of British Minister, 206–7 ; 208 ; Shiraz, 209–12, 217, 221–3, 225, reinforced, 228, 234 ; 230–2, appointment officially recognised, 232 ; 234–5, 238–9, 244, operations of mission, 247–51, 262–6, 278–80 ; 257, 262, 266, leaves for India, 267, returns, 292 ; 281, 286, 288, 293, 297–8, 309, 311–12, 317–19, under orders of C-in-C. India, 320, 324 ; 325, 330–1, 336–7, 341, 345, 351, 353–4, 373, 414, leaves for India, 456
Synge, Col. M., 406

Tabriz, Turks occupy, 50, driven out, 53, re-occupy, 323
Talaat Pasha, 381
Tanner, Brig.-Gen. C. O. O., relieves Gen. Dyer, 214, 215 ; 227, 241, succeeded by Gen. Dale, 242
Tehran, enemy representatives leave, 123 ; British women and children leave, 199
Tejend, occupation of, 397
Thacker, Capt. W. C. H., 304–5
Thomson, Major-Gen. W. M., 365, 370, 380, 385, 389, 419, 421, 423–4, 431, 435
Thornton, 2nd Lt. L. I. L., killed, 110
Topography, 1–3, 91–2, Bushire peninsula, 101 ; Sarhad, 155–6 ; Sar-i-Drukan valley, 186 ; Dasht-i-Arjan area, 218 ; Shiraz, 326
Townley, Sir Walter, 45, 50–1, 53–4, 57–8, 60–1 ; succeeded by Sir Charles Marling, 63
Townshend, Maj.-Gen. C. V. F., 112, 117, 128, 382
Trans-Caspia, British withdraw from, 450
Treaties, Anglo-Persian, (1800), 22, (1814), 23, revised, 24, Russo-Persian, (1813), 23–4, (1828), 24 ; proposed Alliance with Russia, 139–40 ; Brest-Litovsk, 283, 384, 419 ; Russian, denounced, 350. See also " Agreements "; " Concessions "; " Conventions "

Trebizond, Turks recapture, 284
Trevor, Major A. P., 124–5, 161, 178–9, 240
Tribes, description of, 12–13, 156
Trotski, M., 254
'Turkestan Union, The ", anti-Bolshevik, subsidised, 347, 349; defeat Bolsheviks, 348; failure of, 356; 358, 392
Turkey, aims of, in Persia, 29, 33; attitude of, Aug.–Oct. 1914, 45–6; effect of entry into war, 48–51; relations with Germans, 128; peace with, 380–2, 386; Committee of Union and Progress, 384. *See also* "Policy"
Twigg, Lt.-Col. E. F., 177, 217–21, 226
Tytler, Col. H. C., 413

Ukraine, German peace with, 282
Urmia, 59, Russians re-occupy, 69; Turks capture, 356
Ushnu, Russians occupy, 126

Vali of Pusht-i-Kuh, 132, 138, loyalty of, 154
Van, Russians reach, 69, evacuate, 98
Vanrenen, Lt.-Col. G. R., 228, 328–30, 458
Versen, Major von, (enemy agent), 116, 147
Voight, (enemy agent), 80 81, captured, 171; 191
Vossuk-ud-Daula, 199–200, 204, 232–3, 269, 270, 272, 300–3, 321–2, 332, 343, 345, 350, 352–5, 367, 369–71, 377, 381–3, 385, 466, 468–9, 471

Wagner, (enemy agent), 71–2, 79, 83, 90, 94–6, 171, 216, 267
Wagstaff, Capt. L. C., 203, 207–8, 212
Wahl, 2nd Lt. B. W., killed, 214–15
Wake, Capt. D. St. A., R.N., Dilbar, 98–101; Bushire, 108–11
Waldmann, (enemy agent), 147
Wallace, Capt., 410–13

Wapshare, Gen. R., 372–3, 396, 402, 451
Ward, Major C. H., Bushire, 109
Washington, Capt. B. G., R.N., 385, 419, 422–3
Wassmuss, (enemy agent), 55–6, 58, 61, 64, 66–7, 70, 72–3, 75–84, 87, 89, 102–3, 125, 150, 160, 179, 212, 240, 261, 298, 310, 324, 336, 373–4, 409, 453–4, 461
Water, scarcity of, 187–9, 404; in Northern Fars, 308; Bushire, 375
Wedig, H. (enemy agent), 94–5, 147–8, 150, 158, taken prisoner, 159
Weldon, Capt. G. H., 218–19
Wetherall, Capt. F. C. B., 314–17
Wikeley, Lt.-Col. J. M., 93, 97, 114–15, 129, strength of force under, 130, 145; 137, 146, 148–9
Will, Capt. A. W., 309–11, 313–17, death, of 317
Williams, Lt.-Col. V. P. B., 247–50, 265, 309–10, 340, 345, 351, 354
Willis, Capt. C. R., 313–17
Winkelmann, Lt., (enemy agent), 81, 113–14, 129, captured, 146; 147
Wintle, Major C. E. H., Dilbar, 98–101
Wise, Capt. A. D., 165–6, 191
Wittkugel, Capt. A. F., mortally wounded, 219, 221
Wonckhaus, (enemy agent), 55
Wooldridge, Col. W. H., 73
Wustrow, (enemy agent), 103, 150

Yezd, Consuls leave, 133; 137, Sykes's mission reaches, 200, leaves 202
Young, Dr. M. Y., 133

Zafar, Sirdar, subsidised, 354
Zair Khidar, 87, 374, 376, 408–9, 414, 455
Ziarat, affair of, 306–7
Zil-es-Sultan, 196, 206
Zugmayer, (enemy agent), 61, 71, 74–84, 90, 96, 113, 115, 137, 147–50, abandons Baluchistan expedition, 158; taken prisoner, 159; 162

PERSIA.

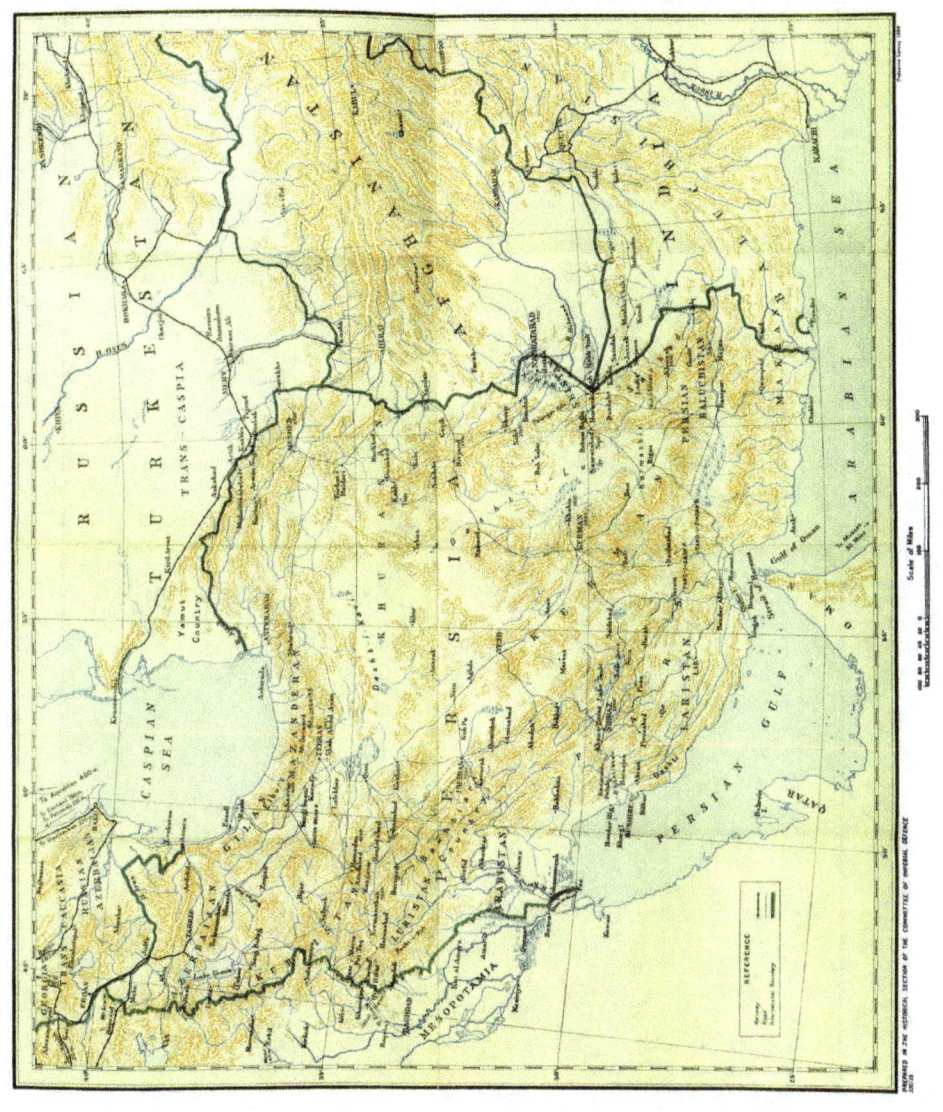

TO ILLUSTRATE OPERATIONS AT BUSHIRE.

1915.

Piquet Posts of outpost line shown in Red.

MAP 1

PREPARED IN THE HISTORICAL SECTION OF THE COMMITTEE OF IMPERIAL DEFENCE.

520/29.

Ordnance Survey 1929.

SCALE OF MILES.

¾ ½ ¼ 0 1 2

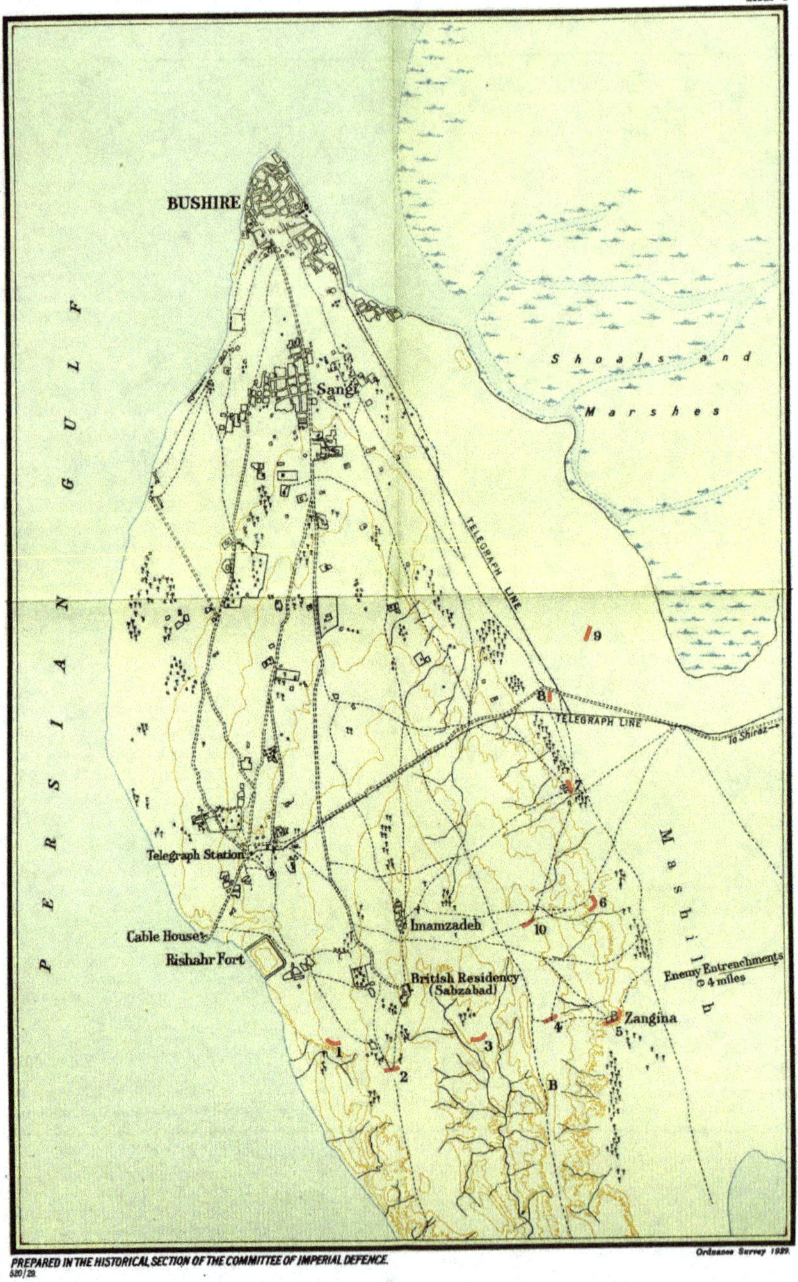

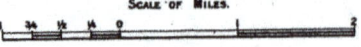

PORTION OF PERSO-AFGHAN FRONTIER.

MAP 2

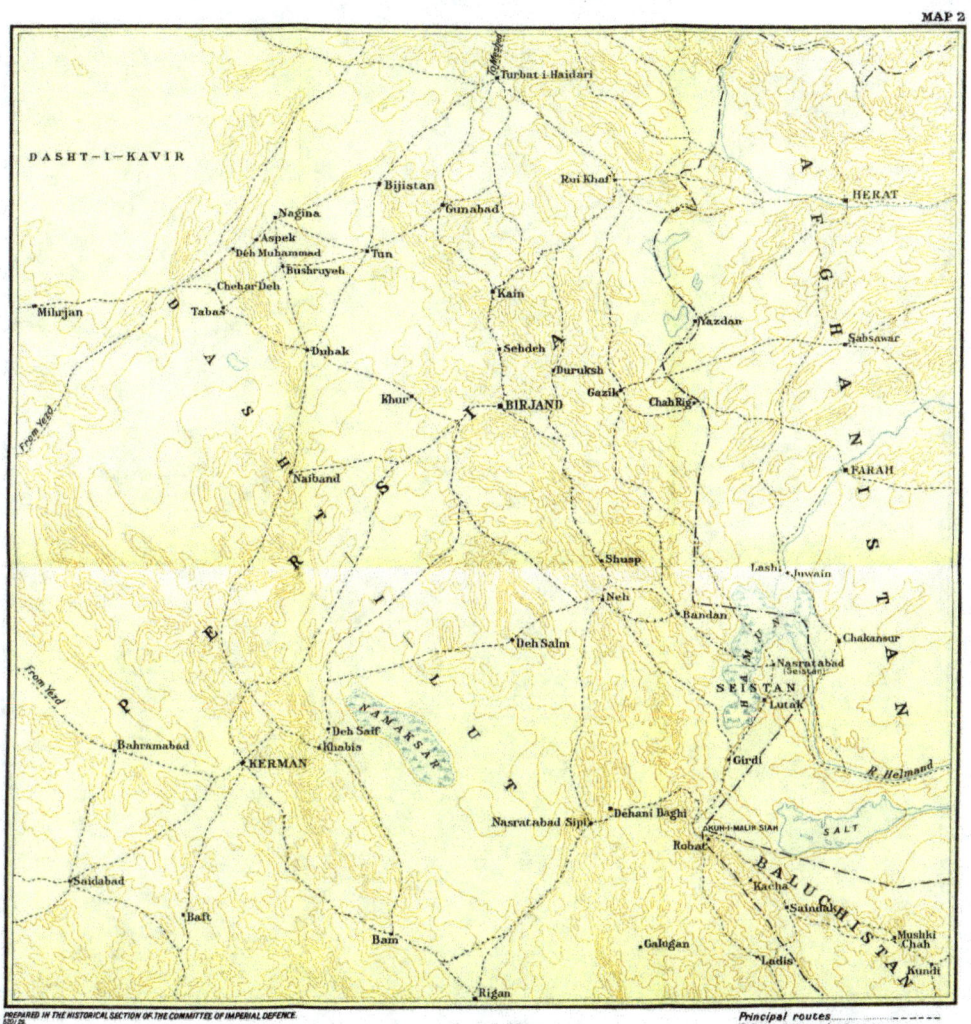

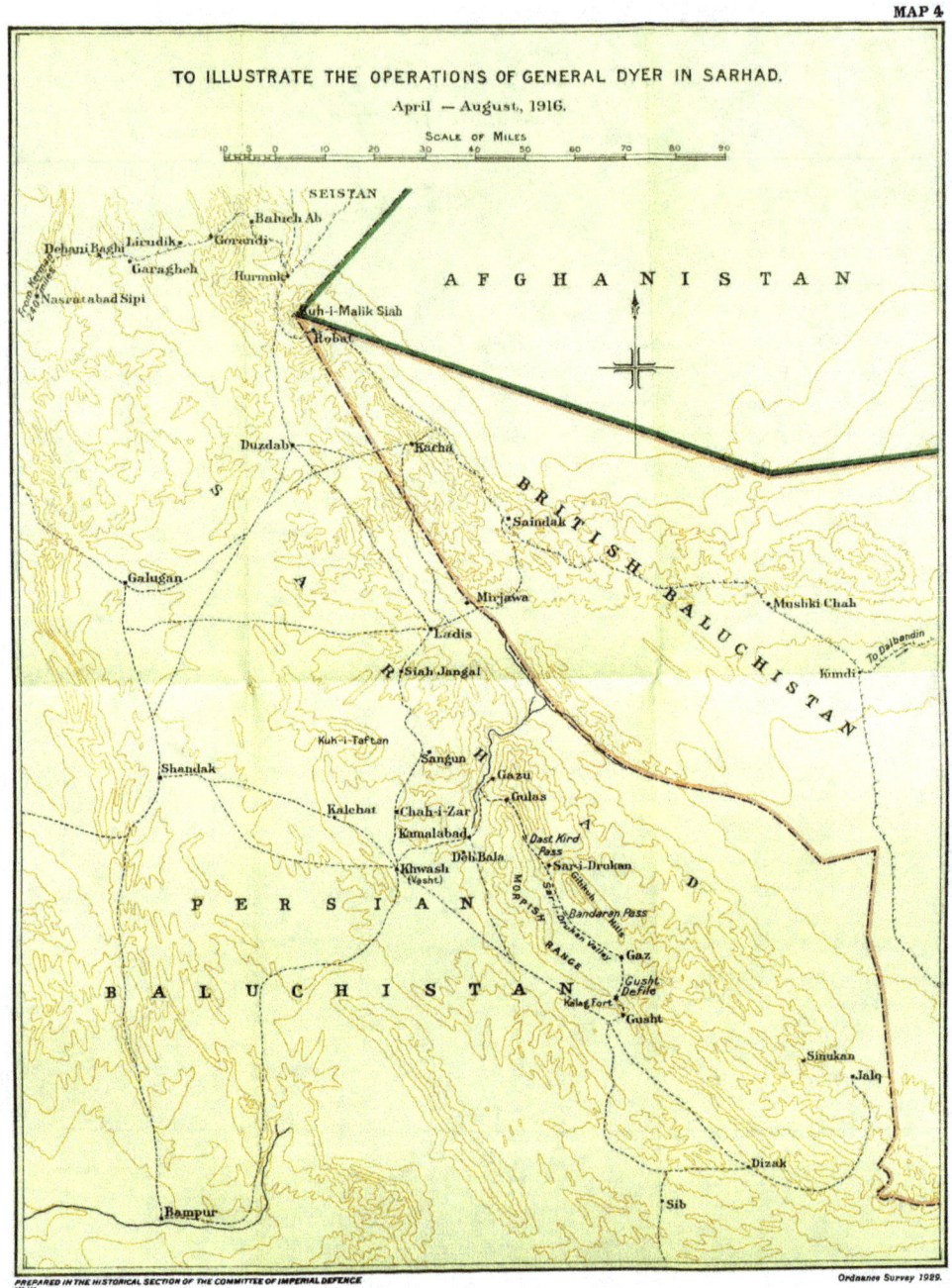

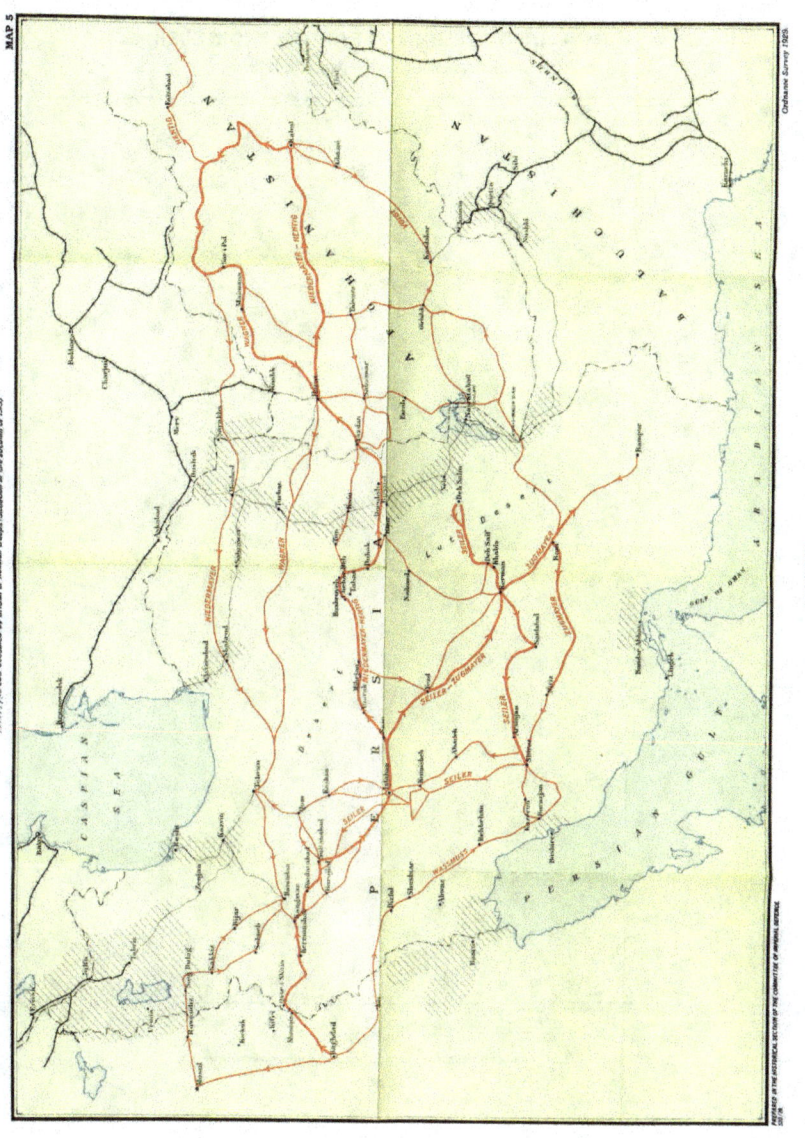

TO ILLUSTRATE THE OPERATIONS FROM BUSHIRE.
September, 1918 — January, 1919.

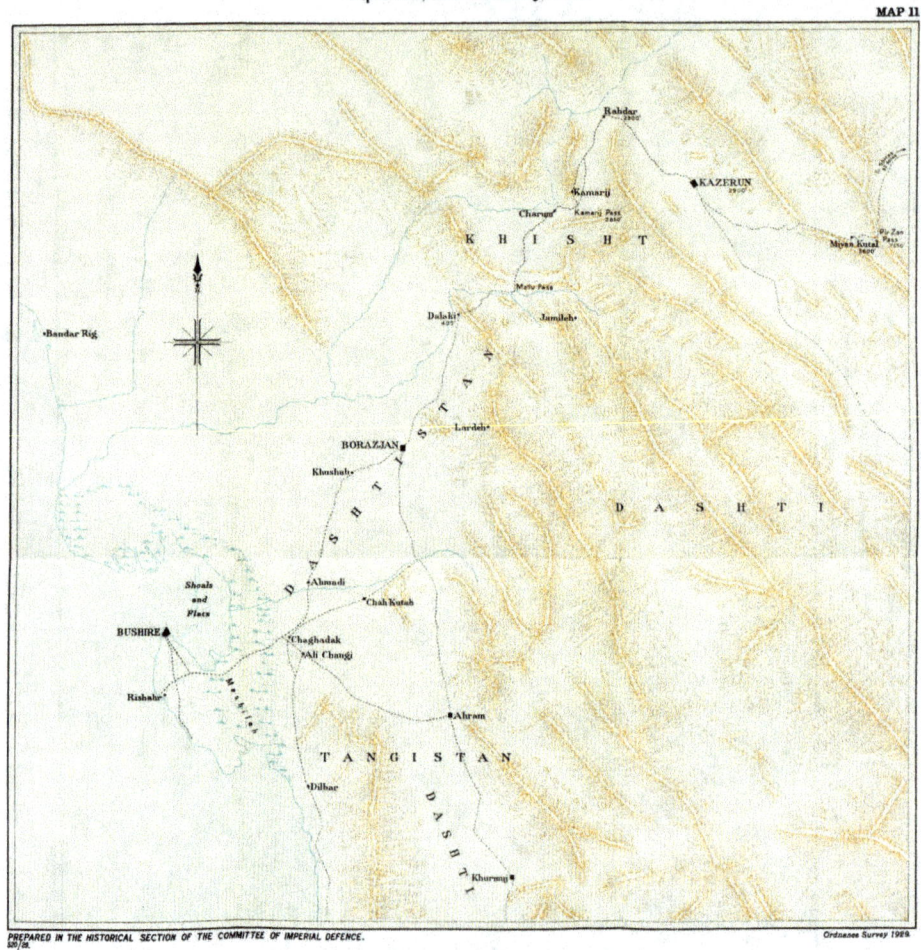

www.ingramcontent.com/pod-product-compliance
Lightning Source LLC
Chambersburg PA
CBHW070754300426
44111CB00014B/2403